Children and the European Court of Human Rights

Children and the European Court of Human Rights

CLAIRE FENTON-GLYNN

OXFORD
UNIVERSITY PRESS

OXFORD
UNIVERSITY PRESS

Great Clarendon Street, Oxford, OX2 6DP,
United Kingdom

Oxford University Press is a department of the University of Oxford.
It furthers the University's objective of excellence in research, scholarship,
and education by publishing worldwide. Oxford is a registered trade mark of
Oxford University Press in the UK and in certain other countries

First Edition published in 2021

Published in the United States of America by Oxford University Press
198 Madison Avenue, New York, NY 10016, United States of America

British Library Cataloguing in Publication Data

Data available

Library of Congress Control Number: 2020942399

ISBN 978–0–19–878751–8

DOI: 10.1093/oso/9780198787518.001.0001

Printed and bound in Great Britain by
Clays Ltd, Elcograf S.p.A.

To Nuala Mole and the AIRE Centre,

who have done so much to advance the rights of all people in Europe

Contents

Convention for the Protection of Human Rights and Fundamental Freedoms (Extracts)

Article 1 Obligation to respect human rights

The High Contracting Parties shall secure to everyone within their jurisdiction the rights and freedoms defined in Section I of this Convention.

Section I Rights and freedoms

Article 2 Right to life

1. Everyone's right to life shall be protected by law. No one shall be deprived of his life intentionally save in the execution of a sentence of a court following his conviction of a crime for which this penalty is provided by law.
2. Deprivation of life shall not be regarded as inflicted in contravention of this article when it results from the use of force which is no more than absolutely necessary:
   a. in defence of any person from unlawful violence;
   b. in order to effect a lawful arrest or to prevent the escape of a person lawfully detained;
   c. in action lawfully taken for the purpose of quelling a riot or insurrection.

Article 3 Prohibition of torture

No one shall be subjected to torture or to inhuman or degrading treatment or punishment.

Article 4 Prohibition of slavery and forced labour

1. No one shall be held in slavery or servitude.
2. No one shall be required to perform forced or compulsory labour.
3. For the purpose of this article the term 'forced or compulsory labour' shall not include:

a. any work required to be done in the ordinary course of detention imposed according to the provisions of Article 5 of this Convention or during conditional release from such detention;
b. any service of a military character or, in case of conscientious objectors in countries where they are recognised, service exacted instead of compulsory military service;
c. any service exacted in case of an emergency or calamity threatening the life or well-being of the community;
d. any work or service which forms part of normal civic obligations.

Article 5 Right to liberty and security

1. Everyone has the right to liberty and security of person. No one shall be deprived of his liberty save in the following cases and in accordance with a procedure prescribed by law:
   a. the lawful detention of a person after conviction by a competent court;
   b. the lawful arrest or detention of a person for non-compliance with the lawful order of a court or in order to secure the fulfilment of any obligation prescribed by law;
   c. the lawful arrest or detention of a person effected for the purpose of bringing him before the competent legal authority on reasonable suspicion of having committed an offence or when it is reasonably considered necessary to prevent his committing an offence or fleeing after having done so;
   d. the detention of a minor by lawful order for the purpose of educational supervision or his lawful detention for the purpose of bringing him before the competent legal authority;
   e. the lawful detention of persons for the prevention of the spreading of infectious diseases, of persons of unsound mind, alcoholics or drug addicts or vagrants;
   f. the lawful arrest or detention of a person to prevent his effecting an unauthorised entry into the country or of a person against whom action is being taken with a view to deportation or extradition.
2. Everyone who is arrested shall be informed promptly, in a language which he understands, of the reasons for his arrest and of any charge against him.
3. Everyone arrested or detained in accordance with the provisions of paragraph 1.c of this article shall be brought promptly before a judge or other officer authorised by law to exercise judicial power and shall be entitled to trial within a reasonable time or to release pending trial. Release may be conditioned by guarantees to appear for trial.
4. Everyone who is deprived of his liberty by arrest or detention shall be entitled to take proceedings by which the lawfulness of his detention shall be decided speedily by a court and his release ordered if the detention is not lawful.
5. Everyone who has been the victim of arrest or detention in contravention of the provisions of this article shall have an enforceable right to compensation.

Article 6 Right to a fair trial

1. In the determination of his civil rights and obligations or of any criminal charge against him, everyone is entitled to a fair and public hearing within a reasonable time by an independent and impartial tribunal established by law. Judgment shall be pronounced publicly but the press and public may be excluded from all or part of the trial in the interests of morals, public order or national security in a democratic society, where the interests of juveniles or the protection of the private life of the parties so require, or to the extent strictly necessary in the opinion of the court in special circumstances where publicity would prejudice the interests of justice.
2. Everyone charged with a criminal offence shall be presumed innocent until proved guilty according to law.
3. Everyone charged with a criminal offence has the following minimum rights:
   a. to be informed promptly, in a language which he understands and in detail, of the nature and cause of the accusation against him;
   b. to have adequate time and facilities for the preparation of his defence;
   c. to defend himself in person or through legal assistance of his own choosing or, if he has not sufficient means to pay for legal assistance, to be given it free when the interests of justice so require;
   d. to examine or have examined witnesses against him and to obtain the attendance and examination of witnesses on his behalf under the same conditions as witnesses against him;
   e. to have the free assistance of an interpreter if he cannot understand or speak the language used in court.

Article 7 No punishment without law

1. No one shall be held guilty of any criminal offence on account of any act or omission which did not constitute a criminal offence under national or international law at the time when it was committed. Nor shall a heavier penalty be imposed than the one that was applicable at the time the criminal offence was committed.
2. This article shall not prejudice the trial and punishment of any person for any act or omission which, at the time when it was committed, was criminal according to the general principles of law recognised by civilised nations.

Article 8 Right to respect for private and family life

1. Everyone has the right to respect for his private and family life, his home and his correspondence.
2. There shall be no interference by a public authority with the exercise of this right except such as is in accordance with the law and is necessary in a democratic society in the interests of national security, public safety or the economic

well-being of the country, for the prevention of disorder or crime, for the protection of health or morals, or for the protection of the rights and freedoms of others.

Article 9 Freedom of thought, conscience and religion

1. Everyone has the right to freedom of thought, conscience and religion; this right includes freedom to change his religion or belief and freedom, either alone or in community with others and in public or private, to manifest his religion or belief, in worship, teaching, practice and observance.
2. Freedom to manifest one's religion or beliefs shall be subject only to such limitations as are prescribed by law and are necessary in a democratic society in the interests of public safety, for the protection of public order, health or morals, or for the protection of the rights and freedoms of others.

Article 10 Freedom of expression

1. Everyone has the right to freedom of expression. This right shall include freedom to hold opinions and to receive and impart information and ideas without interference by public authority and regardless of frontiers. This article shall not prevent States from requiring the licensing of broadcasting, television or cinema enterprises.
2. The exercise of these freedoms, since it carries with it duties and responsibilities, may be subject to such formalities, conditions, restrictions or penalties as are prescribed by law and are necessary in a democratic society, in the interests of national security, territorial integrity or public safety, for the prevention of disorder or crime, for the protection of health or morals, for the protection of the reputation or rights of others, for preventing the disclosure of information received in confidence, or for maintaining the authority and impartiality of the judiciary.

Article 11 Freedom of assembly and association

1. Everyone has the right to freedom of peaceful assembly and to freedom of association with others, including the right to form and to join trade unions for the protection of his interests.
2. No restrictions shall be placed on the exercise of these rights other than such as are prescribed by law and are necessary in a democratic society in the interests of national security or public safety, for the prevention of disorder or crime, for the protection of health or morals or for the protection of the rights and freedoms of others. This article shall not prevent the imposition of lawful restrictions on the

exercise of these rights by members of the armed forces, of the police or of the administration of the State.

Article 12 Right to marry

Men and women of marriageable age have the right to marry and to found a family, according to the national laws governing the exercise of this right.

Article 13 Right to an effective remedy

Everyone whose rights and freedoms as set forth in this Convention are violated shall have an effective remedy before a national authority notwithstanding that the violation has been committed by persons acting in an official capacity.

Article 14 Prohibition of discrimination

The enjoyment of the rights and freedoms set forth in this Convention shall be secured without discrimination on any ground such as sex, race, colour, language, religion, political or other opinion, national or social origin, association with a national minority, property, birth or other status.

PROTOCOL 1

Article 1 Protection of property

Every natural or legal person is entitled to the peaceful enjoyment of his possessions. No one shall be deprived of his possessions except in the public interest and subject to the conditions provided for by law and by the general principles of international law.

The preceding provisions shall not, however, in any way impair the right of a State to enforce such laws as it deems necessary to control the use of property in accordance with the general interest or to secure the payment of taxes or other contributions or penalties.

Article 2 Right to education

No person shall be denied the right to education. In the exercise of any functions which it assumes in relation to education and to teaching, the State shall respect the right of parents to ensure such education and teaching in conformity with their own religious and philosophical convictions.

1
Introduction

1.1 Introduction

The European Convention on Human Rights (ECHR) was not drafted with children, still less children's rights, in mind. At the time of drafting, the child rights movement was in its infancy, with children predominantly seen as objects of benevolence and recipients of special protection, rather than subjects holding individual legal rights.[1] Nevertheless, over the past 60 years the European Court of Human Rights (ECtHR) has developed a substantial and ever-growing body of case law concerning children, covering issues ranging from juvenile justice and physical integrity to immigration, education, and religion. Moreover, in the sphere of private and family life the Court has developed a 'whole code of family law',[2] significantly expanding the Convention's scope and influence.

The aim of this book is to provide a detailed overview of the jurisprudence of the Court in relation to children, from its humble and essentially paternalistic beginnings to its recent (though still evolving) recognition of children's individual agency. It is hoped that it will provide a foundation for academics, practitioners, and civil society to better understand the position of the Court in relation to children's rights, and be a helpful tool in advancing their protection under the Convention, both domestically and in Strasbourg.

1.2 Background to the European Convention on Human Rights

On 4 November 1950, the European Convention for the Protection of Human Rights and Fundamental Freedoms was opened for signature. Intended to reflect the 'common desire of the Member States to build a European Union in accordance with the principles of natural law, of humanism and of democracy',[3] the European Convention on Human Rights, as it came to be known, came into force three years later upon the tenth ratification.[4]

[1] See the 1924 League of Nations Geneva Declaration on the Rights of the Child, which included such 'rights' as the 'the right to be among the first to receive relief' and the 'right to understanding and love by parents and society'.

[2] *Marckx v Belgium* (6833/74) 13.06.1979, dissenting opinion of Judge Sir Gerald Fitzmaurice, para. 15.

[3] M. Teitgen, 'Report on the Establishment of a Collective Guarantee of Essential Freedoms and Fundamental Rights' (Consultative Assembly of the Council of Europe, 05.09.1949), para. 2.

[4] By Demark, Germany, Greece, Iceland, Ireland, Luxembourg, Norway, Saarland (which later became part of Germany), Sweden, and the United Kingdom.

Children and the European Court of Human Rights. Claire Fenton-Glynn, Oxford University Press (2021). © Claire Fenton-Glynn.
DOI: 10.1093/oso/9780198787518.003.0001

The Convention was drafted in response to twin concerns on the part of the Allied Powers. First, in the aftermath of the Second World War, the instrument was intended to provide a 'collective guarantee of essential freedoms and fundamental rights',[5] to ensure that such atrocities would never again occur. Second, and related to this, it was a response to the growing influence of communism in Central and Eastern Europe—a statement of values to represent a sense of common identity and to act as an early warning system should a state move towards authoritarianism.[6] As Guido Raimondi, later President of the Court, stated, 'an undemocratic state could not participate in the ECHR system: the protection of democracy goes hand in hand with the protection of rights'.[7]

The text of the Convention was based, 'as far as possible', on the Universal Declaration of Human Rights,[8] proclaimed by the newly formed United Nations two years earlier.[9] It did not directly transpose the provisions of the Declaration, but instead chose those rights that the founding states viewed as most 'fundamental', capable of inclusion in 'an immediate international guarantee'.[10] As a result, the Convention incorporates a tradition of civil liberties and is primarily focused on civil and political rights, which have conventionally been seen as more easily measurable and enforceable.[11]

Notably, the provisions of the Universal Declaration which focus on children—for example, requiring the provision of special care and assistance—were not included. Children are mentioned only twice in the main text of the Convention. First, under Article 5(1)(d)—the right to liberty and security—an exception is permitted for the detention of a minor for the purpose of educational supervision or for bringing him or her before a legal authority. Second, Article 6(1)—the right to a fair trial—allows for the exclusion of the press or public from a trial where the interests of a juvenile so require. Two further provisions relating to children were added in subsequent Protocols to the Convention: Article 2 of Protocol 1, which protects the right to education, and of parents to educate their children in accordance with their philosophical and religious beliefs; and Article 5 of Protocol 7, which protects equality between spouses, with the exception that the state may take such measures 'as are necessary in the interests of children'.[12]

[5] M. Teitgen, 'Report on the Establishment of a Collective Guarantee of Essential Freedoms and Fundamental Rights' (Consultative Assembly of the Council of Europe, 05.09.1949), para. 1.

[6] S. Greer, 'What's Wrong with the European Convention on Human Rights?' (2008) 30(3) *Human Rights Quarterly* 680, 681.

[7] G. Raimondi, 'Immunita Parlamentari e Diritti Umani' (2016) 1 *Dritto Pubblico Europea Rassenga online* 2, 5.

[8] (1948) GA Res 217A.

[9] M. Teitgen, 'Report on the Establishment of a Collective Guarantee of Essential Freedoms and Fundamental Rights' (Consultative Assembly of the Council of Europe, 05.09.1949), para. 1.

[10] ibid., para. 11.

[11] Although these have been interpreted by the Court to incorporate some social and economic dimensions, as is discussed in Chapter 7.

[12] This Article is not discussed further in this book, given the dearth of case law in this area. It has only been discussed by the Court on one occasion—the case of *Chepelev v Russia* (58077/00) 26.07.2007—in which the Court simply stated, in two sentences, that the measures taken were in accordance with the best interests of the child and that having regard to the assessment made under Article 8, there had been no violation of Article 5, Protocol 7. There have been further cases in which the Commission and Court have declared an application under this section inadmissible, but none in which it has been subject to any substantive examination.

The lack of consideration of children's rights in this respect is hardly surprising—it would take another 40 years before such rights were recognised on an international level. Nevertheless, it has meant that the majority of cases that protect the rights of children have in fact fallen under other, broader, *adult*-focused rights—for example, the right to respect for private and family life under Article 8. This has had an inevitable impact on the way in which children's rights have been conceptualised and enforced by the Court. The purpose of Article 8 is to insulate the family unit from outside interference, subjugating children within this private sphere. It has been a long, slow road for the Court to recognise children as their own autonomous beings with separate rights against the state—independent from, and sometimes in conflict with, their parents. This is still a work in progress, as can be seen throughout this volume, but it is at least now a journey the Court (mostly) recognises it is necessary to take.

1.3 The European Court of Human Rights

The success of the European Convention on Human Rights lies not in its provisions, which can be described as conservative rather than radical, but in its enforcement through the European Court of Human Rights. The intention of the drafters was to create an independent judicial body to act as a collective enforcement mechanism of guaranteed rights. This was expected to function primarily as an independent body to adjudicate inter-state complaints; however, provision was also made for individuals to bring a complaint, very much as a secondary apparatus.[13] In reality, only approximately 20 inter-state cases have been brought before the Court in its 60-year history, in contrast to the hundreds of thousands brought by individuals.

It has been this right of individual petition which has distinguished the Convention from other human rights instruments. While today the right of an individual to challenge state practice is a central feature of a large number of regional and international human rights instruments (for example, the African Court on Human and People's Rights, the Inter-American Court of Human Rights, and the majority of United Nations (UN) treaty bodies)[14] this was a significant innovation in 1950, and has been central to the success of the Convention. It has established human rights not solely as obligations between states—as in traditional international treaties—but as obligations towards individuals, facilitating the Convention's status as 'hard, enforceable law'.[15]

Initially, the supervisory function of the Convention was carried out by two bodies. The Commission, which acted as a filtering body, would first evaluate whether the

[13] This was initially optional, but was a de facto requirement for membership of the Council of Europe for some time, before becoming mandatory in 1998, following the coming into force of Protocol 11.

[14] Human Rights Committee; Committee on the Elimination of Discrimination against Women; Committee against Torture; Committee on the Elimination of Racial Discrimination; Committee on Enforced Disappearances; Committee on Economic, Social and Cultural Rights; Committee on the Rights of the Child. The individual complaint mechanism under the Committee on Migrant Workers has not yet entered into force.

[15] Sir Humphrey Waldock (President of the Court), as quoted by E. Myjer, L. Berg, P. Kempees et al. (eds), *The Conscience of Europe: 50 Years of the European Court of Human Rights* (Strasbourg: Council of Europe, 2010), 25.

petition was manifestly ill-founded or whether it should be permitted to proceed for judicial determination before the Court. Following the ratification of Protocol 11, the Commission was abolished, and in 1998 the Court was established as a full-time, permanent institution. Further changes were instituted in 2010 to deal with the significant increase in the Court's workload, allowing admissibility decisions to be made by a single judge,[16] who can forward the case to a Chamber of the Court for further examination on the merits.[17] In addition, following a Chamber judgment, the parties can request that a case be referred to the Grand Chamber for re-hearing—often incorrectly described as an 'appeal'. However, this will only be accepted in cases that are suitable for the development or clarification of the case law, in cases concerning 'new' issues or 'serious issues of general importance', or in 'high-profile cases' in which an authoritative judgment is required.[18]

In the first 30 years of its existence, the Court was a very minor player in the international arena—indeed, between 1960 and 1975 it only delivered 12 judgments on the merits. However, its workload has since grown exponentially, and over the past ten years has averaged over 50,000 applications and 1,000 judgments per year.[19] In this way, and despite its regional nature, it has established itself as arguably the most influential international court in existence in terms of scope, impact, and jurisdiction.

1.4 Principles of interpretation

Throughout its 60-year history, the Court has developed a number of tools and principles to guide its interpretation of the Convention. In doing so, it must walk a fine line between judicial independence and political necessity. On the one hand, the Court must ensure that the Convention guarantees rights that are 'practical and effective', and not merely 'theoretical or illusory'.[20] On the other, it must recognise its role as a supranational body, which gains its legitimacy from the continued adherence and acquiescence of states.

There are four primary principles of interpretation used by the Court: positive obligations; the principle of subsidiarity; the margin of appreciation; and the 'living tree' principle. I provide a brief outline of each below, in order to give a background to the jurisprudence of the Court detailed in later chapters.

[16] Although in cases of doubt, the judge can refer the application to a three-judge committee to decide on admissibility (Protocol 14, Article 7, amending Article 27 of the ECHR).

[17] An exception to this is in cases where a decision can be made on the basis of well-established case law, in which case the judge can refer the case to a three-judge committee, which is empowered to make a decision on the merits (Protocol 14, Article 8, amending Article 28 of the ECHR).

[18] The Grand Chamber will also accept referrals in cases that concern case-law consistency and cases in which it may be called upon to re-examine a development in the case law endorsed by the Chamber. (European Court of Human Rights, 'The General Practice Followed by the Panel of the Grand Chamber When Deciding on Requests for Referral in Accordance with Article 43 of the Convention' (Council of Europe, 2011), https://www.echr.coe.int/Documents/Note_GC_ENG.pdf)

[19] European Court of Human Rights, 'Statistical Overview 1959–2018' (Council of Europe, 2019), https://www.echr.coe.int/Documents/Overview_19592018_ENG.pdf.

[20] See, for example, *Airey v Ireland* (6289/73) 09.10.1979.

1.4.1 Positive obligations

Traditionally, human rights law was considered as giving rise only to negative obligations—that is, individual freedoms that states must *refrain* from interfering with. However, the recognition of positive obligations—i.e. obligations requiring states to *take* action—has been one of the cornerstones of the Court's success.[21] As Starmer has observed, '[i]n many respects, positive obligations are the hallmark of the European Convention on Human Rights'.[22]

Positive obligations are not explicitly set out in the text of the Convention, which is largely framed in proscriptive, rather than prescriptive, language.[23] Rather, they have been carved out by the Court through purposive interpretation. In doing so, it has intentionally declined to establish a comprehensive account of the scope of positive obligations under the Convention, preferring instead to evaluate these on a case-by-case basis.[24] Nevertheless, there are certain broad principles that can be identified.

First, the doctrine of positive obligations involves a recognition that in order to 'secure' the Convention rights to all individuals within their jurisdictions—as is required under Article 1—it is not enough to refrain from acting, but states must also take certain positive steps to ensure their effective enjoyment. This involves both substantive and procedural obligations, including the obligation to provide effective mechanisms for the prevention, detection, and reporting of abuses of Convention rights, as well as to conduct effective investigations in response to any such allegations.

Second, and most importantly, the Court has used the doctrine of positive obligations to provide the Convention with horizontal effect. The state not only has to refrain from violating individual rights itself, but must also put in place appropriate safeguards to protect individuals from infringement on the part of private actors. This principle is of particular importance for children, as it acts as a limit on the action of parents, teachers, and other individuals who may control their day-to-day lives.[25]

While the drafters of the Convention had no intention of creating such positive obligations—focusing purely on the freedom of the individual from 'fascist and communist inquisitorial practices' and state 'horrors, tyranny and vexation'[26] —the Court has clearly rejected an originalist method of interpretation, opting instead for a purposive approach to ensure the Convention's ongoing efficacy and relevance.

[21] For a comprehensive discussion of the doctrine of positive obligations under the European Convention on Human Rights, see K. Starmer, 'Positive Obligations under the Convention', in J. Lowell and J. Cooper (eds), *Understanding Human Rights Principles* (Oxford: Hart, 2001); L. Lavrysen, *Human Rights in a Positive State: Rethinking the Relationship between Positive and Negative Obligations under the European Convention on Human Rights* (Cambridge: Intersentia, 2017); A.R. Mowbray, *The Development of Positive Obligations under the European Convention on Human Rights by the European Court of Human Rights* (Oxford: Hart, 2004).

[22] K. Starmer, 'Positive Obligations under the Convention', in J. Lowell and J. Cooper (eds), *Understanding Human Rights Principles* (Oxford: Hart, 2001), 159.

[23] With the exception of certain rights in Articles 5 and 6: for example, the right to be informed promptly of the reasons for arrest (Article 5(2)); the right to free legal assistance in criminal proceedings where the interests of justice require (Article 6(3)(c)).

[24] See, for example, *Plattform 'Ärzte für das Leben' v Austria* (10126/82) 21.06.1988.

[25] See, for example, the jurisprudence of the Court in the area of corporal punishment, as discussed in Chapter 2.

[26] *Marckx v Belgium* (6833/74) 13.06.1979, dissenting opinion of Judge Sir Gerald Fitzmaurice.

1.4.2 The Convention as a living instrument

In the 70 years since the drafting of the Convention, Europe—and European society—has seen dramatic changes. Advances in technology, changing demographics, and evolving social norms mean that the Court is having to apply the Convention to an ever-expanding range of situations. To respond to these changes, the Court has adopted a dynamic approach to interpretation that recognises the Convention as a 'living instrument', which must be read in light of present-day conditions.[27]

This means that the Court's interpretation of the Convention will change as law and society progresses, with the recognition that the 'failure ... to maintain a dynamic and evolutive approach would risk rendering it a bar to reform or improvement'.[28] Thus, even where an issue has been decided previously, the Court is willing to reassess its prior judgments in light of domestic and international developments. A notable example of this is the characterisation of same-sex relationships under the Convention—once considered as constituting only 'private life', now recognised as 'family life'.[29] Furthermore, treatment that may have constituted 'inhuman and degrading treatment' in the past might cross the threshold into torture in the future, as increasingly high standards are enforced.[30]

As can be seen throughout this volume, for children this has meant that the Court has shifted from a patriarchal understanding of their place in the family and society to a recognition of their individual rights, updating the Convention in line with newly adopted international standards.

1.4.3 The principle of subsidiarity

Despite these expansive interpretative techniques, which have broadened the scope of the Convention beyond the original intention of the drafters, at the heart of the Convention system lies respect for national sovereignty. This respect manifests itself in two separate but interrelated interpretative principles: the principle of subsidiarity and the margin of appreciation.

The principle of subsidiarity requires that the role of the Court be conceived narrowly, only intervening with state practice where necessary. As evidenced by Article 13 (the right to an effective domestic remedy) and Article 35(1) (exhaustion of domestic remedies), the primary responsibility for implementing and enforcing the Convention is placed on states within their domestic legal system. The Court will intercede only when it has failed in this task.[31]

Moreover, subsidiarity requires the Court to adopt a cautious approach to the adjudication of cases. It does not operate as a tribunal of fourth instance, with jurisdiction

[27] *Tyrer v the United Kingdom* (5856/72) 24.04.1978 (Court).
[28] *Stafford v the United Kingdom* (46295/99) 28.05.2002 (GC), para. 68.
[29] See *Schalk and Kopf v Austria* (30141/04) 24.06.2010.
[30] See *Selmouni v France* (25803/94) 28.07.1999 (GC).
[31] *Scordino v Italy (No. 1)* (36813/97) 29.03.2006 (GC).

to review any errors of law or fact alleged against the domestic judgments,[32] but only has the power to review whether the decision was made 'in disregard of fundamental rights.'[33] In doing so, the Court will not re-try the case: it will not investigate the facts, nor hear witnesses and evidence afresh. Nor will it interfere with the interpretation and application of domestic law. Rather, it will accept the determination of the domestic authorities on these issues, unless there is clear evidence of arbitrariness.[34]

These rules are important for the functioning of the Court—it allows this body to focus on its role as a guarantor of fundamental rights, rather than having to undertake a fresh investigation of the entirety of the case, while also ensuring that it does not overstep the boundaries of the powers delegated to it by states.[35] It also recognises that the role of the Court is not to harmonise European laws, but to set common minimum standards. As Lord Hoffman has argued, 'at the level of abstraction, human rights may be universal', but at the level of application they require 'trade-offs and compromises, exercises of judgment which can be made only in the context of a given society and its legal system'.[36]

1.4.4 The margin of appreciation

A corollary of the principle of subsidiary is the doctrine of the margin of appreciation, which governs the interpretation of the substantive rights of the Convention. This phrase, from the French '*marge d'appréciation*', might be more appropriately translated as 'margin of discretion',[37] and provides leeway to national authorities in how they choose to implement Convention rights according to the particular needs, circumstances, and resources of their state. Underlying this doctrine is the recognition of the cultural, social, and legal variety amongst member states,[38] and the understanding that national authorities should be given a certain degree of latitude when resolving conflicts between individual rights and national interests.[39]

[32] See, for example, *Belgian Linguistic Case* (1474/62, 1677/62, 1691/62, 1769/63, 1994/63, 2126/64) 23.07.1968; *Strand Lobben and others v Norway* (37283/13) 10.09.2019 (GC).

[33] M. Teitgen, 'Report on the Establishment of a Collective Guarantee of Essential Freedoms and Fundamental Rights' (Consultative Assembly of the Council of Europe, 05.09.1949), para. 26.

[34] *Sisojeva and others v Latvia* (60654/00) 15.01.2007.

[35] Jurisconsult of the European Court of Human Rights, 'Interlaken Follow-Up. Principle of Subsidiarity' (2010), http://www.echr.coe.int/Documents/2010_Interlaken_Follow-up_ENG.pdf. This is particularly the case following the Brighton Declaration of the High-Level Conference on the Future of the European Court of Human Rights, and Protocol 15 which resulted from it.

[36] Lord Hoffmann, 'The Universality of Human Rights' (Judicial Studies Board Annual Lecture, 19.03.2009), https://www.judiciary.uk/wp-content/uploads/2014/12/Hoffmann_2009_JSB_Annual_Lecture_Universality_of_Human_Rights.pdf, 9.

[37] Greer suggests this could be translated as 'margin of assessment/appraisal/estimation'. (S. Greer, *The Margin of Appreciation: Interpretation and Discretion under the European Convention on Human Rights* (Strasbourg: Council of Europe, 2000), 5)

[38] See F. Matscher, 'Methods of Interpretation of the Convention' in R.S.J. MacDonald, F. Matscher, and H. Petzold, *The European System for the Protection of Human Rights* (Dordrecht: Kluwer, 1993).

[39] See E. Benvenisti, 'Margin of Appreciation, Consensus, and Universal Standards' (1999) 31 *International Law and Politics* 843. For a critique of this principle, see Chapter 12.

This principle is used primarily (though not exclusively) in relation to complaints arising under Articles 8–11—the so called 'qualified rights'.[40] These rights—to respect for private and family life (Article 8), to freedom of religion (Article 9), to freedom of expression (Article 10), and to freedom of assembly (Article 11)—all contain a limitations clause allowing an interference with the right if it is in accordance with the law, pursues a legitimate aim, and is 'necessary in a democratic society'; that is, where there is a relationship of proportionality between the aim and the interference. It is in determining this relationship of proportionality that the Court allows national authorities room for manoeuvre through the doctrine of the 'margin of appreciation'.

The scope of the margin of appreciation is not identical in each case and cannot be reduced to a simple or predictable scientific formula.[41] Indeed, it has been described by Lord Lester as 'slippery and elusive as an eel'.[42] It will depend on a number of factors, including the nature of the right in issue and the object pursued by the interference.[43] Thus, the margin of appreciation will be narrower where the case concerns an intimate aspect of the individual's existence or identity or is crucial to the effective enjoyment of a 'core' value;[44] however, it will be more extensive where the aim of the restriction relates to the protection of morals or invokes social and economic policies.[45] In such cases, the Court considers that national authorities' knowledge of their society and its needs mean that they are better placed to determine what is in the public interest and to decide whether a measure is indeed necessary in the particular circumstances.[46] The Court will also look at whether a consensus exists within the contracting states, either as to the relative importance of the interest at stake or regarding how best to protect it.[47]

The result of this is that the margin of appreciation is an amorphous concept: as Greer has argued, 'its most striking characteristic remains its casuistic, uneven, and largely unpredictable nature'.[48] As is seen throughout this volume, the margin of appreciation often comes into play in areas concerning children and the family, where a large degree of discretion is given to states in the formulation of social policy. This can have its advantages, particularly in securing the ongoing legitimacy of the Court, but it can also have significant drawbacks for a progressive interpretation of children's rights, as is discussed in the substantive chapters.

[40] See J. Kratochvil, 'The Inflation of the Margin of Appreciation by the European Court of Human Rights' (2011) 29(3) *Netherlands Quarterly of Human Rights* 324.

[41] S. Greer, *The Margin of Appreciation: Interpretation and Discretion under the European Convention on Human Rights* (Strasbourg: Council of Europe, 2000), 5.

[42] A. Lester, 'Universality versus Subsidiarity: A Reply' (1998) 1 *European Human Rights Law Review* 73, 75.

[43] See *Dudgeon v the United Kingdom* (7525/76) 22.10.1981.

[44] See ibid.; *S and Marper v the United Kingdom* (30562/04, 30566/04) 04.12.2008 (GC).

[45] *Handyside v the United Kingdom* (5493/72) 07.12.1976; *Buckley v the United Kingdom* (20348/92) 25.09.1996.

[46] *Handyside v the United Kingdom* (5493/72) 07.12.1976; *Dickson v the United Kingdom* (44362/04) 04.12.2007 (GC).

[47] See, for example, *Dickson v the United Kingdom* (44362/04) 04.12.2007 (GC).

[48] S. Greer, *The Margin of Appreciation: Interpretation and Discretion under the European Convention on Human Rights* (Strasbourg: Council of Europe, 2000), 5.

1.5 The use of international instruments

International instruments play an important role in the interpretation of the Convention. In accordance with Article 31 of the Vienna Convention on the Law of Treaties, the Court has held that

> in defining the meaning of terms and notions in the text of the convention, [the Court] can and must take into account elements of international law other than the Convention, the interpretation of such elements by competent organs, and the practice of European States reflecting their common values.[49]

The United Nations Convention on the Rights of the Child[50] has been particularly influential in this regard, recognised by the Court as constituting 'the standards to which all governments must aspire in realising ... rights for all children'.[51] Moreover, the Court has also referred frequently, if not consistently, to other regional and international instruments such as the Hague Conventions on Child Abduction and on Intercountry Adoption,[52] and the European Social Charter,[53] which have thus played a crucial role in its jurisprudence. Importantly, however, the Court has held that it is not necessary for the state in question to have ratified all the international instruments being referred to by the Court,[54] but only that the instruments 'denote a continuous evolution in the norms and principles applied in international law'[55] and that there is common ground in modern societies. In undertaking an analysis of the Court's protection and advancement of children's rights, this book also refers to these applicable standards, examining where they have been noted, affirmed, rejected, or simply ignored by the Court.

1.6 Structure of the book

As stated in the introduction to this chapter, the aim of this book is to provide an overview of the case law of the Court in relation to children. For reasons of space, I do not undertake an extensive analysis of every case that has come before the Court in this area—instead, I attempt to draw out the main threads of the jurisprudence, showing the evolution of the Court's position throughout time and explaining and critiquing its current position. In doing so, I have tried to walk a fine line between breadth of coverage and depth of analysis. I wanted this book to be as comprehensive as possible, so

49 *Demir and Baykara v Turkey* (34503/97) 12.11.2008, para. 85.
50 (1989) 1577 UNTS 3.
51 *Sahin v Germany* (30943/96) 08.07.2003 (GC), para. 39.
52 Hague Convention on the Civil Aspects of International Child Abduction 1980, Hague Convention on the Protection of Children and Co-operation in Respect of Intercountry Adoption 1993.
53 European Social Charter (revised) (1996) CETS 163.
54 For example, in *Marckx v Belgium* (6833/74) 13.06.1979, the Court relied on the European Convention on Legal Status of Children Born out of Wedlock as evidence of emerging consensus, despite the fact that Belgium had not signed or ratified it.
55 *Demir and Baykara* (34503/97) 12.11.2008, para. 86.

that academics, practitioners, and civil society could understand at a glance what the Court has—or has not—said on a topic. At the same time, I did not wish this to be a purely descriptive volume, and have tried to highlight for readers some of the key criticisms that have been levelled at the various cases or lines of jurisprudence.

The book comprises ten substantive chapters, and is organised thematically, rather than by Convention article. Not all issues fall neatly into one section, however, and there is inevitable overlap, particularly where a case has been examined from a number of different perspectives. Nevertheless, I have tried to provide a coherent and logical categorisation of the jurisprudence in a way which will be useful for all readers, whatever their aim in consulting this text.

Following this introductory chapter, Chapter 2 goes on to examine the child's right to freedom from violence and exploitation, including protection from corporal punishment, child abuse, and sexual violence, as well as child marriage, forced labour, and modern slavery. Chapter 3 then analyses the right to respect for private life in the context of privacy, the right to receive information, and the right to individual identity.

Chapter 4 considers the rights of the child in relation to the juvenile justice system, and Chapter 5 the immigration system, including deportation and expulsion, family reunification, and the detention of accompanied and unaccompanied minors. Chapter 6 then examines the jurisprudence in the area of education, and in particular the form and content of schooling, as well as school uniform and religious symbols, followed by an analysis of the Court's approach to social and economic rights in Chapter 7.

The final four substantive chapters relate to the child within the family unit: family life and the establishment of parenthood (Chapter 8); disputes concerning custody and access (Chapter 9); child protection (Chapter 10); and adoption (Chapter 11). Finally, Chapter 12 presents some conclusions of this analysis, highlighting the fields where the Court has made significant advances for children's rights and areas where there remains work to be done.

1.6.1 A note on language

Throughout the book, I refer collectively to the position or jurisprudence of the 'Court' generally to include that of both the European Court of Human Rights and the previous European Commission on Human Rights. However, when discussing individual cases, I make a distinction between the decisions of the Commission and judgments of the Court.

In addition, there are a number of jurisdictions which have changed names, or even formed new countries, during the life of the Convention—notably the Federal Republic of Germany joining with Eastern Germany to become the new country of 'Germany' and the Former Yugoslav Republic of Macedonia ('FYROM') being renamed North Macedonia in 2019. For reasons of consistency and ease of reference, I refer to these jurisdictions by the name they held at the time the case came before the Court.

2
Freedom from Violence and Exploitation

2.1 Introduction

The right of the child to physical integrity is a right that is slowly but surely gaining recognition. While the protection of adults from interpersonal violence is enforced in all societies,[1] when it comes to children, this protection is still a work in progress. Until recently, violence against children was permitted not only by parents, but by teachers and the state for the purposes of discipline, and it still remains socially (and legally) acceptable in many jurisdictions.[2] Moreover, it is only in recent decades that child abuse and mistreatment—both inside and outside the home—has been recognised as a legal, rather than purely social problem.

The jurisprudence of the European Court of Human Rights is also undergoing a gradual, yet encouraging evolution in its approach to the protection of children's physical integrity. It has been recognised as a core element of the child's private life under Article 8, and depending on its severity, an infringement of the prohibition against inhuman and degrading treatment and punishment under Article 3. Moreover, the Court has started to take a child-centred approach to sexual violence, recognising children's vulnerability and the need for enhanced protection. Nevertheless, there is still some way to go before the Convention can be said to truly provide adequate protection for children against all forms of violence, and in all settings.

Cases on physical integrity—and particularly the failure to protect from parental abuse—often overlap with the area of child protection, which is covered in Chapter 10. The reason for providing these cases with their own individual chapter here, and not simply incorporating them into the later chapter, is that the jurisprudence on state responsibility with regard to parental abuse overlaps significantly with issues relating to protection from violence outside the home. Given the approach of the Court to these areas, to separate the cases of violence and abuse involving third parties from cases concerning such practices in a familial setting would be an artificial, and indeed confusing, divide. As such, this chapter considers the issues of corporal punishment, parental child abuse, and sexual violence together, examining the positive and negative obligations placed on states by the Court's growing body of jurisprudence in this area.

[1] Albeit to a greater or lesser extent.
[2] See Global Initiative to End All Corporal Punishment of Children, https://endcorporalpunishment.org.

Children and the European Court of Human Rights. Claire Fenton-Glynn, Oxford University Press (2021). © Claire Fenton-Glynn.
DOI: 10.1093/oso/9780198787518.003.0002

2.2 Corporal punishment

Corporal punishment—which includes any punishment in which physical force is used and intended to cause pain or discomfort to a child—has been recognised by the UN Committee on the Rights of the Child as a violation of human dignity, physical integrity, and children's equal protection before the law.[3] From the early 1990s, the UN Committee has taken a strong stance against this practice, reading into the United Nations Convention on the Rights of the Child an obligation on all states to implement an immediate and complete prohibition, with no exceptions.[4]

The jurisprudence of the European Court of Human Rights in this area has been more equivocal, resting as it does on a margin of appreciation and consensus amongst member states. At the time the Convention was drafted, corporal punishment was legal in all states of the Council of Europe; however, in 1966 Sweden became the first country in the world to prohibit it in all settings, which has since been followed by 33 other European states.[5] It has thus been an important test case for an evolutionary reading of the Convention—starting with *Tyrer v the United Kingdom*.[6]

2.2.1 Judicial corporal punishment

Tyrer concerned a 15-year-old boy sentenced by a juvenile court to 'three strokes of the birch'. The birching raised, but did not cut, his skin, and he was sore for about a week-and-a-half afterwards. The child alleged that this punishment was 'inhuman and degrading', in violation of Article 3 of the Convention.

This was a landmark case from a procedural perspective, as it established the 'living instrument' doctrine, requiring that the Convention be interpreted in a dynamic manner.[7] The Court rejected the originalist argument of the government: that the Convention was intended to protect only such rights as had been 'long accepted by democratic countries', and therefore could not confer a right to immunity from corporal punishment, which had been widely practised at the time of drafting. Instead, it emphasised that the Convention 'must be interpreted in the light of present-day conditions', and the Court's judgment 'influenced by the developments and commonly accepted standards ... of the member States of the Council of Europe in this field'.[8]

While this doctrine has obvious implications for the protection of all individuals under the Convention, it is of particular importance for children. Given their almost complete subjugation within the family unit in the 1950s, an originalist interpretation

[3] United Nations Committee on the Rights of the Child, *General Comment No. 8 (2006): The right of the child to protection from corporal punishment and other cruel or degrading forms of punishment* (CRC/C/GC/8, 02.03.2007).

[4] ibid.

[5] Global Initiative to End All Corporal Punishment of Children, 'Progress Towards Prohibiting All Corporal Punishment in Europe and Central Asia' (January 2020), http://endcorporalpunishment.org/wp-content/uploads/legality-tables/Europe-and-Central-Asia-progress-table-commitment.pdf.

[6] (5856/72) 25.04.1978 (Court).

[7] See Chapter 1.

[8] *Tyrer v the United Kingdom* (5856/72) 25.04.1978 (Court), para. 31.

would have severely restricted the Convention's ability to respond to violations of children's rights, limiting its reach to the public sphere only. As such, this case must be recognised as one of the most significant judgments of the Court's 60-year history.

From a substantive perspective, the judgment was a somewhat pyrrhic victory for children. On the one hand, it recognised that judicial corporal punishment is inherently degrading: it involves the infliction of institutionalised physical violence, where one human being is treated as an object in the power of the authorities. As such, it constitutes an assault on the dignity and physical integrity of the individual, which goes to the heart of the protection of Article 3. Moreover, this degradation could not be militated by assumptions concerning its 'efficacy'. The Court made clear that just because a punishment is, or is perceived to be, 'effective' does not remove it from the scope of Article 3, finding 'it is never permissible to have recourse to punishments that are contrary to Article 3, whatever their deterrent effect may be'.[9]

However, this judgment was based on a generalised discussion of the impact of such treatment: the majority did not discuss the fact that the applicant was a juvenile, nor the implications that this had for its severity. The focus was on the abuse of power by the state, rather than the vulnerability of the individual, which had the (perhaps intended) effect of narrowing the applicability of the judgment to only state punishment, leaving corporal punishment in schools and in the home untouched.[10] Thus, the debate surrounding corporal punishment in these settings continued before the Court for another 30 years—and even now is not finally settled.

2.2.2 Corporal punishment in schools

The issue of corporal punishment in schools has been considered in a line of four cases emanating (again) from the United Kingdom. In three of the four cases, the applicants were successful on the facts, but none managed to achieve a universal ban on corporal punishment in this setting. Instead, the nature, extent, and circumstances of the punishment have simply been progressively narrowed through incremental litigation, while waiting for politics to catch up with new understandings of children's rights.

The first case was *Campbell and Cosans v the United Kingdom*,[11] in which the parents had requested a guarantee that their children would not be subjected to corporal punishment as a disciplinary measure in the state schools they attended. As neither child had been subjected to corporal punishment, there was no violation of Article 3.[12] The

[9] ibid.

[10] cf. the dissenting opinion of Judge Sir Gerald Fitzmaurice, who did focus on the applicant's age—finding, however, that this was a mitigating, rather than an aggravating, factor. He noted that, 'throughout the ages and under all skies, corporal methods have been seen as the obvious and natural way of dealing with juvenile misbehaviour', and 'assuming that corporal punishment does involve some degree of degradation, it has never been seen as doing so for a juvenile to anything approaching the same manner or extent as for an adult'. Relying on a familiar trope, he described his own education, where corporal punishment was regarded as the normal sanction for misbehaviour, and viewed as a matter of 'pride and congratulation' rather than debasement. See also the dissenting opinion of Mr Kevin Mangan in the Commission Report. ((5856/72) 14.12.1976 (ComRep))

[11] (7511/76, 7743/76) 25.02.1982.

[12] The Court also considered whether the threat would be sufficient, but found in this case that it would not.

Court therefore shifted away from an analysis of the children's rights, and considered the matter under the parents' right to have their children educated in line with their philosophical convictions, under Article 2, Protocol 1.[13] The Court found that an objection to corporal punishment could constitute a 'philosophical conviction' as it related to a weighty and substantial aspect of human life and behaviour, specifically the integrity of the person and the distress which the risk of such punishment entails. The authorities have a duty to respect these convictions, and must allow parents to object to corporal punishment by the school.[14] In this way, this case provided protection for parents from state interference with their philosophical beliefs, but provided no independent protection for children from physical violence.

The second case of *Warwick v United Kingdom*[15] went one step further. Here, a 16-year-old had been given one stroke of the cane by the headmaster, in the presence of the deputy head, which caused large bruises on her hand. In this case, the Court distinguished institutional violence by the state—as prohibited in all circumstances following *Tyrer*—from violence by individual school authorities, which must be decided on a case-by-case basis. On a positive note, the Court looked at the particular circumstances of the applicant—inflicted on a young woman by a man, in the presence of another man. Unfortunately, however, rather than noting that the girl was a minor, the Court based its finding of humiliation on the fact that at 16 the girl was 'a woman of marriageable age', therefore reducing her to a sexual object whose humiliation must be traced back to her desirability to the opposite sex. Nevertheless, this case was an important landmark as it recognised that corporal punishment at school could, in certain circumstances, violate Article 3.[16]

Third, in *Y v the United Kingdom*[17] a 15-year-old boy was caned at school, causing wheals to appear, as well as swelling and bruising. The Commission found that such injuries were unacceptable no matter who inflicted the punishment—be that parent or teacher—and thus there was a violation of Article 3. This created an important precedent on the limits of adult power over children, even if inflicted for disciplinary purposes, but still fell short of achieving a total prohibition of corporal punishment in schools: it depended on the seriousness of the violence, rather than the characterisation of the child as a human being deserving of protection of physical integrity. The fact that the case was decided under Article 3 was positive as it recognised the seriousness of the conduct, but it nevertheless meant that the Court failed to grapple with the deeper issue of whether adults should be permitted to exercise physical power over children in *any* circumstances.

[13] Although the Court considered the applicant Cosans's own claim that he had been denied the right to education because he was suspended until he accepted punishment, the Court held that return to school could only be secured if his parents acted contrary to their convictions, thus bringing the matter back within an adult-focused lens.

[14] This aspect of the case is discussed further in Chapter 6.

[15] (9471/81) 18.07.1986 (ComRep).

[16] Though see the partially dissenting opinion of Messrs Schermes, Batliner, Vandenberghe, and Sir Basil Hall, where it was argued that the school was acting 'in loco parentis' and therefore had not violated the child's rights.

[17] (14229/88) 08.10.1991 (ComRep).

It wasn't until the final case in this line—*Costello-Roberts v the United Kingdom*[18]—that the Court was in fact forced to confront this issue head on, with disappointing results. This case involved a seven-year-old child given three 'whacks' on his bottom by a teacher, through his shorts and with a rubber-soled gym shoe. There was no visible bruising, as the physical force was moderate, but instead the case was brought on the fact that there had been an assault on the child's dignity and physical integrity. That is, the applicants argued that it was irrelevant whether there was any physical harm to the child; the very fact of violence inflicted by an adult was a violation of his rights.

The Commission accepted this argument, finding that corporal punishment constitutes an interference with physical integrity, and a lack of respect for private life under Article 8(1). While parents could give consent to corporal punishment, thus removing the practice from Article 8, the scope of consent could not be unlimited, and the state was under an obligation to provide safeguards. Turning to Article 8(2), the government was not able to give any social, educational, health, or moral justification, and thus the Commission held that there was a violation of the Convention.

On referral to the Court, however, the majority fell back on a requirement of a minimum level of severity to invoke the protection of the Convention, and the comprehensive protection given to children by the Commission was overturned. The Court found that as there was no evidence of severe or long-lasting effects, the punishment did not pass the minimum threshold to fall within the scope of Article 3. Moreover, although it acknowledged that there was an interference with the moral and physical integrity of the child, there were not sufficient adverse effects to bring it within the scope of Article 8.

The dissent of Mr Loucaides in the Commission judgment is notable for progressive understanding of children's rights, and worth quoting at length:

> In principle I believe that any school corporal punishment amounts to a breach of Art 3 bearing in mind present day values regarding human dignity and human personality. Corporal punishment is nothing less than a deliberate assault on a person's dignity and physical integrity in an organised manner. Beating any person as a method of punishment for whatever wrong doing on his part, be that a criminal offence or otherwise, is nowadays generally an unacceptable form of punishment and it amounts, in my view, to inhuman and degrading treatment. This is all the more so when such punishment is applied to children by adults in authority like in the present case. The inferior and helpless position of children in such circumstances, as well as their sensitivity, aggravates the inhuman and degrading elements of this kind of punishment. The number, intensity or hardness of the strokes, or the fact that they do or do not cause physical injuries are, in my view, immaterial factors in determining whether corporal punishment amounts to inhuman and degrading treatment.[19]

Despite these strong words, almost 30 years on from *Costello-Roberts* the Court has still not found that corporal punishment in schools is, absolutely and without

[18] (13134/87) 25.03.1993 (Court).
[19] (13134/87) 08.10.1991 (ComRep).

exception, contrary to children's rights under the Convention—although prohibition has now been achieved across Europe in this setting in any case. While it is laudable that the jurisprudence has evolved with time to provide greater protection in this field, the focus on the physical effects of the treatment, rather than the right to physical integrity, exposes a weakness in the Court's understanding of children's rights.

2.2.3 Corporal punishment in the home

As with corporal punishment in schools, the Court's jurisprudence on corporal punishment within the home is imperfect. While it has upheld the prerogative of states to prohibit corporal punishment, and to remove children from the home where this occurs, where a child has complained of a violation of their physical integrity the Court has failed to take a robust approach. Instead, it has only stopped violence from going 'too far', leaving the infliction of corporal punishment as a permissible practice—at least in so far as it does not reach the levels of Article 3.

Importantly, two of the key cases in this area have been brought by parents who wished to continue to practice corporal punishment, against the restrictions placed by the state. In *7 Individuals v Sweden*,[20] the Swedish government had introduced a clause in the Code on Parenthood stating that 'the child shall not be subjected to corporal punishment or any other form of humiliating treatment'. This was not accompanied by any criminal sanctions, nor were there any other legal implications for the family. The applicant parents argued that this interfered with their rights under Article 2, Protocol 1, as they practised a 'traditional' means of bringing up their children, and as an aspect of their religious doctrine, believed in the necessity of physical punishment.

The Commission examined the case from an adult-focused perspective, stating that the evaluation 'must start from the premise that parental rights and choices in the upbringing and education of their children are paramount as against the state'.[21] However, they concluded that this right was not infringed upon, as the applicants had not been directly subjected to any enforcement or other procedure arising from their disagreement with the Code. Furthermore, the Commission noted 'that the actual effects of the law [were] to encourage a positive review of the punishment of children by their parents, to discourage abuse and prevent excesses which could properly be described as violence against children'.[22]

On a positive note, the Commission also rejected the argument that a violation arose as the law gave parents no greater immunity from criminal sanction in inflicting physical chastisement on their own children than they would have if the same acts were committed on an adult stranger. The Commission found that there was no interference with the right to respect for private and family life in this respect, noting that the Swedish law of assault and molestation was a normal measure for the control of violence. Its extension to apply to the physical chastisement of children by their parents was simply intended to protect potentially weak and vulnerable members of society.

[20] (8811/79) 13.05.1982 (dec.).
[21] ibid., para. 111.
[22] ibid., para. 113.

The Court returned to this issue—albeit in a slightly different context—in the recent case of *Tlapak and others v Germany*.[23] In this case, the applicants *had* been directly subjected to legal proceedings: their children were removed into state care, and their parental authority removed, based on their use of physical punishment (caning and physical restraint). The parents complained that the decision to withdraw their parental authority was disproportionate, and a violation of their right to raise their children in compliance with their religious beliefs.

The Court in this case spoke out strongly against corporal punishment. Noting that the UN Committee on the Rights of the Child has stated clearly that 'all forms of violence against children, however light, are unacceptable',[24] the Court considered it 'commendable' if states prohibited in law all forms of corporal punishment of children. In doing so, it described corporal punishment as 'a form of institutionalised violence against minors', and endorsed the children's removal as being based on a risk of inhuman or degrading treatment, as prohibited by Article 3.

While these were strong statements from the Court, the protection that this case provides for children's rights is limited. It affirmed that the Convention *permits* state interference with parental authority on this basis, but does not *require* it, leaving children at the continued mercy of domestic decision-making in this respect. Moreover, when the Court has been asked to consider an application brought by a child who had been subjected to corporal punishment, the protection provided by the Court has still fallen short of absolute prohibition.

A v the United Kingdom[25] was a challenge to the English law allowing a defence of 'reasonable chastisement' to a charge of assault. The child in question had been beaten by his stepfather with a garden cane with 'considerable force', leaving bruises that were deemed sufficiently serious by the authorities to merit the initiation of criminal proceedings. Nevertheless, the stepfather was acquitted, with the judge stating that 'it is a perfectly good defence that the alleged assault was merely the correcting of a child by its parent ... provided that the correction be moderate in the manner, the instrument and the quantity of it'.[26]

The Court considered that the treatment suffered by the boy at the hands of his stepfather reached the level of severity prohibited by Article 3, and in permitting such treatment under domestic law, the authorities had failed to provide adequate protection for the child's rights. Having dealt with the issue under Article 3, the Court did not consider it necessary to discuss the applicability of Article 8. And this is where the case does not go far enough. While it established that children must be protected from corporal punishment which reaches the level of torture, or inhuman or degrading treatment or punishment, it left unclear whether corporal punishment that does not meet this standard is nevertheless contrary to the Convention. The Commission—which had also found a violation under Article 3—went so far as to emphasise in the final paragraph of its judgment that its finding 'does not mean that Article 3 is to be

23 (11308/16, 11344/16) 22.03.2018.
24 ibid., para. 86.
25 (25599/94) 23.09.1998 (Court).
26 ibid., para. 10.

interpreted as imposing an obligation on States to protect, through their criminal law, against any form of physical rebuke, however mild, by a parent of a child'.[27]

This finding overlooks the fact that any corporal punishment inflicted by an adult on a child is inherently degrading. As Judge Loucaides pointed out so early in the jurisprudence, it is its nature, not its severity, which infringes the child's rights. But it was not until 2017, in the case of *DMD v Romania*,[28] that the Court finally accepted this, bringing the Convention in line with international standards:

> It is also to be noted that the overriding concern in the 1989 United Nations Convention on the Rights of the Child is dignity. Such a value is consistent with both evolving international law on human rights and the developing psychological perspective in jurisprudence. Respect for the dignity of children is consonant with provision of those elements important to their growth as full members of the community. Assuring basic dignity to the child means that there can be no compromise in condemning violence against children, whether accepted as 'tradition' or disguised as 'discipline'. Children's uniqueness—their potential and vulnerability, their dependence on adults—makes it imperative that they have more, not less, protection from violence, including from domestic corporal punishment, the latter being invariably degrading. It is thus clear that respect for children's dignity cannot be ensured if the domestic courts were to accept any form of justification of acts of ill-treatment, including corporal punishment, prohibited under Article 3.
>
> It is thus clear that respect for children's dignity cannot be ensured if the domestic courts were to accept any form of justification of acts of ill-treatment, including corporal punishment, prohibited under Article 3. In this context, the Court considers that Member States should strive to expressly and comprehensively protect children's dignity which in turn requires in practice an adequate legal framework affording protection of children against domestic violence falling within the scope of Article 3, including a) effective deterrence against such serious breaches of personal integrity, b) reasonable steps to prevent ill-treatment of which the authorities had, or ought to have had, knowledge, and c) effective official investigations where an individual raises an arguable claim of ill-treatment.[29]

This firmly places *any* form of corporal punishment as contrary to Article 3, as a violation of physical integrity, and thus basic human dignity. In addition, the Court criticised the decisions of the lower domestic courts for the finding that 'isolated and random' acts of violence could be tolerated within the family, making clear that this was not compatible with the Convention.[30]

However, as Judges de Gaetano, Pinto de Albuquerque, and Motoc suggested in their joint concurring opinion, the obligation placed on member states in this respect was rather weak. They argued that the Court

[27] *A v the United Kingdom* (25599/94) 18.09.1997 (ComRep), para. 55.
[28] (23022/13) 03.10.2017.
[29] ibid., paras. 50–51 (citations omitted).
[30] See also *OCI and others v Romania* (49450/17) 21.05.2019 discussed in Chapter 9.

> should have stated, in more principled and clearer terms, that member States of the Council of Europe have a positive obligation under the European Convention on Human Rights to prohibit all forms of violence against children in all settings, and to effectively investigate, prosecute and punish those responsible for such violence.[31]

For these judges, the expression 'should strive' used by the majority did not adequately reflect states' obligations, which must be held to a higher standard in light of current understandings of children's rights.

Moreover, when the Court considered *Tlapak* the following year, it described the prohibition of corporal punishment by states merely as 'commendable', rather than as a requirement under Article 3. This leads us to question whether the Court remains somewhat hesitant to take a strong and principled stand against corporal punishment, particularly in light of social practices still prevalent in many member states. As such, while *DMD* brings hope of a new era of child rights jurisprudence under the Convention, it remains two steps forward, one step back.[32]

2.3 Protection of children from parental abuse

In Chapter 10, the jurisprudence of the Court regarding the obligations on states when removing children from their families is discussed in detail. However, this section examines the converse of these obligations—the positive duty to act to protect children from abuse where they know, or ought to know, it is occurring.

As minors, children fall within the group of 'vulnerable individuals' entitled to especial state protection.[33] This protection extends beyond the physical to sexual and psychological abuse also, and like corporal punishment, may fall within the scope of Article 8 (right to respect for private life) or Article 3 (freedom from inhuman or degrading treatment), depending on its severity.

The threshold to trigger Article 8 is quite low—all that is required is interference with physical or psychological integrity, which is clearly the case in situations of child abuse.[34] Article 3, however, requires a higher degree of severity. In relation to physical abuse, the applicant will have to show that the treatment is inhuman or degrading either because of its severity (severe or long-lasting effects)[35] or the circumstances in which it was inflicted (institutionalised violence, or causing humiliation or debasement of the individual).[36] Sexual abuse, on the other hand, is more firmly entrenched as a violation of Article 3, and the Court has rightly accepted, without further examination, that this falls within the protection against inhuman or degrading treatment.[37]

[31] ibid., joint concurring opinion of Judges de Gaetano, Pinto de Albuquerque, and Motoc, para. 5.
[32] On this point, see C. O'Mahony, 'Is Time Running Out for Corporal Punishment under the ECHR?' (2019) 24(1) EHRLR 55.
[33] *A v the United Kingdom* (25599/94) 23.09.1998 (Court).
[34] Although see *Costello-Roberts v the United Kingdom* (13134/87) 25.03.1993 (Court).
[35] ibid.
[36] *Tyrer v the United Kingdom* (5856/72) 25.04.1978 (Court); *Warwick v the United Kingdom* (9471/81) 18.07.1986 (ComRep).
[37] *DP and JC v the United Kingdom* (38719/97) 10.10.2002; *E and others v the United Kingdom* (33218/96) 26.11.2002; *MC v Bulgaria* (39272/98) 04.12.2003.

The most difficult of all are allegations of psychological abuse, where the question asked by the Court is whether the treatment causes its victims feelings of fear, anguish, or inferiority, or if it humiliates or debases them.[38] In determining the severity of the interference, the effects of the abuse—of whatever kind—will not be taken in isolation, but instead viewed cumulatively, to evaluate the totality of the situation. The Court will take into account all the circumstances of the case, including the nature and context of the treatment; its duration; its physical and mental effects; and the sex, age, and state of health of the victim.[39]

2.3.1 The positive obligation to protect against harm

The landmark case which established the positive duty on the state in relation to child abuse was *Z v the United Kingdom*,[40] brought by four children who had suffered severe neglect at the hands of their parents. Health professionals, teachers, and neighbours all expressed concerns to the authorities over a period of several years, and when visiting the house, police had reported that the conditions were 'not fit for [the] children to live in'. Even the mother herself had informed social services that the children would be better off living in care. Despite this, the authorities initially concluded that as the parents were not wilfully neglecting their children—and were indeed doing the best they could—the children should remain within the family. It was not until some time, and many complaints, later that the children were eventually removed, by which time they had suffered many years of severe neglect.

Before the Commission, they argued, inter alia, that the state was responsible for the inhuman and degrading treatment they had suffered at the hands of their parents, as the authorities had known that it was occurring, but had failed to act. The Commission accepted this argument, finding that the state has a positive obligation to protect children from abuse and neglect, not just from strangers, but also from parents. Relying on Article 19 of the UN Convention on the Rights of the Child, and the obligation to take all appropriate measures 'to protect the child from all forms of physical and mental violence, injury or abuse', the Commission concluded:

> [T]he protection of children who by reason of their age and vulnerability are not capable of protecting themselves requires not merely that the criminal law provides protection against Article 3 treatment but that, additionally, this provision will in appropriate circumstances imply a positive obligation on the authorities to take preventive measures to protect a child who is at risk from another individual.[41]

As such, the Commission concluded that the state had a duty 'to take those steps that could be reasonably expected of them to avoid a real and immediate risk of ill-treatment

[38] *M and M v Croatia* (10161/13) 03.09.2015.
[39] *Ireland v the United Kingdom* (5310/71) 18.01.1978 (GC).
[40] (29392/95) 10.05.2001 (GC).
[41] *Z v the United Kingdom* (29392/95) 10.09.1999 (ComRep), para. 93 (citations omitted). This does not necessarily mean removing the child from the home—in some circumstances, it may oblige the state to remove the perpetrator: see, for example, *ES and others v Slovakia* (8227/04) 15.09.2009.

contrary to Article 3 of which they knew or ought to have had knowledge'.[42] While the authorities were initially justified in taking steps to maintain the family unit by giving support to the family, the Commission found that the gravity of the circumstances required that effective steps be taken to safeguard the children's welfare when the situation failed to show 'a significant and reasonably timeous improvement'.[43]

This case was a watershed moment for children's rights, substantially extending the obligations on states in this area. While previously the Convention had only required that the state impose appropriate penalties on parents who breach the Article 3 rights of the child,[44] *Z* now extended this to a duty to prevent abuse happening in the first place—at least where they knew, or ought to have known, about it.[45]

2.3.2 Constructive knowledge and causation

When determining the extent of the state's liability in this respect, the Court has been careful not to place too great a burden on the authorities. This is obviously a difficult balance to strike—authorities are at risk of violating the children's (and parents' rights) by removing the children from the home too early, but likewise are liable if they are left in the home too long. The Court has acknowledged the 'difficult and sensitive' decisions facing authorities in this area, and will not impose this duty lightly.[46]

This was seen in the case of *DP and JC v the United Kingdom*,[47] where the social services were heavily involved with a family for many years concerning a multitude of issues, including chronic financial problems, housing problems, family violence, one of the applicants soiling himself on a regular basis, and concerns about truanting. However, during this time, they failed to identify that sexual abuse was ongoing within the household. Based on the case of *Z*, the applicants complained that the authorities should have identified this, and acted to protect the children.

The Court took a cautious approach to this case. It noted that, unlike *Z*, there were no facts that revealed a clear pattern of victimisation or abuse, or which should have led social services to suspect a deeper, more insidious problem in the family. Because the mother had covered for the father, and the children were silent

[42] *Z v the United Kingdom* (29392/95) 10.09.1999 (ComRep), para. 94 (citations omitted).

[43] ibid., para. 97. The finding on Article 3 was not contested before the Grand Chamber, which focused on Articles 6 and 13: see section 2.3.4 below.

[44] See *A v the United Kingdom* (25599/94) 23.09.1998 (Court).

[45] Having said this, the Court has acknowledged that there are limits to the measures they can take to protect children, especially if they do not desire assistance. In *Ivison v the United Kingdom* (39030/97) 16.04.2002 (dec.), a mother expressed concern that her daughter was involved in sexual relationships with two men who had criminal records. The authorities had worked with the girl to emphasise the risks regarding her behaviour, but the police were unable to bring criminal proceedings against the men as she was not prepared to cooperate with any prosecution. At age 17 she began working as a prostitute on the instruction of the men, and was subsequently killed by a client. The Court dismissed the mother's complaint under Article 2 as manifestly unfounded, emphasising, inter alia, the limits of the measures the state could take in relation to a teenage child: 'Though she was under age and thus vulnerable, this did not give the authorities carte blanche with regard to coercive or more draconian care measures. Considerations of her own individual autonomy cannot be excluded'. (para. 4)

[46] See, for example, *VC v Italy* (54227/14) 01.02.2018.

[47] (38719/97) 10.10.2002.

despite constant contact with professionals, there were no grounds upon which constructive knowledge could be imposed on the authorities. Importantly, the Court emphasised that any obligation to protect the child from abuse must be balanced against the countervailing principle of respecting and preserving family life. Taking the 'draconian' step of permanently removing the children from the family would have required convincing reasons, which were not apparent at the time.

This can be contrasted with the case of *E and others v the United Kingdom*,[48] where the mother's partner was found guilty of sexual assault of her daughters, but spared prison on the condition that he move out of the family home. Despite this, he continued to live there, and committed further sexual assaults. In this case, the Court found that the social services had failed in their duties towards the children: even if they were not aware that he was inflicting abuse at the time, they were under an obligation to monitor an offender's conduct, and should have been aware that the children remained at potential risk. In this way, the authorities had failed to take steps which would have enabled them to discover the exact extent of the problem, and to potentially prevent further abuse taking place.

E and others v the United Kingdom also importantly discussed the issue of causation in attributing liability to the authorities. The government had argued that it had not been shown that the situation would have been any different if they had fulfilled their duty—they would not necessarily have either uncovered the abuse or prevented it. The Court, however, found that Article 3 does not require it to be shown that 'but for' the failing or omission the ill-treatment would not have happened: 'A failure to take reasonably available measures which could have had a real prospect of altering the outcome or mitigating the harm is sufficient to engage the responsibility of the State.'[49]

2.3.3 Investigation and prosecution

The obligation of states under Article 3 relates not simply to the prevention of abuse, where possible, but also to the adequate investigation of allegations of ill-treatment. The Convention itself does not contain an express provision requiring a 'prompt and impartial' investigation, as can be found in Article 12 of the UN Convention against Torture;[50] however, the Court has emphasised that such a requirement is implicit in the notion of an 'effective remedy' under Article 13 of the European Convention on Human Rights, and the positive obligations under Article 3.[51]

To trigger the procedural obligation under Article 3, the abuse does not have to be proven to have occurred: it is sufficient that there is an allegation of *possible* ill-treatment, the severity of which, if proven, would violate Article 3.[52] The relevant

[48] (33218/96) 26.11.2002.
[49] ibid., para. 99.
[50] (1984) 1465 UNTS 85.
[51] *Aydin v Turkey* (23178/94) 25.09.1997 (GC).
[52] *MP and others v Bulgaria* (22457/08) 15.11.2011.

threshold that has been given by the Court is that the allegations be 'credible',[53] 'arguable',[54] or 'raise a reasonable suspicion'.[55]

Once the obligation is triggered, domestic authorities must undertake a speedy and effective investigation. The investigation must be independent, impartial, and subject to public scrutiny, and it must be undertaken promptly, and with reasonable expedition.[56] It must be capable of leading to the establishment of the facts of the case, and to the identification and punishment of those responsible.[57]

The obligation on states in this respect is not one of results, but of means:[58] an investigation is judged by the procedure undertaken, not the outcome achieved. To be deemed 'effective', the conclusion reached by the authorities does not have to accord with the claimant's account of events, nor is there any right to obtain the prosecution or conviction of any particular person.[59] When investigating allegations of child abuse, the Court has recognised that the ascertainment of the truth can be particularly difficult: the accusations often concern situations occurring behind closed doors, and the authorities may be presented with two irreconcilable versions of the facts and inconclusive evidence.[60] This is compounded by the fact that where victims are young children, their testimony must be treated with caution, on account of their age and understanding, but also because of possible influence by adults.[61] However, the Court has emphasised that the obligation on states is not the establishment of the truth, but on an effective investigation. This requires that the authorities take reasonable steps to secure evidence concerning the incident—including inter alia, eyewitness testimony and forensic evidence[62]—and must keep an open mind when assessing this.[63]

Finally, an effective investigation requires that the authorities act with speed in investigating complaints. In *DMD v Romania*,[64] the child's mother complained to

[53] *Đurđević v Croatia* (52442/09) 19.07.2011.
[54] *Afet Süreyya Eren v Turkey* (36617/07) 20.10.2015.
[55] ibid.
[56] *Ay v Turkey* (30951/96) 22.03.2005.
[57] See *Durmaz v Turkey* (3621/07) 13.11.2014; *Mikheyev v Russia* (77617/01) 26.01.2006.
[58] See, for example, *MP and others v Bulgaria* (22457/08) 15.11.2011, para. 111.
[59] *BC v Slovakia* (11079/02) 14.03.2006 (dec.). For example, in *Szula v the United Kingdom* (18727/06) 04.01.2007 (dec.), a young boy was sexually abused by his teacher as part of a wider culture of violence at that school. When this came to light almost 40 years later, a decision was made not to prosecute this particular perpetrator based on his age, the age of the offences, and the state of the evidence. The Commission found that there was no violation of the Convention, as there was nothing to indicate that the authorities failed to take the allegations seriously, nor any lack of diligence or expedition. The criminal law did prohibit the acts in question, and there was no systemic deficiency that prevented prosecution—merely a decision, reviewed on several occasions, that it would not be appropriate to do so given the circumstances and evidence available.
[60] *MP and others v Bulgaria* (22457/08) 15.11.2011.
[61] ibid.
[62] *Tanrikulu v Turkey* (23763/94) 08.07.1999 (GC); *Gül v Turkey* (22676/93) 14.12.2000. In the context of sexual violence against adults, the Court has found that a competent, independent medical examination may be necessary, which must be undertaken by medical professionals who have an expertise in this area. (*Aydin v Turkey* (23178/94) 25.09.1997 (GC)) This obligation would no doubt also extent to child victims, with the added requirement that the professionals have expertise in examining children.
[63] *Durmaz v Turkey* (3621/07) 13.11.2014. In assessing the acceptability of medical reports, the Court has referred to the standards set out by the Council of Europe Committee for the Prevention of Torture, as well as the Istanbul Protocol. (*Dilek Aslan v Turkey* (34364/08) 20.10.2015)
[64] (23022/13) 03.10.2017.

the police on five occasions that her husband was abusing her son, before the authorities launched a criminal investigation. Three-and-a-half years later, the father was indicted, and overall the investigation and court proceedings took eight years and four months. The Court noted that this length of time was excessive according to the Court's standards under Article 6 (the right to a fair trial), but this would not be sufficient, in and of itself, to render the investigation ineffective for the purposes of Article 3. Under Article 3, the length of proceedings is merely one element that must be considered in a holistic analysis of whether the investigation was effective. On the facts of the case, the Court found that there *were* shortcomings in the proceedings which undermined its overall effectiveness, noting in particular the fact that the domestic courts had taken into account the length of proceedings when sentencing the father, but failed to offer comparable compensation to the child himself. Thus the lengthy proceedings contributed to the finding of a procedural violation under Article 3.

Judges de Gaetano, Pinto de Albuquerque, and Motoc issued an important joint concurring opinion in this case, which emphasised the vulnerability of child victims of abuse, and suggested that states should be held to a higher standard in such cases. They argued that any proceedings, civil or criminal, which directly involve minors must automatically attract not so much a 'special diligence' requirement as an 'exceptional diligence' requirement.[65]

Having said all this, it is important to remember that the European Court of Human Rights is not a court of appeal, but an international body. It cannot substitute its own findings of fact for that of the domestic courts, nor can it re-examine the evidence presented. Its role is supervisory, with states given a margin of appreciation: the question is not whether the authorities did the best job possible, but whether it was deficient to such an extent as to violate the state's human rights obligations.[66]

2.3.4 The right to an effective remedy

The final procedural right for children who have suffered parental abuse is the right to an effective remedy. Article 13 of the Convention requires the availability of a domestic mechanism for establishing the liability of state authorities for acts or omissions involving a breach of Convention rights. This obligation applies whether or not it is eventually determined that there has been a violation of the Convention: if there is an arguable claim, there must be the prospect of a procedure that can establish the facts and determine the conduct that could be reasonably expected of the authorities.[67]

For example, the Court in *Z v the United Kingdom*[68] found a violation of Article 13 where domestic law shielded social welfare authorities from claims by children to whom they were providing services. The Court found that the inability to bring a negligence complaint against the authorities deprived the children of a domestic remedy,

[65] ibid., joint concurring opinion of Judges de Gaetano, Pinto de Albuquerque, and Motoc, para. 2.
[66] See, for example, *MP and others v Bulgaria* (22457/08) 15.11.2011.
[67] *DP and JC v the United Kingdom* (38719/97) 10.10.2002.
[68] (29392/95) 10.05.2001 (GC).

as there were no appropriate means available of obtaining a determination of their allegations that the authorities had failed to protect them.

In addition to imposing an obligation that children have access to an adequate procedure, Article 13 also requires—in principle at least—that compensation be available as part of the range of available remedies. This was discussed in *ES and others v Slovakia*,[69] where the Constitutional Court had held that a finding of a violation of the children's rights in itself provided just satisfaction, and therefore awarded no compensation. Moreover, the state argued that the criminal conviction of the father, and the subsequent amendment to the law, provided adequate redress. The Court rejected these arguments, and made clear that such measures were not adequate to address the failure to offer the children protection from an abusive parent for almost two years. In such a case, financial compensation was necessary.[70]

This does not mean, however, that compensation must be made available for every victim of abuse. This requirement rests on the (in this case, indirect) responsibility of the state for the damage inflicted, and is not a general obligation applicable to all victims. In *Stuart v the United Kingdom*,[71] the applicant had suffered repeated and systematic sexual abuse at the hands of her stepfather. There was no suggestion that the state was in any way liable for the abuse, but the United Kingdom had available a general governmental scheme that provided compensation to victims of crimes, to which she applied. Her claim under this scheme was rejected, however, as she did not meet the necessary criteria. She complained under Articles 3 and 8 that the state's positive obligation to provide effective protection against abuse extended to the provision of compensation where it could not be obtained from the perpetrator.

The Court rejected this argument as manifestly ill-founded. It held that deterrent sanctions were in existence—in the form of criminal penalties—and civil remedies were also available. Article 8 does not require states to provide unlimited civil remedies where criminal sanctions are in operation, and nor is there an obligation on the state to provide compensation to victims of ill-treatment perpetrated by private individuals where the state has no additional responsibility.

2.3.5 Conclusions on protection of children from parental abuse

The recognition of a positive obligation on states to protect children from parental abuse has been one of the most progressive, and important, contributions of the European Court of Human Rights. It is a significant obligation to impose on states: on the one hand, they cannot remove children from their family precipitously, as this would breach their rights under Article 8 (as discussed in Chapter 10), but nor can they leave children in a home where they are at risk of suffering harm without careful consideration and close monitoring of the situation. Nevertheless, this strict duty is to be applauded: children are in an incredibly vulnerable position vis-à-vis their parents,

[69] (8227/04) 15.09.2009.
[70] See also *Kontrova v Slovakia* (7510/04) 31.05.2007.
[71] (41903/98) 06.07.1999 (dec.).

subject to their power behind closed doors. If child rights are to mean anything, the state must be willing and able to breach this private sphere in order to ensure adequate protection of their physical and emotional integrity.

2.4 Protection from sexual violence

As with parental child abuse, the state has a positive obligation to protect children against sexual violence perpetrated by private individuals. Cases concerning sexual violence are generally brought under Articles 3 and 8 jointly, and the Court often does not draw a clear distinction between the two.[72] This is to be regretted, as the provisions encompass complementary, but separate, aspects of the child's rights. As Judge Tulkens has pointed out, '[r]ape infringes not only the right to personal integrity (both physical and psychological) as guaranteed by Article 3, but also the right to autonomy as a component of the right to respect for private life as guaranteed by Article 8'.[73]

The obligations in this area mirror those discussed in section 2.3 above in relation to child abuse under Article 3—an adequate legal framework, effective investigation and prosecution, and adequate legal remedies—although their interpretation inevitably differs due to the different nature of the offence. Although much of the jurisprudence in this area has built on principles already derived from adult cases, the contribution of cases concerning minors has nevertheless been significant. Importantly, the Court has taken a child-sensitive approach in this area, recognising the particular vulnerability of certain classes of victims—including children, and those with a disability—as a source of additional accountability, and requiring special measures by the authorities.

2.4.1 The need for an adequate legal framework

The first, and foremost, obligation on states is to have in place an adequate legal framework for the protection of individuals from third-party violence. The Court has made clear that in cases of rape and sexual violence, this protection must involve the criminal law—civil penalties will not be sufficient. This was established in the seminal case of *X and Y v the Netherlands*,[74] involving a 16-year-old girl suffering from a mental disability. She was living in a group home for children with such disabilities when she was forced to have sex with the son of the Director of the institution. Her father filed a complaint, asking for criminal proceedings to be instituted, and since his daughter was not able to sign the complaint herself because of her mental condition, he did so on her behalf. The prosecutor decided not to open proceedings, finding that a charge of rape would only be possible if the victim herself had taken action. The father's

[72] Connor O'Mahony provides an excellent analysis of this issue in 'Child Protection and the ECHR: Making Sense of Positive and Procedural Obligations' (2019) 27 *International Journal of Children's Rights* 660.
[73] *MC v Bulgaria* (39272/98) 04.12.2003, concurring opinion of Judge Tulkens, para. 1.
[74] (8978/80) 26.03.1985.

complaint could not be regarded as an acceptable substitute, even if the child herself was incapable.

The applicant complained (through her father) that the impossibility of having criminal proceedings instituted against her rapist violated her rights under Article 8. Although civil remedies were available, for a young girl like the applicant, the requisite degree of protection against such wrongdoing could only be provided by the criminal law. The Court agreed. It found that 'in a case where fundamental values and essential aspects of private life are at stake', effective deterrence is indispensable.[75] Only the criminal law can provide sufficient protection.

2.4.2 Consent

2.4.2.1 The age of consent

From an early stage of its jurisprudence, the Court has made clear that a person's sexual life is part of their private life protected by Article 8, and cannot be interfered with without sufficient justification. Nevertheless, it has recognised that states may legitimately set an age of consent to sexual activity for the protection of the child's sexual autonomy.[76]

Originally, such cases were argued in the context of homosexual activity: the 'sexual autonomy' referred to related to the protection of children from 'undesirable and harmful pressures and attentions' and the risk that children would be influenced into the development of homosexual tendencies.[77] The Court found that not only were states justified in setting age limits for participation in sexual activity—for example, 19 in Austria,[78] or even 21 in the United Kingdom[79]—but the authorities could also legitimately distinguish between homosexual and heterosexual sexual activity in setting such limits. In *X v the Federal Republic of Germany*, the Commission justified this difference in treatment on the basis of the increased vulnerability of young men, drawing on studies of 'psychologists, sociologists and specialists in social protection', which they claimed demonstrated

> the existence of a specific social danger in the case of masculine homosexuality. This danger results from the fact that masculine homosexuals often constitute a distinct socio-cultural group with a clear tendency to proselytise adolescents and that the social isolation in which it involves the latter is particularly marked.[80]

Thankfully, this position was revised—albeit not until two decades later—in *Sutherland v the United Kingdom*,[81] where the Commission found that there was no

[75] ibid., para. 27.
[76] *X v the Federal Republic of Germany* (5935/72) 30.09.1975 (dec.).
[77] ibid. See also *X v the United Kingdom* (7215/75) 12.10.1978 (ComRep); *Dudgeon v the United Kingdom* (7525/76) 22.10.1981.
[78] *Zukrigl v Austria* (17279/90) 13.05.1992 (dec.).
[79] *X v the United Kingdom* (7215/75) 12.10.1978 (ComRep).
[80] *X v the Federal Republic of Germany* (5935/72) 30.09.1975 (dec.), p. 56. See also *X v the United Kingdom* (7215/75) 12.10.1978 (ComRep).
[81] (25186/94) 01.07.1997 (ComRep).

objective and reasonable justification for differentiating between homosexual and heterosexual relationships in this respect.

Despite this unsavoury backdrop, some important principles can be salvaged from this line of cases: namely that some degree of control over sexual activity is legitimate in a democratic society in order to safeguard children against exploitation. Moreover, it falls to the national authorities in the first instance to fix the age under which young people should have the protection of the criminal law.[82]

This issue has not been directly addressed by the Court in relation to heterosexual sexual activity. The closest that the Court has come was the recent case of *MGC v Romania*,[83] concerning an 11-year-old girl who alleged that she had been raped by her 52-year-old neighbour. He was charged with sexual intercourse with a minor, but not rape, as the authorities concluded that she had consented. The applicant argued that by permitting the possibility that an 11-year-old child could express valid consent to sex, the Romanian law failed to effectively protect her against rape.

As is discussed further in section 2.4.2.2 below, the Court made clear that the law must take a child-sensitive approach to the evaluation of consent, and in particular, should have considered the age difference between the victim and the accused and the impact this would have on the child's possible reactions to the assault. Nevertheless, the Court failed to engage with the underlying question concerning the protection of children from exploitation through the imposition of an appropriate age of consent. By tacitly accepting that an 11-year-old child can ever give valid consent to sex with an adult, the Court failed to take a vital opportunity to provide real and significant protection to children who are victims of sexual violence.

2.4.2.2 The definition of consent

While the Court has been equivocal about setting an age of consent of children to intercourse, where it has excelled is in the imposition of strong obligations on states to interpret consent in a child-friendly manner.

This was seen in the landmark case of *MC v Bulgaria*,[84] where the Court made clear that authorities cannot impose a requirement of force or physical resistance for cases of rape, and must instead focus on the existence of consent. While this case has wider significance for sexual offences against adults, it is of particular importance for children, as it recognised the different ways in which they might react to sexual violence.

The applicant in this case was a 14-year-old girl, who alleged that she had been raped by two men. Although the authorities acknowledged that the young age of the applicant and lack of experience in life meant that she was unable to firmly demonstrate her unwillingness to have sex, they concluded that there could be no prosecution for rape unless she had shown resistance. The applicant complained that the requirement of physical resistance left certain acts of rape unpunished—and particularly those against children, where the majority displayed passive psychological reactions of panic—in violation of Articles 3 and 8 of the Convention.

[82] See *Dudgeon v the United Kingdom* (7525/76) 22.10.1981.
[83] (61495/11) 15.03.2016.
[84] (39272/98) 04.12.2003.

The Court recognised that, historically, proof of physical force and physical resistance were required in rape cases in many jurisdictions, but noted that there had recently been a 'clear and steady trend ... towards abandoning formalistic definitions and narrow interpretations of the law in this area'.[85] Drawing on both comparative law and international instruments, it identified a universal movement towards regarding lack of consent as the essential element of rape, rather than physical resistance. The Court referred to the jurisprudence of the International Criminal Tribunal for the former Yugoslavia, which had recognised that force is not an element of rape, as well as the statement of the Council of Europe Committee of Ministers, who had affirmed that penalising non-consensual acts, including those where the victim does not show signs of resistance, is necessary for the effective protection of women against violence.

In this light, the rigid approach of the Bulgarian authorities to the definition of rape jeopardised the effective protection of the individual's sexual autonomy. The Court endorsed an evolving understanding of the manner in which rape is experienced by victims, and criticised the domestic authorities for not attaching sufficient weight 'to the particular vulnerability of young persons and the special psychological factors involved in cases concerning the rape of minors'.[86] The Convention must be read as requiring the penalisation and prosecution of any non-consensual sexual act, even in the absence of physical resistance.[87]

The Court returned to this issue in *MGC v Romania*,[88] discussed in section 2.4.2.1 above, concerning an 11-year-old girl who alleged that she had been raped by a 52-year-old man.[89] However, he was only charged with the lesser offence of sexual intercourse with a minor on the grounds that she was deemed to have consented—that is, she failed to physically resist, and after the alleged abuse, she continued to return to the house to play with her friends.

The Court held that the authorities had failed to take a child-sensitive approach to the assessment of consent. Surveying the Romanian case law concerning rape, it

[85] ibid., para. 156 (citations omitted).

[86] ibid., para. 183.

[87] Ironically, this case was decided in the same year as one of the least child-friendly judgments relating to sexual abuse: *August v the United Kingdom* (36505/02) 21.01.2003 (dec.). This case involved a 13-year-old boy, who had gone to a public bathroom to seek out someone to pay him for 'homosexual activity'. The man he engaged in those activities with was convicted, but had his sentence reduced based on the fact that the child was 'a willing and active participant'. As a result, his application for compensation as the victim of a crime was rejected on the grounds that his own conduct had contributed to the incident. He complained under Article 8 that his right to respect for private life was violated by the finding that he had consented to the sexual offences committed against him, and that he was not the victim of a crime. The Commission found that it was not inconsistent to view the applicant as a vulnerable child who required help, and to find that he was an active participant, rather than a victim of violence. In such circumstances, the Convention did not require compensation to be provided. This decision is from 2003, although it reads as if it is from a much earlier era. To define a 13-year-old child as a 'willing and active participant' presents a regressive understanding of child sexual abuse. Moreover, it must be questioned whether the same decision would have been reached—either by the domestic authorities, or the Commission—if a young woman had been the victim or the sexual activity had been between individuals of the opposite sex. While the principle that the state does not have an obligation to provide compensation for crimes committed by private individuals is acceptable, the characterisation of the child abuse that occurred in this case is not.

[88] (61495/11) 15.03.2016.

[89] The applicant was also allegedly raped by several younger boys, who were also given administrative fines for the same offence.

found that the majority of convictions for rape of children involved physical violence. Conversely, in a significant number of cases where the authorities had concluded that consent had been present, this was inferred from facts that indicated child-specific reactions to trauma—for example, that the victim did not scream for help, or did not tell their parents. In less than half of cases had the courts ordered an expert opinion as to the capacity of the victim to give valid consent, and in only a handful of these did the courts consider that the victim could not express consent due to their age (ranging from six to 12 years old). In the case at hand, the courts had given no consideration to the difference in age between the victim and the accused, instead giving weight to the applicant's reactions to the incident, which were consistent with a child's possible reaction to a stressful event. As a result, the Court found that the authorities had failed to attach sufficient weight to the particular vulnerability of young persons, and the special psychological factors involved in cases of rape against minors.

Thus, it can be seen that Articles 3 and 8 require that domestic law and practice concerning consent to sexual activity be adequately tailored to respond to the reality of victim's experiences and responses. The existence of consent must be assessed taking into account the circumstances of the individual, including their age, any disability, and physical or psychological condition.[90]

2.4.3 Investigation and prosecution

Of course, a law is only as good as its implementation: the relevant offences must be effectively investigated and appropriately prosecuted. In order for the state to fulfil its positive obligations in this respect, authorities must take reasonable steps to secure the evidence concerning the incident, including interviewing witnesses and examining the physical evidence in an independent and impartial manner.

In relation to sexual violence against children, three particular procedural obligations have been raised: the necessity of a child-sensitive process; the need for speed and efficiency; and the impact of statutory time limits.

The most significant contribution of the Court in this area is the focus on child-friendly procedures. In particular, the Court has emphasised that when considering allegations made by a child, the authorities must take into account the vulnerable position of minors who have been victims of sexual violence. The ability and willingness of a child victim to make a complaint is often compromised, and therefore they must be provided with increased protection.[91]

This was seen in *GU v Turkey*,[92] where the Court made clear that the state's obligations under Articles 3 and 8 require that the best interests of the child be respected,

[90] See *IC v Romania* (36934/08) 24.05.2016, concerning a 14-year-old girl with a slight intellectual disability (an IQ of 68). The Court recognised that the applicant's age and disability placed her in a heightened state of vulnerability, which required increased diligence on the part of both the investigative authorities and the domestic courts. The Court found that authorities should have ordered a psychological evaluation for the purposes of analysing the applicant's reactions, and the validity of her consent should have been considered in light of her age and her mental and physical development, as well as the circumstances in which the incident took place.

[91] See, for example, *RIP and DLP v Romania* (27782/10) 10.05.2012.

[92] (16143/10) 18.10.2016. See also *MMB v Slovakia* (6318/17) 26.11.2019.

and the right to dignity and psychological integrity requires particular attention when the victim is a child. In this case, the Court first found that the authorities had failed to hear a 17-year-old victim in a manner that reflected her youth and experience of sexual violence. During the investigation, and in order to obtain her evidence, she was interviewed by two male police officers, neither of whom were specialised in cases concerning the sexual abuse of minors. Furthermore, during the trial, and while she was still a minor, the applicant had to testify in open court. Neither the investigating authorities, nor the judges, took into account her particular vulnerability as a child victim, nor the psychological factors specific to the rape of minors committed in the home, which could have explained the reluctance both to report the violence and to describe the facts.[93] The Court noted the 'traumatising nature of the publicity of the proceedings',[94] which was likely to undermine both her dignity and her private life.[95]

Second, and in common with other areas where procedural obligations arise, the Court has found that implicit in the obligation to undertake an effective investigation and prosecution is the requirement of promptness and reasonable expedition. However, in relation to sexual violence against children, the Court has also indicated that the assessment of the length of proceedings must be interpreted in light of the allegations in question: for example, in *PM v Bulgaria*,[96] involving a 13-year-old child, the Court took into account the gravity of the offence and the victim's age at the relevant time in finding that an eight-year investigation was not 'effective'.[97]

Having said this, in *PM* it is likely that the Court would have come to the same decision notwithstanding the fact that the victim was a child: eight years must be considered excessive for any investigation of sexual violence. However, the case of *CAS and CS v Romania*[98] provides a good example of the Court analysing the efficiency of the authorities over much shorter periods. This case involved the rape of a seven-year-old boy over a period of several months. The Court noted with concern that despite the gravity of the allegations and the vulnerability of the victim, the investigations did not start promptly: following his complaint to the police, it took the authorities three weeks to order a medical examination of the victim, and almost two months to question the main suspect.[99] Such delays contributed to the finding that there had been a violation of Articles 3 and 8.

The final issue that has been raised in relation to the positive obligation to conduct an effective investigation and prosecution in relation to sexual violence against children is that of statutory time limits. In relation to criminal prosecution, such time

[93] *GU v Turkey* (16143/10) 18.10.2016, para. 72.

[94] ibid., para. 71.

[95] In addition to the procedural violation concerning the taking of evidence, the Court also noted the considerable delays in the proceedings. The domestic courts had sought an expert medical opinion concerning the stepfather (who had alleged that he was impotent and therefore could not have committed the crime), but it was more than four years before this was conducted. Following this, it took another four-and-a-half years for the courts to hear an appeal against the accused's acquittal.

[96] (49669/07) 24.01.2012.

[97] See also *RIP and DLP v Romania* (27782/10) 10.05.2012, where the Court held that a seven-year investigation was excessively long, 'given that this is an alleged rape case involving minors'.

[98] (26692/05) 20.03.2012.

[99] The Court then went on to criticise the additional delays in the case—five years for the investigation and seven years from the date of the alleged incidents that the accused was acquitted.

limits have been considered as a peripheral issue in the cases concerning length of proceedings—for example, in *PM*, where the inaction of the authorities had led to prosecution becoming time barred, thus contributing to a violation of Article 3.

However, in relation to civil remedies, the Court has given considerably more leeway to states, allowing reasonable time limits to be imposed on victims seeking compensation. This was seen in *Stubbings and others v the United Kingdom*,[100] involving several women who had been allegedly abused as children. They wished to bring a claim for damages under civil law; however, they were unable to do so as such claims became time barred six years after their eighteenth birthday. They argued that they had not understood the relationship between the alleged abuse and their subsequent psychiatric difficulties until later in life, and that their claim for damages became time barred before they even realised that they had a cause of action.

The Court found that the right of access to a court under Article 6(1) is not absolute, and may be subject to limitations, as long as these do not restrict or reduce access to such an extent that the very essence of the right is impaired. It noted that limitation periods serve the important purpose of providing legal certainty and finality, and prevent potential injustice where courts are required to decide on events that took place in the distant past, with unreliable and incomplete evidence because of the passage of time. In this case, the six-year period was not unduly short, and was proportionate to these aims: even if the cases were brought within the limitation period, the domestic courts would have been required to adjudicate on events that had taken place 20 years earlier. The Court also emphasised that while civil proceedings may be time barred, a criminal prosecution could be brought at any time, and a compensation order made in connection with this. In light of these considerations and the margin of appreciation given to states in this regard, there was no violation of the right to a fair trial under Article 6(1).

2.4.4 The involvement of children in proceedings

Where sexual violence against children has led to domestic prosecution, the Court has considered the involvement of children in proceedings. On the one hand, the defendant has the right to a fair and public hearing (Article 6(1)), and to examine (or have examined) witnesses against him (Article 6(3)(d)). On the other hand, the Court must take into account the rights of the child and the need to protect them from further victimisation.[101]

[100] (22983/93, 22095/93) 22.10.1996.

[101] Although the Court has not directly imposed an obligation to provide psychological support and assistance to children who have been victims of sexual violence, in the case of *CAS and CS v Romania* (26692/05) 20.03.2012, the Court criticised the domestic authorities for never offering counselling to the child, nor providing a qualified psychologist during the proceedings, or afterwards. Drawing on the obligations undertaken by the Romanian state under international children's rights instruments—although the UN Convention on the Rights of the Child is not explicitly mentioned in the reasoning, its provisions in this respect are set out as 'Relevant Domestic and International Law'—the Court found that such lack of support could not constitute an adequate measure for 'recovery and reintegration' of child victims. Although this was linked with other procedural failures, and it is unclear whether it would constitute a violation in and of itself, it is nevertheless an important recognition of the wide scope of positive obligations that the state has towards children exposed to sexual violence.

The Commission discussed this balance in *Vanhatalo v Finland*.[102] Here, a man had been accused of sexually abusing his stepdaughter, R. Before the District Court, R had given evidence in the presence of the applicant's counsel, but when the case was appealed to the Supreme Court, the applicant and his counsel were excluded from the courtroom when she was called to give evidence. He was, however, permitted to listen to an audio recording of R's evidence, and had the opportunity to put questions to her on the basis of this, but declined to do so. Following his conviction, he complained to the Court that the exclusion of both himself and his counsel from the courtroom during the evidence of the complainant meant that he had not had an adequate opportunity to examine the witnesses against him, contrary to Article 6(3)(d).

The Commission in this case took a laudably child-sensitive approach to the balance between the competing rights of the accused and the child victim. It noted the 'special features of criminal proceedings concerning sexual offences', emphasising that they are often conceived of as an ordeal by the victim, especially when unwillingly confronted with the defendant. The Commission further had regard to the fact that the complainant was a minor at the time of the hearing and had psychological problems, meaning that she was more in need of assistance than a complainant generally would be. The purpose of the hearing in the Supreme Court was to give the judges a chance to observe her demeanour without being affected by the presence of her stepfather in any way, and to make sure that she could tell everything she knew about the case without fear. Having regard to the nature of the case, and the victim's circumstances, there had been no violation of Article 6.[103]

In this case, the child's testimony was not the sole basis of conviction, as a number of other witnesses and experts had provided evidence. This can be contrasted with *SN v Sweden*,[104] where statements made by the child were virtually the sole evidence on which guilt was based. Nevertheless, even here the Court found that there is no absolute right to secure the appearance of a witness in court—it is for the domestic authorities to decide whether it is necessary or advisable to hear a witness. The Court acknowledged that, as a rule, the defendant must be given an adequate and proper opportunity to challenge and question a witness against him, either when the statements were originally made or at a later stage in the proceedings. However, the Convention does not require in all cases that questions be put directly by the accused (or his counsel) through cross-examination in the court room. Instead, the Court found that it was sufficient that the defendant had been able to give questions to the police, to be asked by the officer conducting the interview with the child.

Having found that such a system was adequate, the Court imposed an important caveat: in cases where evidence is obtained under conditions in which the rights of the defence are not secured to the extent normally required by the Convention, this evidence should be treated with extreme care. The Court was satisfied that the domestic authorities had done so in this case.[105]

102 (22692/93) 18.10.1995 (dec.).

103 See also *Finkensieper v the Netherlands* (19525/92) 17.05.1995 (dec.); *Hols v the Netherlands* (25206/94) 19.10.1995 (dec.).

104 (34209/96) 02.07.2002.

105 See also *B v Finland* (17122/02) 24.04.2007.

SN v Sweden can be contrasted with *W v Finland*,[106] which likewise involved a conviction based almost solely on the statement of the child victims. In this case, however, the applicant was not given the chance at any stage to have his questions put to the children who he was alleged to have sexually abused. The evidence was given through a video recording of the children's statements, and the applicant's request that they be interviewed again, and his questions put to them, was refused. In such circumstances, the Court found that the applicant could not have been said to have received a fair trial.[107] Likewise, in *F and M v Finland*,[108] the child—who had neurological problems, and whose mental development was below normal—was never questioned in the course of the investigation. The only evidence implicating the defendant was the child's statement given to the psychologist, which was not recorded on audio or video tape. The Court found that there were no circumstances that would have prevented a recorded interview, during which the defendant was able to have questions put to the child, and as a result, his rights of defence had been limited to such an extent that he could not be said to have received a fair trial.

These cases highlight two requirements that must be met by the domestic authorities: first, that there is an opportunity for the defendant to have questions put to child witnesses, either directly or indirectly; and second, that there is an opportunity to see or hear the evidence given by the child witness, in some form—so that their demeanour under questioning can be observed and an impression of their reliability can be gained.[109]

All the above cases were brought by the accused, bringing forward arguments concerning their right to a fair trial under Article 6. While these rights were carefully balanced against the rights of the child witnesses concerned, the case of *Y v Slovenia*[110] is important for its explicit consideration of the Convention rights of a child to protection of personal integrity when involved in such proceedings. This case concerned the alleged rape of a 14-year-old girl, whose alleged rapist was permitted to cross-examine her directly during the trial. She argued that the proceedings had exposed her to traumatic experiences violating her personal integrity, contrary to Article 8.

As her testimony was the only direct evidence in the case, the Court found that the interests of a fair trial required the defence to be given the opportunity to cross-examine the victim, who by that time was no longer a minor. However, the right to defend oneself does not provide an unlimited right to use any defence arguments, and the manner of questioning must strike a fair balance between the victim's right to personal integrity, and the defence's rights. In this light, the Court found that

> since a direct confrontation between the defendants charged with criminal offences of sexual violence and their alleged victims involves a risk of further traumatisation on the latter's part, in the Court's opinion personal cross-examination by defendants

[106] (14151/02) 24.04.2007.
[107] See also *Kovac v Croatia* (503/05) 12.07.2007; *AL v Finland* (23220/04) 27.01.2009.
[108] (22508/02) 17.07.2007.
[109] *Bocos-Cuesta v the Netherlands* (54789/00) 10.11.2005.
[110] (41107/10) 28.05.2015.

should be subject to most careful assessment by the national courts, the more so the more intimate the questions are.[111]

On the facts of the case, the victim had been questioned in four hearings, over the course of seven months. At two of those hearings the accused personally cross-examined the victim himself, asking questions of a 'distinctly personal nature', as well as those which were meant to denigrate her character. The Court held that the domestic authorities had not sufficiently taken into account the sensitivity of the situation—the applicant was directly questioned, at length and in detail, by a man accused of sexually assaulting her. Such a situation required the judge to oversee the form and content of the questions, and to intervene if necessary. The pre-existing relationship between the applicant and defendant, the intimate nature of the offence, and the young age of the applicant at the time of the offence required a sensitive approach on the part of the authorities in conducting the criminal proceedings. This was not adequately achieved, with the cumulative effect that the proceedings substantially exceeded the level of discomfort inherent in giving evidence as a victim of alleged sexual assault, and could not be justified by the requirements of a fair trial.

2.4.5 Conclusions on sexual violence against children

The Court's approach to sexual violence against children has been largely positive. Although there has not been any clear decision on the *age* of consent, the child-sensitive approach to the *assessment* of consent has set a high standard for states, while the strong procedural safeguards, adjusted in light of the child's age and the gravity of the offence, are commendable. Combined with the nuanced approach to the involvement of children in proceedings, the Court's jurisprudence in this area makes a valuable contribution.

2.5 Child marriage

Although the UN Convention on the Rights of the Child does not explicitly discuss child marriage, the Committee has made clear that the marriage of a child under 18 should be prohibited as a form of forced marriage, as a child cannot give full, free, and informed consent. Nevertheless, an exception is permitted for a mature and capable child above the age of 16, where there is judicial authorisation.[112] The majority of member states of the Council of Europe set the minimum age of marriage at 18 in compliance with this standard; however, many also allow exceptions for younger children where there is parental consent, thus opening the door for abusive practices and parental pressure.

[111] ibid., para. 106.

[112] United Nations Committee on the Elimination of Discrimination against Women and Committee on the Rights of the Child, *Joint General Recommendation No. 31/General Comment No. 18 (2014) on Harmful Practices* (CEDAW/C/GC/31-CRC/C/GC/18, 14.11.2014), para. 20.

The European Court of Human Rights has only directly confronted the issue of child marriage on two occasions,[113] starting with the 1986 decision of *Khan v the United Kingdom*.[114] This case concerned a 21-year-old Muslim man and a 14-year-old girl. The girl left home with the applicant's assistance, and they underwent an Islamic marriage ceremony.[115] The applicant was charged with 'abduction of a girl from the possession of her father', and sexual intercourse with a girl under the age of 16. He claimed that he was prevented from manifesting his religion through his marriage under Islamic law, contrary to Article 9, and that he had been prevented from consummating his marriage and founding a family, contrary to Article 12. He further argued that he was discriminated against as the judge failed to take into account his religion, under which the marriage was lawful.

The Commission held that the protection of religious 'practices' under Article 9 does not cover every act that might be motivated or influenced by a religion or belief. Marriage cannot be considered simply as a form of expression of thought, conscience, or religion—as is evidenced by the inclusion of a specific article of the Convention to govern it. The right to marry and found a family under Article 12 is expressly subject to internal laws governing access to this right, and as such, the application was manifestly ill-founded.

Unfortunately, as an admissibility decision, and thus barely two pages long, there was no discussion of why the protection afforded under domestic law may be important, or the rights of the girl herself not to be subject to a forced marriage, something that was partly rectified by the Court 30 years later in *ZH and RH v Switzerland*.[116] This case concerned two Afghani asylum seekers who had entered into a religious marriage in Iran when they were aged 14 (female) and 18 (male). The ceremony took place in a familial setting, without the presence or participation of religious functionaries, and therefore was not registered with the authorities.

When they applied for asylum in Switzerland, the domestic courts refused to recognise their marriage for two reasons: first, because it would have been illegal under the Afghan Civil Code (which prohibits marriage for women under 15); and second, as it was manifestly incompatible with the Swiss *ordre public*, where having intercourse with a child under 16 is a crime. For this reason, the authorities found that the applicants could not be considered as members of the same family under the Dublin II Regulation,[117] nor could they claim the right to respect for family life under Article 8 of the Convention. The applicants complained that the authorities wrongly refused to recognise their married status, and therefore they had been separated, and their right to respect for family life as a married couple violated.

[113] Child marriage was also considered indirectly in the case of *M and others v Italy and Bulgaria* (40020/03) 31.07.2012. The parents alleged that their daughter had been kidnapped, while the authorities alleged that it was in fact an arranged child marriage. The case before the Court concerned procedural obligations to investigate alleged rape and violence that occurred during the child's alleged kidnapping, and the prohibition of child marriage was not discussed.

[114] (11579/85) 07.07.1986 (dec.).

[115] Under Islamic law, a girl can marry without her parents' consent at 12 years old.

[116] (60119/12) 08.12.2015.

[117] European Union Regulation No. 343/2003/EC, which governs the responsible state for determining asylum applications. This regulation had been triggered as the applicants had previously submitted an application for asylum in Italy.

The Court found that Article 8 cannot be interpreted as imposing an obligation to recognise a marriage—religious or otherwise—contracted by a 14-year-old child. Nor can such an obligation be derived from Article 12, which expressly provides for the regulation of marriage by national law. Importantly, the Court went on to note the sensitive moral choices concerned, and the 'importance to be attached to the protection of children and the fostering of secure family environments'.[118] For this reason, the domestic authorities were justified in finding that the applicants were not married, and there was no violation of the Convention.

In a concurring opinion, Judge Nicolaou criticised the domestic authorities (and by implication, the majority) for focusing on form, rather than function. He pointed out that a determination of whether someone is a 'family member' under the Dublin II Regulation is different from whether there was 'family life' under the Convention. While the former requires a formal status, the latter incorporates de facto relationships between individuals. As such, he argued that the Court should have recognised the 'family life' between the two applicants, even if they did not recognise the existence of the marriage for public policy reasons. This argument was strengthened by the fact that the authorities had in practice treated them as a couple; providing joint accommodation with just one bed, and referring to them as husband and wife in official documents. Moreover, despite the fact that intercourse with a child under 16 is a crime—relied on in determining the marriage as contrary to the Swiss *ordre public*—no charges were brought in this respect.

Ultimately the recognition of 'family life' under Article 8(1) was not determinative for Judge Nicolaou, as he found that any interference was justified under Article 8(2). Nevertheless, his opinion raises an interesting dilemma. Should the Court focus purely on the function of the family, and recognise familial bonds no matter how they have arisen? Or should it refuse, on principle, to recognise 'family life' resulting from what is perceived under law as an exploitative and abusive situation?

An obvious concern is that any judgment on the moral status of the family tie will lead to a lack of recognition of relationships that are deemed morally suspect by the majority. An obvious example here lies in the non-recognition of 'family life' between an unwed mother and her child,[119] or more recently, in the long fight for recognition of same-sex relationships as a form of 'family life' under the Convention.[120] One solution might be to do as Judge Nicolaou did and recognise the relationship as 'family life', but then limit the protection given depending on the constitution of the particular 'family'. This would have the advantage of at least giving important recognition to existing familial links, and require justification for interfering with these. On the other hand, undertaking a balancing process under Article 8(2) necessarily involves judging some families as more worthy of protection, and others where interference is more justified, which brings us back to the same position in any case.

Another solution is to focus not on moral judgements concerning the type of family, and instead focus on issues of vulnerability and exploitation. This is where a real

[118] *ZH and RH v Switzerland* (60119/12) 08.12.2015, para. 44.

[119] *Marckx v Belgium* (6833/74) 13.06.1979.

[120] See *Mata Estevez v Spain* (56501/00) 10.05.2001 (dec.); *Schalk and Kopf v Austria* (30141/04) 24.06.2010.

distinction can be drawn between same-sex relationships and child marriage. Same-sex relationships involve two equal partners, who have formed a life together: they have entered into this relationship with full capacity and consented to its formation. Any failure to recognise this as a 'family' rests on moral judgements concerning homosexuality. On the other hand, as discussed above, the United Nations has made clear that child marriage is a form of forced marriage. It involves exploiting the vulnerability of children, who cannot consent to the formation of the relationship.[121]

For these reasons, although the domestic authorities did treat the couple as husband and wife, the Court was correct to take a strong stance in refusing to recognise 'family life' between them—at least while the child lacked the maturity and capability to consent to such a relationship.

2.6 Forced or compulsory labour, servitude, and slavery

The jurisprudence of the Court concerning forced labour is still in its infancy—to this date there have only been a handful of cases where the Court has found a violation of the prohibition of slavery, forced or compulsory labour, and servitude found in Article 4 of the Convention.[122] There are two strands of jurisprudence concerning children in this area: the first concerning military service and civic duties performed for the state; the second concerning labour extracted by private individuals, from which the state has failed to protect.

2.6.1 Military service

The majority of jurisprudence concerning service performed for the state has been in regard to adults. Cases have arisen concerning the requirement to pay taxes;[123] to perform compulsory jury service;[124] to participate in the medical emergency service;[125] or to perform work while in detention.[126]

One aspect of the case law that has concerned minors has been that of military service. Once an individual has entered the military, states often require a compulsory

[121] This debate has also arisen in relation to illegal surrogacy arrangements, and is discussed in this context in Chapter 8.

[122] For an excellent discussion of the Court's approach in this broad area, see V. Stoyanova, *Human Trafficking and Slavery Reconsidered: Conceptual Limits and States' Positive Obligations in European Law* (Cambridge: Cambridge University Press, 2017); V. Stoyanova, 'Dancing on the Borders of Article 4: Human Trafficking and the European Court of Human Rights in the *Rantsev* Case' (2012) 30 *Netherlands Quarterly of Human Rights* 2; J. Allain, 'Ranstev v Cyrpus and Russia: The European Court of Human Rights and trafficking as slavery' (2010) 10(3) *Human Rights Law Review* 546–557.

[123] See, for example, *Karlheinz Schmidt v Germany* (13580/88) 18.07.1994, which concerned compulsory state service and taxes (the requirement that all men pay a fire service levy, but not women).

[124] *Zarb Adami v* Malta (17209/02) 20.06.2006.

[125] *Steindel v Germany* (29878/07) 14.09.2010 (dec.).

[126] *Stummer v Austria* (37452/02) 07.07.2011 (GC); *Van Droogenbroeck v Belgium* (7906/77) 24.06.1982; *De Wilde, Ooms and Versyp v Belgium* (2832/66, 2835/66, 2899/66) 18.06.1971; *Floroiu v Romania* (15303/10) 12.03.2013 (dec.).

period to be completed before an individual can be discharged from such service. The question that has been raised before the Court is whether individuals can be bound by such commitments made as children.

This was explored in *W, X, Y, and Z v the United Kingdom*,[127] where the applicants had enlisted into the military services aged 15 and 16, with the consent of their parents. This involved a commitment for a period of nine years, to be calculated from the time they reached 18. For various reasons, they sought to be discharged from this obligation, which was refused.

The first hurdle that had to be passed by the applicants related to the text of the Convention. Article 4 divides the prohibited practices into two categories: slavery and servitude under Article 4(1), regarding which the prohibition is absolute; and forced or compulsory labour, under Article 4(2), which is subject to exceptions listed in Article 4(3). In particular, Article 4(3)(b) excludes 'any service of a military character or ... service exacted instead of compulsory military service', from the scope of 'forced or compulsory labour'.

The Commission rejected the government's argument that the exclusion of military service from the meaning of forced and compulsory labour removed such service from the scope of Article 4 as a whole. It observed that while the practices prohibited under Article 4(1) and those under Article 4(2) must often overlap, they cannot be treated as equivalent. As the applicants argued, the practices are conceptually different—'servitude' is not merely a more oppressive form of 'forced or compulsory labour', but involves different constituent elements.[128]

Nevertheless, despite acknowledging that military service can in principle constitute a breach of the prohibition of 'servitude' in Article 4(1), the Commission found that it did not do so in this case. In doing so, the Commission focused on the issue of consent: the children entered into military service voluntarily, and with parental consent. As the government had argued, they chose that course freely from amongst the various forms of employment available to them. The fact that they were minors could not transform the normal conditions of a soldier into servitude.

In coming to its decision, the Commission focused purely on the capacity of the applicants to agree to recruitment, and did not consider whether they could—as minors—sign themselves up for a period of up to 12 years (in the case of the youngest applicant). In the view of the Commission, it was enough that they did so with parental consent, which was sufficient to take into account the special vulnerability of minors.

This was an admissibility decision, handed down over 50 years ago, so it is difficult to draw any general conclusions from it as to how the Court would treat such an issue today. Some indication can be drawn, however, from the approach the Court has taken in relation to adult recruits in subsequent—and substantially more recent—cases.

For example, in *Chitlos v Greece*,[129] the Court found that while it was legitimate for states to require a period of compulsory service for army officers after their studies in order to recover the costs associated with their education, this could not be so

[127] (3435/67–3438/67) 19.07.1968 (dec.).

[128] It was in fact not until some decades later that the Court really came to grips with the different meanings of the terms included in Article 4: see section 2.6.2 below.

[129] (51637/12) 04.06.2015.

burdensome as to constrain the actions of the individual. This case concerned an applicant who had received his medical training through the military. Military medical officers were entitled to privileges not available to civilian medical students, including not only free training, but also job security and the payment of a salary throughout their training. In return for this, they were obliged to complete a certain number of years of service after completion of their studies, or alternatively 'buy back' the remaining years of service (that is, pay a sum of money to be relieved of this obligation).

The Court in this case found that such an obligation was not disproportionate in theory—in fact, it was viewed as 'an integral part of the duties they assume'.[130] However, it emphasised that there must be a balance between the interests involved, and a disproportionate burden cannot be imposed. Here, the applicant had been required either to serve for another nine years or pay approximately 50,000 euros. This was then subject to interest of between 12 and 13 per cent. This burden was so onerous as to oblige the applicant under constraint to act, contrary to Article 4.

It is important to note that the legitimacy of a compulsory period of service was predicated solely on the fact that the applicant had been provided with specific training, as well as privileges that would not otherwise be available to ordinary medical students. It was only when the burden was so great—in terms of length of service or compensation to be paid to avoid this—as to outweigh these benefits that a violation was found.[131] This can be contrasted with the situation of the applicants in *W, X, Y and Z*, who were locked into their service for a longer period of time than the applicant in *Chitlos*,[132] without receiving the additional benefits of specialist training. This provides a strong suggestion that the decision in *W, X, Y and Z* would be decided differently if it came before the Court today.

Crucially, the Court in *Chitlos* also found that the limitation under Article 4(3), removing military service from the scope of 'forced and compulsory labour' only applied to *compulsory* military service, and not to ordinary service voluntarily entered into. This was obviously important, as the criteria for establishing 'forced or compulsory labour' is a lesser hurdle than that of 'servitude' or 'slavery', as is discussed below.

2.6.2 Modern slavery

While children have been at the periphery of the case law concerning civil obligations under Article 4, they have been at the heart of the development of jurisprudence concerning modern slavery and the actions of private individuals. Importantly, the first case where the Court found a violation of Article 4—*Siliadin v France*[133]—concerned a child, and bears discussion in detail: first, because it is the first case to fully explore the meaning of forced or compulsory labour, servitude, and slavery; and second, because of the importance placed by the Court on the victim's status as a child in coming to its decision.

[130] ibid., para. 94.
[131] cf. *Lazaridis v Greece* (61838/14) 12.01.2016 (dec.).
[132] After training was completed.
[133] (73316/01) 26.07.2005.

In this case, a 15-year-old girl (A) arrived in France from Togo on a tourist visa. Her father had agreed with a Mrs D that A would work in her home until the cost of her air ticket had been reimbursed, and that Mrs D would regularise her immigration status and find her a place at school. In fact, A became an unpaid housemaid: her passport was taken from her, and she did not attend school. Approximately six months later, Mrs D 'lent' A to Mr and Mrs B, where she worked for 15 hours a day, seven days a week, as an unpaid housemaid and child minder. She did not have her own room, and she was required to sleep on the floor of the baby's bedroom.

Mr and Mrs B were charged with having obtained the performance of services without payment or in exchange for payment that was manifestly disproportionate to the work carried out, by taking advantage of that person's vulnerability or state of dependence, and with having subjected an individual to working and living conditions that were incompatible with human dignity by taking advantage of her vulnerability or state of dependence. They were found guilty at first instance, but the Court of Appeal found that although she had not been paid, it had not been established that she was being kept in working or living conditions that were incompatible with human dignity. They held that it had not been established that A was in a state of vulnerability or dependence, as she went shopping and took the children out unsupervised, and was able to contact her family. She had once taken the opportunity to leave, but had later returned 'on the advice' of her uncle.

Following a successful challenge, the case was remitted to the Versailles Court of Appeal, which found Mr and Mrs B guilty of having obtained A's services without payment, by taking advantage of her vulnerability and dependence. However, it maintained that she had not been kept in conditions incompatible with human dignity—carrying out household tasks and looking after children could not be considered as such, as it is what falls to many mothers. Moreover, the fact that she did not have a bedroom to herself was not conclusive, since Mr and Mrs B's own children shared a bedroom.

The applicant complained before the Court that there had been a violation of Article 4, as the domestic law was inadequate to prevent practices prohibited under this article, nor effectively punish perpetrators. The Court considered separately the three offences under Article 4—forced or compulsory labour, servitude, and slavery—defining for the first time the limits of each of these terms, and their constituent elements.

The Court defined 'forced or compulsory labour' in line with the ILO Forced Labour Convention, as including 'all work or service which is exacted from any person under the menace of any penalty and for which the said person has not offered himself voluntarily'.[134] In this case, although A was not directly threatened by a 'penalty', she was in an equivalent situation in terms of the perceived seriousness of the threat. The Court emphasised the importance of her age in this respect, and noted that she was an adolescent in a foreign land, unlawfully present and in fear of arrest: a fear that was nurtured by Mr and Mrs B. Moreover, the Court found that it could not be seriously maintained that she worked of her own free will. On the contrary, it was evident that

[134] Forced Labour Convention of 1930 (No. 29).

she was not given any choice, and therefore must be recognised as a victim of forced labour.

The Court then turned to the question of servitude and slavery. Relying on the 1927 Slavery Convention, it defined slavery as 'the status or condition of a person over whom any or all of the powers attaching to the right of ownership are exercised'.[135] As the Court pointed out, this is a 'classic' definition of slavery, as it was practised for centuries. Despite recognising this, and despite noting the importance of interpreting the Convention as a living instrument in light of present-day conditions, the Court seemed unwilling to extend the understanding of slavery beyond the idea of a 'genuine right of legal ownership', and thus found it did not apply in this case.

This narrow definition not only fails to consider the modern permutations of slavery, but also falls back on a negative obligation on the state. If only legal ownership is recognised as slavery, then the state can simply legislate to prevent one individual 'owning' another, and their obligation is fulfilled. As such, it does not consider de facto ownership, derived not from law, but from reducing a human being to an object to be traded and bartered between private individuals. Here, A had been 'lent' by Mrs D to Mr and Mrs B, treating her as a possession that could be passed around at will.

Finally, the Court considered the concept of 'servitude' as involving a threefold test: (i) the obligation to perform services for others (by use of coercion); (ii) the obligation to live on another's property; and (iii) the impossibility for the individual to alter their condition. Here, again, the Court noted A's status as a minor child as an important factor in amplifying her vulnerability and dependency. She had been brought to France by a relative of her father, and with his consent. As a minor, she had no resources, was vulnerable and isolated. She had no means of living elsewhere than with Mr and Mrs B, and was entirely at their mercy, her papers having been confiscated. She had no freedom of movement and no free time. With this in mind, the Court concluded that A, 'a minor at the relevant time', had been held in servitude.

Turning to the positive obligations of the French authorities, the Court noted that 'children and other vulnerable individuals, in particular, are entitled to State protection, in the form of effective deterrence, against such serious breaches of personal integrity'.[136] The possibility of a civil remedy was not sufficient in a case of wrongdoing of this kind—this could only be achieved by the application of the criminal law. In these circumstances, the domestic law did not afford A practical and effective protections against the actions of which she was a victim.

The second case concerning a child also involved France, this time relating to two French nationals who were born in Burundi. *CN and V v France*[137] concerned two sisters, CN (aged 16) and V (aged ten), who were brought to France by their aunt and uncle—Mr and Mrs M. The girls were subjected to verbal and physical harassment, forced to live in the basement with no bathroom and makeshift toilets, and were required to carry out domestic chores. Over a period of five years they were not paid, nor were they given any days off. The situation of the applicants did differ in one respect: while CN was kept in the house all day and was required to care for the disabled

[135] (1927) 60 LNTS 254.
[136] *Siliadin v France* (73316/01) 26.07.2005, para. 143.
[137] (67724/09) 11.10.2012.

son of Mr and Mrs M, V was sent to school, and helped her sister with the domestic chores after she came home.

The domestic courts found that while the living and working conditions of the girls were 'poor, uncomfortable and blameworthy', they could not be seen as degrading in the context, given the circumstances of 'family solidarity', and the fact that there was no intention of economic gain or exploitation. They were not intended to debase them as human beings, but 'obeyed a duty to help them'. The housework undertaken by CN was described as 'repayment for her having been permanently taken into the home and care of an already large family'.[138]

In contrast, when the case came to Strasbourg, the Court found that there had been a violation of Article 4 in relation to the work performed by CN, but not by V. CN worked seven days a week, was responsible for all the household chores, and had no time for leisure activities. On the contrary, V attended school, had time to do her homework, and only then did she help with household chores. The Court noted that not all work extracted under the threat of penalty will be 'forced or compulsory labour': instead, the type and amount of work must be taken into account. As such, it distinguished between 'forced labour' and 'a helping hand which can reasonably be expected of other family members or people sharing accommodation'.[139] In the case of CN, without her aid, Mr and Mrs M would have had to employ and pay a professional housemaid. On the other hand, V was not found to have contributed 'in any excessive measure' to the upkeep of the household.

Turning to the issue of 'servitude', the Court noted that it was an aggravated form of forced or compulsory labour, the distinguishing feature lying in the victim's feeling that their condition is permanent and unlikely to change. This feeling may be based on objective criteria, or may be something brought about or kept alive by those responsible for enslaving the victim. CN was convinced that her immigration status depended on her living with Mr and Mrs M, and that she could not free herself without placing herself in an illegal situation. She did not attend school, and received no training that would give her hope of finding work outside the home of Mr and Mrs M. As she was not given any time off, she had no possibility of meeting people from whom she might seek help. The situation started when she was a minor and continued for four years. She was therefore effectively kept in a state of servitude.

What is interesting about this case is the conceptualisation of the child as a member of a wider family network, with associated obligations. The Court suggests that requiring a lot of housework from a child is acceptable, as long as they are also given outside opportunities—for example, attending school. What is not discussed, however, is the difference in treatment between V and the seven children of Mr and Mrs M, nor the position of vulnerability of a child who is being housed by a relative, and whose sole dependence (and immigration status) is on them. The facts are not entirely clear as to what tasks exactly V was expected to undertake, whether she had to work at weekends, and whether she was allowed out of the house except for school. This would

[138] ibid., para. 47.
[139] ibid., para. 74.

seem to be key here—whether she was attending school, and doing some chores on the side; or whether she was there to perform chores, but also permitted to attend school.

This is an area of the Court's jurisprudence which needs significantly greater development, especially in relation to children within a familial setting. While the Court has been swift to note the special situation of dependence of children in a wider setting, it has not equally recognised the impact of familial coercion, and the way in which notions of duty and obedience can play a part in subjugating children.[140] This is not to suggest that the Court should open the door to children being able to challenge any kind of household chores—merely that there needs to be a clearer discussion of the type and amount of work that can be deemed as acceptable, and a recognition of the kind of pressures that can be brought to bear within that setting.

2.7 Conclusion

The Court's approach to the child's right to physical integrity and protection from exploitation has come a long way from the early decisions on corporal punishment. There has been a clear development in the way it has addressed issues of violence against children—including physical, sexual, and psychological abuse—driven by increasing recognition of international and regional instruments in this area.

The positive and procedural obligations that the Court has placed on states across the last 30 years of jurisprudence have created a strong foundation for the protection of children. The requirements of an adequate legal framework, an effective investigation, and an effective remedy provide significant safeguards for children, while the increasing focus on child-sensitive procedures are to be applauded. While these are only minimum standards, the expansive approach to state responsibilities have laid the groundwork for the wider protection of children's rights in Europe, which is largely in line with the obligations in Article 19 of the UN Convention on the Rights of the Child.[141]

This is not to say that no difficulties exist within these lines of jurisprudence. The failure to conclusively declare corporal punishment to be a violation of children's rights is particularly problematic, representing as it does a continuing deference to parental authority and the family unit. Moreover, while important steps have been taken in the area of children exposed to exploitative practices, there is considerable scope for expansion in this area. Not only can the jurisprudence in relation to child marriage and compulsory labour be strengthened, but issues such as child trafficking, forced marriage, and even the sale of children could gain significant protection from a progressive approach to positive obligations in this area. Of course, this requires such issues to be brought before the Court in the first place, and is clearly an area which would benefit from strategic litigation.

In addition, while the Court has focused on direct violence against children—in the form of child abuse or sexual violence—it is only just starting to come to terms

[140] See, for example, *Osman v Denmark* (38058/09) 14.06.2011.

[141] C. O'Mahony, 'Child Protection and the ECHR: Making Sense of Positive and Procedural Obligations' (2019) 27 *International Journal of Children's Rights* 660.

with the impact of indirect violence: for example, where children are witnesses to violence perpetrated against other individuals. There is a rich vein of jurisprudence concerning the protection of women from domestic violence, which has been the subject of considerable academic discourse,[142] but the impact of this on children must also be acknowledged. The Court has taken some small steps in this regard: in *Eremia v the Republic of Moldova*[143] the Court found a violation of Article 8 on the basis that the children's psychological well-being had been adversely affected by witnessing their mother being physically and verbally abused in their home and being unable to help.[144] However, this is an area of the Court's jurisprudence that is still in its infancy—in part because this is still not universally recognised socially, let alone legally.

Hopefully, in future editions of this book there will be more to say on this topic, as the Court expands its case law in this area.

[142] S. Choudhry and J. Herring, 'Righting Domestic Violence' (2006) 20 *International Journal of Law, Policy and the Family* 95; L. Hasselbacher, 'State Obligations Regarding Domestic Violence: The European Court of Human Rights, Due Diligence, and International Legal Minimums of Protection' (2010) 8(2) *Northwestern Journal of International Human Rights* 190; B. Rudolf and A. Eriksson, 'Women's Rights under International Human Rights Treaties: Issues of Rape, Domestic Slavery, Abortion and Domestic Violence' (2007) 5(3) *I-Con* 507; R.J.A. McQuigg, 'Domestic Violence as a Human Rights Issue: Rumor v Italy' (2016) 26(4) *European Journal of International Law* 1009.

[143] (3564/11) 28.05.2013.

[144] See also *TM and CM v the Republic of Moldova* (26608/11) 28.01.2014.

3
The Right to Respect for Private Life

3.1 Introduction

The concept of 'private life' under the Convention is imprecise and ambiguous—and intentionally so. As the British Lord Chancellor said at the time of drafting:

> Vague and indefinite terms have been used just because they were vague and indefinite, so that all parties, hoping and expecting that the terms will be construed according to their separate points of view could be induced to sign them.[1]

As a result, it is not susceptible to exhaustive definition, and covers issues as diverse as reproductive rights,[2] environmental issues,[3] sexual orientation,[4] data protection,[5] police surveillance,[6] and assisted suicide.[7] What unites these concepts is the underlying intention of the provision: 'to ensure the development, without outside interference, of the personality of each individual in his or her relations with other human beings'.[8]

This chapter considers the child's right to respect for private life from the perspective of three interrelated, but distinct, aspects. First, it considers the Court's case law concerning the right to privacy and the protection of one's image. Second, it examines the development of the Court's approach to the right to receive information—from rather conservative and paternalistic beginnings to a more robust protection of freedom of expression. And finally, it analyses the Court's jurisprudence concerning the right to identity, including the right to information on origins and rights concerning the naming of children and citizenship.

3.2 The right to privacy

The ability to control knowledge relating to oneself is inherent in the right to privacy—both in terms of quantity and quality.[9] As Fried has pointed out, '[p]rivacy is not

[1] Cabinet Office Memo CAB/130/64, as cited by Lord Steyn in *R (Pretty) v the Director of Public Prosecutions* [2002] 1 AC 800, para. 56.
[2] See, for example, *A, B and C v Ireland* (25579/05) 16.12.2010 (GC).
[3] See, for example, *López Ostra v Spain* (16798/90) 09.12.1994.
[4] See, for example, *Dudgeon v the United Kingdom* (7525/76) 22.10.1981.
[5] See, for example, *Rotaru v Romania* (28341/95) 04.05.2000 (GC).
[6] See, for example, *Halford v the United Kingdom* (20605/92) 25.06.1997.
[7] See, for example, *Pretty v the United Kingdom* (2346/02) 29.04.2002.
[8] *Couderc and Hachette Filipacchi Associés v France* (40454/07) 10.11.2015, para. 83.
[9] C. Fried, 'Privacy' (1968) 77 *Yale Law Journal* 475.

Children and the European Court of Human Rights. Claire Fenton-Glynn, Oxford University Press (2021). © Claire Fenton-Glynn.
DOI: 10.1093/oso/9780198787518.003.0003

simply an absence of information about us in the minds of others; rather it is the *control* we have over information about ourselves'[10]—it allows us to grant or deny access to others.[11] The right to privacy relates not only to information, but also to the protection of a person's image, which the Court has recognised 'constitutes one of the chief attributes of his or her personality, as it reveals the person's unique characteristics and distinguishes the person from his or her peers'.[12] The right to control that image—including whether to publish it, where, and in what context—falls within the scope of the right to respect for private life under Article 8.

The Court has discussed the right to privacy of children in four different contexts. First, the child's right has been asserted against the wider public in relation to court proceedings, which is discussed in detail in Chapter 4 (on juvenile justice), and Chapter 9 (on child custody). Second, the right has been asserted against the media where personal information or images have been published in the press. Third, it has been asserted in relation to private individuals in cases of filming or photography without consent. And finally, the right to privacy has been asserted against the state where it has collected personal information or genetic material from an individual. These latter perspectives are discussed below.

3.2.1 Intrusion by the media

In all cases concerning the publication by the media of personal information—be that of an adult or a child—the Court must engage in a balancing exercise between the right to freedom of expression under Article 10, on the one hand, and the right to respect for private life under Article 8, on the other. The Court has emphasised on numerous occasions the importance of the free press in ensuring the proper functioning of a democratic society: not only the right of the press to impart information and ideas, but also the right of the public to receive them.[13]

Nevertheless, the publication of photographs has been held to a higher level of scrutiny than that of purely textual information. In *Von Hannover v Germany*,[14] the Court held that although freedom of expression also extends to the publication of photos, a distinction must be drawn between the dissemination of 'ideas' and the publication of images concerning intimate 'information' about an individual. In this context, the rights and reputation of others—one of the express limitations on the right under Article 10(2)—takes on special importance, particularly when the images appear in the tabloid press, where images are often taken in a climate of harassment, intrusion, and even persecution.[15]

[10] ibid., 482.

[11] ibid.

[12] *Couderc and Hachette Filipacchi Associés v France* (40454/07) 10.11.2015, para. 85.

[13] See, for example, *Bladet Tromso and Stensaas v Norway* (21980/93) 20.05.1999; *Pedersen and Baadsgaard v Denmark* (49017/99) 17.12.2004 (GC); *Von Hannover v Germany (No. 2)* (40660/08, 60641/08) 07.02.2012 (GC).

[14] (59320/00) 24.06.2004.

[15] ibid., para. 59.

This is exemplified by the case of *Krone Verlag GMBH v Austria*,[16] which concerned the publication of 13 articles over the course of two months in relation to a custody dispute regarding an eight-year-old boy. Custody had been awarded to the mother, but the father refused to comply and had gone into hiding with the child. When court officials tried to enforce the order by seizing the child, he cried and resisted. The articles revealed the child's identity, gave details of his family life, his health and emotional state, and were accompanied by photographs in which he was clearly identifiable. The mother and child brought proceedings against the publisher, who was ordered to pay damages. The publisher complained to the Court that the articles covered a matter of public importance—namely the conduct of the courts and authorities when enforcing decisions to transfer custody—and thus the judgment violated their right to freedom of expression under Article 10. They argued that they had to incorporate 'entertaining' components to reach the public, and in order to show the anguish and shock that the authorities' approach had produced in the child, it was necessary to show a photograph.

The Court found that although the articles did deal with a matter of public concern, the disclosure of the child's identity was not essential for understanding the particulars of the case. It was acceptable to report on all the relevant details of the case, but not to publish a picture of the child, nor reveal intimate facts about him. He was not a public figure; he entered into the public sphere merely by becoming the victim of a custody dispute which had attracted public attention. Drawing on the earlier *Von Hannover* decision, the Court noted that, '[t]he publication of photographs and articles the sole purpose of which is to satisfy the curiosity of a particular readership regarding the details of a public figure's private life cannot be deemed to contribute to any debate of general interest to society'.[17] This doctrine was held to apply equally—if not more so—to persons who are not public figures, especially minors who require particular protection on account of their vulnerable position. In particular, the number of articles, and the corresponding numerous photographs, was capable of creating a climate of continual harassment and was an intrusion into the private life of the child.

The sensitive approach to the child's rights in this case can be contrasted with the case of *Couderc and Hachette Filipacchi Associés v France*,[18] which concerned the biological child of the Prince of Monaco, who had been born out of wedlock and whose father had not legally or publicly recognised him. The child's mother had participated in an interview with a newspaper and provided photographs of the Prince and his son. The domestic courts found the publisher liable for infringing the privacy of the Prince and ordered them to pay damages.

The publisher complained that this penalty violated their right to freedom of expression, which was accepted by the Court. It held that given the dynastic implications of the birth and the information it conveyed about a public figure, the story was of public interest, and this therefore outweighed the right to respect for private life of the Prince.

[16] (27306/07) 19.06.2012.
[17] ibid., para. 48.
[18] (40454/07) 10.11.2015.

In coming to this conclusion, the focus of the Court was solely on the Prince. At no stage was the child's right to privacy examined. Indeed, the only mention of the child's rights was by the publisher: concerning the right of the child to be recognised as the son of the Prince—a fact which the Prince had not previously acknowledged, and that the mother sought to precipitate by going to the press. This deficiency may be explained partly by the fact that it was the child's mother, who held parental responsibility, who shared the information about the child and his images. Indeed, the interview was described as a 'means of expression for the [mother] *and* her son',[19] despite the fact that the child was not yet two years old at the time. The second possible reason behind the failure to recognise the child's individual rights was that the case before the Court concerned a dispute between the newspaper and the state. The child was not involved directly with the proceedings, nor indeed were he or his mother involved on a domestic level. Nevertheless, in its analysis of whether the state could restrict the right of the newspaper to freedom of expression, it is telling that the interests of the child were never mentioned as a relevant factor by the government.[20]

It is not only the traditional print media, however, who are now publishing information concerning, and images of, children. The advent of the internet has created a multitude of new avenues for publication—and thus intrusion—into children's lives. While there have not as yet been any cases before the Court concerning the more pernicious aspects of the internet—for example, child pornography,[21] child sexual exploitation online, or revenge pornography—the Court has had to deal with cases concerning the use of a child's image without their consent. In *KU v Finland*,[22] an unknown individual posted an advertisement on an internet dating site in the name of a 12-year-old boy, without his knowledge or permission. It included his age, description, and a link to a website where his picture and telephone number were posted. It also said that he was looking for an intimate relationship with a boy his age or older 'to show him the way'. The service provider refused to tell the police the identity of the person who had placed the advertisement, and the domestic courts found there was no legal provision authorising them to order the provider to disclose it. The child complained to the Court that he had no means of redress or protection against a breach of privacy under domestic law.

The Court highlighted the potential threat to the child's welfare brought about by the situation, emphasising his particular vulnerability due to his young age. It held that

[19] ibid., para. 127 (my emphasis).

[20] Despite its lack of sensitivity to child rights, the Court in *Couderc* made a very important clarification of the right to privacy in relation to the birth of a child. It noted that while birth is an event of an intimate nature, it does not fall solely within the private sphere, since it must be accompanied by a public statement (in the form of a birth certificate or civil-status document) and the establishment of a legal relationship between parent and child. This brings it necessarily within the public sphere, where the purely private and family interest is supplemented by a public aspect related to social and legal structures of kinship. In this sense, the Court held that a news report about a birth cannot be seen as a publication purely concerning private life.

[21] While there have been some limited cases concerning individuals accused of participating in, or publishing, child pornography, the crime in question has not been central to the complaint or judgment: see, for example, *Nordisk Films and TV A/S v Denmark* (40485/02) 08.12.2005 (dec.), concerning the revelation of journalistic sources; *Shannon v Latvia* (32214/03) 24.11.2009, concerning detention on remand; and *Treptow v Romania* (30358/03) 20.05.2008 (dec.), concerning conditions of detention).

[22] (2872/02) 02.12.2008.

states have a positive obligation inherent in Article 8 to criminalise offences against the person, including sexual abuse, and where the physical and moral welfare of a child is threatened this requirement assumes even greater importance. The guarantee of privacy and freedom of expression for users of telecommunications and internet services is important, but is not absolute, and is overridden by the protection of the rights and freedoms of others in this case.

While this decision was a positive one in many respects, it set a low bar for the protection of the child's privacy. It was not the publication of the child's description and personal information itself which posed the problem, but the fact that it was accompanied by misinformation that was potentially harmful. This focus on the purpose of the publication, rather than the protection of the child's image, was also seen in *Bogomolova v Russia*,[23] concerning the unauthorised publication of a photograph of a child in a print campaign. The publisher of the brochure—which was entitled 'Children Need a Family', and concerned the provision of alternative care and support for orphans—had found the photograph of the child on the internet and had not sought permission for its use. The domestic authorities dismissed the mother's complaints on the grounds that the publication had a positive scope, aimed at providing information, and did not contain any defamatory details which diminished her reputation. The Court found that the domestic authorities had incorrectly focused on whether the mother had given permission for the photograph to be taken, rather than on whether she had given her consent to its use in the publication. As the publication had implied that her son was an orphan, the Court held that this could prejudice the public perception of the family and the relationship between the mother and son, and therefore there had been a violation of Article 8.

As with *Couderc*, the focus was on the mother's permission, the mother's reputation, and the perception of the mother's family relationships. While the application was also brought on behalf of her son, his rights were not mentioned in the analysis, leaving a purely adult-focused discussion of a misuse of a child's personal information.[24]

3.2.2 Intrusion by private individuals

Unlike the jurisprudence concerning intrusion of privacy by the media, intrusions of privacy by private individuals have not come before the Court on many occasions. Where it has, the cases have related solely to images obtained without consent.

For example, in the case of *Reklos and Davourlis v Greece*,[25] a professional photographer took photos of a child shortly after birth, in a place where only medical staff had access. The child's parents complained that their consent had not been sought and requested the negatives, but this was refused. The domestic courts dismissed

[23] (13812/09) 20.06.2017.

[24] See also *Ageyevy v Russia* (7075/10) 18.04.2013, where hospital officials had permitted media and government officials to take photos of an injured child, and provided them with information concerning his identity and medical condition. The Court found a violation of Article 8 on the basis that there was no provision in domestic law which permitted this, and thus the case fell at the first hurdle without further discussion of the child's (or parents') rights.

[25] (1234/05) 15.01.2009.

their complaint, reasoning that the mental maturity of a one-day-old child was not sufficiently developed for him to perceive any infringement of his personality rights. Before the Court, the government further argued that since there had been no publication of the photos—they were intended solely for the child's parents to purchase if they so wished—the private life of the child had not been interfered with.

The Court dismissed this argument, finding that the substance of the right to the protection of one's image requires that the consent of the individual is obtained at the time the picture is taken, not simply if and when it is published—at least where the individual 'did not knowingly or accidentally lay himself open to the possibility of having his photograph taken in the context of an activity that was likely to be recorded or reported in a public manner'.[26] The Court held that as a minor, the exercise of the right to protection of his image was overseen by his parents, and their consent to the taking of the photograph was indispensable. Importantly, and unlike the cases concerning intrusion of privacy by the media, the Court also noted that the key issue is not the nature of the representation of the child in the photograph—degrading, harmless, or otherwise—but the fact that the photos were taken at all.

The second case in this area—known as *ES v Sweden*[27] at the Chamber level, and *Söderman v Sweden*[28] before the Grand Chamber—unfortunately lacked the clarity of analysis present in *Recklos*. This case concerned a 14-year-old girl who discovered that her stepfather had attempted to film her naked by hiding a video camera in the bathroom. Her mother immediately destroyed the recorded film, and it was not until two years later that the incident was reported to police. The stepfather admitted having tried to film her, but was acquitted on appeal because there was no general prohibition against filming an individual without their consent, and the act could not be covered by the provision on sexual molestation as the law stood. The girl complained to the Court that the state had failed to provide her with a remedy against the violation of her personal integrity, as is required by Article 8.

The Fifth Chamber, by a vote of four to three, found that there had been no violation of Article 8. The majority emphasised that only significant flaws in legislation and practice, and their application, can constitute a breach of the state's positive obligations. Here, they found that even despite the lack of specific legislation, there was a legal framework in place that could—at least in theory—cover such acts: for example, child pornography.

The case was subsequently referred to the Grand Chamber, which decided, by 16 votes to 1, that there had in fact been a violation of the state's positive obligations under Article 8. These obligations included a duty to maintain and apply in practice an adequate legal framework affording protection against acts of violence by private individuals. The measures in place must be aimed at preventing ill-treatment and provide effective deterrence against serious breaches of personal integrity, ensuring respect for human dignity and protecting the best interests of the child.

In overturning the test of 'significant flaw' relied on by the Chamber, the Grand Chamber emphasised that this only applied in the context of investigations, rather

[26] ibid., para. 37.
[27] (5786/08) 21.06.2012 (Ch).
[28] (5786/08) 12.11.2013 (GC).

than the assessment of whether the state had in place an adequate legal framework. The sole question before the Court was whether the law afforded an acceptable level of protection to the victim of such circumstances. Unlike the Chamber, it dismissed the possibility of a conviction for child pornography as theoretical, rather than practical. As such, it found that neither criminal nor civil remedy existed under domestic law to obtain effective protection in her case, leading to a finding of a violation of Article 8.

While this is a welcome clarification from the Grand Chamber, the reasoning as to why this case did not fall under Article 3 is of concern.[29] The Grand Chamber acknowledged that the stepfather's conduct constituted a violation of the girl's personal integrity, and affected her in highly intimate aspects of her private life. This was aggravated by the fact that she was a minor, that the incident took place in her own home, where she was supposed to feel safe, and that the offender was a family member who she was entitled to trust. Nevertheless, due to the lack of *physical* violence or abuse, the Grand Chamber found it did not reach the level of severity required to infringe Article 3. This is a disappointing conclusion, given the severe psychological implications of a child being covertly filmed in a sexual manner, but also because sexual abuse does not require a physical aspect to constitute a serious violation of personal integrity. This is not to say that the girl in this particular case was affected to such a degree as to invoke Article 3—it may be that she was mercifully not so affected—merely that the test should not be predicated on the presence of physical violence.

3.2.3 Intrusion by the state

The final aspect of the child's right to privacy discussed before the Court has been the gathering of information by the state authorities. In all states, the authorities will collect, and hold, a wide range of personal information concerning an individual, including, for example, gender, parenthood, and civil status. The Court has made clear that this kind of information has a public function, conveying legal rights and responsibilities, and therefore cannot be seen as falling solely within the private sphere.[30]

Nevertheless, the power of the government to collect and retain personal information regarding its citizens is not unlimited, as was explored in *S and Marper v the United Kingdom*.[31] This case involved an 11-year-old who had been charged with attempted robbery, leading to his fingerprints and DNA samples being taken. He was later acquitted, but the police refused his request to destroy the records of the fingerprints, the cellular samples, or the DNA profiles generated from this. He (and another, adult, applicant) complained that this was an intrusion into his private life under Article 8.

The Court found that the mere storing of data relating to the private life of an individual amounts to an interference under Article 8(1). The subsequent use—or

[29] The applicant herself characterised the case as a violation of physical integrity under Article 8, but the Court of its own accord discussed why this would not meet the test of seriousness needed to invoke Article 3.

[30] *Couderc and Hachette Filipacchi Associés v France* (40454/07) 10.11.2015.

[31] (30562/04, 30566/04) 04.12.2008.

not—of the information has no bearing on this finding. Nor does it matter that the information is only intelligible with the use of computer technology, or capable of being interpreted by a limited number of people. The Court held that all three types of data—fingerprints, cellular samples, and DNA profiles—contained highly personal, sensitive, and unique information about an individual, which brings them within the scope of an individual's private life.

In order to ensure that the interference with private life is justified under Article 8(2), the state must put in place a clear framework for the storing and use of personal information, including ensuring that the data is relevant and not excessive in relation to the purposes for which it is stored; that it is preserved in a form which permits identification of the data subjects for no longer than is required for this purpose; and affords adequate guarantees to protect data subjects from misuse and abuse.

In this case, there was a blanket and indiscriminate power of retention, with the personal information being retained irrespective of the nature or gravity of the offence or the age of the offender. This, as the Court noted, could be especially harmful in the case of minors, given their vulnerable situation and the importance of their development and integration in society. It emphasised the special position of minors in the area of criminal justice, and found that particular attention should be paid to the protection of juveniles from any detriment that may result from retention of their data following an acquittal. The Court also noted that the government policy had led to over-representation in the database of young people and ethnic minorities who had not been convicted of any crime, all of which contributed to a finding of a violation of Article 8.

3.2.4 Conclusions on the right to privacy

The applications brought before the Court concerning the privacy of children, and in particular the publication of their image, have produced largely positive results for the individuals in question. However, the reasoning used by the Court has at times been problematic. Despite taking a child-sensitive approach in relation to the impact of the publication of the image—with the lamentable exception of *Söderman*—the focus on the nature of the publication and on parental decision-making fail to come to grips with the core principle underpinning the right to privacy: that of individual control.

In the digital age, this is an area that is only going to grow in importance—in relation to images, personal information, and biological data. The Court must ensure that it adopts an approach to interpretation that is capable of providing rights that are 'practical and effective' in this new era.

3.3 The right to receive information

Childhood is a time for learning and developing, and as such, the right to receive information is a crucial one. Article 10 of the Convention provides an important guarantee for children in protecting freedom of expression, including the right to hold opinions and to receive and impart information and ideas. However, this right is not absolute, and is subject to limitations on the grounds of, inter alia, national security or public safety, the prevention of disorder or crime, and for the protection of health or morals.

It has been this last limitation that has been invoked in order to censor certain materials that may be deemed 'injurious' to children, as was first discussed in the 1963 case of *X and the German Association of Z v the Federal Republic of Germany*[32] concerning a magazine liable to 'have a corrupting influence on young persons'. The description of the material is somewhat amusing to read 70 years later, and in the age of tabloid media. It included

> a colour photograph of the film star Lana Turner who, dressed as an oriental dancer, behind a gossamer-thin curtain, 'seemed to be looking straight at the reader and beckoning to him'; the veil-like curtain 'threw into relief rather than concealed the charms of the lower part of the body' … [accompanied by text which] described the 'extravagance, frivolity, looseness and profligacy' of filmstars' lives, and thus presented a grave danger to adolescents who were much more prone than adults to seek models to imitate and emulate.

The Commission found, without more, that the German authorities had 'in no way exceeded' their margin of appreciation, since the measures were necessary 'for the protection of morals' of young persons. Sadly, there was no more detailed examination of what exactly was being protected, and against what danger, nor was there any discussion of the proportionality of this measure.

This more critical engagement with the issue had to wait another 15 years, when the Court decided the landmark case of *Handyside v the United Kingdom*.[33] This case was important for procedural reasons, as it was the first detailed discussion of the subsidiarity position of the Court and the doctrine of the margin of appreciation. However, it was also important from a substantive perspective, as for many decades it was the leading case on the restriction of information to children.

The case concerned the publication of 'The Little Red Schoolbook', a book which contained information on sex and sexuality, including subsections on, inter alia, masturbation, intercourse, contraceptives, wet dreams, menstruation, pornography, homosexuality, venereal diseases, and abortion. In one section, it also discussed smoking cannabis. The book was seized and destroyed, and the publisher convicted of possessing an 'obscene book' for publication.

There was no question that these measures were in accordance with the law, nor that they pursued a legitimate aim of the protection of morals. The only question was whether they were 'necessary' in a democratic society. The Court observed that it is not possible to identify a uniform European conception of morals: these will vary 'from time to time and from place to place'.[34] Invoking the margin of appreciation, it held that domestic authorities will be in a better position than an international judge

[32] (1167/61) 16.12.1963 (dec.).
[33] (5493/72) 07.12.1976.
[34] ibid., para. 48.

to decide the exact content of the requirements of morals and the necessity of a restriction to meet them.

However, this margin of appreciation is not absolute, and is subject to supervision by the Court, which includes giving primary place to the principles characterising a democratic society—of which freedom of expression is one such. This freedom applies not only to information or ideas that are favourably received, or regarded as inoffensive, 'but also to those that offend, shock or disturb the State or any sector of the population. Such are the demands of that pluralism, tolerance and broadmindedness without which there is no "democratic society".'[35]

Crucial to the Court's determination of whether the state had surpassed its margin of appreciation was the readership of the book—it was aimed at children and adolescents from 12–18, and its style made it 'easily within the comprehension of even the youngest of such readers'.[36] Although the majority of the book was purely factual, and 'often useful', the Court noted that there were passages that 'young people at a critical stage of their development could have interpreted as an encouragement to indulge in precocious activities harmful for them or even to commit certain criminal offences'.[37] In light of this, the authorities were entitled to determine that the book would have 'pernicious effects on the morals of many of the children and adolescents who would read it'.[38]

While not a surprising judgment, given the era in which it was decided, the fact that this has long been considered the leading judgment in this area is deeply worrying from a child rights perspective. It relies on the paternalistic position of protecting children 'for their own good', denying them the ability to receive information—even if it is 'purely factual'—and thus the ability to make their own informed choices. This is not to say that no restrictions should be applied, but that the ability to receive factual, objective, and age-appropriate information is a foundation upon which all other children's rights are built.[39]

Moreover, restrictions on information are often concerned with promoting 'appropriate' behaviour, thus marginalising minority groups and practices, and legitimising discrimination—as was seen clearly in *Bayev and others v Russia*.[40]

This case concerned the (in)famous Russian 'Law on Protection of the Morality of Children', which prohibited public activities aimed at the promotion of homosexuality amongst minors. The applicants were convicted of attending demonstrations in which they held banners with slogans such as, 'I am proud of my homosexuality'; 'Children have the right to know. Great people are also sometimes gay; gay people also become great. Homosexuality is natural and normal'; and 'Russia has the world's highest rate of teenage suicide. This number includes a large proportion of homosexuals. They take this step because of the lack of information about their nature. Deputies are child-killers. Homosexuality is good!'

[35] ibid., para. 49.
[36] ibid., para. 52.
[37] ibid., para. 52.
[38] ibid., para. 52.
[39] See Child Rights International Network, 'Access Denied: Protect Rights—Unblock Children's Access to Information' (2014), https://archive.crin.org/sites/default/files/access_to_information_final_layout.pdf.
[40] (67667/09, 44092/12, 56717/12) 20.06.2017.

The government argued that the restriction on the applicants' free speech was justified for the protection of children from information, propaganda, and activism which are harmful to their health and moral and spiritual development. In their view, the applicants were not expressing views, or informing others in a neutral manner, but were engaged in propaganda, targeting an underage audience, so as to impose a homosexual lifestyle and corrupt their vision of traditional family values.

The Court firmly rejected the government's argument that there was any incompatibility between maintaining family values as the foundation of society and acknowledging the social acceptance of homosexuality. There is a clear European consensus regarding the right to openly identify as gay, and same-sex couples are recognised as having 'family life' under the Convention. Importantly, although the Court acknowledged that the majority of Russians disapprove of homosexuality, it emphasised that it would be incompatible with the underlying values of Convention if the exercise of rights by a minority were made conditional on it being acceptable to majority. Moreover, the Court rejected the assertion that the promotion of homosexuality poses a risk to public health, finding, on the contrary, that disseminating knowledge and raising awareness of associated risks was an indispensable part of risk prevention.

Turning to the specific situation of minors, the Court also dismissed the government's claim that the ban was necessary to shield minors against information which could convey a positive image of homosexuality, as a precaution against their 'conversion' to a homosexual lifestyle that would be detrimental to their development. There was no explanation of how a minor could be 'enticed' into a homosexual lifestyle, nor any evidence presented that sexual orientation was susceptible to change under external influence.[41]

The Court further rejected the government's argument that parents should have the right to decide on appropriate forms of education and means of ensuring the moral and intellectual development of their children—a right which, according to the government at least, the promotion of homosexuality infringed upon. The Court held that the applicants had not sought to interact with minors, nor intrude on their private space. There was nothing in the banners they produced that could be interpreted as a proposal to provide tuition or guidance on issues of sexuality. Even if the obligation of the authorities to respect parents' religious and philosophical views could be extended beyond the classroom and the setting of curricula, the Court found that it would be unrealistic for parents' beliefs to be given automatic priority, in every situation. It held that:

> In sensitive matters such as public discussion of sex education, where parental views, educational policies and the right of third parties to freedom of expression must be balanced, the authorities have no choice but to resort to the criteria of objectivity,

[41] This is in stark contrast to the early cases on the age of consent to sexual activity, discussed in section 2.4.2 above.

pluralism, scientific accuracy and, ultimately, the usefulness of a particular type of information to the young audience.[42]

In conclusion, the Court noted that the messages of the applicants were not inaccurate, nor were they sexually explicit or aggressive, and did not advocate any sexual behaviour. Contrary to the position that they were harming children, they were exposing them 'to the ideas of diversity, equality and tolerance' and 'the adoption of these views could only be conducive to social cohesion'.[43]

Thus, in *Bayev* the Court displayed a much more robust approach to the censorship of materials for children's 'own good', examining the underlying aim of the measures and questioning their legitimacy. This was helped considerably by the nature of the restriction, with LGBT rights now being widely recognised at an international level. It is not clear whether the same scrutiny would now be applied to other, less clear-cut, 'moral' issues—for example, the issues described in the Little Red School Book, such as drug taking or non-discriminatory sexual education. Nevertheless, it is a step forward for children's rights in this important area.

3.4 The right to identity

The right to an identity has been recognised as an essential condition of the right to autonomy and development, and as such, lies within the inner core of the right to respect for private life.[44] This right has been characterised by Eekelaar as comprising two concepts: individual identity—concerning individual personal characteristics and linked to the development of personality and self-perception; and communal identity—concerning the individual's identification with others and the relationship with those around them.[45]

Both concepts of identity have been recognised by the Court: the former, in cases concerning information on origins and genetic relationships;[46] the latter, in the context of a person's name, gender,[47] citizenship, or ethnic identity.[48]

3.4.1 Access to information on biological origins

In Chapter 8, the right of a parent and child to establish their biological relationship is discussed, in the context of the determination of legal parenthood and the right to respect for family life. However, the Court has also recognised another important right in this regard: the right of the child to access information on their biological origins as

[42] *Bayev and others v Russia* (67667/09, 44092/12, 56717/12) 20.06.2017, para. 82.
[43] ibid.
[44] See, for example, *Odièvre v France* (42326/98) 13.02.2003 (GC), dissenting opinion of Judges Wildhaber, Sir Nicolas Bratza, Bonello, Loucaides, Cabral Barreto, Tulkens, and Pellonpää.
[45] J. Eekelaar, 'Family Law and Identity' (2018) 38(4) *Oxford Journal of Legal Studies* 822.
[46] See, for example, *Jäggi v Switzerland* (58757/00) 13.07.2006; *Odièvre v France* (42326/98) 13.02.2003.
[47] See, for example, *Christine Goodwin v the United Kingdom* (28957/95) 11.07.2002 (GC).
[48] See, for example, *Ciubotaru v the Republic of Moldova* (27138/04) 27.04.2010.

a part of the development of their identity. This does not necessarily relate to the determination of legal ties—although it can do—but instead concerns a separate right: the right to identity, which the Court has identified as a central tenet of the right to respect for private life.

The seminal case in this area is *Mikulić v Croatia*,[49] where the child and her mother had filed a paternity suit before the courts to establish the identity of her father. The courts ordered a DNA test, but the putative father failed to attend on numerous occasions and, as a consequence, the courts held that paternity could not be established. The child brought an application before the Court,[50] arguing that the lack of mechanism to determine a biological connection with their putative father infringed on her right to respect for private life.

On the one hand, the Court held that people in the applicant's situation had a vital interest, protected by the Convention, in receiving the information necessary to uncover the truth about an important aspect of their personal identity. On the other hand, it also acknowledged that there must equally be protection of third persons to preclude their being compelled to make themselves available for medical tests—including DNA tests—that they did not want to undertake. The Court made clear that the domestic authorities were required to strike a fair balance between the rights of the putative father and those of the child, while having regard to the basic principle of the child's best interests. In this light, the Court found that the lack of any procedural measure in Croatian law to compel the alleged father to comply with the court order was only in conformity with the principle of proportionality if it provided alternative means enabling an independent authority to determine the paternity claim speedily.[51] No such procedure was available to the applicant in the present case, and as such, there was a violation of Article 8.[52]

The Court returned to this issue in *Jäggi v Switzerland*,[53] which did not concern a child—the applicant was over 60 before the case was decided—but is nevertheless of great importance in this line of jurisprudence. This case involved a man seeking to have the identity of his father established; however, the person who he believed to be his father was already dead. During his lifetime he had always refused to submit to tests to establish his paternity, but after his death, the applicant had applied for a DNA test on his remains. The Swiss Federal Court linked the 'right to know one's parents' with 'the right to be raised by them': as the applicant was 60 years old by the time of the case, it held that he had 'been able to develop his personality and pursue a large

[49] (53176/99) 07.02.2002.

[50] While procedurally this was a case brought by the child herself, she was two months old when the proceedings commenced before the domestic courts, three years old when the application was made to the Court, and five-and-a-half years old when the Court handed down its decision. As such, from a practical perspective, it was her mother driving the litigation. This is not a problem in and of itself, as children will often require an adult to enforce their rights on their behalf. A difficulty arises, however, when adults use a claim based on the 'child's rights' simply to further their own position, as is discussed in Chapter 9.

[51] The requirement that an alternative means be provided to determine the paternity 'speedily' was emphasised in *Jevremovic v Serbia* (3150/05) 17.07.2007, where the Court found that proceedings lasting eight years violated the child's rights under Article 8. Likewise in *Ebru and Tayfun Engin Çolak v Turkey* (60176/00) 30.05.2006, the Court found that proceedings lasting for almost nine years, and heard at five levels of jurisdiction, violated Article 6(1).

[52] See also *Canonne v France* (22037/13) 02.06.2015.

[53] (58757/00) 13.07.2006.

portion of his existence without suffering any medically attested damage to his physical or mental health as a result of his uncertainty as to his parentage'.[54]

The Court did not agree with this analysis, finding a violation of Article 8. It held that the right to identity, which includes the right to know one's biological parentage, is an integral part of the notion of private life, and therefore particularly rigorous scrutiny is called for when weighing up competing interests. It acknowledged, as the Swiss Federal Court had done, that the applicant had been able to develop his personality even in the absence of certainty. However, the Court emphasised that an individual's interest in discovering their parentage does not disappear with age—quite the reverse. The applicant had tried throughout his life to obtain conclusive information on the subject, and the Court found that such conduct implies mental and psychological suffering, even if this had not been medically attested.

In both of these cases, the identity of the parent was not a 'secret', it was simply unestablished. Indeed, a particular man had been identified, and the only question was whether DNA tests could be undertaken. When the Court has considered the right of the child to discover information concerning their origins which has been concealed by law, however, a different approach has been taken. This issue has arisen in the context of anonymous birth, where a mother has asked for her identity to be kept secret, and therefore she is indicated on the birth certificate by a simple letter 'X'. The question is whether a child, who had subsequently been adopted, is entitled to pierce this veil, and be given information about their biological parent.

In the first case of this kind, *Odièvre v France*,[55] the child in question—by this time, an adult—complained that although she could obtain non-identifying information about her natural family, her inability to obtain identifying information prevented her from finding out her personal history, in violation of Article 8 of the Convention. As with many other adoption decisions, the Court in *Odièvre* was divided—in this case, ten votes to seven. The majority found that '[b]irth, and in particular the circumstances in which a child is born, forms part of a child's, and subsequently the adult's, private life guaranteed by Article 8 of the Convention',[56] and recognised that all people 'have a vital interest, protected by the Convention, in receiving the information necessary to know and to understand their childhood and early development'.[57] However, the majority made clear that this was not a case where it was trying to reconcile the rights of a child with those of an adult—instead, the conflict was characterised as one between two adults, 'each endowed with her own free will'.[58]

The majority distinguished the situation of an adopted child seeking information about their origins and the identity of their natural parents and cases concerning the establishment of paternity. They emphasised that Article 8 refers to the right of 'everyone' to respect for private life, which must include the natural mother, who expressly requested that information about the birth remain confidential. Ultimately, the majority found that the French government had a wide margin of appreciation, 'in view

[54] ibid., para. 19.
[55] (42326/98) 13.02.2003.
[56] ibid., para. 29.
[57] ibid., para. 42.
[58] ibid., para. 44.

of the complex and sensitive nature of the issue of access to information about one's origins, an issue that concerns the right to know one's personal history, the choices of the natural parents, the existing family ties and the adoptive parents'[59] and had not overstepped this margin when deciding how to balance these competing interests.

A different approach was taken by Judge Greve in his concurring opinion, who characterised the conflict not as between two adults, nor even between a parent and their child, but between the competing rights of the child themself.[60] If mothers were denied the right to give birth anonymously, he argued, then they may try to hide their pregnancy, and even the birth itself, which would be detrimental to the child. He asserted that '[t]he primary interest of the child is to be born and born under circumstances where its health is not unnecessarily put at risk by birth in circumstances in which its mother tries to secure secrecy even when that means that she will be deprived of professional assistance when in labour'.[61] Moreover, he suggested that at the prenatal stage, the rights and interests of the mother and child converge: in these circumstances, he held that it is in the best interests of the child to be born in a safe environment, without putting either the child's or the mother's life in jeopardy, even if it meant that this came at the expense of having information concerning their origins.

The seven judges in dissent, on the other hand, strongly rejected the conclusion of the majority that there had been a balance achieved between the competing interests. Drawing on the United Nations Convention on the Rights of the Child, they argued that no balancing of interests is possible where a birth had been registered anonymously, as French law allowed the mother's decision to constitute 'an absolute defence to any requests for information by the applicant, irrespective of the reasons for or legitimacy of that decision. In all circumstances, the mother's refusal is definitively binding on the child, who has no legal means at its disposal to challenge the mother's unilateral decision.'[62] As such, they argued that the effect of the mother's rights, as recognised by the majority, is that the rights of the child 'are entirely neglected and forgotten', and, in an (in)famously emotive statement, opined: 'The mother thus has a discretionary right to bring a suffering child into the world and to condemn it to lifelong ignorance.'[63]

These different opinions are particularly interesting for the way in which the rights are conceptualised. For the majority, the case concerned the competing rights of two adults; for the minority, the tension lay between the rights of the child and those of the mother; and for Judge Greve, between the child's competing rights. This is of crucial importance, as the approach taken will necessarily affect the conclusion arrived at—there is no 'neutral' option in this respect.

A key aspect of the French system, relied on by the majority, was the fact that the applicant was able to access non-identifying information, which would enable her to trace some of her roots. Moreover, it was emphasised that the French system permitted

[59] ibid., para. 49.

[60] This has been how the debate has been framed in Belgium, where a debate on anonymous birth began as a result of the large number of women crossing the border into France to give birth anonymously: see ibid., para. 19.

[61] ibid.

[62] *Odièvre v France* (42326/98) 13.02.2003, joint dissenting opinion of Judges Wildhaber, Sir Nicholas Bratza, Bonello, Loucaides, Cabral Barreto, Tulkens and Pellonpää, para. 7.

[63] ibid.

the mother to change her mind and decide to release her information at a later date, which the majority held introduced an element of balance. The importance of these provisions was confirmed in the subsequent case of *Godelli v Italy*.[64] In this case, the Court found that the Italian system was in violation of the Convention, as a child whose mother had claimed anonymity was neither provided with non-identifying information, nor could the mother's identity be disclosed, even with her later consent. The Court found that such restrictions prevented any balancing of interests, giving blind preference to the birth mother, in contrast to the French system endorsed in *Odièvre*. This is a somewhat odd decision: it is difficult to see how the mother's ability to change her mind creates a balance between the mother's and child's rights. Instead, it appears simply to continue to leave the decision as to whether the child's rights will be respected to the mother herself. However, this appears now to be the settled approach of the Court in this area.

While the decision of *Godelli* is a (small) step in the right direction, the Court nevertheless continues to judicially approve a system that denies the child the right to information concerning a fundamental aspect of their identity, without any possibility of an independent balancing process. While the protection of women is an important consideration, particularly those who feel that they have no choice but to go through an anonymous birth, it is equally important that there is some mechanism available to assess the rights of all parties involved, rather than a system where the scales are automatically weighed against the child.

3.4.2 Legal recognition of biological parenthood

A second aspect of the child's identity as it relates to biological parenthood concerns not the discovery of a parent, but their legal recognition. Again, this is discussed in Chapter 8 in the context of 'family life', but it also raises issues concerning the child's right to identity, which are worthy of mention in this chapter.

The leading case in this respect is *Mennesson v France*,[65] which involved a cross-border surrogacy arrangement undertaken by a French couple in the United States. As surrogacy is prohibited in France, the French authorities refused to enter the births on the register for births, marriages, and deaths, leaving the parents and child with no recognition of their relationship under French law. The Court found that the interference with the parents' family life had not been disproportionate—there was no danger that the family would be separated and they were able to continue their life together unimpeded. However, it went on to observe that the establishment of parental ties comprises an important aspect of the child's identity, and is thus protected by the right to respect for private life under Article 8. The Court emphasised that 'it cannot be said to be in the interests of the child to deprive him or her of a legal relationship of this nature where the biological reality of that relationship has been established and the child and parent concerned demand full recognition thereof'.[66]

[64] (33783/09) 25.09.2012.
[65] (65192/11) 26.06.2014. See also *Labassee v France* (65941/11) 26.06.2014, decided on the same day.
[66] *Mennesson v France* (65192/11) 26.06.2014, para. 100.

The child therefore had the right to have a legal relationship with their biological parent recognised.[67] Of course, this is not an absolute right, and there may be other competing factors—and indeed other competing parental ties—which might outweigh this biological link. Nevertheless, this case was a huge step forward for the Court, recognising that the *status* of parenthood is of equal importance to the *function* of parenting. It is not enough that the child will not be separated from their family—they have a right to recognition of their identity through this vital legal status.

3.4.3 Access to information on upbringing

When considering the right to identity, it is not only parenthood and biological origins that are important, but also an individual's personal history. The Court has recognised that individuals have a right to access information concerning their childhood and upbringing in order to be able to understand their past.

This was first recognised in *Gaskin v United Kingdom*,[68] where the applicant had been taken into public care at a young age. He wished to obtain the details of where he was kept, by whom, and in what conditions, but this was refused by the authorities, who argued that the disclosure would be contrary to the public interest. Contributions to public care records were made by doctors, teachers, police, social workers, and foster parents, and had been made in the strictest confidence. It was in the public interest that such records should be as full and frank as possible, without fear that they would be published at a later date. The applicant complained that the refusal to allow him access to these records was in breach of his right to respect for private and family life under Article 8.

The government argued that the file did not form part of the applicant's private life—it was simply information compiled for and by the authorities. The Court disagreed. It held that 'the file provided a substitute record for the memories and experience of the parents of the child who is not in care'.[69] It contained information concerning highly personal aspects of his childhood, development, and history and was his principal source of information about his past and formative years.

While the Court recognised that the confidentiality of the file contributed to the effective operation of the care system, it found that individuals have a vital interest in receiving information necessary to know and understand their childhood and development. These interests must be balanced: a system that makes access to records dependent on the consent of the contributor is compatible with the Convention, as long as there is an independent authority which can order disclosure if the contributor is not available, or improperly refuses consent.[70]

The age and vulnerability of the child played an important role in the finding of a violation in this case. The records in question covered a period in which his own

[67] See also *Foulon and Bouvet v France* (9063/14; 10410/14) 21.07.2016 (dec.); *Laborie v France* (44024/13) 19.01.2017 (dec.).
[68] (10454/83) 07.07.1989.
[69] ibid., para. 36 (quoting the earlier Commission Report).
[70] See also *MG v the United Kingdom* (39393/98) 24.09.2002.

memories could not provide a 'reliable or adequate source of information',[71] and provided information concerning his 'basic identity'.[72] This can be contrasted with the case of *Martin v the United Kingdom*,[73] concerning the medical records of a young man who had undergone psychiatric treatment from the age of 19. Although the Commission recognised that Mr Martin's records also contained information of a personal nature, and related to personally significant incidents in his life, the case was distinguished from *Gaskin*. The records related to a four-year period, starting when he was already an adult, and therefore the question of reconstituting information relating to childhood did not arise. He had not demonstrated that there was no other source of information available to him—unlike Mr Gaskin, whose care lasted for almost the entirety of his minority, and who would have otherwise been unable to trace his entire childhood.

3.4.4 The right to a name

The naming of a child is a core component of communal identity.[74] It identifies the individual within society and can be an indicator of other communal characteristics, for example, gender. It can also be an important outward sign of a bond between family members and a natural link between them.[75] Nevertheless, it must also be recognised as relating to individual identity. The way that someone chooses to identify themselves to others—especially if they are changing their name to something of their own choosing—is a central aspect of an individual's personality and self-perception.[76] This dual nature can be seen in the cases concerning a change of name associated with gender identity: it both reflects how an individual perceives themselves, and equally how others will perceive them.[77]

Having said this, the Court was initially reluctant to recognise that a refusal to register a child's forename, as chosen by their parents, constituted an interference of sufficient severity to bring it within the scope of the Convention. In *Guillot v France*,[78] the applicants wished to give their daughter the name 'Fleur de Marie', but this was refused on the grounds that it did not appear in any calendar of saints' days. The law was

[71] *Gaskin v the United Kingdom* (10454/83) 13.11.1987 (ComRep), para. 90.
[72] ibid.
[73] (27533/95) 28.02.1996.
[74] It should also be noted that there is a large body of jurisprudence concerning the choice of surnames for adults: in relation to married couples (for example, *X v Netherlands* (9250/81) 03.05.1983 (dec.); *Burghartz v Switzerland* (16213/90) 22.02.1994; *Ünal Tekeli v Turkey* (29865/96) 16.11.2004; *Losonci Rose and Rose v Switzerland* (664/06) 09.11.2010; *Henry Kismoun v France* (32265/10) 05.12.2013), and also in relation to pejorative connotations from a particular name in a given language (*Siskina and Siskins v Estonia* (59727/00) 08.11.2001 (dec.); *Macalin Moxamed Sed Dahir v Switzerland* (12209/10) 15.09.2015).
[75] See *Petersen v Germany* (31178/96) 06.12.2001 (dec.).
[76] See, for example, *Stjerna v Finland* (18131/91) 25.11.1994, where the applicant wanted to change his surname to that borne by a paternal ancestor. He argued that the strength of his relationship to this ancestor was primarily a matter to be assessed by himself, and not the authorities. The Court held, however, that the ancestor had died more than 200 years before, and therefore lived so far back in time that no significant weight could be given to that link for the purposes of Article 8(1).
[77] *SV v Italy* (55216/08) 11.10.2018.
[78] (22500/93) 24.10.1996.

intended to 'prevent parents from choosing forenames which are excessively whimsical and so eccentric that the child is likely to be the first victim'.[79] The applicants claimed that the refusal to register their choice of name amounted to a violation of their right to respect for private and family life.

The Court held that names constitute a means of identifying persons within their family and community, and the choice of a child's name by its parents is a personal, emotional matter that falls within the sphere of Article 8. Nevertheless, it held that the inconvenience caused was not sufficient to constitute an 'interference' under Article 8(1). The child could still use the parents' chosen forename socially, and in all her private dealings, other than in official documents, and therefore neither the parents nor child were sufficiently affected to have suffered an 'interference'.[80]

Likewise, in *Salonen v Finland*,[81] the Commission found that the refusal of the Finnish authorities to register the name 'Ainut Vain Marjaana' (The One and Only Marjaana) did not show a lack of 'respect' for the private and family life of the parents. Instead, it held that it is in the interests of society to regulate the choice of names in order to protect the child from 'possible inconveniences' caused by a name that might be considered inappropriate by others. On the facts, the Commission held that the decision of the authorities could not be considered unreasonable, given its aim, and the fact that the forename could still be used by friends and family if they so wished.

This approach was not universally accepted, however. In a short but strong dissenting opinion in *Guillot*, Judges MacDonald and de Meyer held that the right to respect for private and family life 'without any doubt' includes the right to choose a name for one's child. As such, the restriction of this freedom constituted an interference under Article 8(1). Turning to Article 8(2), they concluded that while the law pursued a legitimate aim of protecting the child's interests, the interference had not been shown to be necessary to protect this aim, particularly as there was no evidence that the name 'Fleur de Marie' could cause any harm.

It was this line of reasoning that was followed in the later case of *Johansson v Finland*.[82] Here, the applicants wished to call their child 'Axl', but the authorities refused to register the name as that form of spelling did not comply with Finnish name practice. Under domestic law, a name that was incompatible with domestic name practice could only be accepted if the person had a connection with a foreign state, and the name was in accordance with the naming practice of that state, or 'for other valid reasons'.

Rather than relying on whether the applicants had been inconvenienced to such an extent as to constitute an 'interference' under Article 8(1), the Court focused on whether the case involved the state's positive or negative obligation. In this context, it noted that not all regulation of names will necessarily constitute an interference, but that there may nevertheless be positive obligations inherent in the respect for private

[79] ibid., para. 10.
[80] See also the dissenting opinions of Judge Vilhjálmsson, Judges Pettiti and Valticos, and Judge Russo, in *Burghartz v Switzerland* (16213/90) 22.02.1994; *X v Netherlands* (9250/81) 03.05.1983.
[81] (27868/95) 02.07.1997 (dec.).
[82] (10163/02) 06.09.2007.

and family life. In either case, the issue will be whether a fair balance has been struck between the public and private interests involved.

The Court accepted that the protection of a child from an unsuitable name—for example, those that are 'ridiculous or whimsical'—was in the public interest. However, the name 'Axl' did not qualify as such, nor was it contended in either the domestic or Strasbourg proceedings that he would suffer prejudice, or that it was in any way inappropriate or contrary to the child's interests. The second rationale put forward by the government—that of maintaining a distinctive naming practice in a small country like Finland—was also accepted as a legitimate public interest. In this case, however, the name appeared on the official Population Information System for three other people at the time of the child's birth, and subsequently at least two other children had been given that name. The Court found that the name had therefore already gained acceptance in Finland, without any negative consequences for the preservation of cultural and linguistic identity of the country. For these reasons, neither the child's interests nor those of the public could outweigh the interests claimed by the parents to have their child registered under a name of their own choosing.

In addition to disputes concerning the choice of the child's forename, the Court has also considered whether parents have the right to choose their child's surname, in accordance with their own preferences. In *Cusan and Fazzo v Italy*,[83] the applicants (a married couple) wished to register their child with the mother's family name. This was refused on the grounds that although there is no rule of law that obliges a child born to a married couple to be registered under the father's name, it is a principle rooted in social consciousness and Italian history. The applicants complained that this decision was a discriminatory interference with their private and family life, contrary to Article 14 in conjunction with Article 8. The Court agreed, finding that in the context of handing down the family name, the child's mother and father were treated differently. Unlike the father, and in spite of agreement between spouses, the mother had no opportunity to give her family name. The Court reiterated the importance of moving towards gender equality and eradicating all discrimination on the grounds of sex in the choice of surname. While tradition can be respected, it cannot justify discrimination.

3.4.5 Citizenship

The final aspect of identity that has been considered by the Court in relation to children has been that of citizenship. In *Genovese v Malta*,[84] the Court recognised that citizenship is an important aspect of a person's social identity, and therefore fell within the ambit of Article 8.

This case concerned a British citizen who had been born out of wedlock to a British mother and a Maltese father. His application for Maltese citizenship was rejected on the grounds that a child born out of wedlock is only eligible for Maltese citizenship if the mother is Maltese. He complained that this law discriminated against him as a

[83] (77/07) 07.01.2014.
[84] (53124/09) 11.10.2011.

child born out of wedlock (as children with a Maltese father and foreign mother who were married were granted citizenship), as well as on the basis of the sex of his Maltese parent (if his mother had been Maltese and his father foreign, he would have been entitled to citizenship).

The Court found that the applicant was in an analogous situation to other children with a Maltese father and foreign mother, and weighty reasons must be advanced to justify a difference in treatment on the basis of birth outside wedlock. The government argued that while the mother of the child was always certain, the father was not, and absent a marriage, there was no identifiable link between the child and parent—and consequently, Malta. Thus, the law was objectively justified on the basis of social reality. This was swiftly dismissed by the Court, who found that it was precisely this type of distinction that Article 14 was intended to protect against, and found that the applicant's Convention rights had been breached.

As *Genovese* concerned a complaint under Article 14, it was sufficient that the application fell within the *scope* of private life, and did not have to meet the higher standard finding that there was an *interference*. However, Judge Valenzia in his dissenting opinion, argued that the issue did not even meet this standard: the majority did not define social identity, nor did it explain how citizenship might affect this. He observed that the concept of private life is interpreted so vastly that it embraces everything, and that the facts in the case did not warrant the Court pushing the concept too far. Quoting the words of Rosalind English, he stated: 'The jaws of Article 8 have already been opened wide enough.'

3.5 Conclusion

The right of the child to respect for private life is still a right under construction before the Court. The child's right to privacy has not been examined in any great depth by the Court, and where it has arisen, it has been interpreted largely from the perspective of parental interests, and subject to parental control. However, the jurisprudence concerning the right to identity is somewhat more developed, and in particular, the recent jurisprudence concerning the establishment of parenthood as an aspect of the child's identity has been influential in domestic law across Europe.[85]

The future challenges for the Court in this area are many and varied.

The child's right to privacy will continue to gain importance in coming years. We have entered a digital age, and the invasion of privacy will continue to take on new dimensions. The growth of social media platforms, and children's engagement with them, involves a paradigm shift—no longer is children's private information filtered solely through their parents, but children themselves are able to dictate what they share with the outside world. This requires the Court to re-evaluate the way in which they conceptualise the child's right to privacy, and in particular, the weight given to parental acquiescence to any interference with this right.[86] Such platforms also open

[85] France, Germany, and Spain now all allow the registration of a child born through surrogacy by an intended parent, provided there is a genetic link.

[86] It is notable that children have already expressed disapproval of their parents posting pictures of them online without their consent: see, for example, K. Lyons, 'Apple Martin Tells of Mother Gwyneth Paltrow

up new opportunities for exploitation and harassment. The Court has recently considered a complaint concerning cyber-surveillance and cyber-bullying of a woman by her former husband, who had hacked her social media accounts to access private conversations and photographs.[87] This is an area in which children are particularly vulnerable—revenge porn is another—and there is no doubt that other such cases will follow.

Another further challenge for the Court will come in relation to mechanisms by which children receive information. Advertising is now ubiquitous in our daily lives, and the impact of this on children's rights is gaining recognition. The Court has recognised that protecting children from indirect advertising is a legitimate justification for a restriction of freedom of expression of broadcasters,[88] but has not yet engaged with this as a positive obligation.

Finally, while the Court has engaged with the child's right to a name and citizenship, it has not yet had to grapple with the issue of gender identity for children. There is a growing body of jurisprudence concerning the right to gender identity for adults,[89] but children have been absent from this debate at a European level—something that will no doubt change in the near future.

Of all the areas covered in this book, this is perhaps the one in which the jurisprudence is the least developed, and the opportunity for future impact the greatest. It is to be hoped that the Court can rise to the challenge.

for Sharing Photo without Consent' (*The Guardian*, 29.03.2019), https://www.theguardian.com/film/2019/mar/29/apple-martin-tells-mother-gwyneth-paltrow-off-for-sharing-photo-without-consent).

[87] *Buturugă v Romania* (56867/15) 11.02.2020.

[88] *Nederlandse Omroeprogramma Stichting v the Netherlands* (16844/90) 13.10.1993 (dec.).

[89] See, for example, *Christine Goodwin v the United Kingdom* (28957/95) 11.07.2002 (GC); *Van Kuck v Germany* (35968/97) 12.06.2003; *Grant v the United Kingdom* (32570/03) 23.05.06; *Hämäläinen v Finland* (37359/09) 16.07.2014 (GC); *YY v Turkey* (14793/08) 10.03.2015; *AP, Garçon and Nicot v France* (79885/12, 52471/13, 52596/13) 06.04.2017.

4
Juvenile Justice

4.1 Introduction

Criminal justice is an area in which the Court has been particularly active: nearly 40 per cent of all violations found by the Court from its inception in 1959 to 2018 have concerned Article 6—the most of any article—while Article 5 takes second place with 13 per cent.[1]

Articles 5 and 6 are both significantly more detailed than other articles in the Convention. This provides a clearer structure for complaints, and as a result, does not require the same level of judicial activism as, for example, the determination of the scope and protection of Article 8. This does not mean, however, that no judicial interpretation is necessary. Although both Articles 5 and 6 have specific provisions concerning children, allowing for the deprivation of liberty for the purposes of educational supervision and the limitation on public trials for juveniles, neither of them fully considers the need of children for greater protection than adults in the field of juvenile justice. This has meant that the Court has been left to devise safeguards as best it can, through an expansive definition of terms such as 'fair', 'lawful', and 'reasonable'.

The jurisprudence in this area significantly overlaps with that concerning adults involved with the criminal justice system. This chapter does not attempt to detail the entirety of this framework: whole books could be (and indeed have been) written about Article 6 criminal trial rights alone.[2] Instead, the chapter discusses the cases that have specifically concerned children, in order to continue this book's aim of analysing the approach of the Court to children's rights.

4.2 Differences in treatment between adults and juveniles

The intent of developing separate rules, and indeed often a separate system, for children involved in the criminal justice system is protective, intended to ensure stricter procedural safeguards to account for the current vulnerability of children, while also providing greater flexibility in response to their evolving capacities. Such a separate

[1] European Court of Human Rights, 'Statistical Overview 1959–2018' (Council of Europe, 2019), https://www.echr.coe.int/Documents/Overview_19592018_ENG.pdf.

Although of course not all decisions under these articles concern criminal justice.

[2] See, for example, R. Goss, *Criminal Fair Trial Rights: Article 6 of the European Convention on Human Rights* (Oxford: Hart, 2014).

Children and the European Court of Human Rights. Claire Fenton-Glynn, Oxford University Press (2021). © Claire Fenton-Glynn.
DOI: 10.1093/oso/9780198787518.003.0004

system has, nevertheless, led to challenges under Article 14 where juveniles have been treated differently to adults being dealt with as part of the criminal process.

In most cases, this line of argument has been swiftly dismissed by the Court, finding that any difference in treatment stems from the protective, rather than punitive, nature of the juvenile justice system, and therefore is based on an objective and reasonable justification.[3] However, there are a number of cases worth noting where this principle has been discussed in more detail.

The first, *X v Switzerland*,[4] involved a 15-year-old who was sent to a specialist centre for behavioural monitoring pending his trial, where he was compelled to undertake work as a cabinet maker, for which he was paid a small wage. He complained under Article 14 in conjunction with Article 4 that this work was discriminatory, as adults were not required to undertake work when detained pending trial. The Commission noted that a difference in treatment is only discriminatory if it distinguishes between groups of people considered comparable and where it lacks objective and reasonable justification. However, it concluded that a minor's position in law is fundamentally different to that of an adult, and especially where this relates to the justice system. When implementing a juvenile justice system, states provide a much wider choice of measures which may be taken, and greater emphasis is placed on the development of the child's personality and on education and training, as is reflected in the very text of Article 5(1)(d) of the Convention. As a result, the Commission found that the appropriate comparator was not an adult who had entered the criminal justice system, but another minor—in which case, there was no difference in treatment.

The difference in approach to adult and minor offenders was again emphasised by the Commission in *Nelson v the United Kingdom*.[5] In this case, a 15-year-old who had been convicted of attempted murder was sentenced to nine years' imprisonment under a statute which dealt specifically with the detention of minors. While adult sentences at the time were eligible for remission—a system under which their sentence would be reduced by one-third unless the prisoner violated prison rules—a sentence under this statute was not.

The applicant complained that his ineligibility for remission resulted in a heavier penalty, effectively imposed on him due to his age, in violation of Article 14 in conjunction with Article 5. Unlike *X v Switzerland*, the Commission in this case did not focus on the relevant comparator, but instead examined the justification for the difference in treatment. It found that 'obviously' the penal law of a state cannot be expected to treat child and adult offenders in the same way, and the different sentencing options must be examined in this light. The Commission acknowledged that children can change greatly over the course of their sentence and viewed flexibility as an important prerequisite to any such measure. The purpose of the juvenile justice system was not to punish children, but to subject them to appropriate programmes of care and supervision. The fact that the applicant did not benefit from earlier release did not detract

[3] See, for example, *Bouamar v Belgium* (9106/80) 29.02.1988; *DG v Ireland* (39474/98) 16.05.2002.
[4] (8500/79) 14.12.1979 (dec.).
[5] (11077/84) 13.10.1986 (dec.).

from the distinctive nature of this regime, the purpose of which was to deal more flexibly with juvenile offenders.[6]

Likewise, in *Khamtokhu and Aksenchik v Russia*[7] the Court found that adult offenders were in an analogous situation with juveniles who had committed the same offence, but that the difference in treatment was justified. This case was brought by adults who had been given a life sentence after having been found guilty of certain crimes. However, a person under 18 convicted of the same offence would not have been given a life sentence, as statute explicitly excluded this punishment for juveniles. The Court found that the exemption of juvenile offenders from life imprisonment was common to the legal systems of all member states, and consistent with the recommendations of the UN Committee on the Rights of the Child. Where young offenders are held accountable, this must be done with due regard to their mental and emotional immaturity, the greater malleability of their personality, and their capability for rehabilitation and reformation.[8]

Nevertheless, despite this important acknowledgement that states are *justified* in creating different criminal justice systems for juveniles, the Court has not recognised a *positive obligation* for them to do so. No case has yet been brought arguing that the state has failed to establish appropriate mechanisms for dealing with juvenile offending, which are separate and distinct from the system in place for adults. The arguments that have been made have concerned a failure to take specific measures to mitigate the adult system, rather than a challenge to the entire system itself.[9]

4.3 The age of criminal responsibility

Across Europe, the age at which children can be found criminally responsible for their actions varies greatly. While in some states, there is no age of criminal responsibility, and any child capable of 'discernment' can be found criminally liable (France, Luxembourg), those that do have an age limit range from a low of ten

[6] On a factual level, the Commission also found that the applicant had not established that he would have benefited from being sentenced as an adult, even with remission, as the judge had made clear that had he been older, his sentence would have been considerably heavier.

[7] (60367/08, 961/11) 24.01.2017 (GC).

[8] Interestingly in this case, the applicants complained that there was discrimination based on sex as well as age, as life imprisonment was prohibited where the offender was female, or over 65. The Court found that there were relevant differences between male offenders and female offenders, and between offenders over and under the age of 65, such as to justify a difference of treatment. However, this justification was rather thinly argued, perhaps due to the acknowledgment of the Court that while desirable, there was no European consensus which would oblige states to prohibit life sentences in all situations. Russia's move to abolish these sentences in *some* circumstances was thus viewed as a positive move. However, Russia had indicated that if a violation of Article 14 was found in this case, then it would simply re-apply life imprisonment to all categories of offenders. Unlike other provisions of the Convention, where a violation requires the state to improve its practices, a violation of Article 14 gives states two options: 'they can either take away the privilege of one group or grant the privilege to the other group as well'. (ibid., concurring opinion of Judge Nussberger, para. 3) Rather than advancing human rights, a finding of a violation in this case would have set them back. Although it is not ideal that all do not have the optimum protection, as Nussberger argued in her concurring opinion, 'a State should not be punished for taking one step in a good direction merely because the second step does not follow'. (ibid., para. 6)

[9] See *T v the United Kingdom* (24724/94) 16.12.1999 (GC).

(England and Wales, Northern Ireland, and Switzerland), to 12 (Andorra, Belgium, Ireland,[10] Netherlands, San Marino, Turkey, Scotland), 13 (Greece, Monaco), 14 (Albania, Austria, Bosnia and Herzegovina, Bulgaria, Croatia, Cyprus, Estonia, Georgia, Germany, Hungary,[11] Latvia, Lichtenstein, the Former Yugoslav Republic of Macedonia (FYROM), Malta, Montenegro, Romania, Serbia, Slovakia, Slovenia, Spain), 15 (Czech Republic, Denmark, Finland, Iceland, Italy, Norway, Sweden), 16 (Armenia, Azerbaijan Lithuania, the Republic of Moldova, Portugal, Russia, Ukraine),[12] and 17 (Poland).[13] Interestingly, no European state sets the age of criminal responsibility at the age of majority: 18.[14]

Unsurprisingly, given this range of responses, the European Court of Human Rights has been reluctant to interfere in this area, even in cases concerning states at the very low end of the spectrum—as was seen in *T v the United Kingdom*.[15] In this case, concerning one of two ten-year-old boys who were convicted of the murder of a toddler,[16] the applicant argued that the attribution of criminal responsibility at such a low age—in combination with other features of the trial, discussed below—gave rise to a breach of Article 3, as it constituted inhuman and degrading treatment.

The Court noted that there was no commonly accepted minimum age for criminal responsibility in Europe—while admittedly, most European states had adopted a higher age, four states at the time attributed criminal responsibility at a younger age. As such, the minimum age adopted by England was not considered so low as to differ disproportionately from other states. The Court also rejected the applicant's argument that there was a clear developing trend at an international level towards higher ages, noting that the UN Convention on the Rights of the Child merely requires states to set a minimum level, without specifying what this should be, while the United Nations Standard Minimum Rules for the Administration of Juvenile Justice (Beijing Rules)[17] merely advise states not to set it too low. As a result, the Court found that the attribution of criminal responsibility to a ten-year-old did not in itself give rise to a breach of Article 3.

The concurring opinion of Lord Reed went into more detail on this point, and is worth citing at length:

> [T]he purpose of attributing criminal responsibility to a child of a given age is not to cause that child suffering or humiliation, but to reflect a consensus in the society in question as to the appropriate age at which a child is sufficiently mature to be held criminally responsible for his or her conduct. Since perceptions of childhood reflect

[10] Though this is lowered to ten for murder, manslaughter, rape, or aggravated sexual assault.

[11] The age is 12 for the offences of homicide, manslaughter, battery, robbery, and plundering.

[12] Although in all these jurisdictions save Portugal, this age is lowered to 14 for certain named offences.

[13] The age is 15 for certain named offences.

[14] All information obtained from Child Rights International Network, 'Minimum Ages of Criminal Responsibility in Europe', https://archive.crin.org/en/home/ages/europe.html.

[15] (24724/94) 16.12.1999 (GC).

[16] See also *V v the United Kingdom* (24888/94) 16.12.1999, which concerned his co-defendant, also ten years old. The reasoning applied by the Court is the same in both cases, with only a small variation for some specific differences in the circumstances of the two defendants.

[17] (1985) GA Res 40/3.

> social, cultural and historical circumstances, and are subject to change over time, it is unsurprising that different States should have different ages of responsibility…
>
> [A]lthough the attribution of criminal responsibility to a child of ten will have consequences which may cause distress to the child concerned, it is necessary to bear in mind that the treatment of a child who has behaved in the same way in a State with a higher age of criminal responsibility may also cause distress. Whether a child who has intentionally killed another child is regarded as criminally responsible or not, any society is likely to require some form of inquiry to establish whether the child has in fact behaved in the manner alleged and, if so, some form of measures for the protection of the public and the care and treatment of the child in question.

This case, although now over 20 years old, is still the leading authority on the age of criminal responsibility under the Convention. However, it is far from clear that the same decision would be reached today. The decision of the Court in this respect was by no means unanimous, with Judges Pastor Ridruejo, Ress, Makarczyk, Tulkens, and Butkevych dissenting on this point. In particular, they disputed the finding of the majority that there was no clear consensus on the appropriate age of criminal responsibility, stating:

> We have no doubt that there is a general standard amongst the member States of the Council of Europe under which there is a system of relative criminal responsibility beginning at the age of thirteen or fourteen—with special court proceedings for juveniles—and providing for full criminal responsibility at the age of eighteen or above. Where children aged from ten to about thirteen or fourteen have committed crimes, educational measures are imposed to try to integrate the young offender into society. Even if Rule 4 of the Beijing Rules does not specify a minimum age of criminal responsibility, the very warning that the age should not be fixed too low indicates that criminal responsibility and maturity are related concepts. It is clearly the view of the vast majority of the Contracting States that this kind of maturity is not present in children below the age of thirteen or fourteen.

This argument has only grown more powerful with the passage of time. Three of the four states relied on by the majority to show that the English approach was not disproportionate—Cyprus, Ireland, and Lichtenstein—now all have higher minimum ages (14, 12, and 14, respectively) leaving England and Wales, Northern Ireland, and Switzerland as outliers at two years younger than any other state.[18] Moreover, despite the lack of explicit guidance in Article 40(3)(a) of the UN Convention on the Rights of the Child as to the appropriate age of criminal responsibility, the UN Committee on the Rights of the Child has since declared that an age of less than 12 years is not 'internationally acceptable',[19] and encouraged it to be set at at least 14 years of age.[20] It is thus

[18] Although in Ireland, the age of criminal responsibility is lowered to ten for some crimes, including murder, which is relevant on the facts of *T v the United Kingdom* (24724/94) 16.12.1999 (GC).

[19] United Nations Committee on the Rights of the Child, *General Comment No. 10 (2007), Children's Rights in Juvenile Justice* (CRC/C/GC/10, 25.04.2007), para. 32.

[20] United Nations Committee on the Rights of the Child, *General Comment No. 24 (2019) on Children's Rights in the Child Justice System* (CRC/C/GC/24, 18.09.2019), para. 22.

clear that both European consensus and international guidance, would now view the criminal prosecution of a ten-year-old child as a violation of their rights.[21]

4.4 Deprivation of liberty

Article 5 protects the right to liberty and security of the person. Any restrictions on this freedom must fall within one of the six enumerated grounds in Article 5(1). In summary, these are:

(a) detention following conviction by a court;
(b) arrest or detention for non-compliance with a court order, or in order to secure the fulfilment of a legal obligation;
(c) arrest or detention on suspicion of having committed an offence;
(d) detention of a minor for the purpose of educational supervision, or to bring him before a competent legal authority;
(e) detention for the prevention of 'spreading of infectious diseases, of persons of unsound mind, alcoholics or drug addicts or vagrants';
(f) arrest or detention to prevent unauthorised entry into a country or of a person who is to be deported.

The detention of children in the context of immigration is discussed in Chapter 5, while restrictions of liberty as an exercise of parental authority are discussed in Chapter 9. This section considers the detention of children by state actors in the context of the juvenile justice system, both in terms of educational supervision (Article 5(1)(d)) and arrest and detention on suspicion of having committed an offence (Article 5(1)(c)). It then goes on to analyse the procedural safeguards that accompany such detention, as well as the Court's case law surrounding the conditions in which children can be held.

4.4.1 Educational supervision

4.4.1.1 Educational supervision and juvenile justice

In one of the few direct references to children in the text of the Convention, Article 5(1)(d) contains a special provision for the detention of minors 'for the purpose of educational supervision'. The purpose of this provision was to enable states to adopt a different response to adult and juvenile offending, recognising children's vulnerability.[22] It allows

[21] For further discussion of this topic, see D. Cipriani, *Children's Rights and the Minimum Age of Criminal Responsibility* (Abingdon: Routledge, 2009); B. Goldson, 'Difficult to Understand or Defend: A Reasoned Case for Raising the Age of Criminal Responsibility' (2009) 48(5) *Howard Journal of Criminal Justice* 514; G. Maher, 'Age and Criminal Responsibility' (2004) 2 *Ohio State Journal of Criminal Law* 493; E. Delmage, 'The Minimum Age of Criminal Responsibility: A Medico-Legal Perspective' (2013) 13(2) *Youth Justice* 102; E. Farmer, 'The Age of Criminal Responsibility: Developmental Science and Human Rights Perspectives' (2011) 6(2) *Journal of Children's Services* 86.

[22] See U. Kilkelly, *The Child and the European Convention on Human Rights* (Farnham, Surrey: Ashgate, 1999), 44–45.

children to be diverted from the criminal justice system, and provides rehabilitation rather than punishment.

Despite this, the Court has not been called on to consider whether any specific diversion into educational supervision has been justified in a particular case, or in relation to a specific offence. Nor has it considered whether there is a positive obligation to impose educational supervision rather than a prison sentence. Instead, the focus of the jurisprudence has been on whether the conditions of detention are such that could qualify as 'educational supervision'.

The leading case in this area is *Bouamar v Belgium*,[23] concerning a 15-year-old who was suspected of various offences. The Juvenile Court ordered his detention, using legislation intended to divert young offenders from the criminal justice system and into specialised reform facilities. However, these provisions also permitted detention in a remand prison for up to 15 days where it was 'materially impossible' to find an institution able to accept the child immediately. In fact, it was *factually* impossible to do so, as Belgium—despite passing this legislation—had not yet established such facilities. The applicant was therefore placed in remand prison on nine occasions over the course of a year, for a total of 119 days. The applicant challenged the lawfulness of his detention under Article 5(1), arguing that an interim order for custody in a remand prison, which could not last for more than 15 days, could not be regarded as having been made for the purpose of 'educational supervision'.

The Court held that confinement in a remand prison does not necessarily contravene Article 5(1)(d), even if it does not itself provide 'educational supervision'. Article 5(1)(d) does not preclude the use of an interim placement as a preliminary measure prior to a regime of supervised education, but this must truly be temporary, and be speedily followed by such a regime in a setting designed for that purpose. In this case, the Court found that the placements became 'less and less lawful' as they progressed, categorising nine such placements as 'fruitless repetition'.

The Court noted that there was no obligation under the Convention to divert juveniles from the criminal justice system, nor to provide educational supervision as an alternative, and recognised the 'liberal spirit' of the Belgian law in this regard. However, once Belgium chose the system of educational supervision, it was under an obligation to put in place appropriate institutional facilities to fulfil the demands of Article 5(1)(d).[24] This it had failed to do.

When assessing whether a particular regime can be considered 'educational supervision', the Court has emphasised that this term must not be equated rigidly with notions of classroom teaching.[25] Indeed, in *Blokhin v Russia*,[26] the Court held that attendance at school whilst being detained was not sufficient to make the detention itself 'for the purpose' of educational supervision. Schooling in line with the normal school curriculum should be standard practice for all minors deprived of their liberty, and therefore there must be further justification to bring the detention within the scope of Article 5(1)(d). Instead, 'educational supervision' is more closely aligned with an

[23] (9106/80) 29.02.1988.
[24] See also *DG v Ireland* (39474/98) 16.05.2002.
[25] See *Koniarska v the United Kingdom* (33670/96) 12.10.2000 (dec.), discussed below.
[26] (47152/06) 23.03.2016.

exercise of parental responsibility—providing guidance and protection for children, through a process of assessment, treatment, and rehabilitation.[27]

As such, the authorities must make sure that any placement is capable of meeting these aims and the conditions of detention consistent with this. For example, a 30-day temporary measure cannot offer any meaningful opportunity to provide appropriate treatment aimed towards changing the child's behaviour, and therefore cannot constitute 'educational supervision'.[28] Nor can the holding of a child in conditions of virtual isolation be considered as furthering any educational aim.[29] Rather, the Court will expect to see 'regular or systematic' activities, that are clearly prescribed, and with appropriate staff to carry them out.[30]

In this way, the Court has interpreted Article 5(1)(d) relatively strictly in the field of juvenile justice, though not particularly progressively—states which use a system of educational supervision must ensure facilities that are fit for purpose, and provide appropriate educational activities to justify the restriction on liberty, but there is no positive obligation to establish such a system in the first place.

4.4.1.2 Educational supervision for the protection of the child

Educational supervision is not limited to the juvenile justice system, however. Article 5(1)(d) provides for the deprivation of liberty in the interests of the child regardless of whether they are suspected of having committed a crime, or whether they are simply a child 'at risk'.[31] In cases concerning children at risk, the Court has made clear that the measure will only be lawful under Article 5(1)(d) if it constitutes a proportionate response: it must be in the child's best interests and be aimed at preventing serious risks for the child's development.[32]

The Court discussed the obligations on the authorities in this area in the decision of *Koniarska v the United Kingdom*.[33] Despite being an admissibility decision, and almost 25 years old, it remains the leading case in this area. The case involved a 17-year-old who was placed in a specialist residential facility for 'seriously disturbed minors', on the grounds that she was a danger to herself and others. While she was there, a study programme was available to her, but she only took limited part in this—for example, classes in social skills. She complained that her deprivation of liberty was unlawful, not only because she did not actually receive education while in detention, but also because at 17, she was beyond the age where she was required by law to be in schooling.

The Court in this case drew a clear distinction between 'education' in terms of schooling and the concept of 'educational supervision', which embraced a much wider range of activities. As discussed above in relation to educational supervision in the context of juvenile justice, this phrase should not be equated rigidly with notions of classroom teaching, but rather encompasses various aspects of the exercise of parental

[27] See also *A and others v Bulgaria* (51776/08) 29.11.2011; *DL v Bulgaria* (7472/14) 19.05.2016.

[28] *Blokhin v Russia* (47152/06) 23.03.2016.

[29] *Bouamar v Belgium* (9106/80) 29.02.1988.

[30] See ibid.; *Ichin and others v Ukraine* (28189/04, 28192/04) 21.12.2010; *Blokhin v Russia* (47152/06) 23.03.2016.

[31] *A and others v Bulgaria* (51776/08) 29.11.2011.

[32] *DL v Bulgaria* (7472/14) 19.05.2016.

[33] (33670/96) 12.10.2000 (dec.).

rights for the benefit and protection of the child. For this reason, the fact that the child could not have been required to attend ordinary school under domestic law was not relevant, nor was the fact that she chose not to attend many classes: it was sufficient that the placement was intended to provide her with protection and guidance, and that such opportunities were offered to her.

The Court has also emphasised that proportionality requires that detention for educational supervision be ordered as a last resort, and only where less stringent measures have proven inadequate. For example, in *A and others v Bulgaria*,[34] the Court found that the placement of children in a young offenders' institution on account of 'antisocial behaviour'—running away from home, truancy, vagrancy, and/or prostitution—fell within Article 5(1)(d), as it had been ordered to provide them with a more favourable environment and a more structured upbringing. Despite the fact that the institution also housed minors who had committed criminal offences, it had not been intended as a punishment, and was only implemented when other measures and alternative placements had been insufficient.[35]

Likewise, in *DG v Ireland*,[36] the Court found that the placement of a homeless child in a penal institution was justified, despite the fact that he had not been charged or convicted of any offence, on the grounds that there was no other placement that could meet his needs and secure his welfare. The Court rejected his argument that the placement violated his rights under Article 3, as he was a minor in special need of care, not punishment, finding that the placement had been for his own safety, and the safety of others, and the intention of the authorities had been protective. The Court went on to note that the mere placement in a penal institution could not be considered inhuman and degrading in and of itself, and no evidence had been put forward to indicate any adverse mental or physical impact. The significant proportion of detainees were the same age as, or close in age to, the applicant, the prison regime was adapted to juvenile detainees, and educational and recreational activities were available. As such, the fact that he was subject to prison discipline did not give rise to an issue under Article 3.

These cases establish a very wide mandate for authorities in this area—as long as the detention provides protection for the child, the 'educational' aspect of the placement is interpreted broadly to include any kind of benefit for personal development. At first glance, this breadth of discretion may appear problematic, especially where there is a significant cross-over between the juvenile justice system and the protective function of the state. As was seen in *A* and *DG*, it allows children who are in additional need of care to be placed in penal institutions with children who have committed offences. However, it reflects the wider function of a specialised juvenile justice system, which recognises that children who have committed offences are also children in additional need of care: the state's role in both cases should be to provide support and assistance to children. While it is important that this discretion is not too broad, the requirement that a protective placement is made only

[34] (51776/08) 29.11.2011.
[35] See also *DL v Bulgaria* (7472/14) 19.05.2016.
[36] (39474/98) 16.05.2002.

where no lesser measure is available, and where it is in the child's best interests, provides an adequate check on state practice.[37]

4.4.2 Bringing a minor before a competent legal authority

Article 5(1)(d) not only creates a special avenue of detention for children in the form of educational supervision, but it additionally provides a mechanism for a child's 'lawful detention for the purpose of bringing him before the competent legal authority'. This provision is very similar to Article 5(1)(c), which provides, inter alia, for 'the lawful arrest or detention of a person effected for the purpose of bringing him before the competent legal authority on reasonable suspicion of having committed an offence'. The difference between these two provisions rests in the purpose for which they are designed: Article 5(1)(c) is intended to apply purely to individuals (including children) who are in conflict with the law, while Article 5(1)(d) has a much wider scope. It is not concerned with the determination of a criminal charge—the children who fall within this provision have not necessarily committed an offence—but instead it is intended to provide the authorities with the power to remove children from harmful situations.[38]

This aspect of Article 5(1)(d) has only been discussed on one occasion, in the 1979 Commission decision of *X v Switzerland*.[39] In this case, a 15-year-old boy, who had committed a variety of offences, was placed in a specialist centre pending trial for the purpose of 'studying his behaviour'. Although the Commission accepted that he had been deprived of his liberty for a 'fairly long time'—eight months—it found that this was in conformity with Article 5(1)(d): it had been ordered by a judge, it was required to undertake medical and psychiatric tests, and it had been prompted by the ineffectiveness of previous educative measures.

One early admissibility decision is not much upon which to base an analysis of this provision. It is unclear why it has not been used more frequently: potentially, the expansive approach to educational supervision under the first part of Article 5(1)(d) has removed any need for its use. Indeed, the detention in *X v Switzerland* could have equally been justified on those grounds. While the Commission in this case seemed to indicate quite a wide scope for domestic authorities in the detention of juveniles for the purposes of bringing them before a competent authority,

[37] This does not mean that this power can be used indiscriminately. In *P and S v Poland* (57375/08) 30.10.2012, the Court criticised the authorities for placing a child seeking an abortion in a juvenile detention facility, to determine whether she had made this decision of her own free will. The Court found that it was legitimate for the authorities to attempt to establish with certainty whether she had the opportunity to reach a free and well-informed decision; however, less drastic measures should have been considered than the detention of a young girl in a situation of considerable vulnerability. The true purpose of the authorities, the Court observed, appeared to be to separate the child from her mother, and to prevent the abortion, which could 'by no stretch of the imagination' fall within the justification of 'educational supervision'. (para. 148)

[38] U. Kilkelly, *The Child and the European Convention on Human Rights* (Farnham, Surrey: Ashgate, 1999), 44.

[39] (8500/79) 14.12.1979.

provided that it is proportionate and accompanied by procedural safeguards, a more complete examination is needed of the provision before any firm conclusions can be drawn.

4.4.3 Detention on suspicion of having committed an offence

4.4.3.1 The questioning of child suspects

Although Article 5(1)(d) is the only exception to the right to liberty of the person which explicitly refers to minors, the detention of children is not limited to this provision. A second form of detention which has been frequently challenged before the Court has been that of pre-trial detention under Article 5(1)(c). As discussed in section 4.4.2 above, this provision permits the lawful detention of a person for the purpose of bringing them before a competent legal authority, on reasonable suspicion of them having committed an offence.

From an early stage, the Court has recognised that children can be detained for questioning under this section, even where they are below the age of criminal responsibility for the offence in question. In *X v the Federal Republic of Germany*,[40] a ten-year-old girl was suspected of theft and brought to the police station. She was kept there for two hours, during which time she was questioned, but otherwise kept in an unlocked cell. As she was below the age of criminal responsibility, she was then released without charge. The Commission rejected her claim that she had been deprived of liberty, finding that although she had been questioned, she had been neither arrested nor detained, and therefore the case did not fall within the scope of Article 5.

In concluding that there had been no deprivation of liberty, the Commission endorsed an objective test: considering the concrete situation faced by the individual from the point of view of an objective outsider, taking into account the type of detention, its duration, and effects, and the manner of implementation.[41] The Commission concluded that it was

> regrettable that the children may not have been able to understand the police action and may have felt that they were deprived of their liberty. Nevertheless, in view of an objective appreciation of the information now before the Commission, it considers that in the circumstances of the case the action in question did not constitute a deprivation of liberty in the sense of Article 5(1) of the Convention.[42]

Although this case is consistent with the Court's wider jurisprudence, it raises a dangerous precedent for children. By taking an 'objective appreciation' of the situation, the Commission failed to recognise the subjective vulnerability of the child, who cannot be expected to have the same comprehension of their circumstances as an adult. By

[40] (8819/79) 19.03.1981 (dec.).

[41] See *Engel and others v the Netherlands* (5100/71, 5101/71, 5102/71, 5354/72, 5370/72) 08.06.1976; *Guzzardi v Italy* (7367/76) 06.11.1980; *Nielsen v Denmark* (10929/84) 12.03.1987 (ComRep).

[42] *X v the Federal Republic of Germany* (8819/79) 19.03.1981 (dec.), p. 161.

holding everyone to the same objective standard, the Commission did not adequately reflect the different approach needed for children in conflict with the law.

Moreover, although the Commission did recognise that the interrogation of children must be carried out in a way that respects their age and susceptibility, there was no recognition of the positive obligation of the state to ensure the child's comprehension of her situation. The Commission considered it 'regrettable' that she had not been able to understand the police action, but did not then place any corresponding duty on the state to either ensure that information was provided to her in a manner which she could understand or to inform her parents of the situation, allowing them to provide guidance.

This decision pre-dates both the Beijing Rules and the UN Convention on the Rights of the Child, and seems out of step with the more child-friendly approach now taken by the Court in other areas of juvenile justice. Nevertheless, the principle of objectivity remains the position of the Court, and whether a person has been deprived of liberty is a question of fact, rather than subjective experience, leaving children in a vulnerable position.[43]

4.4.3.2 Pre-trial detention

Article 5(1)(c) permits only 'lawful' detention of a person on reasonable suspicion of having committed an offence. The Court has made clear that in order for this criteria to be fulfilled, the detention must be adequately documented,[44] based on clearly identified legal provisions,[45] and subject to a specified time limit.[46] Moreover, it must be justified on specific grounds, which explain why it is necessary in the particular circumstances.[47]

In addition to these rather obvious obligations inherent in Article 5(1)(c),[48] Article 5(3) sets out explicit procedural requirements that must follow this detention: the individual must be brought promptly before a judge or other officer authorised by law to exercise judicial power and shall be entitled to trial within a reasonable time or to release pending trial.

43 See also *Weeks v the United Kingdom* (9787/82) 02.03.1987, in section 4.6 below.

44 In particular, the authorities must make a record of appropriate matters such as the date and location of the detention, the name of the detainee, the reasons for detention, and the name of the person carrying it out: see *Smolik v Ukraine* (11778/05) 12.02.2012; *Uğur v Turkey* (37308/05) 13.01.2015.

45 *Korneykova v Ukraine* (39884/05) 19.01.2012; *Kuptsov and Kuptsova v Russia* (6110/03) 03.03.2011.

46 *Kuptsov and Kuptsova v Russia* (39884/05) 19.01.2012. In addition to the requirement of lawfulness, Article 5(1)(c) also requires that detention be based on sufficient grounds. While this may seem like an obvious requirement, unfortunately the Court had to reaffirm in *Ipek and others v Turkey* (17019/02, 30070/02) 03.02.2009 that this means that there must at least be 'reasonable grounds' for suspicion. In this case, the two boys were arrested merely on the basis of being at a friend's house at the time of his arrest, a fact the Court found insufficient to satisfy the requirements of Article 5.

47 *Korneykova v Ukraine* (39884/05) 19.01.2012. It is significant to note that although the cases that established these principles concerned juvenile defendants, at no time did the Court refer explicitly to the fact that the applicants were juveniles (at least in relation to this issue). The rights set out are derived from necessary safeguards in the justice system in general, and not from any specific vulnerability of children involved with this system. While obviously adults also require adequate documentation and legal certainty in relation to their detention, the lack of explicit reference to the specific vulnerability of children involved in the justice system is worrying.

48 Sadly not so obvious that the Court has not had to rule on these issues.

The requirement for 'promptness' in relation to review by a judge or judicial officer in the first part of Article 5(3) can be contrasted with the obligation for a trial within a 'reasonable time' in the second part. In relation to the former, the French text, 'aussitôt' has a connotation of immediacy, confirming that the degree of flexibility attached to the notion of 'promptness' is limited.[49] Although the criterion of 'promptness' must be assessed in each case according to its own circumstances, the Court has adopted four days as a rule of thumb for the maximum time before an individual must be brought before a judicial authority.[50] For example, in *Ipek v Turkey*,[51] the Court noted that the applicants were brought before a judge after three days and nine hours, making it '*prima facie* compatible with the requirements of Art 5(3)'.[52] Importantly, however, the Court attached significant weight to the fact that the applicants were minors, detained for over three days without any safeguards against possible arbitrary conduct by the state authorities. In light of their young age, and given that the authorities undertook only limited investigative measures over the three days, there was no justification for keeping them in detention for this length of time.[53]

When the child is brought before the judge or officer exercising judicial authority, a decision must be made as to whether they should be released pending trial. The reasonable suspicion that a person has committed an offence, as required under Article 5(1)(c), is the 'sine qua non' for the validity of detention. However, after a certain period of time this will no longer suffice, and the Court will then consider whether there are other grounds sufficient to justify the deprivation of liberty.[54] In this respect, the Court has made clear that Article 5(3) entails a proportionality requirement: in order to be free from arbitrariness, continued detention must be shown to be necessary in all the circumstances.[55] Indeed, there must be a presumption in favour of release.[56]

This is an area in which significant weight has been placed on the vulnerability of juveniles, and the Court has imposed a higher level of scrutiny in such cases. In particular, the Court has relied on Article 37(b) of the UN Convention on the Rights of the Child, requiring that '[t]he arrest, detention or imprisonment of a child shall ... be used only as a measure of last resort and for the shortest appropriate period of time', adopting this as their standard for review.[57] Although the Court has acknowledged that there may be countervailing interests which require pre-trial detention—that the

[49] See *Brogan and others v the United Kingdom* (11209/84, 11234/84, 11266/84, 11386/85) 29.11.1988.

[50] ibid. See also *McKay v the United Kingdom* (543/03) 03.10.2006.

[51] (17019/02, 30070/02) 03.02.2009.

[52] ibid., para. 36 (original emphasis).

[53] Despite this laudably child-sensitive approach, this case conversely highlights the worrying trend of giving state authorities greater leeway in exercising their powers in the context of terrorism. Here, the Court acknowledged that the investigation of terrorist offences presents authorities with special problems, and in concluding that the authorities had exceeded the requirement of promptness, added the caveat 'even in the context of terrorist investigations'. (ibid., para. 36) While it is encouraging that the Court made clear that authorities do not have *carte blanche* whenever they assert that the arrest relates to terrorism, the fact that states are given a certain degree of latitude when dealing with a particular class of offences is of concern. See also *Brogan and others v the United Kingdom* (11209/84, 11234/84, 11266/84, 11386/85) 29.11.1988; *Murray v the United Kingdom* (14310/88) 28.10.1994; *Dikme v Turkey* (20869/92) 11.07.2000.

[54] See, for example, *Selçuk v Turkey* (21768/02) 10.01.2006, para. 31.

[55] *Korneykova v Ukraine* (39884/05) 19.01.2012.

[56] *McKay v the United Kingdom* (543/03) 03.10.2006.

[57] *Nart v Turkey* (20817/04) 06.05.2008.

defendant would not appear for trial, or would prejudice the administration of justice or commit further offences, as well as the fear of public disorder in light of the gravity of the offences and the public reaction to them—the age of the applicant has been recognised as a 'very important factor' that must be carefully balanced against these.[58]

Even where pre-trial detention is justified, the authorities must then ensure that the child receives a trial within a 'reasonable time'. Article 5(3) does not indicate a maximum length of pre-trial detention, and nor has the Court set any such guideline—this will depend on the particular features of the case. However, the age of the child will be important in undertaking this determination, and the Court has observed that the authorities must display 'special diligence' when dealing with minors.[59]

The proportionality of the length of detention will also depend on what the authorities were trying to achieve within that time frame. The Court has emphasised that the *raison d'etre* of Article 5(3) 'relate[s] to the requirements of an investigation which is to be conducted with expedition'.[60] This was seen in *Assenov and others v Bulgaria*,[61] where the Court held that the authorities had breached Article 5(3) in detaining a 14-year-old on remand for two years. While the government had argued that the case was particularly complex, the Court noted that during a period of one year, virtually no action had been taken in the investigation,

On the other hand, in *JM v Denmark*,[62] the Court found that the Danish authorities *were* justified in keeping the 15-year-old applicant on remand for 16 months while undertaking investigations concerning his mental health. In order to determine an appropriate sanction, it was vital to obtain accurate information concerning his psychiatric condition, and the period taken to achieve this could not be considered excessive. In coming to this conclusion, the Court attached weight to the fact that there were no periods of inactivity of any significance, and that whenever the domestic courts extended the detention, they gave detailed and specific reasons for doing so. Moreover, the authorities had considered his young age when ordering the ongoing detention, and decided to place him in an appropriate home or institution, followed by a secure institution for young offenders. The Court was thus satisfied that the domestic courts had adequately adapted the measures in light of the applicant's individual age and situation.

[58] *Korneykova v Ukraine* (39884/05) 19.01.2012; *Selçuk v Turkey* (21768/02) 10.01.2006.

[59] *Assenov and others v Bulgaria* (24760/94) 28.10.1998, para. 157. See also, for example, *Selçuk v Turkey* (21768/02) 10.01.2006, where the Court held that four months' detention for a 16-year-old exceeded a 'reasonable' time; while in *Nart v Turkey* (20817/04) 06.05.2008, the Court found that the detention of a 17-year-old for 48 days violated his rights under Article 5(3), particularly as he was kept with adult prisoners during that time. Similarly, in *Güveç v Turkey* (70337/01) 20.01.2009, there was definitely a violation of the applicant's rights when he was detained for four-and-a-half years, from the age of 15.

[60] *Bezicheri v Italy* (11400/85) 25.10.1989, para. 21.

[61] (24760/94) 28.10.1998.

[62] (34421/09) 13.11.2012.

4.4.4 The opportunity to challenge lawfulness of detention

The final safeguard in relation to arrest and detention is found in Article 5(4), providing that anyone deprived of his liberty is entitled to take proceedings by which the lawfulness of his detention can be decided speedily by a court. This is an ongoing obligation—it is not sufficient that the applicant is given a single opportunity to submit a challenge to their detention, but must be able to review the continuing lawfulness of the detention on an ongoing basis.[63] Given that pre-trial detention is intended to be of limited duration, periodic reviews at short intervals are required.[64]

Although the procedure under Article 5(4) does not necessarily have to be attended by the same guarantees as those under the right to a fair trial in Article 6(1), it nevertheless must have a judicial character, and provide guarantees appropriate to the kind of deprivation of liberty in question.[65] This means that the scope of the obligation is not identical in all circumstances, or for every kind of restriction on liberty.[66]

In the context of pre-trial detention, the Court has made clear that there must be an oral hearing: for example, in *Assenov and others v Bulgaria*,[67] the Court found a violation of Article 5(4) when the prosecutor made a decision on the papers, while in *Bouamar v Belgium*,[68] there was no *inter partes* hearing, and the judge was free to take a decision on the basis of what he considered adequate information. Moreover, the child must have the effective assistance of a lawyer for any such proceedings: in *Bouamar*, the Court emphasised that the mere fact that the child himself appeared in person did not afford the necessary safeguards, particularly given the applicant's 'very young' age.

Moreover, the system of review must be practical and effective, capable of providing substantive relief. While Article 5(4) does not require the court to be empowered to substitute its own discretion for that of the decision-maker, the review must be wide enough to be able to consider the conditions that are essential for deciding the 'lawfulness' of detention. This includes not only an examination of compliance with the procedural requirements in domestic law, but also consideration of the reasonableness of the suspicion grounding the arrest and the legitimacy of the purpose pursued by the ensuing detention.[69] The proceedings must also be efficient—particularly where the detention is of a short duration, the review must be completed before the period of detention ends, in order to ensure that they provide practical protection for the individual's rights.[70]

Interestingly, the Court has indicated that a different regime for the review of the detention of children than that available to adults will not violate the Convention. In *Bouamar*, the child complained that he could not benefit from the procedure available

[63] *Assenov and others v Bulgaria* (24760/94) 28.10.1998.
[64] ibid. See also *Bezicheri v Italy* (11400/85) 25.10.1989.
[65] See *Megyeri v Germany* (13770/88) 12.05.1992.
[66] See section 4.6 below for a discussion of the application of Article 5(4) in the context of sentencing.
[67] (24760/94) 28.10.1998.
[68] (9106/80) 29.02.1988.
[69] See *Nikolova v Bulgaria* (31195/96) 25.03.1999; *Grabowski v Poland* (57722/12) 30.06.2015.
[70] *Bouamar v Belgium* (9106/80) 29.02.1988.

to adults, which required their detention to be reviewed within five days of their arrest. The Court held that this difference in treatment did not amount to discrimination, as it stemmed from the protective, rather than punitive, nature of the procedure applicable to children. While the adults in question were subject to criminal proceedings against them, the minors were detained as part of an educational programme, which did not have a punitive element. In light of the different purpose of the detention, it was justifiable to have a different mechanism for review.

The requirements of Article 5(4) are discussed in further detail in section 4.6.2 below in relation to sentencing, and in particular, the need for an independent body, with adequate procedural safeguards, capable of providing an effective remedy.

4.4.5 Conditions of detention

4.4.5.1 Material conditions of detention

There is a large body of jurisprudence from the Court relating to the material conditions of detention, and in particular, whether they are such as to breach the prohibition of inhuman and degrading treatment and punishment under Article 3. In undertaking this evaluation, the Court will examine the situation as a whole, to determine whether the conditions of detention have subjected the applicant, in view of the length of his imprisonment, to hardship of an intensity exceeding the unavoidable level of suffering inherent in detention.

When considering the detention of children—whether for educational supervision, pre-trial detention, or detention following a conviction—their age will be a relevant factor in deciding whether the treatment has crossed the threshold of Article 3.[71] However, the mere fact that a child is detained in a penal institution will be insufficient, in and of itself, to constitute inhuman and degrading treatment—there must be some aggravating factor that accompanies it.[72] Factors which have been found to contribute to a violation under Article 3 include issues such as overcrowding and cramped conditions,[73] lighting,[74] temperature and ventilation,[75] sanitary facilities,[76] access to running water,[77] insect infestation,[78] availability of physical exercise,[79] and lack of outside

[71] *Kuptsov and Kuptsova v Russia* (6110/03) 03.03.2011.

[72] See *DG v Ireland* (39474/98) 16.05.2002.

[73] *Kalashnikov v Russia* (47095/99) 15.07.2002; *Florea v Romania* (37186/03) 14.09.2010; *Ananyev and others v Russia* (42525/07, 60800/08) 10.01.2012; *Orchowski v Poland* (17885/04) 22.10.2009; *Mandić and Jović v Slovenia* (5774/10, 5985/10) 20.10.2011.

[74] *Modarca v the Republic of Moldova* (14437/05) 10.05.2007; *Mandić and Jović v Slovenia* (5774/10, 5985/10) 20.10.2011; *Torreggiani and others v Italy* (43517/09, 46882/09, 55400/09, 57875/09, 61535/09, 35315/10, 37818/10) 08.01.2013.

[75] *Peers v Greece* (28524/95) 19.04.2001.

[76] ibid.

[77] *Vasilescu v Belgium* (64682/12) 25.11.2014; *Pocasovschi and Mihaila v the Republic of Moldova and Russia* (1089/09) 29.05.2018.

[78] *Varga and others v Hungary* (14097/12, 45135/12, 73712/12, 34001/13, 44055/13, 64586/13) 10.03.2015; *Kalashnikov v Russia* (47095/99) 15.07.2002.

[79] *Ananyev and others v Russia* (42525/07, 60800/08) 10.01.2012; *Clasens v Belgium* (26564/16) 28.05.2019.

contact.[80]

One such factor that has been identified by the Court that relates specifically to juveniles is detention with adults. While the Court has not imposed an absolute prohibition on such detention, as it has always been just one of a number of factors considered in a particular case, there are strong indications that this would be the case.

The leading decision on this issue is *Güveç v Turkey*,[81] concerning a 15-year-old boy who was arrested on suspicion of being a member of the Kurdistan Workers' Party (PKK). He was detained on remand for five years in an adult prison, during which time he suffered psychological problems, which worsened over the course of his stay. For the first six months he had no access to legal representation, and indeed did not have adequate representation for the duration of the five years' detention. This, coupled with the fact that for 18 months he was being tried for a crime that carried a sentence of death, created a situation of uncertainty which 'undoubtedly' caused his psychological problems. The Court found that having regard to his age, the length of his detention in prison together with adults, the failure of the authorities to provide adequate medical care for his psychological problems, and the failure to take steps to prevent his repeated attempts to commit suicide, there had been a violation of the applicant's rights under Article 3.

As such, although this case has been cited for the proposition that children cannot be detained with adults, in reality, this was simply one factor amongst many leading to a violation of the Convention. This is partly because the focus of the Court in such cases is the psychological state of the detainee that results from these conditions, rather than the conditions themselves.[82] As a result, most applications will depend on a variety of different factors, all combining to produce a loss of dignity.

This issue of detention of children with adults has also arisen in relation to Article 2, and the positive obligation on states to take adequate steps to protect the life of individuals within their care. In *Çoşelav v Turkey*,[83] the Court found that the state had failed to fulfil its obligations in this regard with respect to a 16-year-old boy who committed suicide in prison, where he was being kept in an adult wing. In response to the government's argument that the boy's transfer to the adult wing came at his request, the Court '[found] it surprising that such a request was considered without any verification of his age, and considers that decision to be a clear illustration of the prison authorities' lack of respect for both the domestic regulations and the international instruments regulating the detention of juvenile prisoners'.[84] Nevertheless, the Court failed to take the next step and find that such conditions of detention were, in and of themselves, a violation of the Convention, instead focusing on the lack of appropriate medical treatment and protection for the boy.

This again leaves a gap in protection for children involved with the justice system. As the Court has rightly pointed out, the detention of children with adults is prohibited

[80] *Clasens v Belgium* (26564/16) 28.05.2019. See also cases on solitary confinement, for example *Ilaşcu and others v the Republic of Moldova and Russia* (48787/99) 08.07.2004; *Piechowicz v Poland* (20071/07) 17.04.2012.

[81] (70337/01) 20.01.2009.

[82] On this, see N. Mavronicola, 'Bouyid v Belgium: The "Minimum Level of Severity" and Human Dignity's Role in Article 3 ECHR' (2016) *Cyprus Human Rights Law Review* 1.

[83] (1413/07) 09.10.2012.

[84] ibid., para. 59.

under international law: Article 37(c) of the UN Convention on the Rights of the Child states that 'every child deprived of liberty shall be separated from adults unless it is considered in the child's best interest not to do so', while the Beijing Rules require that juveniles must be detained separately from adults.[85] In light of these clear international rules, this is an area that the Court could have taken a much stronger stance and provided much more robust protection for children's rights.

4.4.5.2 The provision of medical treatment

In addition to complaints concerning detention with adults, both *Güveç* and *Çoşelav* raised allegations concerning the inadequacy of medical treatment during their confinement. The Court has recognised that prisoners are in a vulnerable position, as they are under the exclusive control of the state, and thus there is a correlative duty to ensure that they are provided with appropriate care and assistance, including medical treatment.[86]

In *Güveç v Turkey*,[87] the 15-year-old child suffered psychiatric problems during his five-year-detention, and made several suicide attempts. The Court found that not only were the national authorities directly responsible for his psychological state, as a result of his detention in inhuman and degrading conditions, but that they also manifestly failed to provide adequate medical care for him. When the domestic court received a report stating that the applicant required treatment in a psychiatric hospital, they failed to act on this: instead, their only action was to refer him for examination to see whether he had the necessary criminal capacity when allegedly committing the offence. Moreover, despite repeated suicide attempts, the authorities took no action to protect or assist the applicant.[88]

Importantly, the Court observed that in addition to not providing medical care themselves, the authorities had also prevented his family from doing so by refusing to release him on bail. The Court noted that although Article 3 cannot be construed as imposing an obligation to release detainees on health grounds, it does require the state to safeguard the physical and emotional well-being of individuals deprived of their liberty. Taking into consideration the applicant's age, the failure to provide medical care and to prevent his repeated attempts to commit suicide amounted to inhuman and degrading treatment contrary to Article 3.[89]

The most comprehensive examination of the level and standard of medical care that states are obliged to provide was provided in *Blokhin v Russia*,[90] concerning a 12-year-old who suffered from attention deficit hyperactivity disorder (ADHD), neurosis, and enuresis. He was placed in a temporary detention centre for 30 days, during

[85] Rules 13(4) and 26(3).
[86] *Çoşelav v Turkey* (1413/07) 09.10.2012.
[87] (70337/01) 20.01.2009.
[88] See also *Çoşelav v Turkey* (1413/07) 09.10.2012, where the Court held that sufficient steps had not been taken by the authorities to provide the applicant with adequate protection and assistance. He needed urgent specialist care, yet despite repeated requests for help and attempts to take his own life, the authorities' response was to bring disciplinary proceedings against him for setting a bad example.
[89] In finding this violation, the Court also noted the length of his detention in prison together with adults, as discussed in section 4.4.5.1 above.
[90] (47152/06) 23.03.2016.

which time he did not receive medical care for his conditions. The Court held that the standard of health care required must be compatible with the human dignity of a detainee, taking into account the practical demands of imprisonment. Drawing on the UN Convention on the Rights of the Child, the UN Rules for the Protection of Juveniles Deprived of their Liberty (Havana Rules),[91] and the Council of Europe Rules for juvenile offenders,[92] the Court held that juveniles deprived of their liberty must be safeguarded according to recognised medical standards applicable in the wider community. The child must be guaranteed proper care and protection, guided always by their best interests. In determining whether the minimum level of severity has been attained to come within the scope of Article 3, the Court emphasised the age of the applicant and his state of health, noting that they left him in a particularly vulnerable situation. The authorities were aware of his medical condition, and that he was in need of treatment, yet failed to act on this—as was evidenced by the fact that he required hospitalisation the day after his release, and was kept there for almost three weeks for treatment.

The Court went further, however, requiring that when considering deprivation of liberty, authorities must undertake a medical assessment of the child's health to determine whether or not he can be placed in a juvenile detention centre. This is a strong statement from the Court. While in *Güveç*, the Court was quick to note that there was no obligation to release detainees on health grounds, in *Blokhin*, the Court indicated that juveniles should not be detained *at all* if their state of health so indicates. While the facts of this case involved a young child below the age of criminal responsibility who had a number of mental and physical issues, thus making it a more clear-cut issue than many other cases, it sets an important precedent, recognising the double vulnerability of children who also suffer from health problems.

4.4.5.3 Medical examinations in detention

While there is an obligation on states to provide adequate medical treatment for children in detention, any examination or treatment must correspond to medical necessity, and should only be undertaken with appropriate consent. This issue has arisen in a number of cases taken against the Turkish authorities, in relation to their practice of forcing female detainees to undergo a gynaecological examination. For example, in *Salmanoğlu and Polattaş v Turkey*,[93] the applicants alleged that while in custody they were examined by a medical expert to determine their virginity status, and whether they had recently had sexual relations. The government argued that the applicants had consented to the tests; however, the Court found that even if this were the case, in assessing the validity of any purported consent, it could not overlook the fact that one of the applicants was 16 years old at the relevant time. Even if the consent was valid, there was no medical or legal necessity justifying such an intrusive examination, and the tests therefore constituted discriminatory and degrading treatment.

[91] (1990) GA Res 45/113.

[92] Recommendation of the Committee of Ministers to member states on the European Rules for juvenile offenders subject to sanctions or measures (CM/Rec(2008)11).

[93] (15828/03) 17.03.2009.

The compatibility of these tests with Article 3 was further considered in *Yazgül Yilmaz v Turkey*,[94] also concerning a 16-year-old detainee. The police superintendent ordered a gynaecological exam, which was undertaken without the applicant's consent, to establish whether there was evidence of assault during police custody, and whether her hymen was broken. The Court held that obtaining a minor's consent should have been surrounded by minimum guarantees commensurate with the importance of a gynaecological examination. A gynaecological examination can be traumatising—particularly for a minor—who must be afforded additional guarantees and precautions, including ensuring that consent is given at all stages, allowing her to be accompanied during the procedure, allowing her to choose between a male or female doctor, informing her of the reason for the exam, its organisation and results, and respecting her dignity. In failing to provide these fundamental safeguards, the applicant had suffered extreme anxiety and deep distress, which the authorities could not have failed to be aware of, given her young age and the fact that she was unaccompanied. Moreover, the Court criticised the automatic nature of the examination. It did not relate to any allegation brought by the applicant, nor was it a medical necessity, but instead was an automatic process for the purpose of avoiding false sexual assault accusations against police officers. As such, it failed to take into account the rights of the detained women and constituted degrading treatment contrary to Article 3.

While these may seem like quite basic requirements—that any tests must be necessary, and accompanied by appropriate consent—these cases are worth noting for the additional scrutiny placed on states when the individual is a minor. In particular, the Court's comments—albeit brief—about the validity of a 16-year-old's consent to an invasive medical procedure while in detention are of importance, as is the recognition of the age of the child as a factor to be considered in determining the impact of the procedure.

4.4.6 Conclusions on deprivation of liberty in the context of juvenile justice

The Court's jurisprudence as it relates to the deprivation of liberty of children is very inconsistent. In some circumstances (for example, with regard to the length and proportionality of pre-trial detention), it has placed significant weight on the vulnerable situation of juveniles and the need for greater scrutiny in such cases. However, in other areas, the child's age is barely mentioned and the Court's reasoning simply mirrors that relating to adults.

Moreover, while the special accommodation made for juvenile detention in the form of educational supervision is of benefit, the conservative way in which it has been interpreted—as imposing a negative obligation only—means that many children continue to be subject to detention systems designed for adults, with no positive obligation to provide a specialised system of juvenile detention to accommodate their different needs.

[94] (36369/06) 01.02.2011.

It is to be hoped that the Court will continue to expand its jurisprudence in this area, relying in particular on the multitude of international standards in this field. The unique position of children in conflict with the law must be considered in all cases concerning minors, not just where it suits the Court. Only then can it be considered a child-friendly system of justice.

4.5 The right to a fair trial

The fair trial guarantees under Article 6 are both explicit and implicit. Explicit in the wording of Article 6 are the right to a fair and public hearing (though this is subject to some exceptions, notably for juveniles), a trial within a reasonable time, an independent and impartial tribunal, and access to a lawyer. The Court has added to these guarantees by interpreting an extra safeguard into the right to fair trial under Article 6(1): the right to effective participation.

Before discussing these guarantees, however, it is first important to note that Article 6 only applies '[i]n the determination of [an individual's] civil rights and obligations or of any criminal charge against him'. Moreover, the requirements of this provision will be different depending on whether the proceedings are civil or criminal, with criminal proceedings requiring a number of additional safeguards for the defendant. As a result, before considering the substance of the complaint, the Court must first determine whether they should be characterised as civil or criminal.

This was examined at length in *Blokhin v Russia*,[95] concerning a 12-year-old child accused of extortion, but who was not prosecuted as he was below the age of criminal responsibility. Instead, he was placed in a temporary detention centre for 30 days for the purposes of 'behavioural correction'. The government argued that the proceedings placing the applicant in detention were not proceedings concerning a 'criminal charge'; the purpose of the order was to prevent him from committing further offences, and did not establish his guilt in respect of a crime, nor punish him for offences already committed. Therefore, the authorities argued that the process should be construed as a type of civil proceedings, in line with their designation at domestic law, meaning that the applicant could not complain regarding the lack of legal representation, nor that he had not had an opportunity to cross-examine witnesses.

The Court held that the classification of proceedings under domestic law was relevant, but not determinative. Applying the *Engel* criteria,[96] it held that the nature of the alleged act, and the penalty that might be imposed, must also be considered when deciding whether the proceedings were civil or criminal. In this case, the alleged act corresponded to an offence under ordinary criminal law. However, the Court did not find it necessary to conclude whether, despite the indisputably criminal nature of the offence, the fact that criminal prosecution was legally impossible removed the proceedings from the scope of the criminal limb of Article 6. Instead, it concentrated on the third criterion: the nature and degree of severity of the penalty that the applicant

[95] (47152/06) 23.03.2016.

[96] *Engel and others v Netherlands* (5100/71, 5101/71, 5102/71, 5354/72, 5370/72) 08.06.1976.

risked incurring. Placement in a detention centre involves a deprivation of liberty, raising the presumption that the proceedings will be criminal. This is only rebuttable in 'entirely exceptional circumstances', if deprivation of liberty cannot be considered 'appreciably detrimental' given its nature, duration, and manner of execution.[97] Here, although the authorities stated that the placement was to correct behaviour and deter future acts of delinquency, the Court looked beyond appearances and the language used and concentrated on the factual circumstances faced by the applicant: he was detained for 30 days, in a closed and guarded centre, under constant supervision, and subject to a strict disciplinary regime. Although the authorities had stated that the placement was not a punishment, there was no doubt it contained punitive elements, as well as prevention and deterrence. As a result, it was classified as criminal proceedings for the purposes of Article 6.[98]

This decision is of particular importance for children, given the nature of the juvenile justice system. The philosophy behind this system is social welfare, rather than criminal justice, and the authorities are to some extent exercising a *parens patriae* jurisdiction—seeking to determine the needs of the child, focusing on guidance and rehabilitation, rather than solely on criminal responsibility, guilt, and punishment.[99] As the proceedings are predominantly protective, rather than penal, this can lead to them being categorised as civil, rather than criminal, meaning that the child is deprived of important safeguards. The Court's judgment made clear that the protective function of the domestic courts should not deprive children of their procedural rights.

4.5.1 Effective participation in proceedings

The most important safeguard that the Court has developed for the protection of the rights of juveniles undergoing due process is the requirement of 'effective participation'. The overriding obligation on states is that criminal proceedings must be organised to respect the best interests of the child, and proceedings adapted to ensure that they are able to understand and participate in proceedings.

The first time the Court was called upon to consider how the guarantees in Article 6(1) apply to criminal proceedings concerning children was in *T v the United Kingdom*.[100] This case concerned high-profile criminal proceedings in England relating to two ten-year-old boys who were charged with the murder of a toddler. In addition to challenges concerning the low age of criminal responsibility in England (section 4.3 above) and the length of their sentence (section 4.6 below), the applicant also complained of the trial process itself, arguing that it breached his right to fair

97 See also *Ezeh and Connors v the United Kingdom* (39665/98, 40086/98) 09.10.2003 (GC).

98 This decision was not unanimous, however. In their partially dissenting opinion, Judges Speilmann, Nicolaou, Bianku, Keller, Spanó, and Motoc suggested that the majority relied too heavily on the punitive elements of the 30-day detention, and overestimated the significance of the connection between the alleged criminal act and the subsequent detention. If this became the general rule, they argued that this would result in almost all temporary measures involving deprivation of liberty being considered criminal under Article 6.

99 See *Blokhin v Russia* (47152/06) 23.03.2016, dissenting opinion of Judge Zupančič.

100 (24724/94) 16.12.1999 (GC).

trial (Article 6(1)) and constituted inhuman and degrading treatment (Article 3). The question before the Court was whether procedures which are generally considered to safeguard the rights of adults on trial should be abrogated in respect of children to promote their understanding and participation.

The applicant argued that the right to fair trial under Article 6(1) contains an implicit requirement that the defendant can participate effectively in the conduct of his case. In this case, the applicant suffered from post-traumatic stress, which combined with the lack of therapeutic work since the offence, limited his ability to instruct his lawyers and testify adequately in his own defence.

The Court found that, in and of itself, the trial on criminal charges of a child could not be said to violate the fair trial guarantee under Article 6(1)—even for a child as young as 11 (as the child was by that time). However, any child charged with an offence must be dealt with in a manner that takes full account of his age, level of maturity, and intellectual and emotional capacity, and steps must be taken to ensure that he is able to understand and participate in proceedings.

Here, the domestic authorities had taken special measures to promote the child's understanding of the proceedings: the trial procedure had been explained to him, he had been taken to see the courtroom in advance to gain familiarity with it, and hearing times had been shortened to mirror the schedule of a normal school day. The dock where the defendant sat was raised so that he could see what was going on in the courtroom, and the court adjourned for a break whenever counsel indicated that the child (or his co-defendant) needed it. Despite all these measures, however, the Court found that the applicant had been unable to effectively participate in proceedings. It observed that the very formality and ritual of the Crown Court must have seemed incomprehensible and intimidating, inhibiting him from participating freely. Even some of the measures designed to assist the defendant had the opposite impact—the raised dock did allow him to see what was going on, but also exposed him to the scrutiny of the press and public, increasing his sense of discomfort.

Furthermore, although the applicant was represented by skilled and experienced lawyers, the Court found that this was insufficient in the circumstances to remedy the lack of participation by the defendant himself. It held that it was highly unlikely that the child would have felt sufficiently uninhibited—given the tense courtroom, and under public scrutiny—to have consulted with his lawyers during the proceedings. In addition, given the defendant's immaturity and disturbed emotional state, the Court doubted that he would have been capable of cooperating with lawyers outside the courtroom, and able to give them information for the purposes of his defence. As a result, the child had been denied the opportunity to participate effectively, and thus denied a fair hearing under Article 6.

Judge Baka dissented on this point, finding that representation by a highly trained legal professional was sufficient to protect the child's right to participation. He argued that the child's position was objectively no different from that of an accused who is lacking legal knowledge, suffering from a mental disorder, or of low intelligence. Such individuals can be said to be subjects of the criminal justice system, rather than active participants. It is illusory to expect them to be able to give any legally relevant instructions or facilitate their defence—instead, we must trust lawyers to perform this function for them.

This is a regressive understanding of the position of children, reducing them to objects of the legal system, rather than active subjects with enforceable rights. By placing their defence in the hands of others, Judge Baka falls back on the idea of children in need of protection and fails to recognise their individual agency. While it is true that others may be in similar, difficult, positions when participating in proceedings, the answer is to provide enhanced protection to *all* these groups, rather than none of them.

Despite this dissent from Judge Baka, *T v the United Kingdom* has become the leading case in evaluating the fairness of criminal proceedings from a child rights perspective. However, the case did not provide detailed guidance on what was required to achieve a trial for children which was compatible with Article 6(1), only what was not acceptable, and it has been left to subsequent cases to fill in the gaps.

Most important in this respect has been *SC v the United Kingdom*,[101] concerning an 11-year-old boy who was charged with attempted robbery. He was diagnosed as having learning difficulties (with an intellectual capacity of between six and eight years old) and a very short attention span. In light of this, the trial proceedings were modified to create a more informal environment—he wasn't required to sit in the dock, the judges and lawyers did not wear wigs and gowns, and he was accompanied by a social worker with whom he conferred frequently in order for him to explain what was happening. Despite these amendments to the procedure, he argued that he had not been able to effectively participate in the trial.

The Court reiterated that effective participation includes not only the right to be present during proceedings, but also to be able to adequately follow them. However, this does not require that the child should understand—or even be capable of understanding—every point of law or evidential detail. Instead, it presupposes that the child has a broad understanding of the nature of the trial process, including the significance of the penalty that may be imposed. This means that he should be able—with the assistance of an interpreter, lawyer, social worker, or friend—to understand the general thrust of what is being said in court, including the case being put forward by the prosecution, and what is said by their witnesses. In response to this, he should then be capable of explaining to his lawyer his own version of events, pointing out any statements with which he disagrees, and making them aware of any facts that should be put forward in his defence.[102]

On the facts of the case, the child seemed to have little comprehension of his situation, of the role of the jury, or that he risked a custodial sentence. The Court dismissed the government's argument that there had been a failure to exhaust domestic remedies, on the grounds that he had not argued at trial that he was unfit to plead. It held that being unfit to plead requires that the accused be so intellectually impaired that he was unable to understand whether he was guilty—it was not incompatible to find that he could understand this, but nonetheless be unable to participate effectively for the purposes of Article 6(1).

[101] (60958/00) 15.06.2004.

[102] See also *Güveç v Turkey* (70337/01) 20.01.2009.

In this regard, the Court made the following, important statement:

> [W]hen the decision is taken to deal with a child, such as the applicant, who risks not being able to participate effectively because of his young age and limited intellectual capacity, by way of criminal proceedings rather than some other form of disposal directed primarily at determining the child's best interests and those of the community, it is essential that he be tried in a specialist tribunal which is able to give full consideration to, and make proper allowance for, the handicaps under which he labours, and adapt its procedure accordingly.[103]

SC thus overcame one of the major problems inherent with the decision in *T*. As Judges Pastor Ridruejo, Ress, Makarczyk, Tulkens, and Butkevych pointed out in their partial dissent in *T*, by focusing on whether these children could participate effectively in adult procedures the majority had failed to sufficiently address the suffering that such a procedure would inevitably entail for them. Even though the domestic authorities did everything they could to accommodate the vulnerability of the child, it was operating within a system which, both in principle and practice, was in breach of Article 3. The very fact of being tried in accordance with the same criminal procedures as adults—even with modifications to make them more informal and less intimidating—must be qualified as inhuman treatment.

In requiring that a separate, specially adapted, system of justice be implemented to accommodate the particular situation of juveniles, Article 6(1) provides one of the most important safeguards imposed by the Convention in the area of juvenile justice. While further cases are needed to fully elaborate the requirements of such a system, and the procedures within it, it is nevertheless an area of the Court's jurisprudence that is to be applauded.

4.5.2 The right to a public hearing

One of the specific safeguards for minors contained in the text of Article 6(1) is the recognition that the press or public may be excluded from all or part of a trial where the interests of juveniles so require. This was considered in *T*, where the case had given rise to widespread media attention, courtrooms were packed with public and media, and hostile crowds surrounded the court and met the defendants as they arrived each day.

The Court considered the impact this environment could have on the ability of the child to participate effectively. It noted that for a young child charged with a grave offence, which attracted high levels of public interest, it would be necessary to conduct the hearing in such a way as to reduce as far as possible any feelings of intimidation and inhibition. The Court observed that in England, for less serious crimes, children were dealt with in special youth courts, from which the public is excluded and there

[103] *SC v the United Kingdom* (60958/00) 15.06.2004, para. 35.

are automatic reporting restrictions. However, the applicants had been subject to an open trial, attended by the public, and the media.

The government argued that public trials serve the general interest of ensuring the open administration of justice. While the Court acknowledged this justification, it considered that such interests could be satisfied by a modified procedure providing for 'selected attendance rights and judicial reporting',[104] and thus the publicity of the hearing contributed to the finding of a violation of Article 6(1).

This was further explored by Lord Reed in his concurring opinion, where he recognised that the authorities were being asked to draw a balance between 'countervailing, and incommensurable, values': the importance of safeguarding the wellbeing and future of the child, as well as promoting their later rehabilitation and reintegration against the public interest in the open administration of justice and freedom of information. In England, the balance is usually held to be in favour of the child's welfare, requiring trials in private, and it is only when the child is accused of a very serious offence that the pendulum swings in the other direction. As Lord Reed pointed out, this is 'not because of indifference towards their welfare, or a lack of respect for human dignity, let alone any intention to cause suffering or humiliation', merely that in such cases, the public interest weighs heavier in the balance.

Lord Reed also observed that the judge had instructed the jury, when assessing witness testimony, to bear in mind that witnesses had had to give evidence in a large court room packed with people. However, no such instruction was given in relation to the children, who were the primary focus of this attention and hostility, and would be likely to find it even more difficult to cope with. He concluded that if holding a public trial is incompatible with holding a fair trial, it is the latter which must take priority. However, like the majority, he noted that it is possible to put restrictions on attendance and reporting, thus protecting the interests of the child, without fully excluding the public interest in the open administration of justice. The failure to achieve such a balance violated the rights of the child under Article 6.

While the publicity surrounding the trial was found to contribute to an unfair trial, the Court rejected the submission of the applicants that it had created an environment of inhuman and degrading treatment, contrary to Article 3. The Court referred to the international instruments, noting that one of the minimum guarantees of the UN Convention on the Rights of the Child in the field of juvenile justice is that children accused of crimes should have their privacy fully respected at all stages of the proceedings,[105] which was binding on the United Kingdom and all other member states of the Council of Europe. Furthermore, the Beijing Rules require that a 'juvenile's privacy shall be respected at all stages' and that 'in principle, no information that may lead to the identification of a juvenile offender shall be published'.[106] In this light, the Court acknowledged a clear international trend in favour of the protection of the privacy of juvenile defendants. However, the Court found that while the existence of an international trend is one factor to take into account when assessing whether treatment violates the European Convention on Human Rights, it cannot be determinative.

[104] *T v the United Kingdom* (24724/94) 16.12.1999 (GC), para. 85.
[105] Article 40(2)(b).
[106] Rule 8.

The Court then shifted the focus to the subjective intent of the authorities. It found that the criminal proceedings were not motivated by any intention on the part of the authorities to humiliate the defendant or to cause his suffering. In a somewhat callous conclusion, it held that any proceedings to determine the circumstances surrounding the commission of a brutal murder would have provoked feelings of guilt, distress, and fear, whether they were carried out in public or private. Since the defendant already showed signs of post-traumatic stress disorder *before* the trial, the Court was not convinced that the conduct of the proceedings added to this to any significant degree.

This case is thus simultaneously encouraging and disheartening. On the positive side, the ruling that a fair trial under Article 6(1) requires that the child be given some degree of privacy is an important step forward. On the other hand, the dismissal of the UN Convention on the Rights of the Child standards in this respect is to be regretted. While obviously a breach of another international instrument does not necessarily imply a corresponding violation of the ECHR, this is one of the few areas in which there are clear international standards, accepted by all member states of the Council of Europe. As such, this represents a missed opportunity by the Court to take a strong stance on children's rights.

4.5.3 The right to an independent and impartial tribunal

The right to a fair trial under Article 6(1) requires that the case is heard by 'an independent and impartial tribunal'. This requirement has been discussed extensively in relation to adults, but rarely for children. Where it has arisen, the Court has failed to adequately differentiate the application of this principle for juveniles, relying instead on adult principles, without any further consideration.

This was demonstrated in *Nortier v the Netherlands*,[107] concerning a 14-year-old accused of attempted rape. Judge M, the investigating judge, ordered that he be placed in initial detention on remand, and that he undergo a psychiatric evaluation. When the case came to trial, Judge M was again the presiding judge. The applicant argued that he had not received a hearing before an impartial tribunal, as his case had been dealt with by the same judge throughout. The same judge had on four occasions ordered his detention on remand, which implied that he had already reached the conclusion that there were serious indications that the applicant had committed the crime. Moreover, he argued that Judge M must have already formed an idea of the likely sentence, as law required him to ascertain that it was unlikely that the detention on remand would last longer than any sentence.

The Court reiterated that what is decisive are not the subjective apprehensions of the suspect, but whether, in the particular circumstances of the case, his fears are objectively justified. It held that the mere fact that a judge made pre-trial decisions, including those relating to detention on remand, cannot be taken as in itself justifying fears as to his impartiality: what matters is the scope and nature of these decisions.

[107] (13924/88) 24.08.1993.

In this case, Judge M had not made use of his investigative powers, save for the order for a psychiatric examination. Moreover, the question he was being asked to decide when ordering remand was of a different nature than those at issue when making his final judgment. In the former, he only had to find that the prosecution had prima facie grounds for the charge against the applicant. There was therefore no objective justification for an allegation of impartiality, and no violation of Article 6.

Unfortunately, by narrowing its conclusions to the application of the particular case, the Court failed to engage with the more fundamental issue: whether Article 6 should be applied to juvenile criminal procedure in the same way as to adult criminal procedure. This was left to Judge Morenilla in his concurring opinion. Unlike the majority, who focused on the nature and scope of decision-making, Judge Morenilla considered the age of the defendant as the issue of decisive importance: the function and purpose of the juvenile justice system is fundamentally different from that of the adult justice system, and the role of the judge must be evaluated in this light. He held that although minors are entitled to the same protection of fundamental rights as adults, the developing state of their personality—and consequently, their limited social responsibility—should be taken into account in applying Article 6. The right to be heard by an 'impartial tribunal' should not be seen as incompatible with the protective treatment of juveniles, and Article 6 should not be interpreted so as to hinder measures aimed at ensuring the full development of minors. States should be given a margin of appreciation to organise their juvenile justice system to protect both the interests of the child and of society. In many cases, this is achieved by setting up juvenile courts which focus on correction and re-education, and the qualifications and functions of judges are tailored to reflect that function. In light of this, the organisation of the system so that one judge deals with the case the whole way through is intended to develop a relationship of trust between the judge on the one hand, and the minor and his parents on the other. This, according to Judge Morenilla, was not only reasonable, but commendable.

The acceptance by the Court of the judge's ongoing involvement in the *Nortier* case can be contrasted with *Adamkiewicz v Poland*,[108] where a 15-year-old boy had been arrested for murder. He was brought before a family affairs judge, who directed the investigation, and ultimately committed him for trial before the Youth Court on the basis that 'the evidence gathered during the investigation indicated that the applicant had committed the crime'. This same judge later sat on the Youth Court, which found him guilty. The applicant complained that he had not been heard by an impartial tribunal, contrary to Article 6(1).

In this case, the Court held that, unlike *Nortier*, the issue on which the judge had ruled during the investigation coincided in large measure with the question on which he subsequently had to rule as president of the trial bench. This gave rise to a concern regarding the impartiality of the judge, as he already had a pre-conceived idea concerning the question of guilt. Moreover, during the investigation, he had made broad use of the powers available to him, including ordering the opening of proceedings, directing the evidence-gathering, and deciding to commit the applicant to trial. The

[108] (54729/00) 02.03.2010.

Court accepted that because of the different functions of the juvenile and adult justice systems, there must necessarily be differences in procedure. However, it did not consider that the presence on the trial bench of a judge who had been responsible for the investigation, and who had previously committed him to trial on the basis of probable guilt, could be seen to be in the best interests of the child.[109]

4.5.4 Access to legal representation

Article 6(3)(c) of the Convention provides the right of everyone to defend themselves in person, or through legal assistance of his own choosing. If he does not have sufficient means to pay for legal assistance, this must be provided by the state free of charge where the interests of justice so require. In cases concerning juveniles, this provision has been read expansively, and the Court has emphasised that in light of the vulnerability of children, and in particular their level of maturity and intellectual and emotional capacities, it is of fundamental importance that they are provided with the assistance of a lawyer.

The seminal case on legal representation under Article 6—both for adults and juveniles—is *Salduz v Turkey*.[110] Here, a 17-year-old applicant was suspected of having participated in an unlawful demonstration supporting the PKK. His right to access a lawyer was restricted, as he was accused of an offence falling within the jurisdiction of the State Security Courts, and he did not have representation when he made statements to the police, the prosecutor, or the investigative judge.

The Court found that, as a rule, the rights of the defence will be irretrievably prejudiced when incriminating statements made without access to a lawyer are used for conviction.[111] Although he had access to a lawyer following his detention on remand, the investigation was in large part completed by that stage, and the damage to his right to fair trial had already occurred. Neither the assistance provided subsequently by a lawyer, nor the adversarial nature of the ensuing proceedings could cure defects which occurred during police custody.

While the majority found that, as a general principle, access to a lawyer should be provided from the first interrogation of a suspect by the police, Judge Bratza felt that this did not go far enough. In his concurring opinion, he suggested that the Court should have used the opportunity to state in clear terms that the fairness of criminal proceedings under Article 6 requires that a suspect should be granted access to legal advice from the moment he is taken into police custody or pre-trial detention. Likewise, the concurring opinion of Judge Zagrebelsky, joined by Judges Casadevall and Türmen, argued that providing a lawyer from the point of questioning was not sufficient. They held that

[109] See also *Romenskiy v Russia* (22875/02) 13.06.2013, where a 16-year-old was refused release prior to trial on the grounds that 'he has committed a serious crime'. The Court found that the wording not only described a state of suspicion, but implied he was already considered guilty.

[110] (36391/02) 27.11.2008 (GC).

[111] Though see *Ibrahim and others v the United Kingdom* (50541/08, 50571/08, 50573/08, 40351/09) 13.09.2016 (GC), where the Court accepted a delay in access to legal advice in the light of an exceptionally serious and imminent threat to public safety.

> the fairness of proceedings against an accused person in custody also requires that he be able to obtain (and that defence counsel be able to provide) the whole wide range of services specifically associated with legal assistance, including discussion of the case, organisation of the defence, collection of evidence favourable to the accused, preparation for questioning, support to an accused in distress, checking his conditions of detention and so on.[112]

As such, they argued that Article 6 required that an accused person be entitled to access representation from the moment of custody or detention, in order to discuss everything concerning his defence and legitimate needs.

This position was accepted by the Court in later cases, where it was held that the protections afforded by Article 6(3)(c) apply from the moment that someone is subject to a 'criminal charge'. This means that from the moment that an individual is notified by the competent authority of an allegation that he has committed a criminal offence, or from the time at which his situation has been substantially affected by the actions taken by the authorities as a result of suspicion against him, he will have the right of access to a lawyer.[113] This applies whether or not that person is interviewed or participates in any other investigative measure during that period.[114]

Although *Salduz* concerned a juvenile, this was not a central feature of this case, and instead the Court dealt with the principles at stake in a general manner. However, the Court returned to this issue in *Blokhin v Russia*,[115] where it elaborated in significant detail the additional obligations on states in relation to child suspects. In this case, concerning a 12-year-old boy with ADHD and neurosis, the Court found that the particular vulnerability of the child at the initial stages of police questioning could only be compensated for by the assistance of a lawyer. The task of the lawyer must be to ensure the respect of the right of the accused not to incriminate himself, but also to protect him from coercion on the part of the authorities, to prevent a miscarriage of justice, and to ensure the equality of arms. The Court noted that the child was well below the age of criminal responsibility under domestic law, and therefore was in need of special treatment by the authorities. This was exacerbated by his disability, which made him particularly vulnerable and in need of protection. Relying on the UN Convention on the Rights of the Child, the Beijing Rules, and Council of Europe Guidelines on child-friendly justice, the Court emphasised that any measures against him should have been based on his best interests, and from the time of his apprehension he should have been guaranteed *at least* the same legal rights and safeguards as those provided to adults.

This was an issue of particular concern for the Court. In this case, the restrictions on the child's rights under Article 6 were due to the fact that he was below the age of criminal responsibility, and therefore he fell outside the protection offered by the procedural guarantees provided for adults under the Code of Criminal Procedure. The

[112] *Salduz v Turkey* (36391/02) 27.11.2008 (GC), concurring opinion of Judge Zagrebelsky, joined by Judges Casadevall and Türmen.

[113] *Salduz v Turkey* (36391/02) 27.11.2008 (GC); *Beuze v Belgium* (71409/10) 09.11.2018 (GC).

[114] *Simeonovi v Bulgaria* (21980/04) 12.05.2017 (GC).

[115] (47152/06) 23.03.2016.

applicable Minors Act provided significantly restricted procedural safeguards, as it was intended to be protective, rather than punitive. As such, the legislature's intention to protect children came into conflict with the child's rights, where the child could be deprived of liberty without the procedural rights to defend himself. In this regard, the Court held that minors deserve support and assistance whenever coercive measures are applied, even if they relate to educational measures. To find otherwise would put children at a clear disadvantage with adults in the same situation. This does not mean that they should be subjected to a full criminal trial, merely that 'their rights should be secured in an adapted and age-appropriate setting in line with international standards, in particular the Convention on the Rights of the Child'.[116]

Importantly, Article 6(3)(c) provides not only an *entitlement* to legal representation, but places a positive obligation on the state to ensure that the accused understands this entitlement and fully comprehends the nature of this right. While this right applies to all individuals, this is particularly important for children who come into conflict with the law, who may have less awareness of their rights and less comprehension of the consequences of a lack of legal representation.

In *Panovits v Cyprus*,[117] the applicant was a 17-year-old suspected of murder, who was not informed of his right to legal assistance until after his confession. The authorities argued that there was no violation of Article 6(3)(c) in this case, as they had been willing to allow him access to a lawyer if he so requested and had not placed any obstacle in the way of this. However, the Court held that such a passive approach wasn't sufficient to fulfil the *positive* obligation on the state to provide the applicant with information regarding his rights. The applicant was unlikely to be aware of his entitlement to legal representation, nor would a mere caution as routinely provided to defendants have been enough to enable him to sufficiently comprehend the nature of his right to remain silent. Moreover, given the lack of assistance by a lawyer or guardian, he was unlikely to be able to appreciate the consequences of being questioned without a lawyer in a murder investigation.[118]

An important question arose in this case as to whether a parent can waive the right to legal representation on behalf of their child. While the applicant was being questioned by police, his father was asked if he wanted to be with his son or appoint a lawyer. He declined both options. The majority found that the waiver of a Convention right—as far as it is permissible—must not run counter to any important public interest and must be attended by minimum safeguards commensurate to the waiver's importance.

[116] ibid., para. 219.

[117] (4268/04) 11.12.2008. See also *Adamkiewicz v Poland* (54729/00) 02.03.2010, where the Court found that given the age of the applicant, and the fact that he had no criminal record, it could not be assumed that he knew that he had a right to request legal representation, nor that he knew the consequences of a lack of representation.

[118] This conclusion was criticised by Judge Erotocritou, who in his dissenting opinion drew a distinction between the denial of a right to access legal assistance and a failure to inform the individual of the existence of such a right. Although a right to be informed might exist under certain circumstances, this should be established on the facts of the case as a whole. Moreover, he contested the majority's conclusion that a mere caution was not enough to enable the applicant to comprehend the nature of the right. In his opinion, the applicant was of sufficient maturity to understand the nature and implications of the caution, and in the absence of special factors or some form of incapacity, there should be no duty placed on the investigative authorities to take further steps to make sure an individual understands the caution given.

Further, before an accused can be said to have waived a right under Article 6 implicitly through his conduct, it must be shown that he could have reasonably foreseen what the consequences of this would be. In light of the vulnerability of minors suspected of crimes and the imbalance of power inherent in the very nature of criminal proceedings, a waiver of such an important right as the right to legal representation can only be accepted where it is expressed in an unequivocal manner. Moreover, this can only occur after the authorities have taken all reasonable steps to ensure that the individual is fully aware of their rights of defence and can appreciate, as far as possible, the consequence of their conduct. This was not the case here. The majority noted that the authorities wavered between treating the applicant as a child—addressing his father to explain the seriousness of the case and to describe the evidence—and treating him as an adult capable of being questioned in the absence of his guardian, without informing him of the right to legal assistance.

However, the majority avoided the question of whether the father could have validly waived the applicant's rights under Article 6(3)(c) by noting that the authorities only informed the father of the right to obtain a lawyer after questioning had already begun, by which time it was too late.[119] Although the Court failed to make an explicit finding in this case, it appears inconceivable that a parent should be able to waive the right to legal representation on behalf of a child. As the majority pointed out, if the child is old enough to be treated as an adult and capable of being questioned in the absence of his guardian, then he must be treated as old enough to be directly offered legal assistance. In a case in which the child is not deemed sufficiently capable of being questioned without the presence of an adult, this would seem equally to require that legal assistance be given to the child, unless the child has unequivocally, and with full understanding, rejected this. It is not sufficient that the parent rejects legal assistance on the child's behalf: it is the child, not the parent, who is potentially going to be subject to detention or discipline. A parent should not be able to waive a fundamental right of the child where it has otherwise been held that the interests of justice require legal advice. While this is not explicitly stated in *Panovits*, it would be consistent with the finding of the majority that any waiver of a Convention right must not run counter to an important public interest, and must be attended by minimum safeguards commensurate with the waiver's importance. Thus, it can only be accepted where the authorities have ensured that the child is fully aware of his rights and can appreciate the consequences of refusal. If the child is not sufficiently capable of comprehending this, then the answer is not to turn to the parent to decide whether to waive the right on his behalf: the default should instead be that the right cannot be waived.

Putting aside the issue of the waiver of rights, the positive obligation in *Panovits* is of crucial importance for children, as it ensures that they are not denied access to their rights simply because they are not sufficiently aware of what they are. Importantly, this positive obligation goes beyond simply informing the defendant of their right to representation,

[119] On the other hand, Judge Erotocritou in dissent argued that the father's waiver was valid, and the authorities could not be blamed for their inactivity in this regard. The father was informed that it was advisable to find a lawyer, and had ample time to do so. However, he remained inactive. In this way, he argued that there was 'no doubt that ... the father waived any right that [the son] may have had'. (*Panovits v Cyprus* (4268/04) 11.12.2008, para. 2)

but includes also taking steps to intervene if the chosen representative is not performing their functions. In *Güveç v Turkey*,[120] a 15-year-old was charged with being a member of the PKK. The lawyer who claimed to be representing him failed to attend 17 of the 25 hearings in his trial, and attended only one of the 16 hearings during the retrial. While the Court acknowledged that the state cannot normally be held responsible for the actions or decisions of a lawyer, where there is a manifest failure by the counsel appointed under the legal aid scheme to provide effective representation the authorities are under a positive obligation to intervene. Under Article 6(3)(c), the accused is entitled to have a lawyer assigned by the court of its own motion 'when the interests of justice so require'.[121] Here, given the applicant's young age, and the seriousness of the offences with which he was charged, the failure of the lawyer to represent him properly and his many absences from hearings should have led the trial court to consider that he urgently needed alternative representation. As such, there was a violation of Article 6(1) in conjunction with Article 6(3)(c).[122]

The final issue that arises under Article 6(3)(c) relates not to the right to access legal representation, but to the right to be able to *choose* who that legal representation will be. In *Martin v Estonia*,[123] a 17-year-old was first interviewed as a witness to murder. His parents signed an agreement with a lawyer, J, to act as his counsel, who was also to defend two schoolmates who were suspects in the crime. Soon after, however, the police suspected the child of involvement also, and he was arrested on suspicion of murder. At this time, the applicant alleged that he was pressured by the authorities to terminate J's services on account of a conflict of interest between the applicant and his schoolmates. He complained that the legal aid lawyer who replaced him, R, served the interests of the authorities rather than the applicant. It was in R's presence that he confessed to the murder, on the basis of which the trial judge found him guilty. On appeal, the Court of Appeal declared that his confession was inadmissible, as it was obtained in contravention of his rights, but nevertheless found his conviction safe based on 'general knowledge': that is, the fact that he *had* confessed, even if the actual confessions themselves were not admissible.[124]

The Court noted that the right to be defended by counsel of one's own choosing is not an absolute one and the defendant's wishes can be overridden if it is necessary in the interests of justice. Nevertheless, if the authorities believed that there was a conflict of interest arising from J's representation of the other suspects, they failed to use the formal procedure for removal of counsel in such circumstances. This would have allowed J to present his position and would have ensured that no pressure had been exerted on the applicant. A court would have independently and impartially examined the matter, and procedures and decisions taken could have been properly documented. Instead, it appears that unrecorded discussions took place between the applicant and investigators, in the absence of counsel, in which it was 'explained' to him that it would

[120] (70337/01) 20.01.2009. This case also raised an issue that the applicant was not represented during the first six months after his arrest, including during his questioning by police, a prosecutor, a judge, and the trial court.
[121] See *Vaudelle v France* (35683/97) 30.01.2001.
[122] See also *Kuptsov and Kuptsova v Russia* (6110/03) 03.03.2011.
[123] (35985/09) 30.05.2013.
[124] This, in and of itself, is an extraordinary conclusion!

be reasonable to terminate J's services. The Court found that this reliance on informal practice gave rise to a concern regarding the applicant's rights of defence and freedom from self-incrimination. Moreover, the legal aid counsel subsequently appointed to the applicant was not chosen by the Bar Association but by the police investigator, raising doubts as to his impartiality. Coupled with the applicant's age and apparent instability, the Court was not satisfied that his wish to replace counsel of his own choosing could be considered genuine in the circumstances, and there was thus an infringement of Article 6(3)(c). The fact that the Court of Appeal relied on the fact that he had confessed showed that the consequences of the breach of his defence rights had not been totally undone, even if the confessions themselves were ruled inadmissible.

Of particular importance in this case was the way in which the Court discussed the applicant's age and the impact this had on the protections guaranteed to him. The applicant was 17 at the time of the alleged murder, but turned 18 three weeks before his arrest. The Court held that

> the reasons for which the special treatment of minors is required—such as the person's level of maturity and intellectual and emotional capacities—do not cease immediately once the legal age is reached. Therefore, the considerations based on those factors could maintain some of their relevance, although their importance decreased as time passed.[125]

This acknowledgement that 'vulnerable' children do not suddenly mature into fully competent adults once they reach the age of 18 is of crucial importance. It recognises the arbitrary nature of the division between children and adults and the resulting need for protection for individuals on both sides of the boundary. This is especially important for children involved in the justice system, where cases can go on for years, and safeguards cannot stop simply because a child has reached the legal age of maturity during this period.

4.5.5 Conclusions on the right to a fair trial

This is an area of the case law where the Court has taken an encouragingly child-friendly approach. With the exception of the right to an independent and impartial tribunal, the Court has demonstrated a strong child rights focus, adapting the general requirements under Article 6 to the specific vulnerabilities of children involved in the criminal justice system.

Moreover, the use of the international instruments—not only the UN Convention on the Rights of the Child , but also the Beijing Rules and the Council of Europe Guidelines on child-friendly justice—has been critical in creating a coherent framework for the protection of children's rights. The only stain on the Court's record in this respect is the unfortunate approach to the application of the prohibition of inhuman and degrading treatment on the child's right to privacy during criminal law

[125] *Martin v Estonia* (35985/09) 30.05.2013, para. 92.

proceedings. The Court's dismissal of the international instruments and the clear international trend are out of keeping with its otherwise progressive approach in this area of law.

4.6 Sentencing

4.6.1 The proportionality of sentencing

The Court will not generally review the severity of the punishment imposed on an offender, as the Convention does not provide a right to call into question the length of a sentence imposed by a competent court.[126] Nevertheless, this does not mean that sentencing falls wholly outside the competence of the Court. First, as discussed in section 4.2 above, where a sentencing policy appears to affect individuals in a discriminatory fashion, this may raise issues under Article 14 in conjunction with Article 5. Second, as is examined in this section, the Court will consider whether the sentence is manifestly disproportionate, and thus contrary to the prohibition on inhuman and degrading treatment under Article 3.

Cases involving juveniles give rise to difficult issues in this regard, where the protective function of juvenile justice wars with wider societal concerns. The question of how to balance the (at times competing) principles of punishment, retribution, and rehabilitation is particularly acute in relation to children, whose personalities and behaviour are still developing, and therefore may call for a different response.

The issue of the proportionality of a sentence arose in the case of *Weeks v the United Kingdom*,[127] where the applicant was sentenced to life imprisonment for entering a shop armed with a starting pistol loaded with blank cartridges, and stealing 35 pence—which sum was later found on the shop floor. Under English law at the time, a person sentenced to life imprisonment could be released from detention at any time by the Secretary of State (a government minister), subject to such conditions as that individual may determine.

Having regard to the applicant's age and the offence committed, the Court found that such a sentence would have been so disproportionate as to raise serious doubts as to its compatibility with Article 3, were it not for the fact that it was imposed as a 'mercy'. Rather than imposing a lengthy, determinate sentence, all of which would have to be served, the judge held that an indeterminate sentence would be more appropriate, as it left the length of sentence in the hands of the Secretary of State, who could release him 'if and when those who have been watching him and examining him believe that with the passage of years he has become responsible'. The sentencing judge noted that this might not take long, or change might not occur for some time, but that this sentence, though it might seem 'terrible', actually allowed for greater flexibility in reacting to the changing circumstances of a young offender.

[126] See *X v the United Kingdom* (5871/72) 30.09.1974 (dec.).
[127] (9787/82) 02.03.1987.

The Court returned to this issue in *T v the United Kingdom*[128]—a case that was also discussed in sections 4.3 and 4.5 above. The applicant in this case argued that given his age at the time of the offence (ten years old) a sentence of 'detention during Her Majesty's pleasure' was 'severely disproportionate', in breach of Article 3. This sentence required that the Secretary of State set a 'tariff' period, which determined the number of years' detention necessary to satisfy the requirements of retribution and deterrence. After this 'tariff' was served, it would only be legitimate to detain the offender if it appeared necessary for the protection of the public. If not, then the offender would be eligible for parole, but even if that were granted, they would be liable to be recalled to prison for the rest of their life. The tariff in this case had initially been set at 15 years, but after being quashed on appeal, no new, lower tariff had been set.

The Court noted that Article 37 of the UN Convention on the Rights of the Child prohibits life imprisonment without the possibility of release for offences committed by persons below the age of 18, and provides that detention of a child should be a measure of last resort, and for the shortest period possible. However, states also have a duty under the Convention to take measures to protect the public from violent crime. As such, it did not consider that including a punitive element inherent in the tariff gave rise to a beach of Article 3, in and of itself. Nor does the Convention prevent states from subjecting a child or young person convicted of a serious crime to an indeterminate sentence, allowing for continued detention, or recall to detention following release where necessary for the protection of the public.[129]

With regard to the length of the punitive sentence, the Court noted that the applicant had only been detained for six years so far, which could not be said to amount to inhuman or degrading treatment, given the crime committed. Until the new tariff was set, and thus the length of the sentence imposed for the purposes of retribution and deterrence determined, it was not possible to draw any conclusions as to whether or when this would be breached in the future.

The Court did note, however, that an unjustifiable and persistent failure to fix a tariff, leaving the applicant in uncertainty over his future, might itself violate Article 3. This was particularly the case in relation to a child as young as the applicant at the time of his conviction. However, given the 'relatively short' time in which there had been no tariff set, the Court found that issue did not yet arise. With regard to this conclusion, it might be wondered how long a child should be left in a state of uncertainty regarding his sentence. By the time the case came before the Court, it had been five years since the Secretary of State had set the initial tariff, and over two years since this had been found unlawful on appeal. For a child of 17, this must be seen as a very long time to not know the minimum length of detention.

This criticism of the majority decision was raised by Judges Rozakis and Costa in their partially dissenting opinion. They acknowledged that it is difficult to determine the dividing line between what is 'inhuman and degrading' within the meaning of Article 3 and what is not. However, they argued that the crucial factor must be the extreme youth and immaturity of the applicant at the time he committed the crime.

[128] (24724/94) 16.12.1999 (GC).

[129] See also *Hussain v the United Kingdom* (21928/93) 21.02.1996.

The majority only assessed the period of time that had *objectively* elapsed, rather than considering it from the *subjective* perspective of the applicant. He was ten years old at the time of the crime, and now, at 17, he still did not know how much of his sentence he would have to serve before he would become eligible for release. Such uncertainty must have caused him considerable distress, which Judges Rozakis and Costa believed crossed the threshold of severity necessary to invoke Article 3. Likewise, Judges Pastor Ridruejo, Ress, Makarczyk, Tulkens, and Butkevych in their partially dissenting opinion argued that the problem with the sentence lay in its indefinite nature: 'the uncertainty and anxiety for persons as vulnerable as children inevitably adds another element of suffering', leading to a violation of Article 3.[130]

The applicant in *T* also challenged the fact that the tariff was set by the Secretary of State—a government minister—rather than a tribunal meeting the requirements of Article 6(1). He argued that the setting of the tariff amounted to a sentencing exercise, and as such, should attract the safeguards of Article 6. The government, on the other hand, argued that Article 6 was not applicable at all: the applicant had been sentenced by a competent court on conviction to 'detention during Her Majesty's pleasure'. The fixing of the tariff was merely an aspect of the administration of the sentence, the substance of which had already been imposed by the court.

The Court held that in contrast to the mandatory life sentence imposed on adults convicted of murder, 'detention during Her Majesty's pleasure' is an open-ended sentence. The tariff represents the period of detention to satisfy the requirements of retribution and deterrence, and thereafter the offender must be released unless his continued detention is necessary for the protection of the public. As such, where the juvenile is not perceived to be dangerous, the tariff represents the maximum period of detention he can be required to serve. As such, the Court held that the setting of the tariff constitutes a sentencing exercise, which falls within the scope of Article 6. By leaving the setting of the tariff in the hands of the Secretary of State—a member of the executive branch of government—the procedure failed to comply with the requirement for an 'independent and impartial tribunal' under Article 6(1).

4.6.2 Parole and recall to prison

A secondary issue that arises in relation to sentencing is the possibility of parole, and the conditions under which this is granted. As discussed in section 4.4.4 above, Article 5(4) requires that individuals are able to bring proceedings to challenge the lawfulness of their detention, and the question has been raised as to how this applies to juveniles who have been detained 'during her Majesty's pleasure'.

The case of *Hussain v the United Kingdom*[131] involved a 16-year-old convicted of murder. He was given a sentence of 'detention during Her Majesty's pleasure', with the tariff set by the Secretary of State at 15 years. On four occasions, the Parole Board considered whether to recommend release, and on each of these occasions this was

[130] These judges did not consider the issue of the sentence separately, but instead considered this in conjunction with the low age of criminal responsibility and their prosecution in an adult court.

[131] *Hussain v the United Kingdom* (21928/93) 21.02.1996.

refused. By the time the case came before the Court in Strasbourg, he had been detained for 17 years.

The Court reiterated that in cases involving determinate life sentences, the requirements of Article 5(4) are satisfied by the original trial proceedings.[132] However, where the sentence is indeterminate and discretionary, for example being based on ongoing dangerousness, the lawfulness of continued detention must be examined by a body satisfying Article 5(4) requirements. As discussed above in section 4.6.1, 'detention during Her Majesty's pleasure', contains a punitive element (the tariff), but detention after this constitutes an indeterminate sentence that could only be justified by considerations relating to the need to protect the public. When assessing this, the authorities must take into account the development of the offender's personality and attitude, which may be susceptible to change with the passage of time. As such, while ongoing revision may not be necessary during the tariff period, the Court found that after this has been completed, new issues of lawfulness will arise on a periodic basis, and therefore continued assessment is necessary.

In undertaking this assessment, Article 5(4) requires examination by a court, or court-like body, which the Court has on several occasions made clear that the English Parole Board as it existed at the time could not be considered to be. In *Weeks v the United Kingdom*,[133] the Court noted that this body did not have the power to order the release of the applicant, merely to advise the Secretary of State in this regard. Its decisions took the form of 'recommendations', and indeed, the Secretary of State was free not to accept these. This purely advisory function—both in law and substance—meant that the Board could not be regarded as satisfying the requirements of Article 5(4). Separately, the Court found that the lack of adversarial proceedings also precluded its designation as a court-like body. The Board decided cases based on documents, and did not provide an oral hearing or an adversarial procedure. Moreover, the prisoner was not entitled to full disclosure of the adverse material in the possession of the Board. The Court observed that the procedure thus followed did not allow proper participation of the prisoner in the decision-making process, and therefore could not be regarded as judicial in character. This was reaffirmed in *Hussain*, where the Court held that

> where a substantial term of imprisonment may be at stake and where characteristics pertaining to his personality and level of maturity are of importance in deciding on his dangerousness, Article 5 para. 4 requires an oral hearing in the context of an adversarial procedure involving legal representation and the possibility of calling and questioning witnesses.[134]

In *Weeks*, the government argued that the availability of 'judicial review' provided a supplement to the procedure before the Parole Board, allowing the ordinary courts to scrutinise the decisions of the Board itself and the Secretary of State. While the Court recognised that apparent shortcomings in one procedure may be remedied

[132] See *Wynne v the United Kingdom* (15484/89) 18.07.1994.
[133] (9787/82) 02.03.1987.
[134] *Hussain v the United Kingdom* (21928/93) 21.02.1996, para. 60.

by safeguards available in others, it found that the process of judicial review as practised in England—allowing the court to overturn a decision of the Parole Board on the grounds of illegality, irrationality, or procedural irregularity—did not meet the requirements of accessibility and effectiveness under Article 5(4). While there is no right to judicial control such as to empower a court, or court-like body, to substitute its own discretion for that of the decision-making authority, the review must be wide enough to determine the lawfulness of detention, both under domestic law and in accordance with Article 5(1), which was not the case in relation to judicial review.[135]

It is important to note that even where an individual has been released on parole, the procedural requirements under Article 5 do not cease. In *Weeks*, the applicant—who had been sentenced to life imprisonment for crimes committed as a 17-year-old—was released on parole, but recalled to prison after committing various other offences. He argued before the Court that his detention subsequent to the revocation of his parole was not in accordance with Article 5.

The Court dismissed the government's central submission, which was that the applicant's recall to prison had not deprived him of liberty, because that right had been taken away from him for the rest of his life following his life sentence. All persons, whether at liberty or in detention, are entitled to the protection of Article 5. Whether he retained his liberty on release was a question of fact: although his freedom was more circumscribed and precarious than that of an ordinary citizen, this didn't prevent it being qualified as a state of liberty for the purposes of Article 5. As such, the Court found that when recalling the applicant to prison, the authorities were ordering his removal from an actual state of liberty.

When deciding whether this removal of liberty was lawful, the Court held that a formal legal connection between the original conviction and the recall is not on its own sufficient to justify continued detention—there must be a factual connection between the objectives of the sentencing judge and the reasons for recall. In this case, the indeterminate life sentence was imposed due to fears of an unstable personality, and disturbed and aggressive behaviour, which were susceptible by their very nature to change with the passage of time. There were sufficient grounds to conclude that, in light of his subsequent offences, he constituted a danger to the public and to himself, and recall could not be regarded as unreasonable in terms of the objective of the sentence imposed on him.

4.7 Conclusion

Juvenile justice is an area where there is much to be applauded in the Court's incorporation of children's rights. In particular, its use of the international instruments has been extensive: Article 37 of the UN Convention on the Rights of the Child, the Beijing Rules, and numerous Council of Europe Recommendations have all been referred to in framing the standards set by the Court. While the Court has made clear that a violation of these international instruments does not, in and of itself,

[135] See also *Singh v the United Kingdom* (23389/94) 21.02.1996.

automatically constitute a violation of the Convention, it is an important indicator by which the Court (usually) sets significant store.

However, the jurisprudence is limited by the Court's role as a supervisory body, subject to the margin of appreciation. Cases in this area are very fact specific, with the Court largely restricting itself to narrow decisions which place a band-aid over the worst practices without addressing wider systemic or underlying issues—for example, a lack of alternative and specialised system for minors in conflict with the law. Coupled with the reluctance of the Court to determine a minimum age of criminal responsibility, this leaves a significant gap in the protection of children's rights in this area.

The future challenges for the Court lie in developing strong positive obligations, rather than bare minimum standards. It has already begun to do so in relation to 'effective participation' under Article 6, but this must be extended to all areas of juvenile justice. In particular, decisions concerning the proportionality of detention and the consideration of appropriate alternatives is an area ripe for development. Likewise, the conditions of detention and its ability to meet educational and rehabilitative aims.

Overall, there is much to be hopeful for, particularly if the Court continues to refer to, and rely on, the international standards. The Court's interpretation of the Convention is a long way from establishing a child-friendly system of justice, but it is at least on the right track.

5
Children and the Immigration System

5.1 Introduction

The intervention of the Court in cases concerning refugees, migration, and deportation has been one of, if not the most controversial areas of its jurisprudence. States have expressed concern regarding the obligations imposed by the Court's expansive jurisprudence under Article 8 in respect of both private and family life,[1] yet conversely, critics argue that this does not go far enough.[2] This tension is partly because immigration (at least as currently conceived) and human rights are uneasy bedfellows: as Thym points out, '[i]mmigration law has long been characterised by its orientation towards the public interest ... Conversely, human rights pose a direct challenge to state sovereignty with their orientation towards the individual.'[3]

Strangely for a body focused on individual rights, the Court has paid great deference to state interests in restricting immigration. Unlike other areas of its case law, where the Court starts with the right of an individual and then discusses interference, where immigration issues are at stake, the Court begins with a statement of the *state's* rights, namely:

> [T]he Court reiterates that a State is entitled, as a matter of well-established international law and subject to its treaty obligations, to control the entry of aliens into its territory and their residence there. The Convention does not guarantee the right of an alien to enter or to reside in a particular country.[4]

In addition to the elevated degree of deference given to the state in cases concerning immigration, a second limitation is placed on the protection of children's rights in this area. In common with cases concerning child protection, immigration cases

[1] For example, in arguing that the United Kingdom Human Rights Act—which incorporates the Convention into domestic law—needed to be abolished, Theresa May, then Home Secretary (later Prime Minister), claimed that an illegal immigrant could not be deported because of his pet cat. (BBC Online, 'Theresa May under Fire over Deportation Cat Claim' (BBC News, 04.10.2011), https://www.bbc.co.uk/news/uk-politics-15160326)

[2] See, for example, A. Farahat, 'The Exclusiveness of Inclusion: On the Boundaries of Human Rights in Protecting Transnational and Second Generation Migrants' (2009) 11(3) *European Journal of Migration and Law* 253; C. Murphy, 'The Concept of Integration in the Jurisprudence of the European Court of Human Rights' (2010) 12(1) *European Journal of Migration and Law* 23.

[3] D. Thym, 'Residence as De Facto Citizenship? Protection of Long-Term Residence under Article 8 ECHR' in R. Rubio-Marin (ed.), *Human Rights and Immigration* (Oxford: Oxford University Press, 2014), 143.

[4] *Butt v Norway* (47017/09) 04.12.2012. See also *Abdulaziz, Cabales, and Balkandali v the United Kingdom* (9214/80, 9473/81, 9474/81) 28.05.1985; *Nunez v Norway* (55597/09) 28.06.2011.

Children and the European Court of Human Rights. Claire Fenton-Glynn, Oxford University Press (2021). © Claire Fenton-Glynn.
DOI: 10.1093/oso/9780198787518.003.0005

concerning children have largely revolved around their separation from their parents. However, unlike in family law cases, it is usually the *parents* being removed from the children, not children from their parents. As a result, children's interests have not been so central to the analysis of the Court, and are often subjugated to the general societal interest of immigration control.

As with the decisions discussed in Chapter 4 on the juvenile justice system, the cases in this area are very fact specific, relying on the balancing of a variety of factors, and in light of a wide margin of appreciation. Nevertheless, this section attempts to draw out some of the key considerations that can be seen running through these judgments, starting with the existence of 'family life' in the context of immigration control.

5.2 'Family life' in immigration disputes

While the Court's interpretation of the nature of 'family life' is discussed at length in Chapter 8, it is important to make a few short comments about its application in the context of immigration. On a number of occasions, the government has attempted to argue before the Court that no 'family life' exists between the applicant parent and their child, meaning that Article 8 cannot be invoked to require family reunification or to block deportation. The Court has developed a clear and consistent line of jurisprudence in this regard: where there is a committed relationship between the parents at the time of conception—demonstrated either through marriage or cohabitation—there will automatically be 'family life' between the parents and the child.[5] Absent this committed relationship between the parents, the Court will have to look further to determine whether there nevertheless exists a 'close personal relationship' between the parent and child, sufficient to trigger the protection of Article 8.[6]

However, even if 'family life' does exist, the Court has indicated that in exceptional circumstances this tie can be broken.[7] This has been discussed almost exclusively in the context of immigration—where the government has argued that deportation of a parent should be permitted to proceed, as they have not shown sufficient dedication to the family whose interests they are invoking to halt it.[8] However, while this has been raised in a number of cases, none have been successful, and as a result it is not clear what it would take for the Court to rule that this has occurred.

This issue first arose in *Berrehab v the Netherlands*[9] where, following his divorce, the father saw his daughter four times a week for several hours. The government argued that in the absence of cohabitation, 'family life' did not exist, and thus there was no bar to the father's deportation. This was swiftly rejected by the Court, which found that the child had been born from a lawful marriage, and thus, from the moment of birth, 'family life' existed between her and her parents. After her parents separated, the

[5] See *Berrehab v the Netherlands* (10730/84) 21.06.1988; *Keegan v Ireland* (16969/90) 26.05.1994.
[6] See *Anayo v Germany* (20578/07) 21.12.2010.
[7] See, for example, *Boughanemi v France* (22070/93) 24.04.1996.
[8] The termination of 'family life' has also been discussed in the context of adoption: see section 11.9.
[9] (10730/84) 21.06.1988.

frequency and regularity of contact between the father and daughter demonstrated that he valued this relationship greatly, and therefore 'family life' had not been broken.

This case sets quite a formidable precedent of regular and frequent contact, but subsequent cases have shown that this is not necessary. In *Ciliz v the Netherlands*,[10] the father had only irregular contact with his child, and the Court acknowledged that after separation it could not be said that at all times he demonstrated that he valued meetings with his son. He made no attempts to see him, and failed to keep appointments when they were set up. However, contact was later re-established, if not regularly then frequently, and the Court found that this was sufficient to retain the ties of 'family life'. Likewise, in *Boughanemi v France*,[11] the applicant did not recognise his child until ten months after his birth. He did not provide for him financially, nor did he contribute to his education, and he did not exercise parental rights. The Court acknowledged that doubts as to the existence of family ties were not wholly unfounded, but held that neither the belated recognition nor his subsequent conduct were sufficiently 'exceptional'.[12]

In a similar vein, even prolonged absences from the child's life will not sever the family tie. In *Gül v Switzerland*,[13] the fact that the applicant father left Turkey when his child was only three months old was insufficient to break the bond, especially as he had made various visits to see him; while in *Ejimson v Germany*[14] 'family life' continued to exist despite not seeing his child for four years while he was imprisoned. In the latter case, the Court gave weight to the fact that he had continued to hold joint custody rights during this time, and had re-established a relationship since his release.

From these cases we can see that the relationship of 'family life' under Article 8(1) between a minor child and their parents, once formed, is difficult—if not virtually impossible—to break.[15] However, once the child reaches adulthood, the analysis shifts, and the relationship will only fall within the notion of 'family life' where the adult child can demonstrate additional elements of dependency, involving more than the normal emotional familial ties.[16]

In undertaking this examination, the Court considers the financial relationship between the parties: for example, in *B v Switzerland*[17] and *S and S v The United Kingdom*[18] the Commission relied on a lack of economic dependence in finding that there were not sufficiently close links between a parent and their adult child to be considered 'family'. Material and social dependence will also be considered; however, the bar has been set very high in this respect. In *Senchishak v Finland*,[19] the Court found that even

[10] (29192/95) 11.07.2000.

[11] (22070/93) 24.04.1996.

[12] See also *C v Belgium* (21794/93) 07.08.1996, where the fact that the applicant had been imprisoned and deported, and his son taken in by his sister, did not constitute exceptional circumstances.

[13] *Gül v Switzerland* (23218/94) 19.02.1996.

[14] (58681/12) 01.03.2018.

[15] The Court has left open whether 'family life' is terminated upon the dissolution of legal ties, as occurs in the case of an adoption. (*IS v Germany* (31021/08) 05.06.2014))

[16] See, for example, *Kwakye-Nti and Dufie v the Netherlands* (31519/96) 07.11.2000 (dec.); cf. *Emonet and others v Switzerland* (39051/03) 13.12.2007.

[17] (16249/90) 01.10.1990 (dec.).

[18] (10375/83) 10.12.1984 (dec.).

[19] (5049/12) 18.11.2014.

assuming that the elderly mother was dependent on outside help to cope with her daily life, this did not mean that she was reliant on her daughter specifically. Instead, it was somewhat callously suggested that it was possible to hire external help or to place the mother in a care home.

One area in which 'family life' *has* been found between adult children and their parents is where the adult child is still living with their parents and has not yet started a family of their own. This was seen in relation to an 18-year-old in *Maslov v Austria*;[20] a 20-year-old in *Moustaquim v Belgium*;[21] a 24-year-old in *Bousarra v France*;[22] and a 28-year-old in *Boujlifa v France*.[23]

The focus of the Court on 'dependence' when assessing the 'family life' of adult children has been criticised on a number of occasions. *In Slivenko v Latvia*,[24] Judge Kovler complained that the majority had opted 'for the traditional concept of a family based on the conjugal covenant—that is to say, a conjugal family consisting of a father, a mother and their children below the age of majority, while adult children and grandparents are excluded from the circle'.[25] Likewise, Judge Spielmann pointed out in *Shevanova v Latvia*,[26] that the Court has prioritised dependency to the detriment of normal ties of affection, creating an artificial understanding of 'family life', thereby impoverishing the concept.

What is clear, however, is that absent exceptional circumstances, while minor children and parents enjoy protection of Article 8, adult children and their parents do not. Of course, this does not mean that deportation may not be subsequently justified under Article 8(2), merely that the relationship is prima facie provided the protection of this article.

5.3 Deportation and expulsion without a right to reside

Once family life has been recognised, the authorities must show that the refusal to allow the applicant to stay pursues a legitimate aim and is necessary in a democratic society. The legitimate aim being pursued will have a direct impact on the proportionality analysis, and therefore a distinction must be drawn between a refusal to allow someone to stay based on the prevention of disorder—for example, where the applicant has committed a criminal offence—and the preservation of the country's economic well-being—that is, where the applicant does not fulfil the requirements of the immigration rules.

The Court has adopted different criteria when considering a refusal to grant a (further) residence permit on the one hand, and the withdrawal of leave to remain and

[20] (1638/03) 23.06.2008 (GC).
[21] (12313/86) 18.02.1991. See also *Bouchelkia v France* (23078/93) 29.01.1997.
[22] (25672/07) 23.09.2010. This was also raised in *AA v the United Kingdom* (8000/08) 20.09.2011 in relation to a 24-year-old adult child, but the Court did not find it necessary to decide the question in this case.
[23] (25404/94) 21.10.1997.
[24] (48321/99) 09.10.2003 (GC).
[25] ibid., para. 4.
[26] (58822/00) 15.06.2006 (Ch).

expulsion on the other. In expulsion cases, the starting point is that the individual has the right to remain in the jurisdiction, and the state must show grounds justifying their removal—though in cases involving criminal offences, this is not a difficult hurdle to pass. In cases concerning a refusal to grant a residence permit, however, the Court starts from the understanding that Article 8 does not entail an obligation on the state to respect families' choices concerning the country of their residence, and the individual will have to show why their particular circumstances place a positive obligation on the state to allow them to remain.

5.3.1 The obligation to grant a residence permit to a parent

5.3.1.1 Where family life has been formed during legal residence

Where the family life between a parent and child has been established while the parent was lawfully resident within the jurisdiction, the Court has provided this relationship with strong protection, recognising a positive obligation to grant them continuing permission to remain where this is necessary to maintain their familial relationship.

The high point of the Court's jurisprudence in this respect was *Berrehab v the Netherlands*,[27] concerning a Moroccan man who had been given permission to stay in the Netherlands for the sole purpose of enabling him to live with his Dutch wife. They soon separated, and his wife gave birth to their daughter. Upon their divorce, the father was made an 'auxiliary guardian' of the child, and the parents concluded a contact agreement granting him regular, frequent contact with her. However, the father was refused a further residence permit, as his marriage was no longer subsisting, and he was deported. He complained that there had been an interference with his right to respect for family life.

The Court recognised the state's legitimate aim of regulating the labour market, and thus preserving the economic well-being of the country, but found that the authorities had failed to achieve a proper balance with individual rights. There was no pressing social need to exclude the applicant—he had lived in the Netherlands lawfully for several years, he had a home and a job there, and the government did not claim to have any complaint against him. The sole reason for refusing a further residence permit was that he was no longer married to his wife. On the other hand, there had been very close ties between the father and daughter for many years, and the refusal of a residence permit threatened to break these. These interferences were seen by the Court as all the more serious as the child was very young, and needed to remain in contact with her father. As such, there had been a violation of Article 8.

While this was a strong judgment, the right to remain is not automatic, and will depend greatly on the quality of the family life at issue. In *M v the Federal Republic of Germany*,[28] the Commission declared inadmissible the application of a father whose immigration status was very similar to Mr Berrehab: he had been given a residence

[27] (10730/84) 21.06.1988.
[28] (12411/86) 04.03.1987 (dec.).

permit to live with his wife, with whom he had had a child, but following divorce, his application for a prolongation of his residence was refused. The Commission held that a parent's interest in maintaining regular contact with a child in the care of the other parent doesn't necessarily entitle them to take up residence in that country. In order to establish whether such a right exists in a particular case, the character of the relations between the parent and child must be examined and balanced against the general interest which calls for restrictions regarding immigration. On the facts, the Commission noted that the father and son had only lived together for two years, and the divorce judgment didn't provide him with a right of visitation. Coupled with a complaint brought by the ex-wife concerning molestation, the Commission held that the measure was proportionate.

Despite seeming to row back from *Berrehab*, this case is important for the way in which the relevant principles were expressed by the Commission. In particular, it stated that as a matter of principle, particular regard must be had to the interests of the child, and when assessing the proportionality of a measure, authorities must take sufficient account of the 'interest to continue existing, extensive contacts between them'.

5.3.1.2 Where family life has been formed during illegal residence

In contrast to cases where family life has been created during legal residence, where the relationship has been created at a time when immigration status is precarious, the Court has held that it will only be in the most exceptional circumstances that the removal will constitute a violation:[29] namely, a significant rupturing of family ties, the particular vulnerability of the child, or proof that the authorities have tolerated the parent's ongoing presence.

5.3.1.2.1 Significant rupturing of family ties

The strongest argument that a parent can put forward to prevent their removal—at least in relation to 'family life'—is the risk of a significant rupturing of ties with their child. Where the parent's deportation would terminate all forms of contact between the child and the parent, the Court has recognised a positive obligation on the state to allow them to remain. However, this is not an easy hurdle to pass—the applicant will have to show why the child cannot simply return with the parent to their country of origin, or if the child remains, why they cannot continue to have contact with them through occasional visits.

One successful case in this respect was *Rodrigues Da Silva and Hoogkamer v the Netherlands*,[30] where the applicant mother, who had until that time been living in the Netherlands illegally, challenged the refusal of a residence permit. This refusal meant she would have to return to Brazil, leaving behind her Dutch national child. The child, who was three years old, lived with her paternal grandparents, although she stayed with her mother at weekends and maintained very strong ties with her. If the applicant were to return to Brazil, she would have to leave her child behind, as her father,

[29] See, for example, *Charfa v Sweden* (20002/92) 05.04.1995; *Mitchell v the United Kingdom* (40447/98) 24.11.1998 (GC); *Rodrigues Da Silva and Hoogkamer v the Netherlands* (50435/99) 31.01.2006; *Nunez v Norway* (55597/09) 28.06.2011.

[30] (50435/99) 31.01.2006.

who held parental authority and to whom the courts had awarded custody, would not permit her to go.

The Court noted that the refusal of a residence permit would in effect break off ties between the mother and daughter, as it would be impossible to maintain regular contact. This was all the more serious given the age of the child and the need to remain in close contact with her mother. Weight was also given to the fact that although she had been unlawfully resident in the Netherlands, she was eligible for a residence permit if she had applied for it, on the basis of her relationship with the child's father. As such, the Court distinguished this from cases where the applicants could not at any time have reasonably expected to be able to continue family life in the host country. The Court concluded that due to the far-reaching consequences that the expulsion would have on her responsibilities as a mother, and that it was clearly in the interests of the child that she should stay, the economic well-being of the state could not outweigh the applicants' rights under Article 8.

This can be contrasted with the case of *Darren Omoregie and others v Norway*,[31] where the Court was satisfied that the mother and child could visit the father in Nigeria, should he be expelled. The links between father and child were arguably equally strong in this case (they were living as a family unit); however, unlike *Rodrigues Da Silva*, there was a possibility that the mother and child might join the father in Nigeria, the child being of an 'adaptable age' and there being no 'insurmountable obstacles' in the way of their developing family life there. In this light, not only was the expulsion not in violation of Article 8, but the Court also found that the state was within its margin of appreciation to impose a five-year re-entry ban.

This test of 'insurmountable obstacles' is also seen in cases concerning family reunification discussed below, and is of great importance. Where the family unit is still intact, the Court will usually expect that they continue their family life in the other jurisdiction, unless there is something weighty preventing this. The very language of 'insurmountable', coupled with the 'exceptional circumstances' test that applies in this area generally, makes it very difficult for a family to demonstrate that they should be permitted to continue to live in the host country rather than elsewhere.

This difficulty was demonstrated in *Antwi and others v Norway*,[32] where the Court held that there would be no 'insurmountable obstacles' to a ten-year-old child born in Norway, who only spoke Norwegian and was fully integrated there, moving to Ghana, a place she had only visited three times, and had little knowledge of the languages spoken. Alternatively, the Court found that she could remain in Norway with her mother and maintain regular contact with her father after he was deported to Ghana, despite the fact that the father was her primary carer, playing an important role in her daily care and upbringing, and to whom she was strongly attached. The 'exceptional circumstances' test was not met even though the domestic authorities held that it would be detrimental for the child that the father be deported.

This finding was criticised in the dissenting opinion of Judge Sicilianos, joined by Judge Lazarova Trajkovska. Quoting the UN Committee on the Rights of the Child,

[31] (265/07) 31.07.2008.
[32] (26940/10) 14.02.2012.

Judge Sicilianos noted that '[e]very legislative, administrative and judicial body or institution is required to apply the best interests principle by systematically considering how children's rights and interests are or will be affected by their decisions and actions'.[33] In this way, he argued that Article 3 of the United Nations Convention on the Rights of the Child 'imposes[s] a burden of proof on those seeking to put the interests of the child aside to demonstrate that, under the circumstances, other feasible and acceptable alternatives do not exist'.[34] Judge Sicilianos noted that the domestic authorities in this case admitted that the deportation was 'clearly not' in—that is, against—the child's best interests, yet the majority was satisfied that sufficient weight had been attached to these. This, he argued, paid lip service to a guiding human rights principle, which was recognised in both European and international instruments.

This case exposes the limitations of the best interests principle: as an expression of children's *interests*, rather than basing a decision on children's individual *rights*, children run the risk of being subjugated to adult interests. The child is an innocent party, yet it will not be a violation of the Convention to deprive them of the benefit of family life, even if it is contrary to their welfare.[35] Here, the choice for the child was between losing her primary carer and moving to a country she had little connection with.

It may be that there is also some gender bias at play in these cases: even where the mother was not the primary carer in *Rodrigues Da Silva*, her presence was deemed essential, while in *Antwi*, the Court was willing to allow the father to be deported despite his primary caring role. The Court appears to assume that the emotional disruption of removing a father is less than in removing a mother, irrespective of their role in the child's life, while women are also seen as more capable of uprooting their lives to follow their husband to another country. It may be that the Court has one rule for mothers and another for fathers.[36]

5.3.1.2.2 Particular vulnerability of the children

In addition to the significant rupture of ties between parent and child, a second factor that will create 'exceptional circumstances' is the particular vulnerability of the child or children in question. This was established in the landmark decision of *Nunez v Norway*,[37] where the Court took a laudably child-centred approach to the evaluation of the mother's deportation. In this case, the mother had given birth to two children while living illegally in Norway, and when she separated from the children's father,

[33] United Nations Committee on the Rights of the Child, *General Comment No. 5 (2003), General Measures of Implementation of the Convention on the Rights of the Child* (CRC/GC/2003/5, 03.10.2003).

[34] ibid., para. 3.

[35] This argument was made by the applicant child in *Rodrigues Da Silva and Hoogkamer v the Netherlands* (50435/99) 31.01.2006, who argued that she 'had her own, individual, interests which also required consideration: it could not and should not be held against her that she had been conceived while her mother was not lawfully resident'. (para. 31)

[36] See also *Nunez v Norway* (55597/09) 28.06.2011, discussed below, where the domestic authorities had transferred custody to the children's father, clearly satisfied that he could care for them in the mother's absence, but the Court nevertheless found the mother's deportation violation of Article 8. This can be contrasted by the decision in *Antwi and others v Norway* (26940/10) 14.02.2012, where the father was the primary carer, yet the Court accepted that the children could be cared for by the mother alone, if he were deported.

[37] (55597/09) 28.06.2011.

she was given primary responsibility for their care and upbringing. Upon discovering her illegal status, the authorities ordered that she be deported and banned from re-entering Norway for two years. Sole parental responsibility was subsequently transferred to the children's father, largely on the basis of her pending deportation. She complained that the expulsion and ban on re-entry would breach her right to respect for family life as it would separate her from her small children, aged three and four at the time of the final domestic decision.

The Court noted all the features of the case which supported deportation: she had arrived as an adult, having lived all her life in the Dominican Republic; she had entered the country on a false passport; and her family life had been established while she was staying illegally. However, the Court emphasised that these factors must be balanced against the best interests of the children. In particular, the Court observed that the children were particularly vulnerable—they had experienced great stress due to the risk of their mother's expulsion, as well as from the disruption of their care situation, first following the separation of their parents, then being moved from their mother's home to live with their father.

The Court further noted the critical time in the children's life—the applicant's expulsion and re-entry ban would mean the children would in all likelihood be separated from their mother for two years, a very long period for children of that age. Furthermore, they would have difficulty in understanding why they were separated from their mother, who had been their primary carer until the risk of expulsion motivated the courts to transfer custody to the father. Drawing on the UN Convention on the Rights of the Child, the Court concluded that in light of the long-lasting and close bonds to their mother, and the disruption and stress already experienced, the decision of the domestic courts did not sufficiently protect the best interests of the children.

What makes this judgment so important from a child rights perspective was that it was clear that on her own part, the expulsion of the mother would not have been disproportionate. Although the children were not themselves party to the case, their rights were indirectly protected, and dictated the outcome of the case. Having said this, it is difficult to see how these children were more vulnerable than any others whose parents were at risk of deportation—for example, the children in *Darren Omoregie* or *Antwi* discussed above. As quoted by Judge Jebens in his concurring opinion, the UN Committee on the Rights of the Child has made clear that

> [y]oung children are especially vulnerable to adverse consequences of separations because of their physical dependence on and emotional attachment to their parents/primary caregivers. They are also less able to comprehend the circumstances of any separation. Situations which are most likely to impact negatively on young children include ... situations where children experience disrupted relationships (including enforced separations).[38]

5.3.1.2.3 *Tolerance of presence*

The third and final factor that the Court has recognised as giving rise to an 'exceptional circumstance' is tolerance by the authorities of the presence of the individual

[38] United Nations Committee on the Rights of the Child, *General Comment No. 7 (2005), Implementing Child Rights in Early Childhood* (CRC/C/GC/7/Rev.1, 20.09.2006), para. 18.

in the host country. Where the authorities have failed to take steps to remove an individual, in effect enabling the establishment and development of family ties, the Court has given less latitude to the state in subsequently ordering expulsion.

This principle was established in the seminal case of *Jeunesse v the Netherlands*,[39] concerning a Surinamese national who lived in the Netherlands for 13 years on an expired tourist visa. She married a Dutch national and the couple had three children together. She applied unsuccessfully for a residence permit on five occasions between 1997 and 2010, but these were refused. Nevertheless, and despite her address being known to the authorities at all times, no steps were taken to remove her until 2010.

The Court held that by permitting an individual to remain within the jurisdiction whilst awaiting a decision concerning a residence permit, the state allows them to take part in society, form relationships, and create a family. The fact that the applicant's presence in the Netherlands had been tolerated for over a decade, during which time her address had always been known to the authorities, distinguished the case from others where the authorities were simply presented with family life as a fait accompli. This opened the door for wider consideration of the rupture of family ties—as the state had been partially responsible for allowing them to exist, they must give greater weight to them when deciding to deport.[40]

The Court reiterated that children's best interests must be of paramount importance, and although they cannot be decisive, national authorities should 'advert to and assess evidence in respect of the practicality, feasibility and proportionality of any removal of a non-national parent in order to give effective protection and sufficient weight to the best interests of the children directly affected by it'.[41]

The Court found that here were no insurmountable obstacles to the family moving as a unit to Suriname; however, it was likely that they would experience a degree of hardship. Although the husband was originally from Suriname, the children had no direct link to the country, and had never been there. Their best interests were not served by disrupting their present circumstances by either a forced relocation or by separating them from their primary caregiver. A fair balance had not been struck between the interests of the state and the impact of removal on the children.

The facts in this case were not unique by any means—similar fact patterns had arisen in other cases, if not all at the same time. For example, in *Useinov v the Netherlands*[42] the Dutch authorities had similarly appeared to tolerate the applicant's presence within the jurisdiction (albeit for a shorter time period), yet in that case the Court observed that such tolerance did not mean that the applicant had been given any assurances that he could expect to remain in the country. Likewise, it is not unusual for other family members to all have the nationality of the state in question.[43] What had changed was

[39] (12738/10) 03.10.2014.

[40] The passage of time was also noted in *Nunez v Norway* (55597/09) 28.06.2011, where the Court noted that the expulsion was not ordered until four years after the unlawful nature of the mother's stay had been brought to the attention of the authorities. This long period of time taken to come to a decision did not fulfil the need for swiftness and efficiency, thus contributing to the finding that there had been a violation of Article 8.

[41] *Jeunesse v the Netherlands* (12738/10) 03.10.2014, para. 109.

[42] (61292/00) 11.04.2006 (dec.).

[43] See, for example, *O and OL v the United Kingdom* (11970/86) 13.07.1987 (dec.).

the weight given to the child's best interests, which assumed greater impetus, in line with other areas of the Court's jurisprudence.[44]

This increased emphasis on the best interests of the child was not universally accepted, however. The joint dissenting opinion of Judges Villiger, Mahoney, and Silvis criticised the majority for improperly elevating this factor above all others, and moving away from the subsidiary role assigned to the Court by the Convention. They focused on the issue of parental choice and questioned the responsibility of the state for the consequences on children of deliberate acts of parents. Citing examples of imprisonment of parents and of divorce, they noted that children are liable to suffer from such decisions, yet the rupture of family life is not attributed to the state. Likewise, where a family chooses to move their children to another country, even where it would be contrary to what is best for them, the state generally has no positive obligation to intervene. Rather, it is understood that the best interests of the child are served by accepting the (lawful) choices of parents, unless the fundamental rights of the child are violated. The threshold they set, therefore, was Article 3—inhuman or degrading treatment. This appears to be in line with the jurisprudence concerning corporal punishment—parental authority prevails unless it crosses the threshold of Article 3.[45]

This dissenting judgment shows the lingering influence on the Court of the traditional understanding of 'family rights'. One of the drawbacks of the Convention for children is the way in which their rights are subsumed within the family structure, with a barrier erected between the child as the rights holder and the state as the duty bearer.[46] Such an approach further entrenches the structural problem, ignoring children's individuality and autonomy. Overall, however, *Jeunesse* is a step in the right direction for the Court. While it did not involve any shift in the principles of analysis of the Court—the usual emphasis was still placed on the state's right to control immigration and residence—it does indicate an expansion of the understanding of 'exceptional circumstances', with a greater focus on the impact of immigration decisions on children.

5.3.2 Constructive deportation

Despite the laudable approach of the majority in *Jeunesse*, the cases considered so far have been adult-centred: brought by adults, and argued from their perspective. Although children's interests are discussed, this is in the balancing exercise, rather than a separate consideration of their Convention rights. However, there have been a number of cases that have been argued from the perspective of children themselves, on the basis that separating them from their parents, or forcing them to leave their country of citizenship, would breach their rights under Article 8. Even though these cases are nominally brought 'by children', it remains doubtful that the children were the principal protagonists, and is more likely a litigation strategy, albeit one that has not been successful.

44 See, for example, *Neulinger and Shuruk v Switzerland* (41615/07) 06.07.2010 (GC).
45 See Chapter 2.
46 See Chapter 8.

An example of this is seen in *O and OL v the United Kingdom*,[47] where the applicants were two children born in the United Kingdom to illegal immigrants. They acquired British nationality by birth, but their parents, when discovered, were deported back to Cyprus. The children submitted that this deportation breached their rights under Article 8: they were not of a sufficiently adaptable age to follow their parents without severe damage to their development. They had no substantial family ties in Cyprus apart from their parents, they did not speak the language, and had no cultural or social identity with Cyprus, and therefore it would be unreasonable to expect them to follow their parents there.

The Commission found that the nationality of children cannot in itself confer a right of abode on parents, particularly where the parents were residing illegally in the host country at the time of the birth. The parents themselves created the situation, and it is they who must be held responsible for the separation from their children. Importantly, the Commission noted that there would have been no obstacle for the parents to take the children back with them to Cyprus when they were younger, and therefore more adaptable.

Despite this case being ostensibly about the rights of the children, there was no consideration of what was in their best interests. This may be indicative of the time at which the case was decided—two years before the UN Convention on the Rights of the Child —but it again highlights the 'sins of the father' approach discussed above in the dissenting opinion in *Jeunesse*.[48] Children's rights are not violated as long as the situation results from a 'choice' made by their parents.

The issue was further explored in *Ajayi and others v the United Kingdom*.[49] The applicants argued that the expulsion of a mother to Nigeria would constitute 'constructive deportation' of her child from her country of birth and of which she was a citizen, in breach of Article 3. They claimed that Nigeria had none of the advantages of the United Kingdom, and obliging the child to live there would constitute inhuman and degrading treatment. On the other hand, if the child remained in the United Kingdom, the enforced separation from her mother would also violate Article 3, as it would leave her without parental care, given her father's abandonment of the family. The Commission, very simply, found that the minimum level of suffering required to invoke Article 3 was not present—no evidence had been submitted to indicate the degree or nature of the alleged hardship. Likewise, the Commission rejected the application under Article 2, Protocol 1, where the child had argued that she would be deprived of her education in British schools, and she would be unable to afford schools of a similar standard in Nigeria. The Commission found that the child was not required to move to Nigeria, relying on the argument of the government that the situation arose because of the mother's choice to take the child with her, not because of the deportation.

This conclusion completely ignores the reality of children's lives: while the authorities were not forcing her to move to Nigeria, the only other option would be to be placed in alternative care in the United Kingdom, separated from her mother. The

[47] (11970/86) 13.07.1987 (dec.).
[48] See also *Poku and others v the United Kingdom* (26985/95) 15.05.1996.
[49] (27663/95) 22.06.1999 (dec.).

mother's 'choice' in this respect was no real choice at all. Nevertheless, and despite the flaws in the Court's reasoning, it is clear that the constructive deportation of children holding citizenship will not in itself be considered a violation of the Convention, unless the facts are such as to indicate there will be inhuman and degrading treatment—in the traditional sense—in the country of deportation.[50]

5.3.3 Conclusions on deportation without a right to reside

It is clear that in this area the odds are stacked against applicants. The Court has recognised a positive obligation to allow family life to continue within the jurisdiction where it has been established during legal residence, and where deportation would rupture family ties. However, where family life has been created when the parent is in the country illegally, it is only in exceptional cases that the rights of the family will be sufficient to overcome the interests of the state. There are a few rays of hope in this jurisprudence, however. In particular, both *Nunez* and *Jeunesse* point the way towards a more child-friendly approach in this area, which recognises the vulnerability of children to the consequences of separation from their caregivers, and the paramountcy of their interests in this respect. It is to be hoped that these cases signal a new era of jurisprudence for the Court.

5.4 Expulsion following a criminal offence

5.4.1 Expulsion of a parent following a criminal offence

The cases in section 5.3 above all concern the removal of individuals who had no ongoing right to remain in the host country, thus placing the burden on the applicants to show that the state had a positive obligation to allow them to remain in their particular circumstances. The cases in this section, however, concern expulsion of individuals who were living in the country legally, but who faced deportation as a result of criminal offences.

The Court has made clear that the expulsion of third-country nationals following criminal offences does not constitute discrimination on the grounds of nationality, contrary to Article 14 of the Convention. In *Mostaquim v Belgium*,[51] the applicant argued that his deportation was discriminatory, as individuals who had citizenship of the host country did not face deportation following their offences, nor did nationals

[50] And this is the case no matter how, or in what circumstances, the children acquired citizenship. The applicants in *Sorabjee v the United Kingdom* (23938/94) 23.10.1995 (dec.) tried to distinguish between children who had acquired citizenship by being born on British soil, while their parents were there illegally—that is, *ius soli*—and those who had acquired citizenship as a result of *ius sanguinis*, as they had, by virtue of their British father. The Commission rejected this argument, finding that the method of acquiring citizenship made no difference: the question was whether there were obstacles to the children accompanying the parents. See also *Jaramillo v the United Kingdom* (24865/94) 23.10.1995 (dec.).

[51] (12313/86) 18.02.1991.

of another country within the European Union. The Court held that a third-party national could not be considered in a similar position to a citizen of the host state, as the latter have a right to abode in their own country and are protected from expulsion by the Convention.[52] On the other hand, third-party nationals were in a similar position as individuals who were citizens of other EU countries, but a difference in treatment had an objective and reasonable justification given the special legal order that the EU created.

Applicants must therefore rely on a violation of a substantive Convention right, which for the purposes of this volume, is the disruption of family life between the individual and their child(ren), who would either remain in the country without their parent or have to leave the jurisdiction where they may have nationality. In such circumstances, the Court has developed a set of guiding principles to examine whether the deportation can be considered necessary in a democratic society. These principles were first set out in *Boultif v Switzerland*,[53] concerning the deportation of an Algerian national who had been found guilty of charges relating to robbery and damage to property. In deciding whether his deportation was proportionate, notwithstanding the impact that it would have on his family, the Court set out the following criteria to be considered:

- the nature and seriousness of the offence;
- the duration of the applicant's stay in the country from which he is being expelled;
- the time elapsed since the commission of the offence, and the applicant's conduct during that period;
- the nationalities of those concerned;
- the applicant's family situation, for example, the length of their marriage;
- other factors revealing whether the couple had real and genuine family life;
- whether the spouse knew of the offence when they entered into the family relationship;
- whether there are children of the relationship, and if so, their age;
- the difficulties the spouse is likely to encounter in the new country, although the mere fact they might face difficulties in accompanying the applicant cannot in itself preclude expulsion.

While children were mentioned in these criteria, they were not a key consideration—the couple in this case were childless, and the decision was based purely on the difficulties faced by the applicant's wife in moving to Algeria. However, the Court returned to this issue five years later in *Üner v The Netherlands*,[54] in a case concerning the expulsion of an applicant with not only a wife, but also two young children. In this case, the Court made explicit two additional criteria, which it considered already implicit in those identified in *Boultif*:

[52] As confirmed by Article 3, Protocol 4: 'No one shall be expelled, by means either of an individual or of a collective measure, from the territory of the State of which he is a national.'
[53] (54273/00) 02.08.2001.
[54] (46410/99) 18.10.2006 (GC).

- the best interests and well-being of the children, and in particular, the seriousness of the difficulties they are likely to encounter in the country to which applicant is expelled;
- the solidity of social, cultural, and family ties with the host country and that of the country of destination.

On the facts, the existence of children made little difference: at the time the exclusion order became final, they were aged 18 months and 6 years old respectively, and thus deemed to be of an 'adaptable age'.[55] Moreover, the Court noted that the applicant had only lived with his elder son for a short period, and had never lived with his second son, meaning 'the disruption of their family life would not have the same impact as it would [have had] if they had been living together as a family for a much longer time'.[56]

Key to this case was the fact that there were no insurmountable obstacles preventing the applicant's partner and children following him to Turkey. This can be contrasted with *Udeh v Switzerland*,[57] where the applicant had separated from his wife, with whom he had two daughters. The Court noted that the children's mother could not be expected to follow the applicant to Nigeria if he were expelled, meaning that the removal would entail a significant rupture of the father's ties with his children. The Court acknowledged that it was in the children's best interests to grow up with both parents, and the only way to maintain regular contact with both would be for the father to be permitted to remain in the country.

In the recent case of *Ejimson v Germany*,[58] however, the Court took a much harsher line concerning contact between the father and his children. This case also concerned a father being deported to Nigeria, where the mother could not be expected to follow. However, in this case the Court noted that contact could be maintained by telephone and 'different forms of electronic communication'. Moreover, after an initial exclusion period of a year, the father could enter Germany twice a year to visit his daughter.

The difference here lies in the age of the children. In *Udeh*, the children were seven at the time of the deportation order, and ten by the time the case came before the Strasbourg Court. However, in *Ejimson*, despite being arrested when his daughter was 7 months old, his expulsion order had been suspended on several occasions, and by the time the Strasbourg judgment became final, the child would be almost 18. The Court thus found that she would not be deprived of a 'lived' relationship with her father, as they had enjoyed family life together for the majority of her childhood (barring his time in prison).

This case also demonstrated the importance of the timing of the offence in relation to the creation of family life. In this case, the applicant had two family units—his wife and two children with whom he was living at the time of his offence, and the partner and child he cohabited with after his imprisonment. In deciding whether the applicant

[55] See also *Arvelo Aponte v the Netherlands* (28770/05) 03.11.2011.

[56] *Üner v The Netherlands* (46410/99) 18.10.2006 (GC), para. 62. This can be contrasted with *Mehemi v France* (25017/94) 26.09.1997, where the Commission found that moving to Italy would mean radical upheaval for the couple's children, leading to a violation of Article 8.

[57] (12020/09) 16.04.2013.

[58] (58681/12) 01.03.2018.

could be deported, the Court held that regard could be had to the family life with his wife and children from the marriage, as this was established before the offence was committed. However, the family life with his new girlfriend and the child from that relationship could not be taken into consideration, given that they occurred at a time when his residence was already insecure.[59]

Focusing as they do on the sole issue of separation from children, these cases only provide a snapshot of the vast case law in this area. What is clear from this line of jurisprudence, however, is that the interests of children have gradually gained increasing importance, and although they are not considered decisive, must at least be given significant weight. While the state maintains a wide margin of appreciation in this area, the Court has made clear that the national authorities must explicitly address the impact that the removal of their parent will have on the children and ensure that their best interests are given effective protection.

5.4.2 Expulsion following a criminal offence by a child

The Court has not only considered the expulsion of parents following the commission of a criminal offence, but has also examined the situation of immigrant children in conflict with the law. Where offences committed by a child underlie a deportation order, the usual *Boultif/Üner* principles must be supplemented by a consideration of the best interests of the offender and the requirement that expulsion be a last resort.[60]

This is particularly the case where the deportation is to be carried out while the individual is still a child. In *Jakupovic v Austria*,[61] the Court held that the decision of the Austrian authorities to deport a 16-year-old boy to Bosnia was a disproportionate interference with his right to respect for family life under Article 8. He had arrived in Austria aged 11, and aged 14 was the subject of a criminal complaint concerning a burglary. While the criminal proceedings were dropped in relation to this charge, a year later he was convicted of committing 50 further burglaries, for which he was given a suspended sentence, and issued with a deportation order. He was deported aged 16.

The Court noted that the applicant had only been in Austria for four years at the time of his expulsion, distinguishing his situation from that of a second-generation immigrant who was born in the country. He had attended school in Bosnia, and must have been well acquainted with its language and culture. However, his only family in Bosnia would be his father, who had in fact been reported missing since the war, and in any case, whom he had not seen since he was nine years old. The Court found that 'very weighty reasons' would have to be put forward to justify the expulsion of a 16-year-old to a country which had recently had a period of armed conflict, and with no evidence of close relatives living there. On the facts, his offences were not deemed particularly serious: they did not involve violence, and he was given only suspended

[59] See also *El Boujaïdi v France* (25613/94) 26.09.1997.
[60] *Maslov v Austria* (1638/03) 23.06.2008 (GC).
[61] (36757/97) 06.02.2003.

sentences. As such, they were not of sufficient gravity to outweigh the interference with the applicant's family life.

While the outcome is commendable, this judgment is notable for its lack of discussion of children's rights. There is little discussion of the fact that the applicant was a minor at the time of the deportation order, and no consideration of whether it can ever be justified to remove a child from the country in which his or her only close family are living. The reasoning in this case could, and indeed should, have been much stronger.

Somewhat counterintuitively, where the offences were committed as a juvenile, but the deportation was carried out as an adult, there has been greater emphasis on children's rights, best seen in *Maslov v Austria*.[62] In this case, a Bulgarian national had moved with his family to Austria when he was six. Aged 15, he was convicted of a series of offences, including aggravated burglary, extortion, and assault, and sentenced to 18 months' imprisonment (13 of which were suspended). Following his release, he was again convicted on a number of counts of aggravated burglary, and sentenced to 15 months' imprisonment. While serving this sentence, he was issued with a ten-year exclusion order, which was carried out on his release: that is, after he had reached the age of majority.

Unlike *Jakupovic*, the Court in *Maslov* did draw heavily on the international instruments, noting that in cases where the reason for expulsion rests on offences committed while the individual was a minor, both EU law and Article 3 of the UN Convention on the Rights of the Child require the state to have regard to the best interests of the child. Further, Article 40 of the UN Convention on the Rights of the Child makes reintegration an aim of the juvenile justice system, and the Court observed that this could not be achieved by severing family or social ties through expulsion. As such, the Court made clear that expulsion must be a last resort in the case of a juvenile offender—no lesser measure can suffice. This will be particularly important where the deportation is coupled with an exclusion order, prohibiting the individual from returning to the jurisdiction within a set period of time. In such cases, the authorities must show not only that the exclusion itself is warranted, but that its length is also proportionate.[63]

This sets a very high bar for domestic authorities to meet. Rather than the individual having to show insurmountable obstacles to leaving the country, the authorities have to show something in the nature of the offence that is so serious it justifies removal. In undertaking this evaluation, the Court in *Maslov* identified four factors to be taken into account where the person to be expelled is a young adult, who has not yet founded a family of his own:

(i) the nature and seriousness of the offence;
(ii) the length of the applicant's stay in the country from which they are being expelled;
(iii) the time that has lapsed since the offence was committed, and the applicant's conduct during that time; and

[62] (1638/03) 23.06.2008 (GC).
[63] See *Radovanovic v Austria* (42703/98) 22.04.2004.

(iv) the solidity of social, cultural, and family ties that the applicant has with host country and with the country of destination.[64]

In assessing the nature and seriousness of the offences committed, the Court observed that although the Convention does not prevent individuals from being expelled for offences committed while a minor, only 'very serious violent offences' can justify this. Property offences, no matter how often repeated, do not seem to be sufficient in this regard: the Court in both *Maslov* and *Jakupovic* highlighting the lack of violence involved in the offences committed. On the other hand, offences against the person, including rape, will weigh heavier in the balance. In *Bouchelkia v France*,[65] the Court found that deportation was not disproportionate following an aggravated rape committed by a 17-year-old. This was despite the fact that the individual had arrived in France aged two and lived there almost his entire life. Likewise, in *Ferhat Kilic v Denmark*,[66] the Court declared inadmissible a complaint brought concerning the exclusion order placed on a 16-year-old who had been convicted of aggravated assault and manslaughter.

The Court will also take account of the fact that juvenile offences do not necessarily indicate that the individual will constitute a danger to society once they reach adulthood. In *Emre v Switzerland*,[67] when evaluating the 30 offences that the applicant had committed as a child—including robbery, theft, property damage, and serious bodily harm—the Court referred to the UN Guidelines for the Prevention of Juvenile Delinquency (Riyadh Guidelines),[68] noting that experience shows that juvenile delinquency tends to disappear in most individuals with the transition to adulthood.[69]

The importance of the second criteria in *Maslov*—the length of the applicant's residence in the country from which he is being expelled—lies in the assumption that the longer a person resides in a particular country, the stronger his ties with that country will be, and the weaker his ties with his country of origin will become.[70] In this way, it is linked to the fourth *Maslov* factor, which looks directly at the solidity of social, cultural, and family ties with the host country, as opposed to his country of origin.

Factors that the Court will consider in this respect include the age at which the child came to the host country;[71] where they received their schooling;[72] how often they have visited their country of origin,[73] and what family they have living there;[74] and

[64] These factors were in fact used in the earlier case of *Emre v Switzerland* (42034/04) 22.05.2008, decided the month before *Maslov*. Nevertheless, *Maslov* remains the leading authority cited for these principles.

[65] (23078/93) 29.01.1997.

[66] (20730/05) 22.01.2007 (dec.). See also *Hizir Kilic v Denmark* (20277/05) 22.01.2007 (dec.), concerning the applicant's 17-year-old cousin, who was also charged with the same offences.

[67] (42034/04) 22.05.2008.

[68] (1990) GA Res 45/112.

[69] See also *Maslov v Austria* (1638/03) 23.06.2008 (GC), where the Court emphasised that the offences in question could be characterised as acts of juvenile delinquency.

[70] See *Emre v Switzerland* (42034/04) 22.05.2008.

[71] See, for example, *Mostaquim v Belgium* (12313/86) 18.02.1991; *Radovanovic v Austria* (42703/98) 22.04.2004; *Jakupovic v Austria* (36757/97) 06.02.2003; *Emre v Switzerland* (42034/04) 22.05.2008.

[72] See, for example, *Jakupovic v Austria* (36757/97) 06.02.2003; *Emre v Switzerland* (42034/04) 22.05.2008.

[73] See, for example, *Mostaquim v Belgium* (12313/86) 18.02.1991.

[74] See, for example, *Jakupovic v Austria* (36757/97) 06.02.2003.

what languages they are able to speak.[75] Nevertheless, even the strongest of profiles in this respect can be outweighed by the seriousness of the offence committed—as noted above, in *Bouchelkia*, the individual had arrived aged two, received his schooling in France, did not speak the national language in the country to which he was being deported, and had no close relatives there, and yet deportation was still permitted.

The final criteria in *Maslov* is the time that has lapsed since the offence was committed and the applicant's conduct during that time. This is crucial given that the expulsion must pursue a legitimate aim under Article 8(2), and the authorities have an obligation to show why the measure is necessary to achieve that aim. This was explored in *AA v the United Kingdom*,[76] involving a 15-year-old convicted of rape in 2002. He was sentenced to four years' detention, but released after two years and four months. In 2004, during his detention, he was served with a deportation order, but this was appealed several times, and it was not until 2007 that appeals were exhausted. In 2010, the authorities wrote to the applicant to inform him that they were considering whether they should enforce the deportation order.

The Court rejected the government's argument that the interference with the applicant's family life pursued the legitimate aim of 'public safety'. He had only committed a single offence, and the domestic courts had acknowledged that his risk of reoffending was low. Instead, the Court characterised the deportation as pursuing the aim of 'prevention of disorder and crime'. As a result, the task of the Court was to determine the extent to which the applicant could be expected to cause disorder or to engage in criminal activities.

While the fact that he was a minor when he committed the offence did not preclude deportation, given the seriousness of the offence, this had to be weighed against the applicant's subsequent conduct. In the seven years since his release from prison, the applicant's behaviour had been 'exemplary' and he had demonstrated 'commendable efforts to rehabilitate himself and to reintegrate into society'.[77] He could not therefore reasonably be expected to cause disorder or engage in criminal activities, such as would make it necessary in a democratic society to deport him.[78]

The Court thus takes a decidedly child-friendly approach to the expulsion of individuals based on an offence committed as a juvenile—whether or not the child has reached adulthood by the time the deportation is carried out. Its reference to the international materials and recognition of the nature of juvenile offending has created commendably strong protection for children in this area.

[75] See, for example, *Emre v Switzerland* (42034/04) 22.05.2008.

[76] (8000/08) 20.09.2011.

[77] ibid., para. 68.

[78] This principle was also seen in *Mostaquim v Belgium* (12313/86) 18.02.1991, where there had been a four-year delay between the offence and deportation order. During 16 months of this, the applicant was in jail; but for the other 23 months he had been at liberty and had not committed further offences. Combined with the applicant's strong ties to the jurisdiction (he had moved there at age two and only visited his country of nationality twice since then on holiday), the Court found that the deportation was disproportionate.

5.5 Family reunification

5.5.1 The obligation to allow 'essential' reunification

The situation of family reunification is slightly different from that of deportation and expulsion. In this case, the family has already been separated through the immigration of one or both of the parents. The question before the Court is whether there is a positive obligation on the state to allow the child to enter the jurisdiction, in order to respect their family life.

The issue of family reunification was first authoritatively discussed in *Abdulaziz, Cabales and Balkandali v the United Kingdom*[79] concerning the refusal to permit the husbands of the applicants to either join them in the United Kingdom or remain there. This was the first time the Court had been called on to consider the extent of the state's obligations under Article 8 in respect of immigration, and it set the foundations for all cases that followed.[80]

Although the Court rejected the government's argument that matters of immigration control lie outside the scope of Article 8, it set out its now well-established mantra concerning the limits of its application: that the starting point for cases concerning family reunification is that states have the right, without prejudice to their treaty obligations, to control the entry of non-nationals into their territory. It further affirmed that the extent of the obligation to admit the family of immigrants depends on the situation of the persons concerned, and on the general interest, but Article 8 cannot be interpreted as imposing a general obligation to respect the choice of families as to where they choose to establish their family life.[81]

The central question that the Court asked itself was whether there was any obstacle to the couples establishing family life in the applicants' own, or their husbands', home countries. Only then would the Convention impose a positive obligation on the state of residence to allow family reunification within their territory. While this case concerned only adults, these principles have provided the basis for family reunification cases concerning parents and children: an obligation to allow entry will only arise under Article 8 where this is essential for the promotion of family life.[82]

This was further explored in *Gül v Switzerland*,[83] which is the leading case to focus specifically on the reunification of children with their parents. This case involved a father who had left Turkey when his son was three months old, in order to apply for political asylum in Switzerland. Although his asylum application was rejected, he was nevertheless given a residence permit, and was joined by his wife. Some time later he sought to have his son—now six years old—join them also. He argued before the

[79] (9214/80, 9473/81, 9474/81) 28.05.1985.

[80] This had been considered by the Commission in admissibility decisions, and in its Report on the *East African's Case* (*East African Asians v the United Kingdom* (4403/70–4419/70, 4422/70, 4423/70, 4434/70, 4443/70, 4476/70–4478/70, 4486/70, 4501/70, and 4526/70–4530/70) 14.12.1973 (ComRep)). However, this was the first occasion upon which it had been addressed by the Court.

[81] See also *Gül v Switzerland* (23218/94) 19.02.1996; *Ahmut v the Netherlands* (21702/93) 28.11.1996.

[82] *Gül v Switzerland* (23218/94) 19.02.1996.

[83] ibid.

Court that the refusal of the Swiss authorities to allow this constituted a violation of Article 8.

The Court found that its task was to determine to what extent the son's move to Switzerland would be the only way for the applicant to develop family life with his son. The Court placed great emphasis on the fact that the father had himself 'caused' the rupture of family life by leaving his son in Turkey. The Court concluded that given the length of time he and his wife had lived in Switzerland, it would not be easy for them to return to Turkey, but there were, 'strictly speaking, no obstacles preventing them from developing family life' there.[84]

The case was thus treated in the same way as reunification between two adult spouses—there was no evaluation of the best interests of the child, and indeed the child himself was barely discussed in the judgment. The only mention of the child's situation was in noting that he had always lived in Turkey, and had grown up in that cultural and linguistic environment. The child was very much an object in these proceedings, rather than a subject in his own right.

The dissenting opinion of Judge Martens, approved by Judge Russo, is of significance. Again, it focuses on the rights of the adults, rather than the child involved, but takes a much more 'family-centred' approach. For the majority, the scales were weighed heavily in favour of the state's right to enforce immigration controls, with the applicant needing to meet a high evidential burden to displace this. Judge Martens, on the other hand, viewed the competing interests as operating on a much more even scale. On the one hand, he placed the government's 'harsh, political objectives' to serve the interests of the economic well-being of the country;[85] on the other, 'a fundamental element of an elementary human right, the right to care for your own children'.[86]

He drew a distinction between families that had been formed *while* the individual was living as an immigrant in a foreign country—for example, the spouses in *Abdulaziz*—and families that already existed before immigration and were seeking reunification. In the latter case, he argued that 'it is per se unreasonable, if not inhumane to give [the parents] the choice between giving up the position which they have acquired in the country of settlement or to renounce the mutual enjoyment by parent and child of each other's company which constitutes a fundamental element of family life'.[87]

Much was made in this case by both the government and by the majority judgment of the fact that the parents were resident in Switzerland on humanitarian residence permits, and therefore did not have permanent settled status. This focus on form, rather than function, ignores the private life that the applicants had established within the jurisdiction, which was highlighted by Judge Martens in dissent. No matter under what guise the father came to the country, he had been there for seven years, developed social ties, and integrated into the life of his 'new homeland'.

[84] ibid., para. 42. Despite the fact that he had claimed asylum, he had been unable to prove he had been a victim of persecution, and he had in fact been back several times to visit his son, so this was not seen as a valid reason not to return.

[85] ibid., para. 9.

[86] ibid., para. 12.

[87] ibid., para. 14.

Despite this criticism, when the Court returned to the issue of family reunification later that year, in the case of *Ahmut v the Netherlands*,[88] it in fact hardened its stance. In this case, the father had moved to the Netherlands, leaving behind his children to be cared for by his ex-wife in Morocco. When she died, he sought to bring his youngest son to live with him (aged nine), but this was refused. Despite the fact that he had by this time gained Dutch nationality, the Court found that the authorities' refusal to allow reunification in the Netherlands did not violate Article 8. Instead, it noted that the father had retained his Moroccan nationality, and there was no obstacle to his returning to that jurisdiction. Moreover, alternative care with family members or at boarding school was available if he chose not to return.

This case was narrowly decided, by a margin of five votes to four, and Judge Martens once again dissented (joined by Judge Lõhmus). He argued that the availability of alternative care for the child was immaterial, as long as his father was ready, willing, and able to care for him: 'If a father who is a Netherlands national wants to live with and care for his nine-year-old child in the Netherlands both father and child are, in principle, entitled to have that decision respected.'[89]

This focus on nationality was shared by the other judges in dissent. Judge Morenilla held that '[t]he fact that [the applicant] is a national of the Netherlands, and his child's age at the time of the refusal, are in my view, decisive in finding a violation in the present case',[90] while Judge Valticos went so far as to raise the issue of racial discrimination, arguing that

> in any country, a national is entitled to have his son join him, even if the son does not have the same nationality. How does it come about that in the present case this right was refused him? I cannot think that it is because the Dutch father was called 'Ahmut'. However, the suspicion of discrimination must inevitably lurk in people's minds.[91]

Judge Valticos' dissent was similarly impassioned in other respects. He proclaimed that:

> Few human rights are as important as a father's right to have his son by him, to guide him, to supervise his education and training and to help him choose and begin a career and as it were to prepare the projection of his own life into the future by contributing to a happy and productive life for his child. Similarly, few rights are as important as an adolescent son's right to live with his father and to take advantage of the atmosphere of affection as well as of the father's help and advice.[92]

These few words were the only real consideration of the rights of the child in either the majority judgment or by the judges in dissent, tacked on as they were as a corollary to the father's rights. As in *Gül*, the discussion of the rights of the child by the majority was restricted to noting that he had lived in Morocco all his life and had strong links

88 (21702/93) 28.11.1996.
89 ibid., para. 7.
90 ibid., para. 4.
91 ibid., dissenting opinion of Judge Valticos.
92 ibid.

and wider family there. While these cases must be read in the context of the parent applicant, the lack of discussion around the individual rights, interests, and needs of the child is nevertheless striking.

This is somewhat remedied in later jurisprudence, in line with the Court's growing recognition in all areas of jurisprudence of the importance of children's individual rights and interests. There was no one landmark case that heralded this change from the perspective of immigration cases, but it is noticeable that after the child abduction case of *Neulinger and Shuruk v Switzerland*,[93] the Court started to include in its judgments an explicit statement concerning the paramountcy of children's best interests.

However, in the field of immigration at least, paramountcy does not imply determination: the Court has made clear that the child's best interests cannot be seen as a 'trump card' which requires the admission of all children who would be better off living in a contracting state.[94] Indeed, in *IAA and others v the United Kingdom*, despite the domestic authorities acknowledging that reunification would be in the children's best interests, and describing their situation as 'unenviable', the Court was satisfied that a refusal to grant them permission to enter struck a fair balance between immigration control and the family life of the applicants. As such, despite the strong language used by the Court, the child's best interests continue to be just one factor amongst many, easily outweighed by state interests.

Having said this, the Court has imposed an important procedural protection concerning the best interests of children. In coming to their decision, the domestic authorities must demonstrate that they have placed the child's interests at the centre of their balancing exercise and reasoning, and failure to do so will constitute a violation of Article 8. For example, in the case of *El Ghatet v Swtizerland*,[95] the Court noted that the domestic courts had only considered the child's interests in a brief manner and put forward summary reasoning in this regard, leading to a breach of the Convention. However, this case provides a paradigm example of the Court giving with one hand, while taking with the other: in giving its judgment, the Court indicated that had the domestic authorities engaged in a thorough balancing exercise and given relevant and sufficient reasons for their decision, it would have found the decision within the state's margin of appreciation. What is important is the procedure, not the outcome.

5.5.2 Relevant factors for family reunification

As set out in *Gül v Switzerland*,[96] the question before the Court will be whether the entry of the child into the country is *essential* for the development or promotion of family life. In undertaking this assessment, the Court will look at a variety of factors, including the age of the child, the conduct and intention of the parents, their ability to return to their country of origin, and what level of care would be available to the child if they were unable to do so.

[93] (41615/07) 06.07.2010 (GC).
[94] *IAA and others v the United Kingdom* (25960/13) 08.03.2016 (dec.).
[95] (56971/10) 08.11.2016.
[96] (23218/94) 19.02.1996.

5.5.2.1 The age of the child

The Court has sporadically used the age of the child to assess whether family reunification is essential, looking in particular at whether their age indicates a need for parental care. For example, in *Sen v the Netherlands*,[97] the Court noted that the daughter in question, at nine years of age, was still a young child, and there was a particular need to integrate her into her parents' family unit. However, this can be contrasted with *Ahmut*, which involved a child of the same age, where the Court was satisfied that the child could be cared for by relatives, or even sent to boarding school.

In practice, the age of the children and their dependency (or lack thereof) is more frequently used as a reason *not* to find a violation of Article 8, rather than being used to support reunification. For example, in *El Ghatet*, the Court suggested that at 15 years of age, the applicant's son was not as much in need of care as a younger child would be.[98] Likewise, in *IAA*, the Court noted that the applicants were no longer young children (at 21, 20, 19, 14, and 13 years old) and had reached an age where they were 'increasingly able to fend for themselves'.[99]

The use of age in this way was criticised by the dissenting opinion of Judges Jočienė and Karakaş in *Berisha v Switzerland*.[100] As in previous judgments, the majority had concluded that the elder two children—who were 19 and 17 years old at the time of the judgment—could be expected to care for themselves in the country of origin, and therefore family reunification was not necessary. However, Judges Jočienė and Karakaş noted that at the time of the domestic proceedings, the children were 14 and 15, and asked: 'Who can in reality prove the thesis relied on by the Swiss authorities in this case, to the effect that a child of fifteen or fourteen has less need of the parents' care than a child of seven?'[101]

While this has not been picked up by the majority in subsequent cases, it makes a very important point. The definition of 'children' under the UN Convention on the Rights of the Child includes everyone up to the age of 18.[102] While we cannot ignore the differences between the needs of a child at the age of nine and at the age of 17, nor can we simply dismiss a teenage child as able to 'fend for themselves'. In European culture, we would expect the majority of children of this age to still be at school, with few having moved into their own accommodation and away from parental care. The Court's decisions in this area thus force adulthood on children prematurely, undermining the protection due to them.

5.5.2.2 The conduct and intentions of parents

On the other side of the coin, the Court has been critical of parents who have left their children when they are young, passing what seems to be a moral judgement on their decision. In *Ramos Andrade v the Netherlands*,[103] the Court noted that the mother 'decided voluntarily to leave behind her daughters, who were five and three years'

[97] (31465/96) 21.12.2001.
[98] (56971/10) 08.11.2016. See also *Chandra and others v the Netherlands* (53102/99) 13.05.2003 (dec.).
[99] (25960/13) 08.03.2016 (dec.), para. 46.
[100] (948/12) 30.07.2013.
[101] ibid., para. 5.
[102] Article 1.
[103] (53675/00) 06.07.2004 (dec.).

old respectively at that time and completely dependent on others'.[104] It therefore gave short shrift to her application for reunification three years later. This leads to another factor on which the Court has placed significant weight: the conduct and intentions of the parents. In particular, the Court will look to the circumstances in which the parent emigrated, and the reasons for which they left the child behind.[105]

Where the reason is economic, the Court has maintained that the parent has left their child of their own free will, and thus must take responsibility for the rupture of family life. As discussed above, the majority in *Gül* placed great emphasis on the fact that the applicant father had himself caused the separation from his son by leaving Turkey to seek work in Switzerland.[106] However, where the parent in question has arrived seeking asylum, the Court has been much more lenient. This was seen in one of the few successful family reunification cases, *Tuquabo-Tekle and others v the Netherlands*,[107] where the mother had fled civil war and settled in the Netherlands. Despite the fact that her application for asylum had been rejected, the Court observed that it was questionable that she had left her country of origin of 'her own free will', and instead focused on her lawful residence in the Netherlands for a number of years and her acquisition of Dutch citizenship. This can be contrasted with *Ahmut v the Netherlands*,[108] where the applicant had also lived in the Netherlands for some time, and acquired citizenship, but had emigrated for economic reasons.

The decision in *Tuquabo-Tekle* was made even more significant by the fact that it involved a child of 16 years. As discussed above, the Court has usually rejected cases where the child in question has reached an age where they are able to fend for themselves, and are—at least in the Court's opinion—not much in need of parental care. Moreover, here there were relatives (an uncle and grandmother) who were able and willing to care for her—usually a weighty factor.[109] However, the Court found that in this case, the girl's age made her more, not less, dependent on her mother. In accordance with Eritrean culture, the child had reached an age where she could be married off, and her grandmother had removed her from schooling. Although her mother disagreed with this decision, she could not do anything about it while her daughter remained in Eritrea, making reunification necessary.

While this was an encouraging decision, we should be cautious in placing too much significance on it. Rather than opening the door for a more flexible approach to family reunification, instead it has been used to set a higher standard. For example, in *El Ghatet*, the Court distinguished the situation of the child from *Tuquabo-Tekle*, as there was no similar 'major threat to [the child's] best interests in the country of origin'.[110]

A further factor in favour of reunification in *Tuquabo-Tekle* was that the mother always intended that her child would eventually join her in the host country. As soon as she had settled, she took steps for them to be reunited, and the fact that she could not do so immediately was due to circumstances beyond her control. This can be

[104] ibid.
[105] See, for example, ibid.; *Adnane v the Netherlands* (50568/99) 06.11.2001 (dec.).
[106] *Gül v Switzerland* (23218/94) 19.02.1996 .
[107] (60665/00) 01.12.2005.
[108] (21702/93) 28.11.1996.
[109] See section 5.5.2.4.
[110] (56971/10) 08.11.2016, para. 51.

contrasted with *IAA*,[111] where the Court found no evidence that the mother always intended that the children would join her. She made a conscious decision to leave the children to live in the United Kingdom with her new husband, knowing that he would not agree to the children joining them. Even after her divorce, she waited another two years before applying for reunification. Likewise, in *Adnane v the Netherlands*,[112] the Court noted that when the father was awarded custody of his son, who was then living in Morocco, he did not seek immediate reunification in the Netherlands, but left the child with his grandparents for a year before seeking a residence permit for him.[113]

5.5.2.3 The ability of a parent to return to the country of origin

The third factor that the Court has focused on when deciding whether there is a duty to allow family reunification is whether there is any reason the parent cannot simply return to the country of origin to care for the child.[114] As discussed above, a positive obligation to allow entry will only arise under Article 8 where entry into the host state is the only way for family life to develop.

In the majority of cases, the Court has found that there is no obstacle to returning to the country of origin. Even if the parent in question has substantial ties in the host country, or even gained citizenship, the Court has observed that while it may not be *desirable*, relocation is not *impossible*. For example, in *Chandra and others v the Netherlands*,[115] the mother told the Court that she was afraid of her abusive ex-husband and his family, and had submitted evidence that a return to Indonesia would be traumatic for her. In rejecting her application, the Court stated that there was no reason why the mother could not settle in another part of Indonesia, away from her ex-husband.

The few cases where return has been found to be impossible have involved parents who have established new families in the host country. The leading authority on this is *Sen v the Netherlands*,[116] where the parents left their three-year-old child (M) in Turkey while they moved to the Netherlands to seek employment. Whilst there, they had two further children. The Court found that despite the fact that the separation was the result of a deliberate decision taken by the parents, the refusal to allow M—now nine years old—to join them in the Netherlands was a violation of Article 8.

The Court held that parents who have left children behind while they have settled abroad cannot be assumed to have irrevocably decided that those children are to remain in the country of origin, and to have thereby abandoned any idea of a future family reunion. Even if they had not financially supported M for the last six years while she lived with relatives, she was still a young child, and there was a particular

[111] (25960/13) 08.03.2016 (dec.).

[112] (50568/99) 06.11.2001 (dec.).

[113] See also *Ramos Andrade v the Netherlands* (53675/00) 06.07.2004 (dec.), where the Court noted that mother had left the children behind to join her partner in the Netherlands, and even when the relationship broke down, chose not to return to her children, but remained in the Netherlands instead.

[114] See, for example, *Ramos Andrade v the Netherlands* (53675/00) 06.07.2004 (dec.); *Chandra and others v the Netherlands* (53102/99) 13.05.2003 (dec.).

[115] (53102/99) 13.05.2003 (dec.).

[116] (31465/96) 21.12.2001.

need to integrate her into her parents' family unit where they were willing and able to look after her.

Moreover, the two younger children, despite having Turkish nationality, had no further links with that country. They had been raised in the Netherlands, received their schooling there, and were integrated into that environment. As such, the most appropriate way to develop family life between the applicants was for M to move to the Netherlands. By leaving the parents with the choice of abandoning the situation they had acquired in the Netherlands or giving up the company of their eldest daughter, the state had failed to strike an appropriate balance between immigration control and the right to respect for family life.[117]

This can be contrasted with *Gül v Switzerland*,[118] where the parents had also had a child in the host country, but had placed her in alternative care as they were not able to look after her due to the mother's illness. In that case, the majority did not even mention the effect that returning to Turkey would have on the couple's daughter or their relationship with her.[119]

Sen thus represents an important step forward in the jurisprudence, and was followed in *Tuquabo-Tekle*, where the mother also had started a new family in the Netherlands. However, it must not be read to stand for the proposition that simply because an immigrant has had further children in the host country, family reunification must be permitted with the left-behind child. Rather, this will depend on the age of the child with whom the family wish to reunite and the availability of care in the country of origin.

An example of this was seen in *El Ghatet v Switzerland*,[120] where a father in Switzerland wished to be reunited with his 15-year-old son, who was at that time living with his mother in Egypt. The Court distinguished the facts from *Sen* and *Tuquabo-Tekle*, as they had involved family reunification where there were no other parents available to care for the child.[121] In *El Ghatet*, however, the mother was still willing and able to care for the child. Although the case was ultimately decided in the applicant's favour on procedural rather than substantive grounds—the domestic authorities had failed to adequately consider the best interests of the child in their decision-making process—the case demonstrates the Court's cautious and restrictive approach to the *Sen* principle.

5.5.2.4 Availability of care in the country of origin

The case of *El Ghatet* also brings us to the final important feature recognised in the balancing process—the availability of care in the country of origin. In determining

[117] This line of reasoning was also an important factor in *Tuquabo-Tekle and others v the Netherlands* (60665/00) 01.12.2005, where the mother had two children with Dutch nationality, and who had always lived in that cultural and linguistic environment, and therefore could not be expected to move with their mother to Somalia.

[118] (23218/94) 19.02.1996.

[119] This was briefly discussed by Judge Martens in his dissenting opinion, however, when he noted that the parents were being given the choice between 'renouncing' their son, or their daughter, who on the facts would have to be left behind in Switzerland.

[120] (56971/10) 08.11.2016.

[121] In *Sen* (31465/96) 21.12.2001, both parents were in the Netherlands, while in *Tuquabo-Tekle* (60665/00) 01.12.2005, the other parent was dead.

whether family reunification is necessary under Article 8, the Court will look to whether the child can continue to live in the country of origin, if necessary, in the care of another family member. Here, the Court will look to practical solutions, relying on function rather than form. In *El Ghatet*, the Court held that the fact that the father had custody was not decisive: the child's mother could care for him adequately in Kuwait (where she now lived), or a grandparent could assume his care in Egypt.

Other examples of this principle can be seen in *IAA*,[122] where the Court had regard to the fact that the older siblings (21, 20, and 19) could look after the younger (14 and 13), rather than requiring reunification with the mother, and in *Benamar v the Netherlands*,[123] where the Court found that there was no reason why the eldest child—at 18—could not look after her younger siblings (16, 14, and 12), 'if need be with the financial support of their mother'.[124] The Court then went on to note: 'It further appears that the children have a maternal aunt living in Morocco.'[125] The Court went furthest of all in *Ahmut v the Netherlands*,[126] where it held that the child could simply continue living at boarding school in the country of origin.

The Court is thus not looking at who can provide the *best* care for the children—indeed, in *IAA* the Court noted that continuing in their current situation was not in their best interests. Rather, they are deciding whether the situation the children are left in is so deficient as to outweigh the state's right to control immigration into their territory, taking into account the latitude given in this respect by the margin of appreciation.

In making this determination, the Court will be heavily influenced by the status quo, in terms of who is currently providing care to the children. Where the parent has voluntarily left the child in the care of a third party—be that a grandparent, aunt and uncle, or sibling—the Court has required strong reasons to be shown why that care simply cannot continue. This has an impact not only on the perceived suitability of the care in the third country, but also on how the Court quantifies the level of interference in family life under Article 8.

In *Ahmut*, the applicant father had left his children in Morocco to be cared for by his ex-wife. After her death, he sought to bring the youngest child to live with him in the Netherlands, claiming that a failure to permit this was an interference with his family life. The Court noted that he was not prevented from maintaining the degree of family life that *he himself* had opted for when moving to the Netherlands. While he might 'prefer to maintain and intensify his family links' in the Netherlands, 'Article 8 does not guarantee a right to choose the most suitable place to develop family life.'[127] This was also the basis of the Commission's reasoning in the earlier case of *X and Y v Switzerland*,[128] where the father was prohibited from entering Lichtenstein, where his mistress and two children lived. The Court noted that the relationship between the

[122] (25960/13) 08.03.2016 (dec.).
[123] (43786/04) 05.04.2005 (dec).
[124] ibid.
[125] ibid.
[126] (21702/93) 28.11.1996.
[127] ibid., para. 71.
[128] (7289/75, 7349/76) 14.07.1977 (dec.).

applicants consisted of rather loose ties, and occasional visits, which could be carried out in neighbouring Germany (where the father lived with his wife).

The leading case on this issue is *Berisha v Switzerland*,[129] which stands out even amongst the otherwise strict and conservative judgments in this area. The father in this case lived in Switzerland (married to another woman), while the mother—with whom he continued to have a relationship—remained in Kosovo with their children. Ten years later, and following the breakdown of the father's marriage, the mother joined him in Switzerland, and they sought permission for their children to join them also. When this was refused, the children moved to Switzerland clandestinely. When the Swiss authorities sought to expel the children three years later, the applicants challenged this decision.

The Court held that the applicants had maintained a degree of family life for many years before the mother moved to Switzerland, with the father visiting them in Kosovo regularly, and supporting them financially. There was nothing stopping them from continuing to exercise family life in this way. By the time of the case, the eldest two children were 19 and 17, and could be supported from a distance, as they were of an age that they could be expected to look after themselves. The youngest child, however, was only seven years old, and therefore clearly in a different situation. Nevertheless, the Court found that there was nothing to prevent the parents from travelling to visit her in Kosovo, or alternatively, moving there themselves, to ensure that she was provided with the necessary care to promote her best interests.

The Court thus placed the emphasis firmly back on the parents—they must be responsible for protecting the child's welfare, and it was up to them to choose the best available option to do so. This removed the responsibility from the state, which therefore had no separate obligation to the child. The discussion of the child's situation was limited to one single sentence, with no further consideration of what might be required by her own rights and interests, and this deficiency was the focus of the dissenting opinion of Judges Jočienė and Karakaş. They noted that at the age of seven, the child was still dependent on her parents, and it could not be expected that her elder siblings would take care of her in Kosovo. Moreover, she had lived in Switzerland almost half her life, and most of her schooling was in that country. While acknowledging that the children had been brought to the country illegally, the judges emphasised that the best interests of the child cannot be jeopardised simply because of the wrongful conduct of the parents: 'children cannot be held responsible or suffer for their parents' incorrect or illegal behaviour'.[130]

5.5.3 Conclusions on family reunification

The jurisprudence of the Court in this area—as with other areas concerning immigration—is decidedly conservative and state-centric. Rather than balancing a variety of different factors to determine whether family reunification is necessary,

[129] (948/12) 30.07.2013.
[130] ibid., para. 4.

the Court instead appears to search for any factor that could relieve the state of that 'burden'. The age of the children and degree of dependence; the voluntariness of separation; the intention of the parents when immigrating in relation to reunification; whether the parents could return to the country of origin; the availability of alternative care; and whether the current level of family life could be maintained absent reunification: any of these factors will be sufficient for the Court to reject the application.

The rights of the children involved are rarely discussed, let alone given any weight. The decision is framed as a battle between the state's interests in immigration control on the one hand, and the parents' right to respect for family life on the other. The children are merely collateral.

5.6 Children in immigration detention

While the previous sections have examined the right of a parent or child to either remain within, or enter, a country for the purposes of maintaining their family life, we now turn to a different category of cases: immigration detention. Here, the question is not whether the child should be permitted within the jurisdiction, but under what conditions they may be detained pending deportation.

Much of the Court's case law on children in detention is relatively recent, with the majority of cases dating from the mid-2000s onwards. One advantage of this is that by this stage, the Court had already begun to show greater awareness of children's rights, which they incorporated into the jurisprudence on this issue from the very beginning. This has meant that the decisions in this area are encouragingly robust, with significant reliance on international instruments, as well as evidence gathered by non-governmental organisations. The Court has recognised that the child's extreme vulnerability must be the decisive factor and takes precedence over considerations relating to the legality of the migration: in stark contrast to cases in other areas of immigration law.[131] This may be partly a consequence of the articles of the Convention involved: unlike cases concerning family reunification or deportation, which rely predominantly on Article 8, cases on detention have largely focused on Articles 3 and 5. While Article 8 allows balancing between state interests and individual rights, Articles 3 is absolute, and no justification on the basis of legitimate aims or pressing interests is possible.

This does not mean that there is not significant discretion in deciding whether Article 3 can be invoked. In principle, whether the threshold has been crossed depends on all the circumstances of the case, including the nature and context of the treatment, its duration, its physical and mental effects, and the sex, age, and state of health of the victim.[132] However, this is such an imprecise test, relying on a case-by-case evaluation of an individual applicant, that the Court has considerable discretion as to where the line is drawn. What may be inhuman and degrading treatment for one person may not be for the next. Conditions that may be tolerable for five days may not be tolerable for six. The intent is not to criticise this approach—an individual evaluation of the case

[131] See *Mubilanzila Mayeka and Kaniki Mitunga v Belgium* (13178/03) 12.10.2006; *Popov v France* (39472/07, 9474/07) 19.01.2012.

[132] *Ireland v the United Kingdom* (5310/71) 18.01.1978 (GC).

is necessary, and such lines cannot be drawn with precision—but rather to highlight the *choice* made by the Court to hold authorities who have detained children to a very high standard, in line with the requirements of the UN Convention on the Rights of the Child.

Having said this, state obligations concerning the protection of migrant minors in detention may be different depending on whether they are accompanied or not, and for this reason, the cases below are divided on this basis.[133]

5.6.1 Unaccompanied minors

The case law on detention of unaccompanied minors has been dominated by the decision in *Mubilanzila Mayeka and Kaniki Mitunga v Belgium*[134]—and indeed its influence on decisions concerning accompanied minors has also been profound. For this reason, it is worth exploring at some length. It involved a five-year-old girl, who arrived alone in Brussels from the Democratic Republic of Congo (DRC). Her uncle was to care for her in the Netherlands until she could continue on to Canada, where her mother was seeking asylum. When she arrived in Brussels without the necessary travel and immigration papers, she was refused entry, and placed in a detention centre for two months pending removal. From there, and despite the fact that no family member had been identified to care for her, she was deported to the DRC. She argued that her detention and subsequent deportation constituted inhuman and degrading treatment under Article 3, that the separation from her family infringed her rights under Article 8, and that her deprivation of liberty was unlawful under Article 5.

In relation to her detention, the Court observed that she had been kept for two months in a closed centre for adults. No facilities for children existed, no arrangements were made to attend to her needs, and no measures were taken to ensure that she received proper counselling and educational assistance. As a five-year-old child, she was clearly dependant on adults, with no ability to look after herself, yet there was no staff member or specialist assigned to look after her; rather, it was the other detainees who cared for her. The Court noted that her position

> was characterised by her very young age, the fact that she was an illegal immigrant in a foreign land and the fact that she was unaccompanied by her family from whom she had become separated so that she was effectively left to her own devices. She was thus in an extremely vulnerable situation.[135]

[133] It should be noted that parents have also brought cases to the Court concerning a violation of *their own* rights as a result of their children's detention. While some have been successful (notably, *Mubilanzila Mayeka and Kaniki Mitunga v Belgium* (13178/03) 12.10.2006; *Mahmundi and others v Greece* (4902/10) 31.07.2012), for the most part, the Court has found that whilst the detention of parents with their children could have created a feeling of powerlessness, anxiety, and frustration, the fact they weren't separated must have provided relief such that the threshold under Article 3 was not reached. (see *Muskhadzhiyeva and others v Belgium* (41442/07) 19.01.2010; *Popov v France* (39472/07, 9474/07) 19.01.2012)

[134] (13178/03) 12.10.2006.

[135] ibid., para. 51.

Importantly, the Court made clear that the fact that she was in an extremely vulnerable situation must take precedence over considerations relating to her status as an illegal immigrant. She indisputably came within the class of highly vulnerable people to whom the authorities have a positive obligation to provide care and protection under Article 3. The Court noted that the state could not have failed to be aware of the severe psychological effect her situation would have, yet they put her in detention in conditions which 'demonstrated a lack of humanity to such a degree that it amounted to inhuman treatment', in violation of Article 3.[136]

Turning to her deportation, the Court stated that it was 'struck by the failure to provide adequate preparation, supervision and safeguards for her deportation'.[137] She travelled alone back to the DRC, where there was no one there to meet her. The authorities did not seek to ensure that she would be properly looked after, nor have regard to the situation she was likely to encounter. The conditions of her deportation were 'bound to cause her extreme anxiety and demonstrated such a total lack of humanity towards someone of her age and in her situation as an unaccompanied minor as to amount to inhuman treatment.'[138]

In relation to the state's obligations under Article 8 to respect the family life of the child, the Court held that detention pending deportation will only be acceptable where it is intended to combat illegal immigration, and must in all cases comply with the state's international obligations, including under the European Convention on Human Rights and the UN Convention on the Rights of the Child. The effect of the detention was to separate her from her uncle, in whose care she had been placed, and to significantly delay—and in fact hinder—reunification with her mother, in violation of her right to respect for family life under Article 8. The Court did not stop there, however. It held that the private life of the child had also been violated, as her physical and mental integrity were compromised by her detention. There was no risk that she would evade the authorities, making detention in a closed centre unnecessary, and the Court concluded that other measures could have been taken that would have been 'more conducive to the higher interest of the child guaranteed by Article 3 of the Convention on the Rights of the Child'—for example, placement with foster parents. Likewise, in relation to her deportation, the Court found that the state had failed in its positive obligation under Article 8 to ensure she would be looked after in the DRC.

The final aspect of the child's claim related to the lawfulness of her deprivation of liberty, under Article 5(1)(f). This Article provides an exception to the right to liberty and security in the context of 'the lawful arrest or detention of a person to prevent his effecting an unauthorised entry into the country or of a person against whom action is being taken with a view to deportation or extradition'. While the detention of the applicant obviously fell within this provision, the Court held that this was not sufficient. Instead, the authorities must prove that there is a relationship between the ground of detention relied on, and the place and conditions of detention. In this case, the child

[136] ibid., para. 58.
[137] ibid., para. 66.
[138] ibid., para. 69.

was kept in a closed centre for adults, in conditions which were not adapted to her position of extreme vulnerability as an unaccompanied minor. As such, there had been a violation of Article 5(1).

This was a comprehensive and far-reaching judgment, with findings of violations in respect of all aspects of the child's complaint,[139] and can be contrasted with the case of *Nsona v The Netherlands*,[140] decided ten years earlier. In this case, the applicant, BN, was a Zairean national residing legally in the Netherlands. On one occasion, after a trip to Zaire, she returned with a nine-year-old child, FN, who she claimed to be her daughter, and later, her niece. As FN did not have an entry permit, she was told that she would be returned to Zaire. BN decided not to travel with her, and FN was returned to Zaire alone. Since her relatives could not be contacted, she was met by a business relation of the airline, who then entrusted her to the immigration authorities. After spending a night at the home of an immigration officer, she was taken to friends, with whom she had stayed prior to travelling to the Netherlands. Unlike in *Mubilanzila Mayeka*, the Court held that the separation of BN and FN could not be attributed to the state—BN could have simply travelled back with her. Likewise, the arrangements for her return were deemed sufficient: the airline had made arrangements for her to be met at the airport, and these had proved 'adequate'. While the Court did question the apparent willingness of the Dutch authorities to hand over all responsibility for her welfare to others (including the airline), and in a case involving a nine-year-old such an attitude was open to criticism, it was held that it did not pass the threshold of inhuman and degrading treatment under Article 3.

Although the two cases can be distinguished on the facts—the age of the children, the length of time of detention, the ability of the guardian to return with the child—it is the difference in the language and approach of the Court that is most striking. In *Nsona*, the focus was on the conduct of BN, in trying to deceive the authorities, and in deciding not to return to Zaire with the child. In *Mubilanzila Mayeka*, the focus was on the child herself, and the impact of the situation on someone who was clearly extremely vulnerable.

This focus on the vulnerability of unaccompanied migrant children has carried through in the subsequent jurisprudence, although the cases that have followed have all involved much older teenagers. Drawing on the provisions of the UN Convention on the Rights of the Child, in these cases the Court has made clear that the best interests of the child must be a primary consideration (Article 3) and that detention must be considered only as a last resort (Article 37), no matter what the age of the child.[141]

[139] There was also a complaint by the child's mother regarding Article 5(1), but this was not upheld, as she could not claim to be a victim for the purposes of Article 34 of the Convention.

[140] (23366/94) 28.11.1996.

[141] This has not been without criticism, however. In the case of *Abdullahi Elmi and Aweys Abubakar v Malta* (25794/13, 28151/13) 22.11.2016, Judge Sajó in his concurring opinion objected to the majority's reliance on the applicant's age, and their reference to the Court's previous case law requiring special standards of care with regard to the detention of migrant children. Those cases, he argued, were about small children, as opposed to the 17-year-old applicants in *Abdullahi Elmi*. While Judge Sajó may be correct that the case law on young children is not directly and automatically applicable to older adolescents on the cusp of adulthood, his objection to the majority 'considering [the applicants] to be children'—as they are, after

In relation to older unaccompanied migrant children, the focus has largely been on the length and conditions of detention, interpreted in light of their age and situation, rather than on the detention in and of itself. In determining whether such detention constitutes inhuman or degrading treatment under Article 3, the Court has considered the amount of personal space available; access to outdoor exercise; the isolation of the applicants; the availability of natural light or air, and of adequate ventilation; the effect of extremes of heat or cold; and compliance with basic sanitary and hygiene requirements.[142] Most importantly, however, the Court has made clear that unaccompanied children—even if they are approaching 18—should not be detained with adults. This was emphasised in *Rahimi v Greece*,[143] where the 15-year-old applicant was detained for two days in a centre with adults. The centre was designed to hold 300 people, yet housed over 700, meaning that people were forced to share mattresses, or sleep on the floor, and there was only one toilet and one shower between 150 people. Despite the fact that his stay was very short, the Court held that the child's age and personal situation placed him in a position of extreme vulnerability, and the conditions of detention were so serious that they 'undermined the very meaning of human dignity'.[144]

Article 3 is not the only hurdle the state has to pass, however. Even if the length and conditions of detention are not so severe as to pass the threshold of severity for Article 3, they can influence the Court's interpretation of the state's compliance with Article 5(1)(f). In *Abdullahi Elmi and Aweys Abubakar v Malta*,[145] the Court made clear that in order for the state to satisfy its obligations in this regard, the conditions of detention must be appropriate, and the length of detention must not exceed what is reasonably required for the purpose pursued. In this case, the applicants were detained in less than ideal conditions while awaiting an age assessment. The Court held that detention of more than seven months for a process that entailed one or two interviews and an x-ray was so significant that it 'raise[d] serious doubts as to the authorities' good faith'.[146] There is also a procedural requirement entailed in Article 5(1): as held in *Rahimi*, in order for detention to be justified under this provision, the authorities must have explored the possibility of replacing detention with a less drastic measure.[147]

It must also be noted that the responsibility of the state does not end when the child is released from detention. In *Rahimi*,[148] a violation of Article 3 was found where the authorities had failed to provide accommodation after the child's release. There was no policy with regard to finding children's families, nor for protecting them from possible violence or exploitation. Rather, the child in question was abandoned to fend for himself. The Court found that as an unaccompanied minor, the applicant was one of the

all, according to the (almost) universally accepted definition in the UN Convention on the Rights of the Child —is somewhat extraordinary, not to mention disheartening.

[142] See, for example, *Karalevicius v Lithuania* (53254/99) 07.04.2005; *Ananyev and others v Russia* (42525/07, 60800/08) 10.01.2012; *Abdullahi Elmi and Aweys Abubakar v Malta* (25794/13, 28151/13) 22.11.2016 ; *ShD and others v Greece, Austria, Croatia, Hungary, North Macedonia, Serbia and Slovenia* (14165/16) 13.06.2019.

[143] (8687/08) 05.04.2011.

[144] ibid., para. 86.

[145] (25794/13, 28151/13) 22.11.2016.

[146] ibid., para. 146.

[147] *Rahimi v Greece* (8687/08) 05.04.2011. See also the cases below on accompanied minors.

[148] ibid.

most highly vulnerable members of society, and the authorities were required to take adequate measures to provide him with care and protection.[149]

We can thus see that the Court has placed strict and far-reaching obligations on states in relation to unaccompanied minors, under a number of different provisions of the Convention. Perhaps the most promising indication comes from the concurring opinion of Judge Pinto de Albuquerque in *Abdullahi Elmi*: 'Any form of detention is ill-suited to the vulnerability of children, be it before or after the asylum application assessment decision has been taken. Unaccompanied or separated children must never be detained.'[150] Let us hope that this is a portent of the future direction of the Court.[151]

5.6.2 Children detained with their parents

While the Court has taken a strong position on the detention of unaccompanied minors, the jurisprudence concerning the detention of accompanied migrant children is no less rigorous. As the Court has consistently held, the fact that children are accompanied by their parents does not exempt the authorities from their duties under the Convention.

The case of *Muskhadzhiyeva and others v Belgium*[152] involved the same transit centre as the child was detained in *Mubilanzila Mayeka*. In this case, however, the children—aged seven, five, three, and seven months—were detained for a month, along with their mother. The Court held that the presence of their mother was not sufficient to mitigate the suffering of the children. They were held for a considerable period in a centre unsuitable for children, and had shown serious psychological and psycho-traumatic symptoms. The Court invoked Article 22 of the UN Convention on the Rights of the Child, which requires states to take appropriate measures to ensure that refugees and asylum seekers enjoy appropriate protection and assistance, whether or not they are accompanied by their parents. In view of the children's age, the length of their detention, and evidence given concerning their state of health, the Court held that their detention reached the threshold of gravity required by Article 3. When considering the detention under Article 5(1), importantly, the Court saw no reason to depart from the previous findings in *Mubilanzila Mayeke*, despite the fact that the children had been accompanied by their mother.

This judgment was followed shortly by a third case also concerning the same transit centre: *Kanagaratnam and others v Belgium*.[153] This case differed from those that had gone before it, however: the children were much older (13, 11, and eight), and although they were detained for a longer period (four months), no evidence was

[149] See also *VM and others v Belgium* (60125/11) 07.07.2015, which concerned a family with young children who had to live on the streets for four weeks following their removal from a reception centre. The Court similarly found that there had been a violation of Article 3 in these circumstances.

[150] (25794/13, 28151/13) 22.11.2016, para. 14 (citations omitted).

[151] It should also be noted that detention should not be the only option for unaccompanied minors, and the authorities have an obligation to provide appropriate care outside of this setting, (see, for example, *Khan v France* (12267/16) 28.02.2019, concerning the 'Calais jungle'.

[152] (41442/07) 19.01.2010.

[153] (15297/09) 13.12.2011.

provided concerning the psychological effects of the detention. However, the Court held that these elements were not decisive. Even in the absence of specific evidence, it started from the assumption that the children were vulnerable, both because of their childhood itself and because of their personal history—having been separated from their father, and having left their home country in the grip of civil war. The Court reiterated that the children's best interests must prevail, even in the context of expulsion, and their placement in a closed detention centre designed for adults constituted inhuman and degrading treatment under Article 3 ECHR. Moreover, by placing them in conditions that were ill-suited to their extreme vulnerability as minors, the authorities had not sufficiently guaranteed their right to their liberty under Article 5(1).

The assumption of vulnerability, and indeed psychological trauma, even in the absence of specific evidence, is of particular importance in this case. The Court found that by placing children in closed detention centres they are presumptively exposed to anxiety and inferiority, which it is not necessary to quantify to invoke Article 3.[154] This opened the door wide for future applicants, removing a significant hurdle they had previously faced. However, this was criticised by Judge Sajó in his concurring opinion in *Abdullahi Elmi and Aweys Abubakar v Malta*.[155] He noted that the applicants were considered 'vulnerable individuals' on account of the 'traumatic experiences they were likely to have endured previously', yet no specific information concerning these experiences was provided, and indeed, not even the applicants themselves had alleged any such experiences.[156]

Despite this criticism, this must be seen as a move in the right direction for the Court. Children must be recognised as vulnerable members of society, even without specific evidence to this effect. With regards to evidence of *further* grounds of vulnerability, the expansive interpretation of the Court does not automatically result in a finding of trauma, but simply shifts the burden of proof from the individual to the state. This rebalancing goes some way to addressing the power imbalance between the parties, requiring the party with greater strength and resources to prove that their treatment of a vulnerable individual has not caused harm.

In any event, the jurisprudence that followed *Kanagaratnam* has continued to expand the reach of the Court, narrowing the circumstances in which children can be placed in detention to a significant degree.

A second factor that will be considered in conjunction with the conditions of detention will be the length of time for which they are detained. *Popov v France*[157] was the first time that the Court considered a much shorter period of detention—in this case, two weeks. The Court observed that while this was objectively a short period of time, for the children—aged five months, and three years—it would be perceived as neverending. This was particularly the case as they were being held in an adult environment, with a strong police presence, and without any activities to keep them occupied.

[154] See, for example, *AB and others v France* (11593/12) 12.07.2016.

[155] (25794/13, 28151/13) 22.11.2016.

[156] *Abdullah, Elmi and Aweys Abubakar v Malta* (25794113, 28151/13) 22.11.2016, concurring opinion of Judge Sajó.

[157] (39472/07, 9474/07) 19.01.2012.

The Court held that the domestic authorities failed to take into account the inevitably harmful consequences for the children, and thus found a violation of Article 3.

Interestingly, the Court also examined the case under Article 8—something that it had refused to do two years earlier in *Muskhadzhivyeva*, when they declared this aspect of the complaint inadmissible. It noted that since that case, there had been developments in the case law concerning the primacy of children's best interests in the context of immigration detention,[158] and a different approach was justified. In this light, the Court found that protecting children's best interests involves not only keeping the family together as far as possible, but requires that the authorities ensure that the detention of minors is only used as a measure of last resort. In this case, there was no indication that any other options had been considered, and thus there was a violation of Article 8.

This principle was further explored in *AB and others v France*[159] in the context of Article 5(1). The Court noted that the situation of children is intrinsically linked to that of their parents, from whom they should not be separated, yet this has the consequence that when parents are placed in detention, the children themselves are de facto deprived of liberty. While the Court acknowledged that this deprivation of liberty stemmed from a legitimate decision on the part of the parents, who could otherwise entrust the children to a third party, this did not negate the fact that the children found themselves in an environment that was a source of anxiety and tension, which could cause them serious harm. As such, the requirements of Article 5(1)(f) will only be met where the domestic authorities can establish that that no other measure involving a lesser restriction of their freedom could have been implemented.[160]

AB is also important as it demonstrates the Court's increasingly strict approach to detention under Article 3. In this case, a four-year-old child was detained for 18 days in a detention centre that was adapted to children, but was built next to an airport, on land classified as an 'area unsuitable for building'. While the Court found that the conditions were not such that they would be sufficient, in and of themselves, to cross the threshold of Article 3, in cases where the detention was of longer duration, the repetition and accumulation of mental and emotional stress would have harmful consequences for a young child. Eighteen days was sufficient to cross this threshold in this case, and in a line of cases decided on the same day, the same detention facility was found to violate the rights of a 15-month-old child held for nine days;[161] a two-year-old held for ten days;[162] and a seven-month-old for seven days.[163]

As such, even in cases of detention for quite a short period of time, a lack of adequately child-friendly facilities will cross the threshold required to violate Article 3. The most

[158] See, for example, *Rahimi v Greece* (8687/08) 05.04.2011.

[159] (11593/12) 12.07.2016.

[160] See also *Popov v France* (39472/07, 9474/07) 19.01.2012.

[161] *RK and others v France* (68264/14) 12.07.2016.

[162] *RC and VC v France* (76491/14) 12.07.2016

[163] *RM and others v France* (33201/11) 12.07.2016. See also *GB and others v Turkey* (4633/15) 17.10.2019, where the family had rarely been permitted to go outside, had constantly been exposed to cigarette smoke from other detainees, and had not been given food suitable for children. The Court found that the detention of the family in these conditions—including a six-year old, a two-year-old, and a one-year-old—violated Article 3.

extreme example of this was *SF and others v Bulgaria*,[164] where the applicants—a family, including a 16-year-old, an 11-year-old and an 18-month-old child—were detained between 32 hours (on the government's calculation) and 41 hours (on the applicants' calculations). In either case, the Court held that there had been a violation of Article 3. It noted that the time period involved was considerably shorter than other cases where a violation had been found, but the conditions were considerably worse. The cell was dirty and run-down, there was limited access to the toilet, forcing them to urinate on the floor of the cell, and they were not provided with food or drink for 19 hours—a situation which was described as having 'particularly nefarious effects' on the 18-month-old child.

5.7 Conclusion

From the perspective of child rights, immigration cases can be split into two distinct categories. First, deportation, expulsion, and family reunification, where the state's interests largely prevail and children's rights, while considered, are demoted to a secondary position. This is not to say they are not important—indeed, children's rights have been one of the key factors which have triggered a finding of a violation of family and private life in these cases. However, as suggested by Beduschi, this seems to be instrumentalised by the Court, being used only when it is convenient for finding a violation of the Convention, rather than as a systematic tool for evaluation of state action.[165]

In contrast, the cases on detention show a strong children's rights focus, with significant protection carved out for children within Article 3. Their particular vulnerability—both as children and as migrants, as well as further vulnerabilities relating to trauma they may have experienced—has been affirmed by the Court on numerous occasions. Nevertheless, the Court has stopped short of prohibiting detention of migrant children altogether, despite recognising its negative effects on both short- and long-term health.

It is important that the Court continues to come to grips with children's enhanced vulnerability in the migration context—not only in relation to detention, but in decisions concerning deportation and family reunification also. Too often in this area, the Court allows children to suffer for the 'sins' of their parents, and the harm to the child is swept away by the overpowering 'public interest'. In this light, greater reliance on the international instruments—and in particular the work of the UN Committee on the Rights of the Child—would be beneficial to ensure a more robust approach by the Court. The 'best interests' principle has been imported by the Court from the UN Convention on the Rights of the Child, but it has often failed to seek further guidance on what this actually means in the context of immigration.

[164] (8138/16) 07.12.2017.

[165] A. Beduschi, 'Vulnerability on Trial: Protection of Migrant Children's Rights in the Jurisprudence of the International Human Rights Courts' (2018) 36(1) *Boston University International Law Journal* 55.

6
The Right to Education

6.1 Introduction

The right to education is the only child-focused right in the European Convention on Human Rights.[1] Article 2, Protocol 1 provides that:

> *No person shall be denied the right to education.*
>
> *In the exercise of any functions which it assumes in relation to education and to teaching, the State shall respect the right of parents to ensure such education and teaching in conformity with their own religious and philosophical convictions.*

This provision is unique for a number of reasons. The first sentence, starting '[n]o person shall be denied', is formulated in a negative manner, in contrast to the majority of rights under the Convention which have a positive formulation: 'Everyone has the right to . . .'. In the first case which considered this article—the *Belgian Linguistic Case*[2]—the Belgian government argued that this formulation was inspired by the 'classic conception of freedoms, in contrast to rights', and was evidence of an intention of the contracting parties to undertake 'purely negative duties' in this respect.[3] This argument was rejected by the Court, who confirmed that positive obligations could arise under this article. Nevertheless, the Court recognised that the right to education under Article 2, Protocol 1 does not require states to establish education of any particular type, or at any particular level—merely that individuals within the jurisdiction can access the means of instruction existing at any given time.

As a result, it is rare for the right under the first sentence to be breached, leaving the second sentence—the right of parents to ensure education in conformity with their convictions—to do the majority of the work in this area. But this second sentence is also unusual. As Judge Rozakis has pointed out, this right, although linked with the right to education, does not vest in the basic recipient of that right. Instead, it vests in parents, whose direct right to education is not at stake.[4] Moreover, this parental control extends beyond just the classroom and the school curriculum: it applies '[i]n the exercise of any functions which [the state] assumes in relation to education and to teaching', encompassing school administration and organisation, as well as discipline. The concept of 'education' and 'teaching' have likewise been given very wide

[1] Although it also applies to adults (see section 6.8 on Higher Education) the jurisprudence of the Court has focused almost exclusively on the education of children.

[2] (1474/62, 1677/62, 1691/62, 1769/63, 2126/64) 23.07.1968.

[3] ibid., para. 1.

[4] *Lautsi v Italy* (30814/06) 18.03.2011, concurring opinion of Judge Rozakis, joined by Judge Vajić.

Children and the European Court of Human Rights. Claire Fenton-Glynn, Oxford University Press (2021). © Claire Fenton-Glynn.
DOI: 10.1093/oso/9780198787518.003.0006

interpretations—with the former connoting 'the whole process whereby, in any society, adults endeavour to transmit their beliefs, culture and other values to the young', while the latter refers 'to the transmission of knowledge and to intellectual development'.[5]

Despite these limitations, the Court has provided strong protection for children's rights in this area, recognising the parasitic nature of the second sentence of Article 2, Protocol 1, allowing parental convictions to prevail only where they do not impinge on the primary right of the child to education. Thus, while the jurisprudence in this area is largely predicated on cases brought by parents complaining of the infringement on *their* rights, the Court has managed to ensure that the rights of children are not forgotten.

6.2 Form of education

6.2.1 State versus private schooling

There have been a myriad of cases before the Court regarding the parental assertion of education in conformity with their convictions—challenging both the form of education and the content. In relation to the former, the Court has been asked to decide whether the state has the right to establish a public education system, and if so, how systems of private education and home schooling fit within this framework.

First, and unsurprisingly, Article 2, Protocol 1 does not prevent the state from establishing a system of public education. In a somewhat unusual case, *40 Mothers v Sweden*,[6] the applicants argued that their right to ensure their children's education in conformity with their religious convictions was violated by the decision of the Swedish government to set up public nursery schools for all children from age six. Although attendance was voluntary, the parents argued that once municipal schools were created, private religious schools would be jeopardised for lack of public financial support. In a short and swift admissibility decision, the Commission found that a system of state education was not incompatible with the Convention, particularly where there was no obligation for children to attend, and thus the complaint was manifestly ill-founded.

While this case determined that the state has the *right* to establish a system of public education, this does not mean that the state has an *obligation* to do so. As discussed in section 6.1 above, the Court has made clear that Article 2, Protocol 1 does not require states to establish education of any particular type, or at any particular level.[7] Instead, the obligation on the state is to permit individuals to benefit from any education system that the state chooses to provide.

Having said this, the obligation to permit individuals to benefit from a state-run system does not mean that parents can demand that their child attend any particular school. In *W and D, M and HI v United Kingdom*,[8] the state system provided for

[5] *Campbell and Cosans v the United Kingdom* (7511/76, 7743/76) 25.02.1982, para. 33.
[6] (6853/74) 09.03.1977 (dec.).
[7] *Belgian Linguistic Case* (1474/62, 1677/62, 1691/62, 1769/63, 2126/64) 23.07.1968.
[8] (10228/82, 10229/82) 06.03.1984 (dec.).

both single-sex, selective grammar schools and mixed-sex comprehensive schools. The parents wished to send their children to the grammar school, but there were no places available. The parents argued that the choice of a grammar school rather than a comprehensive was based on a philosophical objection to the latter, which they claimed imposed a vision of a classless, egalitarian society, in sharp contradistinction to the parents' notions of relations between the sexes and sex roles in society. The Commission noted first that Article 2, Protocol 1 requires that parents' views be *respected*, but not necessarily *reflected* in the state school system. There was no allegation that the parents were denied a major role in the education of their children, nor that the children were being indoctrinated at the comprehensive school. The Commission also noted that other options were available to the parents—including private education and home schooling—and the mere fact that they could not afford this was not sufficient to conflict with the requirements of Article 2, Protocol 1.

Second, while the state has the right to create a public education system, the Court has also made clear that parents (and other organisations) must have the opportunity to establish alternative schools if they so wish: in *Kjeldsen, Busk Madsen and Pedersen v Denmark* the Court found that the *travaux preparatoires* 'indisputably demonstrate ... [the] freedom to establish private schools'.[9] While this system can be subject to regulation in order to ensure a proper education system as a whole—for example, a requirement that the education provided meets a certain objective level[10]—any restrictions cannot infringe on the substance of the right to education.[11]

Despite the obligation to *allow* private schools to be set up, Article 2, Protocol 1 does not oblige states to *subsidise* such institutions, and a refusal to grant public funds for the establishment and running of private education is not incompatible with this provision.[12] Of course, any difference in funding between private and state education must meet the requirements of Article 14: the Court must determine whether the schools are in a relevantly comparable situation, and if so, whether the difference in treatment is a proportionate means of pursuing a legitimate aim.

This was challenged in *X v the United Kingdom*,[13] concerning the funding provisions for private schools in Northern Ireland. For those wishing to set up a school, the state agreed to cover 85 per cent of capital expenditure and 100 per cent of recurrent costs—leaving 15 per cent to be covered by others. The applicant complained that a failure to provide private schools with 100 per cent funding (which was given to state-run schools) was a violation of Article 14 in conjunction with Article 2, Protocol 1. The Commission held that private and public schools are in a different situation—the state exercises substantial control in the ownership and management of public schools, and

[9] (5095/71, 5920/72, 5926/72) 07.12.1976, para. 50.

[10] See *Ingrid Jordebo Foundation of Christian Schools and Ingrid Jordebo v Sweden* (11533/85) 06.03.1987 (dec.), where the school was given permission to run classes in lower-year levels, but not for the final years of school, based on a finding that the school did not provide knowledge and skill of such a nature and level that corresponded with public schooling. The Commission found that such a restriction was compatible with Article 2, Protocol 1.

[11] *Leuffen v the Federal Republic of Germany* (19844/92) 09.07.1992 (dec.).

[12] *40 Mothers v Sweden* (6853/74) 09.03.1977 (dec.). See also *Simpson v the United Kingdom* (14688/89) 04.12.1989 (dec.), concerning the paying of private tuition fees for a child with disabilities.

[13] (7782/77) 02.05.1978 (dec.).

thus a 100 per cent subsidy was legitimate. Conversely, where a private body seeks ownership and decisive control over the management of a school, it is reasonable for the state to require a financial contribution to this.

Likewise, the Court has recognised that states may be permitted to vary the level of funding they provide to different types of private schools, as long as this is based on reasonable and objective grounds. For example, in *Verein Gemeinsam Lernen v Austria*,[14] the state awarded subsidies for staff costs to Church schools, but schools run by other organisations had to show that there was a 'need' for the schools before funding was granted. The Commission dismissed the complaint under Article 14 in conjunction with Article 2, Protocol 1: Church schools were long established and widespread, and if the educational duties they shouldered fell to the state, there would be a considerable burden. The test applied to other schools for funding—what would be the burden on the state if the private school did not operate—was the same.

The oversight of the Court in this area is thus very light touch—the state has a right, though not an obligation, to set up schools within its jurisdiction, but they must allow private individuals and groups to do so also, subject to appropriate and non-discriminatory restrictions.

6.2.2 Home schooling

While the Convention requires that states allow private schools to operate within their jurisdiction, in line with respect for parents' beliefs and convictions, the Court has made clear that this does not prevent the state from establishing a system of compulsory school attendance: there is no requirement that parents be permitted to home school their children.

This was examined in *Konrad v Germany*,[15] in relation to the system of compulsory primary schooling in Germany. In this case, the applicants wished to educate their children at home, as no state or private school currently in operation was compatible with their convictions. However, their application for an exemption from compulsory school attendance was rejected by the domestic authorities on the grounds that the parents' wishes could not take precedence over the children's rights: children have an interest in attending school with children from all backgrounds, which enables them to gain their first experiences of society and acquire social skills. The domestic authorities further concluded that parents do not have an *exclusive* right to educate their children—the state's obligation to provide children with an education must be regarded as on an equal footing with parents' right in this respect.

The parents' complaint under Article 2, Protocol 1 was dismissed, with the Court finding that the second sentence of Article 2, Protocol 1—granting rights to parents—must be read in conjunction with, and as subsidiary to, the first sentence, protecting the child's right to education: 'It is on to this fundamental right that is grafted the right of parents to respect for their religious and philosophical convictions.'[16] As such, the

[14] (23419/94) 06.09.1995 (dec.).
[15] (35504/03) 11.09.2006 (dec.).
[16] ibid., para. 1.

Court found that respect is only due to convictions on the part to parents that do not conflict with the child's right to education.

Relying on the lack of consensus amongst contracting states with regard to compulsory attendance at primary school, the Court found that the decision of the German authorities that home schooling could not meet the objectives of integration and experiences of society falls within the margin of appreciation in setting up and interpreting rules for their education systems. The Court also emphasised that the parents were free to educate their children as they wished after school and at weekends. Compulsory school attendance did not deprive them of the right to educate their child in conformity with their religious convictions, but merely restricted it to outside school hours.

Where home schooling is permitted within the state, the Court has also recognised the right of the authorities to require that certain minimum standards be met in this respect. For example, in *Family H v the United Kingdom*,[17] the Commission emphasised that the state had the right to ensure that the education provided to the children—in whatever setting—met a certain standard; while in *Leuffen v the Federal Republic of Germany*,[18] the Commission recognised that the authorities are entitled to assess the ability of the parent to provide adequate education, and thus determine whether home schooling should be permitted.

Finally, where parents refuse to comply with their obligations in relation to their children's schooling, the Court has accepted that the authorities can take strong enforcement measures against parents to ensure school attendance. In *Wunderlich v Germany*,[19] the Court found that there was no violation of Article 8 where the authorities had removed parental authority from parents who persistently refused to send their children to school. The Court observed that the authorities had reasonably assumed that the children's best interests were endangered as they were growing up in a 'parallel world', isolated from everyone outside their family, and concerns had been raised regarding physical abuse. Lesser measures, such as fines, had been attempted, but the parents continued to refuse to cooperate with the authorities, meaning that the drastic measure of removing the children from the family was justified in the circumstances.[20]

These are strong decisions for children's rights: recognising that when parents' convictions conflict with children's rights it is the latter that must prevail.[21] Interestingly, the parents in *Konrad* had tried to avoid this clash of rights by aligning the interests of the children with those of the parents. The application alleging a violation of Article 2, Protocol 1 was filed not only on the parents' own part, but also on behalf of the children—meaning that technically, the 'children' were also arguing they had a right to be educated in accordance with their parents' beliefs. However, the Court relied on the young age of

[17] (10233/83) 06.03.1984 (dec.).

[18] (19844/92) 09.07.1992 (dec.).

[19] (18925/15) 10.01.2019.

[20] The children were returned to the home three weeks later, when the parents agreed to a learning assessment, and for the children to attend school. See also *Family H v the United Kingdom* (10233/83) 06.03.1984 (dec.), where the Commission implicitly accepted the criminal conviction of parents who had failed to provide their children with adequate education.

[21] See also *BN and SN v Sweden* (17678/91) 30.06.1993 (dec.).

the children—ten and 11 at the time of the application—to find that they were unable to foresee the consequences of their parents' decision to opt for home education.

In some ways, this is commendable: it prevents parents from being the exclusive arbiter of the child's interests and ensures that there is judicial scrutiny in this respect. On the other hand, there is no indication that there was any true investigation of the children's capacity for decision-making, or any analysis of the point at which children's wishes *may* become determinative in the field of education—if ever.[22]

6.3 Specialised and segregated schooling

6.3.1 Children with disabilities

The schooling of children with disabilities has been an issue that has arisen on several occasions before both the Commission and before the Court. The primary question has been the extent to which domestic authorities must mainstream their education and adapt facilities and education to their needs, and whether placement in a separate school is acceptable.

In general, the Court has deferred to the decisions of the domestic authorities in this respect, finding that it is not its role to re-assess which type of schooling is more appropriate, as long as it is not discriminatory or patently unsatisfactory. This was seen in the early case of *PD and LD v the United Kingdom*,[23] where the parents argued that they held deep philosophical convictions about the type of schooling best suited to their daughter's needs and believed segregated education inappropriate and harmful in the long term. The Commission left open the question of whether disagreement with the authorities about the most appropriate school could be based on deep-founded philosophical convictions, rather than simply reflecting a difference of view as to the best way of providing a child with education.[24] However, even if the form of schooling could fall under this provision, the Commission held that states have a wide margin of discretion as to how to make the best possible use of the resources available to them in the interests of children with disabilities generally. As such, Article 2,

[22] There was some minimal discussion of this issue in the earlier case of *Kramelius v Sweden* (21062/92) 17.01.1996 (dec.), although the majority of the reasoning in the case relied on other grounds. In this case, a 16-year-old child was removed from her family and placed in public care. It was decided that she should not attend lessons at school, as her behaviour made learning difficult for others, but instead to receive individual lessons at home. However, she refused to cooperate, and thus her education ceased. Her mother complained that the child was not provided with any effective possibility of completing her compulsory education, contrary to the Convention. In dismissing the application as inadmissible, the Commission held that Article 2, Protocol 1 guarantees a right of access to educational establishments existing at a given time. However, it cannot be interpreted so as to impose an absolute obligation on a state to provide schooling for someone who does not wish to make use of this right. Having said this, this complaint was made in the context of a child who was 16—past the age of compulsory schooling in many jurisdictions. It is unclear how this would be dealt with where a younger child was refusing to attend classes—either at school, or as individual lessons at home.

[23] (14135/88) 02.10.1989 (dec.).

[24] See also *Simpson v the United Kingdom* (14688/89) 04.12.1989 (dec.); *SP v the United Kingdom* (28915/95) 17.01.1997 (dec.); *Graeme v the United Kingdom* (13887/88) 05.02.1990 (dec.).

Protocol 1 cannot be said to require the placing of a child with disabilities in a general school rather than in an available place in a special school.[25]

However, in recent years, a shift can be seen in the Court's approach to children with disabilities, and a more progressive position has been taken. This was epitomised in the case of *Cam v Turkey*,[26] where the applicant—who was blind—had successfully applied for entrance to the Turkish National Music Academy. However, the Academy withdrew the offer after discovering the extent of her disability, explaining that they did not have the facilities to cater to her 'special needs'. In examining the complaint under Article 14 in conjunction with Article 2, Protocol 1, the Court noted the importance of universality and non-discrimination in education and noted that international instruments have recognised inclusive education as the most appropriate way to secure children's rights in this area.

The Court found that there must be reasonable accommodation of the applicants' needs, understood as necessary and appropriate modifications and adjustments not imposing a disproportionate or undue burden. This may take a variety of forms, 'whether physical or non-physical, educational or organisational, in terms of the architectural accessibility of school buildings, teacher training, curricular adaptation or appropriate facilities'.[27] A refusal to provide such reasonable accommodation constitutes discrimination contrary to the Convention.[28] On the facts, the Academy never attempted to identify the applicants' needs, nor to consider what adaptations may be possible to facilitate these. As such, there had been a violation of Article 14 in conjunction with Article 2, Protocol 1.[29]

This case seemed to herald a new era of rights for children with disabilities with regard to their education. Inclusivity and non-discrimination were the touchstones of this judgment, with a strong emphasis on the rights set out in the UN Convention on the Rights of Persons with Disabilities.[30] However, the Court seems to have retreated from this position somewhat in its most recent decision of *Dupin v France*.[31] This case involved a child with an autism spectrum disorder, whose mother wished

[25] See also *Dahlberg and Dahlberg v Sweden* (18511/91) 02.03.1994 (dec.), where the parents wanted their child placed in a particular special school, rather than the one chosen by the authorities. The Commission found that the child had not been denied the right to education, but only the opportunity to be placed in a particular school, which the authorities considered did not have necessary facilities to provide for his needs. Such a decision fell within the state's margin of appreciation. See also *Klerks v the Netherlands* (25212/94) 04.07.1995 (dec.).

[26] (51500/08) 23.02.2016.

[27] ibid., para. 66.

[28] This does not mean, however, that the provision must be exactly the same, only that reasonable accommodation is made. In *McIntyre v the United Kingdom* (29046/95) 21.10.1998 (dec.), a child suffering from a physical disability could not access classrooms on the upper levels of her school—including science laboratories—which her able-bodied classmates used. She argued that the failure to provide a lift amounted to a discriminatory restriction on her right to education. The Commission found that the school had arranged a fixed classroom on the ground floor, and allocated additional resources to accommodate her disability. The state was entitled to balance the cost of installing the lift with other demands on its finances, and the response was proportionate, given the aim of a practical and efficient use of resources. See also *Stoian v Romania* (289/14) 25.06.2019.

[29] See also *Enver Şahin v Turkey* (23065/12) 30.01.2018, concerning access to university facilities by a paraplegic student.

[30] (2006) 2515 UNTS 3.

[31] (2282/17) 18.12.2018 (dec.).

for him to be educated in a general school rather than a specialised institution. The Court observed that inclusive education was the priority in the French system, but acknowledged that in the particular circumstances, the authorities did not feel it was the correct approach for this individual child. The Court was thus satisfied that the child had not been denied the right to education—his placement had not been a default option on account of a lack of resources or means of special assistance in mainstream schools, but a decision based on his individual situation.

While on the facts of the case, this may have been a justified conclusion, the reasoning of the Court in this respect is of great concern. Unlike *Cam*, there is no mention of the UN Convention on the Rights of Persons with Disabilities, either in the judgment itself or in the list of relevant domestic and international materials.[32] Nor is there any consideration of the potentially discriminatory effects on a child with disabilities of being excluded from mainstream education, with the Court focusing on absolute deprivation, rather than relative.[33] It may have been that the Court was willing to take a strong stance on the inclusion of children with physical disabilities, as in *Cam*, but less receptive of the arguments brought on behalf of children with mental disabilities, which may require greater adjustment in terms of teaching methods. Whatever the reason, as Lievens and Spinoy have correctly argued: 'It is almost as if the Court considers inclusive education as a favour accorded by the State, rather than as the priority scenario to which children with a disability are entitled.'[34]

6.3.2 Ethnic minorities

As with cases concerning children with disabilities, cases concerning the education of ethnic minorities have largely revolved around their segregation into different classrooms and different schools. This has arisen particularly in relation to Roma children, confronting a systemic issue in many Central and Eastern European states. Social exclusion and discrimination often impede the access of Roma children to quality education, with significant gaps in both school attendance and attainment when compared to non-Roma children.[35]

In a series of cases from 2007 onwards, the Court has challenged the compatibility of segregated education for Roma children with the Convention, developing a strong line of jurisprudence in this area. These cases are of paramount importance, not just for the children directly affected by the judgments, but also because they have changed the way in which the Court approaches discrimination cases in general.

[32] See J. Lievens and M. Spinoy, 'Dupin v France: The ECtHR Going Old School in Its Appraisal of Inclusive Education?' (Strasbourg Observers, 11.02.2019), https://strasbourgobservers.com/2019/02/11/dupin-v-france-the-ecthr-going-old-school-in-its-appraisal-of-inclusive-education/.

[33] cf. *Cam v Turkey* (51500/08) 23.02.2016.

[34] J. Lievens and M. Spinoy, 'Dupin v France: The ECtHR Going Old School in Its Appraisal of Inclusive Education?' (Strasbourg Observers, 11.02.2019), https://strasbourgobservers.com/2019/02/11/dupin-v-france-the-ecthr-going-old-school-in-its-appraisal-of-inclusive-education/.

[35] See European Union Agency for Fundamental Rights, 'Education: The Situation of Roma in 11 EU Member States' (2014), https://fra.europa.eu/sites/default/files/fra-2014_roma-survey_education_tk0113748enc.pdf.

The first, and most important, case on this issue was *DH and others v the Czech Republic*,[36] concerning so-called 'special schools', intended for children with 'mental deficiencies', and which followed a more basic curriculum than 'ordinary' schools. The decision to place a child in a special school was taken by the head teacher on the basis of results of tests to measure intellectual capacity carried out in an educational psychology centre. However, parental consent was needed before the placement could be made. In the town where the applicants lived, 56 per cent of pupils in special schools were Roma, despite only making up 2.26 per cent of the population, and 50.3 per cent of all Roma students were placed there. The applicants alleged that the placement of their children in these special schools amounted to discrimination on the basis of race or ethnic origin, contrary to Article 14 in conjunction with Article 2, Protocol 1.

The Court acknowledged that the wording in the statute was neutral and that the schools were not introduced solely to cater for Roma children. The rules governing placement did not refer to pupils' ethnic origins, but pursued the aim of adapting the education system to the needs, aptitudes, and disabilities of children. Nevertheless, the statistics revealed that in practice, a disproportionate number of Roma children were placed in special schools, and thus the measure had considerably more impact on them than on non-Roma children. In light of this, the Court held that it was not necessary to show discriminatory intent on the part of the authorities—it was enough to show a prejudicial effect.

Although the placement was based on a test that was sat by all students, this very neutrality was criticised by the Court. The questions on the test were conceived for the majority population and did not take into account the linguistic and cultural differences of Roma children. The results were thus not capable of constituting an objective and reasonable justification for the placement, unless they were analysed in light of the particularities and special characteristics of the Roma children who sat them. As a result, the Court held that the arrangements for the placements were not attended by safeguards that would ensure that the state took into account the special needs of Roma as members of a disadvantaged class. They received an education that compounded their difficulties, rather than helping them integrate into ordinary schools and develop skills that would facilitate life amongst the majority population.

The government put forward the argument that because parental consent was needed, it was the parents, not the authorities, who were ultimately responsible for their child's placement. As such, there could be no discrimination. This was rejected by the Court, which found that it is not possible to consent to discriminatory treatment, as this would amount to a waiver of the right not to be discriminated against. Further, the Court noted that the parents were members of a disadvantaged community, and often poorly educated themselves, and for this reason, it was not satisfied that they were capable of weighing up all the aspects of the situation and the consequences of consent.

This reasoning was questioned by Judge Borrego Borrego. In his dissenting opinion, he criticised the majority for questioning the capacity of Roma parents to perform their parental duty, finding that '[s]uch assertions are unduly harsh, superfluous and,

[36] (57325/00) 13.11.2007 (GC).

above all, unwarranted'.[37] He argued that the hearing room at the Court had become 'an ivory tower', divorced from the lives of the applicants, and the reality of the situation. Likewise, Judge Jungwiert, also in dissent, argued that although the situation was 'far from ideal and leaves room for improvement',[38] a distinction must be drawn between what is desirable and what is 'realistic, possible or simply feasible'.[39]

Despite these criticisms, *DH* has been recognised as a landmark judgment. It was the first case in which the Court was willing to recognise the concept of indirect discrimination—where a difference in treatment flows from a policy that is neutral on its face, but results in disproportionately prejudicial effects for a certain group. Moreover, this case was ground-breaking as it relied on systemic discrimination, where there was a pattern of discrimination in a particular sphere of public life—in this case, education—rather than a specific act impacting on one individual.

These changes in approach were not universally approved, however, with Judge Borrego Borrego stating that: 'The Grand Chamber has in this judgment behaved like a Formula One car, hurtling at high speed into the new and difficult terrain of education and, in so doing, has inevitably strayed far from the line normally followed by the Court.'[40] Nevertheless, *DH* introduced a revitalisation of the right to freedom from discrimination before the Court, and in the educational sphere the reasoning has formed the basis of findings against Greece, Croatia, and Hungary. In particular, when examining allegations of de facto segregation of school children on the basis of ethnic origin, the Court has identified from *DH* two crucial factors that will guide its evaluation.

First, any test for segregating students must be capable of objectively determining their aptitude and be appropriately tailored to students from different ethnic backgrounds. This was examined in *Horváth and Kiss v Hungary*,[41] where the facts were remarkably similar to *DH*. The applicants were Hungarian nationals of Roma origin who, following a diagnosis of 'mild mental disability' by a governmental panel, were placed in remedial schools whose student body comprised 40–50 per cent Roma children. The applicants complained that their placement in a remedial school represented ethnic discrimination, as the tests used were culturally biased and knowledge-based, putting Roma children at a disadvantage. The Court noted that the burden of proof fell on the state to demonstrate that the tests, and their application, were capable of determining fairly and objectively the aptitude and mental capacity of the applicants. They had failed to meet this burden: the Court found that the test had a prejudicial effect on children from socially disadvantaged groups, based on expert reports that Roma children could have performed better in the IQ tests if they had not been designed for children belonging to the ethnic majority.

Second, the education received in the segregated classrooms must pursue the aim of reintegrating students within the mainstream student population. The leading case in this respect is *Oršuš and others v Croatia*,[42] where again, the applicants attended

[37] ibid., dissenting opinion of Judge Borrego Borrego, para. 13.
[38] ibid., dissenting opinion of Judge Jungwiert, para. 12.
[39] ibid., para. 13.
[40] ibid., dissenting opinion of Judge Borrego Borrego, para. 2.
[41] (11146/11) 29.01.2013.
[42] (15766/03) 16.03.2010 (GC).

classes comprising only Roma pupils, which the government claimed was for the purpose of improving their Croatian language skills. The Court found that temporary placement in a separate class based on a lack of language skills can be a legitimate aim, but must be accompanied by appropriate safeguards. In particular, the Court will examine whether adequate steps were taken by school authorities to ensure the applicant's speedy progress in remedying the perceived educational difficulties, and once this was achieved, immediate integration into mixed classes.

On the facts, however, the government's assertion that the children were placed on the basis of language difficulties was undermined. The placement in separate classes on the basis of insufficient command of Croatian applied only to Roma children, and the tests for deciding whether to assign children to this class were not specifically designed to test command of the Croatian language. Moreover, the curriculum followed by the class was reduced by 30 per cent in comparison with ordinary classes, which the Court did not consider was an appropriate way to address a supposed lack of proficiency in Croatian. The Court concluded that if the concern really was language, the state had an obligation to take appropriate positive measures to assist applicants in acquiring such skills in the shortest time possible, by means of special language lessons, so that they could be quickly integrated into mixed classes. This they had failed to do.

Likewise, in *Sampanis and others v Greece*,[43] the authorities had visited Roma camps with the purpose of enrolling all children of school age in school. However, the newly enrolled Roma children were placed in 'preparatory classes', held in classrooms in an annex separated from the main school building. As with *Oršuš*, the stated aim of the preparatory classes was to bring students up to a standard level in order to integrate them into ordinary schooling. However, the school could offer no examples of students who had swapped over, nor were there any tests in place to enable the school to assess their aptitude to integrate. The Court thus held that the difference in treatment was not based on objective and reasonable justification, and there had been a violation of Article 2, Protocol 1.[44]

This is a very promising line of jurisprudence from the Court, recognising the dual vulnerabilities of children from ethnic minorities—both because of their status as children and as members of a subordinated social group—and the need to ensure robust safeguards against both de jure and de facto racial segregation. However, there is an additional factor of vulnerability involved in these cases that has also been recognised

[43] (32526/05) 05.06.2008.

[44] Four years later, the Court was called to re-examine the situation arising in this community, in *Sampani and others v Greece* (59608/09) 11.12.2012. The applicants complained that despite the decision in *Sampanis*, Roma children continued to be placed—purely based on their ethnicity—in a school which had been separated from those attended by non-Roma students. Although the annex had been renamed as a separate school ('12th School'), intended to cater for both Roma and non-Roma pupils, and a Presidential Decree required all children in the catchment area to transfer there, only Roma children were attendance. The Court found that by not enforcing the Presidential Decree, the authorities had allowed the school to become a 'ghetto school'. Moreover, the authorities had failed to allocate sufficient resources for the school, meaning that the students were being educated in material conditions that rendered it, if not impossible, at least very difficult, to pursue their schooling. See also *Lavida and others v Greece* (7973/10) 30.05.2013, where the Court held that continuing the education of Roma children in a state school attended exclusively by children belonging to the Roma community and the failure to implement anti-segregation measures violated Article 14 in conjunction with Article 2, Protocol 1.

by the Court—that of special educational needs. In *Horváth*, the Court observed that segregation of children with mental disabilities and who have developmental challenges into specialised schools in itself presents a human rights problem—even if these difficulties are correctly diagnosed.[45] It is interesting that it is only here, when the primary focus is on racial discrimination, that the Court has questioned the use of segregated schooling for children with mental disabilities, given the wide margin of appreciation afforded to states in cases brought directly concerning this issue.

6.3.3 Migrant children

The third group of children whose education has been specifically discussed by the Court is migrant children. Here, two questions have arisen: first, relating to immigration law and whether individuals should be permitted to enter, or remain, in the country to undertake study; second, relating to freedom from discrimination and whether those living in the country should be able to access education on the same basis as citizens.

In relation to the former, the Commission has made clear that Article 2, Protocol 1 does not grant the right for a foreign national to stay in any particular country. In *15 Foreign Students v the United Kingdom*,[46] the applicants were foreign university students who were refused permission to remain in the United Kingdom to complete their studies. They argued that where a refusal to allow them to remain would constitute a denial of the right to education, they could not be removed. The Commission maintained that the refusal of permission to remain cannot be regarded as an interference with the right to education, but only as a control of immigration—the right to education is independent of any right of an alien to enter, or stay, in the country.

Similarly, in *Jaramillo v United Kingdom*,[47] the mother of a British citizen child was being removed to Colombia. Due to his young age (he was four at the time of the application), he would have to go with her, which 'he'[48] argued would interfere with his rights under Article 2, Protocol 1. He submitted that if he were forced to move with his mother to Columbia, he would be deprived of education in British schools and unable to afford education of a similar standard in Colombia. The Commission dismissed this argument, stating that his departure to accompany his mother, who was being deported pursuant to a legitimate measure of immigration control, could not be construed as a deprivation of the right to education.[49]

While this line of reasoning has been firmly rejected by the Court, applicants have had more success in relation to claims of *equal* access to education while they are lawfully within the jurisdiction. In particular, in *Ponomaryovi v Bulgaria*,[50] the Court held that it was a violation of Article 14 in conjunction with Article 2, Protocol 1 to set

[45] (11146/11) 29.01.2013, para. 113.
[46] (7671/76) 19.05.1977 (dec.).
[47] (24865/94) 23.10.1995 (dec.).
[48] Or at least, his mother submitted on his behalf.
[49] See also *Dabhi v the United Kingdom* (28627/95) 17.01.1997 (dec.); *Ajayi and others v the United Kingdom* (27663/95) 22.06.1999 (dec.).
[50] (5335/05) 21.06.2011.

different levels of fees for children with citizenship or permanent residence and those without. In this case, the children were residing legally within the jurisdiction, but were charged higher fees to attend secondary school as they were on temporary visas.

This decision is important not so much for the outcome (as it rested on the specific facts of the case), but for the way in which the Court characterised the right to education. The Court acknowledged that the state may have a legitimate reason for curtailing the use of 'resource-hungry public services' by short-term and illegal immigrants, and may even in certain circumstances differentiate between different categories of aliens (for example, preferential treatment for EU nationals). However, the Court emphasised that education falls into a different category. As with other public services, it is expensive to run, and the resources that can be allocated to it are necessarily finite. On the other hand, education is a very particular type of public service that not only benefits the individuals using it, but also serves a broader societal function. Moreover, it is a right that is directly protected under the Convention.

The Court also differentiated between different levels of education, finding that 'the State's margin of appreciation in this domain increases with the level of education, in inverse proportion to the importance of that education for those concerned and for society at large'.[51] While differentiated fees may be legitimate at university level, the same is not true for primary schooling, which provides not only basic literacy and numeracy, but also integration into society. The Court saw secondary education falling between these two extremes, but noted that it plays an increasingly important role in modern society, and without it, individuals will experience barriers to personal and professional development.

On the facts of the case, the applicants were not living in Bulgaria unlawfully, nor were they trying to abuse the system. As such, considerations such as the need to stem illegal immigration clearly did not apply. The requirement to pay fees on account of their nationality and immigration status was not justified.[52]

6.3.4 Conclusions on specialised and segregated schooling

The jurisprudence of the Court in relation to ethnic and national discrimination in the field of education has been highly encouraging, taking an expansive approach to the concept of discrimination and recognising the insidious ways in which it can manifest in seemingly 'neutral' laws. There is now acknowledgement that discrimination can arise not only when children in analogous situations are treated differently, but also when the state fails to treat differently children whose situations are significantly different.

However, the Court's approach to segregated schooling for children with disabilities—and in particular, mental disabilities—continues to afford states far too much discretion

[51] ibid., para. 56.

[52] See also *Timishev v Russia* (55762/00, 55974/00) 13.12.2005, where the Court found a violation of Article 2, Protocol 1 when children were denied admission to a school on the grounds that the father was no longer resident in the relevant town.

in its decision-making. Inclusive education has become the touchstone for children with physical disabilities—and rightly so—yet this has not translated into the jurisprudence for children with mental disabilities, whose equal treatment continues to be subject to the availability of resources, and at the discretion of states.[53]

6.4 Content of education

While the case law on the form of education and specialised schooling is of great importance, the majority of the Court's jurisprudence has focused on another, albeit related, issue: the content of education provided. Where children do attend state-run schools, the Court has been asked to examine the extent to which parents can direct or dictate the material taught or the manner of its teaching. This has arisen in respect to the language of instruction, sexual education, and most extensively, religious education.

6.4.1 Education in a chosen language

The case *'Relating to Certain Aspects of the Laws on the Use of Languages in Education in Belgium'*,[54] known as the *Belgian Linguistic Case*—was the first to examine the content and scope of Article 2, Protocol 1, and is still the basis for much of the Court's jurisprudence today. This case concerned French-speaking Belgian citizens, living in regions considered by Belgian law as majority Dutch-speaking. They complained that the state did not provide any French-language education where they lived, and although they were permitted to establish private schools teaching in French, these were not subsidised by the state.

As discussed in section 6.1 above, the Court found that there is no obligation on the state to establish a general and official system of education, merely that they allow all persons access to the means of instruction existing at a given time. In particular, it found that '[t]he Convention lays down no specific obligations concerning the extent of these means and the manner of their organisation or subsidisation'.[55] With regard to the first sentence of Article 2, Protocol 1, the Court found that although it does not specify the language in which education must be conducted, the right to education would be meaningless if it did not imply a right to be educated in the national language—or in one of the national languages. But this right does not extend to allowing the parents free choice as to the language of education: Article 2, Protocol 1 only refers to respect for parents' religious and philosophical convictions, and it would be a distortion of the ordinary and usual meaning of the words to read linguistic

[53] See C. Cojocariu, 'Stoian v Romania: The Court's Drift on Disability Rights Intensifies' (Strasbourg Observers, 15.09.2019), https://strasbourgobservers.com/2019/09/05/stoian-v-romania-the-courts-drift-on-disability-rights-intensifies/#more-4406.

[54] (1474/62, 1677/62, 1691/62, 1769/63, 2126/64) 23.07.1968.

[55] ibid., para. 3.

preferences into this. As such, the Court found that there is no guarantee of the right to be educated in the language of one's parents by the public authorities, or with their aid.

Nevertheless, there may be an exception to this, where the territory in question is subject to occupation and the government authorities not internationally recognised. Where this is the case, the Court has scrutinised the provision of education in the minority language more closely. This was seen in the case of *Cyprus v Turkey*,[56] which concerned the situation arising out of Turkish military operations in Northern Cyprus in the 1970s, and the division of the territory into the 'Turkish Republic of Northern Cyprus' (TRNC). The Cypriot government—who was the applicant in this rare inter-state case—complained of a violation of Article 2, Protocol 1 on account of the lack of Greek-language secondary education available to the children of Greek-Cypriot parents living in northern Cyprus, which had been abolished by the Turkish-Cypriot authorities.

The Court found that there was no denial of the right to education '[i]n the strict sense', as the children could attend Turkish- or English-language secondary schools in the north, and Article 2, Protocol 1 does not specify the language in which education must be conducted. However, the Court also noted that the children had received primary school education in a Greek-language school, and the authorities would be aware that the parents would wish for this to continue through to secondary schooling. Thus, '[h]aving assumed responsibility for the provision of Greek-language primary schooling, the failure of the TRNC authorities to make continuing provision for it at the secondary-school level must be considered in effect to be a denial of the substance of the right at issue'.[57]

While technically this was a victory for the Cypriot government and the Greek-speaking minority in northern Cyprus, the reasoning employed by the Court undermines its impact. Based as it was on the fact that Greek-language primary schools were provided, and so secondary schools must be too, the simple solution for authorities facing such a situation would be to remove both. As the Court said, 'in the strict sense', there would be no violation of Article 2, Protocol 1 in that case.

Likewise, the Court found a violation of Article 2, Protocol 1 in the case of *Catan and others v the Republic of Moldova and Russia*,[58] involving the Moldavian Republic of Transdniestria (MRT). This territory—part of Moldova, but with strong Russian/Ukrainian influence due to migration—declared independence in 1990, but has not been recognised by the international community. The official languages of the MRT were declared as Russian, Ukraine, and 'Moldavian'—Moldovan/Romanian written with a Cyrillic alphabet. Schools teaching in Moldovan, using the Latin script, were closed down. The applicants, who attended one such school, complained that the forced closure violated their right to education under Article 2, Protocol 1—a complaint that was upheld by the Court.

[56] (25781/94) 10.05.2001 (GC).

[57] ibid., para. 278. Although it was possible for children to travel to southern Cyprus in order to obtain Greek-language secondary education, the Court found that this would involve an disproportionate interference with their right to respect for family life: schoolchildren from northern Cyprus attending school in the south were not allowed to return permanently to the north after reaching 16 (males) or 18 (females).

[58] (43370/04, 8252/05, 18454/06) 19.10.2012 (GC).

Relying on the decision in the *Belgian Linguistic Case*, the Court found that there had been a violation of the Convention. The school in question was registered with the Moldovan Ministry of Education and provided instruction in the first official language of Moldova—even if it was not an official language of the MRT. The forced closure of the school based on the MRT law on languages interfered with the pupil's rights of access to educational institutions existing at a given time and to be educated in their national language.

The Court then turned to the parents' rights under the second sentence of Article 2, Protocol 1, finding that these too had been violated. Unlike in the *Belgian Linguistic Case*, where the decision to allow teaching in only one of the national languages in particular regions pursued a legitimate aim, achieving linguistic unity within regions, and based on a public interest to ensure all state schools conduct teaching in the language of the region, the MRT law was aimed at the Russification of the language and culture of the Moldovan community, with the overall aim of separating the region from Moldova, and uniting it with Russia. The Court held that given the importance of education for each child's development, 'it was impermissible to interrupt these children's schooling … with the sole purpose of entrenching the separatist ideology'.[59]

The joint partly dissenting opinion of Judges Tulkens, Vajić, Berro-Lefèvre, Bianku, Poalelungi, and Keller is important for the emphasis placed on Article 8, and the rights of the child in this respect. The majority had dismissed this aspect of the argument, finding it was sufficient to consider the complaint under Article 2, Protocol 1, but the partly dissenting judges maintained that Article 8 brings in an important aspect that is not dealt with under Article 2, Protocol 1—the right to cultural identity. They noted that Article 8 encompasses the right to recognition of one's language as a component of cultural identity, which in turn is an essential factor in personal development and social interaction. Relying on Article 29 of the United Nations Convention on the Rights of the Child, which requires that education be directed to respect for the identity, language, and values of the country in which the child is living, the judges found that the laws surrounding schooling were aimed at undermining the linguistic heritage of the Moldovan population, forcing them to adopt a new identity.[60] This is an important opinion, as it recognises language as an essential vehicle for education and a tool for both inclusion and exclusion. While still a long way from recognition of linguistic preferences as an aspect of parents' right to pass on their own identity, it is a step in the direction of recognising the collective rights of minority communities to cultural identity—an area that has been long overlooked by the Court.

6.4.2 Sexual education

In addition to the language of education, the Court has also considered the content of particular classes, largely in the area of sexual and religious education. The leading case on sexual education in public schools is *Kjeldsen, Busk Madsen and Pedersen v*

[59] ibid., para. 144.
[60] See also *Iovcev and others v the Republic of Moldova and Russia* (40942/14) 17.09.2019.

Denmark,[61] dating from 1976. The applicant parents asked for their child to be exempted from the compulsory classes, but this was denied, giving rise to their complaint under Article 2, Protocol 1. The Court's decision in this case set out principles that extend far beyond sexual education, which have been central to the jurisprudence of the Court for the past 40 years, and is therefore worth discussing at length.

First, the Danish government had argued that by allowing parents to educate their children at home or to send them to private schools, they discharged their obligations under the second sentence of Article 2, Protocol 1. If the parents chose to send their children to state-run schools, they could not complain about the curriculum. This argument was swiftly dismissed by the Court. It held that Article 2, Protocol 1 is binding on states in the exercise of each and every function that they undertake in the sphere of education and teaching, including the organisation and financing of public education. Where the state establishes public schooling, it must continue to respect the rights of parents in its provision. Nevertheless, the fact that parents can have recourse to private schools as an alternative should not be disregarded, as it provides an avenue through which parents can disassociate their children from sex education.[62]

Second, the government argued that by referring to 'religious and philosophical convictions', the second sentence of Article 2, Protocol 1 implies a right of parents to have their children exempted from classes offering religious instruction, and not a wider right concerning other parts of the curriculum. This too was rejected by the Court. Article 2, Protocol 1 applies to all of the state's functions in education and teaching, and requires the state to respect parents' convictions throughout the entire educational programme. No distinction can be made between religious instruction and other subjects in this regard.

Nevertheless, the Court held that in principle, the setting and planning of curriculum fall within competence of states, who have a wide margin of appreciation in this respect. Article 2, Protocol 1 does not prevent states from imparting through teaching or education, information or knowledge of a directly or indirectly religious or philosophical kind, nor does it provide a *right* for parents to dictate the content of education—'otherwise all institutionalised teaching would run the risk of proving impracticable'.[63] The Court acknowledged that any subjects taught at school would have—to a greater or lesser extent—some philosophical complexion or implications. The duty of the state was not to refrain from imparting such knowledge, but merely that in doing so, the information is conveyed in an 'objective, critical and pluralistic manner'.[64] The test is thus whether there has been any attempt at indoctrination by the state authorities. This does not mean that complete neutrality is required—the Danish curriculum included attempts to warn children against birth outside wedlock and abortions—as long as these moral judgments do not entail overstepping the bounds of what a state may regard as the public interest.

The applicants also complained under Article 14 in conjunction with Article 2, Protocol 1 that parents were able to have their children exempted from religious

[61] (5095/71, 5920/72, 5926/72) 07.12.1976.
[62] See also *Jimenez Alonso and Jimenez Merino v Spain* (51188/99) 25.05.2000 (dec.).
[63] *Kjeldsen, Busk Madsen and Pedersen v Denmark* (5095/71, 5920/72, 5926/72) 07.12.1976, para. 53.
[64] ibid.

instruction, but not from sex education. In rejecting this argument, the Court drew a distinction between religious instruction and sex education—while the former disseminates tenets and beliefs, the latter provides knowledge and information.

This idea of objectivity and transmission of knowledge was returned to many years later in *Dojan and others v Germany*.[65] The applicants were fined after they kept their children away from certain classes and events concerning sexual education at the public school they attended, which they claimed were contrary to their religious convictions. The Court declared their application under Article 2, Protocol 1 inadmissible, on the basis that the sexual education classes had aimed at a neutral transmission of knowledge, tailored according to the children's age and maturity, and with the aim of enabling them to develop their own moral views and an independent approach towards their sexuality. These objectives were consistent with the principles of pluralism and objectivity in Article 2, Protocol 1—they had not expressed a preference for any particular belief or approach and had not attempted to indoctrinate the children. While parental beliefs must be respected, the Convention does not guarantee the right not to be confronted with opinions that are opposed to one's own.

While most applications with regard to sexual education have been brought under Article 2, Protocol 1, the recent case of *AR and LR v Switzerland*[66] is an exception. As Switzerland has not ratified Protocol 1, the mother seeking an exemption for her seven-year-old child had to rely on Article 8 instead. This case is significant because the Court had never previously considered whether Article 8 applies to the right of parents to educate their children, having always gone back to Article 2, Protocol 1 as *lex specialis* in the field. Here, the Court found that Article 8(1) is engaged—not only is the concept of 'family life' wide enough to include the freedom and duty of parents to educate and raise their children, the Court did not exclude that the education of children is part of a parent's 'private life', as one of the fundamental aspects of a parent's identity.

As the mother's Article 8(1) rights were interfered with, the question then became whether the interference pursued a legitimate aim and was necessary in a democratic society. The applicant mother in this case did not object to sex education classes in general—merely that they were given to children of such a young age. She argued that the aims of the teaching, of creating conditions for self-determined sexuality, as well as protection against sexually transmitted diseases and involuntary pregnancies, do not concern children aged between four and eight years old. The Court acknowledged that some of the aims pursued may be controversial, especially for children of such a young age, but the protection of health is a legitimate aim under Article 8(2). As such, the Court accepted that the instruction pursued the legitimate aim of the strengthening of a positive relationship with the body, and of preventing sexual violence and exploitation, which poses a direct and real threat to the mental and physical health of children of all ages.

When asking whether the interference was necessary in a democratic society, the Court drew on the case law under Article 2, Protocol 1 and applied it by analogy

[65] (319/08, 2455/08, 7908/10, 8152/10, 8155/10) 22.09.2011.
[66] (22338/15) 19.12.2017 (dec.).

to Article 8. As such, the question that the Court had to ask itself was whether the teaching involved the objective and neutral transmission of knowledge or pursued an aim of indoctrination. The Court in this case gave great deference to parental rights, stating that young children are particularly sensitive and easily influenced, and that the relationship between parent and child is particularly important for the child's development during this time. As such, it is appropriate to grant a particularly high level of protection to parental education for young children. However, relying heavily on the UN Convention on the Rights of the Child, the Court concluded that the protection of parental rights to guide their children's education was not an end in itself, but must always serve the well-being of the child. Given the importance of the issues in question, and the wide margin of appreciation given to states, the Court did not find a violation of Article 8.

From these cases, we can see that parents will have extreme difficulty in obtaining an exemption for their children from sexual education classes. As long as the classes are aimed at the transmission of knowledge and do not cross over into indoctrination, states have a wide margin of appreciation in this respect.

6.4.3 Religious education

The same principles which apply in relation to sexual education also apply in relation to religious education—namely that information is conveyed in an objective, critical, and pluralistic manner. However, parents have had significantly more success in challenging state educational provision in the context of religious teaching than they have in exempting their children from sexual education—although the grounds for this are narrowing as the jurisprudence develops.

6.4.3.1 Exemptions from religious teaching

The seminal case on the ability of parents to seek exemptions for their children from religious education is *Folgerø and others v Norway*,[67] concerning members of the Norwegian Humanist Association whose children attended public schools in Norway. Such schools were required to teach 'Christianity, religion and philosophy': half of the curriculum comprised the transmission of knowledge of the Bible and Christianity; the other half knowledge of other world religions and philosophies. Students could be partially exempted from the parts of the class that were 'clearly religious'—that is, they could be exempted from activities such as reciting from the Bible, singing songs, and saying prayers. If parents wanted to request that a child be exempted from parts of the tuition other than the religious activities listed on the form, they had to give reasons for their request to enable school to consider whether the activity might reasonably be perceived as being contrary to the practice of another religion or adherence to another philosophical conviction. The applicants complained that the refusal to grant full exemption from the classes violated their rights under Article 2, Protocol 1.

[67] (15472/02) 29.06.2007.

The Court held, first, that the second sentence of Article 2, Protocol 1 'does not embody any right of parents that their child be kept ignorant about religion and philosophy in their education'.[68] The fact that knowledge about Christianity represented a greater part of the curriculum than knowledge about other religions cannot, in and of itself, be viewed as a departure from pluralism and objectivity, nor does it amount to indoctrination on the part of the state. In coming to this conclusion, the Court considered the place occupied by Christianity in the history and tradition of Norway, and found that this falls within the state's margin of appreciation in planning and setting the curriculum.[69] The problem, the Court found, was not the *quantitative* difference in the course between Christianity and other convictions, but on the *qualitative* difference applied to the teaching. The objective of the course was to help give pupils a Christian and moral upbringing, which implied something more than mere transmission of knowledge.

The Court also noted that during the course, pupils could be asked to engage in 'religious activities' including prayers, psalms, learning religious texts, participating in religious plays. In this light, it found that 'it can be assumed that participation in at least some of the activities concerned, especially in the case of young children, would be capable of affecting pupils' minds in a manner giving rise to an issue under Article 2 of Protocol No. 1'.[70]

Turning to the possible partial exemption available for parents, the Court noted that this presupposed that parents would be adequately informed of the lesson plans to be able to identify and notify the school in advance of which parts of the teaching that were incompatible with their convictions and beliefs. This was made even more difficult if their objection was to the general Christian leaning of the subject, rather than a specific topic or activity. Even if they were able to identify a particular activity, the exemption only related to *participation*—for example, for hymns and prayers, the law proposed that the student could simply observe, rather than having to actually take part. The Court noted that this meant that the knowledge was still transmitted, and could not be seen as providing sufficient protection for parents' convictions.

As such, the Court found that the partial exemption was capable of subjecting parents to a heavy burden, with risk of undue exposure of their private life, and therefore could not be considered compliant with parents' right to respect for their convictions for the purposes of Article 2, Protocol 1, as interpreted in light of Articles 8 and 9. The fact that parents could send their children to private schools could not relieve the state of its obligation to safeguard pluralism in state schools that are open to everyone.

While this seems to provide a wide prerogative for parents, there are some limits. For example, in *Angeleni v Sweden*,[71] the Commission held that it was legitimate to provide an exemption from religion classes only for those belonging to a 'religious community, which has obtained the permission of the Government to arrange for

[68] *Folgerø and others v Norway* (15472/02) 29.06.2007, para. 89.

[69] At the other end of the scale, the applicants in *Appel-Irrgang and others v Germany* (45216/07) 06.10.2009 (dec.) complained that not enough emphasis was put on Christianity in the syllabus, despite Germany's Christian tradition. The Court found that choice of a neutral course that makes room for different beliefs does not in itself raise an issue under the Convention.

[70] *Folgerø and others v Norway* (15472/02) 29.06.2007, para. 94.

[71] (10491/83) 03.12.1986 (dec.).

religious education as a substitute for the school'. This case concerned Article 9, as Sweden had submitted a reservation in respect to Article 2, Protocol 1, which reserved the ability not to grant parents the right to obtain dispensation from certain parts of education in public schools, including the teaching of Christianity. The Commission found that the pupil had not been obliged to participate in any form of religious worship, or exposed to any religious indoctrination. Moreover, the difference in treatment between atheists and those who are members of religious communities who had been granted exemptions, had an objective and reasonable justification. The government policy was that all children should receive some education about religion, and therefore, an exemption was granted only to those children who would receive satisfactory alternative provision.

Unfortunately, the Commission in this case failed to come to grips with the fact that the very crux of the applicant's argument was that they were atheists, and by very definition did not wish to pursue religious education. As it stands, the Commission's decision protects religious pluralism in the positive sense, but does not engage with what it means to have the right *not* to hold a religion. This was also seen in *Bernard v Luxembourg*,[72] where the government allowed an exemption from 'moral and social education' classes to pupils with a religious belief, but not those who had different philosophical convictions. The Commission held that the government's aim of seeking to reduce the number of pupils who received an exemption was legitimate under Article 2, Protocol 1, in conjunction with Article 14.

Both these cases were decided well before *Folgerø*, and were admissibility decisions rather than Court judgments, so it remains to be seen whether the Court would still take this line today. But in the meantime, the differentiation between religious beliefs and philosophical convictions remains of concern.

6.4.3.2 Religious pluralism

As discussed above in *Folgerø*, it falls within the state's margin of appreciation to choose to focus more on one religion than others in its religious education, in line with the history and tradition of the state in question. A quantitative difference between the treatment of various religions will not trigger the right of parents to seek an exemption for their children. However, a course which focuses exclusively on a specific religion cannot be compulsory, and nor can a 'pluralistic' course ignore a religion followed by a large proportion of the population.

The balance to be drawn in this respect was discussed in the case of *Hasan and Eylem Zengin v Turkey*,[73] brought by a father and daughter who were adherents of Alevism—a branch of Islam. They applied to have the daughter exempted from religious culture and ethics classes on the basis that the teaching was based on the Sunni understanding of Islam, and thus inconsistent with the Alevi faith. The application was refused, on the grounds that it was a general course on different religious cultures, and only Christian and Jewish children were eligible for such an exemption.

[72] (17187/90) 08.09.1993 (dec.).
[73] (1448/04) 09.10.2007.

The Court found that Sunni Islam is the majority religion in Turkey, and therefore the priority given to this faith was not automatically inconsistent with Article 2, Protocol 1. The question that the Court had to ask was whether the compulsory attendance at these classes was likely to influence the minds of young children. The Court found that in this case, the religious diversity which prevails in Turkish society was not taken into account, and there was no teaching on the confessional or ritual specificities of the Alevi faith, although the proportion of the Turkish population belonging to it is very large. This showed a lack of respect for the religious and philosophical convictions of the father, and did not meet the criteria of objectivity and pluralism.[74]

The Court also noted that nearly all member states offer at least one route by which pupils can opt out of religious education classes—either through an exemption, or in attending lessons in a substitute subject. The fact that an exemption was granted only to Christian or Jewish children suggested that the instruction provided in the subject was likely to lead to those categories of pupils having a conflict between religious instruction at school and their parents' convictions. The Court found that if it were in fact a course on different religious cultures, there would be no need to make it compulsory for Muslim children alone—it would not conflict with Christian and Jewish beliefs. On the other hand, if it were a course essentially designed to teach the Muslim religion—and thus an exemption was justified for Christians and Jews—it is a course on a specific religion, and should not be compulsory for anyone.

The Court returned to this issue in *Mansur Yalçin and others v Turkey*,[75] which concerned the same compulsory classes, which had been updated in light of the Court's 2007 judgment. The government contended that the curriculum did not give precedence to any particular faith and adopted a supra-denominational approach, and in light of this, continued not to allow exemptions, except for Christian or Jewish children.

The Court noted the changes in the curriculum, but found that they involved mainly the inclusion about various beliefs existing in Turkey, and did not entail a 'real overhaul of the key components of the syllabus'.[76] In deciding whether the second sentence of Article 2, Protocol 1 had been violated, the Court identified three factors to be taken into account:

(a) whether pupils were obliged to take part in a form of religious worship;
(b) whether they were exposed to any form of religious indoctrination; and
(c) the arrangements for exemptions.

It found that, bearing in mind the particular features of the Alevi faith, as compared with the Sunni understanding of Islam, the applicants could have legitimately considered that the approach was likely to cause their children to face a conflict of allegiance between school and their own values. The discrepancies between the adopted

[74] Children were taught about the Alevi faith in the ninth grade, but this was insufficient to compensate for the absence of instruction in basic elements of this faith in primary and secondary school.
[75] (21163/11) 16.09.2014.
[76] ibid., para. 68.

curriculum and the particular features of their faith were so great that they would scarcely be alleviated by the mere inclusion in textbooks of information about Alevi beliefs and practice: it could only be avoided by an appropriate exemption procedure.

Finally, in relation to religious pluralism, the Court has made clear that there is no obligation on the state to allow children to follow a class in any specific religion. This was examined in *Çiftçi v Turkey*,[77] where a young boy was refused enrolment in Koranic study classes, on the basis of domestic legislation that required pupils to be at least 12 years of age. The Court emphasised that the regulation in the field of education may vary in time and place according to the needs and resources of the community and individuals, and the relevant authorities must be left considerable discretion as to the best use of such resources. The second sentence of Article 2, Protocol 1 was not violated by a refusal to allow the parents to send their child to religious study: it did not constitute an attempt at indoctrination aimed at preventing religious instruction, and in fact was aimed at limiting the possible indoctrination of minors when they may be easily influenced. Furthermore, the parents were not prevented from advising, educating, and guiding their children on religion, even before such study could be commenced. The Court in this case followed the reasoning of earlier decisions concerning instruction in a particular language—there is no positive obligation on the state to permit religious education at schools, nor to allow children to follow any particular class, merely a requirement that where it is offered, it does not amount to indoctrination.[78]

6.4.3.3 The obligation to reveal religious and philosophical convictions

The provision of an exemption procedure will not solve all problems, however. In particular, concerns have been raised about the burden thus placed on children (and parents) to reveal their religious and philosophical convictions.

Initially, such complaints were dismissed at the admissibility stage. For example, in *CJ, JJ and EJ v Poland*,[79] the child was exempted from the class on religion/ethics, but this meant that the school report did not list, or give a mark for, the subject. Her father complained that the lack of mark amounted to a public declaration about his convictions, which infringed upon his right to respect for private life under Article 8. However, the Commission noted that he himself had not been obliged to make any declaration, and his beliefs could not be inferred directly from the behaviour of his daughters in attending a class or not. The child, for her part, complained that the lack of a mark would be seen by future employers, who may discriminate against her on that basis. The Commission dismissed the complaint as manifestly ill-founded: since the subject was not listed, employers would only know it was missing in comparison with other reports. Moreover, the child was only 12 at the time, and it was thus unlikely to adversely affect future employment.

[77] (71860/01) 17.06.2004 (dec.).

[78] See also *X, Y, and Z v the Federal Republic of Germany* (9411/81) 15.07.1982 (dec.), where the parents requested that their son be given the opportunity of taking a course in elementary school arithmetic, instead of the class on 'modern mathematics' taught in his primary school. When this was refused, the parents argued that the inability to have a school education which was suited to their son's abilities and interests violated Article 2, Protocol 1. The Commission dismissed the complaint, finding that the setting and planning of curriculum falls within the competence of the state, as long as there is no evidence of indoctrination.

[79] (23380/94) 16.01.1996 (dec.).

In *Saniewski v Poland*,[80] the applicant likewise complained that the content of his school report would reveal his religious and philosophical convictions, and thus affect his future prospects, in violation of Article 9. In this case, however, 'religion/ethics' was listed as a subject, but the mark simply left blank. The Court left open the question of whether Article 9 guarantees a right to remain silent as to one's religious beliefs, but even if this were guaranteed, there was no evidence that it would have any material impact on his interests: the report covered only one year of school, when he was 16, and there was no indication that he would have to show it to any higher educational body for admission, or to any future employer. The Court also noted that in any case, discrimination on religious grounds is illegal in Poland, so he would have a remedy against the risk of prejudice the school report might engender.

While these cases dismissed the complaints of the applicants quite swiftly, the Court took a very different position in the most recent case of *Grzelak v Poland*.[81] Here, the child had been granted an exemption from religious education, but the school was not able to provide him with an alternative ethics class. As such, the school report listed the class 'religion/ethics' with a line drawn next to it. He alleged a violation of Article 14 in conjunction with Article 9, in that some students had a mark for 'religion/ethics' and some did not.

The Court in this case was willing to go further than *Saniewski*, and declare that individuals have a right not to be required to reveal their faith or beliefs. It held that:

> Article 9 is also a precious asset for non-believers like the third applicant in the present case. It necessarily follows that there will be an interference with the negative aspect of this provision when the State brings about a situation in which individuals are obliged—directly or indirectly—to reveal that they are non-believers. This is all the more important when such obligation occurs in the context of the provision of an important public service such as education.[82]

The Court recognised that the provision for a mark—or lack thereof—for 'religion/ethics' would not infringe Article 14 in conjunction with Article 9, as long as it merely denoted neutral information on the fact that a pupil followed one of the optional courses offered at a school. However, this must be balanced against the right of a pupil not to be compelled, even indirectly, to reveal their religious convictions. In this way, the Court compared school reports to identity cards and documents—in neither case could religious beliefs constitute information that could be used to distinguish an individual in his relations with the state.

In contrast to the reasoning in *CJ, JJ and EJ* and *Saniewski*, the Court found that the absence of a mark on the school report would have a specific connotation, as it would be understood by any reasonable person as indication that child did not follow the classes, and thus was likely to be regarded as a person without religious belief. Thus, the Court found a violation of Article 14 in conjunction with Article 9.

This position was criticised in the partly dissenting opinion of Judge Thór Björgvinsson, who argued that by comparing students who were awarded marks and

[80] (40319/98) 26.06.2001 (dec.).
[81] (7710/02) 15.06.2010.
[82] ibid., para. 87.

those who were not, the majority were not comparing persons in relevantly similar or analogous situations. For the purpose of giving marks for a subject, pupils attending a class are not in the same situation as those who do attend. As such, the school was merely providing neutral information and could not be seen as violating Article 14.[83]

Although Judge Thór Björgvinsson does make some valid criticisms of the reasoning used, overall, the majority decision is to be commended. This case provided an important expansion of the right to privacy—even if it was not argued in such terms—recognising that religion is a matter of individual conscience and should not be something that must be declared to the state.[84]

6.4.3.4 Participation in school activities

Not all education takes place in the classroom. The protection provided by Article 2, Protocol 1 extends to the convictions of parents not only in the content of classes provided by state schools, but '[i]n the exercise of any functions which it assumes in relation to education and to teaching'—including participation in compulsory school activities. However, where the activity in question is not directly religious, the Court has taken a very strict approach, focusing on the facially neutral nature of the activity in order to reject parental objections.

The leading case in this area is *Valsamis v Greece*,[85] which involved a family of Jehovah's Witnesses. The parents asked that their child be exempted from all school religious lessons, Orthodox Mass, and any other event contrary to their religious beliefs, including national holiday celebrations and public processions. An exemption was granted in respect to the lessons and Mass, but not in relation to other events. As such, the student was expected to take part in a procession to celebrate National Day, which commemorates the outbreak of war between Greece and fascist Italy. The parents informed the school that their religious beliefs forbade her joining in the commemoration of war, as pacifism is a central tenet of the Jehovah's Witness faith, and asked for an exemption. This was denied, and when the child failed to attend, she was punished with one day's suspension.

[83] Another point of dissent related to the fact that students received an 'average mark', based on the subjects taken over the school year. The majority had argued that this constituted a real adverse impact on the applicant, as it would be more difficult to increase the average mark if the class was not taken, and students might feel pressured to attend religion class in order to improve their average. However, as Judge Thór Björgvinsson correctly pointed out, students who did not take the religion class were not treated any differently than those who did. The average of each student was calculated on the basis of classes that they did take—any impact on the applicant's average was purely a matter of speculation. In fact, a converse argument could be made that it would be a risk to take the class, as a weak performance could drag the average down.

[84] This line of reasoning can also be seen in cases where *parents* have complained about the disclosure of their religious beliefs, in order to gain exemption for their children from religious education. In *Folgerø and others v Norway* (15472/02) 29.06.2007, the Court noted that where an exemption was sought for an activity that was not 'clearly religious', the parents had to give grounds for their request. It expressed concern that such a requirement of disclosure about personal and religious philosophical convictions, which concern some of the most intimate aspects of private life, may mean parents might avoid asking for an exemption. Likewise in *Hasan and Eylem Zengin v Turkey* (1448/04) 09.10.2007, the Court criticised the government for compelling parents to reveal their religious beliefs in order to gain exemption for their children. It held that religious convictions should be a matter of individual conscience, and as such it was inappropriate to make parents declare them. See also *Papageorgiou and others v Greece* (4762/18, 6140/18) 31.10.2019.

[85] (21787/93) 18.12.1996.

The Court dismissed the parents' complaint that the obligation on their child to participate in this event, and the resulting punishment, had violated their rights under Article 2, Protocol 1. Although it expressed 'surprise' that students can be required to parade outside school precincts on a holiday, it could 'discern nothing, either in the purpose of the parade or in the arrangements for it, which could offend the applicants' pacifist convictions to an extent prohibited by the second sentence of Article 2 of Protocol 1'.[86] In particular, the Court noted that the commemoration of national events serve both pacifist objectives and the public interest, and neither the presence of military representatives, nor the event that was being commemorated, altered the nature of the parade.

Of primary importance to the Court was the fact that *the judges themselves* did not perceive there to be anything objectionable in the parade. In doing so, the Court took an objective approach to the conflict between the parents' convictions and the school activity—evaluating it from an external perspective, rather than from the subjective, internal viewpoint of the applicants.[87] The practices were not viewed from the point of view of an adherent to the Jehovah's Witness faith, but from the perspective of an outsider. This is very problematic: the role of the Court, as well as the domestic authorities, should be to determine whether the religious belief or philosophical conviction is genuinely held, not whether it is reasonable. Once the belief is identified as genuine, it should be respected. The individuals themselves must be seen as the arbiter of whether something is against their belief or not.

As with the cases on sexual education, one of the key tenets of the jurisprudence in this area has been the need to protect the child's right to education from the religious convictions of their parents. This was seen first in *Martins Casimiro and Cerveira Ferreira v Luxembourg*,[88] where Seventh-day Adventists, for whom Saturday is a day of total rest, sought an exemption so that their son would not have to attend school on that day. When this was rejected, they complained to the Court that their rights under Article 9 had been violated. The Court found that the exemption would have had the effect of excluding the child from the normal school timetable, and as such adversely affect the child's right to education protected by Article 2, Protocol 1. The state has a duty to ensure that children are able to exercise their right to education, and where parents' right to respect for religious convictions come into conflict with this, rather than enhancing it, the interests of child must prevail. While professing to reason from the perspective of the rights of the child, it is significant to note that there was no consideration of the *child's* own religious convictions in this case. While it may have made no substantive difference to the outcome—the importance of education to a child may still prevail over the child's religious objections—nevertheless, the lack of consideration given to the child's own position reinforces the adult-centred nature of Court's jurisprudence, whether that adult be the parents or the authorities.

The most recent case on this issue is *Osmanoğlu and Kocabaş v Switzerland*,[89] decided in January 2017. The applicants, devout Muslims, refused to send their daughters

[86] ibid., para. 31.

[87] See C. McCrudden, 'Multiculturalism, Freedom of Religion, Equality, and the British Constitution: The JFS Case Considered' (2011) 9(1) *International Journal of Constitutional Law* 200.

[88] (44888/98) 27.04.1999 (dec.).

[89] (29086/12) 10.01.2017.

to swimming lessons, which formed a compulsory part of the school curriculum, on the grounds that their beliefs prohibited them from allowing them to take part in mixed bathing. They alleged a violation of Article 9, arguing that they were sending their children to private swimming lessons in any case, and their lack of attendance was not likely to restrict their education.

The Court accepted the government's position that the measure was aimed at the integration of 'foreign children' from different cultures and religions, and intended to protect them from social exclusion. Moreover, the compulsory nature ensured that equality between the sexes was promoted within the education system. It found that schools play a 'special' role in the process of social integration, which is all the more decisive where children of 'foreign origin' are concerned, and that 'children's interest in an all-round education, facilitating their successful social integration according to local customs and mores, takes precedence over the parents' wish to have their daughters exempted from mixed swimming lessons'.[90] The value of the lessons thus lay not in learning to swim, but in participating in an activity with all other children, without exception on the basis of the child's origin or parents' religious or philosophical convictions. As such, the state was acting within its margin of appreciation.

It is disheartening to note that the children in the case were referred to as 'foreign children' throughout, despite having been born in Switzerland and having lived there all their lives. This betrays an underlying prepossession on the part of the Court on integration rather than multiculturalism, and the concept of a 'good migrant', who assimilates within the existing community values.[91] As with *Martins Casimiro* above, it may be that the right outcome was reached, but the reasoning remains flawed.

6.4.3.5 The display of religious symbols in school

Another aspect of the wider functions of the state in relation to education and teaching includes the display of religious symbols in schools. This issue has only been considered twice by the Strasbourg Court, and the jurisprudence in this area is dominated by the (in)famous case of *Lautsi v Italy*,[92] which was significant not just in the field of education, but also in the wider jurisprudence, as it explored the tension between freedom *of* religion, and freedom *from* religion.

The case concerned an obligation on state schools in Italy to hang a crucifix on the wall in each classroom. The applicant—a mother of two school-age children—complained that this violated her rights under the second sentence of Article 2, Protocol 1, and infringed the principle of educational pluralism, as it constituted an expression of the state's preference for a particular religion in a place where conscience was formed.

The Second Chamber found in favour of the applicant, ruling that there is an obligation on the state to refrain from imposing beliefs, even indirectly, in places where

[90] ibid., para. 97.

[91] See C. Murphy, 'The Concept of Integration in the Jurisprudence of the European Court of Human Rights' (2010) 12(1) *European Journal of Migration and Law* 23; A. Farahat, 'The Exclusiveness of Inclusion: on the Boundaries of Human Rights in Protecting Transnational and Second Generation Migrants' (2009) 11(3) *European Journal of Migration and Law* 253.

[92] (30814/06) 03.11.2009 (Ch); (30814/06) 18.03.2011 (GC).

persons were dependent on it, or particularly vulnerable.[93] They held that the negative aspect of freedom from religion extended not just to religious services or education, but comprised also practices and symbols expressing a belief, religion, or atheism. The state has a duty to uphold neutrality in public education, and the compulsory and highly visible presence of crucifixes in classrooms is capable of clashing with secular convictions of parents.

This decision was met with widespread, and vigorous, criticism: the Italian Education Minister declared his opposition to the decision, while some state and local officials openly refused to consider removing the crucifixes from classrooms within their jurisdictions.[94] In this strained environment, referral to the Grand Chamber was swiftly approved, and the Court granted requests on behalf of 33 intervenors, including nine other contracting states.[95]

The Grand Chamber, by 15 votes to two, reversed the decision of the Second Chamber, emphasising that the state is not prevented from imparting information or knowledge of a directly or indirectly religious or philosophical kind, but simply requires that this be conveyed in an objective, critical, and pluralistic manner. Students must be free to develop a critical mind 'in a calm atmosphere free of any proselytism'.[96]

The Court supported the government's position that the crucifix is a 'passive' symbol, thus differentiating it from active conduct such as 'didactic speech or participation in religious activities'.[97] It was not associated with compulsory teaching about Christianity, nor was there any proselytising tendency in teaching practices. The mere presence of the crucifix, conferring visibility in the school environment of the majority religion of the state, was not sufficient to denote a process of indoctrination. In particular, the Court found that no evidence had been presented to support the argument that the display of a religious symbol on a classroom wall may have an influence on pupils. As such, it was held that there was no basis for the assertion that it does—or equally does not—influence pupils whose ideas are in the process of being formed. This, combined with the wide margin of appreciation given to states in deciding whether to perpetuate a historical 'tradition'—which was how the government had portrayed the display of the crucifix—meant that there was no violation of Article 2, Protocol 1. The reasoning thus paralleled that concerning religious education: the state can give preference to the majority religion in light of its historical importance, without it being seen as indoctrination.

Interesting, Judge Rozakis in his concurring opinion (joined by Judge Vajić), noted the waning influence of the second sentence of Article 2, Protocol 1. Unlike other guarantees in the Convention, where the Court has been expanding the scope of its protection, he noted that the rights of parents under this provision '[do] not seem realistically to be gaining weight in the balancing exercise of the proportionality test'. This appears to accord with the case law discussed in the sections above, where we can see the rights of children frequently outweighing parental preferences, as well as a wide

[93] (30814/06) 03.11.2009 (Ch).

[94] W.S. Saunders, 'Does Neutrality Equal Secularism? The European Court of Human Rights Decides *Lautsi v. Italy*' (The Federalist Society, 19.12.2011), https://fedsoc.org/commentary/publications/does-neutrality-equal-secularism-the-european-court-of-human-rights-decides-lautsi-v-italy.

[95] Armenia, Bulgaria, Cyprus, Russia, Greece, Lithuania, Malta, Monaco, and San Marino.

[96] (30814/06) 18.03.2011 (GC), para. 62.

[97] ibid., para. 72.

margin of appreciation being given to states in their organisation of curriculum and educational system.

The decision of the majority in the Grand Chamber was not itself without criticism. The dissenting opinion of Judge Malinverni, joined by Judge Kalaydjieva, emphasised that the negative right of freedom from religion deserves special protection if it is the state that displays a religious symbol, and dissenters are placed in a situation from which they cannot extract themselves. Quoting the Chamber judgment, he suggested that 'the compelling power of the State is imposed on minds which still lack the critical capacity which would enable them to keep their distance from the message derived from a preference manifested by the State'.[98]

Academic commentators have also expressed concern regarding the reasoning employed by the majority. For example, Nicolas Hervieu has objected to the majority's conclusion that the state does not promote one religion over another, in support of which they highlighted that Italian school children are allowed to wear the headscarf or other symbols of religious connotation.[99] As he rightly argued, this equates the exercise of freedom of religion by pupils with the state exercising its power to represent a particular religion in classrooms—permitting freedom *of* religion does not compensate for failing to provide freedom *from* religion.

A second criticism has arisen in relation to the conclusion that the symbol of the crucifix, or indeed any symbol, could be 'passive'. As Lorenzo Zucca points out, a symbol can neither be active or passive, as it has no agency of its own. It only gains its meaning from the person who displays it, and the decision by the state authorities to mandate its display in every classroom is an active one, deliberately promoting one religion over others.[100]

The characterisation of the crucifix as 'an essentially passive symbol' must be contrasted with the case of *Dahlab v Switzerland*,[101] where the headscarf worn by a primary school teacher was described as a 'powerful external symbol'.[102] In this case, the Swiss authorities had asked her to stop wearing the headscarf while carrying out her professional duties on the grounds that it constituted 'an obvious means of identification imposed by a teacher on her pupils, especially in a public secular education system'.[103] Teachers had an obligation of denominational neutrality, which the wearing of the headscarf contravened.

Like *Lautsi*, the Court recognised that it was difficult to assess the impact that this symbol would have on young children; however, in *Dahlab*, the Court was prepared to err on the side of caution, finding that 'it cannot be denied outright that the wearing of a headscarf might have some kind of proselytising effect'.[104] Having regard to the

[98] *Lautsi v Italy* (30814/06) 03.11.2009 (GC), para. 48.

[99] N. Hervieu, 'Crucifix dans les salles de classe: la capitulation des droits de l'homme' (Combats pour les droits de l'homme, 21.03.2011), http://combatsdroitshomme.blog.lemonde.fr/2011/03/21/crucifix-dans-les-salles-de-classes-la-capitulation-de-la-cour-europeenne-des-droits-de-l'homme-cour-edh-gc-18-mars-2011-lautsi-c-italie/.

[100] L. Zucca, 'A Comment on Lautsi' (EJILtalk, 19.03.2011), https://www.ejiltalk.org/a-comment-on-lautsi/.

[101] (42393/98) 15.02.2001 (dec.). See also *Kurtulmus v Turkey* (65500/01) 24.01.2006, where a complaint by a university professor was dismissed.

[102] ibid., para. 1.

[103] ibid., part A.

[104] ibid., para. 1.

'tender age' of the children she was teaching—aged four to eight—the Court found that the margin of appreciation had not been exceeded.

A weighty factor for the majority in this case was the importance of teachers as role models for children, who tend to identify with their teachers, on account of daily contact and the hierarchical nature of their relationship. However, it may be questioned whether the influence of an individual teacher would be any greater than the endorsement of the state, where the 'hierarchical' relationship is even more pronounced. While much rests on the margin of appreciation in each of these decisions, it is impossible to ignore the Western, Christian, bias that underpins them both. In *Dahlab*, the wearing of the headscarf is clearly looked at with disfavour by the Court, described as 'hard to square with the principle of gender equality', and 'difficult to reconcile ... with the message of tolerance, respect for others and, above all, equality and non-discrimination that all teachers in a democratic society must convey to their pupils'.[105] On the contrary, in *Lautsi*, the Court accepted that as well as being a religious symbol, the crucifix corresponded to a cultural and historical tradition that the state wished to—and indeed could—perpetuate.

Having said this, it should be noted that the decision in *Dahlab* is consistent with other cases concerning the banning of the headscarf. In particular, it echoes the decision of the Court in *Leyla Sahin v Turkey*[106] and *Dogru v France*,[107] discussed in section 6.5, in which the Court has indicated that the prohibition of the wearing of the headscarf by students within schools and universities is also within the state's margin of appreciation.

6.5 School uniform and dress

From early in its jurisprudence, the Court has established that states have a wide margin of appreciation in prescribing what a child can, or cannot, wear to school. In *Stevens v the United Kingdom*,[108] the Commission held that a state does not violate Article 8 by requiring pupils to wear school uniforms—indeed, any constraint imposed by rules of dress during school hours and on school premises cannot be said to be so serious as to constitute an interference with the right to respect for private and family life under Article 8(1).

The majority of challenges, however, have not concerned an obligation *to wear* certain clothing, but *to refrain from* doing so—in particular, the Islamic headscarf. The first, and still leading, case on this issue—*Leyla Şahin v Turkey*[109]—did not concern a school uniform, but regulations for dress while attending university. In this case, the university prohibited students wearing a headscarf from attending lectures, tutorials, and examinations, and the applicant's refusal to comply led to her expulsion. She alleged that this violated her rights under Article 9, arguing that university students are

105 ibid.
106 (44774/98) 10.11.2005 (GC).
107 (27058/05) 04.12.2008.
108 (11674/85) 03.03.1986 (dec.).
109 (44774/98) 10.11.2005 (GC).

adults who enjoy full legal capacity and are capable of deciding for themselves what is appropriate conduct and dress.

In defining the scope of the margin of appreciation given to the state, the Court characterised the case as one concerning 'the need to protect the rights and freedoms of others, to preserve public order and to secure civil peace and true religious pluralism, which is vital to the survival of a democratic society'.[110] The Court placed great weight on the constitutional principle of secularism as practised in Turkey, requiring not only impartiality by the state, but also the protection of citizens from societal pressure, with the aim of ensuring peaceful coexistence between various faiths and protecting public order. In particular, the Court accepted the justification put forward by the government regarding the prevention of fundamentalist religious movements from exerting pressure on students and the protection of the rights of women. The Court acknowledged that the freedom to manifest one's religion under Article 9 could be restricted in order to defend those values, finding that the wearing of the headscarf, which is presented or perceived as a compulsory religious duty, may have an impact on those who choose not to wear it. In this way, the ban pursued a legitimate aim, and was within the state's margin of appreciation.[111]

In a strong dissent, Judge Tulkens criticised the majority for accepting that the headscarf contravenes the principle of secularism. She argued that the headscarf was not 'ostentatious or aggressive or ... used to exert pressure, to provoke a reaction, to proselytise or to spread propaganda'.[112] Nor was there any suggestion that there was any disruption or disorderly conduct as a result of the wearing of the headscarf. She further questioned the link made by the Turkish government and the majority between the headscarf and religious fundamentalism, finding that:

> Merely wearing the headscarf cannot be associated with fundamentalism and it is vital to distinguish between those who wear the headscarf and 'extremists' who seek to impose the headscarf as they do other religious symbols. Not all women who wear the headscarf are fundamentalists and there is nothing to suggest that the applicant held fundamentalist views.[113]

The issue of gender equality, which was pivotal in Turkey's justification for the ban, as well as the majority's reasoning, was also central to Judge Tulken's dissent. She noted the irony that, by accepting the applicant's expulsion in the name of secularism and equality, the majority had allowed her to be excluded from precisely the type of liberated environment it was seeking to promote. Rather than emancipating young women in the name of gender equality, it was denying them opportunities to participate in

[110] ibid., para. 110.

[111] This was foreshadowed by *Senay Karaduman v Turkey* (16278/90) 3.5.1993 (dec.), where a woman was refused a degree certificate on the grounds that the identity photograph she had provided (which would then be affixed to the degree certificate) showed her wearing a headscarf. The Commission found that manifestation of a religion may constitute pressure on students who do not conform to those beliefs, and that in choosing to attend a secular university, she had agreed to be bound by these rules. Moreover, the purpose of the photograph is to identify the person concerned and could not be used to manifest religious beliefs.

[112] *Leyla Şahin v Turkey* (44774/98) 10.11.2005 (GC), dissenting opinion of Judge Tulkens, para. 8.

[113] ibid., para. 10.

society. Moreover, she was critical of the majority's acceptance that the wearing of the headscarf *did in fact* represent gender inequality. In a scathing passage, she argued that:

> It is not the Court's role to make an appraisal of this type—in this instance a unilateral and negative one—of a religion or religious practice, just as it is not its role to determine in a general and abstract way the signification of wearing the headscarf or to impose its viewpoint on the applicant.[114]

While it was simply a dissenting view at the time, this criticism seems to have gained traction with the Court in later cases. In particular, when France argued in *SAS v France*[115] that its ban on the wearing of the burqa pursued the aim of ensuring gender equality, this was quickly dismissed, with the Court finding that 'a State Party cannot invoke gender equality in order to ban a practice that is defended by women—such as the applicant—in the context of the exercise of the rights enshrined in those provisions'.[116]

While *Leyla Sahin* was controversial when it was decided, the position taken has since been increasingly accepted, and its reasoning applied to cases involving school children, as well as university education. In *Kose and 93 others v Turkey*,[117] the applicants were prevented from entering the school whilst wearing headscarves, and argued that this had violated their right to education under Article 2, Protocol 1 and their right to religious freedom under Article 9. The Court found that the right to education may be subject to limitations—national authorities enjoy a margin of appreciation in defining regulations, although these cannot curtail the right to such an extent as to impair its very essence or deprive it of its effectiveness. In this case, the rules were of a general nature, applying to all pupils regardless of their religious beliefs.[118] They had the legitimate aim of protecting the rights and freedoms of others, and of preserving the neutral character of secondary education, when adolescents are of an impressionable age. Interestingly, the Court seemed to imply that not only do states have the right to protect school children from religious pressure and exclusion, but they may also even have a duty to do so. It stated that

> it is incumbent on the competent authorities to be very careful to ensure, within the bounds of their margin of appreciation, that when, out of respect for pluralism and the freedom of others, they permit students to manifest their religious beliefs on

[114] ibid., para. 12.

[115] (43835/11) 01.07.2014 (GC).

[116] ibid., para. 119. However, the Court found that the ban was proportionate to the legitimate aim of 'living together': on this point, see J. Marshall 'SAS v France: Burqa Bans and the Control of Empowerment of Identities' (2015) 15(2) *Human Rights Law Review* 377.

[117] (26625/02) 24.01.2006 (dec.).

[118] This case was decided the year before *DH v the Czech Republic* (57325/00) 13.11.2007 (GC), which recognised indirect discrimination as constituting a violation of the Convention.

> school premises, such manifestation does not become ostentatious and thus a source of pressure and exclusion.[119]

In this case, the Court noted that no disciplinary measures were imposed on the students, and that they were free to return to school provided they comply with rules on dress. As such, there was no violation of either Article 9 or Article 2, Protocol 1.

However, even in cases where students have been expelled from school for wearing the headscarf, this has not been found to violate the Convention. In *Dogru v France*,[120] the expulsion of a Muslim student after she refused to remove her headscarf during sports class was found to be within the state's margin of appreciation. The Court held that it was not unreasonable for the state to consider that the wearing of the veil was incompatible with sports classes for reasons of health or safety, and observed that the child was able to continue schooling by correspondence, meaning that her right to education was not impinged upon. Likewise, in *Aktas v France*,[121] the expulsion of Muslim girls after they refused to remove their headscarves was found to be within the state's margin of appreciation. While the Court acknowledged that the French law banning the wearing of religious symbols in schools entailed a restriction on the children's rights under Article 9, nevertheless, this restriction fell within the state's margin of appreciation. The Court took the position that the children were not expelled because of any objection to their religious convictions, but in order to pursue the constitutional principle of secularism.

While the jurisprudence in this area has relied largely on the margin of appreciation allowing states to decide whether to allow such religious symbols, rather than imposing any duty or restriction in this respect, this is an area in which Western, Christian bias once again raises its ugly head. The acceptance of this particularly aggressive form of secularism is predicated on a Christian conception of 'neutrality'. If we view 'neutrality' as an absence of external symbols, this preferences those religions—like Christianity—which do not require such a display.[122] The result is the marginalisation of children from different backgrounds, and of different beliefs, and to risk forcing them out of the public sphere. Rather than protecting such children from 'pressure', it may in fact reinforce it.

6.6 Violence, abuse, and neglect

6.6.1 Corporal punishment

The use of corporal punishment against children—in the judicial system, at school, and at home—was discussed in detail in Chapter 2. However, there are specific

[119] *Kose and 93 others v Turkey* (26625/02) 24.01.2006 (dec.), part B.

[120] (27058/05) 04.12.2008. See also *Kervanci v France* (31645/04) 04.12.2008, handed down the same day, which relied on the same reasoning.

[121] (43563/08) 30.06.2009 (dec.).

[122] Though some Christians may choose to do so: see *Eweida and others v the United Kingdom* (48420, 59842/10, 51671/10, 36516/10) 15.10.2013.

elements of the jurisprudence on corporal punishment in schools that deserve especial attention in this chapter, as they relate to the infringement of Article 2, Protocol 1.

Challenges before the Court have arisen both in relation to the first sentence and the second sentence of this Article. Under the first sentence, the central concern is the child—does the use of corporal punishment impinge on their ability to attend school and thus access education? Under the second sentence, the parent becomes the focus—does the use (or not) of corporal punishment constitute a philosophical conviction that the state must respect?

Both these questions were addressed in the joined cases of *Campbell and Cosans v the United Kingdom*.[123] In these cases, two sets of parents with children of compulsory school age complained about the use of corporal punishment as a disciplinary measure in state schools in Scotland. In the case of *Campbell*, the parents sought a guarantee that their children would not be subjected to this measure, which was refused. In *Cosans*, the parents refused to allow their child to be subjected to corporal punishment following wrongdoing, and he was suspended until such time as he and his parents were willing to accept the disciplinary measure.

The government attempted to argue that corporal punishment, as an aspect of discipline, did not fall within the scope of Article 2, Protocol 1: as functions relating to the internal administration of the school, they were ancillary to the 'education' and 'teaching' covered by this Article. The Court rejected this distinction as artificial, finding that while discipline may, in a sense, belong to the internal administration of the school, when it is used, it forms 'an integral part of the process whereby a school seeks to achieve the object for which it was established, including the development and moulding of the character and mental powers of its pupils'.[124]

The government also contended that views on the use of corporal punishment did not amount to 'philosophical convictions': this expression did not extend to opinions on internal school administration, such as discipline, and as such, the parents had no claim under the second sentence of Article 2, Protocol 1. Again, the Court dismissed this position. It held that the word 'philosophical' is not capable of exhaustive definition, and bears numerous meanings—it could 'allude to a fully-fledged system of thought or, rather loosely, to views on more or less trivial matters'.[125] For the purposes of Article 2, Protocol 1, the definition must fall between these two extremes: 'the former would too narrowly restrict the scope of a right that is guaranteed to all parents and the latter might result in the inclusion of matters of insufficient weight or substance'.[126]

Turning to the meaning of 'convictions', the Court held that this should not be read as synonymous with 'opinions and ideas' under Article 10, as this would again be too broad, but should be seen as more akin to 'beliefs' under Article 9: views that attain a certain level of cogency, seriousness, cohesion, and importance. Moreover, 'philosophical convictions' must be consistent with the entirety of the Convention—they must not be incompatible with human dignity, they must not be aimed at the

[123] (7511/76, 7743/76) 25.02.1982.
[124] ibid., para. 33.
[125] ibid., para. 36.
[126] ibid., para. 36.

destruction of other rights and freedoms,[127] and they must not conflict with the fundamental right of the child to education. Applying these principles to the case in hand, the Court found that 'the views relate to a weighty and substantial aspect of human life and behaviour, namely the integrity of the person, the propriety or otherwise of the infliction of corporal punishment, and the exclusion of the distress which the risk of such punishment entails.'[128]

Finally, the government argued that it had fulfilled its obligation to 'respect' parental convictions by adopting a policy of gradually eliminating corporal punishment in schools. The Court made clear that this was simply not sufficient—the duty to respect cannot be overridden by an alleged necessity of striking a balance between conflicting views, nor is a policy to gradually move towards abolition of corporal punishment itself sufficient to comply. For these reasons, the Court found that there was a violation of the second sentence of Article 2, Protocol 1 in both cases.[129]

In addition to relying on parental rights under the second sentence, the child in *Cosans* also relied on his individual right not to be denied education because of the suspension he received. While the Court acknowledged the right of the state to regulate education, as well as the necessity for schools to impose disciplinary measures,[130] it observed that the suspension was motivated by the refusal to accept something that went against his parents' philosophical convictions. As such, the measure fell outside the state's powers of regulation of education under Article 2, Protocol 1: a condition of access to an educational institution that conflicts with another right—in this case, the parents' rights to object to corporal punishment—cannot be described as reasonable.

6.6.2 Sexual and physical abuse

While *Campbell and Cosans* involved the deliberate infliction of corporal punishment in the context of school discipline, the Court has also had to deal with situations where teachers—outside their educational mandate—have physically or sexually abused pupils.

The leading case in this area is *O'Keeffe v Ireland*,[131] where the applicant was sexually abused in the 1970s by a teacher (LH) at her state-funded primary school, which was privately managed by the Catholic Church. Her parents complained to the manager of the school (a priest); however, they did not make a complaint to the police. The teacher went on to teach at other schools, and to abuse other children. In the mid-1990s, in the course of an investigation into a complaint by another student against LH, the applicant made a statement to the police. She applied to the Criminal Injuries Compensation Tribunal, and was awarded damages. But her civil action against LH, the Minister for Education, the Attorney-General, and the Irish state, was dismissed.

[127] See Article 17.

[128] *Campbell and Cosans v the United Kingdom* (7511/76, 7743/76) 25.02.1982, para. 36.

[129] See also *Warwick v the United Kingdom* (9471/81) 18.07.1986 (ComRep), where the government accepted that a failure to provide an undertaking that the child would not be subjected to corporal punishment was in violation of Article 2, Protocol 1.

[130] See section 6.7 below on exclusion from school.

[131] (35810/09) 28.01.2014 (GC).

Before the Court, she argued that the failure of the state to protect her from sexual abuse was in violation of Article 3.

The Court held that there is a positive obligation placed on the government to take measures to protect children from ill-treatment, especially in an educational context, when they are under the exclusive control of school authorities. The state cannot absolve itself of this obligation by delegating to private bodies or individuals. Moreover, the state had to have been aware of the level of sexual crime against minors at the time, for example through the prosecution of such crimes at a significant rate, but continued to entrust the management of the primary education of the vast majority of the population to privately managed schools, without putting in place any mechanism of effective state control to address such risks. In the words of the Court:

> This risk should have been addressed through the adoption of commensurate measures and safeguards. Those should, at a minimum, have included effective mechanisms for the detection and reporting of any ill-treatment by and to a State-controlled body, such procedures being fundamental to the enforcement of the criminal laws, to the prevention of such ill-treatment and, more generally therefore, to the fulfilment of the positive protective obligation of the State.[132]

Although the government argued that there was a reporting process by which the child (or parent) could complain about a teacher, the complainant was directed to the non-state denominational manager (i.e. the Catholic Church), not the state authorities. On the facts, the Court noted that LH had committed over 400 incidents of abuse, and concluded that '[a]ny system of detection and reporting which allowed such extensive and serious ill-conduct to continue for so long must be considered to be ineffective'.[133]

This was disputed by the joint partly dissenting opinion of Judges Zupanćić, Gyulumyan, Kalaydjieva, de Gaetano, and Wojtyczek. Although they recognised that there was a positive obligation on the part of the state, they noted that nothing was ever reported to the police, and they could not be deemed to be constructively aware of the abuse. The decision of the majority implied that the abuse was the result not only of the unpredictable criminal conduct of a private individual, but also of some inherent risk of such treatment arising in the context of education, such that the state 'ought to have had knowledge' of the risk notwithstanding the absence of complaints. The judges in dissent noted that child abuse takes place in both public and private contexts, and were unconvinced that the risk of abuse is necessarily inherent, or higher, in the context of education.

This decision is important, as it was the first time in which the Court was willing to impose a positive obligation in relation to a general risk to unidentified children:[134] previously, states had only been responsible for known risks to identifiable individuals.[135] As it is a relatively recent judgment, it is unclear how this will be interpreted

[132] ibid., para. 162.
[133] ibid., para. 166.
[134] See C. O'Mahony, 'Child Protection and the ECHR: Making Sense of Positive and Procedural Obligations' (2019) 27 *International Journal of Children's Rights* 660.
[135] See Chapter 2 above on the right to freedom from violence and exploitation.

in subsequent cases. However, this extension of liability, shifting the focus from the particular risk posed *to the victim* to the more general risk posed *by the perpetrator*, is to be greatly commended.

6.6.3 Responsibility for student death

Even where the school, or its teachers, are not directly responsible for the harm caused, the Court has extended the positive obligations imposed on states to include a failure to protect from outside risks. This was seen in *Ilbeyi Kemaloğlu and Meriye Kemaloğlu v Turkey*,[136] where a seven-year-old boy died in a heavy snowstorm. He used a free shuttle run by the municipality to travel to and from school, but on the day in question, the school had closed early due to the storm, and had failed to inform the bus drivers. The child tried to walk home by himself, and was found frozen to death the following day.

The Court noted the importance of not imposing an excessive burden on the state, but in the present case, found that 'it cannot be considered as unreasonable to expect the school authorities to take basic precautions to minimize any potential risk and to protect the pupils'.[137] By failing to inform the shuttle service, authorities failed to take sufficient and appropriate measures which might have avoided a risk to life, and therefore were in violation of Article 2.

Moreover, the Court has also held that, in some circumstances, the state has a responsibility to protect third parties from the actions of its students. In *Kayak v Turkey*,[138] a pupil (EG) stabbed another 15-year-old boy (a former pupil) outside the school, with a bread knife he had stolen from the school canteen. Although EG had behavioural problems known to the school, it didn't appear that he had displayed any aggressive or violent behaviour before the incident that would have required special supervision. Nevertheless, the Court found that schools have a primary duty to ensure the health and well-being of pupils, taking into account the vulnerability of their age, and to protect against any form of violence to which they might be subjected while under the school's supervision. While the Court acknowledged that schools could not watch over all students at all times, it found that the entrances and exits to school required heightened surveillance. The school administration had warned authorities about the difficulty of maintaining security around the school, and requested assistance, but none was forthcoming. As such, there was a violation of Article 2.[139]

[136] (19986/06) 10.04.2012.

[137] ibid., para. 41.

[138] (60444/08) 10.07.2012. See also *Đurđević v Croatia* (52442/09) 19.07.2011.

[139] This does not mean, however, that the state is responsible for everything that happens on school grounds, or in the vicinity. In *Molie v Romania* (13754/02) 01.09.2009 (dec.), the Court dismissed as inadmissible a complaint made by the parents of a 15-year-old child, who had died after swinging on the frame of an unsecured goal post on the school sports ground. It found that Article 2 cannot be interpreted as guaranteeing to any person an absolute level of security in all activities of life involving a risk of injury, and in particular, the state cannot be said to have a positive obligation to protect 'imprudent persons'. The child had exposed himself to a significant risk to life, and the state could not be held responsible for the consequences.

This case significantly expands the responsibility of the state in relation to pupils, and coupled with *O'Keeffe*, emphasises that the state does not even have to be aware of the danger to be liable. While extending that awareness to permit constructive knowledge—that the state *ought* to have known—is a legitimate (and important) interpretation of the Convention, the way that it has been interpreted in *Kayak* seems to go a step too far. As the partly dissenting opinion of Judges Sajó and Raimondi points out, simply because EG was a student at the school does not transpose a duty to protect society against him, particularly where there was no background of violent crimes: 'A school cannot control the behaviour of pupils outside its walls, and no state, no matter how paternalistic, is able to control all the actions of its citizens.'[140]

6.7 Exclusion from school

It is clear that the state has the right to discipline students—including expulsion or suspension from school—in accordance with the proper regulation of the education system. However, this regulation cannot interfere with the right of the child to education, and must be implemented fairly and for the minimum period necessary.

This principle was explored in *Ali v United Kingdom*,[141] where the applicant was excluded from school during a police investigation into a fire lit in a classroom. Contrary to domestic statutory requirements, no time limit was placed on the exclusion, nor was he informed of his right to appeal. While he was excluded, he was offered alternative education at home, although this covered only five–15 hours per week, and in a limited range of subjects. The applicant alleged that his indefinite exclusion denied him the right to education, which was not compensated for by the alternative offered during that time.

The Court set out the principles as follows:

> In determining whether or not an exclusion resulted in a denial of the right to education, the Court will have to consider whether a fair balance was struck between the exclusion and the justification given for that measure. It will therefore have regard to factors such as the procedural safeguards in place to challenge the exclusion and to avoid arbitrariness; the duration of the exclusion; the extent of the co-operation shown by the pupil or his parents with respect to attempts to re-integrate him; the efforts of the school authorities to minimise the effects of exclusion and, in particular, the adequacy of alternative education provided by the school during the period of exclusion; and the extent to which the rights of any third parties were engaged.[142]

On the facts, the Court found that the exclusion was in pursuit of a legitimate aim, and was for the minimum period necessary. The applicant was offered alternative education, which, although it did not follow the full national curriculum, was adequate in view of the fact that the exclusion was only temporary. Article 2, Protocol 1 does not

[140] *Kayak v Turkey*(60444/08) 10.07.2012, partly dissenting opinion of Judges Sajó and Raimondi.
[141] (40385/06) 11.01.2011.
[142] ibid., para. 58.

oblige the state to offer the full national curriculum to all pupils temporarily excluded, although it may be different if the exclusion is permanent.[143]

It is not only in relation to discipline that children can be excluded from school, however. For example, in *Memlika v Greece*,[144] the Court found that the state could legitimately prevent students from attending school on public health grounds: in this case, the children were suffering from leprosy. However, any such measure must be proportionate and provide an appropriate balance between the protection of the community and the interests of the children in question. Complete exclusion from school is a particularly restrictive and onerous measure, and should only be kept in place for such time as is strictly required in order to achieve the required aim.[145]

6.8 Higher education

While the majority of cases discussed in this chapter concern primary and secondary education, it is important to note that higher education also falls within the scope of Article 2, Protocol 1.[146] Although the Commission was initially hesitant to recognise this wider scope,[147] in *Leyla Şahin*,[148] the Court noted that while the first sentence of Article 2, Protocol 1 essentially establishes access to primary and secondary education, there is no watertight division separating higher education from the rest of the education system. As such, it cannot be excluded from its scope.

While these cases do not usually concern children directly, it is important to have an understanding of them, as the principles that arise often overlap with those relating to primary and secondary education.

6.8.1 Admission to higher education

A major difference between primary and secondary education on the one hand, and higher education on the other, is the fact that while the former are universal, access to the latter can be restricted. In *X v the United Kingdom*,[149] the Commission made clear that 'where certain, limited, higher education facilities are provided by a State, in principle it is not incompatible with Article 2 of Protocol No 1 to restrict access thereto to those students who have attained the academic level required to most benefit from the courses offered'.[150] As such, states are free to set entrance examinations

143 See also *CP v the United Kingdom* (300/11) 06.09.2016 (dec.), where home tuition was found to be satisfactory to fulfil the state's obligation to an excluded student under Article 2, Protocol 1.

144 (37991/12) 06.10.2015.

145 In this case, the children had recovered from the disease within a month, but were prevented from returning to school for the following six months. As such, the Court found a violation of the children's right to education.

146 *Leyla Şahin v Turkey* (44774/98) 10.11.2005 (GC).

147 In *15 Foreign Students v the United Kingdom* (7671/76) 19.05.1977 (dec.), the Commission held that Article 2, Protocol 1 was concerned primarily with primary education, and not necessarily with advanced studies.

148 *Leyla Şahin v Turkey* (44774/98) 10.11.2005 (GC).

149 (8844/80) 09.12.1980 (dec.).

150 ibid., p. 229.

and impose admissions criteria in order to regulate admission to higher educational institutions.[151]

This does not mean that the state has unlimited discretion, however. In particular, any admissions decisions must have a legal and rational basis, and be reasonably foreseeable.[152] For example, in *Altinay v Turkey*,[153] the Court found a violation of Article 2, Protocol 1 where the rules concerning university admissions were amended, preventing some students from pursuing the course they had been aiming towards. In this case, the applicant was enrolled in vocational high school, intending to go on to study at university. At the time, students holding vocational school diplomas were able to compete on an equal footing with diploma-holders from ordinary high schools to apply for programmes at university, but a new law was introduced applying different weightings to the different forms of high schools. The Court held that in order to ensure that the right to education is not curtailed to such an extent as to impair its very essence, and deprive it of its effectiveness, any restrictions on access must be foreseeable, and pursue a legitimate aim. The regulations themselves were not problematic, as they pursued a legitimate aim of improving the standard of university studies. Moreover, students could choose whether to attend a vocational or an ordinary high school. However, the lack of transitional period meant that for this particular student, who had chosen a vocational high school in good faith, and been adversely affected by a later change of rules, the right of access to higher education had been curtailed.

While this case concerned access to public higher education institutions, the issue of admissions criteria has also been raised in relation to private universities. In *Tarantino and others v Italy*,[154] the applicants complained of government quotas imposed on universities concerning the number of students they could admit. They wished to study medicine and dentistry, but were not admitted after failing the entrance exam. However, they argued that private universities should be permitted to take them on as students if they so wished, and the restriction by the state violated their right to education.

The Court found that the restrictions pursued the legitimate aim of achieving high levels of professionalism by ensuring minimum and adequate education levels in universities. Moreover, assessing candidates through relevant tests in order to identify the most meritorious is a proportionate measure to achieve this. While the Court acknowledged that limiting numbers of students based on society's need for a particular profession is restrictive, it is nevertheless balanced by the entitlement of the government to take action to avoid excessive public expenditure. Resource considerations are clearly relevant, and since certain categories of professionals require a huge

[151] See, for example, *Lukach v Russia* (48041/99) 16.11.1999 (dec.).

[152] See, for example, *Mürsel Eren v Turkey* (60856/00) 07.02.2006, where the applicant's entrance exam results were annulled as they were far better than his previous attempts. The Court found that although there is no positive obligation on the part of the state to provide university education, where it does so access cannot be denied arbitrarily. The government failed to provide any legal basis for annulling the exam results, and the clear wording of the regulation allowed students to form legitimate expectation that they would be able to attend the course for which they had obtained the necessary marks at the exam. The applicant was thus denied his right to education.

[153] (37222/04) 09.07.2013.

[154] (25851/09, 29284/09, 64090/09) 02.04.2013.

investment to train, it is reasonable for the state to aspire that each candidate will be assimilated into the labour market.

Although in private universities, where students pay fees, there is not such a significant burden on the state, such institutions are still partly reliant on state subsidies. Furthermore, the state also has an obligation to regulate private institutions to ensure that access is not available to professions purely on the basis of financial means, irrespective of their qualifications and suitability for the profession. For this reason, the applicants had not been denied a right to education.

The partly dissenting opinion of Judge Pinto de Albuquerque was trenchant in its criticism of this conclusion. In particular, he held that:

> *The right to university education is a human right.* In spite of the negative formulation of Article 2 of Protocol No. 1, States Parties have a positive obligation to provide not only access to the existing schools and educational establishments and official recognition of completed studies, but also to promote access to education for every child, if necessary by creating additional educational possibilities.

Drawing on Italy's international obligations under the UN Convention on the Rights of the Child, and the International Covenant on Economic, Social and Cultural Rights,[155] he argued that states have a duty to make high education equally accessible to all: merit should be the ultimate criterion, not market needs.

Judge Pinto de Albuquerque also argued that while the state had a great deal of control over public education, it must not exercise the same degree of control over private schools. Such institutions must enjoy a greater degree of autonomy—this includes autonomy in the establishment of curriculum; control over admission, evaluation, suspension, and expulsion of students; and selection of staff, budget, and financial organisation. If states were to intervene in the regulation of any of these aspects, the intervention would have to comply with strict requirements of necessity and proportionality.

While this was a dissenting judgment, if picked up in future cases, these principles obviously also have significant implications for primary and secondary education. There has been very limited discussion before the Court of the level of control the state can exercise over private educational institutions, and it remains an area in which there is a considerable level of uncertainty.

6.8.2 Expulsion from higher education

In addition to deciding cases concerning admission to higher education, the Court has also considered the circumstances in which a student can be expelled. As with primary and secondary education, the Court has recognised that the state has the right to take measures to regulate higher education, and Article 2, Protocol 1 does not exclude the imposition of disciplinary penalties on students. For example, it was

[155] (1966) 993 UNTS 3.

held in *Yanasik v Turkey*,[156] that it was not contrary to the Convention for pupils to be suspended or expelled, provided that national regulations did not prevent them from enrolling in another institution to pursue their studies. Three years later, in *Sulak v Turkey*,[157] the Commission was willing to go even further—even where the student was prevented by national regulations from enrolling in another institution (given that he had been expelled for cheating), Article 2, Protocol 1 had not been violated. Here, the Commission noted that the applicant had been given an opportunity to follow his chosen course of study at university, and the state had thus fulfilled their obligations under Article 2, Protocol 1.

Having said this, any disciplinary measures must pursue a legitimate aim, and be proportionate to the aim pursued. In *Irfan Temel and others v Turkey*,[158] the applicants were suspended for two terms following a request that Kurdish language classes be introduced as an optional module. The Court expressed 'serious doubts' as to whether the disciplinary measures pursued a legitimate aim, but preferred to focus on the issue of proportionality. It noted that the applicants were sanctioned merely for submitting a petition, without committing any violence, breach of the peace, or any other 'reprehensible act'. As such, this was an exercise of freedom of expression under Article 10, and could not form the basis of disciplinary measures.

6.9 Conclusion

From the perspective of children's rights, the structure of Article 2, Protocol 1 is far from ideal. Its negative formulation, and the focus on parental interests, provide a much narrower understanding of the right of the child to education than do other international instruments, in particular, the UN Convention on the Rights of the Child. What should be a child's right has been transformed into a battleground for the fight for supremacy between adult interests—both parent and state.

Having said this, the Court has managed to introduce a more child-centred perspective through its recognition that any right of the parent to respect for their beliefs and convictions can be limited by the primary right of the child to receive certain information—for example, through sexual education—and to wider social integration—for example, through compulsory schooling or attendance at certain classes. However, this has always been in the context of the wide margin of appreciation given to states: the Court has yet to recognise that the child *must* have access to these benefits. This is partly because of the way in which cases come before the Court,[159] as it has yet to be faced with a case in which a child is in conflict with their parents, where it has had to confront head on whether there is any independent right of the child in this respect.

Related to this, there is still considerable scope to expand its jurisprudence on the positive obligation to provide education to *all* children. In recent years, the Court

156 (14524/89) 06.01.1993 (dec.).
157 (24515/94) 17.01.1996 (dec.).
158 (36458/02) 03.03.2009.
159 See Chapter 9.

has started to take important steps in relation to children with disabilities, children speaking minority languages, and children from ethnic minorities, but there is still a long way to go before substantive equality is achieved. Likewise, future challenges will no doubt continue to arise in relation to school dress, both for students and teachers, given the controversial nature of the Court's current jurisprudence in the area and ongoing tensions within European society.

7
Social and Economic Rights

7.1 Introduction

As the supervisory body of an instrument focused predominantly on civil and political rights, the Court has been reluctant to enter into any kind of substantive discourse surrounding social and economic rights. This does not mean, however, that they are absent from its jurisprudence. First, and despite its civil and political core, the Convention itself *does* contain some socio-economic rights—for example, the right to property and the right to education, enshrined in Protocol 1—and the Court has used these to impose extensive obligations on state parties. Second, the Court has incrementally developed a social and economic dimension to the existing civil and political rights, through the imposition of extensive positive obligations—in particular under Articles 2, 3, 6, and 8. From as early as 1979 and the case of *Airey*,[1] the Court has recognised that achieving even such classic civil and political rights as the right to a fair trial will inevitably have resource implications. Third, the Court has been able to delineate certain 'civil and political' aspects of traditionally socio-economic rights—for example, the right to respect for physical integrity in consent to medical treatment and the right to privacy of medical information.

This chapter focuses on four social and economic rights which have been invoked in relation to children before the Court: the right to health (care), the right to a healthy environment, the right to property, and the right to social welfare. A fifth socio-economic right, the right to education, was considered in Chapter 6, as its child-centric focus and extensive jurisprudence demanded separate treatment.[2]

7.2 The right to health

From its very early jurisprudence, the Court has rejected a positive obligation on the state to provide any particular level of health or health care. In *X v Ireland*,[3] the Commission found inadmissible a complaint under Article 2 that a severely disabled child was not given access to free health care, on the grounds that she had nevertheless

[1] *Airey v Ireland* (6289/73) 09.10.1979.

[2] The Court has also considered, in a very peripheral manner, the right to an adequate standing of living, through the imposition of positive obligations in relation to children at risk of removal from their family situation due to material deprivation. This is discussed in detail in Chapters 10 and 11, and will therefore not be considered separately here. Likewise, the Court has developed an interesting line of jurisprudence concerning the right to housing, but the rights of children have not been examined in this respect, and thus for reasons of space, it will not be discussed in this volume.

[3] (6839/74) 04.10.1976 (dec.).

Children and the European Court of Human Rights. Claire Fenton-Glynn, Oxford University Press (2021). © Claire Fenton-Glynn.
DOI: 10.1093/oso/9780198787518.003.0007

received assistance from the local health authorities and her life had not been endangered. Likewise, in *La Parola and others v Italy*,[4] the Court rejected a similar claim by Italian parents, since they already received a permanent social assistance benefit. While the Court in this case referred vaguely to the 'scale of the benefit' which showed that the state 'was already discharging its positive obligations', there has not yet been a case where the Court has elaborated on what these obligations might be, nor what minimum standard must be met.[5]

Instead, the majority of the jurisprudence in this area focuses on procedural, rather than substantive, issues: the division of decision-making authority between children, parents, and the state; the right to privacy in relation to medical data; and medical negligence.

7.2.1 Consent to medical procedures

The issue of consent to medical treatment under the Convention can be divided into two separate issues: first, the allocation of decision-making authority between the child and their parents; and second, the relationship between parental authority and state intervention.

7.2.1.1 Children's decision-making capacity

The first question—whether and when a child has the capacity to consent to their own treatment, without the involvement of their parents, or even against their parents' wishes—has only been considered once in the Court's 60-year history, in the seminal decision of *Nielsen v Denmark*.[6] This case involved a 12-year-old child who had been detained in a child psychiatric ward against his wishes. The child had been the subject of a custody dispute, and the mother requested that he be placed in the ward, since it was clear that he did not want to stay with her. He continued to attend the same school he attended before the dispute, and was allowed to leave the ward when he asked for permission. He was not treated with medication, but given 'environmental therapy' (letting him experience relaxed, homelike surroundings with adults who were neutral in relation to the custody dispute) and 'individual talks'. He complained that his placement in the ward for five-and-a-half months constituted a deprivation of liberty, contrary to Article 5(1) of the Convention.

Taking the first tentative steps towards ensuring children's autonomous decision-making as part of their Convention rights, the Commission considered the

[4] (39712/98) 30.11.2000 (dec.).

[5] Having said this, the Court has recognised that there may be an obligation to provide health care where the child is in the control of the state—for example, in a state-run institution. In *Nencheva and others v Bulgaria* (48609/06) 18.06.2013, discussed in detail in Chapter 10, the Court held that where children are under the exclusive control of the domestic authorities, a special and enhanced level of protection is required. In this case, children who suffered from serious mental and physical disorders were 'subjected to the worst living conditions' imaginable: they lacked food, medicines, adequate clothing, and the institution had insufficient heating. As a result, 15 children died in the institution over the space of three months. In this context, the Court found that the state had breached their positive obligations under Article 2, as they failed to protect the lives of vulnerable children placed in their care.

[6] (10929/84) 12.03.1987 (ComRep); (10929/84) 28.11.1988 (Court).

relationship between his mother's decision to place him in the facility and the child's own autonomy. The Commission acknowledged that the Convention presupposes that the holders of parental responsibility are entitled to decide matters concerning their children; however, it emphasised that these are not unlimited, and do not involve unrestricted power over the child and his or her personal decisions. The power of the parent cannot be decisive against the clearly expressed opinions of a child, and in such cases, 'the result will have to depend on a concrete assessment of the maturity of the applicant and his ability to understand his situation and to come to a decision'.[7] It went on to hold:

> The Commission does not find it necessary in this case to set out any fixed age-limit below which the opinion of a minor is of no importance. However, it is evident that the wishes of very young children regarding the question of hospitalisation and treatment in psychiatric wards cannot be decisive. On the other hand a system under which for example a 17-year old minor could be placed in a closed ward with the consent of the holder of the parental rights and against his own wishes could hardly as such be considered a voluntary placement which would not raise any question of deprivation of liberty.[8]

On the facts, the Commission found that the child was a normally developed 12-year-old, who was capable of understanding his situation and expressing his opinion clearly. As such, his detention against his will amounted to a violation of Article 5.

This decision was, however, overturned by the full Court, in what has remained the principal case in determining the extent of a child's decision-making autonomy. The Court held that the child's admission to hospital against his will was not a deprivation of liberty, as this was a responsible exercise by his mother of her custodial rights in the interests of the child.[9] While the Court acknowledged that a parents' decision-making capacity is not unlimited, it considered that the child 'was still of an age at which it would be normal for a decision to be made by the parent even against the wishes of the child'.[10] There was 'no evidence of bad faith on the part of the mother',[11] and the restrictions on the child's liberty were no greater than those of a normal hospital stay for a child with a physical disorder. The Court thus stepped away from the recognition of the evolving capacity of the child, and instead retained the language of parental rights and protectionism.

7.2.1.2 State intervention in medical treatment

While there has only been one case concerning children's decision-making capacity in the field of medical law, there has been greater discussion of the parameters of state intervention in children's medical care. The Court has been clear that parents have the primary decision-making authority in relation to their children's treatment, and it is

[7] (10929/84) 12.03.1987 (ComRep), para. 126.
[8] ibid.
[9] (10929/84) 28.11.1988 (Court), para. 73.
[10] ibid., para. 72.
[11] ibid.

only in exceptional circumstances, prescribed by a clear legal framework, that the state can step in.

This was seen in *MAK and RK v the United Kingdom*,[12] which concerned a nine-year-old child who had been referred to hospital on suspicion of sexual abuse, and social services had been contacted. The parents had given instructions that tests should not be undertaken until they arrived, but the hospital nevertheless went ahead and took blood samples from, and photographs of, the child. The Court held that there had been a violation of the child's right to respect for physical integrity under Article 8: non-emergency medical treatment cannot take place without appropriate consent—which, in the case of a child lacking capacity, means the consent of someone with parental responsibility.[13] If the doctors wished to give treatment without such consent, they would have to seek judicial authorisation.

The interaction between the decision-making authority of parents, doctors, and the state was most comprehensively considered in *Glass v the United Kingdom*.[14] This case concerned a 12-year-old boy who was severely mentally and physically disabled. When discussing possible treatment, there had been disagreement between the mother and the doctors concerning the administration of morphine. The child's condition subsequently deteriorated, to the point where the doctors considered the administration of morphine to be an urgent necessary. They thus administered the drug despite the objections of the mother.

The Court found that the decision to impose treatment on an individual in defiance of their own objections, or the objections of the proxy decision-maker (in this case, his mother), gave rise to an interference with his physical integrity under Article 8. Such interference could only be justified if it was subject to a clear legal framework, which took into account the rights of the parent and the responsibilities of the state. In this case, the Court found that the legal framework was in fact adequate: it respected the rights of parents by requiring their consent to treatment (save in emergency situations) and required judicial intervention in the event that they objected.

However, in the individual circumstances of the case, the hospital had failed to adequately follow this framework. While the Court acknowledged that there had been an emergency situation, the likes of which meant that parental consent was not necessary, the conflict could have been avoided if judicial intervention was sought earlier. The hospital had previously been concerned about the mother's reluctance to approve certain necessary treatment for her child, and had made clinical notes about the possible need to seek the intervention of the court. The Court held that it had not been explained why the hospital did not seek judicial intervention at that stage, when they were left in no doubt that, should the situation arise (as they believed it would), the proposed treatment would not meet with the mother's agreement. In this way, the decision of the authorities to override her objection in the absence of court authorisation resulted in a breach of Article 8.

[12] (45901/05, 40146/05) 23.03.2010.

[13] An exception was also made for treatment in an emergency situation, where seeking consent was not practical.

[14] (61827/00) 09.03.2004.

Despite the approval by the Court of the legal framework in place in the United Kingdom—giving primary responsibility to parents, with possible recourse to the courts if a conflict arose—there was no discussion of the grounds upon which the court could substitute its own decision for that of the parents. Does the court have to respect the decision of parents unless it endangers the child? Or could it simply substitute its own decision according to its determination of the child's best interests?

This question was considered recently in the controversial case of *Gard and others v the United Kingdom*.[15] This case had been the subject of international headlines, prompting the intervention of both the President of the United States and the Catholic Pope. The doctors in this case had concluded that the child's condition was terminal, and it would be best to withdraw treatment: a course of action to which the parents vehemently objected. Under English law, a court can order treatment (or its cessation) for a child if it is deemed to be in their 'best interests'. The parents argued that this test did not provide sufficient protection for their parental rights, and instead the test for judicial intervention should be where the decision of the parents risked 'significant harm' to the child.

In a scantily reasoned admissibility decision, the Court recalled that 'there is broad consensus—including in international law—in support of the idea that in all decisions concerning children, their best interests must be paramount',[16] but held that it did not have to decide this issue: the domestic authorities had concluded that there was a risk of 'significant harm' if the course of treatment sought by the parents were to be pursued, and thus either test was satisfied on the facts.[17]

On the other hand, in *Afiri and Biddarri v France*,[18] the applicants challenged the French legal framework concerning the discontinuance of treatment and end-of-life decisions. While the French law requires several phases of consultation, the decision to withdraw treatment is the sole responsibility of the doctor in charge of the patient. Where the decision concerns a minor, the doctor must obtain the opinion of the child's parents, and attempt to reach an agreement with them, but does not need their consent. The Court found that there had been no violation of the Convention—even if the parents not agree with the decision taken, the process complied with the requirements of Article 2.

We are thus still uncertain as to the exact position of parents vis-a-vis the state when deciding medical treatment for children. We know that 'significant harm' will be sufficient, but whether a lower standard will suffice—for example, a decision based purely on best interests—remains as yet unclear.

[15] (39793/17) 27.06.2017 (dec.).

[16] ibid., para. 118.

[17] A similar test of 'serious health risk' was earlier approved by the Commission in *Wedberg and Hillblom v Sweden* (21607/93) 11.04.1996 (dec.), where it was held that the domestic authorities were justified in removing the child into public care for the purposes of providing medical treatment. The authorities had determined that the parents were subjecting the child to 'serious health risks' by preventing the operation, and thus the Commission concluded that any interference with the parents' rights under Article 8 was justified.

[18] (1828/18) 23.01.2018 (dec.).

7.2.2 Immunisation and disease prevention

In the period from the 1970s to the 1990s the Commission considered a number of cases concerning the state provision of vaccinations to children—either on a voluntary basis, or backed by sanctions. At the time, side effects from certain vaccinations could be quite severe, and there were a number of associations, and individual parents, attempting to limit the power of the state in this regard.

The first case, *Association X v the United Kingdom*,[19] concerned a group of parents whose children had suffered severe damage, or even died, as a result of vaccinations. They alleged that parents had not been informed of the risks involved in vaccinations in a way that would permit them to make a fully informed decision, and as such, had imposed an unjustifiable risk. Invoking Article 2, they argued that there was a causal link between the vaccinations and the subsequent deaths, of which the government was aware. As such, just as there was an intention to benefit the majority through immunisation, there was an intention—reluctant or otherwise—to inflict death on a small minority to achieve this. Moreover, they claimed that due to poor administration of immunisation schemes, and in particular the lack of monitoring of adverse reactions, the right to life of individual children had not been protected.

The Commission rejected these arguments, finding that where a small number of fatalities occur in the context of a scheme whose sole purpose is to protect the health of society and safeguard life, it cannot be said that there has been an intentional deprivation of life under Article 2. While the Commission acknowledged that the government was aware of the risk of adverse reactions, which could involve serious injury or death, this did not mean that they 'intended' them to occur. The scheme as a whole was concerned with avoiding such serious risks, and the Commission noted the wide measure of protection afforded by nationwide programmes of vaccination, including the virtual eradication of diseases like diphtheria and polio. Further, the Commission found that this scheme was appropriately administered, with a clearly established system of control and supervision.

The applicants also claimed that their rights as parents had been violated under Article 8, as they had not been informed of the balance of benefits and disadvantages associated with the vaccinations, or given information concerning contraindications. In this way, they were denied the right to make an informed decision for their child based on proper consent, contrary to the right to respect for private life. The Commission found that in the context of a voluntary scheme, designed to protect the health of society and subject to a proper system of control to minimise the risks involved, there is no interference with the parents' rights under Article 8. The state did not compel vaccination, either directly or indirectly, merely providing facilities for those who wish to do so. It found that 'although the parental decision to have their children vaccinated may not be based on a technical appreciation of the specific risks involved, there exists a general common knowledge that vaccination schemes involve certain risks'.[20]

[19] (7154/75) 12.07.1978 (dec.).
[20] At p. 35.

This case was followed soon after by that of *Godfrey v the United Kingdom*.[21] In 1946, when he was approximately six months old, the applicant's son suffered an adverse reaction to a vaccination, and was left severely disabled, and unable to fend for himself. In 1978, the government introduced a scheme to award payments to certain children who had been severely damaged as a result of vaccinations after 1948 (the date at which the National Health Service was established). The mother complained that this scheme discriminated unfairly against her son, as he was not able to obtain compensation for his injuries, which amounted to a failure to respect his family life under Article 8. The government, on the other hand, argued that neither the vaccination nor the compensation scheme fell within the ambit of Article 8, which should be construed as protecting the individual from arbitrary interference, and not concerned with the provision of a social benefit.

This characterisation of the compensation scheme as social benefit was accepted by the Commission, which emphasised that economic and social rights are not guaranteed under the Convention. The scheme was not instituted because the government had a legal obligation to these children, as vaccination was voluntary, but was instead a benefit extended by the government to certain individuals with disabilities.[22] Further, as the scheme fell outside the scope of Article 8, the Commission could not consider whether the differentiation between children vaccinated before 1948 and those vaccinated after was compatible with Article 14.

Central to both these decisions was the fact that the vaccination scheme in the United Kingdom was voluntary—albeit strongly advocated by the government. However, the Commission has also considered the situation raised by more invasive programmes, in the case of *Boffa and 13 others v San Marino*,[23] where the applicants complained that San Marino's programme of compulsory vaccinations interfered with their right to respect for private life. The Commission found that there was no evidence presented that the vaccination would cause serious problems for that particular child, and relying on *Godfrey*, held that a 'vaccination campaign' does not go beyond the margin of appreciation left to states. However, the Commission failed to differentiate between a general campaign that encourages vaccination and a system of compulsory vaccination with sanctions attached for non-compliance. There is a vast difference between such schemes, which the Commission avoided coming to terms with.

The Commission also failed to grapple with the issue of the right to freedom of thought and conscience, which had been raised by the parents. They argued that the compulsory scheme restricted their ability as parents to freely choose whether or not to vaccinate their children, contrary to Article 9. The Commission found that since the obligation applied to everyone, 'whatever their religion or personal creed', there had been no interference with Article 9. This finding appears to confuse a complaint under Article 9 with one brought under Article 14. Quite obviously, a law or practice

[21] (8542/79) 04.02.1982 (dec.).

[22] This conclusion was reiterated in *Wain v the United Kingdom* (10787/84) 02.12.1985 (dec.), where the applicant father had argued that since the government had recommended vaccination to protect public health in general, it was under a moral and legal duty to compensate those who suffer as a result of vaccination. As in *Godfrey*, the Commission emphasised the nature of the scheme as a social security measure, rather than as a legal obligation.

[23] (26536/95) 15.01.1998 (dec.).

can interfere with an individual's freedom of belief, even if it does apply to everyone. Even if it were a complaint under Article 14, it adopts a narrow view of equality, failing to take into account the disparate impact on certain belief systems—although this accords with the interpretation of Article 14 that was prevalent at the time. For these reasons, it appears likely that the case would be decided differently if it came before the Court again today—if not in outcome, then at least in the way in which the rights were articulated and the decision was reasoned.

The somewhat confused reasoning in *Boffa* can be contrasted with the cases of *JR, GR, RR and YR v Switzerland*[24] and *Acmanne and others v Belgium*.[25] While neither of these cases concerned vaccinations, they both involved compulsory intervention to prevent risks to health, and the Court provided strong reasoning as to why such a scheme could be justified in the interests of a democratic society.

In *JR, GR, RR and YR*, the Swiss Canton required a dental check for all school children at least once a year, and parents were obliged to comply with any treatment recommended as a result of this. A number of parents brought a case before the Commission, complaining that the scheme violated their rights under Article 8, as it required the children to undergo dental treatment with which they as parents did not agree. Unlike other cases in this area, the Commission here placed explicit weight on the vulnerability of the child and the protection of their rights.[26] It noted that there was a public interest in the protection of the health of children, who had limited possibility for protecting their own rights. Importantly for the Commission, however, the parents still had the ability to file an appeal against any decision of the school dentist, and were also free to choose their own dentist to carry out the treatment if they wished to do so.

Acmanne and others v Belgium,[27] on the other hand, concerned compulsory screening for tuberculosis, either by skin reaction test or chest x-ray. The applicants were parents and teachers who were fined for refusing to undergo, or to let their children undergo, such tests, and complained that this was an interference with their private life under Article 8. The Commission acknowledged that there had been such an interference, but found that it was justified in the interests of protecting the health of society as a whole. There had been no evidence provided that the disadvantages of the test outweighed the dangers of tuberculosis, and the Commission thus endorsed the finding of the domestic courts that the individual has a social duty to defer to the general interest, and not endanger the health of others where his life is not in danger.

Although these cases involved less intrusive procedures than vaccination, they nevertheless took a more robust approach to the weighing of individual versus societal interests under the Convention than did *Boffa*. This is an issue that is likely to come before the Court again, especially in light of falling vaccination rates across Europe, and outbreaks of previously virtually eradicated diseases such as measles.[28] The United

[24] (22398/93) 05.04.1995 (dec.).
[25] (10435/83) 10.12.1984 (dec.).
[26] Although this was, in part, because this had been the focus of the decision of the domestic courts.
[27] (10435/83) 10.12.1984 (dec.).
[28] See, for example, V. Saliba, 'Measles Has Been Eliminated in the UK—So Why Do We Still See Cases and Outbreaks?' (Public Health England, 22.01.2018), https://publichealthmatters.blog.gov.uk/2018/01/22/measles-has-been-eliminated-in-the-uk-so-why-do-we-still-see-cases-and-outbreaks/.

Kingdom, for example, has not ruled out a programme of compulsory vaccination if rates continue to drop,[29] while countries such as Austria have linked vaccination with pre-school admission and family assistance payments.[30] All the jurisprudence on this issue have so far been admissibility decisions taken by the Commission, leaving an important gap that the Court needs to fill with a well-reasoned and clearly articulated judgment.

7.2.3 The right to privacy

In Chapter 3, the protection of children's privacy from the intrusion of the media, private individuals, and the state was discussed. The issue of the right to privacy has also arisen in the medical context, concerning the confidentiality of medical information.

In *P and S v Poland*,[31] discussed further in section 7.3.2 below, the Court considered the privacy rights of a 14-year-old child seeking an abortion. The Head of the gynaecological ward where she sought treatment took her to see a Catholic priest, disclosing to him confidential information. The hospital also issued a press release about the case and journalists who contacted the hospital were given details of her situation, and told confidential information. The girl argued that the disclosure of personal data violated her right to respect for private life under Article 8, a complaint contested by the government, who argued that since the availability of legal abortion was the subject of heated debate in Poland, there was a legitimate public interest in the information.

The Court found that the protection of personal data, and especially medical data, is of fundamental importance under Article 8. The exposure of such data can dramatically affect an individual's private life, by exposing them to opprobrium and risk of ostracism, as was the situation in this case. The disclosure did not pursue a legitimate aim: there were no exceptional circumstances in the case to justify the public interest, and it thus could not be considered compatible with Article 8.

This issue was returned to in the case of *Avilkina and others v Russia*[32] concerning a Jehovah's Witness child. The Prosecutor's Office in that area had received complaints concerning the beliefs and practices of Jehovah's Witnesses, claiming that they were a form of extremism, and had thus decided to conduct an investigation. During this investigation, the Prosecutor's Office asked all the city's medical institutions to report every refusal of a blood transfusion by Jehovah's Witnesses, and in this context, reviewed the medical documents and records of a number of Jehovah's Witnesses, including a two-year-old child. The applicants complained that confidential medical information had been disclosed without their consent, and in the absence of any criminal investigation warranting such disclosure. The child's treatment process had been

[29] A. Matthews-King, 'Compulsory Vaccination "Not Ruled Out" in Fight against "Reprehensible" Anti-Vaxxers, Says Health Secretary' (*The Independent*, 04.05.2018), https://www.independent.co.uk/news/health/vaccination-compulsory-uk-matt-hancock-anti-vaxx-measles-nhs-a8899241.html.

[30] G. Finnegan, 'Mandatory Vaccination: Does It Work in Europe?' (*Vaccines Today*, 27.11.2017), https://www.vaccinestoday.eu/stories/mandatory-vaccination-work-europe/.

[31] (57375/08) 30.10.2012.

[32] (1585/09) 06.06.2013.

complicated, and the Prosecutor's interference had obstructed the use of alternative non-blood methods of treatment.

The Court found that respecting the confidentiality of health data is a vital principle in the legal systems of all European states, and the disclosure of such data can seriously affect a person's private and family life. It is crucial not only for the protection of privacy, but also for retaining confidence in the medical profession and ensuring that individuals are not deterred from seeking appropriate treatment. Moreover, the Court found that there was no pressing social need for the disclosure of confidential medical information: as in *MAK and RK* (see section 7.2.1.2 above) the Court emphasised that if the child was at risk, it was open to the authorities to seek judicial authorisation for the treatment. The authorities could also have asked for consent, but as it was, they chose to order disclosure without giving any notice or opportunity to object or agree. As such, there had been a violation of Article 8.

7.2.4 Medical negligence

The final issue related to health care which has been raised before the Court has been that of medical negligence. In line with Article 2, the state must not only refrain from the intentional taking of life, but must also take appropriate steps to safeguard the lives—and indeed, the physical integrity—of those within its jurisdiction. In this light, the Court has made clear that the state has a positive obligation under Article 8 to provide victims of medical negligence with access to proceedings in which they could—where appropriate—obtain compensation for damage.[33]

Importantly, in *Oyal v Turkey*,[34] the Court went one step further, and not only required damages to be made available, but also a specific remedy of ongoing medical treatment free of charge. In this case, a newborn baby received a blood transfusion, from which he contracted HIV. The child's parents claimed that the authorities had failed in their positive obligation to protect the life of the child, but also that they had failed to provide an adequate remedy under Article 2. Although the domestic courts had awarded non-pecuniary damages for the medical negligence, these only covered one year of treatment for the child, and thus the family was left in debt and poverty, unable to meet the cost of continued treatment and medication. The Court acknowledged the positive approach adopted by the domestic authorities in determining responsibility for the negligence, but considered that the most appropriate remedy would have been to order them to pay for the treatment of the child throughout his lifetime. As such, the redress offered was not satisfactory.

The specificity of this remedy—requiring not simply a monetary award, but also ongoing treatment free of charge—seems particularly appropriate for this area of the law. Where the victim is a child who will suffer permanent consequences, a single payment is unlikely to be able to accurately quantify the lifelong medical needs. As such, the

[33] See, for example, *Codarcea v Romania* (31675/04) 02.06.2009; *Jurica v Croatia* (30376/13) 02.05.2017; *Ioniță v Romania* (81270/12) 10.01.2017; *Erdinç Kurt and others v Turkey* (50772/11) 06.06.2017.
[34] (4864/05) 23.03.2010.

willingness of the Court to go beyond its usual principles and think more creatively concerning the adequacy of remedies is to be applauded.

7.3 Abortion

The most prolific area of jurisprudence regarding the right to health has been in the field of abortion. Complaints against abortion laws—either that they are too liberal, or too restrictive—have been brought under almost every article of the Convention: Article 2;[35] Article 3;[36] Article 5;[37] Article 6;[38] Article 7;[39] Article 8;[40] Article 9;[41] Article 10;[42] Article 12;[43] Article 13;[44] and Article 14.[45] They have also been brought by a variety of individuals, and considered in the context of the rights of individual women (pregnant[46] or otherwise[47]), potential fathers[48] and potential grandparents of unborn children,[49] health professionals,[50] medical institutions,[51] vicars,[52] non-governmental organisations,[53] and even 'concerned citizens'.[54]

However, this section intends to focus on one particular aspect of the jurisprudence concerning abortion: the status of the unborn child under the Convention. And despite the large number of cases over a period of over 40 years, the answer to this most important question is still not clear.

[35] See, for example, *WP v the United Kingdom* (8416/78) 13.05.1980 (dec.); *H v Norway* (17004/90) 19.05.1992 (dec.); *Vo v France* (53924/00) 08.07.2004 (GC); *Knudsen v Norway* (11045/84) 08.03.1985 (dec.); *Csoma v Romania* (8759/05) 15.01.2013; *Amy v Belgium* (11684/85) 05.10.1988 (dec.).

[36] *H v Norway* (17004/90) 19.05.1992 (dec.); *Tysiac v Poland* (5410/03) 20.03.2007; *RR v Poland* (27617/04) 26.05.2011.

[37] *WP v the United Kingdom* (8416/78) 13.05.1980 (dec.).

[38] *Csoma v Romania* (8759/05) 15.01.2013; *H v Norway* (17004/90) 19.05.1992 (dec.).

[39] *Silva Monteiro Martins Ribeiro v Portugal* (16471/02) 26.10.2004 (dec.).

[40] *WP v the United Kingdom* (8416/78) 13.05.1980 (dec.); *H v Norway* (17004/90) 19.05.1992 (dec.); *Boso v Italy* (50490/99) 05.09.2002 (dec.); *Brüggemann and Scheuten v the Federal Republic of Germany* (6959/75) 12.07.1977 (dec.); *Open Door and Dublin Well Woman v Ireland* (14234/88, 14235/88) 29.10.1992; *ABC v Ireland* (25579/05) 16.12.2010 (GC); *P and S v Poland* (57375/08) 30.10.2012; *Amy v Belgium* (11684/85) 05.10.1988 (dec.).

[41] *Knudsen v Norway* (11045/84) 08.03.1985 (dec.); *WP v the United Kingdom* (8416/78) 13.05.1980 (dec.); *H v Norway* (17004/90) 19.05.1992 (dec.).

[42] *Open Door and Dublin Well Woman v Ireland* (14234/88, 14235/88) 29.10.1992; *Rommelfanger v the Federal Republic of Germany* (12242/86) 06.09.1989.

[43] *Boso v Italy* (50490/99) 05.09.2002 (dec.).

[44] *H v Norway* (17004/90) 19.05.1992 (dec.); *Csoma v Romania* (8759/05) 15.01.2013.

[45] *H v Norway* (17004/90) 19.05.1992 (dec.).

[46] *Vo v France* (53924/00) 08.07.2004 (GC); *ABC v Ireland* (25579/05) 16.12.2010 (GC); *P and S v Poland* (57375/08) 30.10.2012; *Tysiac v Poland* (5410/03) 20.03.2007; *RR v Poland* (27617/04) 26.05.2011.

[47] *Brüggemann and Scheuten v the Federal Republic of Germany* (6959/75) 12.07.1977 (dec.).

[48] *WP v the United Kingdom* (8416/78) 13.05.1980 (dec.); *Boso v Italy* (50490/99) 05.09.2002 (dec.); *H v Norway* (17004/90) 19.05.1992 (dec.).

[49] *P and S v Poland* (57375/08) 30.10.2012.

[50] *Silva Monteiro Martins Ribeiro v Portugal* (16471/02) 26.10.2004; *Amy v Belgium* (11684/85) 05.10.1988 (dec.).

[51] *Rommelfanger v the Federal Republic of Germany* (12242/86) 06.09.1989.

[52] *Knudsen v Norway* (11045/84) 08.03.1985 (dec.).

[53] *Open Door and Dublin Well Woman v Ireland* (14234/88, 14235/88) 29.10.1992.

[54] *X v Austria* (7045/75) 10.12.1976 (dec.).

7.3.1 Abortion and the rights of the unborn child

The Court first considered the issue of abortion in the case of *Brüggemann and Scheuten v the Federal Republic of Germany*,[55] where the applicants complained of a law which criminalised termination of a pregnancy later than the 13th day after conception. They argued that their private life had been interfered with, as they would either have to abstain from sexual intercourse, use contraception they did not agree with, or carry out a pregnancy against their will.

The Commission found that '[p]regnancy cannot be said to pertain uniquely to the sphere of private life. Whenever a woman is pregnant her private life becomes closely connected with the developing foetus.'[56] As such, Article 8 could not be interpreted as meaning that either the termination, or even the pregnancy itself, was solely a matter for the mother.[57] However, the Commission stopped short of declaring that the foetus itself had rights under the Convention. It held that it was not necessary to decide whether an unborn child is considered as 'life' under Article 2, or whether it could be regarded as an entity which under Article 8(2) could justify an interference 'for the protection of others', leaving the issue open for future adjudication.

This debate continued in *WP v the United Kingdom*,[58] when the husband of a woman seeking an abortion argued, inter alia, that the law of England had violated Article 2 in allowing abortion at all and in denying the foetus any legal rights. The Commission found that the general use of the term 'everyone' in the Convention, and the context in which it is employed in Article 2, supported the view that it does not include the unborn: in nearly all instances, it is such that it can apply only post-natally, and none clearly indicates possible prenatal application.[59] It then turned to the understanding of the term 'life', and whether it only included the life of those already born, or also the 'unborn life' of the foetus. It noted the wide divergence of thinking on the question of when life begins: ranging from conception, to viability, to live birth. However, it failed to come to a conclusion on this point, maintaining instead that the term must be subject to different interpretations in different legal instruments.

When looking at the text of Article 2 itself, the limitations apply, by their very nature, only to persons already born, and cannot include the foetus. Nevertheless, the Commission considered, in the absence of an express limitation concerning the foetus, whether Article 2 should be interpreted (i) as not covering the foetus at all; (ii) as recognising a right to life of the foetus with certain limitations; or (iii) as recognising an absolute right to life of the foetus.

Focusing on interpretation (iii), the Commission found that this could not be the correct interpretation as '[t]he "life" of the foetus is intimately connected with, and cannot be regarded in isolation of, the life of the pregnant woman'.[60] If such an

[55] (6959/75) 12.07.1977 (dec.).

[56] ibid., para. 59.

[57] For a critique of the jurisprudence of the Court in the area of abortion from a feminist perspective, see S. Palmer, 'Abortion and Human Rights' (2014) 6 *European Human Rights Law Review* 596–605.

[58] (8416/78) 13.05.1980 (dec.). Otherwise known as *X v the United Kingdom* or *Paton v the United Kingdom*.

[59] Although the Commission noted that in rare cases (for example, under Article 6(1)), it cannot be entirely excluded.

[60] *WP v the United Kingdom* (8416/78) 13.05.1980 (dec.), para. 19.

interpretation were to be accepted, abortion would have to be prohibited even where continuance of the pregnancy would involve a serious risk to the life of the woman, placing the 'life' of the foetus at a higher value than that of the pregnant woman and subjecting her own right to life to an implied limitation. This is a kind of backwards reasoning—the Commission finding that abortion must be allowed in some circumstances, and therefore the foetus could not have the full protection of Article 2.

Having dismissed this interpretation, the Commission then considered whether Article 2 did not cover the foetus at all, or protected its right to life with certain limitations. It noted that the abortion complained of in this case was carried out in the early stages of pregnancy to avert the risk of injury to the physical or mental health of the woman. Such an abortion must be covered by the implied limitation protecting the life and health of the woman. For this reason, the Commission found it unnecessary to decide whether the foetus's right to life was not protected at all, or subject to limitations, as such an abortion would be compatible with either interpretation.

It was not until almost 25 years later that the Court returned to this issue in *Vo v France*.[61] Although there had been a number of cases on abortion in the intervening years, the Court had consistently declined to reconsider the issue under Article 2, instead simply reiterating the findings in *WP*. The facts in *Vo*, however, forced the Court to confront the issue (or at least discuss it).

In this case, the applicant attended the hospital for a medical examination during her pregnancy. On the same day, another woman with the same surname was due to have a contraceptive coil removed at the same hospital. Noting that the applicant had difficulty understanding French, the doctor sought to remove the coil without examining her beforehand, and in doing so, pierced the amniotic sac and caused the loss of a substantial amount of amniotic fluid. As a result, the pregnancy had to be terminated at 20–21 weeks.

The applicant and her partner lodged a criminal complaint concerning the unintentional homicide of her child, but this was not successful. She complained before the Court that the refusal of the authorities to classify the taking of her child's life as a homicide offence was contrary to the obligation to prevent and punish the taking of life under Article 2. In doing so, she argued that the term 'everyone' in Article 2 of the Convention should be interpreted to mean human beings rather than individuals with the attributes of legal personality, and as such, all forms of abortion, except for therapeutic, were incompatible with Article 2 as an interference with the right to life of the child. On the contrary, the government argued that 'neither metaphysics nor medicine had given a definitive answer to the question whether and from what moment a foetus was a human being'.[62] However, from a legal standpoint, the government argued that the answer was clear: Article 2 did not protect the right to life of the foetus as a person.

The Grand Chamber surveyed the existing jurisprudence, and concluded that the unborn child is not a 'person' directly protected by Article 2, and that if it did have the right to life, it must be implicitly limited by the mother's rights and interests. However, it did not rule out the possibility of certain safeguards being extended to it. Indeed, the

[61] (53924/00) 08.07.2004 (GC).
[62] ibid., para. 51.

Court acknowledged that the issue had always been decided by weighing up the rights and freedoms of the woman in relation to the unborn child.

Turning to the case at hand, the Court considered whether it was 'advisable' to intervene in the debate as to who is a person, and when life begins, concluding that it was not. Given the lack of European consensus, and the fact that such issues have often not been resolved within the states themselves, the question of when the right to life begins comes within the margin of appreciation of domestic authorities. For this reason, the Court concluded 'that it is neither desirable, nor even possible as matters stand, to answer in the abstract the question whether the unborn child is a person for the purposes of Article 2 of the Convention'.[63] It recognised that the foetus belongs to the human race, has the potential and capacity to become a person, and requires protection in the name of human dignity, but was not willing to go one step further and declare it a 'person'.[64]

Judge Rozakis, who issued a separate opinion,[65] criticised the Court for refusing to draw the opposite conclusion—that based on the present state of development of science, law, and morals in Europe, the right to life of an unborn child is not recognised. He argued that even if one accepts that life begins before birth, this does not necessarily confer on this form of life rights corresponding to those enjoyed by a child after birth. It is possible to recognise some protection of certain attributes, which is distinct from, and narrower than, the protection of rights given post-natally.

On the other hand, Judge Costa[66] *would* have found Article 2 applicable. He argued that although there is no consensus amongst ethicists as to what is a person, and who is entitled to the right to life, it is the task of lawyers and judges to interpret the relevant legal instruments. The Court should deal with the terms 'everyone' and the 'right to life' in the same way as it has dealt with other undefined technical concepts under the Convention, such as 'civil rights and obligations', 'criminal charges', and 'tribunals'. He saw 'no good legal reason or decisive policy consideration' for not applying Article 2 to an unborn child. He argued that there is life before birth, and the law must protect this, and if domestic authorities believe that this protection cannot be absolute, then it should only derogate from it within a regulated framework that limits the scope of the derogation.

Likewise Judge Ress, in his dissenting opinion, found that 'the failure to give a clear answer [on whether the foetus is protected under Article 2] can no longer be justified by reasons of procedural economy. Nor can the problem of protecting the embryo through the Convention be solved solely through the protection of the mother's life. As this case illustrates, the embryo and the mother, as two separate "human beings", need separate protection.'[67] He argued that although the structure of Article 2 appears to indicate that rights are only accrued after birth, the aim of the Convention is to provide extended protection. Moreover, the foetus has been recognised as enjoying protection—for example, under Article 8(2), where it has been acknowledged that

[63] ibid., para. 85.

[64] ibid., para. 84.

[65] Joined by Judges Caflisch, Fischbach, Lorenzen, and Thomassen.

[66] Joined by Judge Traja.

[67] *Vo v France* (53924/00) 08.07.2004 (GC), dissenting opinion of Judge Ress, para. 3.

the state has a legitimate interest in limiting the number of abortions.[68] Judge Ress, like Judge Costa and also Judge Mularoni,[69] further argued that the Court and domestic authorities have already implicitly recognised that the foetus contains some rights under Article 2, evidenced by the emphasis of the Court in numerous decisions on the fair balance between the interests of the mother and that of society (that is, the protection of the unborn child). Such a balance would not be necessary, they argued, if Article 2 did not apply to the unborn child. This line of argument seems to confuse the idea of legal rights, enforceable by an individual against the state, and legal interests—for example, legitimate interests that can be pursued by the state to promote a 'good' society. These judges seem to suggest that the foetus has some legal rights, but that they are not the same as those which are acquired after birth. However, they do not explain what these rights may be, or how they would be limited.

And it is in this unsatisfactory state at which the jurisprudence still stands. The foetus does not have rights, but it does not *not* have rights. This is not helped by the multitude of dissenting and concurring opinions issued in cases concerning abortion, all of which support a different method of reasoning, and a different balance between mother, foetus, and society as a whole. Given recent legal movement in Europe in this area,[70] it seems certain that this issue will again arise before the Court in the not-too-distant future.

7.3.2 Effective access to abortion

What is clear is that where abortion *is* permitted, individuals should not be prevented from accessing a lawful procedure, and there must be effective access to reliable and accurate information on its availability and the procedures to be followed.

This arose in the case of *P and S v Poland*,[71] concerning a 14-year-old girl who had fallen pregnant as a result of a rape. In order to obtain an abortion under Polish law, she was required to apply for a certificate from the public prosecutor stating that the pregnancy had resulted from unlawful sexual intercourse. Although she obtained this, she subsequently encountered substantial difficulties in getting access to an abortion. She and her mother received contradictory information from two different hospitals as to who could perform the abortion, who could make a decision, whether there was a waiting period, and whether there were any other conditions that needed to be fulfilled. She was taken to see a Catholic priest, who tried to convince her to change her mind, and was placed in a juvenile shelter, relying on allegations that her mother was pressuring her to have an abortion. While the abortion was eventually performed, the girl and her mother complained that there had been a violation of Article 8 with regard to her inability to access a lawful abortion, and Article 3, in that she had been subjected to inhuman and degrading treatment throughout the process.

[68] *Odièvre v France* (42326/98) 13.02.2003 (GC).
[69] Joined by Judge Strážnická.
[70] In particular, the lifting of the constitutional restriction on abortion in Ireland, and the recent liberalisation of abortion laws in Northern Ireland.
[71] (57375/08) 30.10.2012.

The Court found that while there is no right to abortion, where it is permitted, this right must be accessible in a way that is practical and effective, not theoretical or illusory. The state is under a positive obligation under Article 8 to create a legal framework that will enable a pregnant woman to effectively exercise her right of access to this lawful treatment, which was not present in this case.[72] Furthermore, with regards to Article 3, the Court noted the considerable pressure placed on the girl not to have an abortion. It considered that the age of the child was of 'cardinal importance', and that she had been in a situation of great vulnerability following a forcible rape. Various persons tried to exert pressure on her, a situation which the authorities not only failed to protect her from, but further compounded. As such, she had been subjected to inhuman and degrading treatment.

This is an important judgment in that it provides procedural protection for vulnerable individuals to ensure they are able to effectively exercise their rights. In the field of abortion, where there are many competing—and very active—interest groups trying to influence—or indeed intimidate—those seeking access to lawful treatment, this ruling provides a measure of protection. As the Court recognised, this is especially important for children seeking abortions, who are in a particular situation of vulnerability, on account of their age, the nature of the situation they are in, and the remedy they seek.

7.4 The right to a healthy environment

Drafted in the 1950s and focusing as it does on civil and political rights, the Convention is not well suited to address environmental concerns. Nevertheless, the Court has considered a variety of complaints in this area, ranging from noise from wind turbines[73] and air traffic[74] to passive smoking in detention,[75] water supply contamination,[76] electromagnetic fields caused by power lines,[77] and exposure to nuclear radiation[78]—with varying success.

The only case that has directly related to children, however, has been *López Ostra v Spain*,[79] which recognised that the right to a healthy environment is included in the concept of the right to respect for private and family life under Article 8. In this case, a plant for the treatment of liquid and solid waste was built 12 metres from the house where the applicant lived with her two children, which, owing to a malfunction, released gas fumes, pestilential smells, and contamination, causing health problems and nuisance. The authorities eventually rehoused local residences, but not before the

[72] See also *Tysiąc v Poland* (5410/03) 20.03.2007; *ABC v Ireland* (25579/05) 16.12.2010 (GC); *RR v Poland* (27617/04) 26.05.2011.

[73] *Fägerskiöld v Sweden* (37664/04) 26.02.2008 (dec.).

[74] See, for example, *Powell and Rayner v the United Kingdom* (9310/81) 21.02.1990; *Hatton and others v the United Kingdom* (36022/97) 08.07.2003 (GC).

[75] See, for example, the cases on passive smoking while in detention: *Florea v Romania* (37186/03) 14.09.2019; *Elefteriadis v Romania* (38427/05) 25.01.2011.

[76] *Dzemyuk v Ukraine* (42488/02) 04.09.2014.

[77] *Calancea and others v the Republic of Moldova* (23225/05) 06.02.2018 (dec.)

[78] *LBC v the United Kingdom* (23413/94) 09.06.1998.

[79] (16798/90) 09.12.1994.

child had suffered significant health problems, including nausea, vomiting, allergic reactions, and anorexia, which could only be explained by the pollution from the plant.

The Court observed that '[n]aturally, severe environmental pollution may affect individuals' well-being and prevent them from enjoying their homes in a way as to affect their private and family life adversely, without, however, seriously endangering their health.'[80] The only question was the responsibility of the authorities. In this case, the town council had permitted the plant to be built on their land, and had subsidised its construction. They were aware of the problems that it was causing, and yet failed to take adequate measures to protect the applicant and her family from these. While the Court recognised the state's interest in the town's economic wellbeing, in the form of having a waste-treatment plant, the authorities had failed to strike an appropriate balance between this interest and the right to respect for home and private life.

This was a very conservative judgment—the only mention of the environmental aspect of the case was in the passage quoted in the previous paragraph. Nor was there any discussion—or even reference to—the vulnerability of children to harm as a result of an unhealthy environment, nor of the potential impact of this on their development. Instead, the Court focused on the procedural and planning aspects of the case.

As such, and despite many applications being submitted, this area remains a missed opportunity for the Court. Of course, it is severely limited by the text of the Convention, both the content and the individualism of the rights contained therein hampering its ability to respond to collective environmental concerns. Nevertheless, there is scope for a more progressive position than the Court has been willing to take.

7.5 Property rights

One of only two socio-economic rights explicitly recognised in the text of the Convention is the right to property in Article 1, Protocol 1,[81] which states:

> Every natural or legal person is entitled to the peaceful enjoyment of his possessions. No one shall be deprived of his possessions except in the public interest and subject to the conditions provided for by law and by the general principles of international law.
>
> The preceding provisions shall not, however, in any way impair the right of a State to enforce such laws as it deems necessary to control the use of property in accordance with the general interest or to secure the payment of taxes or other contributions or penalties.

However, issues concerning property and financial obligations can also fall under Article 8—for example, in relation to the expectation of inheritance, or the requirement to pay child maintenance—as well as Article 6 and the right to a fair trial for the protection of such interests.

[80] ibid., para. 51.
[81] The other being the right to education in Article 2, Protocol 1.

7.5.1 Misuse of children's property

The Court has put in place strong safeguards for protection of children's property. This protection not only relates to guarantees to prevent misuse of their property by parents or guardians, but also to ensuring effective remedies where this has occurred.

This was seen in the case of *Lazarev and Lazarev v Russia*,[82] brought by a father who had invested in property and vested the title jointly in his own name and that of his son. When he wished to sell the property, he was prevented from doing so, as the guardianship authority—whose approval was needed—decided that the sale would result in the reduction of the child's property, and therefore would not be in his interests. The father complained to the Court that this restriction interfered with his right to dispose of his property, in violation of Article 1, Protocol 1. Absurdly, the child was also joined as an applicant, with his father as his legal representative, meaning that the 'child' was complaining about his father's inability to deprive him of his property.

The Court held that the restriction pursued the legitimate aim of protecting the child's right to housing: the primary concern of the authorities was to safeguard the child's possessions to the maximum extent possible until he came of age. In the particular context of the Russian real-estate market, the Court noted that children and elderly people were the prime targets of fraudulent transactions concerning their property, making the interest worthy of enhanced protection. This protection applied no matter how these possessions had been obtained: whether by gift, inheritance, or for consideration. As a result, the Court declared the application inadmissible.

Conversely, in *SL and JL v Croatia*,[83] the Court found a violation of Article 1, Protocol 1 where the authorities had failed to provide this robust protection for a child's property. In this case, the children's parent and guardian had agreed to swap the children's property for one of much lower value. Although, as in Russia, the property transaction also had to be approved by the authorities, they had failed to undertake this assessment with the necessary diligence. By 'fail[ing] to evaluate whether the circumstances of the real estate swap agreement complied with the principle of the best interests of the child',[84] the authorities had violated their rights under Article 1, Protocol 1.

The Court has also made clear that children must be afforded an opportunity to challenge misuse of their property once they have come of age. In *Stagno v Belgium*,[85] the children had been paid sums of money as beneficiaries of their father's life insurance policy. The children's mother—as the statutory executor of her children's property—placed the money in accounts for them, but emptied these within a year. When the children came of age, they brought an action against the insurance company,[86] but this was dismissed, as there was a three-year limitation period on any claim arising from an insurance policy. This was held to apply despite the fact that the children had been aged nine and ten when the situation occurred, with their mother—that

[82] (16153/03) 24.11.2005 (dec.).
[83] (13712/11) 07.05.2015.
[84] ibid., para. 83.
[85] (1062/07) 07.07.2009.
[86] They also brought an action against their mother, but this was later dropped.

is, the person who misused their money—being the only legal representative through whom they could have asserted their rights. The Court held that the time bar on claims put the interests of the insurance company first, making it practically impossible for the applicants to defend their property rights, in violation of Article 6.

7.5.2 Inheritance

A second strand of jurisprudence concerning children's property rights relates to inheritance. There is no right to inherit recognised under the Convention, and therefore the cases in this area have been argued in the context of Article 14—namely, the protection from discrimination against children born outside wedlock—and either Article 1, Protocol 1 or Article 8. The difference between these two provisions is important: while Article 1, Protocol 1 only relates to a person's existing possessions and not to their right to acquire possessions in the future, the Court has held that matters of intestate succession between near relatives are intimately connected with family life under Article 8.[87] As such, Article 1, Protocol 1 will only be applicable where the family member is deceased, and the inheritance allocated, while Article 8 can be invoked where the division of assets is prospective.

The leading case in this area is *Marckx v Belgium*,[88] which concerned the requirement that the mother 'recognise' her child born out of wedlock before legal ties were established. One of the consequences of this was that before recognition, the child would have no rights on intestacy. Even once the child was recognised as an 'illegitimate' child, their rights would be less than a 'legitimate' child of the mother. Further, recognition established a legal bond with the mother alone—the child did not become a member of the mother's family, and was excluded from inheritance rights on intestacy from, for example, grandparents. In a landmark judgment, the Court made clear that Article 8 does not entitle a child to some share in the estate of his or her parents (or near relatives), but where the legal system provides such a right, it must be implemented in a non-discriminatory manner. By distinguishing between children born within, and outside, wedlock, the measure was in violation of Article 14 in conjunction with Article 8.[89]

Despite this clear judgment over 40 years ago, governments have continued to attempt to justify differential treatment between 'legitimate' and 'illegitimate' children—none of which have been successful. In *Inze v Austria*,[90] the law required that farms of a certain size not be divided in cases of intestate succession, and one of the heirs must take over the entire property, paying off the others. When choosing which heir should take over, the 'legitimate' heir was given precedence. This was justified on the grounds that legitimate children were more likely to live with their family on the farm, and corresponded to what could be presumed to be the intentions of the deceased. The Court dismissed these arguments, finding that they relied on general and abstract

[87] *Marckx v Belgium* (6833/74) 13.06.1979.
[88] ibid.
[89] See also *Vermeire v Belgium* (12849/87) 29.11.1991.
[90] (8695/79) 28.10.1987.

considerations, and reflected traditional assumptions of family life which may not correspond to the reality of the situation. As such, there had been a breach of Article 14 in conjunction with Article 1, Protocol 1.

While the government in *Inze* at least tried to provide practical justifications for the difference in treatment, in other cases, the discrimination has been more direct. In *Mazurek v France*,[91] the reasoning behind apportioning an 'illegitimate' child half of what he would have been entitled to if he were 'legitimate' was the 'protection of the traditional family'. The Court accepted that this aim was legitimate, but found that the government had failed to show that the difference in treatment was proportionate and appropriate to achieving this aim. Noting the clear trend towards the abolition of discrimination in relation to children born out of wedlock, the Court held that there was no good reason to differentiate based on the circumstances of birth. An illegitimate child could not be punished for events that were not his fault.

The most interesting part of this case is the joint dissenting opinion of Judges Loucaides and Tulkens. While they agreed with the majority concerning a violation of the Convention, they argued that the case should not have been considered as a matter purely under Article 1, Protocol 1, but should have instead also considered Article 8. The applicant had in fact argued his case on the grounds of the latter article, on the basis that the dispute was not about being deprived of money, but about the denigration of the bonds of kinship he had with his mother. He did not want to reduce the issue to a merely pecuniary issue, but wished to complain of the discriminatory status given to 'illegitimate' children. By confining itself to the consequences of status, rather than the status itself, the judges argued that the majority had failed to get to the crux of the issue at hand. The case was about the legal equality of rights conferred by descent, not merely the material equality in the division of an estate.

A third justification put forward by governments for not providing equal inheritance is a practical one, based on the protection of other heirs. Where the estate has already been divided, authorities have emphasised the need to ensure that these heirs do not have their possessions queried many years later when someone comes out of the woodwork to make a claim. The Court has acknowledged that this is a legitimate aim, but has interpreted it strictly: where the other heirs were aware of the child's existence at the time of division, and knew that this might be challenged, then they will not later be able to claim that their rights have been violated. For example, in *Fabris v France*,[92] the applicant was an 'illegitimate' child, whose mother and her husband had distributed their property *inter vivos* between their two 'legitimate' children, while retaining a life interest. After the death of the mother and her husband many years later, the applicant sought a share of the estate, but this was rejected on the grounds that a donation made so long ago could not be challenged. The applicant's complaint under Article 14 in conjunction with Article 1, Protocol 1 was rejected by the Chamber, on the grounds that when the applicant brought his case before the French courts, there had already been an established legal situation in existence for 28 years, and the legitimate aim of guaranteeing legal certainty outweighed the potential discrimination

[91] (34406/97) 01.02.2000. See also *Merger and Cros v France* (68864/01) 22.12.2004.
[92] (16574/08) 21.07.2011 (Ch); (16574/08) 07.02.2013 (GC).

against illegitimate children. This was reversed by the Grand Chamber, on the basis that the other children knew that their rights were liable to be challenged, as they knew that the applicant had been recognised by the courts as their mother's 'illegitimate' child. Moreover, the expectations of heirs who were beneficiaries of *inter vivos* divisions were not, in any case, protected in all circumstances: a legitimate child who was excluded or born after the division would have had a claim. As a result, the legitimate aim of protecting the rights of the half-siblings, and of legal certainty, did not outweigh the applicant's claim to a part of his mother's estate.[93] Likewise, in *Brauer v Germany*,[94] the Court noted that the aim of protecting 'legitimate expectation' must be subordinate to the imperative of equal treatment.[95]

The majority of cases before the Court have concerned succession where the family member has died intestate. However, this does not mean that voluntary distribution is outside the jurisdiction of the Court. *Pla and Puncernau v Andorra*[96] concerned an adopted child, who could not inherit from his paternal grandmother. Her will left the estate to her son, on the basis that he was to pass on his inheritance to a child or grandchild 'from a legitimate and canonical marriage'. The domestic courts held that an adopted child did not fit this description, on the grounds that by choosing not to expressly include adopted children, she must have intended to exclude them.

Before the Court, the government argued that the difference in treatment was not the result of government action, but the private and free will of a testatrix, who had been entirely at liberty to dispose of her property as she wished. This was rejected by the Court, who found that the issue was not the grandmother's free will, but the interpretation of the testamentary will by the domestic courts. The Court noted that adopted children were in the same legal position as a biological child in all respects, and as with cases concerning 'illegitimate' children, any difference in treatment must be justified. However, the government had not put forward any legitimate aim, nor any justification for the difference in treatment, resulting in a violation of Article 14 in conjunction with Article 8.

Thus the issue of inheritance has been an important driver of the jurisprudence that has abolished discrimination on the basis of birth throughout Europe. Given the authoritative judgment of *Marckx* was decided over 40 years ago, it is indeed surprising that there have been so many subsequent cases, where states attempted to circumvent

[93] See also *Camp and Bourimi v Netherlands* (28369/95) 03.10.2000; *Quilichini v France* (38299/15) 14.03.2019.

[94] (3545/04) 28.05.2009.

[95] This case concerned a child outside of marriage in the German Democratic Republic (GDR) in 1948. Upon reunification, equal inheritance rights were only provided for children born after 1949, or for children whose parents were living in the GDR at the time of reunification (which her father was not): see also *Mitzinger v Germany* (29762/10) 09.02.2017. On the other hand, the importance of legal certainty has been used to the advantage of the applicant child when concerning challenges to paternity for the purposes of inheritance rights. In *TÇ and HÇ v Turkey* (34805/06) 26.07.2011, the Court found that there had been a breach of Article 8 where the authorities had permitted a challenge to a child's paternity after her father's death, and outside the legal time limit, which thus affected his inheritance rights. It held that a balance must be struck between the interests of a child to maintain a family relationship with his or her father with the inheritance rights of the other family members, which the Turkish authorities failed to achieve in this case.

[96] (69498/01) 13.07.2004.

the clear rules laid down by the Court—nevertheless, it is hoped that we have now seen the last of this pernicious form of discrimination.

7.5.3 Child maintenance

The final area of jurisprudence concerning children that comes within the scope of Article 1, Protocol 1 relates not to the property of children, but to financial obligations with respect of them. The allocation, quantification, and taxation of child maintenance has been the subject of several cases—predominantly against the United Kingdom—and applicants have tried to argue violations of their rights under Articles 6 and 8, as well as under Article 1, Protocol 1. So far, however, none of these challenges has been successful.

In the first case of this kind, *Burrows v the United Kingdom*,[97] the Commission made clear that requiring payment of child maintenance cannot, in principle, be considered contrary to Article 1, Protocol 1. Legislation governing private relationships between individuals may legitimately include rules which determine the effect of legal relations with respect to property, including compelling a person to surrender possession to another. However, it is the role of the Court to make sure that in doing so, the law does not create such inequality that a person could be seen to be arbitrarily deprived of their property in favour of another. The Commission found that child support measures are not intended solely for the benefit of the children, but also for the benefit of the taxpayer, who bears the burden of paying for single parents who claim social welfare benefits. As such, the aim of reducing taxation and increasing parental responsibility must be considered as in the public interest, for the purposes of Article 1, Protocol 1.

Likewise, a claim under Article 8 is also difficult. When assessing whether there had been interference with family life, the Commission in *Logan v the United Kingdom*[98] found that legislation that seeks to regulate the assessment of maintenance payments does not by its very nature affect family life under Article 8. It is up to the applicant to show that the effect of the operation of the legislation is of such a nature and degree to disclose a lack of respect for his rights. Here, the applicant had argued that the level of maintenance payments was assessed at such a high rate that he could only afford to visit his children once a month, but this was dismissed by the Commission in light of the factual information provided to it. Likewise, in *Burrows*, the Commission found that it was not disproportionate for the applicant to be required to pay 20 per cent of his gross income in child support, taking into account the amount of disposable income he would be left with.

Relying on Article 6, *Logan* also complained that there was no redress for individuals who have been found liable to make a contribution to request for it to be revised in light of their personal circumstances. The relevant tribunal was only able to consider whether the assessment was made correctly within the terms of the legislation, but could not consider the merits of his claim to a lower payment level. The Commission

[97] (27558/95) 27.11.1996 (dec.).
[98] (24875/94) 06.09.1996 (dec.).

emphasised that Article 6 applies only to disputes over rights and obligations which can be said to be recognised under domestic law. In this case, the legislation did not give any scope for costs of access visits to be taken into account, which formed the basis for the applicant's claim for revision. As such, there was no discernible dispute as to a civil right or obligation under domestic law.

The only cases in which there has been any measure of success in the area of child maintenance is where Article 14 has been invoked. In *PM v the United Kingdom*,[99] the applicant complained that although he was under the same obligation to pay child maintenance as a married father, as an unmarried father he was not granted access to the same tax deductions for child maintenance payments. The Court found that there was no reason for treating the applicant any differently from a married father who was now divorced and paying child maintenance for the purposes of tax deductibility of child maintenance. The financial obligation towards the child was the same in each case, and therefore the treatment for tax purposes should be also.

Similarly, in *JM v the United Kingdom*,[100] the applicant was a non-resident parent, liable for child support. If she were living with a new partner in an opposite-sex relationship, her liability for child support would be adjusted—and in her case, reduced[101]—however, the same did not apply for a same-sex partner. The Court found that her maintenance obligation was assessed differently on account of the nature of her new relationship, and thus there had been a difference of treatment on the grounds of sexual orientation. Bearing in mind the purpose of the law, which was to avoid placing excessive financial burdens on the absent parent in their new circumstances, the Court found that there was no reason for treating same-sex and opposite-sex relationships differently.

This does not mean, however, that all differences in treatment are unjustified. In *Burrows*, the father complained that as part of a group of 'separated and second parents' he was subject to a 'hidden method of taxation using a formula and code', which other people were not. The Commission swiftly dismissed this suggestion. It found that the father was seeking to compare himself with taxpayers in general, who were neither separated parents nor second parents, but these groups could not be seen to be in analogous situations. Parents have a responsibility for their children, including a financial responsibility, that taxpayers who are not parents do not have, and as such, the complaint was inadmissible.

The final aspect of child maintenance that has arisen before the Court is in relation to enforcement mechanisms for payments. In *Battista v Italy*,[102] a father was ordered to hand over his passport on the grounds that he was not making maintenance payments, and there was a risk that he would shirk his obligation completely if he were to travel abroad. Relying on Article 2, Protocol 4, which provides that everyone is free to leave any country, including their own, he complained that his freedom of movement had been violated. The Court found that the domestic authorities had not considered

[99] (6638/03) 19.07.2005.
[100] (37060/06) 28.09.2010.
[101] For the purposes of calculating her housing costs, her opposite-sex partner would be taken into account.
[102] (43978/09) 02.12.2014.

the applicant's personal situation, and his ability to pay the sums due, before removing his passport. The measure had been made automatically, and was of indefinite duration, and there had been no consideration of the various means by which debt could be recovered across national borders. As such, the removal of his passport could not be seen to be necessary in a democratic society to protect the property interests of his wife and children.

Battista can be contrasted with the more recent case of *Torresi v Italy*,[103] where the applicant was unable to obtain a passport for over six months because of a failure to make maintenance payments. Unlike *Battista*, the domestic authorities considered the specific situation of the applicant and his ability to pay on a number of occasions, reviewing this in order to ensure that the measure continued to be proportionate. Moreover, the authorities had emphasised the difficulty of recovering maintenance payments outside Europe, noting that Mr Torresi was likely to go to China. The removal of his passport was thus neither automatic nor indefinite, and had been accompanied by sufficient safeguards as to comply with the requirements of Article 2, Protocol 4.

7.5.4 Conclusions on property rights for children

The Court's jurisprudence on the property rights of children is not extensive, but what there is so far is positive. In particular, the case law surrounding inheritance has had a significant impact for children born out of wedlock, going far beyond the domain of property rights, even if the Court has failed to take the final step and recognise that the issue is not simply an economic one, but also a social one. However, as an economic right, and one enshrined in the Convention itself, it is not surprising that the Court has been able to take a strong position on these issues. Where the rights in question are social, however, it has been more of an uphill battle.

7.6 Social security and social welfare

The protection given by the Convention to social security and social welfare measures is unsurprisingly very scant. The Court has consistently maintained that in matters concerning general measures of economic or social strategy, states will enjoy a wide margin of appreciation, as they have direct knowledge of their society and its needs, and will therefore be better placed to determine what is in the public interest on social or economic grounds. As a result, the Court will generally respect the choice of the domestic authorities unless it is 'manifestly without reasonable foundation'.[104]

While this is a high hurdle to pass, applicants have been more successful when bringing a claim under Article 14, following a difference in treatment between different groups of applicants for state benefits. The Court has maintained that the wide

[103] (68957/16) 17.12.2020 (dec.).

[104] See *Dhahbi v Italy* (17120/09) 08.04.2014; *Fábián v Hungary* (78117/13) 05.09.2017 (GC); *JD and A v the United Kingdom* (32949/17, 34614/17) 24.10.2019.

margin of appreciation given to states in the sphere of economic and social policy cannot justify laws or practices that discriminate on protected grounds. In particular, a difference in treatment on the grounds of gender, nationality, or disability will require particularly weighty justification.[105]

7.6.1 Parental leave and allowances

Maternity leave is recognised as a fundamental right by the European Social Charter,[106] intended 'both to grant employed women protection in the case of maternity and to reflect a more general interest in public health'.[107] The Charter also requires that states provide a period of parental leave, available to either parent,[108] with the intention of ensuring that all persons with family responsibilities can engage in employment without discrimination, and as far as possible without conflict between work and family. This inclusion in the European Social Charter, however, does not mean that these rights are wholly outside the jurisdiction of the Court. While the Court has refused to recognise a positive obligation on states to provide financial assistance to parents, or indeed any period of leave,[109] it has nevertheless examined these issues through the lens of Article 14—that is, asking whether there has been discrimination in restricting any benefits that are provided to women only.

The Court initially took a very conservative approach in this regard. In the first case of this kind to come before the Court—*Petrovic v Austria*,[110] decided in 1998—it held that the state had a wide margin of appreciation when deciding whether to extend a parental leave allowance to a father. The Court distinguished between maternity leave and associated allowances—which are primary intended to allow the mother to recover from childbirth—and parental leave and allowances—which are intended to allow the parent to stay at home to care for the infant. The Court started from the premise that mothers and fathers are similarly placed so far as taking care of the child during this period is concerned, and that very weighty reasons would be needed for such a difference in treatment to be compatible with the Convention. Nevertheless, it emphasised that there was no common standard in this field in Europe. While it noted the evolution of social attitudes in this regard, and found that society is gradually moving towards a more equal sharing of child-rearing responsibilities, it observed that the majority of contracting states did not provide for parental leave allowances to be paid to fathers. As such, Austria had not exceeded its margin of appreciation by expanding parental entitlements in a gradual manner.

[105] *Konstantin Markin v Russia* (30078/06) 22.03.2012 (GC); *Guberina v Croatia* (23682/13) 22.03.2016.

[106] Article 8, European Social Charter (Revised) (1996) CETS 163.

[107] European Committee of Social Rights, *Digest of the Case Law of the European Committee of Social Rights* (Strasbourg: Council of Europe, 2018), 116.

[108] Article 27(2), European Social Charter (Revised) (1996) CETS 163.

[109] See *Hasani v Croatia* (20844/09) 30.09.2010 (dec.), where the Court held that the state had not breached a mother's rights under Article 1, Protocol 1 when it reduced the statutory entitlement to maternity leave from three years to one year, cutting short her period of leave and allowances. It noted that a period of one year 'appears satisfactory', and it could not be said that the very essence of her right to maternity allowance (established by statute) was impaired.

[110] (20458/92) 27.03.1998.

The beginnings of a shift in the Court's approach was seen in the 2000s, with cases like *Niedzwiecki v Germany*,[111] where a violation was found in relation to a refusal to grant child benefits to a father on a limited residence permit, in contrast to parents who had more permanent visas. Likewise, in *Weller v Hungary*,[112] the refusal to provide to the father a benefit that was available to mothers, adoptive parents, and guardians, was found to be discriminatory.[113] However, in neither of these cases was it a straight comparison between benefits available to mothers and fathers: the discrimination was based on immigration status (*Niedzwiecki*) and parental status (*Weller*), rather than on sex.

It was therefore not until 2012, in the case of *Konstantin Markin v Russia*,[114] that this issue was confronted head on, and *Petrovic* was relegated to history. In this case, the applicant was employed as a military serviceman,[115] and following a divorce from his wife, it was agreed that the children—including a newborn baby—would live with him. He requested three years' parental leave from his unit, which was rejected, as this duration of leave could only be granted to female personnel.

Before the Court, the government argued that it was in the child's best interests for the mother to take parental leave, as there exists a special biological and psychological connection between a newborn child and their mother. As in *Petrovic*, the Court distinguished maternity leave—for which such considerations would be important—from parental leave, in relation to which both parents were similarly placed. However, it went on to note the significant social and legal advances made in Europe since that decision, which had moved towards equality between men and women with regard to childrearing. In this light, the Court emphasised that difference in treatment cannot be justified by reference to general assumptions or prevailing social attitudes, nor can gender stereotypes—such as the perception of women as primary child-carers and men as primary breadwinners—be relied on for this purpose. Moreover, the Court rejected the argument that restricting parental leave to women was a form of positive discrimination. This treatment, it held, was clearly not intended to correct the disadvantaged position of women in society, but instead had 'the effect of perpetuating gender stereotypes, which is disadvantageous both to women's careers and to men's family life'.[116] In light of this, the Court found that there had been a violation of Article 14 in conjunction with Article 8.

[111] (58453/00) 25.10.2005. See also *Okpisz v Germany* (59140/00) 25.10.2005.

[112] (44399/05) 31.03.2009.

[113] See also *Topčić-Rosenberg v Croatia* (19391/11) 14.11.2013, where the Court held that a refusal to grant an adoptive mother parental leave on the same basis as a biological mother amounted to discrimination under Article 14 in conjunction with Article 8.

[114] (30078/06) 22.03.2012 (GC). See also *Hulea v Romania* (33411/05) 02.10.2012.

[115] Considerable emphasis was placed by the government on the nature of the applicant's work in this case, arguing that military service imposes specific demands on individuals, and taking parental leave by servicemen on a large scale would have a negative effect on the fighting power of the armed forces. The Court accepted that the rights of military personnel may in certain circumstances be restricted to a greater degree than would be possible in relation to private individuals, but that any restrictions must still meet the test of necessity in a democratic society. The government had failed to show that there was a real threat to the operational effectiveness of the armed forces if parental leave was granted to men.

[116] *Konstantin Markin v Russia* (30078/06) 22.03.2012 (GC), para. 141.

While this was a landmark judgment, Judge Pinto de Albuquerque did not feel that it went far enough, arguing that parental leave should be recognised as a freestanding Convention right derived directly from Article 8, which exists independently of any discriminatory infringement of Article 14. It does not only fall within the 'scope' of Article 8, through the promotion of family life, he argued, but is rather a fundamental right that belongs to the core of the human rights of the family. As a result, he considered that Article 8 places a positive obligation on contracting parties to provide for a legal system of parental leave.

While Judge Pinto de Albuquerque was a lone voice in this partly concurring opinion, it is likely to foreshadow the future trajectory of the Court in this area. There is no doubt that this is the direction the law is now developing, and it is only a matter of when, not if. Having said this, this case must be read in the context of parental leave only—a gender-neutral concept. The Court still permits a difference of treatment in relation to specifically gendered types of leave, recognising motherhood and fatherhood as distinct concepts, with different roles to play.[117] For example, in *Hallier and others v France*,[118] the Court drew a distinction between legal fathers and an individual who is the mother's partner, but not a legal parent. This case concerned a same-sex couple, who jointly decided to have a child. When one of them gave birth, her partner applied for paternity leave, but this was denied on the ground that paternity leave could not be granted to a woman. The Court found that the partner was in a comparable situation to a biological father in an opposite-sex couple, but nevertheless found that the difference in treatment did not violate Article 14 in conjunction with Article 8. Paternity leave, they held, was intended to allow fathers to play a great role in their children's lives, and promote a more equal distribution of domestic tasks between men and woman. Moreover, the Court noted that the partner was not a 'parent' of the child, and a man in a similar position, who was not the child's father, would equally not be eligible for paternity leave.

What is noticeable in this case, as with the ones that precede it, is the focus on the entitlement of *parents* to leave and benefits, with little recognition of the rights of children in this regard. This was discussed briefly in *Weller*, where the benefits would have been available to a family comprising a Hungarian mother and foreign father, but not where the father was Hungarian and the mother was foreign. The Court noted that this unjustifiably excluded the children from receiving the benefit of the financial assistance, but this was tacked on as an afterthought, rather than as part of the primary examination of the case. The only real examination of the issue from the perspective of children's rights was by Judge Pinto de Albuquerque in *Konstantin Markin*, who pointed out that parental leave is 'an essential guarantee of the bond between a parent and his or her child at a time of particular vulnerability and special need for the child'.[119] He highlighted the empirical evidence regarding the benefits of parental leave

[117] On this point see also *Alexandru Enache v Romania* (16986/12) 03.10.2017, where the applicant father was sentenced to seven years imprisonment when his child was only a few months old. He applied to defer his sentence to be able to look after the child until their first birthday, but this was refused on the grounds that this could only be requested by mothers. The Court held that motherhood enjoyed special protection, and thus any difference between male and female prisoners was justified.

[118] (46386/10) 12.12.2017 (dec.).

[119] Partly concurring, partly dissenting opinion of Judge Pinto de Albuquerque.

for children—including its impact on infant mortality rates and children's cognitive and socio-emotional outcomes—and noted that if parental leave were not protected, the well-being of the child would be significantly prejudiced.

7.6.2 Access to state benefits

While the Court has recognised the obligation on the authorities to provide family assistance in some circumstances, for example, where this would prevent the necessity of removing a child from the family home,[120] it has not imposed any free-standing right to financial assistance from the state. This was made clear in the early case of *Andersson v Sweden*,[121] where the Commission rejected an application by a mother who wished to stay and home to care for her children. Her husband worked, but his income was insufficient to support the family, and so they applied to the state for financial assistance. The state offered day-care places to the two children to allow the mother to re-enter the workforce, but this was declined on the grounds that she wished to care for the children herself. The Commission dismissed the claim that the refusal to provide financial support violated the family's right to respect for family life, stating:

> [T]he Convention does not as such guarantee the right to public assistance either in the form of financial support to maintain a certain standard of living, or in the form of supplying day home care places. Nor does the right under Art. 8 of the Convention (art. 8) to respect for family life extend so far as to impose on States a general obligation to provide for financial assistance to individuals in order to enable one of two parents to stay at home to take care of children.

However, while no substantive right to financial assistance exists, where it is granted, certain procedural safeguards surround it: for example, access to an impartial tribunal,[122] expeditious proceedings,[123] and non-discrimination. This final criterion has been argued, with varying levels of success, in relation to family benefits and housing assistance.

On the one hand, where states have limited access to benefits on the basis of nationality, they will have to show weighty justification for doing so. For example, in *Dhahbi v Italy*,[124] the Italian authorities provided financial assistance to large families whose income fell below a certain level, but restricted this to Italian and EU citizens. The applicant, a Tunisian national living in Italy on a work permit, complained that his exclusion from such benefits breached his rights under Article 14 in conjunction with Article 8.[125]

[120] See Chapter 11.
[121] (11776/85) 04.03.1986 (dec.).
[122] See, for example, *Kovachev v Bulgaria* (29303/95) 28.10.1997 (dec.).
[123] See, for example, *Mennitto v Italy* (33804/96) 05.10.2000 (GC).
[124] (17120/09) 08.04.2014.
[125] The benefit fell within the scope of Article 8, as it was directed towards large families and was a way in which the state demonstrated its respect for family life.

The Court noted that the applicant was in the same situation as EU workers—he was working in the country lawfully, and paid national insurance contributions on the same basis. While it acknowledged that the protection of budgetary interests is a legitimate aim, there must be a reasonable relationship of proportionality between the aim and the means employed. Here, nationality was the sole criterion used, without any consideration of the applicant's immigration status, or his contributions to the social welfare system. In this respect, the Court emphasised that the applicant 'did not belong to the category of persons who, as a rule, do not contribute to the funding of the public services and in relation to whom a State may have legitimate reasons for curtailing the use of resource-hungry public services such as social insurance schemes, public benefits and health care.'[126]

Likewise, the Court has emphasised that refugees must be treated equally with citizens with regard to access to social assistance. In *Fawsie v Greece*,[127] the applicant—a Syrian refugee—was refused an allowance paid to mothers of large families, as this was only available to families of Greek or EU citizens, or refugees of Greek origin. The Court noted that the Geneva Convention on the Status of Refugees[128] requires that refugees staying lawfully within a contracting state's territory are given the same treatment with respect to public relief and assistance as nationals, and thus the difference in treatment was not reasonably justified.

On the other hand, where the applicant is an economic migrant, admitted to the jurisdiction on the condition of self-sufficiency, the authorities may be permitted to restrict certain types of state assistance that are in short supply—for example, social housing. This was seen in *Bah v the United Kingdom*,[129] which involved a Sierra Leone national living in the United Kingdom, having been granted indefinite leave to remain. Her son was permitted to join her, on the condition that he did not have recourse to public funds. Shortly after her son's arrival, she was asked to leave the accommodation she was renting. She applied to the authorities for priority treatment in obtaining social housing, as a person who was unintentionally homeless with a minor child, but this was refused as her son could not be taken into account as he was not permitted to have recourse to public funds. She argued that this refusal discriminated against her on the basis of her son's nationality.

The Court emphasised that there is no right under the Convention to be provided with housing, but where the state did make provision for social assistance, it must do so in a non-discriminatory manner. However, it rejected the applicant's claim that the discrimination was based on nationality, finding instead that it was based on immigration status. While such a status also falls within the prohibited grounds of discrimination under Article 14, the Court observed that the nature of the protected status would have an impact on the margin of appreciation given to states. Immigration status, unlike nationality, is subject to an element of choice,[130] and therefore the justification required for difference in treatment does not need to be as weighty. This margin of

[126] *Dhahbi v Italy* (17120/09) 08.04.2014, para. 52 (citations omitted).
[127] (40080/07) 28.10.2010. See also *Saidoun v Greece* (40083/07) 28.10.2010.
[128] United Nations Convention relating to the Status of Refugees (1951) 189 UNTS 137.
[129] (56328/07) 27.09.2011.
[130] At least, where the individual was not a refugee.

appreciation was further widened given the subject matter of the decision in question, which was predominantly socio-economic in nature.

The Court accepted that it was 'legitimate to put in place criteria according to which a benefit such as social housing can be allocated, when there is insufficient supply available to satisfy demand, so long as such criteria are not arbitrary or discriminatory'.[131] In the case at hand, the classes of people eligible for social housing couldn't be considered arbitrary or discriminatory: those who had a fixed right to be in the jurisdiction were entitled to assistance, whilst those whose leave to remain was conditional upon the ability to support themselves were not. The difference in treatment thus pursued a legitimate aim, namely the fair allocation of a scarce resource.[132]

All these cases were brought by adults, albeit concerning benefits relating to their children. This can be contrasted with *Santos Hansen v Denmark*,[133] where the complaint was brought by the child herself. In this case, the applicant had been adopted from Brazil by a Danish national, who, as a single woman, was required to satisfy certain financial conditions before adopting. Upon their return to Denmark, the adoptive mother was granted a 'child subsidy', and an 'extra child subsidy' by the government, but her application for a 'special child subsidy'—available for children where paternity had not been established, or where the father had died—was refused. The applicant child argued that this difference in treatment was unjustified: she was in a comparable situation with these children, as she too only had one financial provider, and should be given access to this benefit on an equal basis.

The Court accepted that the government's policy pursued an objective and reasonable aim: the subsidy was intended to provide for children who only had one legal parent as a result of unforeseen circumstances, or where it was not possible to establish in advance that the mother had sufficient means to support herself and the child. In the case of adoption, the situation was different, as it concerned a planned and approved decision, brought about by the parent's own choice, and where there had been prior verification as to their financial situation. Such a deliberate policy choice formed part of the state's economic and social strategy, and thus fell within the margin of appreciation.

This case epitomises the approach of the Court in this area, where the focus is not on deprivation, but on procedural issues such as equality of treatment. Although the latter rights are, of course, of importance, the Court thus ignores the more fundamental and underlying human rights violations. While this is unsurprising, given the rights recognised by the Convention, it does narrow the scope of the Court's protection to an almost negligible level in this area, leaving social assistance largely to the whim of the state.

[131] *Bah v the United Kingdom* (56328/07) 27.09.2011, para. 49.

[132] See also *Okitaloshima Okonda Osungu and Selpa Lokongo v France* (76860/11, 51354/13) 08.09.2015 (dec.), where the Court accepted that the families had been refused family benefits for their children, as they had entered France unlawfully. The complaint was declared inadmissible—the applicants had the opportunity to regularise their situation and thus obtain the benefits, but had not made any effort to do so.

[133] (17949/07) 09.03.2010 (dec.).

7.7 Conclusion

Currently, the jurisprudence in this area is rather sparse and piecemeal in its approach. While *Marckx* has been critical in the abolition of discrimination on the basis of birth, and *Konstantin Markin* has provided important recognition of shared parental responsibilities, on the whole, social and economic rights have largely been a peripheral issue before the Court.

This may in part stem from the nature of the Convention, which focuses on civil and political rights, leaving socio-economic rights to the control of the European Social Charter. This instrument, which includes, inter alia, the right to a decent standard of living, the right to social security, and the right to benefit from social welfare services, provides more fertile ground for complaints in this area—yet it is not as widely ratified as the Convention, nor is there a right of individual petition to the Committee on Social Rights.[134]

As such, a complete delegation of responsibility for this area of law leaves children in a vulnerable position. Child poverty has been recognised as having a significant impact on children's lives—including, for example, a detrimental effect on physical and mental health, social integration, education, and employment opportunities—and yet there is no mechanism to force states to provide adequate assistance to children and their families. This is a significant challenge for the future of children's rights in Europe—the Court must reaffirm the indivisibility of human rights, and the necessity of interpreting the Convention in an expansive manner. It already does this to a certain extent through the doctrine of positive obligations—requiring, for example, legal assistance be provided in order to achieve a fair trial,[135] financial assistance to be provided before a child is removed from their family,[136] and the obligation to provide accommodation and adequate material conditions to vulnerable groups, such as asylum seekers.[137] However, it can, and must go further.

[134] Although non-governmental organisations may bring a collective complaint, upon which the Committee will pass a resolution: see Part IV, European Social Charter (revised) 1996.
[135] See Chapter 9.
[136] See Chapter 10.
[137] *MSS v Greece* (30696/09) 21.01.2011.

8
Family Formation and Parenthood

8.1 Introduction

The European Convention on Human Rights takes a very conservative approach to family life and the interaction between parents and children under Article 8. It is clear from the *travaux preparatoires* that 'family life' under Article 8 was considered as an adjunct to private life, with the drafters expressing concern that 'the father of a family cannot be an independent citizen, cannot feel free within his own country, if he is menaced in his own home and if, every day, the State steals from him his soul, or the conscience of his children'.[1] This deference to the family unit reflects the historical social importance placed on the autonomy of the family and the preservation of family relations, under which parents are granted the liberty to make decisions as to how best raise their child.[2] Article 8 therefore endorses the family as the fundamental unit in society and upholds the power structure within this unit, insulating it from state interference.

This has a significant effect on the way in which Article 8 has been interpreted in relation to children's rights. As a qualified right, states are permitted to interfere with family life so long as it pursues a legitimate aim and is necessary in a democratic society. In general terms, this entails a balancing process between the rights of the individual and the interests of wider society: that is, national security, public safety, and the prevention of crime; the economic well-being of the country; the protection of health or morals; or the protection of the rights and freedoms of others. For children, however, the equation is more difficult. Between the child, as the rights holder, and the state, as the duty bearer, there is an intermediary with the power to dilute and divert their rights. Children's rights—at least in this area—exist within the bubble of the private sphere, controlled by parents, which must be pierced before they can make a claim on the state or before the state can step in to provide protection.

Having said all this, there is no doubt that the jurisprudence of the Court in the field of family law and parenthood has moved the child rights movement in Europe forward. The prohibition of discrimination on the basis of birth, the right of a child to establish his or her identity, and the recognition of the different family forms in which a child may be living have all flowed from Strasbourg judgments. While it may not

[1] M. Teitgen, Rapporteur of the Committee on Legal and Administrative Questions, Consultative Assembly, *Collected Edition of the Travaux Preparatoires* (The Hague: Martinus Nijhoff, 1975), as quoted in G. Douglas, 'The Family and the State under the European Convention on Human Rights' (1988) 2 *International Journal of Law and the Family* 76, 78.

[2] A.R. Appell and B.A. Boyer, 'Parental Rights vs. Best Interests of the Child: A False Dichotomy in the Context of Adoption' (1995) 2 *Duke Journal of Gender Law and Policy* 63, 64.

Children and the European Court of Human Rights. Claire Fenton-Glynn, Oxford University Press (2021). © Claire Fenton-Glynn.
DOI: 10.1093/oso/9780198787518.003.0008

be the optimum instrument for the promotion of children's rights, it nevertheless has significant value.

8.2 The definition of 'family life'

The concept of 'family life' is not easily defined: as the Court has pointed out, 'the institution of the family is not fixed, be it historically, sociologically or even legally'.[3] As a result, there has been significant jurisprudence concerning the existence, or lack thereof, of 'family life', which is continually being re-evaluated in light of current understandings of the nature of the family unit. Establishing the existence of a 'family' relationship is the crucial first step to applications under Article 8—at least in this field of law[4]—and this section considers how this concept has been defined in relation to the child's different relationships: with their mother, with their father, and with wider relatives.

8.2.1 'Family life' between a mother and child

As with many areas of family law under the Convention, the existence (or not) of 'family life' with a child will be decided on different criteria depending on whether it relates to a mother or a father. While a mother is in a strong—indeed almost unassailable—position from the moment of birth, the father will have to demonstrate either commitment, attachment, or motivation[5] to bring himself within the scope of Article 8.

The position of the mother was established in the landmark case of *Marckx v Belgium*.[6] This case is important not simply for the decision itself (although this *was* significant), but also as it interpreted Article 8 for the first time to encompass the wider fields of family law and succession. In this way, it opened the door for the Court to scrutinise domestic family law in ways not previously seen before—much to the chagrin of the judge from the United Kingdom, Sir Gerald Fitzmaurice. Moreover, the majority interpreted the scope of Article 8 to include not just the protection of the family from outside interference, but also as involving positive obligations requiring the state to act to facilitate 'family life', and to establish legal safeguards that 'render possible as from the moment of birth the child's integration in his family'.[7] As Fitzmaurice argued in his dissenting opinion, this amounted to an introduction of a 'whole code of family law' into Article 8,[8] significantly expanding its influence—though for Fitzmaurice, this was not something to be commended. Commenting on the case 40 years later,

[3] *Mazurek v France* (34406/07) 01.02.2000, para. 52.

[4] Article 8 also provides protection to private life, home, and correspondence, which naturally have a different starting point.

[5] To borrow from domestic English law on parental responsibility.

[6] (6833/74) 13.06.1979.

[7] ibid., para. 31.

[8] ibid., dissenting opinion of Judge Sir Gerald Fitzmaurice, para. 15.

Pintens and Scherpe identify it as the beginning of a 'European Family law'[9]—'not merely a landmark case ... a meta-landmark case'.[10]

The case of *Marckx* involved an unmarried mother, Paula Marckx, who gave birth to a baby girl. Under Belgian law at the time, no legal bond arose between an unmarried mother and her child as a result of birth—maternal affiliation of an 'illegitimate' child was only established by subsequent voluntary recognition—or through legal proceedings. Even once affiliation had been established, the child did not legally become a member of the mother's family—for this to be the case, the mother had to 'adopt' her child.

Paula Marckx challenged these laws, claiming that they breached both her rights and those of her child, under Article 8, Article 14 and Article 1, Protocol 1 (in relation to inheritance rights arising from filiation). The Court found that by guaranteeing the right to respect for family life, 'Article 8 presupposes the existence of a family';[11] however, the Convention makes no distinction between a 'legitimate' and 'illegitimate' family in this respect. The refusal to acknowledge Paula Marckx's legal motherhood from the moment of birth was not consonant with 'respect' for family life, in that 'it thwart[ed] and imped[ed] the normal development of such life'.[12]

In this way, 'family life' between a mother and child is established by the fact of the child's birth and flows unquestionably from this. There is no requirement that she show any additional evidence, either in law or fact, to bring her relationship with the child within the ambit of Article 8, and she and the child will automatically benefit from its protection.

8.2.2 'Family life' between a father and child

In contrast to the situation of mothers, a biological relationship between a man and a child will not, in and of itself, constitute 'family life':[13] rather, the Court will consider whether there are legal or factual elements indicating the existence of a 'close personal relationship' in order to attract the protection of Article 8. When examining the jurisprudence of the Court, we can see that 'family life' can be established in one of three ways: (i) by displaying commitment to the family; (ii) by exhibiting attachment to the child; or (iii) by demonstrating the motivation to establish such a relationship.

8.2.2.1 Commitment

The first, and easiest, way for a biological father to establish 'family life' with a child is to show his commitment, either to the child themself, or to the family unit as a whole. As such, where the man in question is married to the child's mother, this legal tie will be sufficient to establish 'family life' with the child.[14] From an early stage, the Court

[9] W. Pintens and J.M. Scherpe, 'The *Marckx Case:* A 'Whole Code of Family Law'?' in S. Gilmore, J. Herring, and R. Probert (eds), *Landmark Cases in Family Law* (2011), 155.

[10] ibid., 156.

[11] *Marckx v Belgium* (6833/74) 13.06.1979, para. 31.

[12] ibid., para. 36.

[13] See *Anayo v Germany* (20578/07) 21.12.2010.

[14] Where there is no biological relationship, the Court will look to the social attachment between the man and child, which is discussed further in section 8.2.2.2 below.

recognised that the relationship between two people in a 'lawful and genuine'[15] marriage will always fall within the scope of Article 8. As the Court stated in *Abdulaziz, Cabales, and Balkandali v the United Kingdom*, '[w]hatever else the word "family" may mean, it must at any rate include the relationship that arises from a lawful and genuine marriage'.[16] Following on from this, the Court has found that 'family life' will automatically extend to any child born of the marriage—'a child born of such a union is ipso jure part of that relationship; ... from the moment of the child's birth and by the very fact of it, there exists between him and his parents a bond amounting to "family life" '.[17] This will be true whether or not the parents continue to live together at the time of the child's birth.[18]

This principle was extended in the case of *Keegan v Ireland*,[19] which recognised that a committed non-marital relationship should be treated as equivalent to marriage for the purposes of establishing 'family life' between a parent and child. This case involved an unmarried cohabiting couple who decided to start a family. When the woman fell pregnant, they became engaged to be married, but the relationship broke down soon after. Following the child's birth, the applicant visited her once, but was afterwards denied permission to see her, and the mother subsequently placed her for adoption. The applicant instituted proceedings to be appointed the child's guardian, which would have enabled him to challenge the adoption;[20] however, the domestic court held that 'although there may be rights of interest or concern arising from the blood link between the father and the child, no constitutional right to guardianship in the father of the child exists'.[21]

Before the Court, the government maintained that the relationship between the applicant and the child's mother did not have the 'minimal levels of seriousness, depth and commitment to cross the threshold into family life within the meaning of Article 8'.[22] This was rejected by the Court, who affirmed that 'family life' encompasses de facto family ties where the parties are living together outside of marriage, in a relationship that bears the 'hallmarks' of family life.[23] Relying on the fact that the parents of the child had been cohabiting, they had planned to marry, and that the child was the result of a deliberate decision, the Court found that, as a matter of fact, a bond amounting to 'family life' between the father and child existed.

We can thus see that 'family life' is recognised between a biological father and his child where the father has shown a commitment to the child's mother—either through marriage or an equivalent de facto relationship. This provides broad protection for the relationship, as it arises whether or not there is an accompanying social relationship.[24]

[15] Where the marriage is not lawful, for example in the case of a child marriage, the Court has found that there is no obligation on the state to recognise it, and it will not, in and of itself, qualify as 'family life': see *ZH and RH v Switzerland* (60119/12) 08.12.2015.

[16] (9214/80, 9473/81, 9474/81) 28.05.1985, para. 62.

[17] *Berrehab v the Netherlands* (10730/84) 21.06.1988, para. 21.

[18] ibid.

[19] (16969/90) 26.05.1994.

[20] While a married man was automatically a guardian of his children, an unmarried man was not unless so appointed by the Court.

[21] *Keegan v Ireland* (16969/90) 26.05.1994, para. 12.

[22] ibid., para. 42.

[23] See also *Johnson and others v Ireland* (9697/82) 18.12.1986.

[24] See *Kroon v Netherlands* (18535/91) 27.10.1994.

Similarly, where the biological father has shown commitment to the child, through recognition as the legal father, 'family life' will be found to exist. This was seen in *Boughanemi v France*,[25] where the Court held that 'family life' was present between a man and a child he had recognised as his, despite the fact that he had little contact with the child, did not support him financially, and had delayed in acknowledging his parenthood until after he received a deportation order. These circumstances notwithstanding, the Court found:

> The concept of family life on which Article 8 is based embraces, even where there is no cohabitation, the tie between a [legal] parent and his or her child, regardless of whether or not the latter is legitimate. Although that tie may be broken by subsequent events, this can only happen in exceptional circumstances. In the present case neither the belated character of the formal recognition nor the applicant's alleged conduct in regard to the child constitutes such a circumstance.[26]

The problem with this reasoning is that it takes an assimilationist approach—using the monogamous, heterosexual, sexual union as the starting point and granting rights to other relationships only where they conform to this norm. In doing so, it risks failing to recognise the plurality of relationships in modern society, excluding from the Convention's protection diverse family forms. However, the limitations in this approach are mitigated by the Court's recognition of other mechanisms to establish 'family life'—most notably, social attachment.

8.2.2.2 Attachment

From an early point in its jurisprudence, the Court made clear that the protection of 'family' under Article 8 extends to situations where the father and child have a social 'parenting' relationship—whether or not this is recognised in domestic law. In this way, the existence of 'family life' is a question of fact, not law,[27] relying on the 'demonstrable interest in and commitment by the father to the child by both before and after the child's birth'.[28] This functional approach to parenthood has facilitated the recognition of a wide range of family relationships, including biological fathers not in a 'steady' relationship with the child's mother, non-biological fathers who have assumed a parenting role, and even foster parents.

As a rule, the Court will require cohabitation in order to recognise a relationship based on social 'attachment', but in *Kroon and others v the Netherlands*,[29] the Court noted that 'exceptionally', other factors might serve to demonstrate that a relationship has sufficient constancy to create de facto family ties—in that case, the fact that the parents had been in a stable relationship was sufficient. While 'exceptionality' appears to set a high threshold, in practice it has not been difficult to pass. In *Sporer v Austria*,[30]

[25] (22070/93) 24.04.1996.
[26] ibid., para. 35 (citations omitted).
[27] *L v the Netherlands* (45582/99) 01.06.2004; *Nylund v Finland* (27110/95) 29.06.1999 (dec.); *MB v the United Kingdom* (22920/93) 06.04.1994 (dec.).
[28] *L v the Netherlands* (45582/99) 01.06.2004; *Nylund v Finland* (27110/95) 29.06.1999 (dec.).
[29] (18535/91) 27.10.1994.
[30] (35637/03) 03.02.2011.

the Court relied on the fact that the father had taken parental leave, the child had been given his surname, and that he had taken care of the child three times a week; while in *Nekvedavicius v Germany*,[31] it was sufficient that the mother had acknowledged the applicant as the biological father of the child, and that he had shown a 'strong desire to have personal contact' with her. Even more tenuously, in *Söderbäck v Sweden*,[32] despite the fact that the father and mother did not have a steady relationship and the father's contact with the child after birth was 'infrequent and limited in character',[33] it was not disputed that 'family life' existed, in light of 'certain ties' between the father and child.

On the other hand, in *Ahrens v Germany*,[34] the Court held that a mere decision to demand a paternity test and bring an action aimed at establishing paternity was insufficient to bring the relationship within the scope of 'family life'—proving that there must be at least some slim relationship to which the Court could attach the label. Likewise, in *JRM v the Netherlands*,[35] a man who had acted as a known sperm donor to a lesbian couple was not found to have 'family life' with the child. Although the donor had had some social relationship with the child—babysitting once a week and visiting regularly for the first seven months of his life—this was not found to be sufficient, either of itself, or in combination with the sperm donation, to bring the relationship within the scope of 'family life'.

All these cases concerned biological fathers wishing for legal recognition of their relationship. However, the Court has also recognised that the notion of 'attachment' can create 'family life' between a child and a non-biological father who is acting in a parental role. In *Söderbäck*,[36] the Court found that in addition to 'family life' existing between the biological father and the child, de facto family ties also existed between the child and her mother's partner, who had been caring for her since she was six months old. This 'family life' did not depend on the child's legal adoption, which 'consolidated and formalised those ties', nor on the partner marrying the child's mother, but existed from the time at which he took over her care as a social parent and began acting as the child's 'father'. Similarly, in *K and T v Finland*,[37] the Court held that notwithstanding the lack of a biological tie between the mother's partner and her child, together they had 'formed a family with the clear intention of continuing their life together'.[38] On the other hand, in *Nazarenko v Russia*,[39] the applicant believed himself to be the father of a child, as she had been born during his marriage to the child's mother and he had been registered as such. However, five years later, when fighting the mother for custody, a paternity test found no genetic connection. Nevertheless, the Court found that 'family life' existed between the man and child on the grounds that they had believed themselves to be father and daughter for many years, and had formed a close emotional bond.

[31] (46165/99) 19.06.2003 (dec.).
[32] (24484/94) 28.10.1998 (Court).
[33] ibid., para. 32.
[34] (45071/09) 22.03.2012.
[35] (16944/90) 08.02.1993 (dec.)
[36] (24484/94) 28.10.1998 (Court).
[37] (25702/94) 12.07.2001 (GC).
[38] ibid., para. 150.
[39] (39438/13) 16.07.2015.

Social attachment between a child and a parental figure—regardless of any legal or genetic relationship—has also been recognised as 'family life' in the context of foster care. In *Moretti and Benedetti v Italy*,[40] a one-month-old baby was temporarily placed with a married couple after her mother had abandoned her. Seventeen months later, the child was moved to a different family for adoption, despite a request for an adoption order being lodged by the foster parents. The Court found that de facto 'family life' existed between the foster parents and child, reiterating that the existence or absence of 'family life' is above all a question of fact and depends on the existence of close family ties. In order to determine the character of the relations between the adults and child, the Court noted a number of factors to be taken into account: the time spent together, the quality of the relationship, and the role played by the adult towards the child. Relying on the fact that the child had lived with the family in the first important stages of her young life; the strong interpersonal relationship between the child, the foster parents, and the foster parents' legal children; and the fact that the foster parents had applied for an adoption order, the Court found that it 'could not rule out' a family tie, notwithstanding 'the absence of any legal relationship of kinship'.[41]

The principle of social attachment has thus been vital in recognising wider familial relationships, even those that do not fit within the traditional family unit. Perhaps the most encouraging use of this principle, however, was seen in relation to the family formed by a female-to-male transgender individual and his female partner, who gave birth to a child who would be raised within their family unit. In *X, Y, and Z v the United Kingdom*,[42] the domestic authorities refused to register the man as the father of the child, as he was still legally female—the legal change of gender not yet permitted in the United Kingdom at this time—which he challenged before the Court.

He submitted that he, his partner, and the child shared 'family life' within the meaning of Article 8, arguing that social reality, rather than formal legal status, should be the decisive criteria. The government, on the other hand, argued that 'family life' could not apply to the relationship between the man and his partner as they were both legally female, and according to the Court jurisprudence at the time, a 'family' could not be based on a same-sex relationship.[43] Moreover, the government argued that the relationship between the child and father could not constitute 'family life' as they were not related by 'blood, marriage or adoption'.

The Court emphasised that when deciding whether a relationship can be said to amount to 'family life', it must consider a range of factors, including whether the couple live together, the length of their relationship, and whether they have demonstrated their commitment to each other by having children together, or by any other means.

[40] (16318/07) 27.04.2010.

[41] ibid., para. 51. This approach was followed in the case of *Kopf and Liberda v Austria* (1598/06) 17.01.2012, where the foster parents had cared for the child for 46 months (from age two to four-and-a-half). The Court found that the foster parents had a 'genuine concern for [the child's] wellbeing, and that an emotional link between [the child] and the [foster parents] similar to the one between parents and children had started to develop'. (para. 37) As such, it was not in dispute between the parties that the relationship fell within the notion of 'family life'. See also *Antkowiak v Poland* (27025/17) 22.05.2018 (dec.); *VD and others v Russia* (72931/10) 09.04.2019.

[42] (21830/93) 22.04.1997 (GC).

[43] This position has since been reversed in the decision of *Schalk and Kopf v Austria* (30141/04) 24.06.2010.

It (somewhat disappointingly)[44] distinguished the situation of the applicants from a same-sex couple, noting that the man had undergone gender reassignment surgery and was to all appearances living with the mother as her male partner. They had applied jointly for artificial reproduction treatment to have a child, and he had acted as his 'father' in every respect since birth. As such, the Court concluded that de facto 'family life' existed between all three parties.[45]

The Court has not been so willing to extend the notion of 'family life' to *all* families formed through reproductive technologies, however. In particular, the existence of 'family life' between commissioning parents and children born through surrogacy has been a contested issue before the Court. Where there is a genetic link between the child and (at least one of) the commissioning parents, and they have been living together as a family unit since the child's birth, the Court has been willing to recognise their relationship as falling within the scope of Article 8.[46] However, in the absence of a genetic tie, the Court has taken a much stricter approach to the examination of the social relationships, and in particular, the context in which these have arisen.

This dilemma was explored in *Paradiso and Campanelli v Italy*,[47] involving an Italian couple who had travelled to Russia to undertake a surrogacy arrangement, as surrogacy was prohibited under Italian law. When they returned with the child to Italy and tried to register the birth, they were charged with 'misrepresentation of civil status', as under Italian law the legal mother is the person who gave birth to the child, contrary to what the couple were trying to register. Furthermore, the Public Prosecutor opened proceedings to free the child for adoption on the grounds that the child had been abandoned. The child's legal mother under Italian law (the surrogate) had ceased to care for him and a DNA test revealed no genetic link between the commissioning father and the child—gametes from other sources having been used in the course of the fertilisation procedure—leaving him with no known genetic parents.

The case before the Court revolved around two issues: first, whether the relationship between the commissioning parents and a non-genetically related surrogate child could fall within the scope of Article 8(1); and second, if it did, whether the interference with the parents' rights, by putting the child in foster care and planning for adoption, could be justified under Article 8(2). The Second Chamber, by a majority of five votes to two, held that there was de facto 'family life' between commissioning parents and the surrogate child, despite the lack of a genetic link, thus bringing the action within the scope of Article 8. As with *Moretti*, the Court relied on the fact that 'the applicants spent time with the child during the important first steps of his young life'[48]—for the first eight months of his life, he had lived with the applicants—and found that

[44] It is disappointing that the Court felt that it was necessary to make this distinction, and was not willing to recognise that these principles apply no matter what the gender of the parents. Moreover, the finding that this family could be recognised because it *appeared* heterosexual is extremely problematic. However, it would be another 13 years before same-sex couples were recognised as having 'family life' before the Court, so the fact that this family was recognised at all is something to be grateful for (even if the reasoning behind it was dubious).

[45] Although the Court found that the refusal to recognise the applicant as the legal father was justified under Article 8(2).

[46] *Mennesson v France* (65192/11) 26.06.2014.

[47] (25358/12) 27.01.2015 (Ch); (25358/12) 24.01.2017 (GC).

[48] (25358/12) 27.01.2015 (Ch), para. 69.

although the period was relatively short, during that time they behaved towards the child as parents, and formed a de facto family unit. The Court emphasised the fact that the applicants wished to care for the child as his parents, and had taken steps to achieve this, and in this way, a parental link was formed between the parents and child.

While this wide and inclusive interpretation may appear attractive on the face of it, it raises the question of the extent to which the Court can, or should, provide legitimacy to relationships which domestic law views as violating fundamental rights. In many jurisdictions, surrogacy is viewed as a violation of human dignity, linked with the exploitation of women.[49] Is a family formed in such circumstances deserving of protection under the Convention? This was the position argued by Judges Raimondi and Spanó, who dissented from the Chamber judgment, arguing that in deciding whether 'family life' exists, the Court should take into account the circumstances in which the child has been placed in the custody of the persons concerned. They emphasised that Article 8(1) cannot be interpreted as protecting 'family life' between a child and people with whom he or she has no genetic link where the facts clearly suggest that the origin of their care is based on an illegal act contrary to public order.

It was this dissenting reasoning that was followed by the Grand Chamber, when it decided the case in January 2017. By a majority of 11 votes to six, the Court held that the removal of the child did not violate Article 8, as there was no relevant 'family life' between the couple and the child. The Court accepted that, in certain situations, de facto 'family life' could arise in the absence of either genetic or legal ties, provided that there were genuine personal ties. In such a case, the Court must consider the quality of the interpersonal ties, the role played by the applicants vis-à-vis the child, and the duration of the cohabitation between them and the child. Although the Court declared that it would be inappropriate to define a minimal duration of cohabitation, it nevertheless identified it as a key factor in the Court's recognition of 'family life'.

The Grand Chamber held that although the termination of their relationship with the child was not directly imputable to the applicants, it was nevertheless the consequences of the legal uncertainty that they themselves had created by engaging in conduct that was contrary to Italian law. As such, the quality of the emotional bonds forged between the applicants and the child was not enough to outweigh the lack of a genetic tie, the short duration of the relationship, and the legal uncertainty of the ties, all of which amounted to an absence of 'family life'. The applicants then had to fall back on the protection of 'private life' under Article 8, interference with which is easier to justify.

This approach, undertaking greater scrutiny of the relationship in question when determining whether or not a 'legitimate' form of family life exists, sets a greater initial barrier for applicants, and allows the Court (and state) to make judgements concerning the acceptability of certain forms of reproduction. It also has the advantage of providing a deterrent to prospective parents in surrogacy, emphasising that they cannot breach the law and expect their family formed as a result of this illegality to be recognised. However, when we consider the position of the child, it becomes more

[49] See J.M. Scherpe, C. Fenton-Glynn, and T. Kaan (eds), *Eastern and Western Perspectives on Surrogacy* (Cambridge: Intersentia, 2019).

complicated. The child was not a party in *Paradiso*, meaning that the case was argued by adults, about adult rights. As discussed in Chapter 2, it may be legitimate to refuse to recognise horizontal de facto family ties where they have arisen as a result of exploitation—for example, in the case of child marriage—but vertical family ties involve different dynamics. In *Paradiso*, the child's right to respect for private and family life was not considered, as he was not a party to the proceedings. An important factor for the Court was the fact that the parents knowingly engaged in an activity that was deemed illegal, due to its exploitative and commodifying nature. If the child were involved in the proceedings, however, it is questionable whether the Court would have been so quick to find that he did not have 'family life' with the only parents he had ever known.[50] While the commissioning couple may have been culpable in breaching domestic law, the child is an innocent party. As such, we have to ask whether 'family life' can be one-directional, flowing only from the child to the putative parents, but not vice versa. Or must 'family life' be reciprocal, and apply equally to all members of the 'family'?

The simple solution, as adopted by the Grand Chamber, is to recognise 'private life' between the parties falling short of a familial relationship. Such an approach has been used in the past by the Court in relation to same-sex relationships, as it is easier to justify interference as necessary and proportionate when characterised as such. While I would argue that this approach was incorrect in relation to same-sex relationships—based as it was on moral objections to homosexuality, rather than legitimate differences between same-sex and opposite-sex relationships—in relation to parenthood achieved through illegal means, the distinction carries greater weight. Opposition to surrogacy is not based solely on morality and social norms (although these do play a part in shaping opinions), but also rests on deeper concerns regarding human trafficking, exploitation, commodification, and a violation of human dignity. As such, a distinction can be drawn between family forms that fall outside current social norms—which we should respect and protect as equal to those falling within more traditional modes—and those family forms that arise as a result of practices that the state views as exploitative and contrary to fundamental rights.

Since *Paradiso* is a very recent case, it is not clear whether the principles that underpin it will form a new line of jurisprudence, or whether instead it will be seen as an outlier, only applying to a very narrow set of (unusual) facts. It does appear that much of the reasoning of the Grand Chamber was driven by an antipathy towards the practice of surrogacy and the fact that the creation of the family was in violation of domestic law. In this way, it shows just how significantly public policy can influence whether 'family life' is recognised—as Judge Pettiti emphasised in *X, Y, and Z v the United Kingdom*: 'A family, in general, cannot be a mere aggregate of the individuals living under one roof. The ethical and social dimension of a family cannot be ignored or underestimated.'[51]

[50] See C. Fenton-Glynn, 'When is a Family Not a Family?' (2017) 47(6) *Family Law* 586.
[51] (21830/93) 22.04.1997 (GC).

8.2.2.3 Motivation

In addition to recognising relationships that already exist—either through a commitment to the family unit or to the child, or through a social attachment—the Court has raised the prospect that 'intended family life' may exceptionally fall within the ambit of Article 8. This form of 'family life' arises where there are no close personal ties between the biological father and child, but where the failure to establish such ties is not attributable to the father.

This possibility was raised in *Anayo v Germany*,[52] where the biological father had had an affair with a married woman, whose husband was registered as the father of the children (twins). Unlike *Keegan*, discussed in section 8.2.2.1 above, the relationship between the mother and biological father did not have great stability, nor had they cohabited, so the father was not able to rely on his commitment to the mother. Moreover, the mother and her husband had refused the father permission to see the children, meaning that he was not able to establish any social attachment between them. Nevertheless, the Court opened the possibility that 'intended family life' can attract the protection of Article 8, where the biological father has demonstrated the motivation to have a relationship with his children—in this case, the Court noted that he had expressed his wish to have contact with the twins even before birth, and repeatedly asked for access. When this was not granted by the mother and her husband, he swiftly brought proceedings before the courts, and the Court found that these factors combined were sufficient to demonstrate his interest in the children and willingness to assume responsibility.

These elements notwithstanding, the Court took a very cautious approach in this case. It '[did] not exclude' that the applicant's intended relationship with his biological children could attract the protection of 'family life' under Article 8, but held that the decision to refuse him contact with his children interfered, 'at least', with his right to respect for private life.[53]

This concept of 'intended family life' has only been applied in one other situation[54]—that of an adoption order that was not enforced. In *Pini and others v Romania*,[55] two Italian couples had entered into intercountry adoptions with regard to Romanian children. The public welfare institutions where the children were living at the time of the adoption challenged the adoption orders, and resisted attempts to implement them. The government argued that the fact that the couples had been acknowledged as the legal adoptive parents should not, in and of itself, bring their cases within the scope of Article 8, as no 'family life' had ever existed in practice—the couples had never met the children in their capacity as parents (and had only done so once before the adoption

[52] (20578/07) 21.12.2010.

[53] ibid., para. 62. See also *Schneider v Germany* (17080/07) 15.09.2011.

[54] Although the Court in *Pini* suggests that this principle is also seen in *Abdulaziz, Cabales and Balkandali v the United Kingdom* (9214/80, 9473/81, 9474/81) 28.05.1985 with regard to a lawful marriage, this should be distinguished on the ground that there was in fact a relationship between the parties, in addition to a legal tie, and the 'intended family life' referred to was simply that they were not able to live together (despite having a legal and social relationship). The Court also referred to *Nylund v Finland* (27110/95) 29.06.1999 (dec.) in relation to the relationship between a biological father and child; however, in *Nylund* the relationship was found *not* to amount to 'family life' and instead only to fall within the concept of 'private life'.

[55] (78028/01, 78030/01) 22.06.2004.

order), the children did not regard them as such, and they had never enjoyed genuine family relations. The Court rejected this argument, finding that although Article 8 presupposes the existence of a family—a requirement that was not met in this case, as they did not live together, nor have sufficiently close de facto ties—this does not mean that all 'intended family life' falls entirely outside its ambit. Drawing on analogies with marriage, the Court held that 'a relationship, arising from a lawful and genuine adoption, may be deemed sufficient to attract such respect as may be due for family life under Article 8 of the Convention'.[56] Importantly, the Court emphasised, as it did six years later in *Anayo*, that the fact that 'family life' had not been fully established was not attributable to the applicants, who were simply following the procedure put in place by the Romanian government for intercountry adoption.[57]

This is thus a narrow ground for attribution of 'family life', recognised only in very particular factual circumstances. Nevertheless, it shows the adaptability of the Court in this area. Rather than being confined by strict rules and rigid interpretations, the Court has been willing to respond flexibly to the demands of differing family situations.

8.2.2.4 Conclusions on 'family life' and fatherhood

From this line of jurisprudence, we can see that while 'family life' for mothers will be straightforward and automatic, for fathers it involves a more difficult calculation. It arises not from one isolated fact, but is a cumulative status, the result of a variety of factors, all of which carry different weight.

The genetic tie is a powerful factor, as can be seen in the cases of unmarried fathers, but it is not enough: something additional, such as a legal commitment or a social relationship, will be needed to bring the relationship within the scope of Article 8. On the other hand, a social relationship without the backing of genetics will have to demonstrate high levels of attachment and commitment before this threshold is passed—for example, having taken on the legal parental role or shown a willingness to do so.

This reflects the wider emphasis of the Court on function, rather than (merely) form. What is important is the role the parent is playing and the factual relationship that exists, rather than simply a biological connection. The genetic tie opens the door to 'family life', but legal or social recognition is needed for it to be confirmed.

[56] ibid., para. 148.

[57] Interestingly, the difference in treatment between adoptive parents and unmarried fathers was one of the reasons that Judge Thomassen (in her dissenting opinion, joined by Judge Jungwiert) argued that 'family life' did not exist in this case:

> To my mind, therefore, what deserves protection under Article 8 is not simply the adoption order itself but what it represents in terms of social reality. To hold otherwise would produce a surprising, and in my view unacceptable, result, namely that the relationship between a biological father and his child, without any additional factors, would not automatically give rise to family life whereas family life would, on the contrary, be created by an adoption order, irrespective of the manner in which adoption had taken place and of the relations between those concerned. (citations omitted)

8.2.3 'Family life' with extended family

In addition to recognising 'family life' between children and their parents or caregivers, the Court has recognised that other types of relationships may also attract the protection of Article 8 in this respect. For example, siblings have been found to have 'family life' with each other both when they are children[58] and as adults.[59] Likewise, in *Marckx*, the Court emphasised that 'family life' within Article 8 'includes at least the ties between near relatives, for instance those between grandparents and grandchildren, since such relatives may play a considerable part in family life'.[60]

What is not clear from the reasoning in *Marckx* is whether the 'family life' with grandparents arose simply as a result of the kinship tie or whether additional evidence of a social relationship was needed. If, for example, the grandparents only had sporadic contact with the child, would 'family life' still exist? The only indication on this matter in *Marckx* was the comment by the Court that 'there is nothing to prove the absence of an actual relationship between [the child] and her grandmother before the latter's death'.[61]

This was clarified in later cases, however, where the Court has made clear that there must exist a situation of 'sufficiently close family ties' to trigger the protection of Article 8 for grandparents. For example, in *Lawlor v the United Kingdom*,[62] the Court noted that the child had lived in the grandparent's home for the first four years of his life, and following the child's removal into care, regular contact was maintained. This was sufficient to bring the relationship within the scope of 'family life' under Article 8: although cohabitation is not a prerequisite, where it has occurred, the relationship between the child and grandparents will normally fall within this definition.[63] Where cohabitation has not taken place, the Court has looked to the existence of a 'close relationship created by frequent contact'. In *TS and JJ v Norway*,[64] the Polish-born child had good contact with his grandmother until he was four years old, and afterwards he continued to return to visit her regularly, and this, the Court found, was sufficient to constitute 'family life' between the pair.

The possibility of 'family life' is not restricted to grandparents, however, and can also extend to other members of the wider family. In *Boyle v the United Kingdom*,[65] the Commission considered whether the relationship between an uncle and nephew fell within the scope of 'family life' under Article 8. The applicant claimed that he enjoyed a very close relationship with his nephew, and acted as a 'father figure' to him in the absence of the child's genetic father. The government, on the other hand, argued that they had never cohabited, and that the bonds of an uncle–nephew relationship in

[58] *Olsson v Sweden (No. 1)* (10465/83) 24.03.1988 (Court); *Mustafa and Armagan Akin v Turkey* (4694/03) 06.04.2010.

[59] *Boughanemi v France* (22070/93) 24.04.1996.

[60] *Marckx v Belgium* (6833/74) 13.06.1979, para. 45. The finding of 'family life' between children and grandparents has since been confirmed in subsequent cases: see, for example, *Bronda v Italy* (22430/93) 09.06.1998; *Nistor v Romania* (14565/05) 02.11.2010; *Manuello and Nevi v Italy* (107/10) 20.01.2015).

[61] *Marckx v Belgium* (6833/74) 13.06.1979, para. 46.

[62] (12763/87) 14.07.1988 (dec.).

[63] See also *Bronda v Italy* (22430/93) 09.06.1998; *Kruškić v Croatia* (10140/13) 25.11.2014 (dec.).

[64] (15633/15) 11.10.2016 (dec.).

[65] (16580/90) 09.02.1993 (ComRep).

themselves were insufficient to constitute 'family life'. The Commission emphasised that cohabitation is simply one factor amongst many to be taken into account when deciding whether family ties exist, and in its absence, focused on the existence of close social ties between the uncle and nephew, emphasising the frequent and regular contact they enjoyed, as well as the fact that the nephew visited for 'weekend stays'. Notably, the Commission characterised the 'family life' of the uncle as existing in lieu of the child's father—finding that 'having regard to the absence of [the child's] father ... there was a significant bond between the applicant and C., and that this relationship fell within the scope of the concept of "family life" '.[66]

Although 'family life' has been found to exist in such circumstances, it is important to note that it differs in both nature and degree from the relationship between a parent and child, and therefore is afforded a lesser degree of protection. For example, in relation to grandparents, this involves only the right to maintain 'a normal grandparent–grandchild relationship', at the discretion of the child's parents.[67] Nevertheless, this line of jurisprudence represents an important acknowledgement by the Court that the protection of Article 8 must stretch further than the nuclear family and reflect the lived reality of children's lives.

8.2.4 When does 'family life' end?

Once 'family life' has been established between a parent and a minor child,[68] it is well established that it continues to exist notwithstanding the parents' separation or divorce,[69] or the fact of the child being taken into public care.[70] However, once the child reaches adulthood, there must be elements of dependency going beyond the normal, emotional ties, in order for 'family life' to exist.[71]

Moreover, the Court has raised the possibility that the tie of 'family life' might be dissolved by subsequent events, for example, the termination of social or legal ties, but has yet to definitively rule that this has occurred. This has arisen primarily in immigration cases, and was discussed in detail in Chapter 5. For example, in *Berrehab v the Netherlands*,[72] the Court suggested that it may be possible for a lack of continued relationship in fact to break the tie between a non-custodial parent and child, but it was

[66] ibid., para. 45.

[67] See *Kruškić v Croatia* (10140/13) 25.11.2014 (dec.), para. 111; *Price v the United Kingdom* (12402/86) 14.07.1988 (dec.).

[68] In relation to an adult child, the Court has held that such relationships do not fall within the scope of Article 8 unless there are additional elements of dependence, other than normal familial relationships (see Chapter 5).

[69] *Hendriks v Netherlands* (8427/78) 08.03.1982 (ComRep).

[70] See, for example, *W v United Kingdom* (9749/82) 08.07.1987; *Olsson v Sweden (No. 1)* (10465/83) 24.03.1988 (Court); *Eriksson v Sweden* (11373/85)) 22.06.1989; *Margareta and Roger Andersson v Sweden* (12963/87) 25.02.1992.

[71] *S and S v the United Kingdom* (10375/83) 10.12.1984 (dec.); *Emonet and others v Switzerland* (39051/03) 13.12.2007. See Chapter 5 for a discussion of 'family life' in the context of immigration.

[72] (10730/84) 21.06.1988, para. 21.

not satisfied on the facts. Indeed, despite numerous attempts by states to pursue this line of reasoning, the Court is yet to recognise any situation where it has occurred.[73]

The more difficult question is whether 'family life' is terminated upon the dissolution of legal ties, as occurs in the case of an adoption. This was considered in *IS v Germany*,[74] where a mother placed for adoption two children conceived as a result of an extramarital affair. When the children were two years old, she commenced proceedings to obtain information about, and have contact with, the children, which were dismissed by the German authorities. She complained to the Court that this refusal amounted to an interference with her right to respect for private and family life under Article 8, arguing that her consent to the placement of her children for adoption did not automatically end her 'family life' under Article 8—she had waived her rights as a legal parent, but not as a natural mother.

The Court acknowledged that the relationship between the mother and her children fell within the protection of Article 8 at the time of the children's birth, but noted that the relationship 'might have ceased to fall within the scope of "family life"' when the mother signed the deed that placed the children for adoption. Drawing on cases concerning unmarried fathers, it observed that a biological relationship alone, without any further legal or factual elements indicating the existence of a close personal relationship, was, in and of itself, insufficient to attract the protection of 'family life',[75] and in this case, 'the existing family relationship was intentionally severed by the applicant'.[76] This seems to indicate, even if it does not say so explicitly, that 'family life' under Article 8 was similarly terminated.[77]

As such, it appears that 'family life' will cease when legal ties between a natural parent and child are dissolved. It should also be noted, however, that this case involved the 'voluntary' termination of legal ties[78] and it is unclear whether the situation would

[73] See *Gül v Switzerland* (23218/94) 19.02.1996; *Boughanemi v France* (22070/93) 24.04.1996; *C v Belgium* (21794/93) 07.08.1996; *Ciliz v the Netherlands* (29192/95) 11.07.2000; *Ejimson v Germany* (58681/12) 01.03.2018. This question has also arisen in relation to a father claiming access to his child. In *Yousef v the Netherlands* (33711/96) 05.11.2002, the Dutch government argued that 'family life' had ceased when a father failed to maintain his commitment to his child born out of wedlock: it was alleged that he failed to stay in touch with his child when he moved abroad for two-and-a-half years, and contact after his return had been sparse and irregular. Nevertheless, the court found that 'family life' existed, citing the undisputed genetic link, the fact of previous cohabitation, and that the father and child continued to 'have contact ... which were considered important' by the domestic courts. (para. 51)

[74] (31021/08) 05.06.2014.

[75] This is an interesting extension of the rule concerning unmarried fathers to also include mothers. No other case has addressed this issue—*Marckx v Belgium* (6833/74) 13.06.1979 only tells us that 'family life' exists from the moment of birth, and mothers must be given automatic recognition, but does not deal with a situation in which the mother does not want a legal relationship. A better analogy would be cases of anonymous birth—but this is not something that has been discussed in the cases that have so far come before the Court.

[76] *IS v Germany* (31021/08) 05.06.2014, para. 69. It is interesting here that the Court distinguished the situation from *Pini and others v Romania* (78028/01, 78030/01) 22.06.2004, and held there could not be 'intended family life' as the mother had voluntarily severed the relationship. However, this ignores the fact that the mother had only agreed to the adoption following a verbal agreement that she would have contact with her children after the adoption order. Even if, as the Court ruled, she knew this was unenforceable in law, she still had an expectation.

[77] However, it did find that the determination of ties between a biological parent and child concern the parent's identity, and thus fall within the scope of 'private life' under Article 8.

[78] See Chapter 11.

be different if the legal ties were terminated through a non-consensual adoption, as a result of child protection proceedings.

8.3 Establishing parenthood

In many ways, the recognition of parenthood overlaps with whether or not 'family life' has been established. As with 'family life', the jurisprudence concerning maternity is relatively straightforward,[79] while the establishment of paternity is significantly more complicated. This may stem from the fact that, traditionally, one woman usually fulfils the role of legal, genetic, and social parent,[80] while different men may perform each of these functions. There have thus been a large number of cases concerning men both seeking to establish and wishing to deny their paternity, raising important questions of what makes a parent.

8.3.1 Mothers

As was discussed in section 8.2.1 above, *Marckx v Belgium*[81] held that 'family life' between a mother and child is established by the fact of the child's birth and flows unquestionably from this. Moreover, Article 8 requires that the domestic legal system implement 'legal safeguards that render possible as from the moment of birth the child's integration in his family'.[82] As such, the birth of the child alone establishes filiation and the domestic authorities must provide a mechanism for this to be recognised in law—automatically and immediately.[83] By refusing to recognise Paula Marckx's maternity from the moment of birth, and by requiring her to establish her parenthood by recognition, the authorities had breached her rights under Article 8. *Marckx* also raised an issue under Article 14 in conjunction with Article 8—namely that while an unmarried mother had to 'recognise' her child for affiliation to be established, a married mother did not. The Court found that this difference in treatment lacked objective and reasonable justification and that there could no longer be any distinction drawn between 'illegitimate' and 'legitimate' children when determining maternal filiation.

Decided in 1979, this case did not have to deal with more difficult issues concerning motherhood arising from artificial reproductive techniques (the first instance of a child being born using IVF having arisen only one year previously), or the even more complex question of surrogacy. The definitive answer to 'Who is a mother?' offered by the Court is therefore liable to future challenge, taking into account the possibility to now split the role of genetic, gestational, and social/intended mother. Until that time, however, the position of the Court remains simple and clear.

[79] With the exception of anonymous birth, discussed in Chapter 3.
[80] Although that is no longer necessarily the case.
[81] (6833/74) 13.06.1979.
[82] ibid., para. 31.
[83] This does not mean, however, that the woman who gives birth cannot *opt out* of being a legal parent, if she so wishes: see Chapter 3 on anonymous birth.

8.3.2 Fathers

8.3.2.1 The legal recognition of paternity

Lacking the simplicity of parturition, nor having achieved the unanimity across contacting states of the attribution of motherhood, the establishment of paternity has generated considerably more case law before the Court. While the Court has made clear that the Convention does not require any one particular man to be designated as a father, leaving a significant margin of appreciation in this area, it has emphasised that any law must not rely on irrebuttable presumptions, but must be sufficiently flexible to adapt to the child's lived reality.

The leading case on the establishment of paternity is *Kroon and others v the Netherlands*.[84] In this case, the mother of the child was a married woman, but she had lived apart from her husband for some time and his whereabouts were unknown. She subsequently entered into a relationship with Z, with whom she had a child. The parents requested that Z be registered as the father of the child, but this was refused on the grounds that unless the husband brought proceedings to deny paternity, recognition of another man was not possible under Dutch law. The Court found that a relationship amounting to 'family life' between the father and child was established, despite not living together—he was the biological father, and in addition to sharing the child's care with the mother, he made financial contributions to his upbringing. Following *Marckx*, the Court held that where such family life is established, the state had a positive obligation to act in a manner calculated to enable that tie to be developed and to render possible, as from the moment of birth, the child's integration in his family. It emphasised that '"respect for family life" requires that biological and social reality prevail over a legal presumption which … flies in the face of both established fact and the wishes of those concerned without actually benefitting anyone'.[85]

In this case, biological and social parenthood rested in the same man—it was only the legal parenthood which remained at odds. More difficult, however, is where social and biological parenthood conflict. In *Różański v Poland*,[86] the domestic law did not allow a putative biological father to bring an action to challenge the paternity of the legal father. This power lay solely in the hands of the public prosecutor, who had wide discretion as to how this should be exercised. The Court found that the fact that the authorities had discretional as to whether to institute proceedings was not, in itself, open to criticism: such a mechanism was clearly designed to safeguard the best interests of the child, which must be balanced against the interests of the putative father. However, this power had been interpreted by the authorities in such a way that the mere fact of legal recognition by another man was sufficient to refuse to bring proceedings. Although the Court acknowledged that recognition by another man was an important consideration, it emphasised that there were also other factual elements

[84] (18535/91) 27.10.1994.

[85] ibid., para. 40. See also *Johnson and others v Ireland* (9697/82) 18.12.1986, where the Court found that an absence of an appropriate legal regime to reflect the family tie between a child and her natural father (who wished to recognise her as his legal daughter) was in violation of Article 8. The Court found that the prohibition on an unmarried father against establishing paternal affiliation denied the 'normal development of the natural family tie' which should be available to children born both within and outside wedlock.

[86] (55339/00) 18.05.2006.

that should have been taken into account. While Article 8 does not require that biology must always prevail, it does require an examination of the circumstances of the individual case and whether the institution of the proceedings would harm the child's interests.

The question of what other elements should be taken into account was answered several years later in *Ahrens v Germany*,[87] where a biological father wished to challenge the acknowledgement of paternity by the mother's cohabiting partner. This was rejected by the domestic courts on the grounds that where a social and family relationship has already been established between the legal father and the child, paternity cannot be challenged. Unlike *Różański* and *Kroon*, there was no relationship amounting to 'family life' between the child and biological father—Mr Ahrens's relationship with the mother was purely sexual, and they did not plan the pregnancy. Nor was there any sign of commitment by Mr Ahrens to the child before he was born. As such, the decision to demand a paternity test was not sufficient to bring the relationship within the scope of 'family life'. Nevertheless, the Court found that Mr Ahrens's 'private life' had been interfered with, as proceedings concerning the establishment of paternity fall within this sphere.

In deciding whether the interference was justified, the Court balanced two competing factors: on the one hand, the biological father had a protected interest in establishing the truth about an important aspect of his private life; on the other, the decision of the authorities was aimed at giving precedence to an existing family relationship between the child and legal father, who was actually living with the child and providing parental care on a daily basis. If the proceedings were successful, all parental links between the child and Mr M—a man who had acknowledged paternity and would continue to perform the role of social father—would have been severed. It was this additional social relationship which distinguished the case from the earlier decision in *Różański*—while simply relying on another man's legal tie did not provide adequate protection of the biological father's interests, the combined recognition of social and legal ties did.[88]

This line of jurisprudence should not, however, be taken to mean that the Court prioritises social over biological parenthood. Rather, it leaves to states a wide margin of appreciation to decide how legal parenthood should be assigned. What is crucial, however, is that there is a mechanism available for an individual assessment of the circumstances of each case, and in particular, the best interest of the child.[89] This was highlighted by the Court's recent decision in *Mandet v France*.[90] Here, and contrary

[87] (45071/09) 22.03.2012. See also *Kautzor v Germany* (23338/09) 22.03.2012, decided the same day.

[88] The decision in this case can be contrasted with that of *Anayo v Germany* (20578/07) 21.12.2010, where the father had been seeking to establish his biological link in order to have contact with the child, rather than to overturn the established legal parenthood. The Court found that *Ahrens* should be considered 'to have a fundamentally different and more far-reaching objective' (para. 67) than *Anayo* did: Article 8 requires that the biological father not be completely excluded from the child's life, unless there are relevant reasons relating to the child's best interests to do so. However, it does not require states to allow the biological father to challenge the legal father's status. The margin of appreciation in respect of the determination of the child's legal status was thus construed as wider than that enjoyed in relation to decisions concerning contact. See also *Yousef v the Netherlands* (33711/96) 05.11.2002.

[89] See also *LD and PK v Bulgaria* (7949/11, 45522/14) 08.12.2016.

[90] (30955/12) 14.01.2016.

to the cases that had come before the Court previously, the French authorities held that despite the fact that the child already had a legal father, who was also his social father, the paternity of the biological father should be recognised. They found that the child's best interests lay in knowing the truth about his origins, rather than in preserving the legal family structure artificially—despite the child's strenuous objections to the contrary. The Court affirmed that while the domestic authorities enjoy a margin of appreciation in this area, the bottom line must always be the best interests of the child. In this case, the child's best interests *had* been placed at the heart of the decision-making—even if the domestic authorities had held that those interests did not lie where the child himself perceived them to lie.

What is notable about all these cases is that they involved unmarried fathers who have been treated differently than they would have been if they had been married to the child's mother. However, the Court has found that such a difference in treatment is justified, on the somewhat dubious grounds that unmarried fathers are less likely to be involved in their child's lives. This was explored in *McMichael v the United Kingdom*,[91] where the applicant complained that while the father who was married to the child's mother was automatically granted parental rights, an unmarried father had to petition a court for these to be awarded. The Court acknowledged that there was a difference in treatment between married and unmarried fathers, but found that this was justified. Echoing the words of the Commission in this case, it held that 'it is axiomatic that the nature of the relationships of natural fathers with their children will inevitably vary, from ignorance and indifference at one end of the spectrum to a close stable relationship indistinguishable from the conventional matrimonial-based family unit at the other'.[92] The aim, then, of the legislation was to 'provide a mechanism for identifying "meritorious" fathers who might be accorded parental rights, thereby protecting the interests of the child and the mother'.[93]

It is interesting to note that this same justification was put forward by the Belgian government in *Marckx v Belgium*, when defending the difference in treatment between married and unmarried mothers, but was soundly rebutted. In this case, the Government had argued that

> whilst the married mother and her husband 'mutually undertake … the obligation to feed, keep and educate their children' (Article 203 of the Civil Code), there is no certainty that the unmarried mother will be willing to bear on her own the responsibilities of motherhood; by leaving the unmarried mother the choice between recognising her child or dissociating herself from him, the law is prompted by a concern for protection of the child, for it would be dangerous to entrust him to the custody and authority of someone who has shown no inclination to care for him; many unmarried mothers do not recognise their child.[94]

[91] (16424/90) 24.02.1995. A similar argument was raised in *Schneider v Germany* (17080/07) 15.09.2011, where the father argued that he was treated differently in the establishment of 'family life' than was a mother or grandparent, but this aspect of the case was not considered by the Court.

[92] *McMichael v the United Kingdom* (16424/90) 24.02.1995, para. 98. This was expressly approved of in *B v the United Kingdom* (39067/97) 14.09.1999.

[93] *McMichael v the United Kingdom* (16424/90) 24.02.1995, para. 98.

[94] *Marckx v Belgium* (6833/74) 13.06.1979, para. 39.

The Court gave short shrift to this argument, finding that 'such an attitude is not a general feature of the relationship between unmarried mothers and their children'.[95] It also pointed out that some married mothers might not wish to bring up their children, and yet their parenthood is automatic.

McMichael is now 25 years old, yet there is no indication that the Court has become more progressive in this area. While there may be legitimate reasons to distinguish between mothers and fathers, and even between unmarried and married fathers,[96] this distinction cannot rest on the assumption that unmarried men are potentially 'unmeritorious'. In this respect, the Court should be not simply be responding to social changes, but leading them. If the Court starts from the assumption that men are potentially uncaring, this legitimates their actions should they in fact be so. Rather, mothers and fathers should be recognised as holding equal responsibilities for children, and rights conferred accordingly.

8.3.2.2 Denying paternity

As was seen in section 8.3.2.1 above, the Convention does not permit paternity to be established through presumption alone, and requires some mechanism for this to be challenged, and a decision made in the best interests of the child. This rule applies equally in relation to the *denial* of paternity as it does to its *establishment*: Article 8 requires that a legal father *must* be able to question his paternity. There is some uncertainty concerning whether this principle falls within the scope of 'family life' under Article 8, but at the very least the determination of the legal relationship between a putative father and child falls within the protection of 'private life'. There was some initial unease with the inclusion of paternity even within this concept: for example, Judge Gersing in *Rasmussen v Denmark*[97] opined that this was 'far too wide an understanding of the right protected by this provision',[98] and 'seem[ed] to imply that any legal problem that has a bearing on a person's private life falls within the scope of Article 8'.[99] However, it is now broadly accepted that the determination of whether someone is, or is not, a father, has direct implications for his private sphere, concerned as it is with entries in the registers of births and marriages, his medical records, and his social identity in a broader sense.[100]

[95] ibid.

[96] For example, that the mother has shown her commitment to the child through carrying it to term, while married fathers have shown their commitment to the family unit through marriage. For an unmarried father, registration is therefore simply a mechanism to demonstrate what these other parties have already established.

[97] (8777/79) 28.11.1984.

[98] ibid., concurring opinion of Judge Gersing, para. 1.

[99] ibid., para. 5.

[100] See *Paulik v Slovakia* (10699/05) 10.10.2006. It should also be noted that the Court has recognised that the establishment of paternity also falls within the scope of 'private life' of the child's mother, who wishes to determine the father of her child. In *Kalacheva v Russia* (3451/05) 07.05.2009, the Court found that recognition of the natural father was important to the mother not only for financial and emotional purposes, but also 'from the point of view of the applicant's social image, her family medical history and the web

When the Court first considered the issue of denial of paternity, it took a very narrow and conservative approach. *X v Sweden*[101] involved a married man who had always believed himself to be the child's biological father, but 24 years later, discovered he was sterile and could not possibly be so. He applied for a declaration that he was not the legal father of the child, but this was denied, as the law required proceedings to be instated within three years from the date on which he received knowledge of the child's birth.[102] The claim was considered under Article 6(1), with the Commission finding that 'it must generally be accepted in the interests of good administration of justice that there are time limits within which prospective proceedings must be instituted'.[103] The Commission also acknowledged that it was legitimate to regard a time limit as final, with no possibility of extension or exception, and that three years was 'not an unreasonable time limit' for instituting paternity proceedings.

This decision appears to be a product of its time, and has not since been cited in the subsequent case law. Instead, the Court now takes a more nuanced approach, requiring that fathers have a 'clear and practical opportunity' to challenge a finding of paternity. This was seen in *Mizzi v Malta*,[104] where a husband was only permitted to challenge his paternity if he could prove adultery on the part of his wife, *and* that the birth had been concealed with him. Furthermore, there was a six-month time limit on any action, which started at the time of the child's birth. This rule was later relaxed to allow an action to be brought if there was evidence of adultery, and of any other fact tending to rule out paternity, but the time limit still remained. When examining whether the applicant had effective access to a court under Article 6(1), the Court found that he never had an opportunity, with reasonable prospects of success, of bringing a claim for disavowal—first being prevented by the concealment requirement, then after the relaxation of the law, by the time limit.

The Court then turned to Article 8, finding that there had also been a violation of the applicant's private life, as the interference had not been shown to be necessary in a democratic society. It had not been shown how society as a whole would benefit from such a 'radical restriction', and that the potential interest of the child in enjoying the 'social reality' of being the daughter of the applicant could not outweigh the legitimate right to have at least the opportunity to deny paternity of a child who, according to scientific evidence, was not his own.

This does not mean that time limits are incompatible with the Convention per se—it will depend on the nature of the time limit and the manner in which it is applied. The most important question is whether the law strikes a clear balance between the interests of the applicant to uncover the truth about an important aspect of their personal identity, the interests of the child to stability, and the general interests of the community as a whole to legal certainty.

of entwined rights and duties between the biological mother, biological father and the child concerned'. (para. 29)

[101] (9707/82) 06.10.1982 (dec.).

[102] For the child, on the other hand, there was no time limit for instituting proceedings for obtaining a declaration that the man was not his father.

[103] *X v Sweden* (9707/82) 06.10.1982 (dec.), p. 226.

[104] (26111/02) 12.01.2006.

As with most issues arising under Article 8, inflexible limitation periods, without any exceptions, will be difficult to justify, as they fail to take into account the individual circumstances of the case. For example, in *Shofman v Russia*,[105] the Court held that a one-year time period, without any exceptions, in which the husband could apply to rebut the presumption of legitimacy was contrary to Article 8. It observed that the government did not give any reason why it should have been 'necessary in a democratic society' to establish an inflexible time limit, with time running irrespective of the putative father's awareness of the circumstances casting doubt on his paternity.[106] This can be contrasted with *Yildirim v Austria*,[107] where the one-year limitation was held to be compatible with Article 8 on the grounds that after that date, the public prosecutor could still commence proceedings if it was necessary in the public interest or in the interests of the child. The Court held that once the limitation period for the applicant had expired, the domestic authorities were justified in giving greater weight to the interests of the child.[108]

Furthermore, the Court has made clear that the Convention does not prevent different time limits being instituted for fathers, as opposed to mothers, children, and third parties. For example, in *Rasmussen v Denmark*,[109] the registered father argued that he had been subject to discriminatory treatment, contrary to Article 14 in conjunction with Article 8, on the grounds that while his ability to contest the paternity of a child born during the marriage was time limited, his former wife and the child in question were entitled to institute paternity proceedings at any time. The Court held that the domestic authorities had a margin of appreciation in this area and were entitled to conclude that the introduction of time limits was necessary to ensure legal certainty and to protect the interests of the child. While the Court acknowledged that wives and husbands were treated differently in this respect, it emphasised that the difference was justified, as time limits were less necessary for wives, since the mother's interests usually coincided with those of the child, as she was usually awarded custody in cases of divorce or separation.

This decision was based on quite narrow facts—where the applicant had the opportunity to disavow his paternity in the five years after the child's birth, as well as for a period of 12 months after the time at which he became cognisant of the facts giving rise to doubts concerning paternity. In subsequent cases, the Court has not been so lenient. In *Mizzi v Malta*,[110] decided 12 years later, the Court distinguished *Rasmussen* on the grounds that although Mr Rasmussen had more limited opportunities to challenge paternity than other parties, the opportunities he had were still adequate. In *Mizzi*, on the other hand, the registered father never had *any* possibility of challenging the presumption, while 'any [other] person interested' could bring an action without time restrictions. As such, there was a violation of Article 14 in conjunction with Article 8.

[105] (74826/01) 24.11.2005.

[106] See also *Doktorov v Bulgaria* (15074/08) 05.04.2018.

[107] (34308/96) 19.10.1999 (dec.).

[108] Here, the Court emphasised that a denial of paternity would jeopardise the child's financial situation, as the registered father would stop paying maintenance, without any realistic prospect of finding the biological parent.

[109] (8777/79) 28.11.1984.

[110] (26111/02) 12.01.2006.

Likewise, in *Paulik v Slovakia*,[111] because the applicant had his paternity declared by a judicial decision, he was not able to subsequently challenge it. In contrast, fathers whose paternity had been presumed (through marriage), or where the man had recognised the child, could later challenge these findings in court. The Court acknowledged that, as a matter of principle, the legitimate interest in ensuring legal certainty and security of family relationships may justify a difference in treatment between fathers whose paternity has been presumed and those who have had paternity determined by a court. However, in the present case, there was no procedure by which the applicant could challenge the ruling and no allowance could be made for the specific circumstances of the applicant's case, leading to a violation of the Convention.

In many ways, this line of jurisprudence under Article 14 adds little to what has already been established under Article 8. Indeed, in *Mizzi* and *Paulik*, the Court had already held that Article 8 had been breached before examining Article 14. What can be seen is that states can legitimately treat fathers differently from mothers and children in challenging paternity. They can even treat differently paternity acquired through different mechanisms. What they cannot do—as with Article 8 standing alone—is to fail to provide any realistic opportunity for a father to challenge his paternity or enforce inflexible rules that do not allow for a consideration of the specific circumstances of the case.

8.3.3 The rights of the child in establishing paternity

The discussion so far has focused on the rights of adults either to establish, or deny, their legal parenthood. While children's interests are a central feature of the Court's analysis of the exercise of such rights, there remains a fundamental difference between a child's interests considered in light of a parents' claim and the child's own free-standing rights.

The right of the child to establish important information concerning their identity is discussed in detail Chapter 3, but it is important to outline here also as it relates to the establishment of paternity. In this respect, the Court has made clear that children have a vital interest, protected by the Convention, in receiving the information necessary to uncover the truth about their biological origins and have their paternity recognised, as an important aspect of their personal identity.

This was first established in *Mikulić v Croatia*[112] concerning a child and her mother who were seeking to establish the identity of the child's father. Despite a court order, the putative father refused to undergo a DNA test, and as a result, the domestic authorities concluded that paternity could not be established. The Court acknowledged that protection for third parties may prevent them from being compelled to make themselves available for medical tests that they did not want to undertake. However, this protection for third parties must be balanced against the right of the child to have any uncertainty as to her personal identity eliminated without unnecessary delay. As

[111] (10699/05) 10.10.2006.
[112] (53176/99) 07.02.2002.

such, it would only be proportionate to allow a refusal to undergo tests if there was an alternative mechanism to enable an independent authority to determine the issue of paternity, absent DNA results.

The principle in *Mikulić* was further expanded in *Jäggi v Switzerland*,[113] where the Court recognised that the right to establish one's biological parentage is an integral part of the notion of private life, and therefore particularly rigorous scrutiny is called for when weighing up competing interests. Importantly, this right does not end when a child reaches majority, but continues to be granted protection as long as it continues to be important to the individual.

In addition to considering the substantive rights of a child to be able to determine their biological origins, the Court has also recognised certain procedural safeguards arising under Article 8. First, as was discussed in *AMM v Romania*,[114] the child must be adequately involved in any proceedings—either directly or indirectly. In this case, the child's mother brought paternity proceedings against the putative father, but later she agreed to forgo DNA tests and the taking of witness evidence, and thus the domestic courts dismissed her claims as unsubstantiated. The Court found that the child's rights under Article 8 had been violated, as the domestic courts had not adequately protected his right to have his interests safeguarded in the paternity proceedings. The Court held that there was a positive obligation on the authorities to act on behalf of the child whose paternity was to be established; however, the guardianship office responsible for protecting the child's own rights had not taken part in proceedings, nor had the child been represented by a lawyer.

Second, as with putative fathers seeking to *deny* their paternity, the Court has considered cases where children have been hindered by restrictive time limits in bringing their applications to *establish* paternity. In *Phinikaridou v Cyprus*,[115] a child could seek a judicial recognition of paternity within three years from the time they reached majority (or if already of majority at the time the law entered into force, three years from that date). The applicant, who had been abandoned at birth, did not find out her father's identity until she was 52—well after this time limit had expired. The Court found that while the provisions of the law may adequately secure the interests of the child who learns of their father's identity within the time period, they did not make allowance for those who did not acquire knowledge of the material facts until a later date. As such, the Court 'ha[d] difficulties' in accepting the inflexible limitation period, with time running irrespective of a child's awareness of the circumstances surrounding their father's identity, and without providing any exceptions.[116] In doing so, the Court drew an analogy with *Kroon v the Netherlands*, discussed in section 8.2.2.2 above, in that the family relationship at stake was regulated by an irrebuttable presumption, with no consideration of the material facts, nor the social reality. Moreover,

[113] (58757/00) 13.07.2006.

[114] (2151/10) 14.02.2012.

[115] (23890/02) 20.12.2007.

[116] cf. *Silva and Mondim Correia v Portugal* (72105/14, 20415/15) 03.10.2017, where the applicants had ten years after the date of achieving majority, with an additional three years' extension if the child became aware after the time limit that paternity should be questioned. The Court held that applicants had waited 20 years and 56 years respectively after reaching the age of majority to institute proceedings, and their interest in establishing biological truth did not exempt them from complying with reasonable time limits.

it had not been shown how the general interest in protecting legal certainty of family relationships, nor the interests of the presumed father and his family, outweighed the child's right to have at least one opportunity to seek judicial determination of paternity.

This was further elaborated upon in *Grönmark v Finland*,[117] where a man had been ordered to pay child support by the District Court, but had never been registered as the legal father, despite all parties being under the impression that paternity had been established when child maintenance had been ordered. It was not until after the man's death that it was revealed that this was not the case. The child initiated proceedings, but these were dismissed on the grounds that paternity proceedings concerning a child born before 1981 had to be initiated within five years of that date, and could not be brought after the death of the father.

The Court found that when balancing competing interests concerning limitation periods of paternity claims, a number of factors have to be considered, including: the point in time that the applicant becomes aware of the biological reality; whether or not alternative means of redress exist if the proceedings are time barred; and whether there are exceptions to the time limit. The Court held that the yardstick against which these factors are measured is whether a legal presumption has been allowed to prevail over biological and social reality, and whether this is compatible with the obligation to ensure effective 'respect' for private and family life.

In this case, the statutory time limit started when the child was eight years old, and finished when she was 13. As a consequence of her age, she needed her mother's authorisation to bring an action, and by the time she was old enough to initiate proceedings without her mother's consent, the time period had elapsed. The Court found that an inflexible limitation period, running irrespective of a child's age and legal capacity, and without providing any exceptions, was not compatible with Article 8. The authorities had 'allowed the legal reality to contradict the biological reality by relying on the absolute nature of the time-limit'.[118] While the fact that the child was a minor when the time period expired was an important factor in *Grönmark*, in *Röman v Finland*, when considering the same legal framework, the Court found that Article 8 had still been violated, even though the child had reached adulthood at the time the limitation period was running.[119]

The final issue that has been discussed by the Court relates not to the right of the child to *establish* information on their origins, but on the right of the child to remain ignorant of this fact. Can the domestic authorities force a child to undergo a DNA test against their wishes? In *Mikulić*, the Court considered that the father had an interest in personal integrity, which may prevent him being forced to undergo a blood test; however, this decision appears to be within the margin of appreciation of states (and required that there be another mechanism to determine paternity). In the more recent case of *Mifsud v Malta*,[120] the Court found that the Maltese law requiring a putative father to provide a genetic sample did not violate his rights under Article 8, as any interference pursued the legitimate aim of protecting the rights of the child. The

[117] (17038/04) 06.07.2010. See also *Backlund v Finland* (36498/05) 06.07.2010.
[118] *Grönmark v Finland* (17038/04) 06.07.2010, para. 56.
[119] (13072/05) 29.01.2013.
[120] (62257/15) 29.01.2019.

Court observed that there is a positive obligation on the state to allow the child to discover the truth concerning the identity of his parents, which outweighed the putative father's right to physical integrity.

Likewise, in a string of cases, the Court has found that it is within the state's margin of appreciation to force a child to undergo medical testing to conclusively determine paternity—whether the objection is to the medical test itself or to the subsequent consequences in terms of overturning the already established parental ties.

This was first considered very early in the Court's jurisprudence in the 1979 decision of *X v Austria*.[121] In this case, the applicant had been registered as the son of a married couple, but when the applicant was 19 years old, the husband brought proceedings to declare that he was not the father. The domestic courts ordered that the applicant undergo a blood test to determine the issue, and when he refused, it was ordered that this be taken by force. The applicant argued that the use of force was not justified in the public interest, as the question of paternity could be determined by other means than forceful interference with his personal integrity.

The Commission found that any compulsory medical intervention, even if it is minor, must be considered as an interference with the right to respect for private life under Article 8. However, this interference is justified in the case of paternity proceedings. Such proceedings determine various family rights, including maintenance payments and rights of succession, and a blood test makes it possible to arrive at a finding in this regard. The public has an interest in the courts having the power to make use of 'harmless scientifically proved methods of obtaining evidence',[122] which must prevail over the applicant's interests in physical integrity.

The Commission thus placed significant weight on the public interest in the establishment of paternity, with no discussion of how the child's best interests may conflict or converge with this. Given the date of the decision, however, this is hardly surprising, and in more recent cases, the Court has taken a much more nuanced approach in this respect.

In *ILV v Romania*,[123] for example, the Court acknowledged that the right of a man to the establishment of paternity is not absolute and must be weighed against the interests of the child. Here, the legal father wished to determine whether he was biologically related to his 14-year-old child, but as the child refused to take a DNA test, the domestic courts dismissed the case. The father complained that the inability to ascertain the truth regarding his paternity violated his rights under Article 8. The Court affirmed that there is no absolute right to verify a biological relationship between two individuals, and the need to protect third parties may exclude the possibility of forcing them to undergo DNA tests. This was all the more so in the case where the third party is a child and the testing would overturn long-established ties of filiation. In such cases, the Court found that it was not unreasonable for the national courts to conclude that the best interests of the child should prevail over the father's wish to verify biological fact.[124]

[121] (8278/78) 13.12.1979 (dec.).
[122] ibid., p.157.
[123] (4901/04) 24.08.2010 (dec.)
[124] See also *MB v the United Kingdom* (22920/93) 06.04.1994 (dec.).

Although only an admissibility decision, this case is important, as it clearly establishes that while the child may have a right to determine their biological relationship with a putative father—for example, in *Mikulić*—any corresponding right of the father may be limited by public policy[125] or the child's best interests.

However, the 'best interests' principle has also been used *against* the child, in order to compel testing, or even to conceal a paternity claim from the child in question. The paternalistic approach of the Court in this respect can be seen in two seemingly contrasting cases, one permitting the enforcement of a DNA test, the other allowing it to be denied, but which both demonstrate the inherent difficulties with the 'best interests' test in denying the child's autonomy and agency.

Frölich v Germany[126] involved an application by a putative biological father for contact and information rights, which was denied on the basis that his paternity had not been established. The domestic courts concluded that ordering a paternity test would not be in the child's best interests, as there was a risk that this would cause the breakdown of the relationship between her mother and her legally recognised father (the mother's husband) and thus endanger the stability of the family unit. In the course of the proceedings, the child—six years old at the time—was heard directly by the court, against the advice of the guardian ad litem. She was told only that there was a dispute regarding contact with the applicant, but was not told the context for this, nor that he was also seeking a paternity test. She indicated that she did not wish for any contact.

In examining an application brought by the putative father, the Court found that the domestic authorities had not exceeded their margin of appreciation—they had undertaken an in-depth examination of the entire family situation and made their decision according to the child's best interests. What is striking about this decision is that the Court appears to tacitly accept that the domestic authorities were entitled to not only directly hear a young child, against the advice of the expert appointed to protect her best interests, but also to lie to the child about the true nature of the proceedings.

This is not to say that all issues should be put to the child directly: there are legitimate reasons not to confront a child with the issues being litigated. In many cases, indirect participation is more appropriate, through expert appraisal of the child's answers to more general questions, or through observation of the child's actions and behaviour. But here, the line between direct and indirect participation has been blurred. The child has been deemed mature enough to directly address the question of contact, thus providing a veneer of autonomy, yet she is being denied the opportunity to provide a substantive response, given that the key to the dispute—the fact that the person wishing for contact was not some random stranger, but her potential biological father—has been obscured. Such an approach appears tokenistic at best, and paternalistic at worst.

This case can be contrasted with *Mandet v France*,[127] which was discussed in section 8.3.2.1 above, involving a 14-year-old child whose putative biological father also sought to overturn the paternity of the mother's husband. In this case, the child clearly stated that he did not wish for the paternity test to be carried out and he wished his

[125] In the form of time limits, as discussed above.
[126] (16112/15) 26.07.2018.
[127] (30955/12) 14.01.2016.

social father, who he had grown up with, to remain his legal parent. This notwithstanding, the domestic courts found that it was in the child's best interests to know the truth about his biological origins, and to have this recognised on his birth certificate.

The Court found that there had been no violation of Article 8 in this respect—the obligation on the domestic authorities was to place the child's best interests at the heart of the decision-making, which they had done. The duty was thus procedural, rather than substantive. The Court would only ascertain whether the child's interests had been appropriately weighed, but would not interfere as to the domestic courts' assessment of their substance.

These cases again demonstrate the 'hands-off' approach of the Court in this area: it is within the margin of appreciation of states to decide whether and how paternity may be established or challenged, as long as the child's best interests have been taken into consideration. The problem lies with the concept of the child's best interests itself: it can mean whatever the domestic decision-makers want it to mean, with apparently no oversight of the Court. Only Judge Nussberger in dissent in *Mandet* was willing to challenge the assessment of the domestic courts in this respect. She emphasised that losing his social and legal father and being forced to accept the alleged biological father as his new legal father was not in the best interests of the child, nor was it justifiable by the interests of the putative father or by other reasons of public order. She further suggested that the domestic court defined the best interests of the child in an abstract and generalised way, without referring to the situation and concrete circumstances of the individual child in question, and in particular taking into his account his views on the matter. She stressed that finding out information on one's biological origins is the *right* of a child, not an *obligation*. This means that a child should also have the right to ignore the truth of his biological paternity if he or she so wishes.

The question then becomes—is there a point at which a state's analysis of the child's best interests will stretch the margin of appreciation too far? Judge Nussberger's scathing dissent suggests that this point has already been reached when domestic authorities act against the clearly expressed wishes of a 14-year-old child. She warned against the concept of 'best interests' being used as a vehicle for the interests of others and of taking an objective view that obscured the true interests of the individual child in question. While it is difficult for a supranational court to undertake an investigation of what would be in the best interests of an individual child, and thus a wide margin of appreciation in this respect is necessary, it is important to ensure that the decision of the domestic authorities is subject to some limitations—safeguarding against arbitrary, capricious, and irrational decisions. It is this that Judge Nussberger is trying to achieve.

8.4 The changing face of the family

With the advent of new reproductive technologies—for example, in vitro fertilisation (IVF) and mitochondrial donation—comes new possibilities for family formation and corresponding challenges for law makers and legal systems. One of the great advantages of the European Convention on Human Rights is its characterisation as a 'living instrument', which must be interpreted according to present-day conditions and reflective of social change.[128] The other side of the coin, however, is the wide margin of appreciation given to states, especially in morally contested areas, which leads to a notoriously slow evolution of ideas.[129] It also means that the Court is rarely at the vanguard of rights protection, but evolves only when domestic authorities themselves have already taken the lead.[130] This is epitomised in the approach taken by the Court in relation to recognition of parenthood in the context of new family forms—for example, same-sex parenting, transgender parenting—and in the use of new technologies—for example, parenthood achieved through surrogacy.

8.4.1 New family forms

8.4.1.1 Same-sex parenting

The Court has taken a very conservative approach to the issue of same-sex parenting, betraying a preoccupation with the 'traditional' family unit based on one man, one woman, and their biological child.

This can clearly be seen in a line of cases, starting with *Kerkhoven and Hinke v Netherlands*.[131] In this case, two women in a same-sex relationship requested that they both be vested with parental authority over a child born to one of them through artificial insemination. In a short judgment, the Commission declared the application inadmissible, finding that the positive obligations of the state under Article 8 do not go so far as to require that the female partner of the mother of a child, who is acting as a social parent, should be entitled to parental rights. Similarly, in *Boeckel and Gessner-Boeckel v Germany*,[132] the Court declared inadmissible an application by two women in a civil partnership to have the mother's partner registered as the child's second parent. They had argued that a husband would automatically be named as the father, regardless of his biological relationship, and that there was no reason to treat children born into a civil partnership any differently from children born in wedlock. The Court found that a same-sex couple in a civil union are not in a relevantly similar position to a married opposite-sex couple. Domestic law worked on the assumption that the husband is the biological parent, even if this did not reflect the child's true descent; however, the same assumption could not be applied to a same-sex couple. There was no

[128] *Tyrer v the United Kingdom* (5856/72) 25.04.1978 (Court). On this point, see G. Letsas, 'The ECHR as a Living Instrument: Its Meaning and Legitimacy' in G. Ulfstein, A. Follesdal, and B. Peters (eds), *Constituting Europe: The European Court of Human Rights in a National, European and Global Context* (Cambridge University Press, 2013).

[129] See, for example, the recognition that same-sex relationships constitute 'family life', rather than simply 'private life'.

[130] This was not always the case. In the so-called 'judicial phase' of the Court, it issued several revolutionary and transformative judgments—for example, *Marckx v Belgium* (6833/74) 13.06.1979; *Dudgeon v the United Kingdom* (7525/76) 22.10.1981—however, this has lessened over the years, with the advent of the 'age of subsidiarity': see R. Spanó, 'Universality or Diversity of Human Rights? Strasbourg in an Age of Subsidiarity' (2014) 14 *Human Rights Law Review* 487.

[131] (15666/89) 19.05.1992 (dec.).

[132] (8017/11) 07.05.2013 (dec.).

factual foundation for a legal presumption that the child descended from the second partner. As such, the case was declared inadmissible.

While these judgments may be contextualised by the time period in which they were decided—*Kerkhoven* over 25 years ago, and even *Boeckel* at six years old may be argued to be outdated due to the rapidly changing social attitudes in this area—more recent judgments show the same conservative attitude towards the 'family life' of same-sex couples. For example, in *Bonnaud and Lecoq v France*,[133] a French same-sex couple—both of whom had given birth to a biological child, whom they jointly raised in a family unit—applied to the domestic courts for the joint exercise of parental authority over each child. This was refused, on the basis that there was no evidence provided as to how this would promote the children's best interests (as opposed to those of the mother). The Court found the application inadmissible, holding that the decision to grant or refuse the delegation of parental authority was based on the factual circumstances in each case, and both same-sex and opposite-sex couples were treated in the same way in this respect. The Court further noted that the applicants had not encountered any practical difficulties flowing from a lack of legal parenthood, and thus the application under Article 14 in conjunction with Article 8 was manifestly ill-founded.

Although the domestic decision does seem to provide formal equality—all parents were treated in the same way, without regard to their sexual orientation—it fails to address the deeper issue: that is, the structural discrimination against same-sex couples regarding parental rights. While it is true that the process of delegating parental authority within a relationship is open to both same-sex and opposite-sex couples, the Court failed to take into account that this was the *only* way in which a same-sex couple could exercise joint parental authority:[134] no other mechanism was available to recognise common parenthood between a same-sex couple. In this way, the seemingly neutral criteria in determining whether it was appropriate to allow delegation of parental authority placed a heavier burden on same-sex couples—if they could not meet this high standard, they had no other option (in contrast to opposite-sex couples, who had other legal mechanisms to which they could turn).

This reliance on formal equality, rather than substantive equity, is a significant flaw in the Court's approach to new forms of families. The question the Court asks itself is whether they fit within, and are analogous to, traditionally recognised family models, rather than acknowledging them as different, yet equally valuable, family forms. While the Court has taken big strides forward in relation to the rights of gay and lesbian individuals and couples in recent years,[135] in this fundamental area of parenthood, one of the most basic and foundational legal statuses, same-sex couples continue to be second-class citizens before the Court.

[133] (6190/11) 06.02.2018 (dec.).

[134] The facts in this case occurred before second-parent adoption within same-sex unions was permitted in France in 2013.

[135] See, for example, *EB v France* (43546/02) 22.01.2008 (GC); *Salgueiro da Silva Mouta v Portugal* (33290/96) 21.12.1999; *Schalk and Kopf v Austria* (30141/04) 24.06.2010; *Gas and Dubois v France* (25951/07) 15.03.2012; *X and others v Austria* (19010/07) 19.02.2013.

8.4.1.2 Transgender parenting

The same is true of transgender parents—although there has only been one case that has come before the Court in this respect. In *X, Y, and Z v the United Kingdom*,[136] a female-to-male transgender individual (X) wished to be recognised as the father of a child born to his partner (Y) through artificial reproductive technology. As was discussed in section 8.2.2.2 above, the Court found that 'family life' existed between X and the child—X and Y had applied jointly for the reproductive treatment, and X had acted as the child's father since birth in every respect. The question remained what steps the domestic authorities had to take to recognise this 'family life' in law. Drawing on earlier cases of *Marckx*, *Keegan*, and *Kroon*, the Court acknowledged that where a family tie has been established, the state must act in a manner calculated to enable that tie to be developed, and legal safeguards must be established to render possible the child's integration into the family. However, it distinguished these cases as they concerned 'family life' existing between biological parents and their children, rather than a child born through artificial reproductive techniques. It emphasised that there was no consensus between member states as to the manner in which the social relationship between a child conceived by artificial reproduction and the person who performs the role of father should be reflected in law.

Moreover, the Court found that there was no consensus with regard to the granting of parental rights to transgender individuals. It observed that it was not clear that it would be to the advantage of the child to recognise X as a legal father and that the state may justifiably be cautious in changing the law, since any amendment might have undesirable and unforeseen ramifications for children, as well as for other areas of family law.[137] As such, the Court came to the tenuous conclusion that because X was not prevented from performing the functions of parenthood, it was not necessary to provide him with formal recognition. He was able to act as the child's social parent, and therefore the lack of legal connection was not deemed to be significant.

This approach confuses the status of parenthood with the more practical notion of parental authority or responsibility. The ability of an individual to exercise the latter does not negate the importance of the former. It harks back to a negative conception of the right to respect for family life, relying on a lack of interference with the parent's role, rather than looking to the positive obligation to fully integrate the child into the family. It also shows that the Court treats differently those families that conform with traditional heterosexual family models and those that challenge the social norms. This could be viewed simply as an unfortunate by-product of the inherent difficulties of a supranational judicial organ: the Court cannot push forward too quickly, as it relies on cooperation to give it authority and ensure compliance with its judgments. On the other hand, it undermines the legitimacy of the Court as an institution which upholds human rights when different rules apply for socially entrenched practices than for those that are newly emerging, or are only practiced by a minority.

Moreover, it also allows children to be treated differently on account of the circumstances of their birth—in direct contravention of Article 2 of the United Nations

[136] (21830/93) 22.04.1997 (GC).

[137] This approach can also be seen in relation to same-sex adoption: see Chapter 11.

Convention on the Rights of the Child. As was seen in *Kroon*, for a child born through natural reproduction to a heterosexual couple, and living with them as a family, legal integration into the family is essential to comply with Article 8. For a child in the same situation born to a same-sex couple, or to a parent who is transgender, it is enough that the state does not interfere with their social relationship, without any obligation to recognise it in law. Of course, *X, Y and Z* is now over 20 years old and it is not clear that the same decision would be made today.[138] However, even if such relationships would now demand recognition, this does not itself solve the problem, as there will always be new forms of relationships, challenging our traditional assumptions of what makes a 'parent'. The Court must not only reconsider the way it views transgender parenthood, but the basis upon which it conceptualises *all* parenthood.

8.4.2 New methods of reproduction

In addition to the impact of new family forms on our understanding of parenthood, another development is of equal importance. The advent of new technologies has extended the possibility of parenthood to individuals and couples who would not otherwise have had the opportunity. Both medical infertility and structural/social infertility can now be overcome through donated egg and sperm, in-vitro fertilisation, and surrogacy. However, with new possibilities also come new challenges, and these developments have raised important legal and ethical questions. Although there is significant case law concerning who can access this technology and these processes, and under what circumstances—for example, *Evans v the United Kingdom*,[139] *Dickson v the United Kingdom*,[140] and *SH and others v Austria*[141]—this book does not consider these adult-focused questions in any detail.[142] Instead, it examines the cases concerning the *children* born from these new technologies, which have centred on the practice of international surrogacy.

The leading case in this field is *Mennesson v France*,[143] which involved a French couple who had travelled to the United States to undertake a surrogacy arrangement (surrogacy being prohibited in France). When they returned to France with the child, the authorities refused to enter the birth onto the French register for births, marriages, and deaths on the grounds that recording such entries would give effect to a surrogacy

[138] In relation to custody, the Court has made clear that an individual being transgender cannot be used to deny access to the child. However, the negative impact on the child of this transition *could* be considered: see *PV v Spain* (35159/09) 30.11.2010.

[139] (6339/05) 10.04.2007 (GC).

[140] (44362/04) 04.12.2007.

[141] (57813/00) 03.11.2011 (GC). See also the admissibility decision of *Charron and Merle-Montet v France* (22612/15) 16.01.2018 (dec.) concerning a same-sex couple seeking access to IVF treatment.

[142] While such decisions inevitably have an impact on children, they have not been argued as such. Another example of this can be seen in cases considering civil claims regarding children born with disabilities: for example, *Draon v France* (1513/03) 06.10.2005 (GC); *AK v Latvia* (33011/08) 24.06.2014. These cases, while they concern the birth of a child, have been examined solely from the perspective of the rights of the adults. In neither of these cases were the children included as applicants, nor were their rights examined. They thus emerge as objects in this line of jurisprudence—the centre of a dispute *about* their lives, yet not recognized as subjects in their own right.

[143] (65192/11) 26.06.2014. See also *Labassee v France* (65941/11) 26.06.2014.

agreement that was null and void under French law, and recognise a practice that the legislature had expressly forbidden.

The Court recognised that surrogacy raises difficult ethical issues, and emphasised the lack of consensus in Europe as to how to respond to this practice, both domestically and abroad. In light of this, the Court held that, in principle, states must be given a wide margin of discretion with regard to the decision of whether or not to allow this method of reproduction, as well as whether to recognise parenthood arising from foreign surrogacy arrangements. However, the Court was also swift to assert that 'the choices made by the State, even within this margin of appreciation, are not beyond the control of the Court'.[144]

The Court found that this refusal to recognise parenthood under French law did not violate the right to respect for family life of the commissioning parents or child: similar to the decision in *X, Y and Z*, the Court observed that despite a lack of legal recognition of parenthood, the family was able to live together in a situation broadly comparable with other families and was not in danger of separation. As such, and in light of the margin of appreciation given to the French authorities, a fair balance had been struck between the interests of the parents and those of the state.

However, the Court did not stop there, and went on to consider separately the right to respect for private life on the part of the child. As discussed in Chapter 3, the Court found that the establishment of paternity relates to an important aspect of the child's identity, which falls within 'private life' under Article 8. The Court emphasised that the children were in a position of legal uncertainty, and that 'it cannot be said to be in the interests of the child to deprive him or her of a legal relationship of this nature where the biological reality of that relationship has been established and the child and parent concerned demand full recognition thereof'.[145] Thus, even if the parents had no right to be recognised in law, the child had a right that they be so.[146]

This judgment follows the reasoning of the Court on the recognition of foreign adoption decisions. In particular, the decision of *Wagner and JMWL v Luxembourg*[147] found that a refusal to recognise an intercountry adoption was a breach of the child's rights under Article 14 in conjunction with Article 8. In this case, the Court noted that where parental ties have been broken in the country of birth, as they also usually are in cases of surrogacy, to deny the formation of new legal ties with the person (or persons) who would now act as parents would be to undermine the child's right to certainty of legal status and to identity.[148]

However, in *Mennsson* a further aspect was emphasised: the Court identified the genetic link as a crucial component in the creation of an interest in private life for the child, once again relying on traditional notions of what 'parenthood' means. The paramountcy of the genetic tie was further reinforced in *Paradiso and Campanelli v Italy*[149]—as discussed in section 8.2.2.2 above—where the Court found that absent

[144] *Mennesson v France* (65192/11) 26.06.2014, para. 60.

[145] ibid., para. 100.

[146] See also *Foulon and Bouvet v France* (9063/14; 10410/14) 21.07.2016 (dec.); *Laborie v France* (44024/13) 19.01.2017 (dec.).

[147] (76240/01) 28.06.2007.

[148] For further discussion on this issue, see C. Fenton-Glynn, 'International Surrogacy before the European Court of Human Rights' (2017) 13(3) *Journal of Private International Law* 546.

[149] (25358/12) 27.01.2015 (Ch); (25358/12) 24.01.2017 (GC).

this connection, no 'family life' existed between the child and the intended parents, notwithstanding the fact that they had cared for the child for the first eight months of his life.

However, this focus on genetics is rather one-sided: while there is an obligation to automatically recognise an intended father who has contributed genetic material, no corresponding obligation exists with regard to the intended mother. This issue was raised by the Cour de Cassation, in the first ever Advisory Opinion of the Court under Protocol 16.[150] Here, the Cour de Cassation noted that although the French authorities now registered the details of the intended father where there was a biological link, it continued to be impossible with regard to the intended mother. If she wished for her parenthood to be recognised, she would instead have to go through an adoption procedure. The Cour de Cassation thus asked the Court the following questions:

1. Was the refusal to register the intended mother as the legal mother contrary to the state's obligations under Article 8? In this connection, should a distinction be drawn according to whether the child was conceived using her eggs?
2. If so, was the possibility of adoption as a means of establishing a parent–child relationship sufficient to ensure compliance with Article 8?

The Court answered both questions in the affirmative. It held that the child's best interests require the legal identification of the persons responsible for raising and caring for the child, and the 'general and absolute' impossibility of achieving this for a child born through surrogacy in relation to the intended mother was incompatible with Article 8 of the Convention. Despite this recognition of intended and social parenthood, however, the hold of biology on the Court's jurisprudence did not disappear entirely. First, it noted that this imperative to provide recognition to the intended mother applied with even greater force in a case where she had provided the genetic material. Second, the Court held that while automatic recognition must be given to the biological intended father, it was sufficient in the case of the intended mother—genetically related or not—for her to be permitted to go through a step-parent adoption. There was no obligation to recognise *ab initio* the parent–child relationship in this case, merely that recognition of that relationship should be established as soon as possible, and at the latest by the time that relationship has become a social reality.

The Court's jurisprudence on surrogacy thus has its high points, as well as its disadvantages. On a positive note, the recognition in *Mennesson* that parenthood must be about the child's experience must be applauded; however, no such child-focused perspective was taken in *Paradiso*. Moreover, the negative formulation of the right to respect for family life seen in *Mennesson* and *X, Y and Z* is of concern, creating a clear distinction between 'conventional' forms of reproduction and new family forms.

This is an issue which will no doubt come before the Court on many more occasions, raising a variety of different, and difficult, human rights concerns. It is to be hoped that the Court will continue to approach the issue from the perspective of the

[150] *Advisory opinion concerning the recognition in domestic law of a legal parent–child relationship between a child born through a gestational surrogacy arrangement abroad and the intended mother* (10.04.2019).

rights of the child, recognising them as individuals in their own right, rather than just collateral in a fight between adults and the state.

8.5 Conclusion

This is an area of the Court's case law that continues to evolve in light of developments in family forms, social norms, and technological advances. But this is an ongoing project—our society is changing rapidly and the Court needs to ensure that it is not left behind.

The law of parenthood is at a crossroads: no longer tied to marriage, or even to intercourse, domestic laws are struggling to adapt. Despite being prohibited in most European jurisdictions, surrogacy has gained an increasing foothold, forcing legislatures and courts to redefine what it means to be a 'mother'. Same-sex parenthood is continuing to push for greater recognition, as is transgender parenthood, and in particular, the question of whether a man who gives birth should be named as the child's 'mother' or 'father'.[151] Moreover, some jurisdictions are starting to recognise *more than* two parents, widening the scope of traditional parenthood to extend to three, or even more, individuals.[152]

Traditionally, the Court has taken a cautious approach to family forms—responding to change only once it has spread sufficiently widely across the continent. But more recently, in the case of surrogacy, the Court has been willing to take a more proactive approach, avoiding questions of ethics in favour of protecting the child's lived reality—at least where there is a biological tie.

This is an important step forward, recognising that parenthood is about children first, and adults second. As the Court said so many years ago in *X, Y and Z v the United Kingdom*, 'the community as a whole has an interest in maintaining a coherent system of family law which places the best interests of the child at the forefront'.[153]

[151] This situation is currently being litigated before the English courts in the case of *TT and YY v the Registrar General* [2019] EWHC 2384; [2020] EWCA Civ 559.

[152] See, for example, Ontario and British Columbia (Canada), Delaware and California (USA).

[153] (21830/93) 22.04.1997 (GC), para. 47.

9
Private Law Child Disputes

9.1 Introduction

One of the most prolific areas of the Court's jurisprudence relates to private law disputes concerning children: the extent of parental authority; custody and residence; access and contact; parental child abduction; as well as the procedural rules that accompany them. This chapter explores how these have come before the Court, and the ways in which children's rights have been conceptualised in both the applications themselves and the Court's decision-making.

There have been attempts—both by government, and by individual judges—to deny the applicability of the Convention in private law child disputes. For example, in *Palau-Martinez v France*, the government argued that, 'in the context of a divorce, court "intervention" was necessary but could not be considered "interference" within the meaning of Article 8(2)'.[1] This was a repetition of an argument made by Judge Mifsud Bonnici in dissent ten years earlier in *Hoffmann v Austria*.[2] In this case, he distinguished between interference and intervention: interference implying 'that action whereby one interposes or meddles in something, without having the right to do so', while intervention constituted 'that action whereby one steps in-between, to prevent or hinder a harm which otherwise will occur'.[3] He argued that since courts are *obliged* to intervene in custody decisions, they cannot then be seen as interferences—rather, they were 'necessary interventions'.[4] In both cases, these arguments were soundly rejected by the majority of the Court. In private law child disputes, a decision of the domestic authorities determines the relationship between the parent and child, which necessarily interferes with their private and family life. The fact that the decision of where the child should live, and with whom they should have contact, was made in the context of a dispute between private individuals made no difference to this conclusion.

As a result, while at a domestic level, these cases are predominantly characterised by a conflict between the parents themselves, at the level of the European Court of Human Rights, they are transformed into a dispute between one of the parents and the state. This in turn leads to a narrowing of the perspectives put before the Court—only one parent will present the case, and as such, it is only one view that will be put forward, making the issue of standing and representation of particular importance.

[1] (64927/01) 16.12.2003, para. 23.
[2] (12875/87) 23.06.1993.
[3] ibid., dissenting opinion of Judge Misfud Bonnici, para. 2.
[4] ibid., dissenting opinion of Judge Misfud Bonnici.

Children and the European Court of Human Rights. Claire Fenton-Glynn, Oxford University Press (2021). © Claire Fenton-Glynn.
DOI: 10.1093/oso/9780198787518.003.0009

9.2 Standing and representation

9.2.1 Standing of a parent

While it is possible for a child to bring a case before the Court in their own right, in practice the very nature of legal claims and court proceedings 'makes it difficult for all but the most confident and competent children to participate effectively'.[5] To address this, the Court permits parents to make an application on behalf of their child, to ensure that they are given effective access to the protection of the Convention.

However, an issue arises in private law disputes where the parents are themselves in conflict. Who then is best placed to bring a case on behalf of the child? In such cases, the Court has taken the starting point that the parent with custody will be the most appropriate person to represent the child, on the assumption that in these circumstances, the interests of the parent and child will align: they will share the concerns of the child, and thus be best placed to enforce their rights.[6]

Unfortunately, however, this assumption is not always correct. A vivid example of the difficulties faced in this area was seen in *Raw and others v France*,[7] where a mother joined her children to her application to the Court regarding the state's failure to enforce her custody in the context of parental child abduction. This was permitted, with no discussion of whether the children themselves were amenable to this, or supported her application. Indeed, one of the children had physically attacked her when faced with return to her custody, and yet, paradoxically, 'he' was complaining to the Court about the failure of the authorities to force him to do so.[8] Judge Nussberger raised this issue in her partly concurring judgment, highlighting the contradiction that this presents to the UN Convention of the Rights of the Child, and the obligation to hear and respect the views and opinions of the child.[9]

Moreover, the Court has also recognised that in the event of a conflict between a natural parent and the parent with custody, there is a danger that some of the child's interests will not be brought to the Court's attention: for example, if only the parent with custody can complain on behalf of the child that custody has been awarded in a discriminatory manner, then it is unlikely that they will do so. As such, the Court has acknowledged that the child will be deprived of effective protection of their rights if a restrictive view on standing is adopted,[10] and has therefore permitted the non-custodial parent to bring an application on the child's behalf where this is necessary to ensure that the child's case is brought before the Court. The approach taken by the Court in this regard was set out in *Eberhard and M v Slovenia*,[11] where it held that:

[5] M. Murch, 'The Voice of the Child in Private Family Law Proceedings in England and Wales' (2005) 8(18) *International Family Law Journal* 8.

[6] *Eberhard and M v Slovenia* (8673/05, 9733/05) 01.12.2009. See also U. Kilkelly, *The Child and the European Convention on Human Rights* (Aldershot: Ashgate 1999), 240.

[7] (10131/11) 07.03.2013.

[8] 'His' application was discontinued on his attaining the age of majority, when he withdrew his consent to its continuance.

[9] Article 12, UN Convention on the Rights of the Child.

[10] See, for example, *Sylvester v Austria* (36812/97, 40104/98) 24.04.2003; *Raban v Romania* (25437/08) 26.10.2010.

[11] (8673/05, 9733/05) 01.12.2009.

> Whether a natural parent has standing to act on his child's behalf in proceedings before the Court is dependent on whether the party who opposes the natural parent and is entitled to represent the child under domestic law can be deemed to effectively protect the child's Convention rights.[12]

This expansive approach to standing is to be applauded, providing as it does important protection for the child through flexible interpretation of the procedural rules. However, systemic issues still remain, the most problematic of which being the conflation by the Court of rules concerning standing and representation. Traditionally, the Court has elided these two concepts, meaning that the parent who has standing to bring the claim before the Court is also responsible for presenting the case on behalf of the child, often while simultaneously arguing for a violation of their own parental rights. As I have argued elsewhere, where a parent brings a case on behalf of themselves *and* on behalf of their child, the child's voice is liable to be drowned out by the stronger, more dominant, party.[13] Where a child and his or her parent are represented by the same person before the Court, it is not surprising that the parent, who will in practice be responsible for the direction of the case, will assume a greater role than the child. This is not to doubt that the parent believes that they are promoting the best interests of the child, but their notion of these interests will necessarily be skewed by their own interests which they wish to forward.

Moreover, where parents are seeking to assist a child in enforcing their rights there has traditionally been a dangerous assumption by the Court that children's interests are identical to those of their parents.[14] While this is starting to shift—as is discussed in section 9.2.3 below—this failure to respect children's individuality is one of the key inadequacies of the Convention: as Fortin has argued, the Court 'has not demonstrated particularly clearly a full understanding that promoting children's rights may be impossible, without acknowledging that they have an existence independent from their parents'.[15]

The difference between children as applicants and children as accessories can be seen in the vastly different approach to children's rights in cases concerning juvenile justice and family law. In the field of juvenile justice, where children do often bring their own individual cases,[16] the Court has a strong record of protecting their rights. However, where parents are the primary litigants, the Court continues to ignore the child's individuality and allows adult interests to dominate decision-making.[17]

[12] ibid., para. 86 (citations omitted).

[13] C. Fenton-Glynn, 'Children, Parents and the European Court of Human Rights' (2019) 6 *European Human Rights Law Review* 643.

[14] See, for example, *D v Germany* (10812/84) 11.07.1985 (dec.), where the Commission held that in general, a mother's interests can be equated with that of the child. The Commission considered that the mother was 'able to introduce the application on behalf of her son without it being necessary for the reciprocal parties to the "family life" question to be made joint applicants'. (para. 1) Although this is an old case, and the child would now be made a joint applicant, the attitude behind this decision remains.

[15] J. Fortin, 'Rights Brought Home for Children' (1999) 62 *Modern Law Review* 350, 354.

[16] Even if adults—including parents—may be key in assisting them to bring the case before the Court, it is only the *child's* rights which are the subject of discussion, so they are the prism that the case is argued through.

[17] J. Fortin, 'A Decade of the HRA and its Impact on Children's Rights' (2011) 41 *Family Law* 176.

9.2.2 Standing of a third party

Despite its flaws, the recognition of an expansive interpretation of parental standing is a step in the right direction. However, this is based on the assumption that the child's interests will align with at least *one* of the parents, which is not a foregone conclusion. As Judges Koskelo, Eicke, and Ilievski pointed out in their concurring opinion in *A and B v Croatia*:

> In highly stressful situations such as e.g. a family break-up it would certainly not be right for this Court to assume that the parent(s) can or should always be the final arbiter of what is in the child's best interest; a conflict of interest will frequently arise.[18]

This arises with even more force in relation to cases concerning child abuse—the parents may in fact be the ones who are inflicting harm on the child and therefore will be unlikely to bring a case before the Court in this respect.

The Court has not been blind to this dilemma and has started to develop new approaches to attempt to ensure that children's rights are adequately represented before the Court. First and foremost amongst these has been to recognise the standing of a third party—including private individuals, lawyers, or even non-governmental organisations—to bring a case before the Court on behalf of a child.

An example of this was seen in *SP, DP and AT v the United Kingdom*,[19] where the Commission permitted an application introduced on behalf of three children by the solicitor who represented them in the domestic proceedings, supported by a letter of authority by the guardian ad litem. The Commission emphasised the vulnerability of the children and the need to adopt flexible solutions to ensure that the safeguards under the Convention are 'practical and effective'. Relying on the UN Convention on the Rights of the Child, it held that a restrictive or technical approach must be avoided, and asked itself four questions:

(i) whether more appropriate representation exists;
(ii) the nature of the link between the representative and the children;
(iii) the object and scope of the application; and
(iv) whether there are any conflicts of interests.

Likewise, the Court in *NTS v Georgia*[20] permitted an application to be lodged by a member of the children's wider family, bypassing the natural parent who had parental responsibility under domestic law. In this case, the three minor boys had lived with their maternal family since the death of their mother, but despite a hostile relationship with their father, and overriding the boys' objections, the domestic authorities had awarded him custody. The boys' aunt submitted an application before the Court in their name, arguing that the national authorities had failed to properly assess the best

[18] (7144/15) 20.06.2019, concurring opinion of Judges Koskelo, Eicke, and Ilievski, para. 18 (citations omitted).
[19] (23715/94) 20.05.1996 (dec.).
[20] (71776/12) 02.02.2016.

interests of the children, and that the children had not been adequately involved in the proceedings. The Georgian government objected that the aunt did not have standing to act on behalf of her nephews, as their father had not been deprived of parental rights and was their sole guardian. However, the Court found that the children were in a vulnerable position, and that the aunt had a sufficiently close link with them—she had been actively involved in their upbringing, and they had lived with her for some period of time—to complain on their behalf. In light of their hostile relationship with their father, there was no closer next of kin who could complain on their behalf, and to hold otherwise would be to deprive them of the practical ability to enforce their rights.

The most recent case of this kind has concerned the involvement of a non-governmental organisation in bringing a case on behalf of a child with mental disabilities. In *LR v North Macedonia*,[21] the child in question had been abandoned by his parents at birth and a social welfare centre appointed as his guardian. Since the case concerned the alleged failures of the social welfare centre, it could not be expected to bring a case on the child's behalf, and instead the case was taken to the Court by the Helsinki Committee for Human Rights in Skopje (HCHR). Unlike in *SP, DP and AT*, HCHR had not represented the child in the domestic proceedings, nor had the child provided written authority for the HCHR to act before the Court, without which only 'exceptional circumstances' could justify that an organisation be permitted to act as a de facto representative of the alleged victim.

Relying on the Grand Chamber decision of *Centre for Legal Resources on behalf of Valentin Campeanu v Romania*,[22] the Court identified the following factors that could contribute to a finding of 'exceptional circumstances':

(i) the victim's vulnerability;
(ii) the nature of the allegations before the Court;
(iii) whether the next of kin or legal guardian was likely to lodge an application;
(iv) whether there had been contact between the direct victim and the representative;
(v) whether the representative was involved in the domestic proceedings, and recognised as having standing there.

On the facts, the Court again noted the extreme vulnerability of the child, who was 'manifestly incapable of expressing any wishes or views regarding his own needs and interests, let alone wishes and views on whether to pursue any remedies'.[23] The allegations concerned serious issues under Article 3 of the Convention, in which the legal guardian was itself implicated. While the HCHR had not represented the child on a domestic level, they had visited him in the institution and contacted the competent authorities about his situation, as well as submitting a criminal complaint to the public prosecutor. In light of all this, the Court accepted that HCHR could act as de facto representation for the child.

[21] (38067/15) 23.01.2020.
[22] (47848/08) 17.07.2014 (GC).
[23] *LR v North Macedonia* (38067/15) 23.01.2020, para. 48.

It must be noted, however, that an NGO is of a different character than a solicitor, or a member of the wider family. As Judge Wojtyczek pointed out in his partly dissenting opinion:

> [N]on-governmental organisations have their own views, objectives and interests, which are not necessarily identical with the best interests of the minor they represent. They are involved in numerous cases and are often engaged in lobbying for the promotion of their views as well as the interests they have decided to defend. Even if, apparently, this did not occur in the instant case, there is a risk that the case of a minor may be instrumentalised for the sake of achieving the organisation's general objectives, for instance for the purposes of strategic litigation, which is by its nature directed towards general issues.

For these reasons, although Judge Wojtyczek endorsed the ability of such organisations to lodge a case with the Court on behalf of a child, he recommended that an independent curator ad litem be appointed to represent the child in the proceedings themselves. This draws an important distinction between standing and representation: while it is important to allow parents and third parties to bring cases concerning children to the attention of the Court, this does not necessarily mean that they should be permitted to represent them.

9.2.3 The need for separate legal representation

Judge Wojtyczek's dissenting opinion echoes earlier statements by other individual judges who have called on the Court to introduce a systemic solution for the representation of children through the appointment of a neutral representative, able to put the child's perspective and interests before the Court. As early as 1994, Judge Bonnici, in the case of *Kroon and others v the Netherlands*, condemned the fact that '[t]he interests of the child were never looked after by an independent person, a "curator ad litem", and in fact they are not mentioned in the judgment. The "interests" of the mother and of the other applicant are the only interests which have really been considered.'[24] Likewise, Judge Pettiti has on several occasions criticised the parent-centred approach to cases before the Court and suggested that lawyers should be instructed specifically to represent the interests of the children in cases that also involve their parents.[25]

However, it was not until 2019 that the Court took decisive action on this front, when for the first time in the Court's history it asked for a separate legal representative to be appointed for the child, so that her interests and views could be separately represented. *A and B v Croatia*[26] involved a complaint brought by a mother on behalf of her child, alleging that the domestic authorities had failed to provide a proper response to the allegations of sexual abuse of the child by her father. However, during the domestic

[24] (18535/91) 27.10.1994, dissenting opinion of Judge Bonnici.

[25] See, for example, *X, Y, and Z v the United Kingdom* (21830/93) 22.04.1997 (GC); *Olsson v Sweden (No. 2)* (13441/87) 30.10.1992.

[26] (7144/15) 20.06.2019.

investigation, the authorities had raised concerns that the child was being manipulated by the mother to present false claims, resulting in emotional abuse. Nevertheless, it was the mother's version of the facts, and the mother's framing of the issues, which was the basis of the case before the Court—the father, who by the time the case was decided had full custody of the child, not only was not invited to participate in the case, but was not even informed of its existence.

This was not the first time such a concern had been raised about potential bias where there is parental conflict. In the child abduction case of *Šneersone and Kampanella v Italy*,[27] the Italian government had objected to the mother being permitted to file a case on behalf of her children. They argued that since both parents had a right to respect for family life together with their son, allowing only one of the parents to represent the child's interests would disrupt parental equality. The Court rejected this argument, stating that the conflict should be characterised as one between the child and the conduct and decisions of the authorities, rather than between two parental rights. In doing so, the Court failed to engage with heart of the issue, namely the disempowerment of the other parent and the one-sided perspective of the issues presented to the Court. In doing so, the Court did not adequately distinguish between standing to bring a case before the Court on behalf of the child—which in private law cases will be limited if only the 'winning' parent is able bring an application—and representation—that is, how the child's rights are put before the Court.

And it was this aspect that the Court finally came to terms with in *A and B*. Here, the Court accepted the mother's *standing* to bring the case, but did not consider her able to appropriately *represent* the child's rights before the Court. In light of these concerns, the Court approached the Croatian Bar Association under Rule 36(4) of the Rules of Court and asked them to name a lawyer who could submit observations on behalf of the child.

This was a revolutionary move by the Court, taking steps of its own motion to protect the interests of the child in the case before it. However, as Judges Koskelo, Eicke, and Ilievski acknowledged in their concurring opinion, simply relying on the Court itself to appoint a representative is, in the majority of cases, too late. The nature of the Court is such that it will only rule on the issues that are brought before it, and the identity of the parent who brings the case will have a significant impact on the way in which the issues are framed. Thus by the time the case comes to the Court, the scope of the case has already been irreversibly constructed without the involvement of the child. This was seen in *A and B* itself, where the appointed representative had sought to introduce a complaint on behalf of the child in relation to the failure of the state to protect from the emotional abuse of the mother. However, because it was not amongst the initial complaints brought before the Court by the mother—for obvious reasons—this aspect of the case could not be examined by the Court, as they were *ultra petitia*.[28]

There is therefore a clear need not only for the child to be separately represented in cases that come before the Court concerning them, but in addition, states must also ensure the involvement of a separate representative for the child well before this: a

[27] (14737/09) 12.07.2011.

[28] This complaint was also outside the six-month time limit for bringing a separate petition. On this point, see also the joint dissenting opinion of Judges Sicilianos, Turković, and Pejchal.

neutral representative, separate from both the parents and the government, must be provided for the child at a domestic level, with the mandate to continue to take the case to the Court, if appropriate. Children should not have to rely on the Court devising ad hoc and stop-gap measures—a systemic response is needed to combat the invisibility of children. Until this occurs, it cannot be said that children have equal and effective access to the protection of the Convention.

9.3 Parental control and authority

The Court has taken a predictably conservative view when it comes to the relationship between parents and their children. As Fortin suggests, Article 8 'appears to assume that as long as families are adequately protected from undue state interference, the regulation of family life can be entrusted to its adult members',[29] aptly demonstrated by the early case of *X and Y v the Netherlands*.[30] This case involved a 14-year-old girl who had run away from home, only to be returned by the police. She alleged that the authorities had interfered with her private life by requiring her to live with her parents. In finding the application manifestly ill-founded, the Commission stated, 'the obligation of children to reside with their parents and to be otherwise subjected to a particular control is necessary for the protection of children's health and morals, although it might constitute, from a particular child's point of view, an interference with his or her private life'.[31]

As this case was decided in 1974, it is unsurprising that it pays so little head to children's rights. However, it was reinforced 14 years later in the (in)famous case of *Nielsen v Denmark*,[32] which again took a very conservative approach to the interaction between parents and children—this time, when discussing the deprivation of liberty under Article 5 as a result of parental authority.

This case involved the compulsory detention in a psychiatric hospital of a 12-year-old boy in the middle of a custody dispute. Although his mother had rights of custody, the child ran away to stay with his father, and together they lived in hiding for three years. When they were located, the father was arrested, and on the advice of the authorities, the mother placed the boy in a psychiatric ward, as it was clear he did not want to stay with her. Although he could leave the ward with permission, the ward was otherwise kept locked and when he left without authorisation, he was located and brought back by police.

The Court held that the child's hospitalisation against his will, and his confinement there for over five months, was not a deprivation of liberty, as it was a responsible exercise by his mother of her custodial rights in the interests of the child.[33] While the Court acknowledged that a parents' decision-making capacity was not unlimited, it considered that the child 'was still of an age at which it would be normal for a decision

[29] J. Fortin, 'Rights Brought Home for Children' (1999) 62 *Modern Law Review* 350, 357.
[30] (6753/74) 19.12.1974 (dec.).
[31] ibid., para. 119. See also *X v Denmark* (6854/74) 29.09.1976 (dec.).
[32] (10929/84) 12.03.1987 (ComRep); (10929/84) 28.11.1988 (Court).
[33] (10929/84) 28.11.1988 (Court), para. 73.

to be made by the parent even against the wishes of the child'.[34] The restrictions imposed on the child were not of a nature or degree similar to the cases of deprivation of liberty specified in Article 5(1), and were no greater than those of a normal hospital stay for a child with a physical disorder. In this way, the state did not even need to prove that one of the exceptions to the prohibition on deprivation of liberty arose—Article 5 simply did not apply as the detention was merely the lawful exercise of parental powers.

This judgment has been widely criticised: indeed, David Feldman described it as narrowing 'the responsibilities of the state, and the protection of the rights of children, almost to a vanishing point'.[35] Nevertheless, it continues to be the leading case on the deprivation of liberty of children as an exercise of parental responsibility, and provides an apt illustration of the way that the Court has traditionally conceptualised the relationship between parents and children.

There is some hope, however, that the Court is starting to recognise the need to weigh children's best interests in any decision concerning the extent of parental authority. In the more recent case of *Osman v Denmark*,[36] the Court considered a complaint by a Somali child who had been sent from her home in Denmark to Kenya by her father, thus losing her Danish residency permit and denying her the right to return to that country. She argued that the authorities had a duty to look past the exercise of parental authority and to recognise that her father was not acting in her best interests.

In evaluating this complaint, the Court retained the language of parental authority, and the right of parents to decide important questions about their children's lives. However, it added an important caveat, holding that

> the exercise of parental rights constitutes a fundamental element of family life, and that the care and upbringing of children normally and necessarily require that the parents decide where the child must reside and also impose, or authorise others to impose, various restrictions on the child's liberty. Nevertheless, in respecting parental rights, the authorities cannot ignore the child's interest including its own right to respect for private and family life.[37]

This is an important decision, especially for the respect given by the Court to both the child's rights and the rights of the parent within the family structure. Although it was unfortunate that the Court did not go further and discuss the implications of the father acting against the child's interests, this reconciliation of the right of a parent to make decisions concerning his or her child with the right of the child to equal recognition and respect is an important step forward for the Court, in line with the UN Convention on the Rights of the Child. Under such an approach, although parental rights are still central to the Court's analysis, the child's own autonomy and individual rights are nevertheless recognised.

[34] ibid., para. 72.
[35] D. Feldman, *Civil Liberties and Human Rights in England and Wales* (2nd edn, Oxford: Oxford University Press, 2002), 459.
[36] (38058/09) 14.06.2011.
[37] ibid., para. 73 (citations omitted).

This question comes before the Court so rarely that it is difficult to draw clear conclusions as to where the jurisprudence will go next. *Osman* was an important step forward, but it was only one case, decided ten years ago, and did not address the issue head on. Given the recent focus by the Court on the paramountcy of the child's best interests, it is to be hoped that this is the direction in which the Court's jurisprudence will continue. It is high time that *Nielsen* was reconsidered, with a focus on the consistency of any parental decision with rights of the child, rather than on what is a 'reasonable' exercise of parental authority.

9.4 Custody and residence

The terms 'custody' and 'residence' are used differently in different jurisdictions, but are used in general to refer to the decision of with whom the child will live. When adjudicating the relationship between parents themselves, the Court has made clear that 'Article 8 does not grant to one or the other parent the right to be given preference as to his claim for the custody of a particular child.'[38] In general, the Court will not interfere with decisions made by domestic authorities concerning custody or residence, giving them a wide margin of appreciation in this area. Instead, the task of the Court is restricted to ascertaining whether the domestic authorities 'conducted an in-depth examination of the entire family situation and a whole series of factors, in particular factors of a factual, emotional, psychological, material and medical nature, and made a balanced and reasonable assessment of the respective interests of each person.'[39]

In undertaking this assessment, the authorities must show that the child's best interests have been a primary consideration. The examination of the child's interests must go beyond simply evaluating whether a parent can provide adequate living conditions, nor can it rely on general considerations—for example, the fact that one party had an extra-marital affair[40] or the parent's religious beliefs.[41] Rather, it must involve an assessment of the parenting abilities of each parent, the children's attachment to each of them, and where best the children will be able to develop and thrive.[42]

The substantive cases in this area can be divided into two categories: disputes between parents and third parties; and cases where the authorities have discriminated against a parent based on a protected characteristic.

9.4.1 Disputes between parents and third parties

While a parent does not have a right to be given preference in a custody dispute concerning the child's other parent, the Court has made clear that their rights must prevail over third parties. The seminal decision in this area is *Görgülü v Germany*,[43] which has

[38] *X v the Federal Republic of Germany* (7770/77) 02.05.1978 (dec.).
[39] *Babayeva v Azerbaijan* (57724/11) 30.01.2020, para. 35.
[40] ibid.
[41] See *Palau-Martinez v France* (64927/01) 16.12.2003, discussed in detail below.
[42] *Zelikha Magomadova v Russia* (58724/14) 08.10.2019; *Babayeva v Azerbaijan* (57724/11) 30.01.2020.
[43] (74969/01) 26.02.2004.

served as a touchstone for the Court in its jurisprudence concerning the importance of maintaining family ties. In this case, the parents separated before the father found out about the pregnancy, but soon after they came to an agreement under which the father would take care of the child when he was born. Before the birth, however, the mother ceased contact with the father, and subsequently placed the child for adoption. When the child was two months old, the father found out about the child's birth and the proposed adoption, and immediately commenced custody proceedings for the child to be transferred to him. While the District Court ordered the child to be returned to his father, the Court of Appeal held that separating the child from his foster family was not in his best interests. It noted that he was now almost two months old and had developed a deep social and emotional bond with his foster parents, meaning that separation from them would lead to severe and irreparable psychological damage.

Before the Court, the father argued that the domestic authorities had violated his right to respect for family life by preventing him from living with his son, although his ability and willingness to care for him was not in dispute. The Court agreed with this position. It acknowledged that instant separation of the child from his foster parents may have had negative effects, but emphasised that the applicant was the child's biological parent, and undisputedly willing and able to care for him, and this carried with it certain positive obligations for the state. It held that 'it is in a child's interest for its family ties to be maintained, as severing such ties means cutting a child off from its roots, which can only be justified in very exceptional circumstances. There is no evidence of such exceptional circumstances in the present case.'[44] Bearing this in mind, the domestic authorities had not adequately considered all possible solutions in order to find a way to reunify the father and son in a way that would minimise these negative effects. They had only focused on the short-term effects of separation from the foster parents, rather than also considering the long-term effects that a permanent separation from his biological father would have, and as such, the father's rights had been violated.

Nevertheless, by the time the case was decided by the Court, the child was five years old—highlighting a significant difficulty with the Convention system. While the Court could order that the state pay 15,000 euros in non-pecuniary damages, it could do little to restore the relationship between the father and child after so much time had passed. While the Court determines the order in which cases are dealt with, having regard to their importance and urgency, and has the power to give priority to particular applications,[45] private law family cases routinely take four to five years before a judgment is handed down. This is despite the oft-cited maxim of the Court that the child's best interests must not be determined by the passage of time.

Görgülü was a case which concerned state intervention—although acting on the request of the mother, it was the state who had placed the child with the foster carers. However, even if the domestic authorities themselves have not been involved in the separation of the parent and child, the duty to take necessary measures to enable

[44] ibid., para. 48.
[45] Rule 41 of the Rules of Court.

family life remains. Such a situation was considered in *Lyubenova v Bulgaria*,[46] where the child was living with the paternal grandparents, while the parents worked abroad. However, after the parents separated, the mother returned to Bulgaria and proposed to take over the care of the child. At this point, the grandparents began to prevent her from seeing her son. When the matter came before the courts, it was held that an order for the return of a child could only be made in cases where both parents had reached a mutual agreement concerning their child's residence. As this was not the case—the father not agreeing to the child's residence with the mother—the child remained with his grandparents and the applicant was deprived of all contact. The Court found that although the applicant had been restricted from exercising custody by the actions of her parents-in-law, rather than by the domestic authorities themselves, there remains a positive obligation on the state to take steps towards reunification of the parent and child. While the obligation is not absolute, as sometimes preparatory measures must be taken before reunification can occur, the state must act precipitously to take such measures. As such, the obligation on the state is not limited to ensuring that the child and parent can be reunited, but also includes the preparatory measures to achieve that result; for example, steps to reintroduce the child and parent through increasing contact.

In fact, a failure to take such preparatory measures before attempting to transfer the child's residence might itself be a violation of the Convention. In *NTS and others v Georgia*,[47] three children who were living with their maternal relatives were ordered to be returned to their father. Despite the fact that the children were diagnosed with suffering separation anxiety disorders, and despite experts recommending that no change be made to their living arrangements, the domestic courts nevertheless ordered their immediate return against their express wishes. Following an application by the children's aunt, the Court held that ordering such a radical measure of forcing the children's return against their will violated their rights under Article 8. The state had a positive obligation to consider transitional measures aimed at assisting the children and their father to rebuild their relationship, before returning them to live with him.

9.4.2 Discriminatory treatment when awarding custody

The second area where the Court has been willing to intervene in custody decisions has been in the context of discriminatory treatment. While initially these cases largely focused on issues of marriage and gender, in recent years we have seen challenges on emerging grounds of discrimination—same-sex parenting, transgender parents, and parents with disabilities.

[46] (13786/04) 18.10.2011. The case of *Hokkanen v Finland* (19823/92) 23.09.1994 also involved the retention of a children by their grandparents; however, in that case the issue before the court was enforcement of rights of contact, rather than custody.
[47] (71776/12) 02.02.2016.

9.4.2.1 Unmarried fathers

The Court's approach to the difference in treatment between married and unmarried fathers, and also between fathers and mothers, has largely reflected the changing social attitudes over the past half-century. The first time it was faced with this issue, in *B, R and J v Germany*,[48] the Commission relied on traditional assumptions concerning the role of men and women in child rearing, noting that an unmarried father may often not be willing to assume any family obligations, and might 'at any moment abandon his "illegitimate" family without having to ask for divorce and without having to face the same consequences as a married father'.[49] On this basis, the Commission argued, the decision to award care and custody only to the mother of a child born out of wedlock protected the child's interests.[50]

This case involved an unmarried, cohabiting couple, bringing up their son together. While the father's paternity was recognised, the mother held the sole right to care and custody. Under German law at the time, the father of a child born out of wedlock could obtain the right to care and custody by marrying the mother, through a declaration of legitimacy, by adoption or appointment as guardian. In all of those circumstances, save marriage, the mother would lose her rights. The Commission acknowledged that Article 8 protects the 'illegitimate' family but nevertheless, by virtue of Article 12 of the Convention, the family based on marriage enjoys greater protection. The Commission placed the responsibility for the lack of rights solely on the shoulders of the adults involved, finding that '[i]t is a consequence of the couple's free decision not to marry that the applicant does not enjoy all the privileges the national family law attributes to a married father'.[51] Moreover, it noted that the parties were 'free to marry and thus to obtain those legal advantages they require. If, however, they choose not to marry in order to avoid the application of marriage and family law, they are themselves responsible for the legal consequences of their choice.'[52]

The issue of joint custody once again came before the Court 25 years later in *Zaunegger v Germany*.[53] By this time, the German law in this respect had changed somewhat—an unmarried mother was still automatically awarded sole custody, but joint custody could be awarded to the father through a joint declaration, marriage, or a court order. Nevertheless, all these mechanisms required the consent of the mother (or in the case of the court order, proof that the mother had threatened the child's well-being through negligence). This position was challenged by Mr Zaunegger—whose ex-partner was not willing to agree to joint custody—arguing that he was treated differently in comparison with the mother, but also in comparison with married or divorced fathers.

[48] (9639/82) 15.03.1984 (dec.).

[49] ibid., para. 5.

[50] This exemplifies the problematic nature of the 'best interests' concept, which can be manipulated to reflect whatever values the decision-makers wish it to. This dilemma is discussed further in Chapter 12.

[51] *B, R, and J v Germany* (9639/82) 15.03.1984 (dec.), para. 4.

[52] ibid. See also *Nylund v Finland* (27110/95) 29.06.1999 (dec.), where the Commission held that '[m]arriage continues to be characterised by a corpus of rights and obligations that differentiate it markedly from the situation of a man and woman who cohabit'.

[53] (22028/04) 03.12.2009.

The Court considered that differences exist in the environments into which children of unmarried parents are born,

> ranging from relationships where the father's identity is not established or where he does not want to take responsibility for the child to those where the father fully participates in the upbringing of the child and where the child grows up in an environment that is practically indistinguishable from an environment based on an intact parental marriage.[54]

In this light, the Court accepted that valid reasons existed to initially attribute parental authority only to the child's mother, in order to ensure that there was a person at birth who could act for them in a legally binding way. Further, the Court acknowledged that there may be valid reasons to deny an unmarried father participation in parental authority—for example, if there may be arguments or lack of communication between the parents such as to jeopardise the child's welfare. However, the Court was not willing to accept that such an attitude was a general feature of the relationship between unmarried fathers and their children—and nor did they accept that that was the case in this situation.

The government had argued before the Court that the domestic legislation took the position that joint custody against the will of the mother is prima facie not in the child's best interests, and that the legislator could legitimately assume that, if the mother refused to agree to joint custody, the case must be an exceptional one in which the mother had serious reasons for the refusal, based on the child's best interests. This was rejected by the Court, however, which held that there was no relationship of proportionality between the exclusion of judicial review of the attribution of sole custody and the protection of the best interests of a child born out of wedlock.

The Court reached a similar conclusion in *Sporer v Austria*.[55] It accepted that the authorities were justified in treating the father of a child born out of wedlock differently from the mother by attributing parental authority initially to the mother, to ensure that there was a person from birth who would act for the child in a legally binding way. However, the Court emphasised that Austrian law provides a full judicial review of attribution of parental authority between separated or divorced parents, and parents retain joint custody unless the court awards sole custody in the child's best interests. It found no reason why an unmarried father should be denied a similar review, deciding where the best interests of the child lay.

From these decisions, we can see the emphasis placed by the Court on individualised decision-making—while states have a wide margin of appreciation in deciding where children's best interests lie, this must not be concluded on the basis of an inflexible legal presumption. This is a theme that runs throughout the jurisprudence of the Court in the field of private family law disputes: the Court is unwilling to dictate what the correct answer should be, but requires that there is an individual consideration of the situation of the particular child.

[54] ibid., para. 54.
[55] (35637/03) 03.02.2011. See also *Leitner v Austria* (55740/10) 08.06.2017.

9.4.2.2 Religion

The need for an individual determination is also seen in the jurisprudence concerning discrimination on the grounds of religion, albeit in a slightly different way. Here, the Court has indicated that decisions on custody cannot rest solely on the religious beliefs of the parent, but must instead be founded on an evaluation of their parenting.

This was examined in the case of *Hoffman v Austria*,[56] where the parents were both Roman Catholics, and the children baptised as such, before the mother converted to become a Jehovah's Witness. Upon separation, the father applied for sole custody of the children, arguing that being brought up in the Jehovah's Witness faith would be contrary to their best interests. He argued that the educational principles of Jehovah's Witnesses were hostile to society, in that they discouraged intercourse with non-members, as well as expressions of patriotism and religious tolerance. Moreover, the father argued that the refusal of the mother to allow the children to have blood transfusions (if needed), based on her faith, may give rise to situations in which their life or health were endangered.

The District and Regional courts awarded custody to the mother, on the basis that she had been caring for the children for the 18 months following the separation and the children had strong emotional ties with her. However, tese decisions were overturned by the Supreme Court, which found that the children would become 'social outcasts' if they lived with their mother, and that the refusal to consent to blood transfusions constituted a danger to their well-being. The Supreme Court considered that it is usually preferable for young children to be taken care of by their mother, but that 'this applies only provided that all other things are equal'. In this case, her religious beliefs meant that they were not.

In a very short judgment, the Court held by five votes to four that this decision violated the mother's rights under Article 14 in conjunction with Article 8. While the majority acknowledged that the factors relied on by the Supreme Court may in themselves be capable of tipping the scales in favour of one parent rather than the other, what had been decisive in this case was the religious faith of the mother. Although the aim of protecting the interests of the children was legitimate, the Court found that 'a distinction based essentially on a difference in religion alone is not acceptable'.[57]

The majority decision was subject to strong dissent, in particular by Judge Walsh. He argued that the 'hazard' identified by the Supreme Court was not the mother's religion, but the possibility of withholding a blood transfusion. Although this was traceable to the mother's religious belief, he held that 'it does not create a situation where the removal of the hazard must necessarily, if at all, be regarded as a discrimination on the grounds of religious belief. The national court's duty was to evaluate or weigh the effects as distinct from the cause'.[58]

Hoffman was followed ten years later in *Palau-Martinez v France*,[59] which provided a more clear-cut example of discrimination. Here, when awarding custody to the father rather than the mother, the domestic courts had found that the childrearing

[56] (12875/87) 23.06.1993.
[57] ibid., para. 36.
[58] ibid., dissenting opinion of Judge Walsh, para. 3.
[59] (64927/01) 16.12.2003.

imposed by Jehovah's Witnesses was characterised by strictness, intolerance, and obligation on children to proselytise. As such, it was held that '[i]t is in children's interests to be free from the constraints and prohibitions imposed by a religion whose structure resembles that of a sect'. The Court criticised the domestic authorities for focusing on generalities, rather than on the individual parenting in question. There was an absence of any direct, concrete evidence demonstrating the influence of the religion on the children's upbringing and daily life, without which the authorities could not have properly concluded what would be in the children's best interests. The authorities attached decisive importance to the principles regarding child rearing espoused by the religion, rather than the actions of the mother herself, in violation of Article 8.

These decisions make clear that while the religious faith of a parent cannot itself be taken into account when deciding custody, its effects on the child's upbringing and well-being can be. This was further emphasised in *Ismailova v Russia*,[60] concerning a mother who converted from non-practising Muslim to Jehovah's Witness. In contrast to *Hoffman* and *Palau-Martinez*, the domestic courts had made their decisions based on the effect that the mother's religion had on the children's upbringing, relying on direct and concrete evidence on the influence that the religion had on the children's daily life, and thus the Court found no violation of the Convention.

In dissent, Judge Hajiyev, joined by Judges Vajić and Steiner, argued that the domestic authorities had failed to strike the correct balance between the interests of the mother and father. Oddly, he criticised the domestic decisions for paying *too* much attention to the specific effects of the mother's religious practices on their daily life. He suggested that there was no evidence to suggest that the mother was generally unfit to care for the children, and argued that a four-year-old girl should not have been removed from her mother 'unless compelling evidence of grave harm to the child was proven'.[61] This is a worrying statement—even if it is in a dissenting opinion—appearing to suggest that there is (or should be) a presumption that young children should be cared for by their mothers, and that fathers have a heavy burden in order to overturn this. Luckily, this has not been the position of the majority of the Court when it has considered the issue: in the parental child abduction case of *Ilker Ensar Uyanik v Turkey*,[62] the Court found a violation of Article 8 where the Turkish authorities had relied solely on the fact that a child at two years of age needs maternal care and affection, on the grounds that this cannot be the only factor that is considered. Nevertheless, the Court has not explicitly ruled out this being *one* factor which is relied on, raising concerns regarding gendered stereotypes relating to parenting.

9.4.2.3 Sexual orientation and transgender parents

The need for 'maternal love' has also been dubiously used by domestic authorities in support of excluding men in same-sex relationships from having custody of their children. In one of its more progressive judgments, the Court in *Salgueiro da Silva Mouta v Portugal*[63] held that such a distinction is a violation of Article 14 in conjunction with Article 8 and cannot be justified on the basis of the child's 'best interests'.

[60] (37614/02) 29.11.2007.
[61] ibid., dissenting opinion of Judge Hajiyev, joined by Judges Vajić and Steiner.
[62] (60328/09) 03.05.2012.
[63] (33290/96) 21.12.1999.

In this case, following separation from his wife, the father began a relationship with another man. The mother was originally awarded custody of their child, but this was transferred to the father, as the mother was not allowing the father access and had shown herself incapable of providing the child with conditions conducive to the life she needed. Following this decision, the mother kidnapped the child and applied for custody. She argued that the child should not remain in the company of the father, as he was cohabiting with another man. The court found that, '[d]espite the importance of paternal love, a young child needs the care which only the mother's love can provide'—relying rather dubiously on the UN Convention on the Rights of the Child to support this proposition. It further went on to declare:

> It is not our task here to determine whether homosexuality is or is not an illness or whether it is a sexual orientation towards persons of the same sex. In both cases it is an abnormality and children should not grow up in the shadow of abnormal situations.[64]

As such, the domestic authorities found that 'an environment of this kind'[65] was not best suited to the child's psychological, social, and mental development.

Despite the government's suggestions that the child's best interests were the only consideration and that the applicant's homosexuality had no direct outcome on the decision, the Court found that this was the decisive factor in awarding custody to the mother. There had been a distinction based on considerations regarding the applicant's sexual orientation, which violated his rights under the Convention. While this judgment was progressive, especially in light of the other jurisprudence of the Court at that point in time[66]—it was nevertheless limited. It did not prohibit domestic authorities from considering sexual orientation as part of a custody determination, merely that it could not be the decisive factor.

This was affirmed in *PV v Spain*,[67] concerning a male-to-female transgender parent—discussed in more detail in section 9.5.2.2 below concerning rights of contact and access. In this case, the domestic authorities focused on the emotional health and development of the child, evidenced by expert opinion, rather than the applicant's gender identity in and of itself, and thus there had been no violation of the Convention.

This may appear to be a step in the right direction. However, this shift in focus towards the child's well-being does not prevent courts from being improperly influenced by the parent's gender identity. The principle of the child's best interests is an amorphous concept that lacks transparency, and which can be stretched to mean anything that someone else thinks is good for you.[68] As Hillary Rodham has argued, the best interests test 'is a rationalization by decision-makers justifying their judgments about a child's future, like an empty vessel into which adult perceptions and prejudices

[64] ibid., para. 14.
[65] ibid.
[66] This was decided two years before the infamous judgment of *Fretté v France* (36515/97) 26.02.2002, where the Court held that the domestic authorities were permitted to reject a woman as a prospective adopter on the grounds of her sexual orientation, and a decade before same-sex couples were recognised as having 'family life' under Article 8: see *Schalk and Kopf v Austria* (30141/04) 24.06.2010.
[67] (35159/09) 30.11.2010.
[68] J. Eekelaar, 'Beyond the Welfare Principle' (2002) 14(3) *Child and Family Law Quarterly* 237.

are poured'[69] and as such, may reinforce preconceived notions of what the family and familial relations should look like.

It is important not only that the Court scrutinise whether the decision has been directly based on the sexual orientation or gender identity of a parent, but it must also ensure that this has not indirectly influenced the analysis of the child's best interests, to eliminate more insidious forms of discrimination.

9.4.2.4 Disability

The final ground of discrimination—that of disability—has only arisen in one case, and unfortunately, was not explored on that basis. In *Mamchur v Ukraine*,[70] sole custody of the child was awarded to the grandmother, as the courts found that the father was unable to provide adequate care due to his disability. The father complained that the decision-making of the domestic courts was flawed and that preference had been given to the grandmother because of his gender and his disability. The Court was able to find a clear violation of Article 8 alone, and therefore did not consider it necessary to examine the complaint under Article 14. Nevertheless, in its discussion of Article 8, the Court made some important observations concerning the emphasis put by the domestic authorities on the father's disabilities. It held that one of the principal arguments on which the custody decision was based—that his disability would prevent him from caring for the child—was not supported by further analysis. There had been no independent analysis of his ability, nor any potential for assistance or support considered, and this contributed to the finding of a violation of Article 8.

It is a pity that a clearer statement was not made by the Court in this respect, and the discriminatory position not considered explicitly under Article 14. It is clear from the facts of the case that the father's disability, rather than his ability to care for the child, was the basis for the decision of the domestic authorities, and that there was no individualised assessment of his capabilities, nor of the interests of the child. The unwillingness of the Court to go beyond the confines of Article 8 alone mean that it missed a valuable opportunity to categorically condemn such discrimination and provide clear guidance in this area of law, particularly on a subject where (thankfully) cases do not come before the Court on a regular basis.

9.5 Contact and access

While questions concerning custody and residence allow a measure of latitude to the domestic authorities to decide with whom it is in the child's best interests to live—meaning most challenges are either based on procedure or consideration of a prohibited ground—the scope of states' margin of appreciation in relation to access and contact is somewhat narrower. While residence disputes usually require a choice between one parent or the other,[71] contact does not create such a dichotomy. From the very beginning of its

[69] H. Rodham, 'Children under the Law' (1973) 43 *Harvard Educational Review* 487, 513.

[70] (10383/09) 16.07.2015.

[71] Although joint custody is now becoming more common, the majority of cases before the Court have been in the context of sole, or primary, custody.

jurisprudence in this area, the Court has made clear that 'the parent who is deprived of the custody of an infant may not be prevented, under Article 8, paragraph (I), from access to that infant unless special circumstances, as defined in paragraph (2) of the same Article, so demand'.[72] This 'special circumstances' test has been strengthened over the years, so that now 'only very serious reasons could justify totally excluding a father from access to his child'[73]—or indeed a mother.

Nevertheless, despite this higher burden, the interests of the child remain at the forefront of the Court's examination. This was seen in *Hendriks v the Netherlands*,[74] where the father's access to his child had been frustrated by the mother. The domestic authorities had concluded that where a conflict existed between the parents, the ordering of a visiting arrangement would lead to tension in the family of the parent to whom residence had been awarded. Since it was in the interests of the child to grow up without such tension, contact should not be ordered. Before the Court, the father argued that even if he behaved in the most reasonable way, without doing harm to the child, the mother could prevent him from seeing his son by simply refusing her co-operation. He contended that it was wrong that only the interests of the child should count, and that his own rights should also be considered. The Commission made clear that although the father does have rights under Article 8(1), 'where … there is a serious conflict between the interests of the child and one of its parents which can only be resolved to the disadvantage of one of them, the interests of the child must, under Art 8(2), prevail'.[75]

When determining where the best interests of the child lie, as with questions of custody and residence, Article 8 imposes a duty on states to undertake an individualistic assessment. The Court has reiterated that the best interests of children cannot be 'truly determined by a general legal presumption', and instead, 'a fair balancing of the rights of all persons involved necessitates an examination of the particular circumstances of each case'.[76]

9.5.1 Who benefits from the right of contact?

As stated above, the Court has emphasised that a parent who is deprived of custody cannot be deprived of access, unless special circumstances so demand. This raises the question of who is a parent for these purposes. Does this apply only to legal parents? Or does it also apply to natural parents wishing to have contact with their biological children?

This question was considered by the Court in *Anayo v Germany*.[77] In this case, the applicant had a two-year relationship with a married woman, during which time she gave birth to his biological twin children. The mother subsequently returned to her

[72] *X v Sweden* (172/56) 20.12.1957 (dec.). See also *Hendriks v the Netherlands* (8427/78) 08.03.1982 (ComRep).

[73] *K v the Netherlands* (9018/80) 04.07.1983 (dec.) (citations omitted).

[74] (8427/78) 08.03.1982 (ComRep).

[75] ibid., para. 124. See also *Garcia v Switzerland* (10148/82) 14.03.1985 (dec.).

[76] *Nazarenko v Russia* (39438/13) 16.07.2015.

[77] (20578/07) 21.12.2010.

husband, who was named as the children's legal father. The mother and her husband were bringing up the children together, and refused the applicant any contact with them. The domestic courts found that the German Civil Code, which provided for the right of a parent to have contact, only applied to legal, not biological parents: as such, it was irrelevant whether contact was in the children's best interests, as the law only protected a biological father's access where a social and family relationship already existed.

As discussed in Chapter 8, the Court found that the natural father did not have existing 'family life' with the children which could be protected under Article 8, as he and the mother had never lived together, he had never met the children, and the relationship did not have sufficient consistency to be defined as such. However, the Court recognised that it was not the fault of the father that he did not have 'family life' with the children, and his efforts to gain access to the children resulted in 'intended family life', which formed an important part of his identity, and thus his private life under Article 8.

Following on from this, the Court found that by refusing the applicant contact with his biological children, irrespective of whether contact was in the children's best interests, the German authorities had not fairly balanced the competing interests of the biological parents, the legal parents, and the child. Contact cannot be denied on the basis of an irrebuttable presumption, and the authorities have a duty to consider the child's best interests.[78]

These principles equally apply to men who have acted in a parental role, but who have no biological connection to the child. In *Nazarenko v Russia*,[79] the applicant's wife gave birth to a child, who was registered as his daughter. They lived as a family for three years before separating, and following the divorce, the child resided alternatively with both parents. However, when the child was five years old, a paternity test requested by the mother showed that the applicant was not the child's biological father. As a result, he lost all parental rights, including the right to maintain contact with the child. Russian law did not include any provisions which would allow a social parent to maintain a relationship with their child—only those on a list set out in legislation (parents, grandparents, brothers, sisters, and 'other relatives') were entitled to maintain contact.

The Court found that the relationship between the applicant and child amounted to 'family life' under Article 8, consisting as it did of a close emotional bond. As such, the state was under an obligation to show that the interference with this relationship was justified under Article 8(2). The Court expressed concern about the inflexibility of the Russian legal provisions governing contact rights—setting out an exhaustive list of persons entitled to maintain contact, without providing for any exceptions to take account of different family situations, nor the best interests of the child. The Court made clear that there must be an individual examination of whether it is in the child's best

[78] This was followed in *Schneider v Germany* (17080/07) 15.09.2011 the following year. The government attempted to distinguish the case on the basis that while in *Anayo*, the applicant was undisputedly the biological father of the children concerned, in *Schneider*, this was unconfirmed. However, the Court found that this difference was not sufficient to demand a different approach.

[79] (39438/13) 16.07.2015.

interests to maintain contact with an individual who has acted in a parental role for a sufficiently long period of time—whether they are biologically related or not.

This rule extends not only to legal parents, but also to others who have cared for the child or form part of their family. In *Kopf and Liberda v Austria*,[80] it was recognised that foster parents who had cared for the child for four years had 'family life' with the child, and thus the domestic authorities had a duty to deal diligently with their request for visiting rights once the child had been returned to his biological mother. Likewise, in *Manuello and Nevi v Italy*,[81] the Court emphasised that ties between grandparents and grandchildren can only be severed in exceptional circumstances.[82]

In addition to contact between adult and child, the Court has also held that there is a positive obligation to maintain contact between siblings also. In *Mustafa and Armağan Akin v Turkey*,[83] the two children of the marriage were separated, with the son living with his father, and the daughter living with her mother. Before the Court the government argued that decisions of courts had not prevented the siblings from seeing each other, as they were both living in the same neighbourhood, and were thus able to keep in contact. The Court, however, held that 'maintaining the ties between the children is too important to be left to the discretion and whim of their parents'.[84]

From these cases, we can see that the right to contact relies not on legal, biological, or social parenthood, but on the existence of 'family life' within the meaning of Article 8. Once 'family life' is established, the emphasis shifts to the state to show that contact is not in the child's best interests, which can only be decided on the basis of individualised decision-making.

9.5.2 Discrimination when deciding contact

9.5.2.1 Fathers

Over the course of ten years, the Court saw a number of cases challenging the German legislation concerning contact between a father and a child born out of wedlock. Under the German law as it stood at the time, a divorced parent was entitled to access unless this would be *contrary* to the child's well-being. On the other hand, the father of a child born out of wedlock was entitled to access only if it was *in the interests* of the child.

The first challenge to this rule, in *Elsholz v Germany*,[85] failed on the grounds that despite the different standards for divorced and unmarried fathers, in the circumstances of the individual case, the father had not shown that a divorced father would have been treated more favourably. It is not the task of the Court to examine domestic legislation in the abstract, but to examine the manner in which it has been applied in the particular circumstances. Here, the domestic courts had found that contact would

[80] (1598/06) 17.01.2012.
[81] (107/10) 20.01.2015.
[82] See also *Price v the United Kingdom* (12402/86) 14.07.1988 (dec.); *GHB v the United Kingdom* (42455/98) 04.05.2000 (dec.)
[83] (4694/03) 06.04.2010.
[84] ibid., para. 24.
[85] (25735/94) 13.07.2000 (GC).

negatively affect the child, so it would have reached the same conclusion whichever rule was applied.

A year later, *Sahin v Germany*[86] provided a better test case in this respect. The Chamber found that German law did not regard contact between a child and a natural father as in the child's best interests, and thus placed a heavy burden of proof on the side of the father. Since the granting of access is an exception to the general statutory rule that the mother determines the relations between the child and father, the mother's negative attitude would be decisive for refusing access. The Chamber was not convinced that this difference in treatment between married and unmarried fathers was justified, and rejected the government's argument that fathers of children born out of wedlock generally lacked an interest in contact with their children. As such, it concluded that there had been a violation of Article 8.

This was affirmed by the Grand Chamber.[87] Distinguishing the case from *Elsholz*, here the Court noted that the domestic authorities had found that in a situation of conflict between the parents, only special circumstances could justify a decision that personal contact with the father would have 'permanently beneficial effects on the child's well-being'.[88] Having regard to the findings by the domestic courts that the father was sincerely attached to his child, had genuine affection for her, and responsible motives for seeking access, the Court found that a heavier burden was placed on the applicant than if he had been a divorced father, in contravention of Article 14 in conjunction with Article 8.[89]

9.5.2.2 Other protected characteristics

In addition to cases brought by unmarried fathers, the Court has also considered discrimination based on other grounds, including religion and disability.

In *Vojnity v Hungary*,[90] the domestic courts restricted the access rights of a father who belonged to a religious group called the 'Congregation of the Faith'. Relying on the child's best interests, the authorities suggested that the applicant had abused his rights by trying to influence the child in his religious beliefs, which triggered anxiety in the child and endangered his development. It also found that his 'irrational worldview' made him incapable of bringing up a child.

The Court held that the father's religious convictions had a direct bearing on the outcome of the case, and that there had been a difference in treatment from other parents in analogous situations. Although the domestic courts had argued that they were protecting the child's psychological health from the stress exerted from the father's efforts to transfer his convictions to him, the Court expressed reservations as

[86] (30943/96) 11.10.2001.
[87] (30943/96) 08.07.2003 (GC).
[88] ibid., para. 92.
[89] Similar reasoning was relied on in *Sommerfeld v Germany* (31871/96) 08.07.2003 (GC), decided by the Grand Chamber the same day. However, in *Sommerfeld*, the facts were not as clear cut, and seven judges dissented on this point, arguing that *Elsholz* should not have been departed from in this case. The judges in dissent criticised the majority for taking an overly formalistic approach, referring to the content of the legislation and the formula of language used in the domestic judgments, instead of the substance of the matter—whether a divorced father would have been treated differently in these circumstances.
[90] (29617/07) 12.02.2013.

to whether this consideration was sufficient to qualify as 'a very weighty reason allowing differential treatment'.[91] In this respect, the Court relied not only on Article 9, but also on Article 2 of Protocol 1, which gives parents the right to communicate and promote their religious convictions in bringing up their children. It held that

> this would be an uncontested right in the case of two married parents sharing the same religious ideas or worldview and promoting them to their child, even in an insistent or overbearing manner, unless this exposes the latter to dangerous practices or to physical or psychological harm, and it sees no reason why the position of a separated or divorced parent who does not have custody of his or her child should be different per se.[92]

The domestic authorities had produced no evidence that the religious convictions of the father involved such dangers, nor that any actual harm had been suffered by the child as opposed to 'mere unease, discomfort or embarrassment which the child may have experienced'.[93]

Moreover, even if the authorities' concerns *did* amount to very weighty reasons for differential treatment, the Court found that the solution chosen by the authorities was not acceptable. As discussed above, 'a measure as radical as the total severance of contact can be justified only in exceptional circumstances',[94] and only after other less severe measures have been considered. In this case, there was no consideration of whether mere suspension of access or other measures would have been sufficient to alleviate the danger identified by the domestic authorities, thus amounting to 'a complete disregard of the principle of proportionality'.[95]

These principles can also be seen in *Kacper Nowakowski v Poland*,[96] concerning a father who was deaf and mute, using sign language to communicate. His wife also suffered from a hearing impairment, but could communicate both orally and through sign language. Together they had a son, who also suffered from a hearing impairment, but was not able to communicate through sign language. Following the parents' divorce, the court ordered that the child's mother should be present during contact visits, since she would be able to translate between the father and son. The father argued that he needed longer visits with his son in order to strengthen their ties, and objected to the mother's presence, as she had attempted to obstruct the relationship and marginalise his role.

[91] ibid., para. 37.

[92] ibid. (original emphasis) This must be contrasted, however, with a complaint that the parent in custody is not bringing up the child in the language, culture, or religion of the other parent. In *X v the Federal Republic of Germany* (2699/65) 01.04.1968 (dec.), the Commission held that

> insofar as the Applicant complains that he has been prevented from educating his son in the Polish language and culture, it is to be observed that the right of education is an integral part of the custody which has been entrusted to the mother and the Applicant therefore no longer has a right to determine the manner in which that education is carried out.

[93] ibid., para. 38.

[94] ibid., para. 41.

[95] ibid., para. 42.

[96] (32407/13) 10.01.2017.

The Court found that the solution imposed by the domestic authorities ignored the animosity between the parents, and the complaints of the applicant about the mother's behaviour. Moreover, the development of a relationship between the applicant and his child required much more time than would be the case in other situations, given the difficulties in direct communication and the necessity of translation, and this had not been adequately considered. The domestic courts should have envisaged additional measures, more adapted to the specific circumstances of the case, having regard to the specifics of the applicant's situation and the nature of his disability.

The Court also noted that the domestic authorities failed to obtain expert evidence from specialists familiar with the problems faced by persons suffering from a hearing impairment. The experts they did hear stressed their limited competence in this area, while the report relied on by the court focused on the barriers faced by the applicant, rather than reflecting on possible means of overcoming them. In this respect, the Court held that the domestic courts have a duty under Article 8 to identify what steps can be taken to remove existing barriers and facilitate contact, which they failed to fulfil in this case.

On the other hand, a positive example of proportionate and adapted measures can be seen in *PV v Spain*,[97] concerning a male-to-female transgender parent. Prior to her gender reassignment, she had a son, with whom she had been granted contact. The child's mother sought to suspend this contact and remove parental authority, arguing that PV was undergoing hormone treatment with a view to gender reassignment, and that she was emotionally unstable. The judge found that PV was undergoing emotional instability (as evidenced by expert reports), which posed a significant risk of disruption to the emotional health and development of the child. Nevertheless, he felt that complete suspension of contact and parental rights was not appropriate. Instead, the judge ordered that contact be temporarily restricted, and gradually extended—with a review every two months—once PV had fully recovered her physical and psychological capacities. In making this order, he stressed that it was not a matter of discrimination, but a question of finding the best solution for the minor's interests, which would enable him to adapt to the new family circumstances.

The Court found that the overriding factor relied on by the domestic courts was the child's best interests, rather than the fact that the applicant was transgender. While there was no doubt a difference of treatment by the Spanish courts—as they adopted a different visitation regime when they became aware of the applicant's gender dysphoria—what was decisive was the repercussions for the child, rather than PV's being transgender itself. The domestic authorities had adopted a flexible and reviewable solution, tailored to the needs of the child.[98]

While these three cases are founded on different protected characteristics, the decisions all reflect the same fundamental principles: individualised decision-making, adapted to the best interests of the child, ensuring the least interference possible with the contact between the parent and child.

[97] (35159/09) 30.11.2010.

[98] Although see the discussion above concerning potential difficulties with relying on the best interests analysis in such controversial cases.

9.5.3 Enforcement of contact arrangements

One of the issues that has attracted the most attention of the Court in this area is that of enforcement of domestic orders on contact and access. This is of vital importance, as where a parent impedes access, the ultimate decision on where the child's best interests lie may be decided according to the mere passage of time. As a result, there is a significant body of jurisprudence concerning the availability of sufficient legal arsenal, the obligations on the state in respect of recalcitrant custodial parents, and the legal framework needed to ensure that the rights to custody and access can be exercised effectively.

9.5.3.1 The obligation to facilitate contact

In order to effectively protect the rights of the parent and child under Article 8, the state has a positive obligation to establish an adequate legal framework to ensure the enforcement of custody and contact decisions. In this respect, it cannot rely on the refusal of the parent to cooperate with proceedings to escape responsibility under the Convention, but instead must have sufficient legal arsenal to ensure compliance with court orders.[99] This may be in the form of mechanisms aimed at fostering cooperation and understanding between the parties, or where this is unsuccessful or inappropriate, more coercive mechanisms.[100]

The Court has stated that it is not its role to assess whether the existing instruments would have been sufficient to resolve the conflict between the parties, or whether they should have been supplemented by legislative reforms. Instead, all it can do is examine whether the domestic authorities sufficiently considered the possibility of existing legal mechanisms which could have facilitated the development of a relationship between the parties.[101] Nevertheless, it has given strong indications of what it believes should be included in the legal framework: for example, in *Cengiz Kılıç v Turkey*,[102] where the Court noted the absence of availability of civil mediation in the national judicial system, which would have aided the cooperation of the parties. The Court then went on to refer to the Council of Europe Recommendation of the Committee of Ministers on Family Mediation, according to which mediation can improve communication, reduce conflict, produce amicable agreements, ensure continuity of personal ties, and reduce the financial and social costs of separation and divorce.[103]

Likewise, 'soft law' mechanisms such as mediation, counselling, and psychological support were considered in the case of *Bergmann v the Czech Republic*,[104] where the Court noted that the reason for contact being discontinued was the lack of bond between the father and child—something that was due to the passage of time, assisted by the lack of enforcement mechanisms of the state, rather than due to any deficiency on the applicant's part. As such, the Court held that the state had failed to adopt all

[99] See, for example, *Santos Nunes v Portugal* (61173/08) 22.05.2012; *AV v Slovenia* (878/13) 09.04.2019.
[100] See *Eberhard and M v Slovenia* (8673/05, 9733/05) 01.12.2009.
[101] *Kacper Nowakowski v Poland* (32407/13) 10.01.2017.
[102] (16192/06) 06.12.2011.
[103] ibid., para. 133. See also *Kacper Nowakowski v Poland* (32407/13) 10.01.2017.
[104] (8857/08) 27.10. 2011.

measures that could be reasonably expected of them to help to develop the relationship between the father and child—noting in particular the lack of mediation offered to reconcile the parties.

Such soft mechanisms cannot be the only mechanism of enforcement, however, and where a parent continues to refuse to cooperate with the authorities, the state must 'take appropriate measures to punish this lack of cooperation'.[105] While the Court has made clear that coercive measures against children are not, in principle, desirable, the use of sanctions in the face of manifestly unlawful conduct by the person looking after the child should not be discarded.

This is not without its own problems. On the one hand, the Court has emphasised that such sanctions must be punitive enough to have a coercive effect—for example, in both *Kuppinger v Germany*[106] and *Z v Poland*,[107] the Court considered that the fines imposed (300 euros and 1000 PLN, respectively) were too low to have a significant impact on the custodial parent. In the former case, the Court noted that this sum was substantially lower than allowed for by the legal framework, which provided for the imposition of fines up to 25,000 euros in each case.

On the other hand, the Court has acknowledged that the imposition of any coercive measures must be considered in light of the child's welfare. In *Moog v Germany*,[108] the Court found that the decision to quash a 3,000 euro fine that had been imposed on the mother was within the margin of appreciation of the domestic authorities, as it was based on the risk that could accrue to the child as a result. Likewise, in *Fourkiotis v Greece*[109] the Court considered that the available measures—namely the institution of fines and the threat of jail—were not adapted to the situation of child custody. Not only are such measures slow, which may deprive the injured parent of contact for a longer period, but they may have a negative effect on the psychological well-being of the child. Furthermore, they may act to ultimately undermine the desired aim, namely the cooperation of the parents in the best interests of the child. Turning in particular to the threat of jail, the Court noted that the use of measures involving the deprivation of liberty of a parent in cases concerning custody or access rights must be regarded as an exceptional measure and must not be used unless all other avenues have been used or explored.

9.5.3.2 Parental participation in enforcement

When enforcing a decision on contact, the Court has found that the applicant parent cannot simply rely on the authorities to enforce their contact rights—they must themselves be proactive and involved in the enforcement attempts.

In *Glaser v the United Kingdom*,[110] the father had argued that the initiative in pursuing enforcement should lie with the domestic courts, once he had presented them with evidence of the mother's refusal to comply with the court order. The Court

[105] *Amănălăchioai v Romania* (4023/04) 27.05.2009, para. 94.
[106] (62198/11) 15.01.2015.
[107] (34694/06) 20.04.2010.
[108] (23280/08, 2334/10) 06.10.2016.
[109] (74758/11) 16.06.2016.
[110] (32346/96) 19.09.2000.

emphatically rejected this argument, referring to widespread practice among member states for plaintiffs in civil proceedings to bear substantial responsibility for their conduct and direction. The Court went on to find:

> It is, after all, their own rights and obligations which are at stake in the proceedings and their active participation can hardly be dispensed with in the normal course of events. Indeed, parental participation in the proceedings concerning children is required by Article 8 in order to ensure protection of their interests.[111]

This obligation goes beyond simply bearing responsibility for the direction of proceedings before the courts, but also extends to the enforcement of proceedings by police and bailiffs. In *Cristescu v Romania*,[112] the Court emphasised that active parental participation in enforcement proceedings is required under Article 8, and that a parent can expect that a long-term commitment and effort will be necessary to re-establish contact with a child. Here, the Court found that simply directing a bailiff to retrieve the child was insufficient—the nature of the obligation that fell to be executed required the father's presence during attempts at enforcement. A bailiff—who was an individual unknown to the child—could not have been expected to go alone to the child's home in order to take him away and deliver him to the applicant's home.

Likewise, in *GB v Lithuania*,[113] police assistance was offered to the applicant so that she could go to her ex-husband's home to retrieve her daughters (after he had unlawfully retained them). She did not avail herself of this opportunity, but chose to ask the bailiff to go in her place. In such a situation, the Court found that she had not taken the opportunities offered to her to remain in contact with her children. This confirmed the authorities' argument that she placed the task of enforcement on the state and municipal institutions, instead of being proactive herself, and thus there had been no violation of her Convention rights.[114]

This line of reasoning was the subject of strident criticism in *Cristescu*, where Judge López Guerra, joined by Judge Myjer, observed that the censure of the behaviour of the parent was unwarranted. They argued that it was not the role of the Court to criticise the father's behaviour, and its appraisal was 'inevitably conjectural and speculative, given that this Court has no such direct knowledge or contact'.[115] Furthermore, they did not feel able to endorse the criticism of the father for lack of effort or sensitivity in a situation in which he had only been able to see his son three times in ten years, despite numerous court proceedings.

As these judges pointed out, the reasoning of the majority in these cases reverses the analysis, contorting it to focus on individual actions, rather than state responsibility. Instead of asking whether the state has undertaken sufficient steps to fulfil their obligations, these cases shift the focus to individuals, and whether they have done enough to secure their own rights. Parents should be able to rely on the state and municipal

111 ibid., para. 70.
112 (13589/07) 10.01.2012.
113 (36137/13) 19.01.2016.
114 See also *Răileanu v Romania* (67304/12) 02.06.2015 (dec.).
115 Concurring opinion of Judge López Guerra, joined by Judge Myjer.

institutions to enforce their own judgments, and although some direction and cooperation may be needed from parents in order to do this, they should not bear primary responsibility in this respect.

9.5.3.3 Reasonable adjustments to contact arrangements

As the Court often states, the Convention must be interpreted in such a way as to give practical and effective rights, and not simply rights that are theoretical or illusory. As such, the national authorities bear an obligation to ensure that parents are able to exercise their right to contact effectively by making reasonable adjustments to the time and place of contact.

This was seen in *Gluhaković v Croatia*,[116] concerning a father who undertook shift work. The national courts ordered that he should see his daughter at a regular time every week, but this was impossible for him due to the nature of his work. He suggested alternative times and arrangements, but these were not accepted by the courts. The Court found that the national authorities had not given any explanation as to why it was not possible to accommodate the father's proposals, and as a result, they had failed to adequately secure his right to respect for family life as regards to effective contact with his daughter. Moreover, the domestic authorities nominated a place for the contact visits—a Counselling Centre—which was not suitable for such meetings (and was acknowledged as such by the Centre itself). Nevertheless, the courts continued to order that visits take place there. When the Centre declared that meetings were no longer possible there, it took a year and three months for a new location to be decided, with no provisional arrangements in the meantime. This likewise indicated a lack of respect for the father's rights under Article 8.

The obligation on the domestic authorities is not limitless, however, and these limits were reached in *Ouinas v France*.[117] In this case, a father was granted the right for his daughter to visit him in jail, if he were held in a certain prison (near where the child was living). He requested to be transferred to this prison, but his request was refused by the authorities. The Commission held that while lawful detention under Article 5 is by its nature a limitation on private and family life, it is an essential part of a prisoner's right to respect for family life that prison authorities assist him in maintaining contact with his close family. It found that it 'cannot ignore the fact' that the prison authorities hadn't done everything in their power to guarantee the father's effective exercise of his right of access, and 'wonder[ed] whether greater efforts' could have been taken. Nevertheless, the Commission held that given the wide margin of appreciation given to national authorities in enforcing prison sentences, the position adopted could not be regarded as disproportionate to the legitimate aim of the prevention of disorder and crime.

The leap from criticism of the domestic authorities to a finding that the complaint was inadmissible in this case was somewhat abrupt, and betrays a lack of coherent reasoning by the Commission. When it has been relied on in future cases, *Ouinas* has stood for the proposition that prison authorities must assist in maintaining contact

[116] (21188/09) 12.04.2011.
[117] (13756/88) 12.03.1990 (dec.).

with close family,[118] despite the decision itself endorsing the lacklustre efforts of the French government. In determining whether reasonable adjustments have been made to support effective contact, *Gluhakovic* provides a much more robust judgment, which aligns with the current emphasis of the Court on the importance of family ties.

9.6 Children's participation in private law cases

Over the past decades, there has been increasing awareness of the right of children to participate in decision-making concerning their lives. Article 12(1) of the UN Convention on the Rights of the Child requires states to ensure that a child who is capable of forming his or her own views has the right to express them freely in all matters affecting them, those views being given due weight in accordance with their age and maturity. Moreover, under Article 12(2), the UN Convention on the Rights of the Child explicitly requires children to be afforded the opportunity to be heard in any judicial or administrative proceedings affecting them, 'either directly, or through a representative or an appropriate body'.

While the Court has been somewhat slow to fully recognise the autonomy of children—particularly within the family setting[119]—its jurisprudence concerning children's involvement in private law disputes has been one area in which it has established strong principles. In particular, the Court has made very clear that domestic authorities *must* seek the opinion of children who are able to formulate their own views on contact with their parents.[120]

This was explained in *M and M v Croatia*,[121] where the Court considered the lack of involvement of a nine-year old girl in custody proceedings. The Court noted that the concept of 'private life' in Article 8 includes the right to personal autonomy, and in particular, the right to self-fulfilment, and stressed the importance for individuals to be able to decide freely how to conduct their private and family life.[122] While for adults, the right to personal autonomy means the right to make choices as to how to lead their lives, provided this does not unjustifiably interfere with the rights and freedoms of others, for children it has a different scope. In the words of the Court:

> [Children] lack the full autonomy of adults but are, nevertheless, subjects of rights. This circumscribed autonomy in cases of children, which gradually increases with their evolving maturity, is exercised through their right to be consulted and heard. As specified in Article 12 of the Convention on the Rights of the Child, a child who is capable of forming his or her own views has the right to express them and the right to have due weight given to those views, in accordance with his or her age and maturity,

[118] See, for example, *Khoroshenko v Russia* (41418/04) 30.06.2015 (GC); *AM v France* (36777/97) 14.03.2000 (dec.); *Descamps v France* (29472/95) 21.05.1997 (dec.).

[119] See C. Fenton-Glynn, 'Children, Parents and the European Court of Human Rights' (2019) 6 *European Human Rights Law Review* 643.

[120] See, for example, *Mustafa and Armağan Akin v Turkey* (4694/03) 06.04.2010; *Płaza v Poland* (18830/07) 25.01.2011; *NTS and others v Georgia* (71776/12) 02.02.2016.

[121] (10161/13) 03.09.2015.

[122] See *Fernández Martínez v Spain* (56030/07) 12.06.2014 (GC).

> and, in particular, has to be provided with the opportunity to be heard in any judicial and administrative proceedings affecting him or her.[123]

In light of this, the Court noted that while Article 8 does not contain any explicit procedural requirements, the decision-making process must be fair, which includes the requirement that parents have been sufficiently involved in the process. Having regard to Article 12 of the UN Convention on the Rights of the Child, the Court found that the same considerations apply *mutatis mutandis* in any judicial or administrative proceedings affecting children's rights under Article 8 of the European Convention on Human Rights: 'in such cases it cannot be said that the children capable of forming their own views were sufficiently involved in the decision-making process if they were not provided with the opportunity to be heard and thus express their views'.[124]

On the facts of this case, the Court endorsed the Croatian law requiring that the child's wishes be respected in custody proceedings, if both parents are equally capable of looking after the child, and the child is—having regard to their age and maturity—capable of forming their own views and expressing them. To decide otherwise, it held, would result in 'the rule that the views of the child must be given due weight [being] rendered meaningless'.[125]

Interestingly, this issue has also been considered from the perspective of Article 6(1) and the right to a fair trial—not for the children, but for the parents themselves. *Iglesias Casarrubios and Cantalapiedra Iglesias v Spain*[126] concerned custody proceedings between divorcing parents. The mother requested that the children—aged almost 15 and 12 at the time of the final proceedings—be heard by the judge, but this was ignored. The Court held that it would be going too far to say that domestic courts are always obliged to hear a child when a right of access is at stake—as this depends on the age and maturity of child concerned—but that Article 6 encompasses the right of parties to present observations that they consider relevant to their case. This includes the right for children to be heard, if they so wish, or at the very least, that the court give reasons for any refusal.

Like *M and M*, this case relied heavily on domestic law that already made provision for children to be heard, but had not been followed in this particular case. As such, the Court has not yet had to rule directly on the question of whether there is a free-standing obligation under the Convention for the participation of the child, that can be enforced notwithstanding domestic laws to the contrary. Nevertheless, these recent judgments provide a strong indication that while the exact age at which the child must be heard may be within the margin of appreciation of states, a failure to allow a competent child to participate in proceedings will constitute a violation of Article 8, and possibly Article 6 also.

The problem with such a position, however, is that it relies on an outdated understanding of child participation—focusing on children who are able to directly participate in proceedings—and therefore ignores the participation rights of younger

[123] *M and M v Croatia* (10161/13) 03.09.2015, para. 171. (citations omitted)

[124] ibid., para. 181.

[125] ibid., para. 185. Despite approving of this rule, however, the Court nevertheless found a violation of Article 8, as the authorities had failed to implement it in practice.

[126] (23298/12) 11.10.2016.

children, whose views and feelings should still be considered. As Article 12 makes clear, all children must benefit from the right to participation—it is only when deciding what weight to give their views that age and maturity become relevant.

9.6.1 Direct versus indirect participation

An important issue that was raised on the facts in *Iglesias Casarrubios*[127] was a request by the younger child to be heard directly by the judge, rather than indirectly by a psychologist, who would then produce a report to be submitted to the court. When this request was rejected, the child refused to participate with the appointed expert. The rejection of this request was not addressed by the Strasbourg Court in its judgment, focusing on the general lack of participation, rather than on the specifics of why it did not occur, or the form it took.

However, the issue of direct versus indirect participation has been examined at length by the Court in the seminal case of *Sahin v Germany*.[128] This case concerned an unmarried father seeking access to his young daughter. Under German law, fathers of children born out of wedlock could only have access to the child if the mother agreed, or if a court ruled that contact was in the child's best interests. It would not be enough that contact was found to be consistent with, or not contrary to, the child's interests—it must be shown to actively serve those interests and promote them. The child in this case was three years and ten months old when proceedings started, and just over five years of age when the case came before the court in question. The regional court did not hear the child directly, on the expert advice that the very process of questioning the child entailed a risk for her psychological health, which could not be avoided by special arrangements. Instead, the court relied on the testimony of the expert concerning her perceptions of the feelings of the child towards her father. These had been ascertained not by directly questioning the child, but by using games and other indirect methods to explore the child's feelings concerning persons and situations. The father challenged this, claiming that the failure of the court to hear the child directly constituted a procedural violation of the Convention.

The Fourth Chamber of the Court found in favour of the applicant, holding that the failure to hear the child revealed an insufficient involvement of the applicant in the proceedings.[129] The Court held:

> It is essential that the competent courts give careful consideration to what lies in the best interests of the child after having had direct contact with the child. The Regional Court should not have been satisfied with the expert's vague statements about the

[127] (23298/12) 11.10.2016.

[128] (30943/96) 11.10.2001 (Ch); (30943/96) 08.07.2003 (GC).

[129] It is interesting to note that the problem identified by the Chamber was not insufficient involvement of the *child* in the decision-making process, but of the *father*. While this in part reflects the fact that it was the father who had taken the case before the Court, the failure to even mention the rights of the child in this regard is problematic.

> risks inherent in questioning the child without even contemplating the possibility to take special arrangements in view of the child's young age.[130]

In this way, the Chamber focused only on *direct* participation, failing to acknowledge that the best interests of some children may require indirect participation. In particular, the expert had been concerned that if the child were heard before the regional court, she would experience feelings of guilt, thinking that she would be responsible for deciding which of her parents to live with. Thankfully, this was corrected by the Grand Chamber, which overturned the Fourth Chamber decision. In doing so, it paid considerable deference to the margin of appreciation given to member states to ascertain all the relevant facts and assess the evidence before them, and thus decide what form of participation best suited the child. It found that:

> It would be going too far to say that domestic courts are always required to hear a child in court on the issue of access to a parent not having custody, but this issue depends on the specific circumstances of each case, having due regard to the age and maturity of the child concerned.[131]

The Grand Chamber thus held that direct participation of the child was unnecessary to fulfil the requirements of Article 8, as long as the wishes of the child were presented to the courts in some manner.

Having said this, domestic authorities must ensure that indirect participation is not forced on children who are old enough to participate directly, and wish to do so. While the Court avoided the issue in *Iglesias Casarrubios*,[132] in *NTS and others v Georgia*,[133] it strongly criticised the national courts for failing to consider the possibility of directly involving the children, instead of only hearing them through a representative assigned by the Social Service Agency. Not only was this found inappropriate given the children's ages—one was 18 by the time the proceedings were completed—but also because the Agency had not shown itself to be adequately representing the children's interests. The Agency only became formally involved in the proceedings from the appeal stage, and even then, it remained ambiguous what their role was, as the legislation did not explicitly state the functions and powers of the representatives. During the two years of proceedings, representatives of the Agency had met the children only a few times, but no regular contact had been maintained, or trusting relationship established. As such, this form of 'participation' was deemed inadequate for the purposes of Article 8.

[130] *Sahin v Germany* (30943/96) 11.10.2001 (Ch), para. 47.
[131] *Sahin v Germany* (30943/96) 08.07.2003 (GC), para. 73.
[132] (23298/12) 11.10.2016.
[133] (71776/12) 02.02.2016.

9.6.2 Weight to be given to children's views

The final—and perhaps most important—question that has faced the Court is the weight to be given to children's views. As was recognised in *M and M v Croatia*, a lack of due weight to children's views renders even the most robust participation mechanisms meaningless,[134] but this does not mean that children's wishes must be followed.

In particular, any refusal of contact by a child must be weighed against the assumption that runs throughout the Court's Article 8 jurisprudence that children's interests normally dictate that their ties with their family be maintained, except in cases where this would harm their health and development.[135] For this reason, the Court has made clear that is not enough to simply accede to whatever the child says they desire, but to consider the child's wishes in the context of their overall best interests. For example, in *C v Finland*,[136] the Court cautioned against giving children 'an unconditional veto power', while in *K v the Netherlands*,[137] the Commission commended the domestic authorities for not simply basing their refusal to allow contact on the child's negative attitude, but for also considering her age and maturity, and her 'serious and not unfounded objections' when deciding what weight to give to this.

In undertaking a determination of the weight to be given to children's wishes and feelings, the Court has emphasised the importance of obtaining expert evidence. This was discussed in *Elsholz v Germany*,[138] where the domestic courts relied on statements made by the child—then aged five—in refusing the father's application for access. Despite the father's request, the domestic court did not find it necessary to seek an expert opinion to evaluate the child's statements and explore the true wishes of the child. The Court found that the refusal to order an independent psychological report was in violation of Article 8.[139]

This does not mean that an expert opinion is always necessary, however. In *Sommerfeld v Germany*, the Court found that '[i]t would be going too far to say that domestic courts are always required to involve a psychological expert on the issue of access to a parent not having custody, but this issue depends on the specific circumstances of each case, having due regard to the age and maturity of the child concerned'.[140] In this case, the judge had obtained expert evidence in the first set of proceedings, but did not do so again two years later when the case came again before him. The Court found that the judge was well placed to evaluate her statements and to decide whether or not she was able to make up her own mind, and his failure to obtain an additional expert opinion did not constitute a flaw in the proceedings. However, the child in this case was considerably older—11 years old (13 in the second proceedings), as opposed to five in *Elsholz*.

This decision was criticised strongly by Judge Ress, joined by Judges Pastro Ridruejo and Türmen, in his partly dissenting opinion. He focused his analysis on

[134] (10161/13) 03.09.2015.
[135] *Neulinger and Shuruk v Switzerland* (41615/07) 06.07.2010 (GC).
[136] (18249/02) 09.05.2006.
[137] (9018/80) 04.07.1983 (dec.).
[138] (25735/94) 13.07.2000 (GC).
[139] See also *C v Finland* (18249/02) 09.05.2006; *Palau-Martinez v France* (64927/01) 16.12.2003.
[140] (31871/96) 08.07.2003 (GC), para. 71.

parental alienation syndrome, and highlighted the importance of judges in considering whether this was present, and what specific consequences this could have on the child's development and on the establishment of what the child's 'true wishes' really were. Noting that the only psychological opinion was a one-page submission in the first proceedings, there was no other expert opinion about the truthfulness of the wishes expressed by the child, nor how far and how strongly she was influenced by her mother and stepfather. As such, he considered that the judge should have required an up-to-date expert opinion to evaluate the child's statements, and to establish whether she was able to make up her own mind.

In this respect, he stated:

> The statements of a ten- or thirteen-year-old girl, whether she is heard in court or not, cannot always be decisive or even indicative of her true wishes. In such a complex situation, where the alienation of the child from her natural father by the strong influence of her mother and her stepfather can be perceived, a more thorough approach has to be taken and an effective and genuine chance of participation has to be given to the natural father.[141]

In addition to assisting judges in ascertaining the children's views and determining where their best interests lie, the Court has also recognised that experts can play an important role in creating the necessary conditions for contact to take place. In this respect, the Court has observed that even where a competent and mature child may resist contact in the short term, this might not preclude contact in the long term, and steps should be taken to attempt to facilitate reconciliation between the child and parent concerned.

This was considered at length in the case of *AV v Slovenia*,[142] which concerned triplet children aged 12 at the start of proceedings, and 15 at the conclusion. Contact between the children and their father was ordered to be held in a social welfare centre, and facilitated by the centre's staff, but the children refused to participate in this, and clearly expressed their wish that contact should not continue. After four sessions, during which the children simply walked out after a few minutes, the centre applied to the courts to change the arrangements on the grounds that they were not in the children's interests. Contact between the children and their father was therefore suspended, and later terminated.

The Court summarised its jurisprudence in this area in the following manner:

> While the Court's case-law requires children's views to be taken into account, those views are not necessarily immutable and children's objections, which must be given due weight, are not necessarily sufficient to override the parents' interests, especially in having regular contact with their child. In particular, the right of a child to express his or her own views should not be interpreted as effectively giving an unconditional veto power to children without any other factors being considered and an examination

141 Partly dissenting opinion of Judge Ress, joined by Judges Pastro Ridruejo and Türmen.
142 (878/13) 09.04.2019.

> being carried out to determine their best interests; such interests normally dictate that the child's ties with his or her family must be maintained, except in cases where this would harm his or her health and development.[143]

The Court went on to note that the involvement of the welfare centre had been ordered by the domestic courts in light of the negative experiences the children had had in the past. Despite these experiences, the courts had determined that contact was still in the children's best interests, and had appointed the welfare centre to assist in overcoming these difficulties, and facilitating contact. This the centre had manifestly failed to do. It had not undertaken a proper assessment of the situation, nor had it drawn up an action plan for dealing with the case. The sessions were not arranged such as to encourage positive relationships, and the children were not offered any help or advice aimed at overcoming the alienation from their father.[144]

While this case sets a strong precedent, requiring a robust response on the part of authorities to reluctance on the part of children to participate in contact, it should not be read to require that contact itself should be enforced against children's wishes. The obligation discussed in *AV* was procedural, rather than substantive—requiring not that contact actually took place, but that the requisite conditions were put in place for it to do so. Where the child nevertheless refuses to take part in contact, the Court has made clear that there will be no violation of the state's obligations in this respect. This was demonstrated most precisely in *Hokkanen v Finland*:[145] while the Court found that the authorities were originally in violation of their obligations for failing to enforce the access arrangements ordered by the courts, from the time that the child was sufficiently mature for her views to be take into account the violation ceased. The positive obligation to facilitate contact terminated once the child herself declared that she did not wish to see her father.[146]

Overall, the Court's jurisprudence in this area is to be commended. It has incorporated the principles of Article 12 UN Convention on the Rights of the Child into its analysis of Article 8 ECHR, by making the child's participation in any private law proceedings a procedural requirement under this provision. It has further recognised the need for discretion in the way in which children are asked to participate, differentiating between direct and indirect participation, and emphasising the role of experts in assisting children in expressing and interpreting their views and opinions. Most importantly, however, the Court has not permitted indirect representation of children's 'best interests' to supplant the direct involvement of children where they so wish, thus ensuring that the requirements of Article 3 UN Convention on the Rights of the Child are not conflated with Article 12.

143 ibid., para. 72 (citations omitted).
144 See also *Amănălăchioai v Romania* (4023/04) 27.05.2009.
145 (19823/92) 23.09.1994.
146 See also *MK v Greece* (51312/16) 01.02.2018.

9.7 Parental child abduction

One of the most prolific areas of the Court's jurisprudence relating to children—and one of its most controversial—has been concerning parental child abduction.[147] This area is governed by private international law instruments at a regional and international level—notably the 1980 Hague Abduction Convention[148] and Brussels IIa Regulation[149]—and the Court therefore has to walk a careful line between recognising and respecting the international obligations of member states under these instruments and enforcing its own standards of protection.

This section does not try to summarise the entire body of the Court's case law in this area, as this is capable of forming a book in and of itself. Instead, it tries to identify and capture the principal trends in decision-making and the key rules that have emerged.

9.7.1 Should there be a full best interests enquiry?

The basic goal of the Hague Abduction Convention is to ensure the swift return of an abducted child to their county of habitual residence. The aim is to re-establish as soon as possible the *status quo ante*, in order to avoid the consolidation of de facto situations that were brought about unlawfully, and to leave issues of custody to be determined by the courts in the place of the child's habitual residence. This is achieved by requiring the domestic authorities in the state where the child has been unlawfully taken or retained to order the return of the child to the state of habitual residence, subject to a number of exceptions. These are: that the child has been living in the new country for over a year, and has settled into his or her new environment (Article 12); that there is a grave risk that the child's return would expose them to physical or psychological harm, or otherwise place the child in an intolerable situation (Article 13(1)(b)); that the child objects to his or her return, and has attained an age and degree of maturity at which it is appropriate to take account of their views (Article 13(2)); or that return is not permitted by the fundamental principles of the state relating to the protection of human rights and fundamental freedoms (Article 20).

The primary area of contention in the Court's jurisprudence relates to the level of review necessary—or appropriate—by a domestic court who is determining whether to order a return. The Court initially took a very cautious approach in this regard, deferring to the assumption under the Hague Convention that the child's best interests lay in ensuring their return without delay.[150] For example, in *Maumousseau and Washington v France*,[151] the Court found no violation in circumstances where the

[147] As of 2019, Simona Florescu counted the number of applications at more than 70. (S. Florescu, 'Parental Child Abduction is Back on the Agenda of the European Court of Human Rights' (Strasbourg Observers, 23.07.2019), https://strasbourgobservers.com/2019/07/23/parental-child-abduction-is-back-on-the-agenda-of-the-european-court-of-human-rights/)

[148] Hague Convention on the Civil Aspects of International Child Abduction 1980 (1980 Convention).

[149] EC Regulation No. 2201/2003 of 27 November 2003 concerning jurisdiction and recognition and enforcement of judgments in matrimonial matters and the matters of parental responsibility [2003] OJ L338/1 (Brussels IIa).

[150] *Paradis and others v Germany* (4783/03) 15.05.2003 (dec.).

[151] (39388/05) 06.12.2007.

domestic authorities had confined their assessment to the limited exceptions in the Hague Convention, rather than examining the child's situation as a whole to determine whether return was in her best interests. The Court noted that the best interests of the child was a primary consideration in the procedures provided for in the Hague Convention, and inherent in this concept was the right not to be wrongfully removed from their country of residence, and their relationship with their other parent disrupted. In expressing itself 'entirely in agreement' with the philosophy underlying the Hague Convention,[152] the Court further opined that this conception of 'best interests' was also compatible with the UN Convention on the Rights of the Child, noting the obligation in Article 11 of that instrument to 'take measures to combat the illicit transfer and non-return of children abroad'. The Court was thus satisfied that domestic authorities may undertake a restricted best interests enquiry in such circumstances, limited to the Hague Convention exceptions, as to require a free-standing investigation of best interests would result in 'both the substance and primary purpose of the Hague Convention ... [being] rendered meaningless'.[153]

When the Grand Chamber came to examine the interaction between Article 8 ECHR and the Hague Convention, however, in the (in)famous decision of *Neulinger and Shuruk v Switzerland*,[154] it was exactly such a free-standing investigation that was mandated. Relying on the reiteration of a passage from *Maumousseau*, it found that the Court must ascertain whether

> the domestic courts conducted an in-depth examination of the entire family situation and of a whole series of factors, in particular of a factual, emotional, psychological, material and medical nature, and made a balanced and reasonable assessment of the respective interests of each person, with a constant concern for determining what the best solution would be for the abducted child in the context of an application for his return to his country of origin.[155]

However, while in *Maumousseau* this was simply a description of the activities the domestic authorities had already carried out, the Court in *Neulinger* turned it into an obligation. In doing so, the Court relied again on the principle of the best interests of the child, noting the 'broad consensus—including in international law—in support of the idea that in all decisions concerning children, their best interests must be paramount'.[156] These interests, the Court found, comprise of two limbs:

> On the one hand, it dictates that the child's ties with its family must be maintained, except in cases where the family has proved particularly unfit. It follows that family ties may only be severed in very exceptional circumstances and that everything must be done to preserve personal relations and, if and when appropriate, to 'rebuild' the family. On the other hand, it is clearly also in the child's interest to ensure its development in a sound

[152] ibid., para. 69.
[153] ibid., para. 73.
[154] (41615/07) 06.07.2010 (GC).
[155] ibid., para. 139.
[156] ibid., para. 135.

environment, and a parent cannot be entitled under Article 8 to have such measures taken as would harm the child's health and development.[157]

In this way, the Court reversed its previous jurisprudence.[158] Rather than taking as its starting point the Hague Convention, and relying on its provisions to protect the child's best interests, in *Neulinger* the Court realigned itself to prioritise 'best interests' itself as the start and end point—although lip service was still paid to the Hague Convention scheme.

In analysing the particular facts of the case, the Court weighed such considerations as the difficulties which the child would encounter in the country of destination; the social, cultural, and family ties both with the host country and with the country of destination; and the seriousness of any difficulties which may be encountered in the destination country by the family members who would be accompanying him. These were balanced against the potential benefits of return, which were limited, given the restrictions on the father's rights of access, and the possibility of criminal proceedings against his mother.[159]

Neulinger was a landmark decision from the perspective of children's rights in general—placing these at the centre of the analysis, heralding a new era of jurisprudence from the Court. However, from the perspective of children's rights in the context of parental child abduction, it represented a significant misstep. By obliging domestic courts to look into the merits of the case, in an assessment 'akin to an examination carried out in a custody decision',[160] the summary return procedure that is so central to the Hague Convention scheme was undermined.[161]

Thankfully, it did not take the Court long to recognise its mistake, and at the next opportunity, the Grand Chamber revised its approach. In *X v Latvia*,[162] decided three years later, the Court stepped back from the requirement of an 'in-depth' examination of the entire family situation, requiring instead that there be an 'effective' examination of any allegations made in relation to a refusal to return under Articles 12, 13, and 20 of the Hague Convention. In order to satisfy this new test, the domestic authorities must fulfil two requirements: first, they must genuinely consider any arguable claims against return; and second, they must give a sufficiently detailed ruling giving specific reasons in light of the circumstances of the case. Furthermore, if return is to be ordered, the domestic authorities must satisfy themselves that adequate safeguards

[157] ibid., para. 136 (citations omitted). Interestingly, and unlike the earlier cases (for example, *Maumousseau and Washington v France* (39388/05) 06.12.2007; *Iglesias Gil and AUI v Spain* (56673/00) 29.04.2003; *Maire v Portugal* (48206/99) 26.06.2003), the Court made no mention of Article 11 of the UN Convention on the Rights of the Child.

[158] Although it did not acknowledge that it did so—see Judge Zupančič in dissent.

[159] See also *Šneersone and Kampanella v Italy* (14737/09) 12.07.2011.

[160] P. Beaumont, K. Trimmings, L. Walker, and J. Holliday, 'Child Abduction: Recent Jurisprudence of the European Court of Human Rights' (2015) 64(1) *International and Comparative Law Quarterly* 39, 43.

[161] Interestingly, in their concurring opinion in *B v Belgium* (4320/11) 10.07.2012, Judges Tulkens and Keller argued that rather than emptying the Hague Convention of its substance, the Court was instead strengthening it: giving it effectiveness and efficiency, by exercising international control which it is otherwise lacking. Unfortunately, such institutional strength came at the expense of substantive content of the Convention, frustrating the procedures for swift return to the point of futility.

[162] (27853/09) 26.11.2013 (GC).

are in place to provide tangible protection against any known risk. Importantly, the Court emphasised that the exceptions in the Hague Convention must be interpreted strictly, and that the term 'grave risk' in Article 13(1)(b) cannot be read to include 'all the inconveniences necessarily linked to the experience of return . . . only the situations which go beyond what a child might reasonably bear'.[163]

This judgment went a long way to recalibrating the approach of the Court in line with the aims and objectives of the Hague Convention. Under this revised approach, it does indeed seem that the Court can play an important role in improving the institutional effectiveness of the Hague Convention, providing it with a mechanism for interpretation and enforcement which is otherwise lacking.[164]

9.7.2 Reasons for non-return

In addition to examining the weight to be given to the child's best interests, and the obligation on domestic authorities to undertake an investigation to this effect, the Court has also considered the interpretation of the specific objections to return: namely, the child's objection and the grave risk to physical harm.

9.7.2.1 The child's objection

As discussed, one of the exceptions to return under the Hague Convention is that the child objects to their return and has attained an age and degree of maturity at which it is appropriate to take account of their views (Article 13(2)). This exception has been considered by the Court on a number of occasions—both in the context of challenges to a failure to give sufficient weight to the wishes of a child to remain with the abducting parent and in cases where parents have argued that *too much* weight has been placed on the children's objections to return, which should have been overridden. In all such cases, the Court has fallen back on the margin of appreciation, giving deference to the domestic courts, who have been in a position to hear the parties directly, and are therefore in a better position to evaluate the child's maturity.[165]

[163] ibid., para. 116. It is important to note that although the judges of the Grand Chamber were unanimous in their revision of the *Neulinger* test, they were nevertheless split nine votes to eight as to its correct application. While the judges in the majority found that the Latvian courts had failed to take into account a report by a psychologist that the child's separation from her mother would be harmful to the child, the judges in dissent considered that since the report considered only separation, it related to custody, not return, and therefore did not need to be taken into account. This demonstrates that although the principles may be clearer, their application still poses difficulties for the Court.

[164] The decision in *X v Latvia* (22643/14) 12.03.2015 notwithstanding, there are still judges who reject the premise of the Hague Convention and have argued for wider exceptions to return. For example, Judge Dedov in *Adžić v Croatia* argued that the summary return mechanism was 'not suitable for the assessment of rights under Article 8 of the Convention, as the Hague Convention does not provide a comprehensive approach to the conduct of the return proceedings'. He emphasised the vulnerability of mothers who were dependent on husbands, and of very young children, for whom separation from their mother would lead to distress, and argued for a broader approach to decisions concerning return. See also the dissenting opinion of Judges Nicolaou, Wojtyczek, and Vehabovic in *RS v Poland* (63777/09) 21.07.2015.

[165] This has also been the case in relation to the decision whether or not to even hear the child in proceedings: see, for example, *Eskinazi and Chelouche v Turkey* (14600/05) 06.12.2005 (dec.); *Maumousseau and Washington v France* (39388/05) 06.12.2007; *Gajtani v Switzerland* (43730/07) 09.09.2014.

Despite this, however, the Court has at times expressed its scepticism at the decisions made by domestic authorities. For example, in *Blaga v Romania*,[166] concerning a refusal to return children of eight and ten years old based on their objections, the Court stated that it would like 'to underline its concern with the fact that only one of the children had been over ten years old at the time', although it was 'prepared to accept' that the conditions had been met for the authorities to rely on the exception in Article 13(2).[167] It went on to remind the authorities that while the Hague Convention recognises the right of a child to have a voice in proceedings, and to have these taken into account if they have achieved a sufficient degree of maturity, it does not make their opinions decisive in deciding the question of return.

More to the Court's liking was the decision of *Gajtani v Switzerland*,[168] where the domestic courts had ordered a 12-year-old boy's return, despite his categorical refusal. This decision was made on the grounds that he was caught in a conflict of loyalties, and his behaviour did not show sufficient maturity for his opinion to be considered sufficiently independent. Likewise, in *Rouiller v Switzerland*,[169] the Court emphasised that the Hague Convention does not give children the freedom to choose where they wish to live, and that objections must relate to sufficiently weighty reasons to justify non-return. In this case, the domestic authorities had distinguished between objections to return and the child's preferences as to her living arrangements, finding that her reasons for wanting to remain in her current situation were not based on sufficiently comprehensible, specific, and strongly asserted grounds. The Court endorsed this approach, finding that there had been no violation of Article 8, as the reasons given by the child for wanting to remain were not such as to justify the application of one of the exceptions to return.

While these cases appropriately navigate the tension between the child's right to participation, the duty on the state to make decisions according to their best interests, and the role of the Court in providing oversight, there is one decision that is notable for its failure to achieve a proper balance in this regard. *Raw and others v France*[170]—discussed in section 9.2.1 above—concerned children aged 12 and 14 who were habitually resident in England, and retained wrongfully by their father in France. Following a return order made by the English courts, a meeting was organised between the children and their mother, but this was unsuccessful on account of the children's negative reaction—one child physically attacked the applicant, the other, shouting and crying, refused to meet her. Following this incident, the French Public Prosecutor refused further attempts to enforce the English judgment, and the mother brought an application before the Strasbourg Court.

The Court found a violation of Article 8, criticising the French authorities for treating the objections of the children to their return as immutable, and reiterating that while their opinions should be taken into account, their objections were not necessarily sufficient to prevent return. This is a questionable conclusion, however, which

166 (54443/10) 01.07.2014.
167 ibid., para. 78.
168 (43730/07) 09.09.2014.
169 (3592/08) 22.07.2014.
170 (10131/11) 07.03.2013.

was seemingly based on the fact that the younger child did eventually go back to live with the mother in later years. It seems contrary to suggest that the domestic authorities had a duty to enforce the return of children who so fundamentally objected to this that they resorted to physical violence and extreme emotional reactions. Indeed, it is not clear why the margin of appreciation given to domestic authorities in other cases, on account of their close contact with the facts and individuals in question, was not similarly extended in this more extreme example of objection.

This case appears to be an outlier, however, and in general, the Court has appropriately recognised the difficult balance to be drawn between participation and best interests in this area.

9.7.2.2 Grave risk of physical harm

In addition to the child's objections, the Court has also considered whether domestic authorities have appropriately evaluated allegations of physical harm in deciding whether to order a child's return. In the recent judgment of *OCI and others v Romania*,[171] the Court took a strong position on this issue, mirroring its jurisprudence concerning corporal punishment in other areas of the law.[172] In this case, the mother had alleged that the father had engaged in physical and psychological violence against the children, including corporal punishment, and provided evidence to support this. The Romanian authorities, however, found that such 'occasional acts of violence' would not reoccur often enough to pose a 'grave risk' as required by Article 13(1)(b) of the Hague Convention, and that the child should not be 'retained in the name of rights linked to his person which are to a larger or lesser extent debatable'.[173]

The Court stated emphatically that '[c]orporal punishment against children cannot be tolerated', and that 'the risk of domestic violence against children cannot pass as a mere inconvenience necessarily linked to the experience of return, but concerns a situation which goes beyond what a child might reasonably bear'.[174] A child therefore could not be returned to a situation where they would face a risk of domestic violence without adequate safeguards in place. It was not sufficient that the Italian authorities would be able to react to such abuse—the Romanian authorities had a positive obligation to protect the child against a known risk.

9.7.3 Effective enforcement

While the Court is somewhat limited in its ability to examine the substance of the return decision, it has been particularly influential in the articulation of positive obligations to achieve reunification between a parent and child once this has been ordered.

First and foremost, states must have an adequate legal framework in place, capable of preventing and punishing parental child abduction. While the Court has noted that the ECHR does not impose an obligation on states to ratify the Hague Convention,

[171] (49450/17) 21.05.2019.
[172] See Chapter 2.
[173] *OCI and others v Romania* (49450/17) 21.05.2019, para. 14.
[174] ibid., para. 43.

they must nevertheless take all necessary measures to ensure the swift return of children who have been wrongfully removed. Moreover, even where the state in question has not ratified the Hague Convention, the Court has nevertheless interpreted the obligations of Article 8 in line with its provisions.[175]

When looking at the specific obligations within such a legal framework, the Court has emphasised that Article 8 must be interpreted in light of Article 7 of the Hague Convention, which sets out of a non-exhaustive list of measures that should be taken to secure the prompt return of children.[176] In particular, in *Ignaccolo-Zenide v Romania*,[177] the Court held that domestic authorities must take adequate and effective steps to facilitate the execution of any return order by creating the necessary conditions for this to occur. This includes not only preparing the children for their return and ensuring regular contact in the meantime,[178] but also ensuring that the authorities have sufficient legal arsenal in place to effect the transfer of custody. In this respect, the domestic authorities have an obligation to consider whether coercive measures against the abducting parent are appropriate: while it has emphasised that such measures are not desirable as against the children themselves, they should not be ruled out against the parent with whom they are living.[179]

For example, the Court has found a violation of Article 8 where the authorities have failed to issue an international search and arrest warrant;[180] where the authorities did not have the power to search the abducting parent's home;[181] where the abducting parent was subject only to a small fine;[182] and where the abducting parent was arrested, but released after several hours without the police having located the child's whereabouts.[183]

Moreover, the Court has recognised that specific streamlined proceedings may be needed for the enforcement of return orders under the Hague Convention. Normal judicial or administrative mechanisms, such as those used for ordinary custody disputes, may not be sufficiently swift, given the nature of child abduction proceedings and the risk that the lapse of time will compromise the position of the non-resident parent irretrievably.[184]

The issue of delay has been central to the Court's jurisprudence concerning parental child abduction. Article 11 of the Hague Convention requires that the domestic authorities act expeditiously in such proceedings, with any delay over six weeks requiring justification. Likewise, the Court has made clear that:

[175] *Bajrami v Albania* (35853/04) 12.12.2006; *Hromadka and Hromadkova v Russia* (22909/10) 11.12.2014.

[176] *Ignaccolo-Zenide v Romania* (31679/96) 25.01.2000; *Monory v Romania and Hungary* (71099/01) 05.04.2005.

[177] *Ignaccolo-Zenide v Romania* (31679/96) 25.01.2000.

[178] See *Bianchi v Switzerland* (7548/04) 22.06.2006.

[179] See also *Maumousseau and Washington v France* (39388/05) 06.12.2007; *Raw and others v France* (10131/11) 07.03.2013; *Severe v Austria* (53661/15) 21.09.2017.

[180] *Iglesias Gil and AUI v Spain* (56673/00) 29.04.2003.

[181] *Maire v Portugal* (48206/99) 26.06.2003.

[182] *Shaw v Hungary* (6457/09) 26.07.2011.

[183] *Cavani v Hungary* (5493/13) 28.10.2014.

[184] *MA v Austria* (4097/13) 15.01.2015.

> In a case of this kind the adequacy of a measure is to be judged by the swiftness of its implementation. Proceedings relating to the granting of parental responsibility, including execution of the decision delivered at the end of them, require urgent handling as the passage of time can have irremediable consequences for relations between the children and the parent who does not live with them.[185]

While it is not possible to identify a specific time period which will be viewed as 'excessive', as each case is so fact specific,[186] the Court has found violations in relation to proceedings lasting, for example, nine months,[187] ten months,[188] 11 months,[189] 13 months,[190] three years,[191] and seven years.[192] It is notable that all these time periods are significantly in excess of the six-week time limit given in the Hague Convention—while the Court consistently refers back to this deadline, it has not applied it strictly, and instead undertakes an evaluation of the whole proceedings, to determine whether they have taken a reasonable length of time. The factors that are considered in undertaking this evaluation are considered in more detail in section 9.8.1 below, concerning the procedural safeguards that are required by the Convention in relation to all private child disputes.

9.8 Procedural rights

Although Article 8 does not contain any explicit procedural requirements, the Court has recognised that the decision-making process 'cannot be devoid of influence on the substance of the decision'.[193] Coupled with the requirements of a fair trial under Article 6, states are required to ensure that the decision-making process is fair and impartial, that the relevant parties are adequately involved, and that the proceedings are independent from political processes.[194] In the area of private law child disputes, complaints have largely related to three issues: the length of proceedings, the privacy requirements of the court process, and the provision of legal assistance.[195]

[185] *Ignaccolo-Zenide v Romania* (31679/96) 25.01.2000, para. 102.

[186] See, for example, *Sylvester v Austria* (36812/97, 40104/08) 24.04.2003; *Bianchi v Switzerland* (7548/04) 22.06.2006; *PP v Poland* (8677/03) 08.01.2008.

[187] *Dore v Portugal* (775/08) 01.02.2011.

[188] *Karadžić v Croatia* (35030/04) 15.12.2005.

[189] *Shaw v Hungary* (6457/09) 26.07.2011.

[190] *Ferrari v Romania* (1714/10) 28.04.2015.

[191] *Adžić v Croatia* (22643/14) 12.03.2015. See also *HN v Poland* (77710/01) 13.09.2005, where the delay was three years and eight months.

[192] *Hoholm v Slovakia* (35632/13) 13.01.2015.

[193] *B v the United Kingdom* (9840/82) 08.07.1987, para. 63.

[194] See, for example, *Rinau v Lithuania* (10926/09) 14.01.2020, in which there had been concerted official efforts to keep the child in Lithuania following Hague Abduction proceedings. Members of Parliament openly questioned the lawfulness of court judgments, the government had made a financial contribution to assist the mother's case before the European Court of Justice, and the President of the Supreme Court had personally intervened in the case. Moreover, pressure was put on the bailiff concerning enforcement, and the child-care service pressurized to change their official opinions. These factors combined led the Court to conclude that the decision-making process had violated the mother and child's rights under Article 8.

[195] The procedural requirements under Article 8 are further discussed in Chapters 10 and 11 as they relate to child protection proceedings and adoption, respectively.

9.8.1 Length of proceedings

As discussed in section 9.7 above in relation to parental child abduction, swift decision-making is of particular importance in the context of custody and access disputes: the relationship between parent and child must not be decided on the mere passage of time.

As each case is so fact specific, this section will not attempt to summarise all circumstances in which the Court has decided that the authorities have exceeded a reasonable length of proceedings. Instead, it discusses the key factors that the Court has identified in undertaking such an evaluation under Article 8, namely: the complexity of the case; the reasons for any delay or period of inaction; and the importance of what is at stake.[196]

When assessing the complexity of the case, the Court will consider not only the difficulty of the legal and factual issues being assessed, but also the number of levels of jurisdiction involved and the number of different parties, experts, and agencies who need to cooperate in the proceedings. As such, the Court has tended to run through a list of each proceeding, and each important piece of evidence waited on, identifying the time that lapsed between each. A passage from *Nuutinen v Finland* gives an indication of what this reasoning looks like:

> The Court further notes that it took four months before a preliminary hearing was held before the Helsinki District Court in the second set of the main proceedings, which the applicant initiated in December 1996. At the preliminary hearing the proceedings were adjourned for a further six months pending the receipt of fresh opinions from the Kuopio and Helsinki social authorities. The Helsinki authority was later granted a two-month extension. Although the opinions had been received by the end of 1997, the main hearing before the District Court took place four months later, in April 1998. Its judgment was rendered the same month, whereas the Court of Appeal dealt with the case in six months and it took the Supreme Court two months to consider the request for leave to appeal.[197]

In addition to the complexity of the case, the Court will also examine carefully the reasons for any delay. In this regard, it is important to note that not all delays are unwarranted—it will depend on what the domestic authorities were doing during this time, and whether this was justified. For example, in *Kuppinger v Germany*[198] the Court differentiated between different periods of delay, based on their different justifications. On the one hand, the Court found that the delay of ten months between the father requesting the imposition of a fine for lack of compliance with the access arrangements and this fine being paid was excessive, as there had been several delays during this period attributable to the German courts. On the other hand, however, a second lengthy delay was justified on the basis that the domestic authorities

[196] See *Hokkanen v Finland* (19823/92) 23.09.1994.

[197] *Nuutinen v Finland* (32842/96) 27.06.2000, para. 113. This is in fact only one of four paragraphs that sets out in detail the exact time frame in which each step of the proceedings was taken.

[198] (62198/11) 15.01.2015.

were undertaking considerable efforts during that time to identify a custodian for the child—the original custodian being objected to by the applicant. This highlights another important consideration for the Court when assessing the reasons for the delay: the conduct of the applicant. If the delay is attributable to the applicant then, obviously, the state will not be in violation of their obligations under Article 8. A notable example of this was *Ancel v Turkey*,[199] where despite proceedings lasting eight years and four months, the Court held that there had been no periods where the authorities had been inactive.

On the other hand, in *K v Slovenia*,[200] the Court found a violation of Article 8 where the civil courts had stayed contact proceedings until the criminal courts could examine a complaint against the father for sexual abuse of the child. It was not until three years later that the criminal charges were finally dismissed and contact considered, a circumstance that the Court found was in breach of the father's rights under Article 8. The fact that the civil court was awaiting the decision of the criminal court before allowing regular contact was not in itself problematic, but it did not release the domestic authorities from their obligation to examine the case promptly, and the length of the criminal case was unreasonable. The state could not rely on unreasonable delays in another part of its own system to justify the length of civil proceedings—it is for the state to organise its judicial system in such a way as to enable all courts to comply with the requirements of the Convention.[201]

The third factor that the Court will consider when evaluating the reasonableness of the length of proceedings is the seriousness of what is at stake for the parent. As was discussed above, any delay is seen as of particular importance in relation to Hague abduction proceedings because of the danger that the child will be integrated into their new environment, and a new *status quo* created. Such a concern also arises in relation to ordinary custody disputes: in *Amănălăchioai v Romania*,[202] the Court found that a ten-week delay between the father filing an application for the child to be returned from the grandparents and the examination of the case violated the father's rights under Article 8. It held that 'the requirement of speed is all the more stringent if, as in the present case, a parent asks for the return of his or her child from a person who holds the child without having the right, and without consent'.[203] By failing to act with due diligence, the national authorities favoured the integration of the child into his new environment, and consequently contributed decisively to the consolidation of a factual situation contrary to the father's rights.[204]

Finally, where proceedings are taking an excessive length of time, there must be effective remedies available to address this. In *Kuppinger v Germany*,[205] the Court

199 (28514/04) 17.02.2009.
200 (41293/05) 07.07.2011.
201 See also *Schaal v Luxembourg* (51773/99) 18.02.2003.
202 (4023/04) 27.05.2009.
203 ibid., para. 93.
204 See also *Eberhard and M v Slovenia* (8673/05, 9733/05) 01.12.2009. It is not only the nature of the dispute that is important in this respect, however—the Court can also consider factual circumstances that make swift proceedings of particular importance. For example, in *Mitovi v the Former Yugoslav Republic of Macedonia* (53565/13) 16.04.2015, the Court noted that delays of between two and five months in dealing with requests for contact orders were particularly excessive in light of the fact that the father had only limited right to stay in the state.
205 (62198/11) 15.01.2015.

emphasised that the ability to lodge a compensation claim was insufficient to effectively expedite proceedings concerning contact rights. Moreover, the provision of domestic law that obliged family courts to treat contact proceedings as a priority and with expedience was merely a recommendation, and without sanction, could equally not be regarded as effective as a remedy against the excessive length of proceedings.

9.8.2 Public hearing and judgment

Article 6(1) of the ECHR provides that the press and public may be excluded from all or part of a trial where the interests of juveniles so require. The Court has made clear that custody disputes following divorce or separation are 'prime examples of cases where the exclusion of the press and public may be justified in order to protect the privacy of the child and parties and to avoid prejudicing the interests of justice'.[206] The judge must be able to gain a full and accurate picture of the situation, including the advantages and disadvantages of various residence and contact options, and in order to do so, parents and other witnesses must feel able to express themselves candidly, without fear of public curiosity or comment.

This was seen in *B and P v the United Kingdom*,[207] which involved fathers who applied to have their residence applications held in open court, with a public pronouncement of the judgment. Domestic law provided that child cases should be held in private unless there is a special direction to the contrary, which would have to be justified by unusual features. In both these cases, the domestic courts held that there was nothing to distinguish the proceedings as 'out of the usual', nor did they raise any issues that would justify a public hearing.

The applicants argued before the Court that the presumption in favour of a private hearing for child law cases should be reversed: they contended that Article 6(1) created a general rule that civil procedures should take place in public, with certain exceptions, and it would be counter to this principle to reverse the presumption for a certain class of cases. This argument was accepted by Judge Loucaides, joined by Judge Tulkens in dissent, who held that the decision to hold a private hearing cannot be decided *in abstracto* or by reference to a category of cases, and must instead be decided on the facts of each individual case that comes before the court. The majority of the Court disagreed, however, finding that it was not inconsistent to designate an entire class of cases as an exception to the general rule, where it was necessary to pursue one of the interests set out in Article 6. Nevertheless, the rule cannot be absolute, and there must be an opportunity for courts to allow for public hearings if the interests of justice require this.[208]

In addition to their complaint concerning the private nature of proceedings, the applicant fathers also complained that the judgments of the courts were not pronounced publicly. In this respect, the applicants made different arguments—while one applicant accepted that, where appropriate, names and other identifying details could be

[206] *B and P v the United Kingdom* (36337/97, 35974/97) 24.04.2001, para. 38.
[207] ibid.
[208] cf. *Moser v Austria* (12643/02) 21.09.2006.

removed from any public judgment, the other argued that if either party wished it, the full, un-anonymised text should be made available.

The Court reiterated that the form of publicity given to a judgment must be assessed in light of the special features of the proceedings and by reference to the object and purpose of Article 6(1). On the facts of the case, , anyone who could establish an interest in the custody proceedings could view the full text of the orders and judgments, and anonymised judgments of the Court of Appeal and of first-instance cases in cases of specific interest were routinely published. As such, the public were able to study the manner in which the courts generally approach such cases, and to examine the principles applied.

For these reasons, the Court considered that a literal interpretation of Article 6(1), which did not allow any exceptions to the publication of judgments, 'would not only be unnecessary for the purposes of public scrutiny but might even frustrate the primary aim of Article 6(1), which is to secure a fair hearing'.[209] This was reiterated by Judge Sir Nicholas Bratza in his concurring opinion, who emphasised that the provision must be read as a whole, and if the public may legitimately be excluded from a hearing under Article 6(1), then 'the requirement that the judgment should be pronounced publicly should not be interpreted in such a way as to undermine that protection'.

9.8.3 Provision of legal assistance

The final procedural obligation that has been examined by the Court in relation to private child law proceedings has been the provision of legal assistance. This was first addressed in the seminal case of *Airey v Ireland*,[210] which was important not only for the specific obligations imposed on states in relation to the issue at hand, but also because it was the first time that the Court recognised the existence of positive obligations of states under Article 6 to ensure a fair trial.

This case was brought by a woman seeking a divorce in Ireland, who had been denied legal aid and had to represent herself before the High Court. The Court found that in litigation of this kind, involving complicated points of law, establishing facts, calling expert witnesses, and entailing a degree of emotional involvement inherent to marital disputes, a person in the applicant's position could not effectively present her own case. More recently, this reasoning was extended to child protection cases in *P, C and S v United Kingdom*,[211] discussed in Chapter 10.

These principles do not, however, extend to all family law disputes. In *NJDB v the United Kingdom*,[212] the father was seeking to appeal a decision by a lower court denying him contact with his child. He was given legal aid to pursue this to the next level of jurisdiction, but his further application for assistance for an appeal to the Supreme Court was denied. The Legal Aid Board found that there was no substantive issue of law arising to merit an appeal, and that no practical benefit to the applicant

[209] *B and P v the United Kingdom* (36337/97, 35974/97) 24.04.2001, para. 48 (citations omitted).
[210] (6289/73) 09.10.1979.
[211] (56547/00) 16.07.2002; cf. *Gnahoré v France* (40031/98) 19.09.2000.
[212] (76760/12) 27.10.2015.

could ensue. The applicant complained that this refusal of legal aid to fund his appeal to the Supreme Court deprived him of effective access to a court, in violation of Article 6(1).

The Court emphasised that the right of access to a court is not absolute, and it may be acceptable to impose conditions on the grant of legal aid, based on, for example, the financial situation of the litigant or his prospects of success. Moreover, it is not incumbent on the state to seek through the use of public funds to ensure total equality of arms between the assisted person and the opposing party, as long as each is afforded a reasonable opportunity to present his case under conditions that do not place him at a substantial disadvantage vis-à-vis his adversary.

In this case, the denial of funding came after the applicant's claims had been thoroughly examined by the domestic courts at two levels of jurisdiction, in which he had received legal aid and been represented by highly qualified solicitors. The Court also took into consideration the fact that the applicant was in any event legally represented by advisers and counsel, who had agreed to act pro bono in the proceedings before the Supreme Court. The Court therefore had no doubt that the applicant was in fact effectively represented in the proceedings before the Supreme Court, notwithstanding the refusal of legal aid. In response to the applicant's argument that the costs had to be borne by his legal team, as they were acting pro bono, the Court held that 'it is not for the Court to concern itself with such private funding arrangements in the absence of evidence that they prevented an applicant from being able to present his case effectively before the court'.[213]

9.9 Conclusion

The European Convention on Human Rights has thus made a significant contribution to the field of private law child disputes in Europe. The prohibition of discrimination in relation to parents in deciding issues of custody and contact, the procedural rights ensuring fairness in decision-making, and the strengthening of the framework provided by the Hague Convention in the field of parental child abduction all provide valuable protection.

However, this protection is provided predominantly to parents, or at most, the family unit. Children's rights are only granted indirect, peripheral protection, flowing from the assertion of adult interests. The cases have largely concerned disputes *over* children:[214] there has been no examination of a free-standing right on the part of the child. This is not to say that important rights have not been carved out for children in this respect—their best interests must be the paramount concern of the domestic authorities, and they must have their wishes and feelings heard if they are capable of expressing them. But the case law has been dominated by adults—adult rights, adult perspectives.

[213] ibid., para. 79.
[214] Although children are sometimes joined as parties by their parents.

This dilemma is compounded by the margin of appreciation given to states in determining where the child's interests lie. Before the Court, this principle becomes purely a procedural right—as long as it has been considered by the domestic authorities, the Court will defer to their judgment, based on their 'direct and continuous contact with the vital forces of their countries'.[215] While this reflects the fact that the 'best interests' principle is a flexible concept that cannot be generalised to apply objectively to all children identically, there must be a point where the Court is willing to step in and declare that the state has wrongly identified what is in the best interests of the child. In this respect, there needs to be greater acknowledgement of the *rights* of children, not simply their *interests*. While the latter can be paternalistic, imposing on children what we think is best, the former respects children as autonomous beings: the subjects, not objects of the law.

Having said this, it does appear that the Court is slowly beginning to recognise the independent rights of children—the most vivid example being the independent representation ordered for the child in *A and B v Croatia*.[216] It is to be hoped that this is the beginning of wider institutional change, not only in relation to the Court, but for domestic systems also. One of the reasons why children's *interests* continue to dominate the jurisprudence of the Court is because children themselves are rarely in a position to assert their *rights*. By providing children with a mechanism to take cases before the Court more easily, or at the very least have separate representation where their parents do so on their behalf, the Court will be forced to confront the issue head on.

[215] *Handyside v the United Kingdom* (5493/72) 07.12.1976, para. 48.
[216] (7144/15) 20.06.2019.

10
Child Protection

10.1 Introduction

From the mid-1990s, there has been a proliferation of cases before the European Court of Human Rights concerning the removal of children into state care.[1] Challenges in this area have been brought under a number of provisions: Article 5, concerning the restriction of children's liberty;[2] Article 6, concerning the right to a fair trial; Article 13, requiring access to an effective remedy; and Article 2, Protocol 1, in relation to the placement of the child in line with philosophical and religious convictions. The majority of cases, however, are examined under Article 8: the right to respect for family life.

This chapter analyses both the substantive and procedural obligations placed on domestic authorities in the field of child protection, including in relation to emergency measures, the removal of the child from the family, their placement in alternative care, and, where appropriate, family reunification. However, before turning to these specific obligations, it is important to examine the way in which the Court has attempted to balance the at times conflicting, at times convergent, rights of parents and children in this area, and in particular, how this has changed across its lifetime.

10.2 Child protection and the child's best interests

The European Court of Human Rights has come a long way in its approach to children's welfare in the field of child protection. From inauspicious beginnings, where children were referred to as 'it',[3] children's interests have developed from a peripheral concern to a central tenet of the Court's jurisprudence. Even the substantive evaluation of the child's welfare has undergone an evolution, from vague statements about the difficulty in ascertaining what is precisely in the child's best interests in *L v Sweden*[4] to the two-limb test famously developed in *Neulinger*.[5]

[1] The cases in this section discuss situations where the state has acted to remove a child from the family. This is in contrast to cases discussed in Chapter 2, where the complaints concerned the failure of the state to protect children, or remove them from a situation where abuse was occurring.

[2] Interestingly, one of the early cases was framed around Article 5, with the parents arguing that the children's placement in a public children's home deprived them of their liberty. However, this was rejected as manifestly ill-founded: see *M, RT and F v Austria* (14013/88) 14.12.1989 (dec.).

[3] *L v Sweden* (10141/82) 03.10.1984 (dec.).

[4] ibid.

[5] *Neulinger and Shuruk v Switzerland* (41615/07) 06.07. 2010 (GC): see Chapter 9.

Children and the European Court of Human Rights. Claire Fenton-Glynn, Oxford University Press (2021). © Claire Fenton-Glynn.
DOI: 10.1093/oso/9780198787518.003.0010

However, the biggest and most important development has been the way that the Court has defined the relationship between parents' rights and children's interests[6] when deciding the necessity and proportionality of removal from the home, contact in care, and family reunification, and the language that has been used in this respect. The approach of the Court in this area can be divided into three stages: (i) parental rights; (ii) competing interests; and (iii) paramount consideration.

The first phase—which I have termed 'parental rights'—was characterised by a strong focus on the autonomy and integrity of the family and the need to protect this from undue interference by the state. This was demonstrated clearly in the early child protection case of *L v Sweden*, where the Commission emphasised that 'the issue in these cases is not only what is the best solution for the child',[7] but whether there are sufficient grounds to interfere with the rights of parents. The focus of the Commission was purely on the parents: what their rights were, and whether there was sufficient justification for these to be interfered with. The child was merely a side note: a reason for interfering with parental rights, rather than an individual with their own rights to be considered.

This conservative approach to the protection of family life from the public sphere was further illustrated in *Olsson (No. 1)*—also decided in the pre-UN Convention on the Rights of the Child era. Despite noting that the children's interests 'must be regarded as an important one',[8] the Commission emphasised that parents have a right under Article 8 to care for, and educate, their children. This right, the Commission held, can only be restricted by the state if they exercise this right in a manner *contrary* to the child's interests. It is not enough that it would be *better* for the child to be taken into alternative care, but that it is *necessary*—that is, that the state demonstrates sufficiently strong reasons for this.[9]

Thus, the language used by the Court at this time was one of parental autonomy. While children's interests were mentioned in passing, these were purely subsidiary. The starting point for the Court was the right of the parent to be free from state interference, and the child's interests had to reach a certain level of importance before they became relevant.[10]

The second phase of cases saw a shift in language and focus from parental rights to competing interests. This began in the early 1990s with the decisions of *Olsson v Sweden (No. 2)*[11] and *Hokkanen v Finland*,[12] where the Court affirmed the obligation of domestic authorities to 'strike a fair balance' between the competing interests of

[6] I use the term 'interests' deliberately. As the discussion below demonstrates, the Court focuses on children's interests, not rights, placing them at a systemic disadvantage.

[7] (10141/82) 03.10.1984 (dec.), p. 151.

[8] (10465/83) 02.12.1986 (ComRep), para. 147.

[9] This is not, of course, to argue that children should be taken away from their parents merely because it might be slightly better for them. The criticism in this respect is not the protection given to the family ties, but the fact that the maintenance of the family unit is seen as a right of the parent, rather than recognising the child's individual rights within this—both to maintain family ties where possible, but also to be protected from harm.

[10] On this point, see J. Eekelaar, 'Beyond the Welfare Principle' (2002) 14(3) *Child and Family Law Quarterly* 237.

[11] (13441/87) 27.11.1992.

[12] (19823/92) 23.09.1994.

parents and children in deciding issues of contact and family reunification. However, the real change came in *Johansen v Norway*,[13] which provided guidance as to how that balance should be struck:

> In carrying out this balancing exercise, the Court will attach particular importance to the best interests of the child, which, depending on their nature and seriousness, may override those of the parent. In particular … the parent cannot be entitled under Article 8 of the Convention to have such measures taken as would harm the child's health and development.[14]

This was a revolutionary judgment, introducing the welfare principle into the Court's jurisprudence for the first time, and placing children on an equal footing with parents. However, it remained an imperfect tool, as judgments continued to be reasoned from the perspective of parents' rights. As Fortin argued:

> There is a significant difference between starting from the premise that a parent's rights must not be infringed unless the court can fulfil the detailed requirements of Article 8(2) and starting from the premise that the outcome of the dispute must be determined by the child's best interests, and then considering the rights of the parties involved.[15]

Thus, although the Court had increased the weight to be given to children in the equation, the equation itself remained the same.

The third phase of the Court's jurisprudence has seen the further elevation of the interests of children from a factor that may outweigh the rights of parents to the paramount consideration in all decisions concerning them. The Court began to use this language as early as 2007,[16] but it was not until *Neulinger and Shuruk v Switzerland*[17] in 2010 that this was firmly established as the relevant test. In this case, which contains perhaps the most comprehensive examination of the Court to date as to the content of, and weight to be given to, the phrase 'best interests of the child', the Court recognised that the child's separation from their parents (in this case, in relation to child abduction), should be viewed from the perspective of the child's own competing rights: on the one hand, the right to have their family ties maintained, where possible, and on the other, the right to ensure their development in a sound environment, free from harm. The starting point for the Court was no longer parental rights, to be weighed against child's interests, but the competing rights of the child themself.

This change of perspective was accompanied by a parallel shift in the weight given to children's interests, as the Court affirmed that 'there is currently a broad

[13] *Johansen v Norway* (17383/90) 07.08.1996.

[14] ibid., para. 78.

[15] J. Fortin, 'Children's Rights: Are the Courts Now Taking Them More Seriously?' (2004) 15 *Kings College Law Journal* 253, 268.

[16] See *Wagner and JMWL v Luxembourg* (76240/01) 28.06.2007; *Kearns v France* (35991/04) 10.01.2008; *EB v France* (43546/02) 22.01.2008 (GC).

[17] (41615/07) 06.07.2010 (GC).

consensus—including in international law—in support of the idea that in all decisions concerning children, their best interests must be paramount'.[18]

As a statement of law, this is, with due respect, incorrect. International law does not recognise the paramountcy of children's interests,[19] only their primary importance. Indeed, in support of this proposition, the Court cited Article 3 of the UN Convention on the Rights of the Child and Article 24(2) of the European Union's Charter of Fundamental Rights, both of which use the term 'primary'. The difference between these two terms is important, particularly since the UN Convention on the Rights of the Child itself uses both to indicate different levels of scrutiny. While 'primary' implies that a particular weight be placed on children's interests as one factor amongst many, 'paramount' connotes supreme importance, determining the issue at hand.

Despite this somewhat dubious foundation, later cases appear to confirm an approach which places children's interests at the centre of decision-making, outweighing any other factor. While *Neulinger* was a parental child abduction case, in *R and H v the United Kingdom*[20] the Court explicitly extended its reasoning to cases concerning child protection and adoption, finding that when balancing the competing interests under Article 8, 'the interests of the biological parents must inevitably give way to that of the child'.[21] This, of course, does not mean that children can simply be removed from their parents where 'better' care is available, as the child too has a right to respect to family life with their parents. However, it does mean that the child's individual rights are respected—it is the child's welfare that will dictate the decision, rather than trying to balance parental rights with children's interests.

This appeared to represent the start of a new era for the Court, and for the decade following there was a consistent emphasis on children at the centre of decision-making in child protection cases. However, in the recent case of *Strand Lobben and others v Norway*,[22] decided in September 2019, the Court seems to have rowed back on this position. This case involved a challenge brought by a biological mother whose child had been removed from her care and adopted. In undertaking its analysis under Article 8, the Court criticised the domestic authorities for focusing on the interests of the child, at the expense of the mother. While acknowledging the 'primordial interest' of the child's interests in the decision-making process, the Court held that the authorities had failed to 'perform a genuine balancing exercise between the interests of the child and his biological family'.[23]

This judgment, coming as it does from the Grand Chamber, sets a new and concerning precedent. To criticise a state for focusing too much on the interests of the child is an astounding position, turning the clock back on the position of children before the Court. As Judges Kjølbro, Poláčková, Koskelo, and Nordén made clear in their

[18] ibid., para. 135 (citations omitted). Interestingly, the Norwegian government in *Johansen* had in fact argued for a test of 'paramountcy', but this was watered down by the Court in its judgment.

[19] Save in adoption cases: see Chapter 11, section 11.3.4.

[20] (35348/06) 31.05.2011.

[21] ibid., para. 77. See also *YC v the United Kingdom* (4547/10) 13.03.2012. For further commentary on this line of cases, see C. Simmonds, 'Paramountcy and the ECHR: A Conflict Resolved?' (2012) 71(3) *Cambridge Law Journal* 498.

[22] (37283/13) 10.09.2019.

[23] ibid., para. 220.

dissenting opinion, the Convention is premised on the balancing of family rights,[24] and the effect of this on children is particularly pernicious: the particular importance given to children's best interests is for the very reason that they are more vulnerable and dependent—their rights are already balanced because of their position in society, and in the family.[25]

It is to be hoped that this case is nothing but an anomaly: a brief deviation from which the Court will soon recover—much like *Neulinger* in relation to the substantive requirements it set for parental child abduction. However, early indications are not good. In *AS v Norway*,[26] decided three months after *Strand Lobben*, the Court had reverted to using the *Johansen* test of 'a fair balance' and 'depending on their nature and seriousness'. The term 'paramount' was not mentioned at any stage.[27]

In light of this, it appears to be a case of two steps forward, one step back for the Court when it comes to protecting children's best interests.

10.3 Emergency measures

Turning to the substance of the obligations on domestic authorities in the field of child protection, it is important to distinguish between emergency measures (and the procedures leading up to them) and 'full' care proceedings. The Court has emphasised that each will be subject to different constraints, and in particular, the procedural protections available to parents under Article 8—discussed further in section 10.6—are not as extensive in relation to emergency measures as they are in other proceedings. Such measures are intended to be temporary, in response to situations of urgent necessity, and as such, procedural safeguards may be curtailed where the situation demands.[28]

This was discussed at length in *K and T v Finland*,[29] which involved a mother who suffered from schizophrenia and paranoia, and who was periodically hospitalised. On the day that the mother gave birth, her child was taken into emergency care in the hospital, without either of the parents being heard. The Court accepted that when making an emergency care order, it may not always be possible to involve the parents of the child in the decision-making process, given the urgency of the situation. Nor may it even be desirable to involve the parents if they are a source of immediate threat to the child, as giving them prior warning may deprive the measure of its effectiveness.[30] It was thus reasonable for the authorities to believe that if the mother had been forewarned, there could have been dangerous consequences for herself, or for her children.

While such dangerous consequences may be a relevant and sufficient reason for excluding parents from the decision-making process—at least initially—a mere concern

[24] *Strand Lobben and others v Norway* (37283/13) 10.09.2019, dissenting opinion of Judges Kjølbro, Poláčková, Koskelo, and Nordén, para. 9.
[25] S. Cretney, *Elements of Family Law* (London: Sweet & Maxwell, 1992), 526.
[26] (60371/15) 17.12.2019.
[27] See also *Abdi Ibrahim v Norway* (15379/16) 17.12.2019.
[28] See *RV and others v Italy* (37748/13) 18.07.2019.
[29] (25702/94) 12.07.2001 (GC).
[30] See also *Covezzi and Morselli v Italy* (52763/99) 09.05.2003; *Hanzelkovi v Czech Republic* (43643/10) 11.12.2014.

that the parent might act 'unpredictably' was found to be inadequate in *Venema v the Netherlands*.[31] In this case, the child had been hospitalised and doctors were concerned that her illness had been caused by her parents. On the basis of a report stating that the child's life was at risk and urgent action was required, a juvenile judge ordered the child's placement away from the family, without the parents being informed of, or in way involved in, the procedures. At no stage did the doctors or the welfare authorities raise with the parents their belief that the child was being abused. The government argued that they had not raised their concerns with the parents because they may have reacted unpredictably if the matter was discussed with them. However, while the Court found that this was a relevant reason, it was not sufficient to exclude the parents from a procedure of immense personal importance to them—particularly as the child was perfectly safe at the hospital and was not in any danger from their (potential) reaction.

In addition to considering the involvement of parents in decision-making, *K and T* also examined the proportionality of the implementation of the care order—particularly in the context of a young child. Here, the Court emphasised that the taking into care of a newborn baby at the time of its birth is 'an extremely harsh measure',[32] and '[t]here must be extraordinarily compelling reasons before a baby can be physically removed from the care of its mother, against her will, immediately after birth as a consequence of a procedure in which neither she nor her partner has been involved'.[33]

The reasons relied on by the domestic authorities were relevant, but they were not sufficient to justify the seriousness of the intervention. In particular, the Court found that the authorities had failed in their positive obligation to examine whether less intrusive interference into family life was possible, and whether there were other mechanisms that could have protected the child short of the drastic measure of removal upon birth. It was acknowledged that precautionary measures may have been necessary, but not such significant ones.

The Court also pointed out that the situation was not an 'emergency' in the sense of it being unforeseen—the authorities had known about the pregnancy for months in advance, and were also aware of the mother's mental health problems. This line of reasoning was followed by the Court in *Haase v Germany*.[34] Here, the Court held that before public authorities have recourse to emergency measures, 'the imminent danger should be actually established'.[35] While in obvious cases of danger it would not be necessary to involve the parents, 'if it is still possible to hear the parents of the children and to discuss with them the necessity of the measure, there should be no room for an emergency action'.[36]

The Court returned to the issue of emergency measures for newborn children in the case of *P, C and S v the United Kingdom*.[37] In this case, the mother had previously been found guilty of endangering her child's health while living in the United States, and

[31] (35731/97) 17.12.2002.
[32] *K and T v Finland* (25702/94) 12.07.2001 (GC), para. 168.
[33] ibid.
[34] (11057/02) 08.04.2004.
[35] ibid., para. 99.
[36] ibid.
[37] (56547/00) 16.07.2002.

was diagnosed as suffering from Munchhausen syndrome by proxy—a disease which in this case manifested in seeking attention by fabricating or inducing illness in her child. She moved to England and commenced a relationship with a man conducting research into cases of women wrongly accused of Munchhausen's, by whom she fell pregnant. The domestic authorities decided to seek an emergency protection order at the child's birth, as they believed that the baby would be at risk of significant harm if left in the care of its parents. The mother was in a state of denial about her condition, and equally, because the father did not accept that she was potentially dangerous, he would not be able to protect the child from the risk posed by her. The child was taken from the hospital on the day of birth and placed with a foster family immediately.

What is most of interest about this case was the nuanced way in which the Court approached the various actions of the domestic authorities. It accepted that it was within the proper role of the authority to obtain an emergency protection order—it had to take appropriate steps to ensure that no harm came to the baby, and to obtain the legal power to prevent the parents or family removing the child from the hospital. However, while *obtaining* the order was based on relevant and sufficient reasons, the *implementation* of it, was not. The Court considered that the removal of the child from hospital, and the placement in foster care, was disproportionate—it was not clear why it was not possible for the child to remain in the hospital under a care order and for the mother to spend at least some time with her under supervision. Even if the mother were a risk of harm to her baby, the Court noted that her capacity and opportunity for doing so, after having just given birth and while there were medical staff present, was limited.

The touchstone for this judgment was proportionality—what was the risk to be guarded against, and what steps needed to be taken to manage this. On the information available, the mother's illness manifested in exaggerating symptoms of ill health in her children and using laxatives to induce diarrhoea. As the Court emphasised, although such harm cannot be underestimated, it was not life-threatening, and was of such a type that supervision could have provided adequate protection. In this way, the Court held that taking legal control of the child was proportionate, but using that power to remove the child from the hospital and the family was not.

10.4 The placement of the child in alternative care

While the authorities are granted certain leeway with regard to emergency measures—given that they are having to make swift decisions concerning the child's immediate safety—the Court has taken a stricter approach concerning 'full' care procedures, where there is time to undertake a full examination of the family's situation.

There is little doubt that where a child is removed from their family in such circumstances, this will constitute an interference within the meaning of Article 8(1)—both of the parents' rights, and those of the child.[38] The key question, therefore, becomes

[38] Not all child protection measures will constitute interference with a parent's right to respect for family life under Article 8. For example, in *W v the United Kingdom* (17071/90) 07.01.1991 (dec.), the Commission held that placing the child on the child protection register did not infringe the mother's right to respect for family life under Article 8. It noted that placing of the child's name on the register did not constitute a finding of fact, nor guilt, and the decision did not affect the mother's custody or access to the children.

whether this interference is justified under Article 8(2): whether it is in accordance with the law, whether it pursues a legitimate aim, and whether it is necessary in a democratic society.

10.4.1 In accordance with the law

In *Olsson v Sweden (No. 1)*, the Court set out three requirements that must be met before a child protection measure can be deemed 'in accordance with the law':

(1) It must be formulated with sufficient precision to enable a citizen (with appropriate advice) to foresee to a reasonable degree the consequences that a given action may entail. However, this does not require absolute precision, as given the need to avoid excessive rigidly and to allow for changing circumstances, many laws in this area are inevitably somewhat vague.
(2) It must be compatible with the rule of law, meaning that there must be a measure of protection against arbitrary interference by public authorities, including in relation to the rights safeguarded by Article 8.
(3) While discretion is not in itself inconsistent with the requirement of foreseeability, the scope of the discretion and the manner of its exercise must be set out with sufficient clarity to give the individual adequate protection against arbitrary interference.[39]

In this case, the Swedish legislation provided that the authorities were obliged to intervene in a family situation if:

> [A] person, not yet eighteen years of age, is maltreated in his home or otherwise treated there in a manner endangering his bodily or mental health, or if his development is jeopardised by the unfitness of his parents or other guardians responsible for his upbringing, or by their inability to raise the child.[40]

In addition, compulsory care was to be provided if:

(1) Lack of care for him or any other condition in the home entails a danger to his health or development; or
(2) The young person is seriously endangering his health or development by abuse of habit-forming agents, criminal behaviour or any other comparable behaviour.[41]

The applicants alleged that these broad provisions set no limits on the discretion they conferred, and were drafted in terms so vague as to render the results unforeseeable. They objected to 'utterly unclear' terms such as 'any other condition in the home' and

[39] (10465/83) 24.03.1988 (Court), para. 61.
[40] ibid., para. 35.
[41] ibid., para. 37.

'unfitness as guardian', arguing that they were written in such a way that an individual could not foresee the consequences of any particular behaviour.[42]

The Court acknowledged that the legislation in question was rather general, and gave a wide measure of discretion to the authorities. However, it considered that the circumstances in which it may be necessary to take a child into care are so variable that it would not be possible to formulate a law to cover every eventuality. Moreover, to confine the ability of the authorities to act to cases where harm has *already occurred* would reduce the effectiveness of the child protection agencies, thus endangering children.

The preparatory work for the legislation provided guidance as to the exercise of discretion, and the exercise of all powers was either entrusted to, or subject to review by, the administrative courts. As such, the scope of the discretion conferred by the law was 'reasonable and acceptable' for the purposes of Article 8.[43]

The reasoning in this case thus set a wide discretion for states in designing child protection legislation. Such legislation does not have to specify the exact conduct which may be of threat to the child: it is enough that the provisions set out in very general terms the types of harm that will trigger state intervention.

10.4.2 Legitimate aim

It is clear that child protection measures pursue the legitimate aim of protecting the health of the child, as well as protecting the child's rights, and in the large majority of cases, this aspect of Article 8(2) will not be contentious.

One case where this has been challenged, however, is *Sabou and Pircalab v Romania*,[44] where the applicant was deprived of his parental rights during his imprisonment. In this case, the applicant was convicted of criminal defamation after publishing a newspaper article concerning the acquisition of land by the mother of a judge, which he alleged was unlawful. He was sentenced to ten months' imprisonment, during which time his parental rights were also suspended. The government argued that this was an accessory punishment, pursuing the legitimate aim of preserving the safety, morals, and education of minors. It emphasised that detention inevitably entails restrictions on family life, and that during detention, a convicted person no longer has the moral authority to exercise parental rights.

The Court reiterated that in cases of this type, an examination of what is in the best interests of the child is of crucial importance, and must come before all other considerations. It observed that the offence for which the applicant was convicted was wholly unrelated to the question of parental authority, and there had been no allegation any deficiencies in his parenting. Under Romanian law at the time, the prohibition on the

[42] (10465/83) 02.12.1986 (ComRep), para. 74.

[43] (10465/83) 24.03.1988 (Court), para. 62. See also *Eriksson v Sweden* (11373/85) 23.02.1989. Interestingly, five judges in *Olsson* gave a separate opinion, arguing that no child should be removed from their family without prior judicial authorisation, except in emergency situations. However, this opinion has not gained any ground in future judgments.

[44] (46572/99) 28.09.2004.

exercise of parental rights following conviction applied automatically and absolutely, without any control by the courts, and without taking into consideration the type of offence or the interests of the children. It was a moral condemnation with the aim of punishing the convicted person, and not a measure to protect the child, and as a result, the Court was not convinced that it pursued a legitimate aim.

This case is exceptional, however, and rests on the lack of connection between the measure and the aim it claimed to pursue. In contrast, in *MD and others v Malta*,[45] where the removal of parental rights was limited to certain offences—namely those where the offender had authority over the child who was the victim of the act—the Court was satisfied that this was sufficiently targeted towards the interests of the children, rather than the punishment of the parents.[46]

10.4.3 Necessary in a democratic society

While the first two criteria under Article 8 have attracted very little debate, it is the third criteria—'necessary in democratic society'—where the majority of cases have been argued. From its earliest jurisprudence, the Court has stated that only the most pressing grounds will justify the disruption of family ties.[47] However, despite these strong words, child protection is an area where a wide margin of appreciation is given to states, at least initially. In this respect, the Court has made clear that it is not its task to substitute itself for the domestic authorities, who have the benefit of direct contact with all persons involved precisely at the time when care measures are being envisaged.

Moreover, this is an area where decisions are largely based on institutional judgement on the suitability of a parent—for example, whether they can look after their child adequately, whether they are sufficiently willing to cooperate with the authorities, or whether the child's welfare requires removal. Although these opinions must be based on objectively established facts, the Commission has noted that, 'it is in the nature of the question at issue that it cannot be established exclusively as a fact that [a parent] is so unable to take care of [their child] as to justify a decision of the taking into public care'.[48] This evaluation requires a judgement call on what is 'adequate' from a parent, what is 'sufficient' cooperation, and what the child 'requires'. In undertaking this evaluation, the Court acknowledges that perceptions as to the appropriateness of intervention by public authorities in the care of children vary from one state to another. Factors such as traditions relating to the role of the family and to state intervention in family affairs, and the availability of resources for public measures in this particular area will affect the decision-making of the domestic authorities, and must be taken into account by the Court.[49]

[45] (64791/10) 17.07.2012.

[46] However, the measure was ultimately found disproportionate, as it applied automatically to everyone convicted of these offences, with no consideration of the interests of justice, nor the best interests of the child.

[47] See, for example, *X and Y v Germany* (8059/77) 03.10.1978 (dec.).

[48] *L v Sweden* (10141/82) 03.01.1984 (dec.).

[49] *L v Finland* (25651/94) 27.04.2000.

As a result of this wide discretion given to member states, the Court has not proven itself a particularly strong tool in challenging the basis of alternative care. Instead, its impact has predominantly been in the enforcement of procedural obligations, examined further in section 10.6 below. Nevertheless, it has set some (very wide) substantive boundaries: namely, that the care order be based on 'relevant' reasons; and that these reasons provide 'sufficient' justification for the measure imposed.[50]

10.4.3.1 Relevant reasons

The first step—relevant reasons—is not a difficult hurdle to pass. The court has accepted as legitimate a wide range of reasons for intervention in family life. These include not only the intentional infliction of abuse—physical,[51] psychological and emotional,[52] and sexual[53]—but also where parents have failed to provide appropriate care, including: cases of neglect;[54] drug addiction;[55] failure to provide medical treatment;[56] educational difficulties;[57] failure to satisfy the need for stimulation;[58] failure to supervise effectively;[59] use of corporal punishment;[60] and failure to protect from other's abuse.[61] These factors can relate to something that the child has already suffered or a risk that they may suffer in the future.[62]

For the removal of a child to be justified, it is not necessary that there is a judicial finding of guilt in respect of parental abuse or neglect. However, the Court has cautioned that in the absence of a conclusive finding in this respect, there is an increased onus on the authorities and courts reviewing the care measure to produce sufficient justification for maintaining it.[63] Having said this, it is important to note that mistaken judgments concerning the need to remove children from the home do not render such a measure incompatible with Article 8 per se. This is a difficult area of law and practice, where mistakes are sometimes made without there having been a breach of an individual's rights. The Court will therefore look at the evidence that was available to the authorities at the time, and whether there was a genuine and reasonably held concern about the safety of a child vis-à-vis members of their family.[64] The removal of a child will only be an infringement of Article 8 where the decision was disproportionate or arbitrary, not simply where it was later proven to be unnecessary.

[50] See *KA v Finland* (27751/95) 14.01.2003.
[51] *AD and OD v the United Kingdom* (28680/06) 16.03.2010.
[52] *P, C and S v the United Kingdom* (56547/00) 16.07.2002.
[53] *KA v Finland* (27751/95) 14.01.2003; *AL v Finland* (23220/04) 27.01.2009.
[54] *MD and others v Malta* (64791/10) 17.07.2012; *YC v the United Kingdom* (4547/10) 13.03.2012; *Pontes v Portugal* (19554/09) 10.04.2012.
[55] *YI v Russia* (68868/14) 25.02.2020.
[56] *Kuimov v Russia* (32147/04) 08.01.2009; *Wedberg and Hillblom v Sweden* (21607/93) 11.04.1996 (dec.).
[57] *Kutzner v Germany* (46544/99) 26.02.2002; *Olsson v Sweden (No. 1)* (10465/83) 24.03.1988 (Court).
[58] *Olsson v Sweden (No. 1)* (10465/83) 24.03.1988 (Court).
[59] *NP v the Republic of Moldova* (58455/13) 06.10.2015; *Buchberger v Austria* (32899/96) 20.12.2001.
[60] *Tlapak and others v Germany* (11308/16, 11344/16) 22.03.2018.
[61] *TP and KM v the United Kingdom* (28945/95) 10.05.2001 (GC); *Covezzi and Morselli v Italy* (52763/99) 09.05.2003; *Jovanovic v Sweden* (10592/12) 22.10.2015.
[62] *P, C and S v the United Kingdom* (56547/00) 16.07.2002.
[63] *KA v Finland* (27751/95) 14.01.2003.
[64] *RK and AK v the United Kingdom* (38000/05) 30.09.2008; *AD and OD v the United Kingdom* (28680/06) 16.03.2010.

There have been very few occasions on which the Court has held that a reason given for the removal of a child from the family is not relevant. One such occasion arose in the case of *Soares de Melo v Portugal*,[65] where the Court was scathing of the attempt of the authorities to require the mother to undergo a sterilisation procedure in order to retain her parental rights. Her ten children had been placed under observation, on the grounds of inadequate physical conditions and neglect, and the mother required to sign a 'protection agreement', which stated that she would retain custody on the condition that she prove, inter alia, that she was preparing to undergo sterilisation. Her failure to go through with this operation was subsequently held against her in the proceedings removing her children. While this was only one issue in a multitude of violations on the part of the Portuguese authorities in this case, the Court made clear that such a requirement should never be made a condition for retaining parental rights.

Likewise, in *Kocherov and Sergeyeva v Russia*,[66] the domestic authorities had refused to allow a father with intellectual disabilities to care for his child, on the grounds that, inter alia, he had only been living outside of a specialist facility for a month, and had no skills or experience in bringing up children or taking care of them. The Court emphasised that the absence of skills and experience in child rearing—no matter the reason for this—could not be regarded as a legitimate ground for restricting parental authority. Nor could prolonged residence in a specialist institution, in and of itself, be a sufficient reason to justify such a restriction. As Judge Keller pointed out in his partially dissenting opinion,[67] this was a case where the government applied a stereotyped view of the applicant as a disabled parent, based on generalised ideas about people with mental disabilities, rather than any analysis of his actual capacity to care for his child or the concrete facts of the case.

However, these cases are few and far between, and for the large part, the Court has been satisfied that the reasons given by the domestic authorities are at least relevant to the question of separation. The more challenging question lies in determining whether they are sufficient.

10.4.3.2 Sufficient justification

In contrast to its rather light-touch approach to the examination of the reasons behind state intervention, the Court has started to exercise greater control in relation to the sufficiency of the reasons given for the particular measure imposed by the domestic authorities. It is not enough that a child would be better cared for if placed in alternative care—the reasons given must be sufficiently strong to break the prima facie right of parents to raise their own children.[68]

This was tested in *Olsson (No. 1)*, where the applicant parents objected to Swedish legislation that permitted the child's removal on the basis of 'danger' to their health and development. They argued that this was a very low standard, as the preparatory text made clear that it was not necessary to establish 'serious' danger, but instead that

[65] (72850/14) 16.02.2016.
[66] (16899/13) 29.03.2016.
[67] He agreed with the majority that there had been a violation of the applicant's rights under Article 8, but considered that the case should also have been examined under Article 14 in conjunction with Article 8.
[68] See, for example, *Olsson v Sweden (No. 1)* (10465/83) 24.03.1988 (Court).

minor danger would suffice. This, they submitted, did not fit with the requirement of 'necessity' under Article 8(2). The Commission noted that the requirement of 'necessity' is not as strong as 'indispensable', but stronger than 'useful', 'reasonable', or 'desirable'.[69] The 'sufficiency' of the measure thus rests on its proportionality—does the severity of the measure correspond to the reason given for the interference with the family? Or could lesser measures suffice?

As discussed above, the Court has traditionally granted a wide margin of appreciation to states in this area, recognising the different approaches to child protection in member states and the advantage of domestic authorities in being in direct contact with the parties involved. However, the Court has started to develop a strong line of jurisprudence in relation to positive obligations on the part of the authorities to show that they have taken adequate steps to allow the family to stay together, and have considered possible alternatives to removal, before a child is taken into care.

10.4.3.2.1 Positive obligations

10.4.3.2.1.1 Material deprivation The development of the Court's jurisprudence on positive obligations has largely been focused on families suffering from material deprivation, particularly inadequate housing. Very early in its history, the Commission made clear that 'only the most pressing grounds can be sufficient in a democratic society to justify the disruption of existing family ties even where the material conditions of the family are poor'.[70] However, it was not until recently that the Court developed more detailed jurisprudence in this area, and in particular laid down the obligations of states to provide material assistance before contemplating the imposition of child protection measures.

In the first case of this kind, *Wallová and Walla v the Czech Republic*,[71] the authorities removed the applicant's children on the grounds that the parents were unable to ensure adequate and appropriate housing, which was compromising the children's health and hygiene. It was acknowledged that the applicants were attempting to rectify this issue, but this was made difficult by their lack of resources. The parents alleged a violation of their right to respect for family life: rather than taking their children into public care, they argued that the family should have been provided with assistance to redress the situation and to find accommodation for them corresponding to their financial resources.

The Court very clearly distinguished this case from other child protection cases that had come before it. It emphasised that there was no issue of ill-treatment on the part of the parents, nor any emotional deficits or psychological imbalance. The educational and emotional capacities of the parents had never been in question, and the authorities had recognised their efforts to overcome their difficulties. The sole reason for taking the children into care was thus the parents' lack of financial resources. This, the Court held, *could* and *should* have been compensated for by the national authorities by means other than the total separation of the family, which should be reserved only for the most serious cases of parental failure. In order to comply with the requirement of

[69] *Olsson v Sweden (No. 1)* (10465/83) 02.12.1986 (ComRep), para. 145.
[70] *X and Y v Germany* (8059/77) 03.10.1978 (dec.).
[71] (23848/04) 26.10.2006.

proportionality under Article 8, the authorities had an obligation to consider less radical measures than the removal of the children.[72]

The Court emphasised that there was a positive obligation on the domestic authorities to find solutions for the family's problems. It noted that domestic law required local authorities to help those in need of social assistance, and that public institutions only intervene in cases where families are temporarily confronted with a difficult situation through no fault of their own. As such, although the interference with the family life of the parents was based on relevant considerations, they were not sufficient to justify the serious action taken.

This decision was followed two years later by *Saviny v Ukraine*.[73] In this case, the family were living in conditions described as 'grossly unsatisfactory'—the house had no drains or hot running water, was dirty, and smelled of excrement. The parents had been given some assistance—including clothing, food, and renovations—but requests to install natural gas to provide heating, the ability to cook, and access to hot water were denied. The children were subsequently taken into care and placed in 'special educational establishments', on the grounds of the 'horrible' living conditions and the parents' 'very poor financial state'.

As in *Wallová*, the Court criticised the domestic authorities for failing to analyse the extent to which the inadequacies in the children's upbringing were attributable to the parents 'irremediable incapacity to provide requisite care, as opposed to their financial difficulties and objective frustrations',[74] which could have been overcome by the provision of financial and social assistance.[75] Importantly, the Court characterised this as a *procedural* obligation. It stated:

> [I]t is not the Court's role to determine whether the promotion of family unity in the case entitled the applicants' family to a particular standard of living at public expense. It is, however, a matter which falls to be discussed by, initially, the relevant public authorities and, subsequently, in the course of the judicial proceedings.[76]

As such, the Court imposed an obligation on authorities to show that they have considered other, less intrusive, measures before a child is removed from the family on the grounds of financial difficulties.

While these cases focused on the proportionality of response, in a recent case the Court has gone one step further. In *Barnea and Caldararu v Italy*,[77] the Court held that material deprivation can *never* be the sole ground for removal of a child. In and of itself, it cannot be sufficient to constitute the 'exceptional circumstances' required

[72] See also *RMS v Spain* (28775/12) 18.06.2013; *Akinnibosun v Italy* (9056/14) 16.07.2015.
[73] (39948/06) 18.12.2008.
[74] ibid., para. 57.
[75] cf. *Achim v Romania* (45959/11) 24.10.2017, where the Court noted with approval that from the beginning the social services had treated the family's material deprivation as distinct from parenting issues.
[76] *Saviny v Ukraine* (39948/06) 18.12.2008, para. 57. See also *NP v the Republic of Moldova* (58455/13) 06.10.2015.
[77] (37931/15) 22.06.2017.

by the Convention to separate a family—there must be other factors such as the psychological conditions of the parents, or their emotional, educational, and pedagogical incapacity.

In this case, the family had left the child in the care of a third party, as they were themselves living in extreme poverty and unable to provide appropriate material conditions. The Court emphasised that before taking the child into care, the authorities had a positive obligation to take concrete steps to enable her to live with her birth family. As the Court stated, the role of the social protection authorities is precisely to help people in such situations, and they should be guiding families in their efforts to overcome poverty, including advising them on the social benefits available, and helping them obtain suitable social housing. This obligation increases when dealing with vulnerable persons—which the applicants clearly were—who must be provided with even greater protection.

10.4.3.2.1.2 Mental health and intellectual disabilities The second area where the Court has recognised positive obligations to provide assistance to families is where the parents are suffering from mental health problems or intellectual disabilities. Where difficulties have arisen in relation to the children's care and upbringing in such families, the Court has emphasised that the authorities should take positive steps to assist parents in fulfilling their parental role, before removing the child from the family.

This was seen in *Kutzner v Germany*,[78] where parents with learning difficulties had their parental rights withdrawn. Their children had late physical and mental development and the guardianship court found that the parents lacked the necessary awareness to answer the children's needs. It held that they were not fit to bring up their children, not through any fault of their own, but because they lacked the requisite intellectual capacity.

The question before the Court was whether the domestic authorities could have provided additional support within the home, rather than removing the children to foster care. The Court reiterated that the fact that a child could be placed in a more beneficial environment would not on its own justify removal; other circumstances must exist that point to the 'necessity' of such an interference under Article 8. It recognised that there were legitimate and relevant reasons for the authorities to be concerned about the late development of the children; however, these reasons were not sufficient to justify the level of intrusion into family life. Rather than the extreme measure of separation, the Court found that the domestic authorities should have given greater consideration to additional measures of support, such as educational assistance. There were no allegations of neglect nor ill-treatment, and greater efforts should have been made to work *with* the parents.

This does not mean that children *cannot* be removed from families where the parents are suffering from intellectual disabilities or mental health difficulties—merely that the authorities have an obligation to consider whether there are less intrusive measures that could be taken to keep the family together. This was addressed in *SS v Slovenia*,[79]

78 (46544/99) 26.02.2002.
79 (40938/16) 30.10.2018.

where the applicant mother—who suffered from paranoid schizophrenia—challenged the removal of her parental rights on the grounds, inter alia, that her neglect of her parental responsibilities had been involuntary, caused by her mental illness.

The Court identified two requirements that must be met in such cases. First, and as seen in section 10.4.3.1 above in *Kocherov and Sergeyeva*, the focus of the authorities must be on the evidence of the parent's child-rearing capacities, and its impact on the child, rather than on the parent's diagnosis. While the two may be connected, this provides not only an important bulwark against discrimination, but also provides procedural protection for the parent—it identifies clearly what aspects of their parenting need improving and what evidence they would need to provide to show that the child was not, or no longer, at risk.

Second, the authorities must consider the extent to which the parents' difficulties can be overcome by targeted social assistance, which would remove the necessity of separating the child from the family.[80]

In this case, both criteria were satisfied. The decision to remove the applicant's parental responsibilities was not based on her diagnosis, but on her inability to care for the child, as confirmed by the expert reports produced for the domestic courts. Furthermore, she had been offered extensive assistance by the social welfare authorities, which had failed to address the situation—not through the fault of the authorities, but as a result of the lack of cooperation by the applicant. In light of this, the Court found that although her behaviour was caused by mental illness, and was involuntary, the child's interests in being provided with permanent care and emotional stability outweighed the applicant's interest in retaining legal ties.

This case was a good example of the positive action taken by authorities to attempt to establish a relationship between the mother and child. Following the child's birth, they had provided the mother with assistance in finding accommodation, as well as various social services, and the assistance of a worker from a psychiatric hospital. While the child was in care, they had approached the mother of their own motion to arrange contact sessions, and offered assistance and counselling, and she had never been refused contact with her child. Despite these efforts, however, there was no emotional connection established between the mother and child, and her understanding of the child's needs was limited, leading the authorities to conclude that it was in the child's best interests to withdraw parental rights.[81] In light of this, the Court found that there had been no violation of Article 8.

10.4.3.2.2 Assessing the proportionality of the choice of intervention

There will, of course, be circumstances where social assistance and support simply is not sufficient, and compulsory measures must be implemented. However, this does not automatically mean that the child must be separated from their family. Before a decision is made to remove a child, less intrusive measures should be considered, including monitoring and assessment.

[80] See *SH v Italy* (52557/14) 13.10.2015, and section 10.4.3.2.1.1 above.

[81] See also *Zambotto Perrin v France* (4962/11) 26.09.2013.

A paradigm example of this principle can be seen in *AD and OD v the United Kingdom*,[82] which concerned a child who doctors believed had suffered physical abuse. The family were required to relocate to a 'Family Assessment Centre', where a risk assessment could be undertaken. In error, the wrong assessment was carried out, and in the absence of the risk assessment, the child was taken into foster care until it could be undertaken. It subsequently emerged that the child suffered from 'brittle bone disease', which was the cause of his broken bones, rather than abuse. Before the Court, the parents argued that there had been insufficient consideration of less intrusive measures, which would have provided adequate protection for the child while minimising interference with their family life.

The Court agreed, stating that it was 'not convinced' that less intrusive measures were unavailable, citing as possible alternatives the extension of the family's stay in the assessment centre or the placement of the child with relatives. It noted that the authorities were required by domestic law to give proper consideration to placing the child within the family, and could only exclude this option if it was not reasonably practicable, or if it would not be in the child's interest. While some concerns about a placement within the family were understandable, the Court found that this option was dismissed too quickly, without proper consideration.

Likewise, in *Moser v Austria*,[83] the authorities ordered that a child should be placed in foster care as the mother lacked appropriate accommodation and financial means, and had an unclear immigration status. The Court stated that a case such as this called for 'a particularly careful examination of possible alternatives'[84] before a child is taken into public care. While the authorities did assess *some* alternatives—including allowing the mother to move into a friend's home with the child—there was a failure to make a *full* assessment of possible alternatives. In particular, there was no positive action to explore possibilities that would have allowed them to stay together—for example, a mother-child foster placement.

However, where the parents are uncooperative with authorities, the Court has acknowledged that this can impact on the level of intervention needed. In *Achim v Romania*,[85] the Court observed that the applicants displayed hostility towards social workers, which had undermined the cooperation between them and the authorities. While less extreme measures than separation are preferable, in light of the lack of cooperation from parents, the Court recognised that it was difficult for the authorities to monitor the children's situation and provide the family with the necessary support.[86]

Even in cases where the Court is satisfied that removal of the child from his or her family is justified, it will go on to carefully scrutinise the form of alternative care chosen. This was seen in *Saviny*, discussed above, where the Court accepted that even if the children would benefit from being placed in an educational institution, this did not require the removal of parental rights, preventing them from taking their children home outside school hours. Likewise, in *Havelka and others v the Czech Republic*,[87]

[82] (28680/06) 16.03.2010.
[83] (12643/02) 21.09.2006.
[84] ibid., para. 69.
[85] (45959/11) 24.10.2017.
[86] cf. *Johansen v Norway* (17383/90) 07.08.1996.
[87] (23499/06) 21.06.2007.

the children were taken into an educational assistance establishment as the father was unable to meet the children's basic needs. The Court found that the Czech authorities had failed to consider appropriate alternatives to complete separation between the father and children: they had not considered the possibility of placing the children in a facility where the father could visit daily, nor did they consider placing the children with the wider family.

While this places an important duty on domestic authorities, as with the obligations placed in relation to social assistance, this duty is procedural, rather than substantive. The Court will not itself determine whether a less intrusive measure should have been chosen, merely whether the domestic authorities had adequately considered the alternatives available. This was made clear in *ML v Norway*,[88] concerning the placement of the child with wider family. In this case, the mother's elder child had been placed with the grandmother and step-grandfather. When a subsequent child was also removed from the mother, she asked that he be placed with his older brother in the care of the grandparents. This was refused. The mother argued before the Court that there had been a violation of Article 8 in the choice of foster home, as there had been a failure to carry out an appropriate examination of less intrusive alternatives. She argued that there was a duty arising from Article 8 that the child be placed with biological family wherever possible, and moreover, that siblings should also be kept together.

The Court reiterated its role as a supervisory body, rather than a court of fourth instance. It noted that its job was to examine whether the authorities had conducted an in-depth examination of the entire family situation and provided relevant and sufficient reasons not to place the child with family. In this light, it found no violation of Article 8, as the domestic courts had weighed the competing factors and decided that the benefits of the child staying with its biological family were outweighed by other concerns.

In this respect, it is interesting to note that there was no discussion by the Court of the importance of biological family, either in considering the prospective carers for the child, nor in the context of the siblings developing a relationship. The analysis of the Court was clearly focused on whether the authorities had taken into account the requisite factors, rather than the ultimate decision they reached.

10.4.4 Conclusions on placement in alternative care

Despite the extensive case law surrounding child protection, very few cases have actually dealt with the substantive basis of removal, which is seen to be something firmly within the state's margin of appreciation. Only the most egregious decisions have been found to breach Article 8—for example, where the decision has not been based on a parent's caring capabilities, but on other considerations (for example, imprisonment, sterilisation, or mental disability). The protection provided by the Convention in this area is thus largely procedural: is the measure taken by the authorities appropriately

[88] (43701/14) 07.09.2017.

suited to the harm concerned? Have less intrusive measures been considered? Would social assistance be adequate?

While these procedural obligations are important, the failure of the Court to discuss the appropriate threshold for state interference is problematic. No guidance has been given as to when the state can step in to remove a child—on one end of the spectrum, we know that it cannot be simply because they could be better cared for elsewhere, and on the other end, it must be before the child's rights under Article 3 are breached. But in between these two extremes is a very wide discretion for states to decide when and why it is 'necessary' to intervene.

As the Court consistently observes, states have differing opinions about the level of interference appropriate in the field of child protection, and for the Court, this means that there should be greater leeway given. But this failure to specify a clear standard undermines the efficacy of the Court in this area.

10.5 Abuse in the care system

In Chapter 2, the positive obligation on the state to protect children from abuse, neglect, and sexual violence from private individuals was examined. This was further expanded on in Chapter 6, concerning the abuse of children in schools. However, this issue also arises in the context of child protection, where children suffer ill-treatment in public care. In this respect, the Court has emphasised that where children are under the exclusive control of the domestic authorities, a special and enhanced level of protection is required.[89]

The seminal case in this area is *Nencheva and others v Bulgaria*,[90] which involved shocking levels of institutional neglect. This case concerned children who suffered from serious mental and physical disorders, and had either been abandoned by their parents or placed in the relevant institution with their parents' consent. This created a dual vulnerability, compounding the degree of control the authorities had over them. They were 'subjected to the worst living conditions' imaginable: they lacked food, medicines, adequate clothing, and the institution had insufficient heating. Concrete evidence concerning the risk to the health and lives of these vulnerable children was brought to the attention of state officials at the highest levels, some months before the first deaths. In the end, 15 children died in the institution over the space of three months. The Court noted that the deaths were not the result of sudden or unforeseen events, as in the case of an event of *force majeure* to which the state might not be able to react. Instead, the authorities had exact knowledge concerning the specific risk to children at this institution, and failed to take any action. This went beyond an ordinary case of negligence—despite having precise knowledge of the real and imminent risks, the authorities failed to take prompt, concrete, and sufficient measures to prevent the deaths reported, in violation of Article 2.

[89] *Nencheva and others v Bulgaria* (48609/06) 18.06.2013; *Centre for Legal Resources on behalf of Valentin Campeanu v Romania* (47848/08) 17.07.2014 (GC).

[90] (48609/06) 18.06.2013.

Moreover, the criminal investigation focused solely on three individual staff members from the institution, and failed to consider responsibility for the deaths at a higher level—for example, the representatives of municipal authorities, or the social assistance workers. As a result, the authorities did not fulfil their positive obligation under Article 2 to protect the lives of vulnerable children placed in their care, nor were there adequate procedural mechanisms to investigate their deaths.

A similar finding was made in *LR v North Macedonia*,[91] regarding a child with mental disabilities. He had been abandoned by his parents at birth, and a social welfare centre was appointed his guardian. At the age of eight, they arranged for him to be placed in a state-run institution for people with physical disabilities, despite this institution repeatedly informing the authorities that they could not accommodate persons with mental disabilities and had no qualified staff to work with him. Over 18 months after his placement, the Ombudsman visited the institution and found the child tied to his bed. The institution stated that this was for safety reasons—namely, to prevent him from running away or putting himself in danger—as they did not have sufficient staff to monitor him at all times.

The Court found a violation of Article 3, both in respect to the child's placement in the institution and his treatment there. The authorities were aware that the institution could not cater for his needs, yet he was nevertheless left in their care for a considerable period. The child was thus not provided with adequate care, leading to a deterioration of his condition. This inadequate treatment was exacerbated by the inhuman and degrading treatment he suffered while he was there.

Here, as in *Nencheva*, the Court noted the vulnerability of the applicant—a disabled eight-year-old child, who was deaf and could not speak, and therefore could not complain about his treatment. The Court emphasised the particular vulnerability of minors in the context of Article 3, given that any inhuman and degrading treatment suffered was liable to have a greater impact on a child than it would on an adult. Also as in *Nencheva*, the Court went on to find a procedural violation of Article 3, on the grounds that although a thorough investigation was carried out by the domestic authorities, it was solely focused on the responsibilities private individuals (i.e. the employees of the institution), rather than a wider examination of the responsibilities of state representatives. The Court differentiated between individual criminal liability and state responsibility for human rights violations, finding that the latter was not confronted by the investigation.

These cases can be contrasted with *X and others v Bulgaria*,[92] concerning allegations of physical and sexual abuse in a Bulgarian orphanage. The applicants in this case, who were three siblings, alleged that the authorities had failed to protect them from physical and sexual abuse inflicted by one of the other children in the institution, and that they had failed to conduct an effective investigation into their complaints. The Court found that the alleged conduct—that the older child 'touched the intimate parts of some of the children and placed his penis in their mouths'—was sufficient to cross the threshold into Article 3, owing to the children's youth and their vulnerability as

[91] (38067/15) 23.01.2020.
[92] (22457/16) 17.01.2019.

children left without parental care in an institution. However, it held that the authorities had fulfilled their obligations to the children under Article 3—general preventative measures were in place to protect children in institutions from abuse, and when informed of the allegations, they responded promptly and with diligence.

In relation to the general duty to take adequate preventative measures, the Court noted that strict rules applied concerning outside visitors, and restrictions were placed on contact between male members of staff and the children in their care. The children were seen regularly by an independent doctor, as well as a psychologist within the institution, and had access to a telephone and phone number for a helpline if they felt in danger.

When they became aware of the specific allegations, the authorities acted swiftly on several fronts—both ordering an inspection of the institution by the social welfare authorities and informing the prosecutor's office concerning possible criminal offences. Authorities visited the institution several times, checking files, and questioning the staff and other persons mentioned in the children's statements. The children in the institution were also questioned using an anonymous questionnaire, as well as being interviewed by police, with the help of a psychologist. As a result, the Court found that the authorities had fulfilled their positive obligations under Article 3—the fact that there was no prosecution did not prevent the investigation from being effective.

10.6 Procedural rights

The most important contribution of the Court to the field of child protection is not the substantive obligations imposed, which are limited by the wide margin of appreciation given to states, but the procedural obligations that accompany them. These are derived from two articles: the right to a fair trial under Article 6 and the right to respect for family life under Article 8.

While often applicants will make a claim under both articles, the nature of the interests protected under Article 6 and Article 8 differ. The purpose of Article 6 is to ensure the proper administration of justice, and therefore relates purely to the judicial proceedings and procedures surrounding it. Moreover, Article 6 does not itself guarantee any particular content for civil rights and obligations in the substantive law of member states—the right must already be recognised under domestic law for Article 6 to be applicable, thus limiting the extent of its protection.

On the other hand, the obligations arising out of Article 8 are ancillary to the wider purpose of ensuring proper respect for private and family life, meaning that the procedural requirements extend far beyond the judicial proceedings (although these are included) and encompass the involvement of parents in the decision-making process as a whole.

The difference between these two provisions can be seen in *McMichael v the United Kingdom*.[93] In this case, an unmarried father wished to access documents in relation to the care proceedings concerning his child. However, under domestic law at the time,

[93] (16424/90) 24.02.1995.

an unmarried father did not automatically acquire parental rights, instead having to apply to obtain them, and as such, he was not joined as a party. He complained under both Article 6 and Article 8 of his insufficient involvement in the proceedings.

His application under Article 6 was dismissed. The Court found that as an unmarried father, to the extent that he could claim 'civil rights' under domestic law, the care proceedings did not involve a determination of any of those rights, since he had not taken the requisite prior step of seeking to obtain legal recognition of his status as father.[94] The right to a fair trial under domestic law only protected legal parents, who held civil rights in relation to their children, and not natural parents without legal status.

However, his claim under Article 8 achieved greater success. As the purpose of Article 8 is the protection of family life, instead of asking whether the father held a recognised civil right, the Court had to determine whether he had the requisite 'family life' with the child. This was established on the basis of his committed relationship with the mother. As a result, the Court found that 'it would not reflect the reality of the situation' to draw a distinction between the procedural rights of the mother and the father under Article 8, as they both held 'family life' with the child, despite the father not having legal recognition. Article 8, unlike Article 6, does not concern itself with legal rights, but instead looks to the de facto substance of the relationship between the parties and what is needed to protect this.[95]

10.6.1 Article 6

In the context of child protection proceedings, Article 6 has been invoked in three main areas: first, access to an impartial tribunal; second, a public hearing and judgment; and finally, the provision of legal assistance to ensure effective access to justice.

10.6.1.1 Access to an independent tribunal

Article 6(1) requires that applicants have access to 'an independent and impartial tribunal established by law'. This does not mean, however, that every dispute must be decided by a court, and authorities are permitted to delegate certain decision-making procedures to administrative authorities. This was seen in *M, RT and F v Austria*,[96] where the children were removed from their parents by an administrative authority and placed in a children's home. They stayed there for four months before their case came before the Youth Court. The parents challenged this under Article 6, arguing

[94] See also *Price v the United Kingdom* (12402/86) 14.07.1988 (dec.), where it was held that the grandparents in question did not have a civil right to contact with their grandchild.

[95] It should be noted, however, that this distinction was criticised by the joint partly dissenting opinion of Judges Ryssdal, Palm, and Sir John Freeland. They argued that the legal circumstances of the father should have been considered for the purposes of Article 8, and it was precisely because he held a different legal status to the mother that the 'incidence of the procedural deficiency is not the same for each of them'. While they agreed that not granting access to documents in the proceedings was a violation of the mother's family life, they considered that it could not be a violation of the father's family life, as he had not asked to be a party to the proceedings.

[96] (14013/88) 14.12.1989 (dec.).

that in view of the immediate effect of the measure, it should have been decided by a court, and not an administrative authority. The Court acknowledged that Article 6 embodies, colloquially, the 'right to a court', but held that this does not obligate domestic authorities to submit disputes to a 'tribunal' meeting the requirements of Article 6 at every stage of the procedure. Indeed, the demands of flexibility and efficiency may justify prior intervention of administrative bodies, which is equally compatible with the Convention. Moreover, the Court referred to Article 5 of the Convention, concerning the deprivation of liberty, and noted that even 'such drastic measures' as this may be effected by administrative authorities without prior authorisation by a court.

However, domestic authorities cannot delegate decision-making authority entirely to the social welfare authorities, and the Court has found that there must always be judicial oversight of decisions. For example, in *MD and others v Malta*,[97] the mother's children were taken into state care as they were being physically abused by her partner. Both the mother and her partner were found guilty of cruelty towards the children—he for physical abuse, and she for failing to report the abuse, and protect the children from it. A care order had been issued by the social policy minister, on the recommendation of the director of social welfare. Subsequently the mother's circumstances changed, and she sought to have the care order revoked. However, under domestic law this could not be considered by a court, as such a revision depended solely on the discretion of the minister who had issued the order. The order was a 'permanent' one, valid until the children reached 18 years of age. Domestic law permitted an objection to this order to be lodged within 21 days of issue, and for this to be determined by the Juvenile Court, but it was not possible to request a revision of the order subsequently, except through the minister.

The government argued that a court was not the appropriate place for continuing evaluation of the care order. They argued that such orders were issued in emergency situations, which often change rapidly. It was thus difficult for a court to evaluate these changing circumstances, and in cases where an order remained in force for several years, a judicial mechanism would not be able to monitor all the developments that occurred. Moreover, the government submitted that the right of access to a court did not imply a right of continuous and repeated petitioning of the courts. It sufficed that the situation was monitored by the welfare service, which was more competent to assess the situation, and reported directly to the minister.

This was rejected unanimously by the Court, which found that the argument that a judicial body would not be the right venue, for such an assessment 'runs counter to the entire basis of Article 6'.[98] The Court emphasised that '[i]t is precisely a tribunal's role to supervise administrative action in any field, and guarantee freedom from arbitrariness'.[99] A review by social workers who reported to the minister was not sufficient to constitute an 'impartial and independent tribunal'. Moreover, there was no legal

[97] (64791/10) 17.07.2012.
[98] ibid., para. 55.
[99] ibid.

framework setting out the process by which the mother could make an application to the minister for review, nor had it been shown that any decision made would be written and made public, in order to provide a possibility for judicial review. As such, the Court found a violation of Article 6(1).[100]

Finally, in *Scozzari and Giunta v Italy*,[101] the Court issued a scathing judgment, censuring the conduct of the Italian authorities in relation to a mother and her two sons. While contact was ordered by the courts, the social services were given complete freedom to decide whether and when meetings should take place, allowing them to alter the practical effect of the judicial decision.

The Court found that the domestic courts had a duty to exercise 'constant vigilance' in this regard, to ensure that the conduct of the social services did not undermine their decisions. The fact that there had been only two visits organised by the social services since the order was made should have prompted the courts to investigate the reasons for the delay, but they merely accepted the conclusions of the social services, without a critical analysis of the facts.

The approach of the authorities was further critiqued by Judge Zupančič in his powerful concurring opinion, who stated that unless the domestic courts were able to assume long-term commitments to monitoring the situation of the children and family, they should not interfere. His opinion on this is worth quoting at length:

> The strictly judicial power of conflict resolution—i.e. the power to resolve further disputes arising out of the initial alternative care arrangements—must not be left to psychiatrists, psychologists, social workers, managers of alternative care institutions, etc. The alternative custody and care arrangements, while in place, will often generate a series of new conflicts between parents and the welfare authorities. In many other cases decided by this Court it was apparent that welfare authorities have a tendency to arrogate to themselves an arbitrary decision-making power far exceeding their judicially granted authority. Undoubtedly, this problem derives from the non-retrospectivity and other idiosyncrasies of child custody and care cases outlined above. However, the fundamental principle of the rule of law requires that the parents' and children's access to court be strictly and continuously maintained.
>
> Too much is at stake here for these grievances to be arbitrarily decided by those authorised only to provide the alternative care. The presumption of their bona fides must remain a rebuttable one, i.e. subject to subsequent legal challenge and uninterrupted access to court. Since this would amount to the so-called khadi-justice, foster parents, social workers, psychologists, psychiatrists, alternative care institutions, etc., cannot be arbiters in situations in which their own decisions are the target of parents' criticism and grievance. Procedurally, such disputes are prima

[100] See also *R v Finland* (34141/96) 30.05.2006; *T v the Czech Republic* (19315/11) 17.07.2014.
[101] (39221/98, 41963/98) 13.07.2000 (GC).

facie admissible, if the issues they raise transcend the strictures of judicial decisions establishing the alternative care arrangements.

This issue goes to the core of the rule of law. The doors of the family court should remain wide open.

10.6.1.2 Public hearing and judgment

The right to an oral hearing is not expressly articulated in the Convention, but the Court has held that it 'constitutes a fundamental principle enshrined in Article 6(1)'.[102] As a general rule, the right to a fair trial means that a party must be entitled to present their arguments orally before a court,[103] although this right is not absolute, and can be dispensed with in exceptional circumstances.

There are no hard-and-fast rules concerning the circumstances in which an oral hearing must be held; rather, it will 'depend on the special features of the proceedings involved'[104] and whether it is necessary to ensure a fair trial for the applicants. In particular, there is no obligation to hold an oral hearing at every level of jurisdiction, and the Court will take into account the entirety of proceedings before the domestic courts, as well as the role of the appellate court within that system.[105]

Having said this, there must at least be an oral hearing at *some* stage. This was seen in *L v Finland*,[106] where the government had argued that the domestic courts should have discretion as to whether an oral hearing was held, and be able to dispense with it where it was manifestly unnecessary given the nature of the case or for some other reason. In this case, the authorities had dealt with cases concerning the same children six times already, and considered that an oral hearing would not bring to light any new evidence. The Court did not accept this argument, finding that in light of the nature of the issues, and what was at stake for the parents, it was not satisfied that there were exceptional circumstances which would have justified dispensing with a hearing. Likewise in *Moser v Austria*,[107] the Court held that the mere production of a witness statement to the court will not be sufficient—there must be an adversarial hearing. It emphasised that there were no exceptional circumstances present, nor did the proceedings concern highly technical issues or purely legal questions that justify a lack of oral hearing.

In *Moser*, in addition to complaining about the lack of oral hearing, the mother also complained that the hearing had been held in private, and the courts had not examined whether there were specific circumstances that justified excluding the public from proceedings. The Court noted that the right to a public hearing under Article 6(1) is not absolute, and expressly permits that

[102] *Jussila v Finland* (73053/01) 23.11.2006 (GC), para. 40.

[103] See *Fredin v Sweden (No. 2)* (18928/91) 23.02.1994.

[104] *Ekbatani v Sweden* (10563/83) 26.05.1988, para. 27.

[105] See, for example, *Hoppe v Germany* (28422/95) 05.12.2002, where the Court held it was sufficient that there had been an oral hearing in the first instance, and a further hearing at the appeal stage would not have added anything of relevance. See also *Sporer v Austria* (35637/03) 03.02.2011.

[106] (25651/94) 27.04.2000.

[107] (12643/02) 21.09.2006.

> the press and public may be excluded from all or part of the trial ... where the interests of juveniles or the private life of the parties so require, or to the extent strictly necessary in the opinion of the court in special circumstances where publicity would prejudice the interests of justice.

However, the Court emphasised that there cannot be a blanket ban on holding any particular type of hearing in public. Under Austrian law, there was no possibility for the judge to allow the case to be heard in public, which the Court found was in violation of Article 6(1). In coming to this conclusion, the Court contrasted *Moser* with *B and P v the United Kingdom*,[108] discussed in Chapter 9. In *B and P*, the Court found that it was not inconsistent with Article 6(1) to designate an entire class of cases as an exception to the general rule of public hearings. However, the English law permitted the judges to examine the facts of the case and consider whether special features merited the proceedings being held in public—something that was not possible under the Austrian law. The Court also underlined the nature of the proceedings in each case—while *B and P* concerned a dispute between parents concerning a child's residence, *Moser* concerned the removal of a child from his family and into public care. In such circumstances, the Court considered that the reasons for excluding a case from public scrutiny must be subject to careful examination, given the public dimension of the proceedings.

The final complaint of the mother in *Moser* was the failure of the court to publicly pronounce the outcome of the proceedings. In this respect, the Court reiterated that despite the wording of Article 6(1), which seems to suggest that reading a judgment in open court is required, other means of rendering a judgment public may be compatible with Article 6(1). As was discussed in Chapter 9, in *B and P* the Court found it sufficient that anyone who could establish an interest in the custody proceedings could view the full text of the orders and judgments, and judgments of the Court of Appeal and of first-instance cases of specific interest were routinely published. However, in *Moser*, this same system was found to be in violation of Article 6(1), given that dispensing with a public hearing was not justified in the first place. This decision does not mean that all child protection judgments must be made public; merely that there must be a mechanism by which the court can consider whether such proceedings should be held in public, and whether the judgment should be subsequently published.

10.6.1.3 Legal assistance

The final obligation under Article 6 that has arisen in relation to child protection proceedings is the obligation to provide appropriate legal assistance where it is required to ensure effective access to a court. The positive obligation on the state to provide legal assistance to ensure a fair trial was first recognised by the Court in *Airey v Ireland*[109] in the context of divorce, but has since been extended to a wide variety of situations, including child protection proceedings.

[108] (36337/97, 35974/97) 24.04.2001.
[109] (6289/73) 09.10.1979.

The seminal case in this area was *P, C and S v United Kingdom*,[110] which concerned a child who had been removed from hospital at the time of birth and placed in a foster family, due to fears that the mother would inflict intentional harm on the child. In addition to challenging the basis for the child's removal under Article 8 (discussed in section 10.3 above), the mother also argued that there had been a violation of Article 6, as in the interests of justice she should have been legally represented in proceedings that had such serious consequences for her.

The Court reiterated that there is no automatic right under the Convention for legal aid or legal representation for proceedings concerning civil rights. However, Article 6 may be engaged in two interrelated circumstances. First, as stated in *Airey*, Article 6 may be violated where the assistance of a lawyer is 'indispensable' for effective access to a court—either because legal representation is compulsory under domestic law for certain types of litigation, or by reason of the complexity of the procedure. The Court will consider whether the applicant would have been able to present their case 'properly and satisfactorily' without the assistance of a lawyer, given 'the complexity of the procedure, the necessity to address complicated points of law or to establish facts, involving expert evidence and the examination of witnesses'.[111] The Court will also look at the nature of the subject matter, and particularly whether it entails an emotional involvement that is compatible with the degree of objectivity required by advocacy in court.

Having said this, the right of access to a court is not absolute, and may be subject to legitimate restrictions. The Court will decide whether the limitation has impaired the very essence of the right, and whether there is a reasonable relationship of proportionality between the means employed and the aim sought to be achieved. In the case of legal aid, of particular relevance will be the limited nature of public funds available for civil actions, which renders a procedure of selection a necessary feature of the system, as long as this is not arbitrary or disproportionate.

The second factor governing the application of Article 6 is that of fairness. Even where the applicant has been able to conduct their case notwithstanding the lack of assistance by a lawyer, the question will nevertheless arise as to whether the procedure was fair. Justice need not just be done, but must also be seen to be done, and ensuring the appearance of the fair administration of justice is of great importance. In this context, the Court will examine the seriousness of what is at stake for the applicant in assessing the adequacy and fairness of procedures.

In *P, C and S*, the mother had been granted legal aid for representation, and both junior and senior counsel appointed. However, three days into the hearing, the lawyers applied to withdraw from proceedings, alleging that they were being asked to conduct the case in an unreasonable manner. The judge allowed the withdrawal, and adjourned the case for four days, but refused to delay this any longer for the mother to seek alternative representation, obliging her to conduct her own case over the bulk of the trial. Moreover, proceedings to free the child for adoption were held merely a week following the care proceedings, with the judge refusing to defer the hearing until the mother had found representation.

[110] (56547/00) 16.07.2002.
[111] ibid., para. 89.

The Court held that these failures had resulted in a violation of Article 6. It noted the exceptional complexity of the case, the voluminous documentation, and the review of highly complex expert evidence which was involved. Moreover, the highly emotive nature of the subject matter—her own alleged disposition to harm her children, together with her personality traits and her relationship with her husband were at the heart of the case—meant that effective access to a court required the assistance of a lawyer.

The Court further rejected the government's argument that legal assistance was not necessary, as the domestic courts had adopted relaxed procedures in order to ensure that the mother did not suffer any prejudice. The Court emphasised that assistance from the counsel of the other parties, and a certain latitude granted by the judge in rules of procedure, was no substitute for competent representation by a lawyer instructed to protect the applicant's rights. Even if a lawyer could not have affected the outcome of the proceedings, this was not decisive to a finding of fairness. There is no requirement to show actual prejudice, as this would deprive the guarantees under Article 6 of their substance.[112]

The Court also addressed the issue of delay, which had been central to the domestic court's refusal to adjourn the case. It was not convinced 'that the importance of proceeding with expedition, which attaches generally to child-care cases, necessitated the draconian action of proceeding to a full and complex hearing, followed within one week by the freeing for adoption application, both without legal assistance being provided to the applicants'.[113] While, as discussed below, it is doubtless desirable that a child's future be settled as soon as possible, the possibility of 'some months' delay' would not be so prejudicial to the child's interests as to justify a procedure that was described by the trial judge as giving an appearance of 'railroading' her parents. The domestic courts were also criticised in this case for placing an arbitrary deadline of settling the child's future by the time she reached one year of age—with the Court describing this as 'a somewhat inflexible and blanket approach, applied without particular consideration for the facts of this individual case'.[114]

The language used by the Court in this case is clear and powerful. Although the factual scenario was on the extreme end of the spectrum in terms of legal and factual complexity, the strength of the language used indicates that it would be rare for a situation to arise where legal representation was not an essential component of fair child protection proceedings under Article 6.

10.6.2 Article 8

In addition to the obligations in relation to the right to a fair trial under Article 6, the Court has made clear that the right to respect for private and family life under Article 8

[112] cf. *Gnahoré v France* (40031/98) 19.09.2000, where cases where legal representation was not compulsory were subject to different rules, as set down in the New Code of Civil Procedure, including 'markedly simpler' rules of procedure.

[113] *P, C and S v the United Kingdom* (56547/00) 16.07.2002, para. 98.

[114] ibid.

also includes inherent procedural safeguards. In order to comply with these safeguards, the authorities must ensure that the decision neither is, nor appears to be, arbitrary, and the decision-making process as a whole adequately involves the relevant parties.

10.6.2.1 The involvement of parents in the decision-making process

The first requirement—that of involvement of the 'relevant parties' in decision-making—has in reality been restricted to consideration of the involvement of parents.[115] As is discussed below, children have largely been seen as objects of the decision-making process, rather than subjects whose involvement is required.

The involvement of parents comprises three, interrelated, aspects: first, that the view of parents be elicited by the authorities, and these views be adequately considered; second, that the parents have sufficient access to the relevant materials in the case; and third, that there is a balanced evaluation of the evidence on file.

These elements were first considered in *W v the United Kingdom*.[116] In this case, the parents were not informed in advance of the decision to place their child with long-term foster parents with a view to adoption. Nor were they consulted in advance of the decision to terminate their contact with their child, only being advised of the decision the following month. The Court noted that the decision-making process has a significant influence on the substance of the decision, most notably by ensuring that it is based on relevant considerations, is not one-sided, and as such, 'neither is nor appears to be arbitrary'.[117] For this reason, the Court is entitled to have regard to the decision-making process to determine that it has been conducted in a fair manner that affords due respect to the interests protected by Article 8.

Having said this, the Court recognised that the domestic authorities could not be required to follow an inflexible procedure, and must be afforded a measure of discretion in this sensitive area. However, given the seriousness of the decisions, and the fact that in many cases they prove to be irreversible, the Court emphasised that this is 'a domain in which there is an even greater call than usual for protection against arbitrary interferences'.[118] For this reason, the relevant considerations to be weighed by domestic authorities in reaching decisions concerning children in their care *must* include the views and interests of the parents. The decision-making process must be such as to ensure that their views and interests are not only elicited, but duly taken into account by the domestic authorities. What has to be determined is 'whether, having regard to the particular circumstances of the case and notably the serious nature of the decisions to be taken, the parents have been involved in the decision-making process, seen as a whole, to a degree sufficient to provide them with the requisite protection of their interests'.[119] If they have not been sufficiently involved, the decision cannot be regarded as 'necessary' within the meaning of Article 8.

The right of parents to involvement in proceedings under Article 8 overlaps with the right to legal representation under Article 6. This is particularly seen in cases

[115] See also Chapter 11, on fairness in adoption decision-making.
[116] (9749/82) 08.07.1987.
[117] ibid., para. 62.
[118] ibid.
[119] ibid., para. 64.

concerning parents with mental health problems or intellectual disabilities, where additional assistance is required to be able to put across their views. For example, in *B v Romania (No. 2)*,[120] the Court emphasised that 'the authorities must display particular vigilance when dealing with vulnerable people and must afford them increased protection as their capacity or will to pursue a complaint will often be impaired'.[121] It noted that despite the mother suffering from a severe mental disorder and having been admitted to psychiatric institutions on numerous occasions, 'no special protective measures were taken in respect of her, for example by assigning a lawyer to represent her during the placement proceedings or appointing a temporary guardian'.[122] The mother was clearly not able to participate in the decision-making process, but there was no evidence of any measures taken by the authorities to ensure that she was able to convey her views, even in an unofficial way. Likewise, in *AK and L v Croatia*,[123] the Court criticised the domestic authorities for using the mother's mild intellectual disability—including a speech impediment and a limited vocabulary—as a reason to remove her child from her, yet failing to recognise that this same disability meant that she required assistance to be adequately involved in the decision-making process.

Importantly, in *X v Croatia*,[124] the Court held that such procedural rights continue to rest in the natural parent, even if they have been divested of the capacity to act due to mental illness (in this case, paranoid schizophrenia). In this case, despite the mother never being divested of her parental rights, her daughter was freed for adoption, and the adoption proceedings completed, all without the participation of the mother in any form—with the exception of one phone call, which summarily informed her of the decision to commence proceedings. The Court maintained that not every person who has been divested of the capacity to act should be automatically excluded from adoption proceedings concerning their child. While her parental rights were still intact, the mother should have been given the opportunity to be heard in the proceedings, and to express her view concerning the potential adoption of her child.

In addition to adequate representation, the obligation of adequate involvement in decision-making requires that parents have sufficient access to relevant materials. In *KA v Finland*,[125] the Court emphasised that parents must be able to access the information that has been relied upon by the authorities in taking the child protection measures. This is relevant not only for the parents' ability to respond to allegations made, but also to enable them to understand and come to terms with the situation.[126]

This obligation arises even where the parent has not themselves requested the relevant information. As the Court explained in *Errico v Italy*,[127] it should not be the sole responsibility of the parent, nor lie at their initiative, to obtain the relevant evidence on which a decision to remove their child is based. The obligation lies on the domestic

[120] (1285/03) 19.02.2013.
[121] ibid., para. 114.
[122] ibid., para. 116.
[123] (37956/11) 08.01.2013.
[124] (11223/04) 17.07.2008.
[125] (27751/95) 14.01.2003.
[126] ibid., para. 105. See also *Buchberger v Austria* (32899/96) 20.12.2001; *P, C and S v the United Kingdom* (56547/00) 16.07.2002.
[127] (29768/05) 24.02.2009.

authorities to protect the interests of the family and to make this material available, even in the absence of any request by the parent.[128] This was also seen in *Moser v Austria*, where the Court held that it was not enough for the applicant to have access to the case file throughout the proceedings. It was not for the applicant, who was unrepresented, to inspect the case file in order to become aware of the information relied on by the state—rather, it was for the court to inform her of this, and provide her with an opportunity to comment on it.[129]

Having said this, the obligation is not absolute and situations may arise where parents cannot claim a right to obtain disclosure of a document presented to the authorities. The example given by the Court in *KA* was a child's statement, if a careful consideration leads to the conclusion that disclosure could place the child at risk;[130] while in *TP and KM v the United Kingdom*,[131] the Court gave the example of a video recording of an interview of the child by a medical professional. Where there are any doubts as to whether the disclosure of material will pose a risk to the welfare of the child, the matter should be submitted to the court, who can make a final determination as to whether this would be appropriate.[132]

The final procedural requirement in respect of the involvement of parents in decision-making is the balanced evaluation of the evidence on file. In *KA v Finland*,[133] the Court made clear that 'Article 8 requires that the decision-making authorities and courts provide such detailed reasons as to enable the parent or custodian to participate in the further decision-making by appealing their decisions adequately'.[134] Any child protection order should 'be capable of convincing an objective observer that the measure is based on a careful and unprejudiced assessment of all evidence on file, with the distinct reasons for the care measure being stated explicitly'.[135] The reasoning in the order 'should reflect the careful scrutiny' of the domestic authorities, 'by weighing the various evidence militating in favour and against the care measure'.[136] In this respect, a mere reference to 'documentation on file' or to 'information' contained in appendices to a decision will not be sufficient to involve the parents adequately. Moreover, a vague description of the considerations taken into account will not provide adequate guidance for appellate bodies to be able to determine whether the measure was based on relevant and sufficient reasons.[137]

[128] ibid., para. 82.
[129] *Moser v Austria* (12643/02) 21.09.2006, para. 87.
[130] (27751/95) 14.01.2003, para. 105.
[131] (28945/95) 10.05.2001 (GC).
[132] See *Errico v Italy* (29768/05) 24.02.2009; *TP and KM v United Kingdom* (28945/95) 10.05.2001 (GC).
[133] (27751/95) 14.01.2003.
[134] ibid., para. 104. See also *McMichael v the United Kingdom* (16424/90) 24.02.1995, where the Court held that 'the lack of disclosure of such vital documents as social reports is capable of affecting the ability of participating parents not only to influence the outcome of the children's hearing in question, but also to assess their prospects of making an appeal to the Sheriff Court'. (para. 80)
[135] *KA v Finland* (27751/95) 14.01.2003, para. 103.
[136] ibid.
[137] See also *Jansen v Norway* (2822/16) 06.09.2018.

10.6.2.2 The involvement of children in the decision-making process

Unlike private law proceedings, where the wishes and feelings of children have assumed a central role in the decision-making process, there is yet to be any real recognition by the Court that children have a procedural right to involvement in child protection cases. It has been a side issue in several cases—for example, in *Kutzner v Germany*,[138] where the Court commented that 'the children themselves have at no stage been heard by the judges'[139]—but such comments were peripheral to the central arguments and to the findings of violations by the domestic authorities.

Interestingly, the cases where this was discussed in most detail were not those where children had not been heard, but those where there had been insufficient expert support to examine their views once they had been expressed. In *Levin v Sweden*,[140] the mother challenged a decision to only allow her to see her children (who had been taken into care) once every six months. The majority of the Court held that this was compatible with the Convention, inter alia, because it corresponded with the children's own opinion about how often they wanted to see their parents. The Court highlighted that the children had expressly stated that they did not want to see the mother more often, and did not want to see her alone, nor to stay with her. This, according to the Court 'cannot . . . be ignored or trivialised'.[141]

However, in a strong dissent, Judge Power-Forde criticised the majority for failing to look behind the views and feelings expressed, to find what the basis for these were, and whether they were influenced by the social welfare authorities. She stated:

> [A]t no stage in the proceedings did the domestic courts hear the children themselves either directly or by way of video link. Whilst the Court of Appeal in 2008 directed that their point of view be obtained, there is a manifest want of independence in the manner in which this 'evidence' was ascertained—the children being interviewed by only one of the parties to the proceedings (the council), in a non-neutral environment and in the presence of their substitute carers. The potential for a conflicted emotional response within the children (then aged 9, 7 and 6) was evident and yet no measures were taken to facilitate a more independent expert assessment of their feelings and wishes.[142]

The consequences of failing to seek expert advice were seen more forcefully in *BB and FB v Germany*.[143] Here, a 12-year-old child told the authorities that her parents were physically abusive, which was corroborated by her eight-year-old brother. There was no physical evidence to support these allegations, and the parents vehemently denied that they had mistreated the children. The domestic courts did not take expert evidence as to the reliability of the children's claims, but accepted them as truth, and ordered that the children be removed into public care. One year later, the children

[138] (46544/99) 26.02.2002.
[139] ibid., para. 77. See also *Saviny v Ukraine* (39948/06) 18.12.2008.
[140] (35141/06) 15.03.2012.
[141] ibid., para. 67.
[142] ibid., dissenting opinion of Judge Power-Forde, para. 8.
[143] (18734/09, 9424/11) 14.03.2013.

admitted that the allegations had been fabricated. The Court found that the interim emergency removal of the children, based on the personal statements given by the children to the Youth Office and the court, was justified. The authorities had an obligation to act swiftly to prevent further abuse, and could not be expected to undertake lengthy examinations while the children were purportedly in danger. However, once the children were safely away from the parents, and the main proceedings had commenced, the courts had an obligation to undertake a more in-depth examination. Here, the Court of Appeal had based its assessment exclusively on the case file, rather than re-hearing the children in person. There was no objective evidence of the alleged abuse, and the facts before the court were capable of casting doubts as to the truthfulness of the children's allegations. The Court noted that the domestic courts had an obligation to carry out on their own motion all investigations necessary to establish the relevant facts, and in this case, there had not been sufficient reason for withdrawing the applicant's parental rights.

This is an area in which there is a lacuna in the Court's jurisprudence. While this can, in some respects, be attributed to the way in which cases have been brought and argued before the Court, this is not the sole contributing factor. The Court itself makes a choice as to what aspects of any case they will focus on, and what features they identify as indispensable to the decision-making process. By failing to include the participation of children within their core requirements, children are relegated to the status of objects over whom parents and the state are fighting, rather than being recognised as the subjects of these decision-making processes.

10.6.2.3 Length of proceedings

The requirement that cases are resolved without significant delay is one that runs through every aspect of the Court's jurisprudence. Unlike Article 6, which relates solely to the judicial proceedings themselves, the procedural requirement under Article 8 requires appropriate speed and efficiency throughout the entirety of the process.

In the context of child protection, the relevant test is whether the authorities acted swiftly, and with 'exceptional diligence'.[144] As in private law child proceedings, there is a danger that any procedural relay will result in the de facto determination of the issue, and the Court must be satisfied that parent–child relations are decided solely in light of all the relevant considerations, and not merely by the passage of time.[145]

This was seen in *RV and others v Italy*,[146] which involved children who were removed from their parents on the basis of emergency measures and not returned for over ten years. The Court noted that the children were removed as a precautionary measure, on the basis that further assessment was necessary concerning the existence of actual harm, yet this assessment was not carried out until 18 months later. In the ten years that followed, only one judicial decision was made by the court entrusted with the task of monitoring the family's situation, ruling on the merits of the care measures and the need to retain them. At one stage, it took three years to decide an urgent

[144] *RV and others v Italy* (37748/13) 18.07.2019.
[145] *W v the United Kingdom* (9749/82) 08.07.1987.
[146] (37748/13) 18.07.2019.

application to revoke the care measures, during which time the children had remained with their alternative carers. While the Court acknowledged the complexity of child protection cases, and the difficulties faced by the authorities in balancing conflicting interests, such a period of time could not be considered reasonable.[147]

The Court further noted that on a number of occasions, the expert appointed by the authorities to undertake assessments far exceeded the time frame given to them. The Court accepted that proceedings sometimes need to be suspended to obtain expert opinion, and that such reports need a certain period of time to be completed, but expressed doubt that an expert who took ten months to do so was acting with appropriate speed or diligence.

The strict scrutiny of the Court in this respect was seen even more clearly in the case of *MAK and RK v the United Kingdom*,[148] where a delay of several days between removing the child and seeking an expert opinion led to a violation of Article 8. On the child's arrival in hospital, the initial doctor had believed that she had been sexually abused, and it was not until the specialist was consulted four days later that the child was found to be suffering from a medical disorder which explained the injuries. The Court found that this delay violated the rights of the parents and child under Article 8: while there were relevant and sufficient reasons for suspecting abuse at the time the child was admitted to hospital, 'the delay in consulting a dermatologist extended the interference with the applicants' family life and was not proportionate to the legitimate aim of protecting the child from harm'.[149]

Having said this, the Court has also acknowledged that certain delays are justifiable. In *Stankūnaitė v Lithuania*,[150] the Court observed that although it took the authorities two years to reach a court decision to return the applicant's daughter to her, this had been for 'uncontestably objective reasons'. The applicant in this case had been accused of being complicit in the sexual abuse of her daughter, and the delay had resulted from the need to conduct a criminal investigation in this regard. Once this was discontinued, the courts had acted with requisite diligence in dealing with the child protection proceedings.

10.7 Family reunification

It is trite law that the natural family relationship is not terminated by the removal of a child into public care.[151] The taking of a child into care should normally be regarded as a temporary measure, to be discontinued as soon as circumstances permit, and the authorities must ensure that the implementation of the care order is compatible with the ultimate aim of family reunification. This obligation is very stringent—the authorities must not only consider the short-term situation of the child, but their best interests in

[147] See also *Covezzi and Morselli v Italy* (52763/99) 09.05.2003.
[148] (45901/05, 40146/06) 23.03.2010.
[149] ibid., para. 73.
[150] (67068/11) 29.10.2019.
[151] See *W v the United Kingdom* (9749/82) 08.07.1987.

the long-term, and only in exceptional circumstances can a complete termination of family ties be contemplated.

A good example of the robust scrutiny of the actions of the authorities was the case of *Barnea and Caldararu v Italy*,[152] where the child had been in foster care from the age of 28 months. Ten days after her removal from her family, the courts ordered that she be placed in foster care with a view to adoption. However, this was overturned on appeal, and at the age of five, the child was ordered to be returned to her family. The courts ordered that a programme be put in place for the gradual reunification of the child with her natural family over the course of six months. The social services did not comply with this, and instead asked the courts to extend the child's placement with the foster family, which was granted, relying on the living conditions of the natural family, the potential difficulties of reintegrating the child, and the strong ties she had developed with the foster carers.

The Court acknowledged that the domestic authorities had been focused on what they considered the best interests of the child, and that she should not be removed from the stable environment that she had lived in from a young age, and into which she was well integrated. However, it emphasised that the future relationship between parents and children cannot be regulated by the simple passage of time, and the reasons given for refusing to return the child did not constitute the required 'very exceptional' circumstances that can justify the separation of a child from their natural family. The Court accepted that a change in the factual situation may exceptionally justify a decision on the care of the child; however, this was only permissible where the essential changes at issue are not the result of action or inaction by the state authorities, and where the competent authorities have made every effort to maintain personal relations and reunify the family. In this case, the passage of time was a consequence of the social services' inertia in beginning the reunification process, and therefore there had been a violation of Article 8.

Having said this, the obligation to facilitate reunification is not an absolute one, and is limited by the best interests of the child. When examining the actions of the domestic authorities, the Court will consider whether they have taken such steps as could be considered 'reasonable in all the circumstances' to maintain and foster the relationship between parents and child.[153] However, the Court has also recognised that after a considerable period of time has passed since the child was removed into care, their interest in not having their de facto family changed again may override the interests of the parents to have their family reunited.[154]

For example, in *Bronda v Italy*,[155] the authorities decided that it would not be in the child's best interests to return her to her natural family, despite the care order being

[152] (37931/15) 22.06.2017.

[153] See, for example, *V v Slovenia* (26971/07) 01.12.2011. For a good overview of the obligations in this area, see Child Law Clinic, University of Cork, 'Research Brief on ECHR Case Law concerning Children in Care and the Obligation to Work Towards Family Reunification' (September 2019), https://www.ucc.ie/en/media/academic/law/childlawclinic/ECHRFamilyReunificationinCareCasesUpdated12September2019.pdf.

[154] See, for example, *U and GF v Germany* (11588/85) 15.05.1986 (dec.); *K and T v Finland* (25702/94) 12.07.2001 (GC); *Hoffman v Germany* (66516/01) 28.08.2007 (dec.); *Mohamed Hasan v Norway* (27496/15) 26.04.2018.

[155] (22430/93) 09.06.1998.

lifted. The child—aged nine—said she did not want to leave the foster home, and showed fear at the prospect of being returned. As a result, the authorities allowed her to stay with her foster family. Her grandparents brought a case before the Court, arguing that the refusal to enforce her return constituted an interference with the right to respect for family life under Article 8. The Court found that a fair balance had been struck between the child's interest in remaining with foster parents and the natural family's interest in having her live with them. The authorities had attached special weight to the overriding interests of the child, who had firmly indicated that she did not wish to return. This interest outweighed that of the natural family.

10.7.1 Contact with children in care

10.7.1.1 The obligation to maintain contact

The maintenance of contact with children in care is closely linked with the issue of family reunification. Where there is limited contact between the parents and the children throughout their separation, it is going to be more difficult for family reunification to take place once the protective measures are lifted. This has led the Court to impose a higher level of scrutiny when considering restrictions on contact. As it stated in *KA v Finland*:

> Whereas the authorities enjoy a wide margin of appreciation in assessing the necessity of taking a child into public care, a stricter scrutiny is called for in respect of any further limitations, such as restrictions placed by those authorities on parental rights of access. Such further limitations entail the danger that the family relations between the parents and a young child are effectively curtailed … The possibilities of reunification will be progressively diminished and eventually destroyed if the biological parents and the child are not allowed to meet each other at all, or only so rarely that no natural bonding between them is likely to occur.[156]

As such, the Court will examine the regime of contact between the parents and the child to ensure that it is consistent with the ultimate aim of family reunification. In this respect, it will consider both de facto and de jure impediments to contact.

The former was seen in the seminal case of *Olsson v Sweden (No. 1)*,[157] where the Court found a violation of Article 8 in circumstances where the children were placed in separate foster homes over 500 kilometres away from their parents, and from each other. While the Court acknowledged that there was nothing to suggest that the Swedish authorities had not acted in good faith, this was not sufficient to render a measure 'necessary' under Article 8. Rather, an objective standard must be met. Although the placement of the children so far away from each other was partly prompted by administrative difficulties, the Court emphasised that in an area so

156 (27751/95) 14.01.2003, para. 139 (citations omitted).
157 (10465/83) 24.03.1988 (Court).

fundamental as family life, such considerations cannot be allowed to play more than a secondary role.[158]

When considering de jure limitations on contact, the Court has made clear that only the most extreme circumstances will be sufficient to justify a complete prohibition on contact between a parent and child. Even where a child has gone through highly traumatic experiences, the authorities must make some effort to allow communication with their parents, unless they plan to permanently sever all ties between them.[159]

An example of this can be seen in *Margareta and Roger Andersson v Sweden*,[160] where the authorities not only placed restrictions on face-to-face meetings between the mother and child, but they were also prohibited from having any contact by mail or telephone for 18 months. The Court noted that these measures were 'particularly far-reaching' and to be compliant with Article 8, must be supported by strong reasons. The reasons given by the government—that the mother was a negative influence on the child, encouraging him to run away from his placement, and to behave inappropriately—were found to be relevant, but not sufficient to deprive the mother and child of almost every means of maintaining contact with one another for such a long period of time. Likewise, in *Jansen v Norway*,[161] the authorities were concerned that the mother or her family may abduct the child from his foster placement if contact were allowed and the identity of the foster family became known. The Court acknowledged that this might make organising contact sessions more difficult, as at any session information about where the child lived could be revealed. However, it noted that it was never foreseen that there would be more than four of such sessions each year, which would decrease the risk of exposure, and reduce the difficulties of the authorities. It found that the domestic authorities had been more concerned about protection from abduction than on family reunification and preparation for the future, and had failed to balance the immediate danger against the long-term effects that permanent separation may have on the child.

In analysing the compliance of a regime of contact with Article 8, the Court will look at both the frequency of contact and the conditions in which it takes place. In *KO and VM v Norway*,[162] the Court maintained that 'family reunification cannot normally be expected to be sufficiently supported if there are intervals of weeks, or even—as in the instant case—as much as months, between each contact session'.[163] Moreover, bearing in mind the purpose of facilitating and strengthening family ties, it found that the decision to allow the child-care authorities to supervise contact between parents and children must be justified on 'special grounds' in every case. Similarly, in *Strand Lobben and others v Norway*,[164] the Court criticised the domestic authorities for

[158] ibid., para. 82. This can be contrasted with *Covezzi and Morselli v Italy* (52763) 09.05.2003, where the Court found that the separation of four siblings into different homes was justified on the basis that they required particularly high levels of support and protection, and indeed did not wish to be placed together.
[159] See *Scozzari and Giunta v Italy* (39221/98, 41963/98) 13.07.2000 (GC).
[160] (12963/87) 25.02.1992.
[161] (2822/16) 06.09.2018.
[162] (64808/16) 19.11.2019.
[163] ibid., para. 69.
[164] (37283/13) 10.09.2019.

organising the contact sessions in a way that was not conducive to letting the mother and child bond, in light of where the sessions were held and who had been present. In both these cases, the Court found that the focus of the contact was not on building the relationship between the parent and child, and thus enhancing the possibility of family reunification, but were instead intended to serve as a means by which the child could become familiar with his roots. As a result, the measures were not in compliance with the state's obligations under Article 8.

It is important to note that the obligation to facilitate contact is not absolute, and nor is there a pre-determined number of visits that a parent can demand. Instead, contact—its frequency, format, location, and duration—will be subject to the overriding interests of the child in question. For example, in *Levin v Sweden*, the mother's contact with her children was reduced following a request from the children's father that he also be permitted to visit. In order to prevent causing anxiety and disruption to the children, the authorities decided not to order additional contact sessions to accommodate the father, but rather that the four existing contact visits per year should be divided between the parents. The Court accepted that this was a logical solution, justified by the need to protect the children's best interests.

Moreover, the child's wishes and feelings will be a compelling factor in deciding whether contact will be permitted, and if so, in what form. For example, in *Asplund v Sweden*,[165] the Commission found that the mother's interest in meeting her 15-year-old son must be outweighed by her son's own wishes, which must be of paramount importance under Article 8.[166] Likewise, in *TS and JJ v Norway*,[167] the authorities restricted a 12-year-old child's contact visits with his grandmother in line with his wishes. The Court noted that there was nothing to prevent him taking the initiative to increase contact at any time in the future if he desired, and in the meantime, the authorities were justified in giving weight to his views as to whether increased contact would be in his best interests.[168]

10.7.1.2 The opportunity to challenge contact decisions

In addition to the substantive requirements concerning the facilitation of contact, the Court has also imposed a procedural requirement on states to ensure the opportunity

[165] (19762/92) 02.09.1994 (dec.). See also *Lundblad v Sweden* (21078/92) 02.09.1994 (dec.), where the Commission held that the expressed wish of a 12-year-old child not to have contact with her mother was a relevant and sufficient reason for the restriction on access.

[166] See also *Dolharmre v Sweden* (67/04) 08.06.2010.

[167] (15633/15) 11.10.2016 (dec.). Note that this case concerned a grandparent, rather than a natural parent. In *Lawlor v the United Kingdom* (12763/87) 14.07.1988 (dec.), the Court made clear that the relationship between grandparents and grandchildren is different in nature and degree from the relationship between parent and child, and a refusal of contact with a child in public care will not necessarily constitute an interference with respect for family life under Article 8. There may be an interference with the grandparents' rights if the domestic authorities diminish contact by refusing them what is, in all the circumstances, reasonable access necessary to preserve a normal grandparent–grandchild relationship, but this can be justified on the basis of the child's best interests. In *Lawlor*, the restriction on contact was justified to achieve the legitimate aim of facilitating the transfer of the child from the foster parents to the adoptive parents, and of establishing her relationship with them.

[168] The views of the children themselves are also an important consideration when facilitating family reunification, and are therefore discussed further in section 10.7 below.

to challenge any decision in this regard. A failure to provide this will run the risk of breaching either Article 6, Article 8, or both.

There was initial resistance to the application of Article 6 in such circumstances. As discussed above, while this provision requires a fair trial in the determination of civil rights and obligations, it does not guarantee any particular content for civil rights and obligations in the substantive law: the right must already be recognised under domestic law for Article 6 to be invoked. It was on these grounds that the government in *W v the United Kingdom*[169] challenged the applicability of Article 6 to a refusal to permit contact, arguing that there was no 'right' to have access to their child—either on a theoretical or on a practical basis.

On a theoretical level, the government argued that the notion of parental 'rights' over children was outmoded, and in any case, the so-called 'right' of access was better described as a right of the child. The Court noted that underlying this conception of parental rights was the view that such rights are derived from parental duties and responsibilities, and exist only so long as they are needed for the protection of the child. The main thrust of this view, they suggested, was not to deny the existence of parental rights, but to recognise that they were not absolute, and in the event of a conflict between the rights of parent and child, the welfare of the child must be the paramount consideration. In this light, the Court found that a parental right did in fact exist, but must be exercised in accordance with the child's welfare.

The government also argued that on a practical level, even if such a parental right did exist, it ceased on the making of a care order, the effect of which was to transfer to the authorities all the rights, powers, and duties of the parent with respect to the child. The authority could then, at its discretion, allow a parent to have access to a child, but this did not constitute a 'right' under domestic law. This was again rejected by the Court, which held that the existence of a discretionary power on the part of the authorities to decide to only allow restricted visits—or even no visits—does not necessarily mean that there is no longer any parental right to contact with their child.

Finally, the Court dismissed the argument that sufficient protection was provided to parents by the ability to challenge the care order itself. While it acknowledged that such proceedings would resolve the question of contact indirectly, the Court maintained they were not directed to the specific issue of access. Whether a child should be in public care and whether his parent should have access to him are matters to which different considerations may well apply: a parent might have no desire to challenge the care order, but might still wish to maintain contact with the child. The ability to launch a judicial review of the decision of the authorities was likewise insufficient, as it only examined whether the authorities had acted illegally, unreasonably, or unfairly. The Court concluded that there was no possibility of a 'determination' with regard to the right of access, in accordance with the requirements of Article 6, unless the parent could have the decision of the authorities reviewed by a tribunal having jurisdiction to examine the issue on its merits.[170]

[169] (9749/82) 08.07.1987. See also *O v United Kingdom* (9276/81) 08.07.1987.
[170] See also *Eriksson v Sweden* (11373/85) 23.02.1989.

10.7.2 The obligation to facilitate family reunification

10.7.2.1 The obligation to respond to changing circumstances

The obligation to facilitate family reunification wherever possible is not limited to contact. Instead, the Court will look to the entirety of the situation in order to determine whether the overall package of measures taken by the authorities are in conformity with the aim of eventually reuniting the child with their family. For example, in *K and T v Finland*,[171] the Court criticised the lack of 'serious and sustained effort' by the authorities to consider or prepare for family reunification. The authorities had consistently assumed that long-term care would be necessary, and in the seven years the children were in care, the sole measure taken by the authorities to prepare for reunification was to once make enquiries as to whether the parents would be able to bond with the children. In finding a violation of Article 8, the Court found that, '[t]he minimum to be expected of the authorities is to examine the situation anew from time to time to see whether there has been any improvement in the family's situation'.[172]

Likewise, in *KA v Finland*,[173] the authorities did not consider reunification as a serious option, and proceeded on the presumption that long-term care would be necessary. As a result, they placed severe restrictions on the visitation rights of the parents, with the intention of diminishing their ties with the children. When the father informed the authorities that he had divorced the children's mother—who was the alleged abuser—he was told that this would have no effect on the authorities' plans for the children, as they had been placed in care 'up to their adulthood'. This blinkered approach to the children's situation, and refusal to consider the father's change in circumstances, resulted in a violation of Article 8.[174]

Of course, to adequately respond to a change in parents' circumstances, the domestic authorities must have access to up-to-date information. In *AS v Norway*,[175] the domestic courts relied on expert reports that were over two years old, while rejecting the request of the mother for an expert to be appointed to assess her parental abilities, and a psychologist to observe her interactions with her child.[176] The Court underscored the importance for authorities to have a sufficiently broad and updated factual basis for reaching such significant decisions as the effective termination of family life between parents and child, and in light of this, found the decision-making process to be in breach of Article 8.

[171] (25702/94) 12.07.2001 (GC).

[172] ibid., para. 179; cf. *Jovanovic v Sweden* (10592/12) 22.10.2015, where the care order was reviewed every six months, and contact rights regularly examined.

[173] (27751/95) 14.01.2003.

[174] This was also seen in the recent case of *Strand Lobben and others v Norway* (37283/13) 10.09.2019 (GC), where the Grand Chamber criticised the domestic authorities for not adequately considering the potential significance of the fact that the mother was going through substantial changes in her life—she got married and had a second child—at the time she applied to have the care order lifted and to be granted extended contact rights. This changing landscape, the Court indicated, undermined the reliability of the decision of the authorities, which was largely based on her inability to provide care.

[175] (60371/15) 17.12.2019. See also *Kocherov and Sergeyeva v Russia* (16899/13) 29.03.2016.

[176] cf. *Achim v Romania* (45959/11) 24.10.2017, where the Court commended the authorities for producing new and updated reports for each proceedings and acknowledged the positive changes in the material situation of the parents, before ultimately deciding to maintain the care order.

In this area, it appears that the Court has adopted the test of 'in-depth assessment of the family situation'—so reviled in *Neulinger*, but now finding a new lease of life when analysing decisions relating to family reunification. In *Haddad v Spain*,[177] the Court noted the 'serious negligence' of the authorities in conducting the proceedings, and in particular in the failure to take into account the change in circumstances of the father—who had been cleared of all charges of abuse against the mother and children, yet not permitted to resume contact with them. While it was acceptable that the children had been placed in care, as the mother had requested this measure, the Court indicated that this should have been swiftly followed by an in-depth assessment of the situation of the children and their relationship with their parents—and if necessary, of their mother and father separately. Instead, the authorities merely reproduced the same decisions, without making new findings or assessing the evolution of the circumstances.[178]

What is perhaps most interesting about this case, however, is that in considering appropriate redress under Article 41 of the Convention, the Court asked the domestic authorities to re-examine the situation of the father and child, and to take appropriate measures in the child's best interests. In doing so, it noted that the most appropriate form of redress would be to ensure that the father's situation was restored as far as possible to what it would have been had the provisions of Article 8 been respected. Even more significantly, the Court observed that Spanish law allows for the possibility of reviewing final decisions which are declared contrary to rights recognised by the Convention in an European Court of Human Rights judgment.[179]

This is in stark contrast to the usual approach of the Court, where it recognises that given the passage of time, the only possible redress can be financial.[180] It seems to indicate that the Court intended the domestic authorities to in fact reunite the father and child—despite the fact that she had been in foster care from the age of 18 months, and was eight years old by the time the Court handed down its judgment.

It is positive that the Court is starting to consider a broader range of remedies, even if this was predicated on the domestic law in question allowing such revision. Financial compensation is scant redress for the damage and the suffering in such cases, and a clear indication from the Court that positive steps must be taken by domestic authorities to redress the harm caused is laudable. Given the length of time that cases take before the Court, it is unlikely that any child can simply be immediately returned to their family in the short term, but that does not mean that steps cannot be taken to support a strong and ongoing relationship that provides the possibility of reunification in the long term.

[177] (16572/17) 18.06.2019.

[178] See also *Strand Lobben and others v Norway* (37283/13) 10.09.2019 (GC).

[179] Provided that this does not prejudice the rights acquired by third parties in good faith. Similar remedies were also suggested in the cases of *Soares de Melo v Portugal* ((72850/14) 16.02.2016) and *RMS v Spain* ((28775/12) 18.06.2013).

[180] See, for example, *Barnea and Caldararu v Italy* (37931/15) 22.06.2017.

10.7.2.2 Preparation for family reunification

The positive duty to take measures to facilitate family reunification as soon as reasonably feasible weighs on domestic authorities with progressively increasing force from the time the child is taken into care.[181] However, family reunification cannot operate in a vacuum, and the Court has recognised that where a child has been separated from their parents for a significant period of time, measures may need to be taken to prepare both the child and parents for their reunion.

This was explored in *Olsson v Sweden (No. 2)*,[182] concerning children who had been removed from their family aged one and three respectively, and remained in foster homes for seven years. Contact between the parents and children during this time was sparse, and at the time that the care order was terminated—as there were no longer sufficiently serious circumstances to warrant its continuation—they had not seen their mother for the previous three years, and had seen their father only once. As such, despite the care order being lifted, the domestic authorities prohibited the children's removal from their foster home. Instead, they ordered that, in the short term, contact should be arranged under such conditions that would make the children feel secure, with a view to reunification in the long term.

The Court found that the restrictions on access were both relevant and sufficient. Both children had expressed a strong wish to remain in their foster homes, and evidence suggested that forcing them to return to their parents would cause long-term psychological harm. Moreover, the parents were free to visit the foster homes as often as they wished—the only restriction was that meetings outside the home were allowed only under 'such conditions as would dispel the children's apprehensions'. The domestic courts were clear that the main responsibility for the necessary preparations for reunification not being made lay with the parents: in order to arrange adequate preparatory contacts, good co-operation between the social welfare authorities, foster parents, and biological parents was essential, yet the biological parents refused to engage in this process. They did not accept the access restrictions, despite knowing that they corresponded with the children's wishes, and visited the children in their foster homes only twice.

The Court affirmed that Article 8 entails the right of the parents to have measures taken with a view to reunification with their children, and an obligation on the national authorities to take such measures. However, where contact would be contrary to the children's interests or interfere with their rights, it is for the national authorities to strike a fair balance. '[W]hat will be decisive', the Court held, 'is whether the national authorities have made such efforts to arrange the necessary preparations for reunion as can reasonably be demanded under the special circumstances of each case.'[183]

This was strongly criticised by Judge Pettiti in his partly dissenting opinion, joined by Judges Matscher and Russo, who considered that there had been a 'serious violation'

[181] *KA v Finland* (27751/95) 14.01.2003.

[182] (13441/87) 27.11.1992.

[183] ibid., para. 90. cf. *Eriksson v Sweden* (11373/85) 22.06.1989, where the refusal to allow contact visits after the lifting of the care order was found to violate Article 8, as it was not in accordance with the law. While the law permitted the authorities to restrict access of children in public care, there was no equivalent provisions to restrict access once the care order had been lifted, but where a prohibition on removal continued in force.

of Article 8 concerning the prohibition on removal and restrictions on access. They considered that in view of the long period of separation, and the relationship between the parents and children, any attempts at contact had no chance of succeeding without adequate psychological preparation—on both sides. For the children, who they considered had been 'conditioned' by the foster family, there should have been psychological preparation, and the progressive organisation of meetings, at first short, then extended to a day, a weekend, a part of the holidays. For the parents, it would have been helpful to prepare them for such progressive stages. Although the judges noted that the attitude of the parents was not always cooperative, the authorities should have made allowances for their frustration, and were under a duty to exert a positive influence, 'by showing understanding and making repeated interventions, instead of reinforcing the differences'.

The approach in *Olsson (No. 2)* was confirmed in *Rieme v Sweden*,[184] decided the same year. In that case, the Court observed that the fact that the child had lived in foster care for seven years, since the age of one, militated in favour of a longer transition period. Although contact was permitted only when arranged by the foster family, the Court found that in view of the child's age and maturity, the length of foster care, emotional ties with foster parents, and the early age that she entered into care, the social welfare authorities were justified in allowing her to set the pace, and providing support to her in doing so.

The obligation of family reunification is thus not absolute, but requires only that the authorities take such steps as can be considered 'reasonable' in the circumstances. The Court will look to whether there were sustained efforts on the part of the authorities, and whether the situation has been regularly examined to be able to respond to changing circumstances, whilst coming to a decision based on the best interests of the child.[185]

10.7.3 Challenging the return of the child to biological parents

The previous sections have focused on the right of the natural parents and their child to be reunited, so that they can enjoy family life together. But what of the foster parents, with whom the child may have established strong familial bonds? Especially where the child has been in care for many years, the return of the child to their natural parents

[184] (12366/86) 22.04.1992.

[185] An example of this was seen in *Achim v Romania* (45959/11) 24.10.2017, where the Court noted with approval that the need to preserve the ties between the parents and children was a constant concern of the authorities. They made genuine efforts to preserve the bond, including providing the parents with fuel for monthly visits, and allowing the children to spend summer holidays with the family. Moreover, the authorities gave advice to the parents on steps they could take to improve their financial situation, and enhance their parenting skills, as well as providing financial assistance to repair the family home and install adequate sanitary facilities. As a result, the Court held that the authorities had done everything that could reasonably have been expected of them to facilitate the children's return to their parents. See also *V v Slovenia* (26971/07) 01.12.2011.

will involve an interference with the rights of the newly formed foster family under Article 8(1)[186]—the only question is whether it is justified.

In *Antkowiak v Poland*,[187] a couple had organised to adopt a baby from a woman they found on the internet. Upon the birth of the child, she signed a declaration agreeing to give her child to the couple for adoption, and the child left the hospital with them. Three weeks later, the mother lodged an application for the return of the child, stating that she had changed her mind. This was granted, finding that there was no reason to deprive her of parental rights. Relying on Articles 8 and 9 of the UN Convention on the Rights of the Child, the domestic courts focused on the right of the child to identity, and a relationship with his natural parents—taking into account his age (he was five years old by the time the case was decided), it was in his best interests to have the ties with the prospective adoptive parents broken, to make way for a new relationship with his biological parents.

The prospective adopters brought a case before the Court, alleging that the return of the child to his natural parents had breached their right to respect for family life. This was rejected by the Court as manifestly ill-founded: the domestic authorities had been faced with a difficult choice between competing interests in a complex case, but the child's best interests had always been their primary consideration. The Court recognised the emotional hardship on the applicants, but found that 'their rights cannot override the best interests of the child'.[188]

This issue arose again in *VD and others v Russia*,[189] where the Court affirmed that the duty on the domestic authorities is to ensure that the child's best interests have been the focus of decision-making, taking into account the competing interests of stability and family reunification. This case concerned a child who suffered from serious medical conditions, requiring him to spend the first eight months of his life in hospital. His parents considered themselves unfit to fulfil his needs, and agreed for him to be put in the care of the applicant, who was an experienced paediatrician. When the child was six years old, his state of health had become more stable, and his parents wished to take him back into their care. This was resisted by his foster mother, and when this was enforced by the authorities, she brought a complaint before the Court. She acknowledged that life in a family environment was a basic need of every child, but disagreed with the government that this right could only be realised when living with his or her natural parents. Instead, she argued, this was something that can be provided by an alternative carer, and indeed had been in this case.

The Court considered that, in view of his special physical psychological conditions, the child was particularly vulnerable, placing an obligation on the domestic authorities to show particular vigilance in assessing his interests, and to afford him increased protection with due regard to his state of health. While the Court acknowledged that the child had spent the first nine years of his life with the foster mother, during which time she was his primary carer and had fully assumed the role of parent, this factor alone could not rule out the possibility of reunification. It recognised that there were

[186] See Chapter 8 on family life between foster parents and children.
[187] (27025/17) 22.05.2018 (dec.).
[188] ibid., para. 72.
[189] (72931/10) 09.04.2019.

many competing factors in this case, but noted in particular that the parents had never renounced their parental authority, and although they had not maintained contact, they had supported him financially and materially while in foster care. The Court found that the domestic authorities had assessed the child's best interests carefully, with due regard to his health and needs, and made them the primary consideration in their decision-making. They had rejected the parents' first claim for reunification, noting that an immediate transfer could compromise the child's development, and that a period of adaption was necessary. It was only a year later, after a programme of preparatory contact, that the transfer was ordered. As a result, there was no violation of Article 8 in this respect.

However, the Court did find that the refusal to allow contact between the foster mother and the child after his return to his natural family *did* constitute a violation of the Convention. The domestic authorities had rejected her application on the grounds that she had no legal or biological link with the child, and therefore, no grounds to seek access. The Court noted that Russian law sets out an exhaustive list of individuals entitled to maintain contact, without exceptions which take into account the variety of family situations.[190] The complete and automatic exclusion of the applicant from the child's life, without giving proper consideration to the child's best interests, failed to respect her rights under Article 8.

10.7.4 Conclusions on family reunification

While the Court may be criticised for its lack of effective oversight in relation to the child's removal from the family, the robust positive obligations imposed on the authorities in relation to family reunification go some way to remedying this. In particular, the strict scrutiny applied to decisions concerning contact, looking at both de jure and de facto limitations, places an appropriately weighty duty on domestic authorities to ensure that the right is practical and effective. Likewise, the requirement of an in-depth and ongoing evaluation of the situation of the child and the family ensures constant vigilance.

Most significantly, however, the Court has recognised the importance of balancing the welfare of the child in the short term with their best interests in the long term. Neither can be allowed to compromise the other, and a careful and nuanced approach is needed by the authorities to ensure that both can co-exist.

10.8 The right to an effective remedy

Under Article 13, everyone has the right to an effective remedy before a national authority for a violation of their Convention rights. This is an important component of the principle of subsidiarity, encouraging the resolution of violations at the domestic level. Not only does this reduce the workload of the Court, but it also acts to entrench

[190] See also *Nazarenko v Russia* (39438/13) 16.07.2015, discussed in section 9.5.1.

human rights protection within national legal systems.[191] This provision has 'close affinity' with Article 35(1), which requires the exhaustion of all domestic remedies before a case can be considered by the Court,[192] as well as Article 6, and the right to a fair trial concerning the determination of civil rights and obligations.

The most comprehensive discussion of the domestic remedies available in relation to child protection is found in *TP and KM v United Kingdom*.[193] This case concerned a child who was taken into care on the basis of suspected sexual abuse. The local authority identified the mother's boyfriend, XY, as the abuser, when in fact the child had indicated that the abuser was X—a man who happened to share the first name. The mother issued proceedings in her own name and on behalf of her daughter, alleging negligence and a breach of statutory duty on the part of the local authority. The House of Lords—at the time, the highest court in the United Kingdom—rejected this claim, on the basis that public policy prohibited the imposition of a liability on the social welfare authorities in the exercise of their child protection functions. Nor did the statutory scheme impose such a liability.

The applicants' case before the Court rested on two grounds. First, they argued that the blanket rule that excluded liability for the social services, irrespective of the harm suffered, the nature and extent of the negligence involved, or the fundamental rights that were at stake constituted a disproportionate restriction on the right of access to a court under Article 6. Second, the rejection of their negligence claim deprived them of any effective remedy within the national legal system, as is required by Article 13.

With regard to the claim under Article 6, the government objected that no right to compensation exists under domestic law, as was made clear by the House of Lords. However, the Court noted that the applicants were claiming damages on the basis of negligence, a tort in English law which is developed through case law. At the outset of the proceedings, there was a serious and genuine dispute about the existence of the right, as was demonstrated by the grant of legal aid, and the fact that the case was argued all the way to the House of Lords. The final decision that there was no duty of care in such cases did not retrospectively remove the arguability of the claim.

Having found that Article 6 was engaged, the Court turned to the applicant's claim that the decision of the House of Lords, which gave immunity from liability of the social welfare authorities, prevented their claims being decided on the facts. The Court noted that the applicants were not prevented from bringing their claims before the domestic courts, which were properly and fairly examined in light of the applicable domestic legal principles. The striking out procedure, which ruled on the existence of a cause of action, did not in and of itself offend the principle of access to the Court.

Under Article 13, the government argued that the return of the child was sufficient redress, and that pecuniary compensation was not necessary to provide an effective remedy. Indeed, they argued that '[t]he harm suffered by the separation of mother

[191] See also the cases on protection of minors from abuse: *A v the United Kingdom* (25599/94) 23.09.1998; *Stubbings and others v the United Kingdom* (22083/93, 22095/93) 22.10.1996; *Z and others v the United Kingdom* (29392/95) 10.05.2001 (GC); *X and Y v the Netherlands* (8978/80) 26.03.1985.

[192] *McFarlane v Ireland* (31333/06) 10.09.2010.

[193] (28945/95) 10.05.2001 (GC). See also *RK and AK v the United Kingdom* (38000/05) 30.09.2008; *MAK and RK v the United Kingdom* (4901/05, 40146/06) 23.03.2010; *AD and OD v the United Kingdom* (28680/06) 16.03.2010.

and child was by its nature likely to be irremediable in terms of damages'.[194] The Court disagreed. It held that the applicants should have had available to them a means of claiming that the authorities were responsible for the damage they had suffered, and to obtain compensation for this. Given that psychiatric damage had occurred, there may have been medical costs to cover, as well as significant pain and suffering to be addressed. The possibility of applying to the ombudsman, or complaining to the Secretary of State, did not provide any enforceable right to compensation, and therefore could not be considered sufficient.

In addition to the legal availability of the remedy, a challenge has also been brought with regard to its practical availability. In *Margareta and Roger Andersson v Sweden*,[195] the question was whether the child's legal guardian—his mother—had been prevented from appealing to Swedish courts on his behalf. Article 13 does not require states to allow a 12-year-old to institute and conduct such proceedings on his own—it is sufficient that someone is able to do this on his behalf. His mother argued that since contact was prohibited, and she had no means of communicating with her child, she was not in a position to learn of any possible infringement, and was therefore prevented from representing him properly. The Court was 'not convinced' by this argument, noting that the mother was able to visit him on a number of occasions, and that they were 'on good terms'. It could not, therefore, be said that she had been prevented from appealing on his behalf.

This judgment is somewhat contradictory. As Kilkelly has pointed out, the contact between the mother and child was so poor—including a prohibition of contact by mail or telephone for 18 months—that the Court found a violation of Article 8, yet it was deemed sufficient for the purposes of representing him under Article 13.[196] As such, it demonstrates the adult-focused nature of the Court's evaluation—as long as the parent can challenge a decision on the child's behalf, there is no need for states to provide such a right for the child themself.

10.9 Conclusion

The Court has made a significant contribution to the promotion of children and parents' rights in the field of child protection. The procedural requirements under Articles 6 and 8 ensure robust decision-making processes, while the strict requirement to strive for family reunification, and the high standards that states must meet in this respect, must be applauded.

However, despite these achievements—or indeed, partly because of them—the Court has failed to set substantive boundaries. Such is the focus on procedure, that the substance has been left behind. Some small steps have been taken in this regard: for example, the development of positive obligations where separation is due to material deprivation, parental disabilities, or mental health. But in all other circumstances, the

194 *TP and KM v the United Kingdom* (28945/95) 10.05.2001 (GC), para. 106.
195 (12963/87) 25.02.1992.
196 U. Kilkelly, *The Child and the European Convention on Human Rights* (Farnham, Surrey: Ashgate, 1999), 290.

Court has left it within the margin of appreciation of states to decide when a family can be separated, and on what grounds.

The challenge for the future will be to see whether the Court progresses in this area, or continues to fall back on procedural violations, leaving the substance unchecked. The signs are not promising—the retreat from the paramountcy of children's interests in *Strand Lobben* raises serious cause for concern, as does the constant pressure on the Court from domestic governments to comply with their perception of 'subsidiarity'.[197] This is not only a problem in the area of child protection: it flows into the question of adoption, and indeed is even more acute in this area, as is discussed in Chapter 11.

197 See the Brighton Declaration of the High Level Conference on the Future of the European Court of Human Rights, and Protocol 15, which resulted from it.

11
Adoption

11.1 Introduction

Europe is a continent with diverse traditions concerning adoption. The prevalence of adoption varies greatly throughout—while in England and Germany there are around 3,000 to 4,000 adoptions per year, in countries such as Bulgaria, Greece, Latvia, Lithuania, and Serbia, they number in the low hundreds only.[1] Further, while some countries have a strong tradition of domestic adoption, others focus predominantly on intercountry placements, either as sending (for example, Russia, Ukraine) or receiving (for example, Denmark, Netherlands, Sweden) states.

This diversity may go some way to explaining why the European Convention on the Adoption of Children of 1967,[2] and its revised 2008 version,[3] have been so ill received, obtaining only 16 and ten ratifications or accessions, respectively.[4] This lack of consensus as to the use of adoption also means that while the European Court of Human Rights has generated a considerable body of jurisprudence concerning adoption, it has been cautious in its approach, leaving a wide margin of appreciation to domestic authorities.

The practice of adoption has many different facets, and has come before the Court in a number of different guises: second-parent adoption; adoption following the removal of the child from the family due to child protection concerns; and intercountry adoption. The Court has had to consider issues concerning parental consent to adoption, the recognition of adoption orders granted in other jurisdictions, the choice of adoptive parents, and the child's right to access information concerning their origins.

Adoption thus provides a compelling case study for the Court's approach to the interaction between parental rights, public policy, and the rights of the children. Unfortunately, as with other areas of the Court's jurisprudence, children are notable more for their absence in the litigation before the Court, and the cases are framed by adults and according to adult interests—even if the welfare of the child is used as a figurehead.

[1] See Hague Conference of Private International Law, 'Adoption Statistics', http://www.hcch.net/index_en.php?act=conventions.publications&dtid=32&cid=69.

[2] European Convention on the Adoption of Children (1967) CETS 58.

[3] European Convention on the Adoption of Children (Revised) (2008) CETS 202.

[4] The 1967 Convention has been renounced by Norway and Sweden, and partially renounced by the United Kingdom.

Children and the European Court of Human Rights. Claire Fenton-Glynn, Oxford University Press (2021). © Claire Fenton-Glynn.
DOI: 10.1093/oso/9780198787518.003.0011

11.2 Second-parent adoption

11.2.1 Consent to second-parent adoption

Second-parent adoption—where a child is adopted by the spouse or partner of their legal parent—is the least controversial of the different types of adoption considered in this chapter, involving as it does a private arrangement, rather than the interference in the family by the child protection authorities. This does not mean that it is without difficulties, however. In particular, the Court has been called upon to decide the relevant test to be applied when a father objects to adoption by the mother's new partner.

In the first case of this kind, *Söderbäck v Sweden*,[5] the Commission applied the same test as it would apply to a child protection case, requiring that the authorities show exceptional circumstances justified by an overriding requirement pertaining to the child's best interests.[6] It noted that the adoption by the mother's husband would totally deprive the father of family life with his daughter, and his personal situation did not warrant the removal of parental rights.

This approach was rejected by the Court, however.[7] The Court distinguished second-parent adoption from a child protection measure, arguing that the former does not concern the severance of links between a mother and child taken into public care, but rather of the links between a natural father and a child who has been in her mother's care since birth. As such, it does not concern a parent who has had custody of the child, or who has in any other capacity assumed care for her.

This distinction appears arbitrary, and seems to reflect an outdated notion of the family, which preferences the stability of the nuclear family unit, rather than recognising the plurality of relationships that characterise modern family forms. Both adoptions following the intervention of child protection authorities and second-parent adoptions involve the severing of family ties without the consent of a parent. The only difference is that in the latter, it is done at the instigation of one of the parents.

Where a father has an existing relationship with the child, it appears incongruous that parental rights should be removed against his will without the authorities needing to show exceptional circumstances. In *Söderbäck*, the father had initially not had contact with the child because of personal difficulties, but had later sought the assistance of the social welfare authorities in arranging access. The case thus involved a father wishing to have a relationship with his child, who was denied this by the child's mother.[8]

Interestingly, the social welfare council in this case, who were ordered to investigate the situation and produce a report for the domestic courts, concluded that adoption was not in the child's best interests. Adoption was not necessary to consolidate the relationship between the child and her mother's husband—he was her psychological

[5] (24484/94) 22.10.1997 (ComRep).

[6] *Johansen v Norway* (17383/90) 07.08.1996.

[7] (24484/94) 28.10.1998 (Court).

[8] This can be contrasted with *Eski v Austria* (21949/03) 25.01.2007, where the father's access rights had been withdrawn as a result of threats towards, and disparagement of, the mother, which were seriously jeopardising the child's well-being.

father, and would probably always remain so, despite the legal situation. On the other hand, it would cut the child off from her origins, and be contrary to her right to know her father and his family.[9]

Unfortunately, however, subsequent cases have followed the Court's reasoning,[10] and it appears settled that the removal of parental authority in order to affect a second-parent adoption will be subject to lesser scrutiny than the same removal in the context of adoption following child protection mechanisms. Indeed, the Court has accepted that domestic law might not even be required to allow the father to contest the adoption. In *Chepelev v Russia*,[11] the Court found no violation of Article 8 in respect of a law which provided that parental consent for adoption was not necessary if, for reasons deemed inadequate, that parent had not been living with the child for more than six months and had failed to care for or support him or her. Unlike *Söderbäck*, the father in this case was not just a natural father, but a legal father as well—the child having been born within wedlock and having lived with both parents until she was 20 months old. Following the parents' divorce, the mother re-married, and the father had had infrequent contact. By the time the mother's new husband applied for an adoption order, the applicant had not seen his daughter in three years—that is, since two months after he moved out of the family home.

The Court noted the existence of strong personal ties between the child and her mother's husband, and that she regarded him as her father. The adoption order could thus be seen as consolidating and formalising existing ties. The domestic courts were of the opinion that the adoption was in the best interests of the child, a decision the Court found fell within the margin of appreciation.

It seems extraordinary that the Court could accept the loss of parental rights on such a basis: this was not a case of the father's consent being overridden—for example, where it was balanced against the child's best interests—he did not even have a right to object. However, this was admittedly not the best test case for this law, given the father's limited relationship with the child and the likelihood that his consent would have been dispensed with in any case.

What it demonstrates, however, is the Court's continuing preference for the conventional family unit—unmarried or divorced fathers can easily lose their parental rights, replaced by the mother's current partner in the formation of a new family. This approach focuses on the consolidation of nuclear family ties, even if it means

[9] On this point, see *Emonet and others v Switzerland* (39051/03) 13.12.2007, concerning a 30-year-old woman who suffered from a serious illness. She required constant care from her mother and her mother's former husband, who had brought her up and who she had always regarded as her father, and it was decided between them that the ex-husband should apply for an adoption order, in order to legalise their relationship and put him on equal footing with the mother in the eyes of the law. This was granted by the courts, but it was only subsequent to this order that the parties realised that in addition to establishing the parent–child relationship between the daughter and her father, it had the effect of terminating the legal parent–child relationship with her mother. The Court rejected the government's argument that the measure was intended to make the child's legal relationships clear, and avoid any conflict of interest that might arise as a result of her new legal status—that of the child of the adoptive parents. While this logic may be valid for minors, it could not be applied equally in a case concerning an adult to whose adoption all the interested parties gave their free and informed consent. As a result, there was a violation of Article 8.

[10] See *Eski v Austria* (21949/03) 25.01.2007.

[11] (58077/00) 26.07.2007.

substituting one member for another. As a result, the Court fails to accommodate and protect the plurality of family forms now existing in modern society. In at least ten member states of the Council of Europe, there are more births outside marriage than within it.[12] Even amongst member states with a lower proportion of births outside marriage, the proportion of such births has risen dramatically in recent decades.[13] At the same time, divorce rates are also increasing, with some European states having a rate of over three in five marriages ending in divorce.[14] It is important that the Court's jurisprudence develops in line with these societal changes, to show that it is, in reality, a 'living instrument'.

11.2.2 Prohibition of second-parent adoption by same-sex partners

With the increasing acceptance and legal recognition of same-sex relationships, the issue of second-parent adoption has taken on an additional dimension. In many European countries, the law traditionally permitted second-parent adoption only by a married partner, thus excluding unmarried couples and civil partners.

This exclusion was challenged in *Gas and Dubois v France*,[15] which concerned a lesbian couple. During the relationship, Ms Dubois gave birth to a daughter, conceived using sperm from an anonymous donor, who was raised from birth as a child of the family. Ms Gas and Ms Dubois subsequently entered into a civil partnership,[16] and Ms Gas applied to adopt the child as a second legal parent. This was refused on the ground that under French law, second-parent adoption is only permitted where the couple is married, which at the time was not possible for same-sex couples in France. The applicants argued that this was a discriminatory interference with their private and family life, in violation of Article 14 in conjunction with Article 8 of the Convention.

The Court rejected the applicants' argument that they were in a comparable situation to a married couple, and therefore should have the same rights in relation to adoption of a partner's child. It noted that the Convention does not require states to grant same-sex couples access to marriage, and where states choose to provide an alternative means of recognition, they enjoy a margin of appreciation as regards to the

[12] Bulgaria, Denmark, Estonia, France, Iceland, the Netherlands, Norway, Portugal, Slovenia, and Sweden. A further nine are between 40 and 50 per cent. (Eurostat, 'Are More Babies Born Inside or Outside Marriage?' (16.04.2018), https://ec.europa.eu/eurostat/web/products-eurostat-news/-/DDN-20180416-1; Organisation for Economic Co-operation and Development (OECD) Family Database, 'SF2.4: Share of Births Outside of Marriage' (29.11.2018), https://www.oecd.org/social/family/SF_2_4_Share_births_outside_marriage.pdf)

[13] For example, the proportion of births outside marriage from 2000 to 2016 has increased eightfold in Cyprus (from 2.3 per cent to 19.1 per cent); tripled in Malta (from 10.6 per cent to 31.8 per cent) and Italy (from 9.7 per cent to 28.0 per cent), and is 2.5 times higher in Spain (from 17.7 per cent to 45.9 per cent) and Greece (from 4.0 per cent to 9.4 per cent). (Eurostat, 'Are More Babies Born Inside or Outside Marriage?' (16.04.2018), https://ec.europa.eu/eurostat/web/products-eurostat-news/-/DDN-20180416-1)

[14] Portugal and Luxembourg. Denmark, Spain, Finland, France, Belgium, Estonia, and the Netherlands are all above 50 per cent. (Statista, 'Divorce Rates in Europe in 2017 by Country' (09.05.2019), https://www.statista.com/statistics/612207/divorce-rates-in-european-countries-per-100-marriages/)

[15] (25951/07) 15.03.2012.

[16] *Pacte civil de solidarité* ('PACS').

exact status conferred. Marriage confers a special status, and has certain social, personal, and legal consequences. Accordingly, the Court found that the applicants' legal situation could not be said to be comparable to that of a married couple.

Instead, the Court compared the applicants to an unmarried opposite-sex couple. Taking a very formalistic approach to the concept of discrimination, it held that since the law applied to all unmarried couples, there was no difference in treatment on the grounds of sexual orientation. It failed, however, to recognise the impact of indirect discrimination—unlike same-sex couples, opposite-sex couples had the opportunity to get married, and therefore be permitted to adopt their partner's children.

This was picked up by Judge Villiger in his dissenting opinion. He argued that the perspective of the judgment was flawed, as it focused on the adults, but not the children whose lives and legal relationships were at the centre of this complaint. In his view, the question that the Court should have asked itself was whether the difference in treatment complained of was justified from the perspective of the child's best interests. He noted that the child of the family was in a comparable situation to that of a child of an opposite-sex couple—in that their parents were in the most committed type of relationship the law permitted—yet under French law the child of a same-sex couple was denied the same opportunities with regard to parenthood. He argued that joint custody is in the best interests of children, and children born into a same-sex relationship should be offered the best possible treatment afforded to children born into an opposite-sex relationship.

The Court returned to this issue the following year in the Grand Chamber decision of *X and others v Austria*.[17] This case was in many ways more straightforward—the Austrian law in question permitted opposite-sex unmarried couples to adopt their partner's child, but not same-sex unmarried couples. As with *Gas and Dubois*, the Court maintained that the applicants were not in a comparable situation to married couples, but *were* in a comparable situation to opposite-sex unmarried couples. By ten votes to seven, the Court found that there had been a violation of Article 14 in conjunction with Article 8: while the Convention does not create an obligation to extend the right to second-parent adoption to unmarried couples, if a state chooses to do so, it cannot be refused on the basis of sexual orientation. The majority further rejected the government's argument that the difference in treatment was justified, as it was aimed at recreating the biological family: although the protection of the traditional family was a legitimate aim, there was no evidence provided to show that it would be detrimental to the child to have two mothers for legal purposes.

For a case that was seemingly so straightforward—following as it does the established case law on the choice of adopters (see section 11.8 below)—the number of dissenting judges is somewhat surprising.[18] Drawing on comparative and international law, they argued that European countries were divided as to whether to allow adoption by same-sex couples, and thus should be given a wide margin of appreciation to decide how best to approach this issue. In this light, these seven judges were highly critical of the majority for what they saw as going beyond the evolutive method of interpretation

[17] (19010/07) 19.02.2013.

[18] They were, in fact, only partly in dissent, as they agreed with the majority that there was no discrimination when compared to married couples.

of the Convention's provisions: they were not reflecting the situation in the member states, but rather anticipating it, and trying to impose their own view on domestic authorities.

This criticism notwithstanding, this judgment should be seen as a strong endorsement of the equality of same-sex couples with opposite-sex unmarried couples. While neither is yet seen as in a similar position to married couples, this judgment suggests that any difference of treatment between unmarried same-sex or opposite-sex couples must be carefully considered. As such, its significance goes beyond second-parent adoption, and may open the door to challenges in relation to 'stranger' adoption, but also wider family law issues. Given the divided nature of the Court, however, such challenges must be approached strategically, and with caution.

11.3 Adoption without parental consent

The Court has long recognised that adoption without parental consent is the most extreme form of interference with family life. As the Court made clear in *Johansen v Norway*, '[s]uch measures should only be applied in exceptional circumstances and could only be justified if they were motivated by an overriding requirement pertaining to the child's best interests'.[19] The Court will therefore in principle require serious justification before allowing an adoption order to be made, and the strictest standard of review will be used. While affording the state a wide margin of appreciation when taking a child into care in the first place,[20] in theory, the Court proclaims to examine much more stringently the need to grant an adoption order.

However, in practice, the 'exceptional circumstances' test has not proved difficult to overcome. When examining whether an adoption order is proportionate and the reasons behind it are relevant and sufficient, the test will be satisfied so long as the state's measures are deemed to be in the best interests of the child.[21] This is coupled with a wide margin of appreciation given to domestic authorities who are in direct contact with the parents and child involved, and are best placed to make a decision concerning the child's welfare.[22]

11.3.1 Positive obligations

The starting point for the Court—as with all cases involving the separation of a parent and child—is the presumption that the interests of the child lie in maintaining ties with their family. This can only be overturned in cases where the family has proved particularly unfit. As discussed in *Gnahoré v France*, 'the interest of the child dictates that family ties may only be severed in very exceptional circumstances and that

[19] (17383/90) 07.08.1996, para. 78.

[20] See Chapter 10.

[21] See S. Choudhry and J. Herring, *European Human Rights and Family Law* (Oxford: Hart 2010), 331–332.

[22] See, for example, *Söderbäck v Sweden* (24484/94) 28.10.1998 (Court).

everything must be done to preserve personal relations and, if and when appropriate, to "rebuild" the family'.[23]

In this way, whether or not adoption without consent will be justified in the circumstances is closely linked to the obligation of family reunification, discussed in Chapter 10. The crucial question is whether the national authorities have taken all the necessary and appropriate measures that could reasonably be expected of them to ensure that the child could lead a normal family life within their own family, before placing them with a view to her adoption. The authorities will have to show that they were justified in permanently severing the bond between parents and child, and that no less radical measure would have been sufficient.

For the most part, the findings of violations by the Court in this area have been on the basis of procedural violations—for example, *Strand Lobben and others v Norway*,[24] discussed in section 11.3.4 below. However, in recent years, the Court has also started to develop a strong line of jurisprudence concerning the proportionality of adoption, in particular where the domestic authorities have failed to provide targeted support to help keep the family together where the child protection concern relates not to direct violence or abuse perpetrated by the parent, but to more indirect causes—for example, financial difficulties within the family.

The positive obligations on domestic authorities regarding children being taken into care as a result of material deprivation were discussed in Chapter 10, and these principles have been found to apply with even more force when the authorities contemplate the permanent dissolution of family ties. For example, in *Soares de Melo v Portugal*,[25] the Court held that as inadequate living conditions and neglect were the main grounds for separation, the authorities should have taken practical steps to allow the children to live with their mother before it had placed them with a view to adoption. The mother was attempting to look after ten children on a monthly state family allowance of €393, a sum that was patently inadequate, yet the authorities did not make any attempt to provide additional financial support. As a result, the adoption was held to violate the parents' rights under Article 8.

Likewise, in *Zhou v Italy*,[26] the child was placed for adoption on the basis that the mother was unable to care for her, having left her in the care of neighbours (who the authorities did not think were appropriate carers) while she was at work. She argued that adoption should be reserved for the most serious cases, and that here, there had been no abandonment or ill-treatment—she was poor, but she was working hard to be able to care for her child. The Court was not convinced that the best interests of the child required adoption. Expert evidence suggested that although the mother was incapable of exercising her role, her conduct was not negative for the child, and as such, the authorities should have taken concrete measures to enable the family tie to be preserved. Adequate measures were not put in place to enable the child to live with his mother—the authorities focused on her difficulties, rather than the means to overcome them.

[23] (40031/98) 19.09.2000, para. 59. See also *Görgülü v Germany* (74969/01) 26.02.2004.
[24] (37283/13) 10.09.2019 (GC).
[25] (72850/14) 16.02.2016.
[26] (33773/11) 21.01.2014.

A similar line of reasoning can also be seen in relation to parents who have suffered mental health problems. The leading case in this area is *SH v Italy*,[27] where the children of a mother suffering from depression were removed from her care, following their hospitalisation on several occasions due to accidentally ingesting her medicine. She admitted that as a consequence of this disease, and the side effects of the medication to treat it, she had difficulties in caring for her children. However, she argued that she would be able to do so with the help of social services and the children's grandfather, and requested that a programme of support be developed to enable the return of the children to the family. The children later returned to the home, but were removed once again when the mother was hospitalised due to a worsening of her illness. Despite the mother arguing that she would soon recover, and in the meantime that the children's father could care for them, the court ordered that the children be placed for adoption.

The Court reiterated that while domestic authorities have considerable discretion in assessing the necessity of taking a child into care, before permanently removing a child from their family they must show that they have carefully assessed the impact that adoption will have on the parents and children, and considered other less drastic solutions.

It emphasised that the children had not been exposed to violence or physical, mental, or sexual abuse, and while it did not doubt the need for intervention to protect the interests of the children, the means of intervention were not appropriate. Solutions other than adoption were feasible: in particular, targeted social assistance would have preserved family ties, whilst ensuring the protection of the best interests of the children. The Court indicated that 'the authorities' role in the social welfare field is, precisely, to help persons in difficulty, to provide them with guidance in their contact with the welfare authorities and to advise them, *inter alia*, on how to overcome their difficulties'.[28] By refusing to consider other less radical solutions that were feasible in this case, the authorities had violated the applicant's rights under Article 8.

This does not mean that the state cannot permanently remove a child on the basis of neglect as a result of mental health difficulties—merely that they must demonstrate that they have taken reasonable steps to help overcome these through targeted social assistance.[29] In doing so, the authorities must be cognisant of the vulnerabilities of the parents—not only in situations of material deprivation and mental health difficulties, but also other sources of vulnerability, for example, where the parent is an immigrant and has little understanding of the legal system.[30]

In light of the obligation on states to remedy transient familial problems, the duty to ensure adequate contact between parents and child bears significant weight. Where conditions in the home have a chance of improving, the authorities must ensure that contact is maintained so that the children can be returned when this occurs. The Court has made clear that the passage of time cannot dictate the necessity of adoption. This

[27] (52557/14) 13.10.2015.

[28] ibid., para. 54 (citations omitted).

[29] See *Zambotto Perrin v France* (4962/11) 26.09.2013; *SS v Slovenia* (40938/16) 30.10.2018, as discussed in Chapter 10.

[30] *KAB v Spain* (59819/08) 10.04.2012; *Akinnibosun v Italy* (9056/14) 16.07.2015; *EP v Italy* (31127/96) 16.11.1999.

was seen in *RMS v Spain*,[31] where the Court found that the decision to place the child in pre-adoption foster care was in violation of Article 8, as this was chosen solely on the ground of lack of contact between mother and child for several years—which was the result of administrative and judicial decisions taken. The child had originally been removed due to the mother's financial difficulties, and the ability of the mother to provide the child with educational and emotional support was not an issue. The refusal to allow any contact between the mother and child breached the positive obligation of the authorities to take measures to reunite the family, and artificially created a situation where adoption was necessary.[32]

A further example is provided by *Pontes v Portugal*.[33] In this case, four of the applicants' children were placed in public care, following reports that the children had been begging and were being neglected by their parents. The three elder children—aged 11, nine, and six at the time of removal—had been placed in a foster home together, and were permitted to return home at weekends. The youngest child, P, aged two, was placed in a separate home 40 kilometres away, where the parents were initially permitted to visit him. Two years later, the elder three children were returned to the care of their parents, but the youngest was placed for adoption, and the parents' contact rights extinguished. Although this adoptive placement was later annulled, by the time this had occurred, the child had been living with his foster family for several years, and had not had contact with his parents during this time. As a result, he had a close relationship with his foster family and no ties with his siblings or parents. In light of this, when the domestic courts came to re-examine the case, it found that it was in the child's interests to be adopted.

The Court found that the authorities were responsible for the progressive deterioration in the relationship between the parents and P, as they failed to take measures to enable the parents to benefit from regular contact with their son. This was particularly the case given the distance between the parents and the home in which the child had been placed.[34] The case of the applicants was strengthened by the fact that the child could be directly compared to his three elder siblings: the domestic authorities had concluded that they could be safely returned to their parents, creating a contradiction in the assessment of the family between the situation of P and his siblings. The Court was not convinced that P was more vulnerable than his brothers and sisters—all had a need for a stable environment for their development, which the authorities had recognised the parents could provide.[35]

The positive obligations on the state are thus two-fold. First, the authorities must ensure that the child is not placed for adoption as a result of difficulties that can be remedied by the reasonable provision of targeted social assistance. Second, contact must be maintained between the parent and child wherever possible, to ensure that adoption does not become necessary merely through the passage of time.

[31] (28775/12) 18.06.2013.
[32] See also *Haddad v Spain* (16572/17) 18.06.2019.
[33] (19554/09) 10.04.2012.
[34] See also *Olsson v Sweden (No. 1)* (10465/83) 24.03.1988 (Court).
[35] cf. partially concurring, partially dissenting opinion of Judges Sajó and Pinto de Albuquerque.

11.3.2 Adoption versus long-term foster care

While the Court starts from the assumption that the child's interests will lie in maintaining their relationship with their family, and in eventual reunification, this position is not absolute. When the child has been in care for a prolonged period, their interest not to have their de facto family situation changed again may override the interests of the parents in family reunification. As long as this situation has not arisen as a result of action (or inaction) by the authorities, and they have taken adequate steps to maintain a relationship between the parents and child, this will not result in a violation of Article 8.

However, in such cases, the question then becomes whether the child should be kept in long-term foster care, thus maintaining the legal tie with the natural family, or whether the child's de facto family ties to their foster parents should be consolidated through adoption, to provide legal protection to the new family.

The leading case on this issue is *Aune v Norway*,[36] where it was clear from the beginning that the parents would not be able to care for their children in the long term. The only question was whether the ties with the foster parents should be formalised. At the core of this case was the threshold for 'necessity'—was it 'necessary' to replace the stable, foster-care arrangements with a more far-reaching measure? What, in such a situation, would constitute 'exceptional circumstances' pertaining to the child's best interests?

On the facts, the Court observed that the social ties between the child and mother were very limited—on account of her own actions and choices—which 'must have implications for the degree of protection that ought to be afforded to her right to respect for family life under paragraph 1 of Article 8 when assessing the necessity of the interference under paragraph 2'.[37] Equally, the expert evidence noted the child's significant need for security and to be certain about his place in the family of his foster parents. In light of this, the Court was satisfied that 'exceptional circumstances' existed in this case.

In *Aune*, the objection of the mother to the finality of adoption was that it would leave contact to the discretion of the adoptive parents.[38] In other cases, the concern of the natural parents has merely been the preservation of the family tie. This was the argument put forward by the mother in *Mohamed Hasan v Norway*,[39] who was not herself unfit to care for her children, but whose husband was physically abusive to both herself and their children. The authorities did not believe that she could protect the children from him, and thus placed them for adoption. Although she did not request that the children be returned to her, the mother did object to the adoption order, on the grounds that the legal tie should be maintained.

The Court acknowledged that the measures taken were far-reaching, but noted that the authorities were clearly motivated by the need to ensure that the children were brought up in a safe environment and by the persons to whom they had become

[36] (52502/07) 28.10.2010.
[37] ibid., para. 69 (citations omitted).
[38] See also *R and H v the United Kingdom* (35348/06) 31.05.2011.
[39] (27496/15) 26.04.2018.

attached. It observed that the domestic courts had compared the advantages of the adoptive placement to permanent foster care, finding that a higher degree of security was important for the children in light of their vulnerability. They had been subject to a number of child welfare measures, including emergency placements, and experienced several broken relationships, and thus their need for a stable and predictable placement was of increased importance. In such a case, the children's best interests outweighed the mother's rights under Article 8.[40]

This can be contrasted with *Abdi Ibrahim v Norway*,[41] which took a very different approach. This case involved a refugee mother who was 16 years old when her child was born. She had challenges caring for him, and he was placed into care as a result of neglect, and a lack of emotional contact and security. The mother did not question that continued foster care was in her child's best interests, but wanted to avoid adoption due to the finality of the measure. Moreover, the foster parents were opposed to post-adoption contact, so adoption would mean that the mother would not be granted the right to have any contact with her child in the future.

As with both *Aune* and *Mohamed Hasan*, the contact that the child had with his mother was very minimal, and the evidence suggested that he would be harmed by removal from the foster family. However, in this case, the Court did not accept the conclusion of the authorities that long-term family reunification was not possible. While accepting that the child could not be returned to his mother in the short or medium term, it criticised the authorities for failing to take 'real measures' to facilitate long-term reunification, before deciding to pursue the most far-reaching measure of adoption. Although the mother had not challenged the contact regime before the Court, it observed of its own accord its minimal nature, and suggested that this was contrary to the principle that contact ought to 'guard, strengthen and develop' family ties. Despite accepting that evidence presented before the domestic courts had indicated that the child had had negative reactions to contact with the mother, the Court criticised the methodology behind this conclusion. It suggested that the sparse contact permitted by the authorities provided limited experience from which to draw clear conclusions in respect of contact in the future, and noted that little had been done to clarify the causes of the child's reactions, whether they could be treated, or whether the quality of contact could be improved. As such, the Court found that there was insufficient evidence to suggest that contact between the mother and child would remain negative on a long-term basis, nor to conclude that a decision to permanently break off all contact would really be in the child's best interests.

The analysis of the Court in this case focused on a particular form of adoption. While the initial stages of the judgment seem to object to the adoption on the grounds that there might be some possibility of future reunification, the latter part appears to suggest that the problem lies with the type of adoption being proposed—that of 'closed adoption', without any continuing post adoption contact. In this context, the Court noted

[40] See also *SS v Slovenia* (40938/16) 30.10.2018.
[41] (15379/16) 17.12.2019.

> the reasons given in the [domestic court's] decision focused largely on the potential effects of removing X from his foster parents and returning him to the applicant rather than on the grounds for terminating all contact between X and the applicant. In this respect, the [domestic court] appears to have given more importance to the foster parents' opposition to 'open adoption' than to the applicant's interest in continued family life with her child.[42]

Either way, this case appears to signal a shift in the Court's approach to such issues, examining the decision-making process and reasoning behind an adoption order in more detail than previously was the case.[43]

11.3.3 Procedural obligations

Although the Court has started to develop stronger jurisprudence in the area of positive obligations, parents still face an uphill battle to succeed on such grounds, in light of the margin of appreciation given to authorities. This is, however, counter-balanced by the robust procedural guarantees inherent in Article 8, the content of which was neatly summarised in *YC v the United Kingdom*:

> [W]hat has to be determined is whether, having regard to the particular circumstances of the case and notably the serious nature of the decisions to be taken, the parents have been involved in the decision-making process, seen as a whole, to a degree sufficient to provide them with the requisite protection of their interests and have been able fully to present their case. Thus it is incumbent upon the Court to ascertain whether the domestic courts conducted an in-depth examination of the entire family situation and of a whole series of factors, in particular of a factual, emotional, psychological, material and medical nature, and made a balanced and reasonable assessment of the respective interests of each person, with a constant concern for determining what would be the best solution for the child. In practice, there is likely to be a degree of overlap in this respect with the need for relevant and sufficient reasons to justify a measure in respect of the care of a child.[44]

The obligations on authorities in this regard mirror those in child protection cases. The right to legal assistance,[45] the right to have access to material relied on by the authorities,[46] and the right to be adequately involved in decision-making[47]—discussed at length in Chapter 10—apply equally to adoption. However, the Court will undertake

[42] ibid., para. 63.
[43] cf. *R and H v the United Kingdom* (35348/06) 31.05.2011.
[44] (4547/10) 13.03.2012, para. 138 (citations omitted).
[45] *P, C and S v the United Kingdom* (56547/00) 16.07.2002; *Soares de Melo v Portugal* (72850/14) 16.02.2016.
[46] *P, C and S v the United Kingdom* (56547/00) 16.07.2002.
[47] *W v the United Kingdom* (9749/82) 08.07.1987.

a higher level of scrutiny of the actions of the authorities when the final outcome of the proceedings is the complete termination of family ties between parent and child.[48]

The Court has found violations of the Convention where the proceedings have been excessively lengthy;[49] but also where they have been completed too quickly, without careful analysis of the impact of the decision on the parties.[50] Procedural violations have also been identified in cases where the authorities have failed to obtain expert evidence on the relationship between the child and parent,[51] or failed to update it,[52] and where the courts have merely reproduced the same decisions without making new findings or assessing the evolution of the circumstances.[53]

While these provide important safeguards for both parents and children, the Court's focus on procedural violations at the expense of a more rigorous evaluation of the substantive issues has been the subject of criticism by commentators and litigants alike.[54] As Lavrysen has argued, there is an increasing reliance on procedural review by the Court, which results in the micromanaging of domestic processes rather than providing guidance on substantive issues.[55] Describing this as an 'organised retreat',[56] he wonders whether the substantive principles espoused by the Court are still worth the paper they are written on, giving their unwillingness to assess the substance of such cases.[57]

This line of reasoning was propounded by the applicants themselves in *Strand Lobben and others v Norway*, who accused the Court of 'hid[ing] behind the margin-of-appreciation concept in a way which could to some extent undermine its control and functions'.[58] *Strand Lobben*, which is discussed further below in relation to the best interests of the child, was a case that was deemed so significant by other states and non-governmental organisations that there was a total of 11 third-party interventions. By focusing on the procedural failings of the authorities—the lack of up-to-date assessments of the mother—the Court side-stepped the crux of the case: the highly interventionalist nature of the domestic child welfare system, permanently removing children from their families far more readily than would other European jurisdictions.[59] The Court thus provided a remedy for the individual mother in

[48] *B v the United Kingdom* (9840/82) 08.07.1987; *YC v the United Kingdom* (4547/10) 13.03.2012.

[49] *EP v Italy* (31127/96) 16.11.1999.

[50] *SH v Italy* (52557/14) 13.10. 2015.

[51] *EP v Italy* (31127/96) 16.11.1999.

[52] *Strand Lobben and others v Norway* (37283/13) 10.09.2019 (GC).

[53] *Haddad v Spain* (16572/17) 18.06.2019.

[54] *Strand Lobben and others v Norway* (37283/13) 10.09.2019 (GC).

[55] L. Lavrysen, 'Strand Lobben and Others v. Norway: From Age of Subsidiarity to Age of Redundancy?' (Strasbourg Observers, 23.10.2019), https://strasbourgobservers.com/2019/10/23/strand-lobben-and-others-v-norway-from-age-of-subsidiarity-to-age-of-redundancy/.

[56] A reference to a phrase coined by O.M. Arnardóttir, 'Organised Retreat? The Move from "Substantive" to "Procedural" Review in the ECtHR's Case Law on the Margin of Appreciation' (2015) 5(4) *European Society of International Law Conference Paper Series* 4/2015.

[57] L. Lavrysen, 'Strand Lobben and Others v. Norway: From Age of Subsidiarity to Age of Redundancy?' (23.10.2019), https://strasbourgobservers.com/2019/10/23/strand-lobben-and-others-v-norway-from-age-of-subsidiarity-to-age-of-redundancy/.

[58] (37283/13) 10.09.2019 (GC), para. 162. See also the third-party intervention of the Government of Bulgaria, who urged the Court to 'go beyond the form' and assess the substance of the case.

[59] See the third-party intervention of the Government of Slovakia, and of the Government of Belgium in *Strand Lobben and others v Norway* (37283/13) 10.09.2019 (GC). See also C. Fenton-Glynn, *Adoption without Consent* (Strasbourg: European Union, 2016), 3.2.6.

question—although as six years had passed between her application and the judgment, this was limited to an award of financial damages—but failed to address the structural issues that were at the heart of the case. The violation could be easily brushed away by the Norwegian authorities as fact specific, a one-off occurrence, obviating the need for wider change on the domestic level.

This does not mean that this decision, and others like it, are devoid of value. While the procedural guarantees that the Court has delineated under Article 8 may seem obvious—up-to-date expert opinions, a thorough and careful analysis of facts, adequately reasoned judgments—the fact that so many cases of this kind have come before the Court is evidence of the important role that it plays in this area. Moreover, there are some indications that the Court might be willing to take a more proactive approach—as discussed in section 11.3 above in relation to adoption on the basis of material deprivation or mental illness.[60] However, for the majority of cases, the Court remains a bit part actor, punishing minor infractions, while ignoring the systemic issues. In the area of child protection, the Court cannot see the wood from the trees.

11.3.4 The best interests of the child

The evolution of the Court's approach to children's rights in the child protection context was discussed in Chapter 10, where the proportionality test under Article 8(2) has progressed from a focus on parental rights, to the balancing of competing interests, and finally, to recognising children's interests as the paramount consideration.

The jurisprudence on adoption plays an important role in this transformation, particularly in the final shift to children as the paramount consideration—in line with the UN Convention on the Rights of the Child.[61] Until 2011, adoption cases were decided on the basis of the *Johansen* test—attaching particular importance to the best interests of the child in question, 'which, depending on their nature and seriousness, may override those of the parent'.[62] While *Neulinger* was a blow to this principle's supremacy, that was a private law case, where the domestic authorities had been deciding between two competing parents: child protection cases, involving a dispute between the parents and the state, are of a different nature.[63] However, *Neulinger* was swiftly followed by the adoption case of *R and H v the United Kingdom*,[64] which firmly placed children's interests at the centre of decision-making in the field of child protection,

[60] While the decision of *Abdi Ibrahim v Norway* (15379/16) 17.12.2019 may at first glance appear to be a move towards stricter scrutiny of the substantive issues, even in this case the Court characterised the violation as a procedural one, noting that the 'decision-making process leading to the impugned decision to withdraw the applicant's parental responsibilities for X and authorise his adoption, was conducted so as to ensure that all views and interests of the applicant were duly taken into account'. (para. 64)

[61] Article 21 on adoption is the only clause of this Convention where children's rights are not merely primary, but paramount.

[62] *Johansen v Norway* (17383/90) 07.08.1996, para. 78.

[63] Of course, by the time the issue comes before the Court, all cases involve a dispute between one individual and the state. Nevertheless, the question at domestic law, and the competing rights that need to be considered, remain relevant to the test applied by the Court.

[64] (35348/06) 31.05.2011.

finding that when balancing the competing interests under Article 8, 'the interests of the biological parents must inevitably give way to that of the child'.[65]

This case involved a child who was taken away from their family at birth, and for whom the domestic court saw no possibility of return. The natural parents did not object to adoption in and of itself, but wanted to be assured that any adoptive parents would agree to post-adoption contact. However, this was not possible due to the nature of the Northern Irish legal system, under which adoption proceedings were divided into two parts. The first step involved the removal of parental rights ('freeing order'), after which prospective adoptive parents would be identified and the child placed with them. The adoption order was then made in a second set of proceedings. The applicants complained that by removing their parental rights, the freeing order prevented them from participating in the subsequent adoption hearing, and was thus contrary to their rights under Article 8.

The Court observed that there were sound practical reasons for the two-stage process in domestic law, given the difficulty of finding suitable adoptive parents and the reluctance of many prospective adopters to consider adoption where birth parents are opposed to it. It held that if there was a pressing need to place the child for adoption, and freeing a child by removing parental rights makes it easier to find adoptive parents, then a freeing order will be in the child's best interests. Moreover, while the Court acknowledged that it would be in the interests of the parents to participate in the adoption proceedings, if the chances of a successful adoption were jeopardised by this, then the interests of the parents must cede to those of the child.[66]

This position was further strengthened by the case of *YC v the United Kingdom*,[67] which concerned an English adoption. England is one of the few jurisdictions in Europe where parental objection to adoption can be overridden on the basis of the child's best interests:[68] in deciding whether to make the adoption order, these must be 'the paramount consideration'.[69] There have been queries whether such a regime, focusing as it does exclusively on children, and without the recognition of any independent parental rights, could be considered compatible with the Convention[70]—queries that were put to rest in this judgment. The Court reiterated that 'in cases

[65] *R and H v the United Kingdom* (35348/06) 31.05.2011, para. 77. See also *YC v the United Kingdom* (4547/10) 13.03.2012. For further commentary on this line of cases, see C. Simmonds, 'Paramountcy and the ECHR: A Conflict Resolved?' (2012) 71(3) *Cambridge Law Journal* 498.

[66] This analysis fails to question whether in fact it was in the child's best interests to be adopted. As Judge Kalaydjieva pointed out in his dissenting opinion, a reasonable determination of a child's best interests can only be based on a comparison between the current situation of the child (and the extent to which it calls for separation from the biological parents) on the one hand, and the extent to which the child's interests would be better met with the candidate adoptive family on the other. Moreover, there were often large gaps of time between the child being freed for adoption and an adoptive placement being found—if one was found at all. This left children in a legal void, deprived of their link with their biological family, but with no other family tie to replace it.

[67] (4547/10) 13.03.2012.

[68] See C. Fenton-Glynn, 'Adoption without Consent: 2016' (European Parliament, 2016), http://www.europarl.europa.eu/RegData/etudes/STUD/2016/556940/IPOL_STU(2016)556940_EN.pdf. Although the authorities must still provide evidence that the threshold criteria for state intervention has been met: that is, that the child is suffering, or likely to suffer, significant harm, attributable to the care given.

[69] Section 1(2) Adoption and Children Act 2002.

[70] J. Herring, 'The Human Rights Act and the Welfare Principle in Family Law—Conflicting or Complementary?' (1999) 11(3) *Child and Family Law Quarterly* 223.

concerning the placing of a child for adoption, which entails the permanent severance of family ties, the best interests of the child are paramount'.[71] In doing so, it referred specifically to the provision of domestic law that requires paramountcy, and stated that the considerations listed in this section 'broadly reflect the various elements inherent in assessing the necessity under Article 8 of a measure placing a child for adoption'.[72]

Although the Court does not examine the law *in abstracto*, and focuses on the particular circumstances of the individual case, this judgment provided a strong endorsement of an adoption system which focuses solely on the rights of children, to the exclusion of parental rights.[73] However, the Court appears to have backtracked on this position in its recent judgment of *Strand Lobben and others v Norway*,[74] where the Court criticised the domestic authorities for focusing on the interests of the child at the expense of the mother. Reverting to the test from *Johansen*,[75] the Court required the authorities to 'perform a genuine balancing exercise between the interests of the child and his biological family'.[76]

As was discussed in Chapter 10, this case represents a severe blow to children's rights under the Convention. This is not to say that parents should not have any rights at all in the process. The protection of parents' procedural rights is particularly important to ensure a bulwark against unnecessary state interference with the family. However, on a substantive level, the child's interests must be determinative. As the Court stated in *Johansen* itself: 'the parent cannot be entitled under Article 8 of the Convention to have such measures taken as would harm the child's health and development'.[77] Family reunification and contact with children in care must occur for the purpose of, and to the extent it promotes, the *child's* best interests. Adoption is the one area under the UN Convention on the Rights of the Child in which children's interests are required to be paramount. Not only is no such 'balancing exercise' needed: no such exercise is warranted.

11.3.5 Recognising fathers in the adoption process

The rights of fathers under the Convention have been largely shaped by two important decisions in the field of adoption. The first, *Keegan v Ireland*,[78] involved an unmarried father whose child was adopted without his knowledge. He had been cohabiting with the child's mother at the time of the pregnancy, and afterwards they became engaged to be married, but the relationship broke down soon after. The applicant visited the child once after her birth, before the mother unilaterally placed her for adoption. As an unmarried father, the applicant had to petition the court to be appointed a guardian

[71] *YC v the United Kingdom* (4547/10) 13.03.2012, para. 134. Although it referenced *Johansen v Norway* in doing so, thus undermining its position somewhat.
[72] ibid., para. 135.
[73] Although the interests of parents are considered, to the extent that they impact on children's welfare.
[74] (37283/13) 10.09.2019.
[75] *Johansen v Norway* (17383/90) 07.08.1996, para. 78.
[76] *Strand Lobben and others v Norway* (37283/13) 10.09.2019, para. 220.
[77] *Johansen v Norway* (17383/90) 07.08.1996, para. 78.
[78] (16969/90) 26.05.1994.

to his child, which would have enabled him to challenge the adoption, but this was denied.

As discussed in Chapter 8, the Court found that 'family life' existed between the father and his child: Article 8 encompasses de facto family ties where the parties are living together outside of marriage, in a relationship that bears the 'hallmarks' of family life. By showing a commitment to the mother—through their cohabitation, decision to start a family, and plan to marry—the Court found that, as a matter of fact, a bond amounting to 'family life' between the father and child existed. It was clear that the secret adoption of his child, without his knowledge or consent, constituted an interference with this family life. The only question was whether this was justified under Article 8(2).

The government argued that the interference pursued the aim of protecting the child's health, as well as her rights and freedoms. In deciding whether to appoint the applicant as a guardian, the first and paramount consideration of the domestic courts was the welfare of the child. The Court accepted this, and was satisfied that the applicant was afforded an opportunity to claim guardianship and custody of his daughter, and that his interests were fairly balanced in the evaluation of her welfare. The problem was not this assessment, however, but the fact that the domestic law permitted the child to be placed for adoption shortly after birth, without his being informed or his consent being sought. Once the child was placed with alternative carers, she began to form new bonds with them, making it more difficult to reverse this decision. By allowing this, the law jeopardised the proper development of the father's ties with his child, but also set in motion a process that was likely to prove irreversible. By the time the case came before the courts, the applicant was at a significant disadvantage in his contest with the prospective adopters for the custody of his child.

While this judgment was a positive step forward for the rights of unmarried fathers, it was a somewhat pyrrhic victory. While acknowledging the right of all fathers to be involved in adoption proceedings concerning their children, the Court implicitly accepted the difference in treatment between unmarried and married fathers in the establishment of parental rights. Under Irish law, married fathers acquired guardianship as of right, whereas unmarried fathers had to seek the permission of the courts. While the Court did not address this issue head on—declining to consider the case under Article 14, and instead focusing on Articles 6 and 8—in accepting the mere possibility for the unmarried father to gain guardianship as satisfactory, the Court tacitly accepted their inferior position.

This implicit acceptance became explicit in the subsequent case of *McMichael v the United Kingdom*,[79] which involved an unmarried father who complained about his insufficient involvement in the child protection proceedings which led to his child's adoption. As with *Keegan*, the domestic law at the time required an unmarried father to apply to obtain parental rights, in contrast to the automatic rights given to a married father. The applicant in this case had not sought an order in this respect, and as a result, was not joined as a party to the child protection proceedings, and was unable to access documents concerning the case.

[79] (16424/90) 24.02.1995.

The Court rejected his complaint under Article 14 in conjunction with both Article 6 and Article 8. In a very conservative judgment, it held that the relationship between unmarried fathers and their children will vary, from 'ignorance and indifference' to a 'close stable relationship indistinguishable from the conventional matrimonial-based family unit'.[80] The domestic authorities were justified in establishing a mechanism to identify 'meritorious' fathers, who were worthy of being granted parental rights, thereby protecting the rights of both the child and the mother.

As discussed in Chapter 10, although a difference of treatment between unmarried and married fathers was found to be justified in respect of assigning parental rights, the Court nevertheless found that—regardless of legal status—the father had a right to involvement in the proceedings. In its initial examination of the case, the Commission had found that the domestic proceedings did not comply with Article 8, in that they failed to disclose relevant documents. While the government accepted this conclusion in respect of the mother, it contended that the father's position was not equivalent—unlike the mother, he had no entitlement to be an associated party in the domestic proceedings.

The Court noted that at the time of the domestic proceedings, the applicant and the child's mother were living together, and leading a joint 'family life', and had acted in concert in their endeavour to recover custody of the child. As such, it would not reflect the reality of the situation to distinguish between the procedural rights of the mother and father, and therefore there had been a violation of both their rights. This difference in treatment was examined purely under Article 8, however, and there was no discussion of a possible violation of Article 14 with regard to this distinction.

While these cases are problematic from the perspective of the establishment of parental rights, they provide a strong framework for the protection of father's rights in relation to adoption proceedings. Even if unmarried fathers do not have to be granted equivalent legal status, they must be involved in the decision-making processes in the same way as any other parent who has established 'family life' with their child.

11.3.6 Conclusions on adoption without consent

Adoption without parental consent is one of the most controversial issues that the Court faces in the field of children's rights. While I have argued that the Court has failed to grasp the opportunity offered to it in this area, by focusing on procedural rights to the exclusion of substantive issues, it has nevertheless developed some important safeguards for children and families.

First, and foremost, the elevation of children's rights to the paramount consideration, and the recognition that when balancing the competing interests in the field of adoption, 'the interests of the biological parents must inevitably give way to that of the child',[81] is of great significance. Although *Strand Lobben* has started to draw back from this principle, reverting to the lesser protection of 'depending on their nature

[80] ibid., para. 98. This was expressly approved of in *B v the United Kingdom* (39067/97) 14.09.1999.
[81] *R and H v the United Kingdom* (35348/06) 31.05.2011, para. 77.

and seriousness',[82] it nevertheless has been an important advancement for children's rights under the Convention.

Second, the Court has placed positive obligations on the authorities to take adequate steps to achieve family reunification. This includes maintaining contact where appropriate so that adoption is not made necessary through the mere passage of time, but also ensuring sufficient assistance to families suffering from transient problems that can be remedied by the reasonable provision of targeted social assistance.

Finally, the procedural obligations developed by the Court have been expansive. The obligation to ensure parents are adequately involved in decision-making—including fathers who enjoy 'family life' with the child—is even more strictly applied in the case of adoption, given that it will involve the complete termination of family ties.

In this way, and despite its significant flaws, the Court has made a positive contribution to the protection of children's rights when involved in an adoption without parental consent.

11.4 Providing consent to adoption

While the majority of cases that have come before the European Court of Human Rights have dealt with non-consensual adoption, there have been a small number of cases that have considered the requisite conditions for giving valid consent to a voluntary adoption. While as yet none of these has been successful, the reasoning of the Court in these cases is important in defining the scope of the positive obligations inherent under Article 8 to ensure that consent is given freely, and is sufficiently formed.[83]

This can be seen especially in the case of *Kearns v France*,[84] which involved an Irish woman who travelled to France and requested an anonymous birth under French law. The day after the child's birth, she signed the record placing the child in state care. Although she did not read or speak French, a nurse and doctor acted as interpreters and explained the process to her. Three months later, the child was placed for adoption with a new family; however, soon after, the mother returned to the hospital seeking the return of her child. When this was refused, as the two-month time period within which she could revoke her consent had passed, she made an application to the Court alleging a violation of her right to respect for family life under Article 8. She argued that the French authorities had a positive obligation to make all necessary arrangements to ensure that she understood the precise implications of her actions, including a clear and accurate translation of the technical legal provisions concerning her.

The Court rejected her argument, noting that she had specifically travelled from Ireland to France to take advantage of the anonymous birth laws in that jurisdiction, which were not available in her home country. She had visited the maternity ward prior to birth, assisted by a lawyer, and the Court found that the presence of this legal

[82] *Johansen v Norway* (17383/90) 07.08.1996.

[83] See Article 21 UN Convention on the Rights of the Child; Article 5(2) European Convention on Adoption (Revised) (2008) CETS 202.

[84] (35991/04) 10.01.2008.

specialist created a presumption that she was provided with legal information even before the birth. Furthermore, it held that the presence of a doctor and nurse with knowledge of English was sufficient: Article 8 cannot be construed as requiring the authorities to ensure the presence of qualified interpreters.

While this application was unsuccessful, this rested in large part on the decision of the applicant, an Irish national, to travel to France, and the fact that she did have the assistance of her own lawyer prior to the child's birth. As such, it leaves the door open to the possibility that the Court may find, in the right factual circumstances, that there is an obligation on the state to take positive measures to ensure that birth parents sufficiently understand the consequences of placing a child for adoption. This case made clear that sufficient information and advice in a language that the parent can understand is still vital, even if these conditions were satisfied in the particular circumstances. It is arguable that a mother who was already living in the country concerned and did not understand the procedure, due to language difficulties or the complicated nature of the law in this area, would be in a strong position to claim a violation of Article 8.

The issue of the state's positive obligations with regard to obtaining valid consent was again raised in *IS v Germany*.[85] In this case, the birth mother had conceived the children (twins) as a result of an extramarital relationship and had been placed under pressure by her husband to have the children adopted. She reported feeling overwhelmed by the situation and the decisions to be taken, and during the pregnancy she received psychological treatment for depression, suicidal tendencies, and panic attacks. The children were placed for adoption shortly after birth, and she gave her consent for their adoption seven months later. While the issue before the Court related to post-adoption contact and no violation was found in this respect, Judge Zupančić in dissent highlighted the positive obligations on the state to ensure independent evidence of the applicant's capacity to consent to the adoption, given that they were aware that she was receiving psychological treatment relating to the difficult decision she was facing. He observed that the authorities 'were obliged to dispel any doubts as to her capacity to make a free and informed consent prior to encouraging and facilitating the adoption of her children', and once on notice of her vulnerability, were obliged to ensure independent expert evidence of her capacity to consent. While this issue was not considered by the majority, given that the mother was not challenging the validity of the adoption, it does open the door for future challenges.

In deciding whether the mechanisms for giving consent are surrounded by appropriate safeguards, the Court has also considered the timing of consent and the opportunity of the mother to be heard by the domestic authorities. This was seen in *Todorova v Italy*,[86] where a mother gave birth to twins, but on the day of their birth requested that she not be legally recognised as their mother, and that her name not be revealed. At the time, she was residing illegally in Italy, alone and unemployed, and was suffering from psychological distress. Four days after this, the mother requested time to reflect before deciding whether or not to recognise her children, and asked that they

[85] (31021/08) 05.06.2014. See also section 11.9.
[86] (33932/06) 13.01.2009.

be placed in a temporary family or placement until she could make a decision. Despite this, 27 days after the children's birth, the courts declared them adoptable, without hearing the mother.

The Court found that it was essential for the applicant to be able to speak to the domestic court and explain the choice to abandon her children. This shortcoming prevented the mother from being sufficiently involved in the entire decision-making process, and meant that there had been a violation of the procedural aspects of Article 8. Although the Court recognised that the interests of the children required that their future be decided as soon as possible, it found that such speed was not necessary in this case, and that the interests of the children did not require 'a measure as radical as the declaration of adoptability 27 days after birth, without hearing the [mother]'.

The Court found that there was a positive obligation on the state under Article 8, stating:

> [I]n disputes of this nature, where the consequences are of extreme importance as they affect the family relationship, the State had a positive obligation to ensure that the consent given by the applicant to the abandonment of her children was informed, and had been surrounded by adequate safeguards.[87]

The mother in this case also relied on Article 5(4) of the European Convention on Adoption (Revised) 2008, which requires that a mother's consent to adoption cannot be given sooner than six weeks after birth, in order for her to recover sufficiently from the effects of giving birth to the child. The government, on the other hand, argued that this was not a case about the validity of the mother's consent, but a case concerning dispensing with the mother's consent on the grounds of abandonment. The Court did not resolve this issue, referring to 'consent to abandonment', and focusing instead on the obligation to ensure the mother could participate in proceedings. However, there remain several countries in Europe that still permit consent to be given to adoption before six weeks has passed,[88] meaning that the issue could arise again in subsequent cases.

The final aspect of parental consent considered by the Court relates not to its provision, but to its revocation. Where consent to adoption has been validly given, in what circumstances may it be revoked? This arose in *Kearns v France*,[89] discussed above. In addition to arguing that she had received insufficient information to allow her to give consent to the adoption, the birth mother also argued that the time period of two months for withdrawing her consent was insufficient, and thus interfered with her right to respect for family life. The Court emphasised the lack of consensus among member states concerning adoption: while some allow consent to be revoked within a certain period, in others, it is automatically binding. As a result, the state has a margin of appreciation in balancing the interests of the biological mother with those of the child; however, in doing so, the child's interests must be paramount. The Court found that it was in the interests of the psychological and legal stability of the child to seek a

[87] ibid., para. 82.
[88] Bulgaria, Slovakia, Slovenia, and Spain.
[89] (35991/04) 10.01.2009.

new family as quickly as possible, and France had not overstepped its margin of appreciation by restricting revocation to two months.

This decision is hardly surprising, as a year previously the Court had found a complaint against Germany manifestly ill-founded, in which a mother challenged a refusal to allow her to revoke her consent. In *VS v Germany*,[90] a 16-year-old girl had given her consent to the adoption of her ten-month-old child, but later wished to revoke this, claiming she had been put under pressure to give her consent and deeply regretted her actions. The Court ruled that although consent was generally irrevocable in Germany, it was possible to annul the consent in certain circumstances, namely if the individual lacked capacity at the time of giving consent, that consent was given within eight weeks after birth, that the individual did not realise what they were consenting to, or that they had been influenced by unlawful threats, or by fraud, to give consent.[91]

Again, the Court considered the variance of practices in European states concerning the revocation of consent. It emphasised that states hold a wide margin of appreciation, and so long as the various interests at stake have been balanced, it will be reluctant to interfere. In this case, the German courts had held extensive hearings into whether the girl's consent had been valid, and the Court found that they had appropriately balanced the interests of the child, the mother, and public policy in this regard. While only an admissibility decision, this case is important, as the revocation laws of Germany are the strictest in Europe in this respect (along with Portugal)—other states allowing for revocation before a certain time period, or before a certain event has occurred—and it thus seems unlikely that other more lenient laws will be found contrary to Article 8.[92]

11.5 Respect for religious and philosophical convictions

One issue that is of great importance in decisions of domestic authorities, but which has received little attention from the Court, is the weight to be given to the child's background in deciding the most appropriate form of alternative care. Article 20(3) of the UN Convention on the Rights of the Child requires that '[w]hen considering solutions, due regard shall be paid to the desirability of continuity in a child's upbringing and to the child's ethnic, religious, cultural and linguistic background', and the issue has been the subject of considerable controversy on a domestic and intergovernmental level.[93] Nevertheless, this issue has not gained traction before the Court, in large part because the nature of the Court as a supranational body and the margin of appreciation given to domestic decisions makes it difficult to draw any clear lines.

[90] (4261/02) 22.05.2007 (dec.).

[91] Article 1760(2) Civil Code.

[92] See C. Fenton-Glynn, *Children's Rights in Intercountry Adoption: A European Perspective* (Cambridge: Intersentia, 2014), 4.1.1.

[93] See C. Fenton-Glynn, 'Adoption without Consent: 2016' (European Parliament, 2016), http://www.europarl.europa.eu/RegData/etudes/STUD/2016/556940/IPOL_STU(2016)556940_EN.pdf.

In early cases, the Court tried to deny the applicability of any Convention right in such cases. For example, in *X v the United Kingdom*,[94] the Commission held that the right enshrined in Article 2, Protocol 1 relates to public education, and so long as the child is not of an age to benefit from this, the right is merely a potential one, and cannot be infringed by the state. As such, the mother of a child who was placed for adoption could not argue that she had been denied the right to bring up the child as she wished.[95]

This was also seen in the private law decision of *X v Sweden*,[96] where a father was denied custody following divorce and was refused all access to his children. He complained that this prevented his children being educated in accordance with his cultural and religious background. The Commission emphasised that 'the right to determine the mode of a child's education is an integral part of the right of custody which in the present case has been removed from the applicant', and thus there was no case for the state to answer.[97]

Later cases have taken a more nuanced approach, recognising that the placement of a child in public care does not nullify the parents' rights under Article 2, Protocol 1 completely. This was discussed by the Commission in *Olsson (No. 1)*,[98] whose conclusion was endorsed by the Court (if not explicitly the reasoning behind it). Here, the Commission considered that the decision to take a child into care is of a different character from the removal of custody—a care order does not imply that the right of custody is removed, simply that the authorities take over the responsibility for the actual care of the child for a period of time. The Commission emphasised that a care order is of a temporary nature, with the aim that the children should eventually be returned to their parents. As a result, the right of the parents under Article 2, Protocol 1 is not removed, but reduced, and authorities still have an obligation to take their wishes into account where possible.[99]

Nevertheless, such an obligation does not require that the placement *conforms* with the parents' convictions, merely that these are taken into account as a relevant factor when deciding where to place the child. As such, they must be balanced against other considerations, which might outweigh them in the particular circumstances. This was illustrated by the case of *Tennenbaum v Sweden*,[100] where the children of a Jewish couple were taken into care and placed in a Protestant foster home. The Commission held that it was sufficient that the authorities had attempted to find a foster home that complied with the parents' religious convictions, but were entitled to conclude that this desire should be balanced against the delay to the

[94] (7626/76) 11.07.1977 (dec.).

[95] The Commission further noted that in the period prior to the adoption, the mother had not appeared to be concerned about the religious and philosophical convictions of the adopters, and expressed the view that in reality, her refusal of consent to the adoption was not based on the adopters' ideas or beliefs, but on her inability to have further children.

[96] (7911/77) 12.12.1977 (dec.).

[97] See also *X v the Federal Republic of Germany* (2699/65) 01.04.1968 (dec.); *X v the United Kingdom* (5608/72) 14.12.1972 (dec.).

[98] (10465/83) 02.12.1986 (ComRep).

[99] See also *Nowacka v Sweden* (12805/87) 13.03.1989 (dec.).

[100] (16031/90) 03.05.1993 (dec.).

placement of the children, and the need to find a home that was not so far away as to prevent the parents having a realistic possibility of maintaining contact.

The most comprehensive examination of the weight to be given to the parents' religious and philosophical beliefs was seen in the Commission decision of *ED v Ireland*.[101] In this case, both the biological father and mother were members of the travelling community, and placed great weight on their culture and heritage. Although the father admitted that neither he nor any member of the child's biological family could adequately care for the child at the current time, he argued that an adoption would mean the loss of the child's access to his 'true' identity. He also argued that he and the child's mother would lose their right to educate the child in traveller culture, history, and identity. Instead, he argued, the state should have placed the child in long-term foster care, where he would have felt the security of a long-term placement without losing his heritage, and upon adulthood he could choose which life he wished to lead.

The Commission held that it was within the state's margin of appreciation to decide that the child's need for a permanent family was greater than the need to maintain his cultural heritage, It observed that the domestic court could have refused the adoption if it believed that the child would have been better in long-term foster care, but had concluded that the benefit to the child of removing any 'residual insecurity in the child by reason of the fear that he might be removed from the foster parents' outweighed any loss of his heritage.

This deferential approach can be contrasted with the recent case of *Abdi Ibrahim v Norway*,[102] involving a Muslim mother who objected to her child being adopted by a Christian family who did not wish for post-adoption contact. She argued that this violated her right to freedom of religion, as it would inevitably involve the child's forced conversion to Christianity. While the Court did not address this issue head on, focusing instead on issues of family reunification, in the second to last paragraph, the Court noted 'other particular reasons that in the instant case militated in favour of maintaining the possibility of some contact between [the child] and the [mother], notably relating to their cultural and religious background'.[103] This is hardly a strong statement of principle, but it is the first time that the Court has indicated that a child's cultural background may be a justification for refusing to allow adoption—or at least requiring post-adoption contact.[104]

[101] (25054/94) 18.10.1995 (dec.).

[102] (15379/16) 17.12.2019.

[103] ibid., para. 64.

[104] The importance of contact for preserving a child's cultural identity was also discussed in *TS and JJ v Norway* (15633/15) 11.10.2016 (dec.), where the grandmother of a child taken into care argued that in limiting her contact, the authorities had failed to duly consider the need to preserve the child's Polish identity. This complaint was dismissed on the grounds that the child had shown little interest in his cultural heritage and did not wish for greater contact with his grandmother, but the Court left the door open for future cases that were stronger on the facts.

11.6 Intercountry adoption

11.6.1 Recognition of foreign judgments

While intercountry adoption did not rise to global prominence until the 1990s, as early as the 1970s the Commission was faced with challenges concerning the recognition of foreign adoption decisions in member states. In *X and Y v the United Kingdom*,[105] the applicant and his wife—both British nationals—adopted their 14-year-old nephew while on a visit to India. However, the British authorities refused the child's entry into the United Kingdom on the grounds that although the adoption was valid under Indian law, it was not recognised in the United Kingdom, as there had been no genuine transfer of parental responsibility. The adoption was performed not because the nephew had no one to care for him, but because the couple were unable to have children of their own. As such, he was refused a visa to return with the couple to the United Kingdom. Even from this early stage, the Commission made clear that Article 8 only protects *existing* family life, and does not oblige a state to grant a foreign citizen entry to its territory for the purposes of establishing a new family relationship there. In deciding whether 'family life' exists, the Commission stated that it will take into account, inter alia, whether the parties have lived together and whether they are financially dependent on each other. In this case, the Commission placed great weight on the fact that the child's natural parents were still willing and able to care for him, and thus the adoption was for the benefit of the parents, not the child.

A different approach has been taken in more recent decisions concerning intercountry adoption, however, most notably in the case of *Wagner and JMWL v Luxembourg*.[106] This case involved a single woman who was a Luxembourg citizen, who travelled to Peru to adopt a child. The adoption order was granted by the Peruvian courts, but the mother's attempt to have this recognised as a full adoption upon her return to Luxembourg failed. The domestic courts noted that the Luxembourg rules of private international law designate that the adoption by a Luxembourg citizen must be governed by Luxembourg law. Since single persons were only able to obtain a simple adoption order under Luxembourg law, the full adoption in Peru could not be recognised.

A claim was brought before the Court by the mother, both for herself, and on behalf of her child. The Court found that there had been a violation of the right to respect for family life under Article 8 of the Convention, as the domestic authorities had failed to take into account the social reality of the child and the family's situation. It noted that there was an advanced stage of harmonisation in member states concerning single-parent adoption—about the only area in which there is consensus in the field of adoption—and as such, the margin of appreciation given to the Luxembourg authorities was narrowed. The Court held that the applicants were suffering disadvantages in their daily lives, and the child was not granted the legal protection that would make it possible for her to be fully integrated into the adoptive family. Taking into

[105] (7229/75) 15.12.1977 (dec.).
[106] (76240/01) 28.06.2007.

account the best interests of the child, which the Court emphasised should prevail in such cases, it was found that the Luxembourg courts could not reasonably disregard the legal status validly created abroad, and the corresponding 'family life' that existed within the meaning of Article 8.[107]

The final case on recognition of foreign adoption, *Negrepontis-Giannisis v Greece*,[108] concerned the adoption of an adult man by his uncle—a bishop in the Greek orthodox church—while he was living in his care in the United States. Subsequently, both returned to Greece, where the adoptive father died. Shortly afterwards, the Greek courts recognised the US adoption order, and found that it was legally enforceable in Greece; a decision that held great importance for the son's inheritance rights. The family of the adoptive father challenged this decision, and the Court of Appeal upheld the appeal on the grounds that monks are prohibited from carrying out legal acts that relate to secular activity such as adoption, as it is incompatible with monastic life and contrary to the principles of Greek public policy, despite there being no provision in law which stated this. The adoptive son applied to the Court, who found that there had been a violation of Article 6, Article 8, Article 14 in conjunction with Article 8, and Article 1, Protocol 1. The Court maintained that although the decision was based on the legitimate aim of protecting public order and morality, it was not proportionate to a pressing social need, as monks were now permitted to marry and found a family. Since a biological child born to the adoptive father could not have been deprived of his rights, nor so could the adopted child. More importantly, for the purposes of this chapter, the Court held that in cases of foreign adoption, national courts cannot reasonably disregard a legal status validly created abroad, nor the corresponding 'family life' under Article 8 to which this legal status gives rise.[109]

11.6.2 The conversion of kafalah to adoption

The practice of kafalah originates in the Sharia, and involves a commitment to maintain, educate, and protect a child in the same way a birth family would. Given the importance of family bonds under Islamic law, kafalah falls short of adoption, providing a long-term alternative care option for children where their biological family can no longer care for them, while preserving the child's family status. As with adoption, kafalah is practised differently in different jurisdictions, but all have in common the assumption of parental responsibility and the obligation of maintenance.

[107] The Court also found a violation of Article 14, in conjunction with Article 8, on the grounds that prior to the applicant's adoption application, all Peruvian adoptions, including those by single parents, were automatically approved. It was only at the time of her application that new rules were applied to strictly scrutinise judgments. The Court found that the child had a right not to be treated differently from other children who had been the subject of a full adoption in Peru, and thus the refusal to recognise a full adoption under Luxembourg law was in violation of the Convention. It is notable that at the time that the facts in this case occurred, the 1993 Hague Convention on Protection of Children and Co-operation in Respect of Intercountry Adoption 1993 was not yet in force between Peru and Luxembourg. Had it been so, the problems arising in this case would have been avoided.

[108] (56759/08) 03.05.2011.

[109] See also Chapter 8 on surrogacy.

Where difficulties arise, however, is where children are entrusted to guardians under a kafalah system in one jurisdiction, who then want to convert this into an adoption order under their own domestic law. This was first addressed in *Harroudj v France*,[110] where the applicant, a French national, was granted an order of kafalah over a three-month-old Algerian child. She subsequently brought the child back to France, and two years later applied to adopt her in that jurisdiction. This was rejected by the French courts on the grounds that the French Civil Code does not permit a child to be adopted where his or her country of origin prohibits the practice—as Algeria does.[111] The applicant complained that the refusal to legally recognise the filial bond established between herself and the child was a violation of her right to respect for family life under Article 8.

Although the Court acknowledged that there was 'family life' between the applicant and the child, it did not accept that there had been any interference with this right. The applicant's parental authority was recognised by French domestic law, and although the child would experience difficulty accessing French nationality and would not have equivalent inheritance rights, the Court found that these problems were not insurmountable. Moreover, the Court considered that the refusal of the adoption order was based on the concern of the domestic authorities to abide by international conventions. In particular, the domestic courts referred to Article 20 of the UN Convention on the Rights of the Child, which expressly recognises kafalah as a form of alternative care, on a par with adoption, and requires that in deciding the most suitable form of alternative care, the child's ethnic, religious, cultural, and linguistic background must be taken into account. The Court held that the French authorities had put in place flexible arrangements that accommodated the law of the child's state of origin and the rights of the child under international law. The law sought to encourage the integration of the child into France without cutting her off from her country of origin, and struck an appropriate balance between cultural pluralism and respect for the mother's family life.

This decision was followed two years later by the case of *Chbihi Loudoudi and others v Belgium*.[112] In this case, a married Belgian couple were entrusted with the care of their niece in Morocco under a kafalah arrangement. A deed of simple adoption was drawn up by a notary in Belgium, but the Belgian courts refused to approve this. The Court of Appeal confirmed that the statutory conditions were not met for an adoption, as the child had not been entrusted to the couple by the competent authorities as required for an intercountry adoption under the 1993 Hague Convention on Intercountry Adoption,[113] and had instead been placed by the child's parents. Furthermore, the requested adoption would create a legal parent–child relationship that was not constituted by the kafalah arrangement, and would therefore create a new legal status. The couple argued before the Court that the Belgian authorities had acted to the detriment of the child's best interests, contrary to their right to respect for private and family life.

[110] (43631/09) 04.10.2012.

[111] Article 46 of the Algerian Family Code.

[112] (52265/10) 16.12.2014.

[113] Hague Convention on Protection of Children and Co-operation in Respect of Intercountry Adoption 1993.

With a narrow majority of four votes to three, the Court held that there had been no violation of the Convention. Although it was acknowledged that the couple and child had been living together in a manner that could not be distinguished from 'family life' in its ordinary meaning, and thus fell within Article 8, the refusal to grant the adoption did not deprive them of all opportunity of establishing a legal relationship, as the procedure of unofficial guardianship was open to them. The applicants had also not identified any practical obstacle they would have to overcome as a result of the situation. The refusal pursued the legitimate aim of preventing the improper use of adoption, and the Belgian authorities were entitled to hold that the refusal was in the child's best interests as it would create a different personal status, and parent–child relationship, in Belgium and Morocco.

In dissent, Judges Karakaş, Vučinić, and Keller pointed out that although kafalah as an institution is largely unknown to the legal orders of the member states of the Council of Europe, in countries where Islamic law is applied, it fulfils a largely similar purpose to that of simple adoption. The functional proximity of kafalah and adoption is reflected in their inclusion in Article 20 of the UN Convention on the Rights of the Child, which deals with both practices as equivalent forms of protection for the care of a child. As such, these judges argued that this situation should have been treated in the same way as the situation in *Wagner and JMWL v Luxembourg*.

This argument is flawed on numerous levels. First, Article 20, in addition to adoption and kafalah, in the same sentence mentions foster placement and the placement of children in institutional care. It is clear that all these options are not considered analogous, and are not substitutable one for another. Second, as discussed above, in *Wagner* a full adoption order had been granted in the foreign jurisdiction, and the question was whether the mother should be given equal rights in Luxembourg, or lesser rights. *Chbihi Loudoudi* involved the converse situation, where only certain limited rights had been granted in the foreign jurisdiction, and the applicants were now seeking greater rights under their own domestic law.

As such, the Court's approach to the conversion of kafalah to adoption appears to strike an appropriate balance between the protection of the original intent of the placement, the laws in the child's country of origin, and the development of new family ties.

11.6.3 The enforcement of an adoption order

The only time the Court has considered the obligations on the state concerning enforcement of an adoption order—either domestic *or* intercountry—involved the case of *Pini and others v Romania*.[114] This case is of particular importance, as it is one of the few where the Court explicitly discusses the balancing of rights between children and adoptive parents—and because it comes down heavily in favour of the children's rights.

This case concerned two young Romanian girls who were adopted by Italian couples. The institution in which the children were living challenged the adoption

[114] (78028/01, 78030/01) 22.06.2004.

order, and applied for a stay of its execution, in a number of proceedings lasting several years. Attempts to enforce the order by bailiffs failed, following obstruction by staff of the institution. The adoptive parents complained before the Court that the failure to enforce the adoption order had breached their right to respect for family life under Article 8, as well as constituting a violation of Article 6.

As discussed in Chapter 8, the Court recognised that 'family life' existed between the applicants and children—even though the applicants had never met the children in the capacity of parents, and did not have close de facto ties with them. It was enough that there was a relationship arising from a lawful and genuine adoption and an intention to create 'family life'. The question was whether the national authorities took the necessary steps to enable this family life to flourish.

In examining this issue, the Court acknowledged the competing interests of the applicant adoptive parents and the adopted children. It recognised the desire of the applicants to create a new family relationship, but maintained that that this could not enjoy absolute protection. It was clear that the children preferred to stay in the institution where they had grown up, into which they were fully integrated, and which was conducive to their physical, emotional, educational, and social development. In light of this, the Court noted that, '[t]here are unquestionably no grounds, from the children's perspective, for creating emotional ties against their will between them and people to whom they are not biologically related and whom they view as strangers'.[115]

The Court 'deplore[d]' the manner in which the adoption proceedings were conducted, and found it 'particularly regrettable' that the children did not receive any support in preparing them for joining their new family, nor had any real, effective contact with the adoptive parents before the order was made. Such measures, the Court suggested, 'would probably have made it possible for the applicants' interests to converge with those of their adopted children, instead of competing with them as occurred in the present case'.[116]

Nevertheless, the Court found that there was no justification for imposing on the Romanian authorities an absolute obligation to ensure that the children joined the adoptive parents against their will. Significantly, and in line with Article 21 of the UN Convention on the Rights of the Child, the Court suggested that in cases of adoption, it was 'even more important that the child's interests should prevail over those of the parents', since, as it has previously held, adoption means 'providing a child with a family, not a family with a child'.[117]

The curious thing about this case was that despite this finding that the authorities did not have an obligation to force the children to join the adoptive parents, the Court nevertheless found a violation of Article 6 in the failure to execute the adoption order. In this respect, the Court reiterated that enforcement of decisions of this kind require urgent handling, as the passage of time can have irremediable consequences. Despite this, the proceedings to enforce the adoption order took four years, and the actions taken by the bailiff were wholly ineffective. The Court held that it is for the state to take the necessary steps to enable bailiffs to carry out their tasks, particularly by ensuring

[115] ibid., para. 153.
[116] ibid., para. 163.
[117] ibid., para. 156 (citations omitted).

effective participation of other authorities that may assist enforcement—for example, the police. It further noted that no sanctions had been taken in respect of the lack of cooperation of the institution, nor were there any repercussions for the Director, who had obstructed the bailiff. As a result, the adoption orders were deprived of their binding force and remained 'mere recommendations', contrary to the rule of law and of legal certainty and in violation of Article 6.

A number of judges in dissent objected to this different approach to the findings under Article 6 and Article 8. Judge Loucaides argued that the Court should have found a violation of both articles, as the problems with enforcement under Article 6 led directly from a failure of the authorities to adequately prepare the children for adoption under Article 8. In contrast, Judge Bîrsan maintained that neither article was breached, as the considerations concerning the children's rights were as relevant to a finding of Article 6 as they were to the dismissal of the claims under Article 8.

It does appear that the Court's approach to Article 8 in this case was out of step with the rest of its jurisprudence. Unlike other cases, which have focused on the procedural failings of the authorities that led to the outcome, the Court focused on the outcome itself, and whether this would be in line with Article 8. It would have been perfectly possible to find that the authorities had violated their obligations to facilitate family life, through a lack of adequate preparation and the failure to enforce the adoption order, without finding that there was an obligation to force the children to join the adoptive parents against their will. What is of real significance here is the weight given to the children's wishes—if not at the time of the adoption order, then at least afterwards.

11.7 The involvement of children in adoption proceedings

The jurisprudence concerning the involvement of children in adoption proceedings is distressingly thin. The only case which has explicitly considered the child's consent to adoption has been that of *Pini and others v Romania*,[118] discussed in section 11.6 above. Even then, this was a peripheral issue—the main concern being their refusal to join the applicants after the adoption proceedings had been completed.

The two girls in this case were nine-and-a-half years old when they were placed in intercountry adoption without their views being sought. Under the law at the time the adoption order was made, the consent of the child was only needed once they reached ten years of age, but by the time the adoptive parents tried to enforce the decision (which was being contested by the orphanage in which the children were living) the girls were between ten and 12. As such, the Court ruled that they 'had reached an age at which it could reasonably be considered that their personality was sufficiently formed and they had attained the necessary maturity to express their opinion as to the surroundings in which they wished to be brought up',[119] and could not be forced against their will to form an alternative family.

[118] (78028/01, 78030/01) 22.06.2004.
[119] ibid., para. 157 (citations omitted).

The part of the judgment concerning the enforcement of the adoption order provides a strong statement on the rights of children. While the Court recognised the desire of the adoptive parents to create a new family relationship with the children, it maintained that this could not enjoy absolute protection, in so far as it conflicted with the children's refusal. Despite this, however, the judgment remains flawed.

In particular, it is notable that the majority of the Court did not question the fact that the children were not asked for their consent to the adoption, other than observing that ten did not appear to be an 'unreasonable' age limit for this. In doing so, the Court relied on the international instruments, suggesting that they provide some discretion as to the age at which children are to be regarded as sufficiently mature for their wishes to be taken into account. This is a somewhat misleading account of the international obligations. While it is true that the issue of the child's consent is left to the discretion of the authorities, there is nevertheless an obligation to give consideration to the child's wishes and feelings, having regard to their age and degree of maturity. As such, although their views need not be determinative, at the very least, they must be elicited and considered. At the time of the order, the girls were only six months away from their consent being obligatory under domestic law, yet they were not even heard in the proceedings. In relation to the enforcement of the order, the Court noted that '[t]here are unquestionably no grounds, from the children's perspective, for creating emotional ties against their will between them and people to whom they are not biologically related and whom they view as strangers'.[120] However, they did not go on to apply this same logic to the order itself.

This was criticised by Judge Thomassen in her dissenting opinion.[121] She noted that:

> It does not appear from the evidence that they were ever asked for their opinion, either directly in an interview with a judge or a counsellor or indirectly through expert assessments which would have provided an opportunity to ascertain their views and feelings about the adoption in practical terms.

Although the ultimate decision in this case was the right one, the methodology was flawed, and reinforced the practice of states in operating on the presumption that children under a certain age lack capacity. The failure to recognise children's evolving capacities, as well as their right to participate in decision-making concerning their lives, has allowed states to continue to maintain patriarchal characterisations of children as needing protection, rather than being deserving of autonomy.

11.8 Selecting adoptive parents

From its earliest cases, the Court has consistently made clear that the Convention does not give individuals a 'right' to a child, and cannot be interpreted as safeguarding the mere desire to found a family—by adoption or any other means.[122] In the case of *X v*

[120] ibid., para. 153.

[121] Joined by Judge Jungwiert.

[122] Nor does a refusal to allow an adoption constitute inhuman and degrading treatment under Article 3: see *X v Netherlands* (8896/80) 10.03.1981 (dec.).

Belgium and the Netherlands[123] in 1975, the Commission observed that adoption is not a 'fundamental right which is analogous to an individual freedom'[124] and therefore there was no requirement that a state provide a process for facilitating adoption. The Commission held that

> a State cannot separate two persons united by an adoption contract, or forbid them to meet, without engaging its responsibilities under Article 8 of the Convention. But one should not deduce from this a positive obligation on the State to grant a particular status—that of adoption—to the applicant and the person in his care.[125]

This case concerned a challenge to a Dutch law which prohibited single persons from adopting, and the applicant relied on Article 12 of the Convention, citing the right to found a family as providing the ground for his claim. The Commission emphasised that Article 12 'does not guarantee the right to have children born out of wedlock', and that the 'right to marry and to found a family' must be seen as one simple right, rather than joint and severable. Moreover, even if this were not the case, the Commission pointed out that Article 12 refers to the right of 'men and women' to have children, and thus the existence of a couple is a fundamental precondition to the exercise of that right. As such, the Commission held that 'the adoption of an adolescent by an unmarried person cannot lead to the existence of a family life in the meaning of the Convention'.[126]

While the decision in this case may appear to be based on outdated notions of the family (and particularly in its reference to 'wedlock'), these basic principles have been a consistent feature of the Court's decision-making ever since—although the language is slightly more nuanced. The most recent case in this respect is *Schwizgebel v Switzerland*,[127] which concerned a single woman seeking to adopt a foreign child. This was refused, on the grounds that the age gap between the prospective mother and the child was too great. Relying on Article 14 in conjunction with Article 8, the prospective adopter complained that she had been discriminated against in comparison with other women of her age, who could give birth on their own. The Court found that there was no difference in treatment in relation to women of the applicant's own age who were able to give birth, as this was a situation over which the state had no control. However, there was a difference in treatment between the applicant and younger or married women, who could adopt. Nevertheless, the Court gave the Swiss authorities a wide margin of appreciation in this case, given the considerable variation between laws concerning single-parent adoption in member states.[128] It was satisfied that the Swiss decision was based on the legitimate aim of protecting the well-being and rights of the child, and was proportionate to achieving that aim.

123 (6482/74) 10.07.1975 (dec.).
124 ibid., p. 77.
125 ibid.
126 ibid. See also *Di Lazzaro v Italy* (31924/96) 10.07.1997 (dec.).
127 (25762/07) 10.06.2010.
128 While this is permitted in all member states, the conditions in which it can occur vary greatly.

While this case was unsuccessful, the application of Article 14 has been crucial in this area of law. Although there is no right to adopt, if the state does permit adoption it must do so on equal terms, without discrimination. This was seen in the 1981 decision of *X v the Netherlands*,[129] where the Commission held that while it is up to national law to determine whether, and subject to what conditions, adoption should be permitted, any conditions on prospective adoptive parents must pursue an objective and reasonable purpose, and be proportionate to achieving that aim. In this case, the difference in regulations between domestic adoptions and intercountry adoptions—which only allowed intercountry adoption when the child was under school age—was justified, as it had the legitimate aim of ensuring that the foreign children could integrate into Dutch society and minimise detrimental effects arising from their removal from their country of origin.[130]

This can be contrasted with *AH and others v Russia*,[131] where the Court found that a blanket ban on intercountry adoption by US nationals was incompatible with Article 14 in conjunction with Article 8. Although the Court did not question the authority of a state to discontinue intercountry adoptions, either partially or completely, it emphasised that it could not do so on a discriminatory basis. Having initiated adoption procedures at a time when Russia permitted US nationals to apply for intercountry adoption, the Court found that applicants could reasonably have believed that their applications would be assessed fairly on the merits. The government failed to show compelling or weighty reasons for a blanket ban, applied retroactively and indiscriminately to all prospective parents for the United States, no matter the status of the adoption proceedings or their individual circumstances.

Importantly from a child rights perspective, the Court noted that no consideration was given by the Russian authorities to the interests of the children concerned. While some were eventually placed in different families, after additional—and unnecessary—periods of time in institutional care, others were still in orphanages at the time of the Strasbourg judgment four years later.

The most significant cases of the Court in this area, however, have focused on the situation of single, homosexual adopters and whether they should be permitted to adopt on an equal basis with single, heterosexual adopters. These cases have been important not just for the field of adoption law, but also for the role they have played in progressing the recognition of LGBTQ rights under the Convention.

The Court has examined this issue on two occasions, coming to vastly different conclusions in each. The first case, *Fretté v France*,[132] concerned an individual who wished to adopt a child as a single man, as was permitted under French law. In its report on the suitability of Mr Fretté as an adoptive parent, the social services report concluded: 'Mr Fretté has undoubted personal qualities and an aptitude for bringing up children.

[129] (8896/90) 10.03.1981 (dec.).

[130] The Commission did leave open, however, whether the requirement that there be an age difference not exceeding 40 years between the prospective adoptive parents and child was compatible with the Convention—a situation the Court has not returned to in the 35 years since, despite the fact that this criteria exists in many European jurisdictions.

[131] (6033/13, 8927/13, 10549/13, 12275/13, 23890/13, 26309/13, 27161/13, 29197/13, 32224/13, 32331/13, 32351/13, 32368/13, 37173/13, 38490/13, 42340/13, 42403/13) 17.01.2017.

[132] (36515/97) 26.02.2002.

A child would probably be happy with him. The question is whether his particular circumstances as a single homosexual man allow him to be entrusted with a child.' The Conseil d'Etat agreed, finding that he 'did not provide the requisite safeguards—from a child-rearing, psychological and family perspective—for adopting a child'. Mr Fretté challenged this before the Court, claiming that his rights under Article 14, in conjunction with Article 8, had been violated by refusing permission to adopt on the grounds of his sexual orientation.

The Court emphasised that a difference in treatment is discriminatory only if it has no objective and reasonable justification, it does not pursue a legitimate aim, or if the means employed to realise this aim are disproportionate. The government argued that the justification for this decision lay in the paramountcy of the child's best interests, which formed the underlying basis for all adoption legislation. As the government pointed out, 'the rights of the child set the limits of the right to have children'.[133] The Court found that states possess a wide margin of appreciation in this area, due to the sensitive social issues that the case raised, and the fact that it was not possible to find any uniform principles in the legal and social orders of member states. It also emphasised that the law was in a transitional phase, and that the scientific community—and particularly experts on childhood, psychiatrists, and psychologists—was divided on the consequences for a child of being adopted by one or more homosexual parent. As such, the Court found that the justification given for the difference in treatment was objective and reasonable, and not discriminatory within the meaning of Article 14.

This decision was incredibly controversial, not least within the Court itself, with three of the seven judges dissenting. In a strongly worded opinion, Judge Sir Nicholas Bratza and Judges Fuhrmann and Tulkens argued that Mr Fretté's application to adopt had been rejected based solely because of his 'choice of lifestyle' and not because this choice would pose any actual threat to a child's interests. They rejected any link between the aim pursued—the protection of the rights of the child—and the specific reasons given for the rejection of the application to adopt, as there was no reference in the case file to anything that would endanger the child. They concluded that there was no reasonable and proportionate relationship between the methods used—the total prohibition of adoption by homosexual parents—and the aim pursued—to protect children. It took the form of an irrebuttable presumption, without any real consideration of the interests at stake, or the situation of the persons concerned, and therefore constituted a violation of Article 14.

It was this dissenting opinion that was endorsed when the Grand Chamber returned to the issue six years later, in the case of *EB v France*.[134] Here, the applicant was an unmarried homosexual woman, but unlike Mr Fretté, Ms EB was in a stable relationship at the time of her application. The refusal of her application to adopt was based on two grounds: first, that her partner was not sufficiently committed to the adoption; and second, that the child would lack a paternal role model in the household.

While the Court accepted that the first ground was a legitimate concern and by itself would justify a refusal, the second ground was more problematic, as it ran the risk

133 ibid., para. 36.
134 (43546/02) 22.01.2008 (GC).

of rendering ineffective the right of single persons to apply for authorisation to adopt. The ground might therefore lead to an arbitrary refusal, and serve as a pretext for rejecting Ms EB's application on the grounds of her sexual orientation. While the lack of a 'paternal referent' may be a legitimate factor to be taken into account in general, where the state permits single parents to adopt, it cannot then rely on this factor. The Court held that where two grounds were relied on to reject an application for adoption, it was sufficient for one of them to be invalid for the decision to be in violation of the Convention.

This reasoning, like that in *Fretté*, was subject to intense criticism—both academic and judicial.[135] In total, seven of the seventeen judges dissented on this judgment, relying on a variety of different reasons. Judge Costa, joined by Judges Türmen, Ugrekhelidze, and Jočienė, argued that although the majority was right in principle—it is a violation of the Convention to prevent a person from seeking to adopt merely on the grounds of his or her sexual orientation—on the facts before the Court, this was not the case. They argued that requiring a male 'referent' was a bizarre requirement, given that single adoption was permitted, but applied equally to heterosexual and homosexual applicants, and was therefore not based on sexual orientation.

Judge Loucaides, on the other hand, objected to the reasoning of the majority on the issue of 'contamination'—that is, that because one ground was invalid, so was the whole decision. He argued that the grounds that led to the decision were separate and autonomous, and its effectiveness was in no way dependent on, or linked to, the other one.

This reasoning is flawed for two reasons. First, it was not possible to separate out the two different grounds in this case—they were not autonomous, as Judge Loucaides suggested, but both played a part in the overall decision to refuse the application. The Court cannot retrospectively try to determine whether, absent the objection to the lack of male referent, the application would still have been refused. Second, even if the grounds were autonomous, this should not preclude the Court deciding that the use of one of those grounds violated the Convention. A nuanced judgment could acknowledge that the domestic authorities were incorrect to rely on the applicant's sexual orientation, and thus were in violation of the Convention in this respect, but that this did not mean that the entire decision was flawed.[136]

Judge Loucaides was also the only judge to argue that refusal to allow a person in a same-sex relationship to adopt actually pursued a legitimate aim—in his view 'the erotic relationship with its inevitable manifestations and the couple's conduct towards each other could legitimately be taken into account as a negative factor in the environment in which the adopted child was expected to live', and he held that there was 'a real risk that the model and image of a family in the context of which the child would have to live and develop his/her personality would be distorted'. Although he accepted that homosexuals, 'like anybody else', have a right to be themselves and should not be the target of discrimination or any other adverse treatment, he argued that they must 'like any other persons with some peculiarity, accept that they may not qualify for certain

135 See, for example, A. Bainham, 'Homosexual Adoption' (2008) 67(3) *Cambridge Law Journal* 479.
136 Although it must be acknowledged that this is not what the majority did.

activities which, by the nature and under some circumstances, are incompatible with their lifestyle or peculiarity'. Judge Loucaides was right, in so far as he argued that personal characteristics might provide a justification for the state to deny them access to a certain activity, if there is evidence to show that there is a connection between that characteristic and their ability to carry out the activity in question. Where his reasoning falls down, however, was in establishing any connection between homosexuality and lack of capacity for child rearing, rather than relying on outdated prejudices.

Finally, Judge Zupančič, in his dissent, argued that adoption is a privilege and not a right. Discrimination in terms of unequal treatment, he argued, is applicable only to situations that involve rights—it is not applicable to situations that concern privileges. He used the analogy of the granting of a prize, claiming it would be bizarre for anyone to claim that they ought to have received a particular award. He did consider that it would be possible to imagine discrimination where a certain prize committee never awarded the prize to applicants of a particular race or nationality; however, for this to be established, statistical evidence would be needed. The Court in this case was dealing with an individual case of discrimination, alleged purely on the basis of a single occurrence. This, Judge Zupančič argued, does not permit the Court to reach the conclusion that there is a general discriminatory attitude in France against homosexuals wishing to adopt a child.

With due respect, the Court was not being asked to identify a general discriminatory attitude in this field, nor should they be required to do so. The application does not need to show that a 'prize' is never awarded to persons with protected characteristics—it is a violation of the Convention if simply one person is denied consideration of a benefit that they would otherwise be eligible to receive.

This case demonstrates a marked shift in attitudes towards homosexual parenting in Europe. While *Fretté* allowed the government to focus on the aim of 'protecting' children from homosexual parents, such arguments were not given any weight by the Court six years later—with the marked exception of Judge Loucaides. Despite the strong, and numerous, dissenting opinions, it now appears well established that where single persons are permitted to adopt (which all European jurisdictions now do), a refusal to allow a single homosexual applicant to do so will violate the Convention.

Overall, what we can see from the cases on the selection of adoptive parents is that a claim based on Article 8 or Article 12 alone will be difficult to substantiate. Even if there is already a de facto relationship between the prospective adoptive parent and child (as there was in *X v Belgium and the Netherlands*), the Court has yet to find that the state has an obligation to legally recognise these ties.[137] On the other hand, a claim under Article 14 in conjunction with Article 8 has greater potential—the Court has now firmly acknowledged that where the state extends a privilege to its citizens, it cannot draw unjustified distinctions in doing so. This is in line with the more recent jurisprudence concerning second-parent adoptions, and in particular, *X and others v Austria*, discussed in section 11.2.2 above.

[137] See also *X, Y, and Z v the United Kingdom* (21830/93) 22.04.1997 (GC).

In the area of adoption, where there is such divergence in domestic law, and states have been consistently afforded a considerable margin of appreciation, the Court may be reluctant to interfere with the criteria for adoptive parents. However, *EB v France* demonstrates that this reluctance has its limits, and states will have to provide strong evidence to show that there is a connection between the criteria used and the paramount interests of children that the criteria aims to protect. Vague and unfounded stereotypes will no longer be accepted.

11.9 Post-adoption contact

Post-adoption contact has become an extremely important issue in recent times, and has been the subject of significant academic debate.[138] However, it is not an issue that has arisen before the Court on many occasions. Where it has been discussed, it has concerned objections to the adoption itself, based on the unwillingness of the adopters to allow post-adoption contact,[139] or alternatively, members of the wider family who wished to maintain contact following an adoption.[140]

The most comprehensive discussion of this issue, however, arose in *IS v Germany*.[141] This case concerned a mother who had fallen pregnant following an extra-marital affair. Her husband threatened to leave her if she did not give the children (twins) up, and she thus consented to their adoption. She later sought contact with the children, but this was resisted by the adoptive parents. She argued before the Court that her consent to the placement of her children for adoption did not automatically end their 'family life': she had waived her rights as a legal parent, but not as a natural mother. At the very least, contact with the children and information about their well-being formed part of her 'private life'.

The Court found that the relationship between the mother and her children did not fall within the scope of 'family life' under Article 8. While 'family life' existed at the time of the child's birth, this had been intentionally and voluntarily severed by the mother when she gave the child up for adoption.[142] However, it mitigated this position by acknowledging that the determination of ties between a biological parent and child will always concern the parent's identity, and thus fall within the scope of 'private life'.

The Court observed that by not providing a right to contact with, and information about, the adopted children, the German authorities pursued the legitimate aim of protecting the adopted child's private and family life, by safeguarding the child's right

[138] See, for example, M. Ryburn, 'A Study of Post-Adoption Contact in Compulsory Adoptions' (1996) 26(5) *British Journal of Social Work* 627; E. Neil, 'Coming to Terms with the Loss of a Child' (2006) 10(1) *Adoption Quarterly* 1; E. Neil, 'Post-Adoption Contact and Openness in Adoptive Parents' Minds: Consequences for Children's Development' (2009) 39(1) *British Journal of Social Work* 5; B. Sloan, 'Post-Adoption Contact Reform: Compounding the State-Ordered Termination of Parenthood?' (2014) 73(2) *Cambridge Law Journal* 378; E. Neil, M. Beek, and E. Ward, *Contact after Adoption* (London: CoramBAAF, 2015).

[139] See section 11.3.2 above.

[140] See, for example, *Price v the United Kingdom* (12402/86) 14.07.1988 (dec.); *GHB v the United Kingdom* (42455/98) 04.05.2000 (dec.).

[141] (31021/08) 05.06.2014.

[142] See Chapter 8 for greater discussion of the dissolution of 'family life'.

to develop and bond with the adoptive parents. The only question was whether a refusal in this case was proportionate. The mother argued that before the adoption took place, the adoptive parents, the authorities, and the applicant had agreed to a 'half open adoption'—where the applicant would be informed of the children's development, and would be able to meet them twice a year—and thus she had a legitimate expectation that this would occur. This was disputed by the government, who emphasised that the arrangement for a 'half open' adoption was a mere declaration of intent, which was not enforceable against the adoptive parents' will—in line with the intention that the adoptive parents should have freedom in the exercise of their custody rights.

The Court accepted this argument, and found that the applicant had understood the nature of these arrangements as unenforceable, and had been informed by an independent lawyer about the legal consequences of the adoption. The German authorities were entitled to attach greater weight to the interests of the adoptive family to enjoy and build a family undisturbed by the attempts of the biological parents to re-establish contact.

The reasoning of the Court in this case relied heavily on the fact that the mother had voluntarily consented to the adoption of her children, and thus had to accept the legal consequences.[143] It is not clear whether similar reasoning would be applied if the child had been placed for adoption contrary to her wishes. The only indication we have in this regard are the cases discussed in section 11.3.2 above, where the ability to continue to have post-adoption contact was considered as a factor in whether adoption without consent was proportionate. There is yet to be a direct challenge by parents to a refusal to grant post-adoption contact following a compulsory adoption, and it will be interesting to see how the Court approaches this difficult issue.

11.10 Revocation of adoption

There have been a number of cases where both parents and children have complained that their adoption has been revoked against their wishes. The first case of this kind, *X v France*,[144] was unusual in that it involved a dispute between the adoptive parent and natural mother. The applicant and his wife had adopted the five-year-old boy, with his mother's consent, but following the wife's death and the applicant's remarriage, he had provisionally entrusted the then 12-year-old child to his natural mother. When he asked for the return of the child two years later, the natural mother refused, and at her request, the applicant's parental authority was withdrawn.

The Commission observed that the relationship between an adoptive parent and child should be afforded the same protection under Article 8 as a natural family. This, the French law did—drawing no distinction between adoptive and natural parents as

[143] cf. *Bogonosovy v Russia* (38201/16) 05.03.2019, where the domestic courts wrongly informed the applicant that he could apply for post-adoption contact with his granddaughter, and seek a court order against the adoptive parents if they hindered this. As this was not the case, and the courts refused to examine his application further, he was completely excluded from his granddaughter's life after her adoption, in violation of his right to respect for family life.

[144] (9993/82) 05.10.1982 (dec.).

regards withdrawal of parental authority, which could be ordered in either case due to a lack of care or direction manifestly endangering the safety, health, or morals of the child. In coming to their decision, the domestic authorities attached particular importance to the best interests of the child, and examined very carefully his situation and his future. The measure could thus be regarded as 'necessary' for the child's health.

This decision is an early admissibility decision, meaning that the Court's reasoning takes up little more than a page, and therefore it is difficult to draw any wide-reaching conclusions. Nevertheless, it appears that the Commission was influenced in this case by the fact that the child was living with his biological parent, with whom he had been voluntarily placed by the applicant. This was not a case where the authorities had removed the child into public care, and in many respects could be seen as more akin to a private law dispute.

A more robust analysis was undertaken in *Ageyevy v Russia*,[145] where two adopted children were removed from their (adoptive) family on suspicion of child abuse, following an injury for which one of the children required treatment in hospital (a burn to his face). Three months later, the adoption was revoked, relying on a medical report from the hospital indicating that both children had untreated illnesses, and on the criminal investigation that had been lodged concerning the child's injury. The father was subsequently acquitted, although the mother was convicted of non-fulfilment of duties relating to the care of minors, as well as the intentional infliction of mild harm to health.

The Court found that the removal of the children from the family was justified by concern for their well-being, and was in their best interests. However, the revocation of the adoption violated the rights of the family under Article 8. In coming to this conclusion, the Court applied its case law concerning the removal of parental authority from natural parents—noting that it could only be done in exceptional circumstances, and justified according to an overriding requirement pertaining to the child's best interests. While the children's injuries and untreated illnesses were of legitimate concern, they were not sufficient to prompt the far-reaching measures imposed. The courts had made a superficial assessment of the allegations, and failed to fully consider whether, and the degree to which, the parents were responsible for the health problems of the children. Moreover, no assessment of the established family bonds between the parents and children was undertaken, nor of the damage to the emotional security and psychological condition of the children that might result from breaking these.

This lack of assessment of the parenting capacity of the adoptive parents, and of the child's interests in maintaining the parental bond, was also seen in *Kurochkin v Ukraine*.[146] This case involved a dispute between a separating husband and wife, who had jointly adopted a child. Upon their separation, the wife requested an annulment of the adoption, as she did not have a positive relationship with the child (then a teenager), and alleged that he had attacked her physically. Although the father did have a good relationship with the child, the mother alleged that he had refused to stop the child's physical attacks against her.

[145] (7075/10) 18.04.2013.
[146] (42276/08) 20.05.2010.

The child and the father did not object to the annulment of the adoption between the mother and child, but wanted to maintain their legal relationship. Despite this, the courts allowed the annulment, maintaining that it was in the child's best interests, regardless of his wish to stay with his father. They found that the father had disregarded the child's aggressive attitude, which had led to him developing a negative attitude towards women and 'misconceptions about normal family relationships'. It was ordered that the child should be removed from his care and transferred to the child welfare authority for subsequent placement, although this never happened, and the child continued to live with father

The Court observed that the domestic authorities had not carried out a careful assessment of the impact the annulment would have on the child's future well-being, or explored any less far-reaching alternatives that would have overcome the alleged deficiency in the child's upbringing and development. It had thus failed in its obligation to promote family reunification, in breach of the father and son's rights under Article 8.

Worryingly, the domestic courts in this case also indicated that the annulment could be 'considered a sanction for [the child's] disgraceful behavior'.[147] The Court mildly suggested that this was not a relevant reason for splitting up a family, but it may be that stronger language would have been more appropriate. The removal of parental authority should never be used as a weapon against a child, or a punishment for their misbehaviour.

The final case on revocation of adoption is very different from those that preceded it. *Zaieț v Romania*,[148] concerned a child who was adopted at the age of 17 by the woman who had cared for her since she was nine years old. Thirty years later, she and her sister (also adopted) jointly inherited land, which had been expropriated from their grandmother many years previously. By this time, their adoptive mother had died, and her sister sought an annulment of the applicant's adoption, claiming that the applicant's only aim in agreeing to the adoption was to obtain inheritance rights. This was accepted by the court, and the adoption annulled.

The Court found that there had been a violation of Article 8, as well as Article 1, Protocol 1. It expressed doubt that the annulment was in accordance with the law, or that it pursued a legitimate aim, and it was clear that it was not supported by relevant and sufficient reasons. The reasons given were vague, and could not provide justification for such a radical measure.

The Court noted that as a general rule, the laws governing adoption are designed primarily for the benefit and protection of children. The annulment of adoption is not envisaged as a measure to be used against an adopted child, and cannot be interpreted to disinherit her 18 years after her mother's death, and 31 years after the order was made. If subsequent evidence reveals that an adoption order was based on fraudulent or misleading evidence, the Court made clear that the interests of the child should remain paramount in deciding what remedy should be pursued.

We can thus see that an adoptive family must be treated in the same manner as any other family. The same protections apply to the child and the parents' right to respect

[147] ibid., para. 56.
[148] (44958/05) 24.03.2015.

for family life, and the same justifications will be needed if the child is to be removed from the family.

11.11 Conclusion

As with the jurisprudence on child protection, this is an area where the Court has offered significant protection for children and families in terms of procedure, but has failed to take the final substantive step to rigorously examine the grounds upon which family ties are permanently severed. When given a choice between an examination of the proportionality of adoption and findings based on procedural violations, the Court has largely opted for the latter.

This does not mean that the Court has not been a force for good in this area: the positive steps it has taken should not be overlooked. It has started to develop a strong line of jurisprudence concerning the positive obligation to provide family assistance where the adoption decision is based not on direct abuse perpetrated by the parent, but more indirect causes (for example, financial difficulties). Moreover, the Court has also signalled a shift towards a stricter scrutiny of the proportionality of adoption measures, and in particular, closed adoption without the possibility of further contact—although this is only one case, and it is early days yet.

Further, adoption has also been an important testing ground for challenges concerning new family forms. Cases concerning adoption have been at the forefront of granting greater rights to unmarried fathers, while the decisions on adoption by single, gay individuals, as well as by same-sex couples, have led the way for wider recognition of LGBTQ rights before the Court, and in Europe more generally. Finally, it has been predominantly in adoption cases that the Court has pushed the boundaries of how children's interests are conceptualised: from its initial focus on parental rights; to a balancing of competing interests; and finally, recognition as the paramount consideration—and now maybe back again.

Overall, there is much to be positive about in the Court's jurisprudence on adoption. We should not let the fact that the glass is half empty blind us to the fact that it is also half full.

12
Conclusions

12.1 The achievements of the Court in the field of children's rights

As an instrument for the protection of children's rights, the European Convention on Human Rights has come a long way from its limited beginnings in 1950. Initially described by the British Lord Chancellor as 'some half-baked scheme to be administered by some unknown court',[1] it has evolved from a rather sparse, adult-centric document, to a mechanism that provides extensive protection across a wide range of rights.

This evolution has not happened overnight. While a number of the early landmark judgments concerned children, it was not until the 1990s that a gradual shift in the Court's jurisprudence can begin to be seen towards an approach that recognised children's unique and individual interests,[2] and later still that the Court started to systematically recognise these as paramount.[3] Despite this progress, the position of children before the Court remains equivocal—much has been achieved, but much is yet to be done.

The Court has been at the forefront of many important advances in children's rights in Europe. Its contribution towards the elimination of violence against children has been particularly laudable—even if it is still hesitant to take the final step of complete prohibition of corporal punishment. Likewise, it has taken huge strides in the fight against discrimination: for children born outside wedlock;[4] for 'non-traditional' families;[5] and for children from minority backgrounds.[6] It has provided safeguards for the right of the child to identity,[7] and has introduced strong procedural guarantees for children in the field of child protection, both in the removal proceedings themselves and in the obligation placed on states to achieve family reunification wherever possible.[8]

[1] As quoted in E. Myjer, L. Berg, P. Kempees et al (eds), *The Conscience of Europe: 50 years of the European Court of Human Rights* (Strasbourg: Council of Europe, 2010), 192.

[2] See, for example, *Johansen v Norway* (17383/90) 07.08.1996; *A v the United Kingdom* (25599/94) 23.09.1998; *T v the United Kingdom* (24724/94) 16.12.1999 (GC).

[3] See, for example, *Neulinger and Shuruk v Switzerland* (41615/07) 06.07.2010 (GC); *YC v the United Kingdom* (4547/10) 13.03.2012.

[4] See, for example, *Marckx v Belgium* (6833/74) 13.06.1979.

[5] See, for example, *Salgueiro da Silva Mouta v Portugal* (33290/96) 21.12.1999; *EB v France* (43546/02) 22.01.2008 (GC); *X and others v Austria* (19010/07) 19.02.2013; *Mennesson v France* (65192/11) 26.06.2014.

[6] See, for example, *DH and others v the Czech Republic* (57325/00) 13.11.2007 (GC).

[7] See, for example, *Gaskin v the United Kingdom* (10454/83) 07.07.1989; *Mikulić v Croatia* (53176/99) 07.02.2002.

[8] See, for example, *P, C and S v the United Kingdom* (56547/00) 16.07.2002; *KA v Finland* (27751/95) 14.01.2003.

Children and the European Court of Human Rights. Claire Fenton-Glynn, Oxford University Press (2021). © Claire Fenton-Glynn.
DOI: 10.1093/oso/9780198787518.003.0012

The Court must also be praised for its adoption of the UN Convention of the Rights of the Child (UNCRC) as a benchmark for the implementation of children's rights. The Court has referred to the UNCRC in numerous and varied cases, ranging from those concerning the right to parental care,[9] custody,[10] and identity[11] to cases on the detention of minors,[12] the right to a fair trial,[13] and corporal punishment.[14] The influence of the UNCRC is particularly strong in the field of adoption,[15] where the Court has held that obligations under Article 8 in relation to adoption *must* be interpreted in this light.[16]

There are limits to this, however. The use of the UNCRC standards is by no means universal, or systematic: there is no guarantee that the UNCRC will be mentioned, let alone followed by the Court. While the latter is understandable—even if not optimal—the former is not. The Court needs to strive for consistency in this area—the UNCRC must be integral to every decision concerning children. Whether or not it is followed, it cannot be ignored.

12.2 The deficiencies of the Court as a child rights instrument

Despite the notable achievements of the Court, this book has laid bare its manifest deficiencies: some substantive, some systemic. This conclusion will not reiterate all the judgments (or areas of law) where the Court has failed to take an appropriately child-rights friendly perspective, but instead looks at the overarching factors that have inhibited its ability to fully integrate children's rights.

12.2.1 Substantive deficiencies

On a substantive level, the lack of strong participation rights for children is particularly problematic. The Court's failure to require that children's wishes and feelings be represented in domestic proceedings concerning them—particularly those concerning child protection and adoption—is inexcusable. Despite requiring strong procedural safeguards for parental involvement in decision-making, this lapse emphasises the paternalistic position towards children evident in many member states—children as objects of protection, but not subjects of rights.

[9] *Keegan v Ireland* (16969/90) 26.05.1994; *K and T v Finland* (25702/94) 12.07.2001 (GC).

[10] *Sahin v Germany* (30943/96) 08.07.2003 (GC); *KT v Norway* (26664/03) 25.09.2008.

[11] *Odievre v France* (42326/98) 13.02.2003.

[12] *Nart v Turkey* (20817/04) 06.05.2008; *Selçuk v Turkey* (21768/02) 10.01.2006.

[13] *T v the United Kingdom* (24724/94) 16.12.1999 (GC).

[14] *Costello-Roberts v the United Kingdom* (13134/87) 25.03.1993 (Court); *A v the United Kingdom* (25599/94) 23.09.1998.

[15] *Emonet and others v Switzerland* (39051/03) 13.12.2007; *EB v France* (43546/02) 22.01.2008 (GC); *Fretté v France* (36515/97) 26.02.2002.

[16] *Pini and others v Romania* (78028/01, 78030/01) 22.06.2004, para. 39. (my emphasis)

This is compounded by the Court's own inadequacies in relation to standing and the representation of children, discussed in Chapter 9. While children *can* take their own cases before the Court, this is rare, and they are more likely to be joined to a parents' application, or at the very least, have their parent driving the litigation. This has inevitably skewed the jurisprudence—the Court can only decide on issues that are brought before it, and the identity of the person bringing the case will impact the way the issues are framed. When cases are presented to the Court through an adult-focused prism, adult-focused jurisprudence will result. While the Court has taken a tiny step in the right direction, through the ad hoc appointment of an individual representative for a child in one case,[17] systemic change is needed.

This raises a second issue with the Convention, namely the subjugation of children within the family. The family unit continues to be the primary recipient of protection, and conservative understandings of parental authority remain strong in the Court's jurisprudence.[18] Children's rights under the Convention exist within the bubble of the private sphere, which must be pierced before a claim can be made on the state, or before the state can step in to provide the child with protection. This lack of recognition of children's autonomy and individualism leads to a tension between the ECHR and the UNCRC. As Judges Kjølbro, Poláčková, Koskelo, and Nordén pointed out in the case of *Strand Lobben v* Norway, 'The ECHR is rooted in the protection, and balancing, of the rights of everyone within a State's jurisdiction, including those who have formed a family, whereas the [UN]CRC is focused on strengthening and protecting children as holders of distinct individual rights.'[19] If the Court is to genuinely protect the rights of children, it must embrace children's individualism, putting behind it traditional notions of the privacy of the family unit. This is not to suggest that the Court should disregard parents altogether—the UNCRC itself recognises that parents have primary responsibility for the upbringing of children.[20] Rather, the Court must recognise that children have their own rights within this framework, which must be clearly articulated, and fully represented, in proceedings.

The third overarching substantive issue raised by the Court's jurisprudence is the best interest principle. Not only has there recently been a row-back on the paramount position given to children's interests by the Court,[21] but there is also a danger that the focus on children's *interests* is coming at the detriment of the recognition of the wider landscape of children's *rights*. The right of the child to have their best interests taken into consideration is merely one of many individual rights that children hold, yet these other substantive rights have been neglected at the expense of 'best interests'.

This is dangerous on two levels. First, the concept of best interests itself is problematic, as an amorphous concept, lacking transparency, that can be used to justify almost any decision. It can potentially be stretched to mean anything that someone else thinks is good for the child,[22] and as such may reinforce preconceived notions

17 *A and B v Croatia* (7144/15) 20.06.2019.
18 See, for example, *Nielsen v Denmark* (10929/84) 28.11.1988 (Court).
19 (37283/13) 10.09.2019, dissenting opinion of Judges Kjølbro, Poláčková, Koskelo, and Nordén, para. 9.
20 Article 5, UN Convention on the Rights of the Child.
21 *Strand Lobben and others v Norway* (37283/13) 10.09.2019 (GC).
22 J. Eekelaar, 'Beyond the Welfare Principle' (2002) 14(3) *Child and Family Law Quarterly* 237.

of what the family and familial relations should look like—as was forcefully brought home in the cases concerning adoption by a homosexual parent. In addition, the lack of defined content to the principle can result in the part that the interests of others play in the decision as to what is in the 'best interests of the child' being obscured. Hillary Rodham argues that the best interests test is 'an empty vessel into which adult perceptions and prejudices are poured',[23] and it is often the case that parental rights and interests are simply reconceptualised in terms of children's welfare, while the rights of children are left unexamined.

Second, the focus on children's interests can result in the balancing process becoming skewed. As Eekelaar has suggested, the Convention approach of applying the rights of adults under Article 8(1), *unless* it can be shown that it is necessary to depart from them in the interests of the welfare of the child under subsection (2), places the interests of the child too low.[24] By recognising the 'rights' of parents, but relegating children to merely having 'interests', an unequal playing field is created.[25]

It follows that where only the rights of parents are considered, in contrast to the interests of the child, there is a subjugation of the child, which suggests a level of paternalism and protectionism, rather than respecting the autonomy of children, their independence, and self-determination. As Bainham puts it, '[p]rotecting children implies that decisions affecting them will be taken for them by others, while the concept of rights visualises that children will either take their own decisions, or at least have a strong say in matters affecting them'.[26]

12.2.2 Systemic difficulties

12.2.2.1 Subsidiarity and the margin of appreciation

In addition to the substantive difficulties, from a structural perspective, the Convention system is not the best mechanism for the protection and advancement of children's rights. This not only relates to the way the rights are formulated—for example, the focus on the family unit as discussed in section 12.2.1 above—but also to the way in which these have been interpreted by the Court.

The Convention system exists in a no man's land between human rights as political norms and human rights as enforceable legal obligations. The Court sits as a judicial body, but it relies on the support of states for its continued validity: it can only operate where states consent to be bound by its strictures, and its enforcement mechanisms rely on states' willingness to implement them.[27] The Convention is thus only ever as strong as the political will behind it.

[23] H. Rodham, 'Children under the Law' (1973) 43 *Harvard Educational Review* 487, 513.
[24] J. Eekelaar, 'Beyond the Welfare Principle' (2002) 14(3) *Child and Family Law Quarterly* 237.
[25] ibid.
[26] A. Bainham, 'Can We Protect Children and Protect Their Rights?' (2002) 32 *Family Law* 279.
[27] Although the Committee of Ministers formally oversees the execution of judgments, as of 2018, there were over 6,000 cases pending implementation (down from over 10,000 from 2010 to 2015). (Council of Europe Committee of Ministers, 'Supervision of the Execution of Judgments and Decisions of the European Court of Human Rights 2018' (Council of Europe, 2019), https://rm.coe.int/annual-report-2018/168093f3da)

This has significant implications for the Court's jurisprudence. It has moved from what Robert Spanó, later Vice President of the Court, called a 'judicial phase', in which the Court issued highly influential and even transformative judgments, to the more sober 'age of subsidiarity', characterised by deference to domestic decision-making and a focus on procedure, rather than substance.[28]

This approach has been particularly evident in cases concerning child protection and adoption. Rather than rigorously examining the grounds upon which the child has been removed from the family, or the proportionality of this measure, the Court has instead focused on the decision-making process: whether the parents were adequately involved, and whether the authorities considered all the appropriate factors. While such an approach is not devoid of merit—as Spanó explains, such strengthening of domestic institutions is democracy-enhancing, and it ensures that human rights norms are embedded in national decision-making[29]—it restricts the scope of the Convention's protection, causing one commentator to wonder whether the substantive principles espoused by the Court in its ubiquitous 'General Principles' section 'are still worth the paper they are written on'.[30]

This focus on procedure rather than substance is coupled with the margin of appreciation—now mandated by Protocol 15 of the Convention. The margin of appreciation is intended to recognise the cultural, social, and legal variety amongst member states, and correspondingly, allows national authorities a degree of discretion when resolving conflicts between individual rights and national interests.[31] However, as Benvenisti argues, this moral relativism is at odds with the concept of the universality of human rights, and can seriously undermine the promise of international human rights regimes.[32] The margin of appreciation is intended to respect democratic principles of domestic authorities, yet the very purpose of human rights law is to protect minorities from being unfairly burdened by the power of the majority.[33]

This is not to say that there should be no discretion given to different ways to *implement* human rights standards. Unfortunately, however, the margin of appreciation is often used to *interpret* these standards. In cases concerning 'sensitive' moral issues—including those concerning children and the family, where traditional attitudes often prevail—states are given a wide margin of appreciation. Despite the living tree doctrine, requiring the Convention to be interpreted in line with present-day standards, the Court will often wait for consensus before moving forward. This can be seen

[28] R. Spanó, 'Universality or Diversity of Human Rights? Strasbourg in an Age of Subsidiarity' (2014) 14 *Human Rights Law Review* 487.

[29] ibid.

[30] L. Lavrysen, 'Strand Lobben and Others v. Norway: From Age of Subsidiarity to Age of Redundancy?' (Strasbourg Observers, 23.10.2019), https://strasbourgobservers.com/2019/10/23/strand-lobben-and-others-v-norway-from-age-of-subsidiarity-to-age-of-redundancy/.

[31] See E. Benvenisti, 'Margin of Appreciation, Consensus, and Universal Standards' (1999) 31 *International Law and Politics* 843.

[32] See F. Matscher, 'Methods of Interpretation of the Convention' in R.S.J. MacDonald, F. Matscher, and H. Petzold (eds), *The European System for the Protection of Human Rights* (Dordrecht: Kluwer, 1993); E. Benvenisti, 'Margin of Appreciation, Consensus, and Universal Standards' (1999) 31 *International Law and Politics* 844.

[33] E. Benvenisti, 'Margin of Appreciation, Consensus, and Universal Standards' (1999) 31 *International Law and Politics* 847–849.

particularly in relation to new family forms, and the reluctance of the Court to take a strong stand in this regard.[34]

12.2.2.2 Workload

Since it was established in 1959, the Court has handed down over 21,600 judgments, and decided on the examination of approximately 841,300 applications.[35] Only 837 of these judgments were delivered between 1959 and 1998—indeed, there was only one case brought before the Court in each of 1960 and 1961, and no cases at all in 1963, 1964, or 1965.[36] However, in the 20 years following the establishment of the permanent Court in 1998, its workload has significantly increased, and it has averaged over 1,000 judgments per year.[37]

Despite this increase in output, there were still 56,350 applications pending as of 31 December 2018,[38] creating a significant delay between the lodging of an application and a final decision. In many cases, the Court process takes three to four years, from start to finish, but it is not unusual for applicants to have to wait five or six years for the resolution of their dispute—especially if the case proceeds to the Grand Chamber,[39] but even sometimes when it does not.[40] Some cases are pending for over a decade before they are finally decided.[41] Ironically, the Court would fail its own requirements for speedy and efficient proceedings.

While this situation is far from ideal for any victim of a human rights violation, for children, it is particularly problematic. By the time the case is decided, many will no longer be children, and the financial remedies habitually provided by the Court will do little to directly address the violation—be that an inability to access appropriate schooling, removal from parental care, conviction following an unfair trial, or refusal to permit entrance to the country to join their family. While the Court has awarded billions in damages in cases concerning corporations,[42] for cases concerning children's rights, the damages awarded are 'more symbolic than instrumental'.[43]

[34] See, for example, *X, Y, and Z v the United Kingdom* (21830/93) 22.04.1997 (GC); *Fretté v France* (36515/97) 26.02.2002.

[35] Through a judgment, decision, or being struck out of the list. (European Court of Human Rights (ECtHR), 'Statistical Overview 1959–2018' (Council of Europe, 2019), https://www.echr.coe.int/Documents/Overview_19592018_ENG.pdf)

[36] E. Myjer, L. Berg, P. Kempees et al (eds), *The Conscience of Europe: 50 years of the European Court of Human Rights* (Strasbourg: Council of Europe, 2010), 193.

[37] ECtHR, 'Statistical Overview 1959–2018' (Council of Europe, 2019), https://www.echr.coe.int/Documents/Overview_19592018_ENG.pdf.

[38] ECtHR, 'The ECHR in Facts and Figures' (Council of Europe, 2019), https://www.echr.coe.int/Documents/Facts_Figures_2018_ENG.pdf.

[39] See, for example, *Maslov v Austria* (1638/03) 23.06.2008 (GC); *Lautsi v Italy* (30814/06) 18.03.2011 (GC); *Paradiso and Campanelli v Italy* (25358/12) 24.01.2017 (GC).

[40] See, for example, *Arvelo Aponte v the Netherlands* (28770/05) 03.11.2011; *MGC v Romania* (61495/11) 15.03.2016.

[41] See, for example, *Adamkiewicz v Poland* (54729/00) 02.03.2010; *Ahmet Ozkan and others v Turkey* (21689/93) 06.04.2004; *Blokhin v Russia* (47152/06) 23.03.2016.

[42] See, for example, *Oao Neftyanaya Kompaniya Yukos v Russia* (14902/04) 31.07.2014 (Just Satisfaction).

[43] In the words of Greer, referring to *all* damages. (S. Greer, 'What's Wrong with the European Convention on Human Rights?' (2008) 30(3) *Human Rights Quarterly* 680, 686)

The problem is thus two-fold—not only the delay in receiving justice, but also the inability of the Court to provide an effective individual remedy. The best that can be hoped for by that stage is that the authorities will adjust their approach to protect the next child, but too often, violations can be dismissed on the basis that it was an isolated problem and individual to the case in question, therefore no systemic change is implemented.[44]

12.3 The future of children's rights before the Court

The European Court of Human Rights has developed an unparalleled body of child rights jurisprudence. It has decided hundreds of cases covering issues as diverse as access to abortion, religious symbols in classrooms, questioning by police, medical care in detention, removal from parental care, financial assistance for struggling families, and international surrogacy arrangements. Yet it has not achieved its full potential, held back by politics, conservatism, and a lack of institutional capacity.

The coming decades will bring a multitude of new challenges for children's rights before the Court. New family forms will further stretch the understanding of 'family life' under Article 8. The question of parenthood arising out of new technology has yet to be fully resolved; recognition of transgender parenthood must be revisited in light of legal and social developments over the last twenty years; and it is surely not long before challenges are made for recognition of multiple parenthood, moving beyond the traditional two-parent model.

The digital revolution will also continue to raise novel human rights issues. The issue of online privacy is ever-present, and the ability of children to control their image and online identity is sure to be tested. Similarly, online violence against children—for example, cyber bullying, revenge porn, and child sexual exploitation—will require the Court to reconceptualise the right to respect for private life under Article 8 and the right to freedom from inhuman or degrading treatment under Article 3.

Likewise, the impact of globalisation will continue to be felt across Europe, and in turn, require adjudication by the Court. Immigration will remain a divisive issue, both in relation to economic migration and refugees. Moreover, as families and individuals cross borders in greater numbers, private international law conflicts concerning children will endure: child abduction, intercountry adoption, and surrogacy have already generated considerable jurisprudence, and this is sure to continue.

Finally, the Court will have to grapple with the protection of socio-economic rights. Child and family poverty, and an associated lack of adequate standard of living, has a significant impact on the ability of children to exercise their rights, and cannot be ignored in the context of education, juvenile justice, and in particular,

[44] L. Lavrysen, 'Strand Lobben and Others v. Norway: From Age of Subsidiarity to Age of Redundancy?' (Strasbourg Observers, 23.10.2019), https://strasbourgobservers.com/2019/10/23/strand-lobben-and-others-v-norway-from-age-of-subsidiarity-to-age-of-redundancy/.

child protection. This is all the more so in the age of austerity, where the most vulnerable are the hardest hit.

Children's rights have now been part of the international human rights framework for over 30 years, and the UN Convention on the Rights of the Child is the most widely ratified human rights treaty in the world, with near-universal acceptance. International children's rights have come of age. It is now time for the Court to embrace them.

Bibliography

Allain, J., 'Ranstev v Cyrpus and Russia: The European Court of Human Rights and Trafficking as Slavery' (2010) 10(3) *Human Rights Law Review* 546.

Appell, A.R. and Boyer, B.A., 'Parental Rights vs. Best Interests of the Child: A False Dichotomy in the Context of Adoption' (1995) 2 *Duke Journal of Gender Law and Policy* 63.

Arnardóttir, O.M., 'Organised Retreat? The Move from "Substantive" to "Procedural" Review in the ECtHR's Case Law on the Margin of Appreciation' (2015) 5(4) *European Society of International Law Conference Paper Series* 4/2015.

Bainham, A., 'Can We Protect Children and Protect Their Rights?' (2002) 32 *Family Law* 279.

Bainham, A., 'Homosexual Adoption' (2008) 67(3) *Cambridge Law Journal* 479.

BBC Online, 'Theresa May under Fire over Deportation Cat Claim' (BBC News, 4 October 2011), https://www.bbc.co.uk/news/uk-politics-15160326.

Beaumont, P., Trimmings, K., Walker, L., and Holliday, J., 'Child Abduction: Recent Jurisprudence of the European Court of Human Rights' (2015) 64(1) *International and Comparative Law Quarterly* 39.

Beduschi, A., 'Vulnerability on Trial: Protection of Migrant Children's Rights in the Jurisprudence of the International Human Rights Courts' (2018) 36(1) *Boston University International Law Journal* 55.

Benvenisti, E., 'Margin of Appreciation, Consensus, and Universal Standards' (1999) 31 *International Law and Politics* 843.

Child Law Clinic, University College Cork, 'Research Brief on ECHR Case Law concerning Children in Care and the Obligation to Work towards Family Reunification' (September 2019), https://www.ucc.ie/en/media/academic/law/childlawclinic/ECHRFamilyReunificationinCareCasesUpdated12September2019.pdf.

Child Rights International Network, 'Access Denied: Protect Rights—Unblock Children's Access to Information' (2014), https://archive.crin.org/sites/default/files/access_to_information_final_layout.pdf.

Child Rights International Network, 'Minimum Ages of Criminal Responsibility in Europe', https://archive.crin.org/en/home/ages/europe.html.

Choudhry, S. and Herring, J., 'Righting Domestic Violence' (2006) 20 *International Journal of Law, Policy and the Family* 95.

Choudhry, S. and Herring, J., *European Human Rights and Family Law* (Oxford: Hart, 2010).

Cipriani, D., *Children's Rights and the Minimum Age of Criminal Responsibility* (London: Routledge, 2009).

Cojocariu, C., 'Stoian v Romania: The Court's Drift on Disability Rights Intensifies' (Strasbourg Observers, 5.10.2019), https://strasbourgobservers.com/2019/09/05/stoian-v-romania-the-courts-drift-on-disability-rights-intensifies/#more-4406.

Consultative Assembly, *Collected Edition of the Travaux Preparatoires* (The Hague: Martinus Nijhoff, 1975).

Council of Europe Committee of Ministers, 'Supervision of the Execution of Judgments and Decisions of the European Court of Human Rights 2018' (Council of Europe, 2019), https://rm.coe.int/annual-report-2018/168093f3da.

Cretney, S., *Elements of Family Law* (London: Sweet & Maxwell, 1992).

Delmage, E., 'The Minimum Age of Criminal Responsibility: A Medico-Legal Perspective' (2013) 13(2) *Youth Justice* 102.

Douglas, G., 'The Family and the State under the European Convention on Human Rights' (1988) 2 *International Journal of Law and the Family* 76.

Eekelaar, J., 'Beyond the Welfare Principle' (2002) 14(3) *Child and Family Law Quarterly* 237.

Eekelaar, J., 'Family Law and Identity' (2018) 38(4) *Oxford Journal of Legal Studies* 822.

European Committee of Social Rights, *Digest of the Case Law of the European Committee of Social Rights* (Strasbourg: Council of Europe, 2018).

European Court of Human Rights, 'The General Practice Followed by the Panel of the Grand Chamber when Deciding on Requests for Referral in Accordance with Article 43 of the Convention' (2011), https://www.echr.coe.int/Documents/Note_GC_ENG.pdf.

European Court of Human Rights, 'Statistical Overview 1959–2018' (Council of Europe, 2019), https://www.echr.coe.int/Documents/Overview_19592018_ENG.pdf.

European Court of Human Rights, 'The ECHR in Facts and Figures' (Council of Europe, 2019), https://www.echr.coe.int/Documents/Facts_Figures_2018_ENG.pdf.

European Union Agency for Fundamental Rights, 'Education: The Situation of Roma in 11 EU Member States' (2014), https://fra.europa.eu/sites/default/files/fra-2014_roma-survey_education_tk0113748enc.pdf.

Eurostat, 'Are More Babies Born Inside or Outside Marriage?' (16.04.2018), https://ec.europa.eu/eurostat/web/products-eurostat-news/-/DDN-20180416-1.

Farahat, A., 'The Exclusiveness of Inclusion: On the Boundaries of Human Rights in Protecting Transnational and Second Generation Migrants' (2009) 11(3) *European Journal of Migration and Law* 253.

Farmer, F., 'The Age of Criminal Responsibility: Developmental Science and Human Rights Perspectives' (2011) 6(2) *Journal of Children's Services* 86.

Feldman, D., *Civil Liberties and Human Rights in England and Wales* (2nd edn, Oxford: Oxford University Press, 2002).

Fenton-Glynn, C., *Children's Rights in Intercountry Adoption: A European Perspective* (Cambridge: Intersentia, 2014).

Fenton-Glynn, C., *Adoption without Consent* (Brussels: European Union, 2016).

Fenton-Glynn, C., 'Adoption without Consent: 2016' (European Parliament, 2016), http://www.europarl.europa.eu/RegData/etudes/STUD/2016/556940/IPOL_STU(2016)556940_EN.pdf.

Fenton-Glynn, C., 'International Surrogacy before the European Court of Human Rights' (2017) 13(3) *Journal of Private International Law* 546.

Fenton-Glynn, C., 'When Is a Family Not a Family?' (2017) 47(6) *Family Law* 586.

Fenton-Glynn, C., 'Children, Parents and the European Court of Human Rights' (2019) 6 *European Human Rights Law Review* 643.

Finnegan, G., 'Mandatory Vaccination: Does It Work in Europe?' (Vaccines Today, 27.11.2017), https://www.vaccinestoday.eu/stories/mandatory-vaccination-work-europe/.

Florescu, S., 'Parental Child Abduction is Back on the Agenda of the European Court of Human Rights' (Strasbourg Observers, 23.07.2019), https://strasbourgobservers.com/2019/07/23/parental-child-abduction-is-back-on-the-agenda-of-the-european-court-of-human-rights/.

Fortin, J., 'Rights Brought Home for Children' (1999) 62 *Modern Law Review* 350.

Fortin, J., 'Children's Rights: Are the Courts Now Taking Them More Seriously?' (2004) 15 *Kings College Law Journal* 253.

Fortin, J., 'A Decade of the HRA and its Impact on Children's Rights' (2011) 41 *Family Law* 176.

Fried, C., 'Privacy' (1968) 77 *Yale Law Journal* 475.

Global Initiative to End All Corporal Punishment of Children, https://endcorporalpunishment.org.

Global Initiative to End All Corporal Punishment of Children, 'Progress towards Prohibiting All Corporal Punishment in Europe and Central Asia' (January 2020), http://endcorporalpunishment.org/wp-content/uploads/legality-tables/Europe-and-Central-Asia-progress-table-commitment.pdf.

Goldson, B., 'Difficult to Understand or Defend: A Reasoned Case for Raising the Age of Criminal Responsibility' (2009) 48(5) *Howard Journal of Criminal Justice* 514.

Goss, R., *Criminal Fair Trial Rights: Article 6 of the European Convention on Human Rights* (Oxford: Hart, 2014).

Greer, S., *The Margin of Appreciation: Interpretation and Discretion under the European Convention on Human Rights* (Strasbourg: Council of Europe, 2000).

Greer, S., 'What's Wrong with the European Convention on Human Rights?' (2008) 30(3) *Human Rights Quarterly* 680.

Hague Conference on Private International Law, 'Adoption Statistics', http://www.hcch.net/index_en.php?act_conventions.publcations&dtid=32&cid=69.

Hasselbacher, L., 'State Obligations Regarding Domestic Violence: The European Court of Human Rights, Due Diligence, and International Legal Minimums of Protection' (2010) 8(2) *Northwestern Journal of International Human Rights* 190.

Herring, J., 'The Human Rights Act and the Welfare Principle in Family Law—Conflicting or Complementary?' (1999) 11(3) *Child and Family Law Quarterly* 223.

Hervieu, N., 'Crucifix dans les salles de classe: la capitulation de la Cour européenne des droits de l'homme' (Combats pour les droits de l'homme, 21.03.2011), http://combatsdroitshomme.blog.lemonde.fr/2011/03/21/crucifix-dans-les-salles-de-classes-la-capitulation-de-la-cour-europeenne-des-droits-de-l'homme-cour-edh-gc-18-mars-2011-lautsi-c-italie/.

Hoffmann, Lord Leonard, 'The Universality of Human Rights' (Judicial Studies Board Annual Lecture, 19.03.2009), https://www.judiciary.uk/wp-content/uploads/2014/12/Hoffmann_2009_JSB_Annual_Lecture_Universality_of_Human_Rights.pdf.

Jurisconsult of the European Court of Human Rights, 'Interlaken Follow-Up. Principle of Subsidiarity' (2010), http://www.echr.coe.int/Documents/2010_Interlaken_Follow-up_ENG.pdf.

Kilkelly, U., *The Child and the European Convention on Human Rights* (Farnham, Surrey: Ashgate, 1999).

Kratochvil, J., 'The Inflation of the Margin of Appreciation by the European Court of Human Rights' (2011) 29(3) *Netherlands Quarterly of Human Rights* 324.

Lavrysen, L., *Human Rights in a Positive State: Rethinking the Relationship between Positive and Negative Obligations under the European Convention on Human Rights* (Cambridge: Intersentia, 2017).

Lavrysen, L., 'Strand Lobben and Others v. Norway: From Age of Subsidiarity to Age of Redundancy?' (Strasbourg Observers, 23.10.2019), https://strasbourgobservers.com/2019/10/23/strand-lobben-and-others-v-norway-from-age-of-subsidiarity-to-age-of-redundancy/.

Lester, A., 'Universality versus Subsidiarity: A Reply' (1998) 1 *European Human Rights Law Review* 73.

Letsas, G., 'The ECHR as a Living Instrument: Its Meaning and Legitimacy' in G. Ulfstein, A. Follesdal, and B. Peters (eds), *Constituting Europe: The European Court of Human Rights in a National, European and Global Context* (Cambridge: Cambridge University Press, 2013).

Lievens, J., and Spinoy, M., 'Dupin v France: The ECtHR Going Old School in Its Appraisal of Inclusive Education?' (Strasbourg Observers, 11.02.2019), https://strasbourgobservers.com/2019/02/11/dupin-v-france-the-ecthr-going-old-school-in-its-appraisal-of-inclusive-education/.

Lyons, K., 'Apple Martin Tells of Mother Gwyneth Paltrow for Sharing Photo without Consent' (The Guardian, 29.03.2019), https://www.theguardian.com/film/2019/mar/29/apple-martin-tells-mother-gwyneth-paltrow-off-for-sharing-photo-without-consent.

Maher, G., 'Age and Criminal Responsibility' (2004) 2 *Ohio State Journal of Criminal Law* 493.

Marshall, J., 'SAS v France: Burqa Bans and the Control of Empowerment of Identities' (2015) 15(2) *Human Rights Law Review* 377.

Matscher, F., 'Methods of Interpretation of the Convention' in R.S.J. MacDonald, F. Matscher, and H. Petzold (eds), *The European System for the Protection of Human Rights* (Dordrecht: Kluwer, 1993).

Matthews-King, A., 'Compulsory Vaccination 'Not Ruled Out' in Fight against 'Reprehensible' Anti-Vaxxers, says Health Secretary' (The Independent, 04.05.2018), https://www.independent.co.uk/news/health/vaccination-compulsory-uk-matt-hancock-anti-vaxx-measles-nhs-a8899241.html.

Mavronicola, N., 'Bouyid v Belgium: The 'Minimum Level of Severity' and Human Dignity's Role in Article 3 ECHR' (2016) *Cyprus Human Rights Law Review* 1.

McCrudden, C., 'Multiculturalism, Freedom of Religion, Equality, and the British Constitution: The JFS Case Considered (2011) 9(1) *International Journal of Constitutional Law* 200.

McQuigg, R.J.A., 'Domestic Violence as a Human Rights Issue: Rumor v Italy' (2016) 26(4) *European Journal of International Law* 1009.

Mowbray, A., 'The Creativity of the European Court of Human Rights' (2005) 5(1) *Human Rights Law Review* 57.

Mowbray, A.R., *The Development of Positive Obligations under the European Convention on Human Rights by the European Court of Human Rights* (Oxford: Hart, 2004).

Murch, M., 'The Voice of the Child in Private Family Law Proceedings in England and Wales' (2005) 8(18) *International Family Law Journal* 8.

Murphy, C., 'The Concept of Integration in the Jurisprudence of the European Court of Human Rights' (2010) 12(1) European Journal of Migration and Law 23.

Myjer, E., Berg, L., Kempees, P. et al. (eds), *The Conscience of Europe: 50 Years of the European Court of Human Rights* (Strasbourg: Council of Europe, 2010).

Neil, E., 'Coming to Terms with the Loss of a Child' (2006) 10(1) *Adoption Quarterly* 1.

Neil, E., 'Post-Adoption Contact and Openness in Adoptive Parents' Minds: Consequences for Children's Development' (2009) 39(1) *British Journal of Social Work* 5.

Neil, E., Beek, M., and Ward, E., *Contact After Adoption* (London: CoramBAAF, 2015).

O'Mahony, C., 'Child Protection and the ECHR: Making Sense of Positive and Procedural Obligations' (2019) 27 *International Journal of Children's Rights* 660.

O'Mahony, C., 'Is Time Running Out for Corporal Punishment under the ECHR?' (2019) 24(1) *European Human Rights Law Review* 55.

OECD Family Database, 'SF2.4: Share of births Outside of Marriage' (29.11.2018), https://www.oecd.org/social/family/SF_2_4_Share_births_outside_marriage.pdf.

Palmer, S., 'Abortion and Human Rights' (2014) 6 *European Human Rights Law Review* 596.

Pintens, W. and Scherpe, J.M., 'The *Marckx Case*: A 'Whole Code of Family Law'?' in S. Gilmore, J. Herring, and R. Probert (eds), *Landmark Cases in Family Law* (2011).

Rodham, R., 'Children under the Law' (1973) 43 *Harvard Educational Review* 487.

Rudolf, B. and Eriksson, A., 'Women's Rights under International Human Rights Treaties: Issues of Rape, Domestic Slavery, Abortion and Domestic Violence' (2007) 5(3) *I-Con* 507.

Ryburn, M., 'A Study of Post-Adoption Contact in Compulsory Adoptions' (1996) 26(5) *British Journal of Social Work* 627.

Saliba, V., 'Measles Has Been Eliminated in the UK—So Why Do We Still See Cases and Outbreaks?' (Public Health England, 22.01.2018), https://publichealthmatters.blog.gov.uk/

2018/01/22/measles-has-been-eliminated-in-the-uk-so-why-do-we-still-see-cases-and-outbreaks/.
Saunders, W.S., 'Does Neutrality Equal Secularism? The European Court of Human Rights Decides Lautsi v. Italy' (The Federalist Society, 19.12.2011), https://fedsoc.org/commentary/publications/does-neutrality-equal-secularism-the-european-court-of-human-rights-decides-lautsi-v-italy.
Schermers, H.G., 'The Eleventh Protocol to the ECHR' (1994) 19 *European Law Review* 367.
Scherpe, J.M., Fenton-Glynn, C., and Kaan, T. (eds), *Eastern and Western Perspectives on Surrogacy* (Cambridge: Intersentia, 2019).
Simmonds, C., 'Paramountcy and the ECHR: A Conflict Resolved?' (2012) 71(3) *Cambridge Law Journal* 498.
Sloan, B., 'Post-Adoption Contact Reform: Compounding the State-Ordered Termination of Parenthood?' (2014) 73(2) *Cambridge Law Journal* 378.
Spanó, R., 'Universality or Diversity of Human Rights? Strasbourg in an Age of Subsidiarity' (2014) 14 *Human Rights Law Review* 487.
Starmer, K. 'Positive Obligations under the Convention', in J. Lowell and J. Cooper (eds), *Understanding Human Rights Principles* (Oxford: Hart, 2001).
Statista, 'Divorce Rates in Europe in 2017 by Country' (09.05.2019), https://www.statista.com/statistics/612207/divorce-rates-in-european-countries-per-100-marriages/.
Stoyanova, V., 'Dancing on the Borders of Article 4: Human Trafficking and the European Court of Human Rights in the *Rantsev* Case' (2012) 30 *Netherlands Quarterly of Human Rights* 2.
Stoyanova, V., *Human Trafficking and Slavery Reconsidered: Conceptual Limits and States' Positive Obligations in European Law* (Cambridge: Cambridge University Press, 2017).
Teitgen, M., 'Report on the Establishment of a Collective Guarantee of Essential Freedoms and Fundamental Rights' (Consultative Assembly of the Council of Europe, 05.09.1949).
Thym, D. 'Residence as De Facto Citizenship? Protection of Long-Term Residence under Article 8 ECHR' in R. Rubio-Marin (ed.), *Human Rights and Immigration* (Oxford: Oxford University Press, 2014).
Van Bueren, G., *International Law on the Rights of the Child* (Leiden: Marinus Nijhoff Publishers, 1995).
Zucca, L., 'A Comment on Lautsi' (EJILtalk, 19.03.2011), https://www.ejiltalk.org/a-comment-on-lautsi/.

Table of Cases

Table of International Instruments

Council of Europe

CONVENTIONS

Recommendations and Guidelines

European Union

Hague Conference on Private International Law

International Labour Organisation

Index

For the benefit of digital users, indexed terms that span two pages (e.g., 52–53) may, on occasion, appear on only one of those pages.